OCCUPIED AM[...]

A HISTORY OF CHICANOS

SECOND EDITION

RODOLFO ACUÑA
California State University at Northridge

HARPER & ROW, PUBLISHERS, New York
Cambridge, Hagerstown, Philadelphia, San Francisco,
London, Mexico City, São Paulo, Sydney

1817

107666

Cover: Mural by Mike Rios, Gallaria de la Raza;
Photo by Karen R. Preuss, Jeroboam.

Sponsoring Editor: John L. Michel
Project Editor: David Nickol
Senior Production Manager: Kewal K. Sharma
Compositor: David E. Seham Inc.
Printer and Binder: Halliday Lithograph Corporation

Occupied America: A History of Chicanos, Second Edition
Copyright © 1981 by Rodolfo Acuña

Library of Congress Cataloging in Publication Data

Acuña, Rodolfo.
    Occupied America.

    Includes index.
    1. Mexican Americans—History. I. Title.
E184.M5A63   1980   973'.046872   80-23573
ISBN 0-06-380352-6

Contents

Preface

The first edition of *Occupied America* followed the current of the times, adopting the internal colonial model that was popular during the late 1960s and early 1970s. The works of Frantz Fanon greatly influenced the tone and direction of the book. Since then, just like the Chicano movement itself, I have undergone dramatic changes. I have reevaluated the internal colonial model and set it aside as a useful paradigm relevant to the nineteenth century but not to the twentieth. After examining a multitude of other paradigms advanced by Chicano scholars in the past ten years, I decided to return to the basics and collect historical data. In this endeavor, I filled over ten thousand five-by-eight note cards. The end result is in many respects a different book.

The second edition of *Occupied America* does not follow the example of most revisions. I refused to tack on two chapters at the end and call it an up-to-date book. This version of *Occupied America* reflects my current understanding of the history of Chicanos. The patterns of repression and injustices are more fully documented than in the first edition; topics overlooked in 1972, such as the role of women and the roots of Chicano labor, have been included. Heavy emphasis is placed on documentation, drawing on a wealth of materials found in the numerous dissertations written by Chicanos and other scholars of the Southwest, as well as in the Arno Series, the Chicano journal *Aztlán*, newspapers such as the *Eastside Sun* and the news-monitoring service published by the *Comité de México y Aztlán* (COMEXAZ), and the newsletters of the American GI *Forum*. The special collections at the Banroft Library at Berkeley, the University of California at Los Angeles, and the University of Arizona were also helpful as were the excellent Chicano Studies libraries at the Universities of California at Los Angeles and Berkeley. I would like to thank collectively all of the workers associated with these publications and institutions.

Because of the amount of documentation and the well-defined patterns illuminated by empirical evidence, I changed the subtitle from *The Chicano's Struggle Toward Liberation* to simply *A History of Chicanos*. The change is subtle, since history is never static and since it reflects struggle. The change also is a reaction to the paradigm rut that so many Chicano scholars have fallen into. Moreover, it is a reaction to the social scientists' utopian flirtation with "pure research," that is, the belief that answers can be found *only* through quantitative studies. To be valid, any and all research must be put into the context of the historical process. To that end, this work represents an attempt to exhaust all available sources in order to make a more exact synthesis.

The second edition of *Occupied America* does not present a political theory. Wherever possible I have attempted to purge polemics. In part this was made necessary by the overwhelming amount of material collected. Hopefully, exposing the patterns of repression and the collective nature of the Chicanos' oppression will help in finding a solution to this monopoly game in which Mexicans in the United States find themselves trapped. I hope that *Occupied America* will provide sufficient data so that readers can arrive at their own conclusions rather than my deducing the conclusions for them.

Unfortunately this text does not include the cultural history of the Chicano. It does not cover the rich artistic renaissance of Chicano painters, the rich literary contributions of Chicano poets and writers, and the coming into its own of the Chicano theatre, for which the Broadway run of Luis Váldez' *Zoot Suit* marks a breakthrough. The advancement of Chicanos in other areas of the media is also significant. My not including these very important components of Chicano life does not represent a lack of appreciation, but merely the constraint of space.

Although *Occupied America* is still divided into two parts, covering first the nineteenth century and then the twentieth, there are substantive changes. In the first part, I have attempted to be more exacting in uncovering the causes of conquest and subjugation, which were essentially economic. I have also attempted to explain how the political process and socialization were used to control and subjugate. In this context, the role of class is explored, with emphasis on the collusion of *los ricos* (the Chicano rich) with Anglo capitalists. The theme of resistance is continued, since Mexicans are no different than any other people—their tolerance reaches a breaking point. Lastly, the linkages between the nineteenth century and twentieth century are strengthened, especially the changes made possible by the railroad network completed in the 1880s.

The second part has been completely redone and is essentially divided into three sections: immigration, labor, and political history. Again, the material reveals clear patterns of repression and resistance. Chapters 6 and 7 are a chronological history of Mexican migration to the United States during the twentieth century. Nativist's reactions are clear and add to the understanding of present-day efforts to make scapegoats of Mexicans for the nation's economic woes. Chapters 8 and 9 deal with Chicanos in the U.S. labor movement, tracing their roots to Mexico, where a tradition of resistance was established that was continued in U.S. mines, factory farms, urban factories, and elsewhere. The last three chapters deal specifically with the Chicanos' efforts to form self-help and advocacy organizations. A significant amount of material is presented dealing with police brutality, urban struggle, and the impact of the Chicanos population explosion during the 1960s and 1970s and its ramifications for the future.

The first edition of *Occupied America* caused considerable controversy. Its challenge of traditional history placed many readers on the defensive. Criticisms of the system were interpreted by many Anglos as a condemnation of themselves. However, it was never the intention to indict collectively any group of people. The book was written to expose past injustices in order to correct present inequities and prevent future ones. The second edition, it is hoped, goes further in seeking the truth by instilling both in Chicanos and others an intolerance for injustice. Also, it is hoped that the second edition gives readers an appreciation for the sacrifices and risks that past generations made, for no progress is possible without sacrifices. We should all realize that our privileges are not of our own making but that we have a debt to the past. We owe it to our ancestors to work for a better future. Most of all, the second edition is intended to strengthen our *amor propio*, self-esteem, along with a feeling of collective responsibility to our fellow workers.

Perhaps this edition can be faulted for its methodology; however, I am sure that it will not be faulted for the amount of work spent on its preparation. I would like to thank again all those who helped make the first edition a success. In this edition, as in the first, my students at California State University/Northridge added to my perspective on history and the contemporary scene. My colleagues all added to the process, especially Jorge García and Raúl Ruiz, with whom I discussed concepts for hours on end. Special thanks to Evelyn Escatiola, who was my assistant on a microfilming project. I am especially indebted to Ricardo Romo, University of California/San Diego, and Mauricio Mazón, University of Southern California, for their careful reading of the rough draft. Their corrections and recommendations contributed greatly to *Occupied America*. Lastly, I dedicate this book to my father and my two sons in name of the working masses who made it possible.

Rodolfo Acuña

Part I
CONQUEST AND COLONIZATION:

An Overview

The history of the Southwest of the United States during the nineteenth century is basically a history of the conflict between the United States and Mexico. The United States made territorial incursions into Mexico and benefited tremendously from the conquest. The Mexicans in the conquered territory became victims of a colonial process in which U.S. troops acted as an army of occupation. This process of conquest and colonization involved violence and brutality on the part of the conquerors, a system of privilege based on racism, and exploitation of the labor of Mexicans and other poor people.

Chapter 1 deals with the invasion of Texas and the rest of Mexico's northwest territory in which the pattern of conquest and the moral and political justifications for conquest were established. Chapters 2 through 5 deal with the colonization of the four major states—Texas, New Mexico, Arizona, and California. The principal theme is the subjugation of Mexicans through the use of the political process. Laws that favored the few were passed, administered, and enforced. They stripped Mexicans of the little wealth they had and relegated them as a class and race to the lowest rung of the economic and social scale. The only exception was a small group of Mexican *ricos* (rich) who collaborated with the conquerors and acted as a broker class. Those in power maintained their superiority through the use of military and police powers.

Government authorities socialized Anglo-Americans and Mexicans alike to accept the new order. History, education, institutions such as the churches and schools, legitimatized those in power. In spite of this, Mexicans resisted. The struggle took the form of primitive forms of rebellion, ranging from social banditry and mob riots to full-scale armed conflict. This era, however, ended abruptly with the arrival of the railroad, which brought large numbers of Anglos to the Southwest ending the region's isolation and undeveloped stage.

Chapter 1
Legacy of Hate: The Conquest of the Southwest

The tragedy of the Mexican cession is that most Anglo-Americans have not accepted the fact that the United States committed an act of violence against the Mexican people when it took Mexico's northwestern territory. Violence was not limited to the taking of the land; Mexico's territory was invaded, her people murdered, her land raped, and her possessions plundered. Memory of this destruction generated a distrust and dislike that is still vivid in the minds of many Mexicans, for the violence of the United States left deep scars. And for Chicanos—Mexicans remaining within the boundaries of the new United States territories—aggression was even more insidious, for the outcome of the Texas and Mexican-American wars made them a conquered people. Anglo-Americans were the conquerors, and they evinced all the arrogance of military victors.[1]

BACKGROUND TO THE INVASION OF TEXAS

An integral part of Anglo rationalizations for the conquest has been either to ignore or to distort events that led up to the initial clash in 1836. To Anglo-Americans, the Texas War resulted because of a tyrannical or, at best, an incompetent Mexican government that was antithetical to the ideals of democracy and justice. The truth is that the roots of the conflict extended back to as early as 1767 when Benjamin Franklin marked Mexico and Cuba for future expansion. Filibusters* from the United States planned expeditions into Texas in the 1790s. The Louisiana Purchase in 1803 stimulated U.S. ambitions in the Southwest and six years later Thomas Jefferson predicted that the Spanish borderlands "are ours the first moment war is forced upon us."[2] The war with Great Britain in 1812 heightened Anglo-American designs on the Spanish territory.

The U.S. experience in Florida set the pattern for expansionist activities in Texas. In 1818 several posts in East Florida were seized in unauthorized, but never officially condemned U.S. military expeditions. Negotiations then in progress with Spain finally terminated in the Adams-Onis or Transcontinental Treaty (1819)

---

*A *filibuster* is an adventurer who engages in insurrectionist or revolutionary activity in a foreign country.

whereby Spain ceded Florida to the United States and the United States renounced its claim to Texas. The treaty set the U.S. boundary at the Sabine River, thereby excluding Texas. When the treaty was ratified in February 1821 Texas was part of Coahuila, a state in the independent Republic of Mexico. Many North Americans claimed that Texas belonged to the United States, pointing to Jefferson's contention that Texas's boundary extended to the Rio Grande and that it was part of the Louisiana Purchase. They condemned the Adams-Onis Treaty. The expanded boundary would have "put several key Mexican posts, notably San Antonio, Albuquerque and Santa Fe inside the United States." Therefore, Anglo-Americans made forays into Texas similar to those they had made into Florida. In 1819 James Long led an abortive invasion to establish the "Republic of Texas." Long, like many Anglos, believed that Texas belonged to the United States and that "Congress had no right or power to sell, exchange, or relinquish an 'American possession.'"[3]

The Mexican government opened Texas, provided settlers agreed to certain conditions and for a time filibustering subsided. Moses Austin was given permission to settle in Texas. He died shortly afterwards, and his son continued his venture. In December 1821 Stephen Austin founded the settlement of San Felipe de Austin. Large numbers followed, many coming to Texas in the 1820s as refugees from the depression of 1819 and in the 1830s as entrepreneurs seeking to profit from the availability of cheap land. By 1830 there were about 20,000 settlers, along with about 2,000 slaves.

Settlers agreed to obey the conditions set by the Mexican government—that all immigrants be Catholics and that they take an oath of allegiance to Mexico. However, Anglo-Americans became resentful when Mexico tried to enforce the agreements and Mexico became increasingly alarmed at the flood of immigrants from the U.S., most of whom retained their Protestant religion.[4]

It soon became apparent that the Anglo-Texans had no intention of obeying Mexican laws. Many settlers considered the native Mexicans to be the intruders in the territory and encroached upon their lands. In a dispute with Mexicans and Indians, as well as Anglo-American settlers, Hayden Edwards arbitrarily attempted to evict settlers from the land before the conflicting claims could be sorted out by the Mexican authorities. As a result the authorities nullified his settlement contract and ordered him to leave the territory. He and his followers seized the town of Nacogdoches and on December 21, 1826, proclaimed the Republic of Fredonia. Mexican officials, who were supported by some Anglo-Americans (such as Stephen Austin), suffocated the Edwards revolt. However, many U.S. newspapers played up the rebellion as "200 Men Against a Nation!" and described Edwards and his followers as "apostles of democracy crushed by an alien civilization."[5]

In 1824 President John Quincy Adams "began putting pressure on Mexico in the hope of persuading her to rectify the frontier. Any of the Texan rivers west of the Sabine—the Brazos, the Colorado, the Nueces—was preferable to the Sabine, though the Rio Grande was the one desired."[6] In 1826 Adams offered to buy Texas for the sum of $1 million. Mexican authorities refused the offer. The United States launched an aggressive foreign policy, attempting to coerce Mexico into selling Texas.

Mexico tried to consolidate its control over Texas, but the number of Anglo-American settlers and the vastness of the territory made it an almost impossible task. Anglo-Americans in Texas had already created a privileged caste, which depended in great part on the economic advantage given to them by their slaves. When Mexico abolished slavery on September 15, 1829, Texans circumvented the law by "freeing" their slaves and then signing them to lifelong contracts as indentured servants. Anglos resented the Mexican order and considered it an invasion of their personal liberties. In 1830 Mexico prohibited further Anglo-American immigration to Texas. Anglos were outraged at the restrictions. Meanwhile, Andrew Jackson increased tensions by attempting to purchase Texas for as much as $5 million.

Mexican authorities grew more nervous as the Anglo-Americans' dominance of Texas increased; they resented the Anglo-Americans' refusal to submit to Mexican laws. Mexico moved reinforcements into Coahuila, and readied them in case of trouble. Anglos viewed this move as a Mexican invasion.

Anglo-Texan colonists grew more defiant and refused to pay customs and actively supported smuggling activities. Armed clashes broke out. When the "war party" rioted at Anahuac in December 1831 it had the popular support of Anglo-Texans. One of its leaders was Sam Houston, who "was a known protégé of Andrew Jackson, now president of the United States. . . . Houston's motivation was to bring Texas into the United States."[7]

In the summer of 1832 a group of Anglos attacked a Mexican garrison and were routed. A state of insurrection existed and Mexican authorities were forced to defend the territory. Matters worsened when the Anglo settlers met at San Félipe in October 1832. At this convention Anglos drafted resolutions sent to the Mexican government and to the state of Coahuila which called for more autonomy for Texas. A second convention was held in January 1833. Significantly, not one Mexican pueblo in Texas participated in either convention, many clearly branding the act sedition. Increasingly it became evident that the war party under Sam Houston was winning out.[8] Sam Houston was elected to direct the course of events and Austin was appointed to submit the grievances and resolutions to Mexico City.

Austin left for Mexico City to press for lifting of restrictions on

Anglo-American immigration and separate statehood. The slave issue also burned in his mind. Austin, anything but conciliatory, wrote to a friend from Mexico City, "If our application is refused . . . I shall be in favor of organizing *without it*. I see no other way of saving the country from total anarchy and ruin. I am totally done with conciliatory measures and, for the future, shall be uncompromising as to Texas."[9]

On October 2, 1833, he wrote a letter to the *ayuntamiento* at San Antonio encouraging it to declare Texas a separate state. He later stated that he had done so "in a moment of irritation and impatience"; nevertheless, his actions were not those of a moderate. Contents of the note fell into the hands of Mexican authorities, who had begun to question Austin's good faith. Subsequently, they imprisoned him, and much of what Austin had accomplished in the way of compromise was undone.

Contributing to the general distrust were actions of U.S. Minister to Mexico Anthony Butler, whose crude attempts to bribe Mexican officials to sell Texas infuriated Mexicans. He offered one official $200,000 to "play ball."[10]

In the autumn of 1834 Henry Smith published a pamphlet entitled *Security for Texas* in which he advocated open defiance of Mexican authority. The agents of Anglo land companies added to the polarization by lobbying in Washington, D.C., and within Texas for a change in governments. The Galveston Bay and Texas Land Company of New York, acting to protect its investments, worked through its agent Anthony Butler, the U.S. Minister to Mexico to bring about the cooperation of the U.S..[11]

According to Dr. Carlos Castañeda:

> The activities of the "Land Companies" after 1834 cannot be ignored. Their widespread advertisement and indiscriminate sale of "landscrip" sent hundreds, perhaps thousands, to Texas under the impression that they had legitimate title to lands equal to the amount of scrip bought. The Galveston Bay and Texas Land Company, which bought the contracts of David S. Burnet, Joseph Vahlein, and Lorenzo de Zavala, and the Nashville Company, which acquired the contract of Robert Leftwich, are the two best known. They first sold scrip at from one to ten cents an acre, calling for a total of seven and one-half million acres. The company was selling only its permit to acquire a given amount of land in Texas, but since an empresario contract was nontransferable, the scrip was, in fact, worthless. . . .[12]

The scrip would be worthless as long as Texas belonged to Mexico.

On July 13, 1835, a general amnesty released Austin from prison. While enroute to Texas, he wrote a letter from New Orleans to a cousin expressing the view that Texas should be Americanized even though it was still a state of Mexico, and indicating that it should one day come under the American flag. In this letter he called for a massive immigration of Anglo-Americans, "*each man with his rifle,"* whom he hoped would come "passports or no passports, *anyhow.*" He continued: "For fourteen years I have had a hard time of it, but nothing shall daunt my courage or abate my . . . object . . . to *Americanize* Texans."[13]

Anglos in Texas saw separation from Mexico and eventual union with the United States as the most profitable political arrangement. Texas-Mexican historian Castañeda notes:

> Trade with New Orleans and other American ports had increased steadily. This development was naturally distasteful to Mexico, for the colonists fostered strong economic ties with . . . the United States rather than with Mexico. Juan H. Almonte in his 1834 report, estimated the total foreign trade of Texas—chiefly with the United States—at more than 1,000,000 pesos, of which imports constituted 630,000 and exports, 500,000. He calculated the exportation of cotton by the settlers in 1833, as approximately 2,000 bales.[14]

Colonel Almonte recognized the fundamental economic conflict reflected in these figures and his report recommended many concessions to the *Tejanos*, but also urged that "the province be well stocked with Mexican troops."[15]

THE INVASION OF TEXAS

Not all the Anglo-Texan settlers favored the conflict. Austin belonged to the peace party, which at first opposed a confrontation with Mexicans. Ultimately, this faction joined the "hawks." Eugene C. Barker states that the immediate cause of the war was "the overthrow of the nominal republic [by Santa Anna] and the substitution of centralized oligarchy," which allegedly would have placed the Texans more strictly under the control of Mexico. Barker admits that "Earnest patriots like Benjamin Lundy, William Ellery Channing, and John Quincy Adams saw in the Texas revolution a disgraceful affair promoted by the sordid slaveholders and land speculators."

Barker draws a parallel between the Texas revolt and the American Revolution, stating: "In each, the general cause of revolt was the same—a sudden effort to extend imperial authority at the expense of local privilege." In fact, in both instances the central governments attempted to enforce existing laws that conflicted with illegal activities of some very articulate men. Barker further attempts to justify the Anglo-Texans' actions by observing: "At the close of summer in 1835 the Texans saw themselves in danger of becoming the alien subjects of a people to whom they deliberately believed themselves morally, intellectually, and politically superior. The racial feeling, indeed, underlay and colored Texan-Mexican relations from the establishment of the first Anglo-American colony in 1821." Therefore, the conflict, according to Barker, was inevitable and, consequently, justified.

Texas history is elusive—a mixture of selected fact and generalized myth. Many historians admit that racism played a leading role in the causes for revolt, that smugglers were upset with Mexico's enforcement of her import laws, that Texans were upset about emancipation laws, and that an increasing number of the new arrivals from the United States actively agitated for independence. But despite these admissions, many historians like Barker refuse to assign guilt to their countrymen. Instead, Barker blamed it on the racial and cultural mistrust between Mexicans and the colonists.[16]

The antipathies of the Texans escalated into a full-scale rebellion. Austin gave the call to arms on September 19, 1835, stating, "War is our only recourse. There is no other remedy."[17] Anglo-Americans enjoyed very real advantages in 1835. They were "defending" terrain with which they were familiar. The 5,000 Mexicans living in the territory did not join them, but the Anglo population had swelled to almost 30,000. The Mexican nation was divided, and the centers of power were thousands of miles away from Texas. From the interior of Mexico Santa Anna led an army of about 6,000 conscripts, many of whom had been forced into the army and then marched hundreds of miles over hot, arid desert land. Many were Mayan and did not speak Spanish. In February 1836 the majority arrived in San Antonio, Texas, sick and ill-prepared to fight. Although the Mexican army outnumbered the Anglo contingent, the latter were much better armed and enjoyed the position of being the defenders. (Until World War I, this was a decided advantage during wartime.) Santa Anna, on the other hand, had overextended his supply lines and was many miles from his base of power.

The defenders of San Antonio took refuge in a former mission, the Alamo. In the days that followed, Texans inflicted heavy casualties on the Mexican forces, but eventually Mexicans' sheer superiority in numbers won out. Much has been written about Mexican cruelty in relation to the Alamo and about the heroics of the doomed men. The result was the creation of the Alamo myth. Within the broad framework of what actually happened—187 Texans barricading themselves in the Alamo in defiance of Santa Anna's force and the eventual triumph of the Mexicans—there has been much distortion.

Walter Lord, in an article entitled "Myths and Realities of the Alamo," sets much of the record straight. Texas mythology portrays the Alamo heroes as freedom-loving defenders of their homes; they were supposedly all good Texans. Actually, two-thirds of the defenders had recently arrived from the United States, and only a half dozen had been in Texas for more than six years. The men in the Alamo were adventurers. William Barret Travis had fled to Texas after killing a man, abandoning his wife and two children. James Bowie, an infamous brawler, made a fortune running slaves and had wandered into Texas searching for lost mines and more money. The fading Davey Crockett, a legend in his own time, fought for the sake of fighting. Many others in the Alamo were men who had come to Texas for riches and glory. These defenders were hardly the sort of men who could be classified as peaceful settlers fighting for their homes.

The folklore of the Alamo goes beyond the legendary names of the defenders. According to Lord, it is riddled with dramatic half-truths that have been accepted as history. Defenders at the Alamo are portrayed as selfless heroes who sacrificed their lives to buy more time for their comrades-in-arms. As the story is told, William Barret Travis told his men that they were doomed; he drew a line in the sand with his sword, saying that all who crossed it would elect to remain and fight to the last. Supposedly all the men there valiantly stepped across the line, with a man in a cot begging to be carried across it. The bravery of the defenders has been *dramatized* in countless Hollywood movies.

In reality the Alamo had little strategic value, it was the best fortified fort west of the Mississippi, and the men fully expected help. The defenders had twenty-one cannons to the Mexicans' eight or ten. They were expert marksmen equipped with rifles with a range of 200 yards, while the Mexicans were inadequately trained and armed with smooth-bore muskets with a range of only 70 yards. The Anglos were protected by the walls and had clear shots, while the Mexicans advanced in the open and fired at concealed targets. In short, ill-prepared, ill-equipped, and ill-fed Mexicans attacked well-armed and professional soldiers. In addition, from all reliable sources, it is doubtful whether Travis ever drew a line in the sand. San Antonio survivors, females and noncombatants, did not tell the story until many years later, when the tale had become well circulated and the myth was a legend. Probably the most widely circulated story was that of the last stand of the aging Davey Crockett who fell "fighting like a tiger," killing Mexicans with his bare hands. This is a myth; seven of the defenders surrendered, and Crockett was among them. They were executed. And, finally, one man, Louis Rose, did escape.[18]

Travis's stand delayed Santa Anna's timetable by only four days, as the Mexicans took San Antonio on March 6, 1836. At first, the stand at the Alamo did not even have propaganda value. Afterwards, Houston's army dwindled, with many volunteers rushing home to help their families flee from the advancing Mexican army. Most Anglo-Texans realized that they had been badly beaten. It did, nevertheless, result in massive aid from the United States in the form of volunteers, arms, and money. The cry of "Remember the Alamo" became a call to arms for Anglo-Americans in both Texas and the United States.[19]

After the Alamo and the defeat of another garrison at Goliad, southeast of San Antonio, Santa Anna was in full control. He ran Sam Houston out of the territory northwest of the San Jacinto River and then camped an army of about 1,100 men near San Jacinto. There, he skirmished with Houston on April 20, 1836, but did not follow up his advantage. Predicting that Houston would attack on April 22, Santa Anna and his men settled down and rested for the anticipated battle. Texans, however, attacked during the *siesta* hour on April 21. Santa Anna had made an incredible blunder. He knew that Houston had an army of 1,000, yet he was lax in his precautionary defenses. The surprise attack caught him totally off guard. Shouts of "Remember the Alamo! Remember Goliad!" filled the air. Houston's successful surprise attack ended the war. He captured Santa Anna, who had no choice and signed the territory away. Although the Mexican Congress repudiated the treaty, Houston was elected president of the Republic of Texas.

The battle of San Jacinto was literally a slaughter of the Mexican forces. Few prisoners were taken. Those who surrendered "were clubbed and stabbed, some on their knees. The slaughter . . . became methodical: the Texan riflemen knelt and poured a steady fire into the packed, jostling ranks. . . ."[20] They shot the "Meskins" down as they fled. The final count showed 630 Mexicans dead versus 2 Texans.

It is commonly believed that after the surrender Texan authorities let Santa Anna off lightly, but, according to Dr. Castañeda, Santa Anna "was mercilessly dragged from the ship he had boarded, subjected to more than six months' mental torture and indignities in Texas prison camps."

The Texas victory paved the way for the Mexican-American War, feeding the growing nationalism of the young Anglo-American nation. Officially the United States had not taken sides, but men, money, and supplies poured in to aid fellow Anglo-Americans. U.S. citizens participated in the invasion of Texas with the open support of their government. Mexico's minister to the United States, Manuel Eduardo Gorostiza, vehemently protested the "arming and shipment of troops and supplies to territory which was part of Mexico, and the dispatch of United States troops into territory clearly defined by treaty as Mexican territory."[21] General Edmund P. Gaines, Southwest Commander, had been sent into Western Louisiana on January 23, 1836; shortly thereafter, he crossed into Texas in an action that was interpreted to be in support of the Anglo-American filibusters in Texas: "The Jackson Administration made it plain to the Mexican minister that it mattered little whether Mexico approved, that the important thing was to protect the border against Indians and Mexicans."[22] U.S. citizens in and out of Texas loudly applauded Jackson's actions. The Mexican minister resigned his post in protest. "The success of the Texas Revolution thrust the

Anglo-American frontier up against the Far Southwest, and the region came at once into the scope of Anglo ambition."[23]

THE INVASION OF MEXICO

The United States during the nineteenth century moved its boundaries westward. In the mid-1840s, Mexico was again the target. Expansion and capitalist development moved together. The two Mexican wars gave U.S. commerce, industry, mining, agriculture, and stockraising a tremendous stimulus. "The truth is that [by the 1840's] the Pacific Coast belonged to the commercial empire that the United States was already building in that ocean."[24]

The United States's population of 17 million people of European extraction and 3 million slaves was considerably larger than Mexico's 7 million, of which 4 million were Indian, and 3 million Mestizo and European. The United States acted arrogantly in foreign affairs, partly because its citizens believed in their inherent cultural and racial superiority. Mexico was plagued with financial problems, internal ethnic conflicts, and poor leadership. General anarchy within the nation conspired against its cohesive development.[25]

By 1844 war with Mexico over Texas and the Southwest was only a matter of time. James K. Polk, who strongly advocated the annexation of Texas and expansionism in general, won the presidency by only a small margin, but his election was interpreted as a mandate for national expansion. Outgoing President Tyler decided to act and called upon Congress to annex Texas by joint resolution; the measure was passed a few days before the inauguration of Polk, who accepted the arrangement. In December 1845, Texas became a state.[26]

Mexico promptly broke off diplomatic relations with the United States, and Polk ordered General Zachary Taylor into Texas to "protect" the border. The location of the border was in doubt. Texas contended it was at the Rio Grande, but based on historical precedent, Mexico claimed it was 150 miles farther north, at the Nueces River.[27] Taylor took his forces across the Nueces into the disputed territory, wanting to provoke an attack.

In November 1845, Polk sent John Slidell on a secret mission to Mexico to negotiate for the disputed area. The presence of Anglo-American troops between the Nueces and the Rio Grande and the annexation of Texas made negotiations an absurdity. They refused to accept Polk's minister's credentials, although they did offer to grant him an ad hoc status.[28] Slidell refused anything less than full acceptance and returned to Washington in March 1846, convinced that Mexico would have to be "chastised" before it would negotiate. By March 28, Taylor had advanced to the Rio Grande with an army of 4,000.

Polk, incensed at Mexico's refusal to meet with Slidell on his terms and at General Mairano Paredes' reaffirmation of his country's claims to all of Texas, began to draft his declaration of war when he learned of a Mexican attack on U.S. troops in the disputed territory. He immediately declared that the United States had been provoked into war, that Mexico had "shed American blood upon the American soil." On May 13, 1846, Congress declared war and authorized the recruitment and supplying of 50,000 troops.[29]

Years later, Ulysses S. Grant said that he believed Polk wanted and planned for war to be provoked and that the annexation of Texas was, in fact, an act of aggression. He added: "I had a horror of the Mexican War . . . only I had not moral courage enough to resign. . . . I considered my supreme duty was to my flag."[30]

The poorly equipped and poorly led Mexican army stood little chance against the thrust of expansion-minded Anglos. Even before the war Polk planned a campaign of three stages: (1) Mexicans would be cleared out of Texas; (2) Anglos would occupy California and New Mexico; and (3) U.S. forces would march to Mexico City to force the beaten government to make peace on Polk's terms. And that was the way the campaign basically went. In the end, at a relatively small cost in men and money, the war netted the United States huge territorial gains. In all, the United States took over 1 million square miles of Mexican lands.[31]

THE RATIONALE FOR CONQUEST

In his *Origins of the War with Mexico: The Polk-Stockton Intrigue*, Glenn W. Price states: "Americans have found it rather more difficult than other peoples to deal rationally with their wars. We have thought of ourselves as unique, and of this society as specially planned and created to avoid the errors of all other nations."[32] In this vein, many Anglo-American historians attempt to dismiss the Mexican-American War by simply stating that it was a "bad war," which took place during the United States' era of Manifest Destiny.

Manifest Destiny had its roots in Puritan ideas, which continue to influence Anglo-American thought to this day. According to the Puritan ethic, salvation is determined by God. The establishment of the City of God on earth is not only the duty of those chosen people predestined for salvation, but is also the proof of their state of grace. This belief carried over to the Anglo-American conviction that God had made them custodians of democracy and that they had a mission, that is, that they were predestined to spread its principles. As the young nation survived its infancy, established its power in the defeat of the British in the War of 1812, expanded westward, and enjoyed both commercial and industrial success, its sense of destiny heightened. Many citizens believed that God had destined them to own and occupy all of the land from ocean to ocean and pole to pole. Their mission, their destiny made manifest, was to spread the principles of democracy and Christianity to the unfortunates of the hemisphere. By dismissing the war simply as part of the era of Manifest Destiny the apologists for the war ignore the consequences of the doctrine.

The Monroe Doctrine of the 1820s told the world that the Americas were no longer open for colonization or conquest; however, it did not say anything about that limitation applying to the United States. Uppermost in the minds of the U.S. government, the military, and much of the public was the acquisition of territory. No one ever intended to leave Mexico without extracting territory. Land was the main motivation.

Further obscuring the issue of planned Anglo-American aggression is what Professor Price exposes as the rhetoric of peace, which the United States has traditionally used to justify its aggressions. The Mexican-American War is a study in the use of this rhetoric.

Consider, for example, Polk's war message of May 11, 1846, in which he gave his reasons for going to war:

> The strong desire to establish peace with Mexico on liberal and honorable terms, and the readiness of this Government to regulate and adjust our boundary and other causes of difference with that power on such fair and equitable principles as would lead to permanent relations of the most friendly nature, induced me in September last to seek reopening of diplomatic relations between the two countries.[33]

He went on to state that the United States had made every effort not to inflame Mexicans, but that the Mexican government had refused to receive an Anglo-American minister. Polk reviewed the events leading to the war and concluded:

> As war exists, and notwithstanding all our efforts to avoid it, exists by the act of Mexico herself, we are called upon by every consideration of duty and patriotism to vindicate with decision the honor, the rights, and the interests of our country.[34]

Historical distance from the events has not reduced the prevalence of this rhetoric. The need to justify has continued. In 1920 Justin F. Smith received a Pulitzer prize in history for a work that blamed the war on Mexico. What is amazing is that Smith allegedly examined more than 100,000 manuscripts, 120,000 books and pamphlets, and 200 or more periodicals to come to this conclusion. It is fair to speculate that he was rewarded for relieving the Anglo-American conscience. His two-volume "study," entitled *The War with Mexico*, used analyses such as the following to support its thesis:

> At the beginning of her independent existence, our people felt ear-
> nestly and enthusiastically anxious to maintain cordial relations with
> our sister republic, and many crossed the line of absurd sentimentality
> in the cause. Friction was inevitable, however. The Americans were
> direct, positive, brusque, angular and pushing; and they would not
> understand their neighbors in the south. The Mexicans were equally
> unable to fathom our goodwill, sincerity, patriotism, resoluteness and
> courage; and certain features of their character and national condition
> made it far from easy to get on with them.[35]

This attitude of righteousness on the part of government officials and historians toward their aggressions spills over to the relationships between the majority society and minority groups. Anglo-
Americans believe that the war was advantageous to the Southwest
and to the Mexicans who remained or later migrated there. They
now had the benefits of democracy and were liberated from their
tyrannical past. In other words, Mexicans should be grateful to the
Anglo-Americans. If Mexicans and the Anglo-Americans clash, the
rationale runs, naturally it is because Mexicans cannot understand
or appreciate the merits of a free society, which must be defended
against ingrates. Therefore, domestic war, or repression, is justified
by the same kind of rhetoric that justifies international aggression.[36]

Professor Gene M. Brack, in the most recent of these works,
attacks those who base their research on Justin Smith's outdated
work: "American historians have consistently praised Justin
Smith's influential and outrageously ethnocentric account."[37]

THE MYTH OF A NONVIOLENT NATION

Most works on the Mexican-American War have dwelt on the
causes and results of the war, sometimes dealing with war strategy.[38] It is necessary, however, to go beyond this point, since the
war left bitterness, and since Anglo-American actions in Mexico are
vividly remembered. Mexicans' attitude toward Anglo-Americans
has been influenced by the war just as the United States' easy
victory conditioned Anglo-American behavior toward Mexicans.
Fortunately, many Anglo-Americans condemned this aggression
and flatly accused their leaders of being insolent, land hungry, and
of having manufactured the war. Abiel Abbott Livermore in *The
War with Mexico Reviewed* accused his country, writing:

> Again, the pride of race has swollen to still greater insolence the pride
> of country, always quite active enough for the due observance of the
> claims of universal brotherhood. The Anglo-Saxons have been appar-
> ently persuaded to think themselves the chosen people, annointed
> race of the Lord, commissioned to drive out the heathen, and plant
> their religion and institutions in every Canaan they could subju-
> gate. . . . Our treatment both of the red man and the black man has
> habituated us to feel our power and forget right. . . . The passion for

land, also, is a leading characteristic of the American people. . . . The god Terminus is an unknown deity in America. Like the hunger of the pauper boy of fiction, the cry had been, 'more, more, give us more.'[39]

Livermore's work, published in 1850, was awarded the American Peace Society prize for "the best review of the Mexican War and the principles of Christianity, and an enlightened statesmanship."

The United States provoked the war and then conducted it violently and brutally. Zachary Taylor's artillery leveled the Mexican city of Matamoros, killing hundreds of innocent civilians with *la bomba* (the bomb). Many Mexicans jumped into the Rio Grande, relieved of their pain by a watery grave.[40] The occupation that followed was even more terrorizing. Taylor's regular army was kept in control, but the volunteers presented another matter:

> The regulars regarded the volunteers, of whom about two thousand had reached Matamoros by the end of May, with impatience and contempt. . . . They robbed Mexicans of their cattle and corn, stole their fences for firewood, got drunk, and killed several inoffensive inhabitants of the town in the streets.[41]

There were numerous eyewitnesses to these incidents. For example, on July 25, 1846, Grant wrote to Julia Dent:

> Since we have been in Matamoros a great many murders have been committed, and what is strange there seemes [sic] to be very week [sic] means made use of to prevent frequent repetitions. Some of the volunteers and about all the Texans seem to think it perfectly right to impose on the people of a conquered City to any extent, and even to murder them where the act can be covered by dark. And how much they seem to enjoy acts of violence too! I would not pretend to guess the number of murders that have been committed upon the persons of poor Mexicans and our soldiers, since we have been here, but the number would startle you.[42]

On July 9, 1846, George Gordon Meade, who like Grant later became a general during the U.S. Civil War, wrote:

> They [the volunteers] have killed five or six innocent people walking in the street, for no other object than their own amusement. . . . They rob and steal the cattle and corn of the poor farmers, and in fact act more like a body of hostile Indians than civilized Whites. Their officers have no command or control over them. . . .[43]

Taylor knew about the atrocities, but Grant observed that Taylor did not restrain his men. In a letter to his superiors, Taylor admitted that "There is scarcely a form of crime that has not been reported to me as committed by them."[44] Taylor requested that they send no further troops from the state of Texas to him. These marauding acts were not limited to Taylor's men. The cannons from U.S. naval ships destroyed much of the civilian sector of Vera Cruz, leveling a hospital, churches, and homes. The bomb did not discriminate as to age or sex. Anglo-American troops destroyed almost every city they invaded; first it was put to the test of fire and then plundered. *Gringo* volunteers had little respect for anything, desecrating churches and abusing priests and nuns.

Military executions were common. Captured soldiers and civilians were hanged for cooperating with the guerillas. Many Irish immigrants, as well as some other Anglos, deserted to the Mexican side, forming the San Patricio Corps.[45] Many of the Irish were Catholics, and they resented treatment of Catholic priests and nuns by the invading Protestants. As many as 260 Anglo-Americans fought with the Mexicans at Churubusco in 1847:

> Some eighty appear to have been captured. . . . A number were found not guilty of deserting and were released. About fifteen, who had deserted before the declaration of war, were merely branded with a "D," and fifty of those taken at Churubusco were executed.[46]

Others received two hundred lashes and were forced to dig graves for their executed comrades.[47]

These acts were similar to those in Monterey when George Meade wrote on December 2, 1846:

> They plunder the poor inhabitants of everything they can lay their hands on, and shoot them when they remonstrate; and if one of their number happens to get into a drunken brawl and is killed, they run over the country, killing all the poor innocent people they find in their way to avenge, as they say, the murder of their brother. . . .[48]

As Scott's army left Monterey, they shot Mexican prisoners of war.[49]

Memoirs, diaries, and news articles written by Anglo-Americans document the reign of terror. Samuel F. Chamberlain's *My Confessions* is a record of Anglo racism and destruction. He was only 17 when he enlisted in the army to fight the "greasers." At the Mexican city of Parras, he wrote:

> We found the patrol had been guilty of many outrages. . . . They had ridden into the church of San José during Mass, the place crowded with kneeling women and children, and with oaths and ribald jest had arrested soldiers who had permission to be present.[50]

On another occasion, he described a massacre by volunteers, mostly from Yell's Cavalry, at a cave:

> On reaching the place we found a "greaser" shot and *scalped,* but still breathing; the poor fellow held in his hands a Rosary and a medal of the "Virgin of Guadalupe," only his feeble motions kept the fierce harpies from falling on him while yet alive. A Sabre thrust was given him in mercy, and on we went at a run. Soon shouts and curses, cries of women and children reached our ears, coming apparently from a cave at the end of the ravine. Climbing over the rocks we reached the entrance, and as soon as we could see in the comparative darkness a horrid sight was before us. The cave was full of our volunteers yelling like fiends, while on the rocky floor lay over twenty Mexicans, dead

and dying in pools of blood. Women and children were clinging to the knees of the murderers shrieking for mercy. . . . Most of the butchered Mexicans had been scalped; only three men were found unharmed. A rough crucifix was fastened to a rock, and some irreverent wretch had crowned the image with a bloody scalp. A sickening smell filled the place. The surviving women and children sent up loud screams on seeing us, thinking we had returned to finish the work! . . . No one was punished for this outrage.[51]

Near Satillo, Chamberlain reported the actions of Texas Rangers. His descriptions were graphic:

[A drunken Anglo] entered the church and tore down a large wooden figure of our Saviour, and making his lariat fast around its neck, he mounted his horse and galloped up and down the *plazuela*, dragging the statue behind. The venerable white-haired Priest, in attempting to rescue it, was thrown down and trampled under the feet of the Ranger's horse.[52]

Mexicans were enraged and attacked the Texan. Meanwhile, the Rangers returned:

As they charged into the square, they saw their miserable comrade hanging to the cross, his skin hanging in strips, surrounded by crowds of Mexicans. With yells of horror, the Rangers charged on the mass with Bowie Knife and revolver, sparing neither age or sex in their terrible fury.[53]

Chamberlain blamed General Taylor not only for collecting over $1 million (from the Mexican people) by force of arms, but also for letting "loose on the country packs of human bloodhounds called Texas Rangers." He goes on to describe the Rangers' brutality at the Rancho de San Francisco on the Camargo road near Agua Fria:

The place was surrounded, the doors forced in, and all the males capable of bearing arms were dragged out, tied to a post and shot!. . . Thirty-six Mexicans were shot at this place, a half hour given for the horrified survivors, women and children, to remove their little household goods, then the torch was applied to the houses, and by the light of the conflagration the ferocious *Tejanos* rode off to fresh scenes of blood.[54]

These wanton acts of cruelty, witnessed by one man, augmented by the reports of other chroniclers, add to the evidence that the United States, through the deeds of its soldiers, left a legacy of hate in Mexico.[55]

THE TREATY OF GUADALUPE HIDALGO

By late August 1847 the war was almost at an end. General Winfield Scott's defeat of Santa Anna in a hard-fought battle at Churubusco put Anglo-Americans at the gates of Mexico City. Santa Anna made overtures for an armistice, and for two weeks negotiations were conducted. Santa Anna reorganized his defenses and, in turn, the Anglo-Americans renewed their offensives. On September 13, 1847, Scott drove into the city. Although Mexicans fought valiantly, the battle left 4,000 of their men dead with another 3,000 taken prisoner. On September 13, before the occupation of Mexico City began, *Los Niños Héroes* (The Boy Heroes) fought off the conquerors and leapt to their deaths rather than surrender. These teenage cadets were Francisco Márquez, Agustin Melgar, Juan Escutia, Fernando Montes Oca, Vicente Suárez, and Juan de la Berrera. They became "a symbol and image of this unrighteous war."[56]

Although beaten, the Mexicans continued fighting. The presidency devolved to the presiding justice of the Supreme Court, Manuel de la Peña y Peña. He knew that Mexico had lost and that he had to salvage as much as possible. Pressure mounted, with U.S. troops in control of much of present-day Mexico.

Nicholas Trist, sent to Mexico to act as peace commissioner, had arrived in Vera Cruz on May 6, 1847, but controversy with Scott over Trist's authority and illness delayed arrangements for an armistice and hostilities continued. After the fall of Mexico City, Secretary of State James Buchanan wanted to revise Trist's instructions. He ordered Trist to break off negotiations and come home.[57] Polk apparently wanted more territory from Mexico while paying less for it. Trist, however, with the support of Winfield Scott, decided to ignore Polk's order, and began negotiations on January 2, 1848, on the original terms. Mexico, badly beaten, her government in a state of turmoil, had no choice but to agree to the Anglo-Americans' proposals.

On February 2, 1848, the Mexicans agreed to the Treaty of Guadalupe Hidalgo, in which Mexico accepted the Rio Grande as the Texas border and ceded the Southwest (which incorporated the present-day states of California, New Mexico, Nevada, and parts of Colorado, Arizona, and Utah) to the United States in return for $15 million.

Polk was furious about the treaty; he considered Trist "contemptibly base" for having ignored his orders. Yet he had no choice but to submit the treaty to the Senate. With the exception of article X, which concerned the rights of Mexicans in the ceded territory, the Senate ratified the treaty on March 10, 1848, by a vote of 28 to 14. To insist on more territory would have meant more fighting, and both Polk and the Senate realized that the war was already unpopular in many sections. The treaty was sent to the Mexican Congress for ratification; although the Congress had difficulty forming a quorum, the agreement was ratified on May 19 by a 52 to 35 vote.[58] Hostilities between the two nations were now officially ended. Trist, however, was branded as a "scoundrel," because Polk was disappointed in the settlement. There was considerable support and fervor in the United States for acquisition of all Mexico.[59]

During the treaty talks Mexican negotiators were concerned about Mexicans left behind and expressed great reservations about these people's being forced to "merge or blend" into Anglo-American culture. They protested the exclusion of provisions that protected Mexican citizens' rights, land titles, and religion.[60] They wanted to know the Mexicans' status, and protect their rights by treaty.

Articles VIII, IX, and X specifically referred to the rights of Mexicans. Under the treaty Mexicans left behind had one year to choose whether to return to Mexico or remain in "occupied Mexico." About 2,000 elected to leave; most remained in what they considered *their* land.

Article IX of the treaty guaranteed Mexicans "the enjoyment of all the rights of citizens of the United States according to the principles of the Constitution; and in the meantime shall be maintained and protected in the free enjoyment of their liberty and property, and secured in the free exercise of their religion without restriction."[61] While Anglo-Americans have respected the Chicanos' religion, their rights of cultural integrity and rights of citizenship have been constantly violated. Lynn I. Perrigo in *The American Southwest* summarizes the guarantees of articles VIII and IX: "In other words, besides the rights and duties of American citizenship, they [the Mexicans] would have some special privileges derived from their previous customs in language, law, and religion."[62]

The omitted article X had comprehensive guarantees protecting "all prior and pending titles to property of every description."[63] When this provision was deleted by the U.S. Senate, Mexican officials protested. Anglo-American emissaries reassured them by drafting a Statement of Protocol on May 26, 1848, which read:

> The American government by suppressing the Xth article of the Treaty of Guadalupe Hidalgo did not in any way intend to annul the grants of lands made by Mexico in the ceded territories. These grants . . . preserve the legal value which they may possess, and the grantees may cause their legitimate (titles) to be acknowledged before the American tribunals.
>
> Conformable to the law of the United States, legitimate titles to every description of property, personal and real, existing in the ceded territories, are those which were legitimate titles under the Mexican law of California and New Mexico up to the 13th of May, 1846, and in Texas up to the 2nd of March, 1836.[64]

Considering the Mexican opposition to the treaty, it is doubtful whether the Mexican Congress would have ratified the treaty without this clarification. The vote was close.

The Statement of Protocol was reinforced by articles VIII and

IX, which guaranteed Mexicans rights of property and protection under the law. In addition, court decisions have generally interpreted the treaty as protecting land titles and water rights. Generally, the treaty was ignored and during the nineteenth century most Mexicans in the United States were considered as a class apart from the dominant race.[65] Nearly every one of the obligations discussed above was violated, confirming the prophecy of Mexican diplomat Manuel Crescion Rejón who, at the time the treaty was signed, commented:

> Our race, our unfortunate people will have to wander in search of hospitality in a strange land, only to be ejected later. Descendants of the Indians that we are, the North Americans hate us, their spokesmen depreciate us, even if they recognize the justice of our cause, and they consider us unworthy to form with them one nation and one society, they clearly manifest that their future expansion begins with the territory that they take from us and pushing [sic] aside our citizens who inhabit the land.[66]

CONCLUSION

As a result of the Texas War and the Anglo-American aggressions of 1845–1848, the occupation of conquered territory began. The attitude of the Anglo, during the period of subjugation following the wars, is reflected in the conclusions of the past-president of the American Historical Association, Walter Prescott Webb:

> A homogenous European society adaptable to new conditions was necessary. This Spain did not have to offer in Arizona, New Mexico, and Texas. Its frontier, as it advanced, depended more and more on an Indian population. . . . This mixture of races meant in time that common soldiers in the Spanish service came largely from pueblo or sedentary Indian stock, whose blood, when compared to that of the plain Indians, was as ditch water. It took more than a little mixture of Spanish blood and mantle of Spanish service to make valiant soldiers of the timid Pueblo Indians.[67]

In material terms in exchange for 12,000 lives and more than $100,000,000 the United States acquired a colony two and a half times as large as France, containing rich farm lands and natural resources such as gold, silver, zinc, copper, oil, and uranium which would make possible its unprecedented industrial boom.[68] It acquired ports on the Pacific which generated further economic expansion across that ocean. Mexico was left with its shrunken resources to face the continued advances of the expanding capitalist force on its border.

NOTES

1. Robert A. Divine, ed., *American Foreign Policy* (New York: World Publishing, 1966), pp. 11–18.

2. Manual Medina Castro, *El Gran Despojo: Texas, Nuevo México, California* (México, D.F.: Editorial Diogenes, 1971), p. 9; Carlos E. Castañeda, *Our Catholic Heritage in Texas, 1519–1933*, vol. 6, *Transition Period: The Fight for Freedom, 1810–1836*, (New York: Arno Press, 1976), p. 86.
3. Richard W. Van Alstyne, *The Rising American Empire* (New York: Norton, 1974), p. 101; T. R. Fehrenbach, *Lone Star: A History of Texas and the Texans* (New York: Macmillan, 1968), p. 128; Castañada, vol. 6, pp. 160–162.
4. Walter Prescott Webb, *The Texas Rangers: A Century of Frontier Defense* (Austin: University of Texas Press, 1965), pp. 21–22.
5. Fehrenbach, pp. 163–164.
6. Van Alstyne, p. 101.
7. Eugene C. Barker, *Mexico and Texas, 1821–1835* (New York: Russell & Russell, 1965), pp. 52, 74–80, 80–82; David J. Weber, ed., *Foreigners in Their Native Land* (Albuquerque: University of New Mexico Press, 1973), p. 89, quoted in Fehrenbach, p. 182.
8. Castañeda, vol. 6, pp. 252–253; Fehrenbach, p. 181.
9. Nathaniel W. Stephenson, *Texas and the Mexican War: A Chronicle of the Winning of the Southwest* (New York: United States Publishing, 1921), p. 51.
10. Stephenson, p. 52; Barker, p. 128. Carlos Castañeda, in vol. 6, on p. 234 refers to Col. Anthony Butler, Jackson's minister to Mexico, as "an unscrupulous, passionate and scheming character . . . ." The new proposal provided final confirmation of the United States' intentions. Gene M. Brack, *Mexico Views Manifest Destiny, 1821–1846: An Essay on the Origins of the Mexican War* (Albuquerque: University of New Mexico Press, 1975) pp. 67–68, states that Jackson told the minister to do anything to get Texas.
11. Stephenson, p. 52.
12. Castañeda, vol. 6, 217–218.
13. Fehrenbach, p. 188. Hutchinson, p. 6, quotes a letter from Austin to Mrs. Mary Austin Holly: "The fact is, we must and ought to become a part of the United States. Money should be no consideration . . . . The more the American population is increased the more readily will the Mexican government give it up . . . . For fourteen years I have had a hard time of it, but nothing shall daunt my courage or abate my exertions to complete the main object of my labors, to *Americanize* Texas."
14. Castañeda, vol. 6, pp. 240–241.
15. Fehrenbach, p. 180.
16. Barker, pp. 146, 147, 148–149, 162.
17. Fehrenbach, p. 189.
18. Walter Lord, "Myths and Realities of the Alamo," *The American West* 5, no. 3 (May 1968): 18, 22, 24.
19. Lord, p. 25.
20. Carlos Castañeda, *Our Catholic Heritage in Texas, 1519–1933*, vol. 7, *The Church in Texas Since Independence, 1836–1950* (New York: Arno Press, 1976), p. 5.
21. Lota M. Spell, "Gorostiza and Texas," *Hispanic American Historical Review*, no. 4 (November 1957): 446.
22. Brack, pp. 74–75.
23. Burl Noggle, "Anglo Observers of the Southwest Borderlands, 1825–1890: The Rise of a Concept," *Arizona and the West* (Summer 1959): 122.
24. Van Alstyne, p. 106.
25. Medina Castro, p. 74, Charles A. Hale, *Mexican Liberalism in the Age of Mora, 1821–1853* (New Haven, Conn.: Yale University Press, 1968), pp. 11–12, 16.
26. On March 1, 1845, Congress passed the joint resolution, but it was not until July 1845 that a convention in Texas voted to accept annexation to the United States. The political maneuverings behind annexation in the U.S. Congress document the economic motive underlying it. Van Alstyne, p. 104, writes: "The pro-annexationists, some of whom like Senator Robert J. Walker of Mississippi had speculated heavily in Texas real estate, managed to influence public opinion in both North and South to the point where, on March 1, 1845, sufficient votes were mustered in Congress to authorize admission to the Union. There was a small margin of votes in each house in favor of annexation: in the House of Representatives, 22; in the Senate, only two."

27. José María Roa Barcena, *Recuerdos de la Invasión Norte Americana (1846–1848)*, ed. I. Antonio Castro Leal (México, D.F.: Editorial Porrua, 1947), pp. 25–27.

28. Albert C. Ramsey, ed. and trans., *The Old Side or Notes for the History of the War Between Mexico and the United States* (reprint ed., New York: Burt Franklin, 1970), pp. 28–29; Ramón Alcaraz et al., *Apuntes para la Historia de la Guerra Entre México y los Estados Unidos* (México, D.F.: Tipografía de Manuel Payno, Hiho, 1848), pp. 27–28. For an excellent account of Slidell's mission see Dennis Eugene Berge, "Mexican Response to United States Expansion, 1841–1848" (Ph.D. dissertation, University of California, 1965). Berge fully documents Slidell's arrogance, stating that at one point he even threatened war.

29. J. D. Richardson, *A Compilation of the Messages and Papers of the Presidents*, 10 vols. (Washington, D.C., 1905) 4:428–442, quoted in Arvin Rappaport, ed., *The War with Mexico: Why Did It Happen?* (Skokie, Ill: Rand McNally 1964), p. 16. Mexican authorities had been requested by Taylor to leave the area; most impartial sources consider his refusal a hostile act, especially since he accompanied it by a naval blockade of Mexican supply ships servicing Matamoros. Troops clashed initially on April 26, 1846; but the first major confrontation did not take place until May 8, 1846, 12 miles north of Matamoros (Berge, pp. 196–297). In short, the movement of U.S. troops forced the war on Mexico (Brack, p. 146).

30. Grady McWhiney and Sue McWhiney, eds., *To Mexico with Taylor and Scott, 1845–1847* (Waltham, Mass.: Praisell, 1969), p. 3.

31. Brack, p. 2.

32. Glen W. Price, *Origins of the War with Mexico: The Polk-Stockton Intrigue* (Austin: University of Texas Press, 1967), p. 7.

33. Rappaport, p. 16.

34. Rappaport, p. 16.

35. Justin H. Smith, *The War with Mexico*, vol. 2, (Gloucester, Mass.: Peter Smith, Publisher, 1963), p. 310.

36. Recently it has become fashionable for political theorists to oversimplify the war by reducing it to the victory of one system of production and land tenure over a less progressive one. This kind of extreme economic determinism results in the same conclusions that Justin Smith arrives at. See Raúl A. Fernández, *The United States-Mexico Border: A Politico-Economic Profile* (Notre Dame, Ind.: University of Notre Dame Press, 1977), p. 7. Seymour V. Connor and Odie B. Faulk, *North America Divided: The Mexican War, 1846–1848* (New York: Oxford University Press, 1971).

37. Brack, p. 185.

38. Brack, p. 10, states that the general view has been that Mexico erred because it chose to fight rather than "negotiate."

39. Abiel Abbott Livermore, *The War with Mexico Reviewed* (Boston: American Peace Society, 1850), pp. 8, 11, 12.

40. T. B. Thorpe, *Our Army on the Rio Grande*, quoted in Livermore, p. 126.

41. Alfred Hoyt Bill, *Rehearsal for Conflict* (New York: Knopf, 1947), p. 122.

42. John Y. Simon, *The Papers of Ulysses S. Grant*, vol. 1 (London, England and Amsterdam: Feffer & Simons, 1967), p. 102.

43. William Starr Meyers, ed., *The Mexican War Diary of General B. Clellan*, vol. 1 (Princeton: Princeton University Press, 1917), pp. 109–110.

44. Quoted in Livermore, pp. 148–149.

45. Smith, vol. 1, p. 550, n. 6.

46. Smith, vol. 2, p. 385, n. 18.

47. Livermore, p. 160.

48. Meyers, vol. 1, pp. 161–162.

49. Winfield Scott, *Memoirs of Lieut.-General Scott*, vol. 2 (New York: Sheldon, 1864), p. 392.

50. Samuel E. Chamberlain, *My Confessions* (New York: Harper & Row, 1956), p. 75.

51. Chamberlain, pp. 87, 88.

52. Chamberlain, p. 174.

53. Chamberlain, p. 174.

54. Chamberlain, pp. 176–177.

55. Stephen B. Oates, *"Los Diablos Tejanos:* The Texas Rangers," in Odie B. Faulk and Joseph A. Stout, Jr., eds., *The Mexican War: Changing Interpretations* (Chicago: Sage, 1973), p. 121.
56. Alonso Zabre, *Guide to the History of Mexico: A Modern Interpretation* (Austin, Tex.: Pemberton Press, 1969), p. 300.
57. Dexter Perkins and Glyndon G. Van Deusen, *The American Democracy: Its Rise to Power* (New York: Macmillan, 1964), p. 273.
58. Robert Self Henry, *The Story of the Mexican War* (New York: Ungar, 1950), p. 390.
59. See John D. P. Fuller, *The Movement for the Acquisition of All Mexico* (New York: DaCapo Press, 1969).
60. Letter from Commissioner Trist to Secretary Buchanan, Mexico, January 25, 1848, *Senate Executive Documents*, no. 52, p. 283.
61. Wayne Moquin et al., eds., *A Documentary History of the Mexican American* (New York: Praeger, 1971), p. 185.
62. Lynn I. Perrigo, *The American Southwest* (New York: Holt, Rinehart and Winston, 1971), p. 176.
63. Perrigo, p. 176.
64. *Compilation of Treaties in Force* (Washington, D.C.: U.S. Government Printing Office, 1899), p. 402, quoted in Perrigo, p. 176.
65. Weber, p. 14, states that the Supreme Court in *McKinney v. Saviego*, 1855, found that the treaty did not apply to Texas.
66. Antonio de la Peña y Reyes, *Algunos Documentos Sobre el Tratado de Guadalupe-Hidalgo* (México, D.F.: Sec de Rel. Ext. 1930), p. 159, quoted in Richard Gonzales, "Commentary on the Treaty of Guadalupe Hidalgo," in Feliciano Rivera, *A Mexican American Source Book* (Menlo Park, Calif.: Educational Consulting Associates, 1970), p. 185.
67. Walter Prescott Webb, *The Great Plains* (New York: Grosset & Dunlap, 1931), pp. 125–126.
68. Leroy B. Hafen and Carl Coke Rister, *Western America*, 2nd ed. (Englewood Cliffs, N.J.: Prentice-Hall, 1950), p. 312.

Chapter 2
Remember the Alamo: The Colonization of Texas

Texan-Mexican hostilities did not end after 1836. Mexico refused to recognize the Republic of Texas. The issue of the prisoners of war continued. Texans kept Mexican soldiers in cages, where many died of starvation and where they suffered untold indignities.[1]

The boundary question also remained an issue, with all the territory between the Rio Grande and the Nueces River in dispute. Anglo-American immigration into the Republic of Texas increased, reaching 100,000 by the 1840s.

To escape racism, Mexicans moved farther into the southern portion of the new republic. Substantial numbers settled in the disputed territory. When hostilities again erupted into war, South Texas became the gateway for Zachary Taylor's invasion of northern Mexico, and the Mexicans in that portion of Texas suffered greatly from Anglo-American violence.

In the years before annexation to the United States, Texans actively warred on the Indians and stepped up their diplomatic front against Mexico. President Mirabeau B. Lamar dreamt of expanding the republic, and in 1839 and 1840, taking advantage of Mexico's problems with France, pressed for a settlement of the boundary question, offering Mexico $5 million if it would accept the Rio Grande as the territorial border. In 1841 he involved himself in Mexican internal affairs by signing a treaty with Yucatán, a southeastern Mexican state, which was attempting to secede from Mexico. That same year Lamar sent the ill-fated Santa Fe Expedition into New Mexico in a scheme to add that area to the republic (see Chapter 3).

During the late 1830s tension was acute along the border. Black Texan slaves who crossed into Mexico to freedom aggravated the situation. By 1855 some 4,000 fugitive slaves had run away to northern Mexico. Texas authorities valued the loss at $3,200,000 and blamed Mexican authorities for encouraging slaves to escape. When owners demanded their return, the Mexican authorities refused. Texans financed several expeditions to recover runaways, greatly adding to border tensions. Their anger at authorities soon was generalized to include all Mexicans; they were all suspected of aiding the Blacks and therefore all subject to attack.[2]

A caste system developed in Texas that condemned Mexicans, because of their race and culture, to the lower stratum. The Texas

Constitution aided in the oppression of Mexicans by excluding from citizenship or ownership of property anyone who had refused to participate in their so-called revolution.[3] Naturally all Mexicans were presumed guilty of supporting the Mexican government which the Texans had overthrown.

THE APOLOGISTS AND THE TEXAS RANGERS

Walter Prescott Webb, until his death in March 1963, was the dean of Texan historians. The most respected professor in history on the faculty of the University of Texas at Austin and past-president of the American Historical Association, he wielded considerable influence among scholars and graduate students. His most important works were *The Texas Rangers, The Great Plains, Divided We Stand,* and *The Great Frontier;* in addition, he wrote countless articles.

Webb's writings have had considerable impact on the historiography of the West. Recently, however, some scholars have begun to question many of his conclusions, implying that they are racist. Among these scholars are Américo Paredes, Llerena B. Friend, and Larry McMurtry.

McMurtry writes of Webb's *The Texas Rangers:* "The flaw in the book is a flaw of attitude. Webb admired the Rangers inordinately, and as a consequence the book mixes homage with history in a manner one can only think sloppy. His own facts about the Rangers contradict again and again his characterization of them as 'quiet, deliberate, gentle' men."[4] McMurtry then points out some of the inconsistencies. He faults Webb's description of the Rangers' role in the siege of Mexico City: "A sneak thief stole a handkerchief from them. They shot him." One Texas Ranger was shot, and the Rangers retaliated by killing 80 Mexicans. McMurtry concludes: "[These] are hardly the actions of men who can accurately be called gentle." McMurtry also questions Webb's description of Ranger Captain L. H. McNeely as a "flame of courage."[5] McMurtry states of McNeely, "He did a brilliant, brave job, and his methods were absolutely ruthless." McNeely tortured Mexicans and shot them down in cold blood. On November 19, 1875, he crossed the border with thirty-one men and attacked a ranch that he thought housed Mexican troops. He was mistaken, and he murdered a number of innocent Mexican workers. When he discovered his error, he merely rode off. Webb's apology for the Rangers is that "Affairs on the border cannot be judged by standards that hold elsewhere." McMurtry responds: "Why they can't is a question apologists for the Rangers have yet to answer. Torture is torture, whether inflicted in Germany, Algiers, or along the Nueces Strip. The Rangers, of course, claimed that their end justified their means, but people who practice torture always claim that."[6]

Webb had ceased being a historian and had become a Ranger by proxy. While he must have recognized the brutality of these violent men, he closed his eyes to it. McMurtry sheds more light on the situation, writing:

> The important point to be made about *The Texas Rangers* is that Webb was writing not as an historian of the frontier, but as a symbolic frontiersman. The tendency to practice symbolic frontiersmanship might almost be said to characterize the twentieth century Texan, whether he be an intellectual, a cowboy, a businessman, or a politician.[7]

McMurtry's work explores the effect of this frontiersmanship. It is also significant that Webb was a scholarly man who did not have evil motives. His works were, however, racist.

By the end of Webb's long career, his viewpoint of the Chicano had changed. When he published an article, in *True West* in October 1962, "The Bandits of Las Cuevas," he received a letter from Enrique Mendiola of Alice, Texas, whose grandfather owned the ranch that Rangers under McNeely, mistakenly attacked. Mendiola stated:

> Most historians have classified these men as cattle thieves, bandits, etc. This might be true of some of the crowd, but most of them, including General Juan Flores, were trying to recover their own cattle that had been taken away from them when they were driven out of their little ranches in South Texas. They were driven out by such men as Mifflin Kenedy, Richard King and [the] Armstrongs.[8]

He stated that there was stealing back and forth. Webb's reply to Mendiola was revealing:

> To get a balanced account, one would need the records from the south side of the river, and these are simply not available. . . . The unfortunate fact is that the Mexicans were not as good at keeping records as were the people on this side. . . . I have often wished that the Mexicans, or some one who had their confidence, would have gone among them and got their stories of the raids and counter raids. I am sure that these stories would take on a different color and tone.[9]

Mexicans did, in fact, record their story in *corridos* (ballads). The *corridos* glorified the deeds of men who stood up to the oppressors and are still sung in the Rio Grande Valley and in other places in the Southwest. *Corridos* to Juan Cortina were composed when he resisted the *gringo* in the 1850s.[10] From those early times to the present, *corridos* have recorded the Mexicans' struggle against racism and injustice.

The traditional view of the Texas Ranger was expressed by Rip Ford, a Ranger himself, who wrote: "A Texas Ranger can ride like a Mexican, trail like an Indian, shoot like a Tennesseean, and fight like the very devil!"[11] T. R. Fehrenbach, in 1968, wrote in his *Lone Star: A History of Texas and Texans:*

To fight Indians and Mexicans, Ranger leaders had to learn to think like both, or at least, to understand what Mexicans and Indians feared. The collision between the Anglo-American and the Mexican on the southern frontier was inevitable, but some aspects of this were unfortunate. Contact did not improve either race; it seemed to strengthen and enhance the vices of both. The Ranger arrived with instinctive Teutonic directness, preferring the honest smash of the bullet to the subtlety of the knife. But against the Mexican, bluntness turned into brutality, because it was almost impossible for the Protestant Anglo-Celt to understand the Hispanic mind. Impatient with Mexican deviousness, the Ranger reacted with straight force. But the Mexican, to keep the records straight, slipped from deviousness to outright treachery; history records that Mexicans killed more Texans by the result of parleys than on all the battlefields. Each side felt themselves justified because of the incomprehensible and despised cultural attributes of the foe. The Rangers seemed barbaric Nordics, void of all gentlemanly intrigue or guile; they saw the Mexicans as treacherous, lying people, who never wanted to do the obvious, which was to call their play and fight.[12]

Webb, who was even less objective in his analysis of cultural differences between the Rangers and the Mexicans, wrote of the Ranger:

> When we see him at his daily task of maintaining law, restoring order, and promoting peace—even though his methods be vigorous—we see him in the proper setting, a man standing alone between a society and its enemies.[13]

Conversely, he wrote of Mexicans:

> Without disparagement it may be said that there is a cruel streak in the Mexican nature, or so the history of Texas would lead one to believe. This cruelty may be a heritage from the Spanish of the Inquisition; it may, and doubtless should, be attributed partly to the Indian blood.[14]

This type of reasoning justified the Rangers' violence to many Anglo-Americans; the "vigorous methods" were necessary in dealing with "savage adversaries."

Américo Paredes gives another perspective of the Rangers. He described them as representatives of Anglo ranchers and merchants who controlled the valley of the Rio Grande. Their commitment was to keep order for an Anglo oligarchy. Violence served the interests of Texas capitalists as a means to maintain a closed social structure that excluded Mexicans from all but the lowest levels. They recruited gunslingers who burned with a hatred of Mexicans, shooting first and asking questions afterwards. Paredes writes: "That the Rangers stirred up more trouble than they put down is an opinion that has been expressed by less partisan sources."[15]

Paredes was one of the first Chicano scholars to attack the Rangers and, by inference, Webb. He expressed how Mexicans felt. His research was based on oral traditions and documents. His findings refuted those of Webb. For example in the murder of the Cerdas, a prominent family near Brownsville in 1902, Paredes wrote:

> The Cerdas were prosperous ranchers near Brownsville, but it was their misfortune to live next to one of the "cattle barons" who was not through expanding yet. One day three Texas Rangers came down from Austin and "executed" the elder Cerda and one of his sons as cattle rustlers. The youngest son fled across the river, and thus the Cerda ranch was vacated. Five months later the remaining son Alfredo Cerda crossed over to Brownsville. He died the same day, shot down by a Ranger's gun.[16]

Paredes' account was based not only on official sources, but on eyewitness accounts. Marcelo Garza, Sr., of Brownsville, a respected businessman, told Paredes that a Ranger shot unarmed Alfredo, stalking him "like a wild animal."

Webb's version was based on Ranger sources. According to Webb, Baker, a Ranger, surprised Ramón De La Cerda branding a calf that belonged to the King Ranch. De La Cerda shot at Baker and the Ranger shot back, killing Ramón in self-defense. The Ranger was cleared at an inquest, but Mexicans did not accept this verdict and disinterred De La Cerda's body and conducted their own inquest. They found:

> "evidence" [quotes are Webb's] . . . to the effect that De La Cerda had been dragged and otherwise maltreated. Public sentiment was sharply divided. . . . The findings of the secret inquest, together with wild rumors growing out of it, only served to inflame the minds of De La Cerda's supporters.[17]

Again, Webb's sources were compromised, and he based his conclusion that the people were being inflamed on Ranger reports. Webb admitted that a double standard of justice operated for Mexicans and Anglos. Therefore, it was natural that they should question findings of the inquest, especially the facts behind this particular shooting. The Cerdas were a well-known and respected family whose land the Kings coveted.

More telling is Webb's quote as to who posted bail for Baker: "Captain Brooks reported that Baker made bail in the sum of ten thousand dollars, and that he was supported by such people as the Kings, Major John Armstrong—McNeely's lieutenant—and the Lyman Brothers."[18]

The historian wonders why Webb did not question the support of the Kings. It is no wonder that Mexicans were inflamed. Shortly afterward Baker shot Alfredo, Ramón's younger brother. The Cerda affair exposed the use of violence to take over land and then legalize murder through the court system. It was not an isolated incident; it represented the activity of Rangers throughout the century.

During the uprising led by Juan Cortina hundreds, if not thousands, of Mexicans were victimized because they were relatives of partisans or because they were suspected of being associated with revolutionaries. Rangers, operating independently of the traditional law enforcement agencies, were proud of their efficiency in dealing with Mexicans. (Further examples of Texas Ranger terrorism are discussed in Chapter 10.)

THE TEXAS ROBBER BARONS

The Texas Rangers facilitated the domination of the area by a handful of unscrupulous and brutal men who corrupted local and state authorities. To gain control, these men assassinated their opposition, stole their homes, and appropriated their cattle.

Before 1848, the valley of the Rio Grande supported many thousands of cattle. It had towns, such as Laredo, Guerrero, Mier, Camargo, and Reynosa, that had been founded before 1755. It supported self-reliant communities in which the people raised corn, beans, melons, and vegetables and also tended sheep and goats. Commerce between the people on both sides of the river helped to bind them together. Life for Mexicans in the other sections of Texas, while not exactly the same, closely resembled the life style of the Rio Grande people. It was not the highly organized and profit-yielding structure Anglos were accustomed to and considered productive. Compared to the technological standards of the United States, the economy of the valley was underdeveloped.

With the Anglo invasion technological changes took place in the region's economy. Class divisions became more marked within the Mexican community as the upper class often aligned themselves with the new elite, either to maintain their privilege or to move vertically within the new system. In many cases rich Mexicans became brokers for the new elite and helped keep the masses of Mexicans in their place. In Brownsville men like Francisco Ytúrria, Jeremiah Galván, and the Spaniard José San Román amassed fortunes by allying themselves with Charles Stillman.[19]

Charles Stillman arrived in the valley in 1846 and started a trading center in a cotton field across the river from Matamoros. Within four years a booming trade with Mexico created the rapidly developing town of Brownsville. This boom drove land prices up and attracted more Anglo-Americans, who came to capitalize on the prosperity.

A substantial number of newcomers were war veterans who still looked upon Mexicans as the losers. They felt that Mexicans had done nothing to improve the land and that they benefited from the Anglo-American occupation. These men did not recognize Mexican land titles and felt few qualms about taking property from them. Racial and nativist arguments justified their chicanery. At first, Stillman and others feared that the state of Texas would protect Mexican land claims, so they attempted to create their own state. They played on the Mexicans' regional feelings and many Mexicans supported the separatist movement.[20] The group enlisted powerful congressional allies such as Henry Clay and William Seward. Separatists were led by Richard King, James O'Donnell, Charles Stillman, Captain Mifflin Kenedy, and Sam Belden—all prominent members of the privileged elite. Their plans for secession proved unnecessary because it was soon evident that the state of Texas supported the Anglos' encroachments.

Conditions in the valley proved to be a bonanza to Stillman. He used unscrupulous means to build up his annual earnings to $50,000. His trading post was built on land that did not belong to him; the land around Brownsville belonged to the descendants of Francisco Cavazos. After 1848 the Cavazos' title to the land was known as the *Espíritu Santo* Grant. Stillman wanted the land, but he did not want to pay for it, so he devised a scheme to create confusion about ownership. Squatters moved onto the Cavazos' land and claimed it on the grounds of veterans' as well as squatters' rights. Ignoring the fact that these actions violated the Treaty of Guadalupe Hidalgo and its Statement of Protocol, Stillman purchased the squatters' claims, as well as other questionable titles, refusing to deal with the Cavazos family and knowing he had the support of the troops at Fort Brown.

The Cavazos family fought Stillman in the courts. Judge Waltrous, the presiding judge, was a friend of Stillman. Moreover, many Anglos believed that the "whole *Espíritu Santo* Grant should be thrown out on the grounds that the owners were Mexicans." Stillman, however, had made many enemies who pressured the judge to decide against Stillman. On January 15, 1852, Judge Waltrous ruled in favor of the Cavazos family, validating their title to the land. Stillman had his lawyers, the firm of Basse and Horde, offer $33,000 for the grant, which in 1850 was evaluated at $214,000.[21] Stillman had made it known that he would appeal the decision, so the Cavazos family accepted the offer; the legal costs to defend the grant would have been prohibitive. Moreover, the Cavazos family knew that Stillman had influence in the political and judicial hierarchy of the state. After the sale the law firm transferred title to Stillman, yet he did not pay the $33,000; neither did the law firm, since it went bankrupt.

During the 1850s, the border became a battleground with U.S. merchants waging an economic war against Mexico. Ranger "Rip" Ford estimates that as much as $10 to 14 million passed by way of the Rio Grande annually.[22] Fierce competition between U.S. and Mexican merchants raged, and violence increased. In 1855, along the Nueces River, eleven Mexicans were lynched. In 1857 in San Antonio Mexican cartmen were literally run out of business by Anglo freighters who were angry because Mexicans carried goods more cheaply and quickly between Indianola and San Antonio; the freighters attacked the Mexican cartmen, murdering an estimated seventy-five.[23] In the same year residents of Uvalde County passed a resolution prohibiting Mexicans from traveling through the county unless they had a passport. At Goliad the townspeople killed several Mexicans because they drove carts on public roads.[24]

In spite of the violence border towns grew. Matamoros went from 18,000 to 50,000 by the end of 1862 and became an international market place with an estimated weekly volume of $2,000,000 in trade during the 1850s.[25] The potential in profits from this growth attracted North American merchants who formed associations to control trade and who openly participated in smuggling, cattle rustling, and other crimes. In 1858 Governor Ramón Guerra of Tamaulipas created *La Zona Libre*, the Free Zone, within which Mexican merchants were exempt from federal tariffs (paying only small municipal taxes and an administrative fee). The purpose of *La Zona* was to combat rampant smuggling from which Anglo-American merchants reaped vast fortunes. The act exempted Matamoros, Reynosa, Camargo, Mier, Guerrero, and Nuevo Leon. In 1861 Mexican federal law extended the zone from the Gulf of Mexico to the Pacific within 12.5 miles of the border with the United States.[26]

U.S. merchants vehemently objected to trade advantages gained by Mexican merchants in Mexico. Brownsville merchants applied political pressure on the U.S. government to intervene and to invade Mexico if necessary. They claimed that they lost from $2 to $6 million annually. They made numerous charges against Mexicans, claiming that they sponsored frequent raids into the United States.

U.S. merchants made the controversy pay off; the claim of the "Mexican threat" justified maintenance of large contingents of U.S. troops along the border. The presence of forts contributed greatly to the economy of the region, for forts meant soldiers, horses, and government contracts. The additional revenues were a bonanza for the merchants and cattlemen along the border. A withdrawal of troops would have caused an economic depression for the valley merchants and ranchers. Increasingly, they relied on the forts and soldiers as a source of revenue which they protected at any cost.[27]

The Mexicans' land and wealth quickly passed into the hands of an oligarchy. By 1860 Anglo-Americans completely dominated the Texas economy. A census taken in that year showed that 263 Texans owned over $100,000 in real property; 57 of these wealthy men lived in southeast Texas; only 2 were of Mexican extraction and their holdings were in Cameron County. Bexar County had 7 wealthy Texans, not one of whom was a Mexican. Of significance is that the real property value and the personal worth of the 261 Texans was roughly in balance, while the 2 Mexicans' personal worth was far below their real wealth.[28]

Stillman's associate, Richard King, was the arch-robber baron of South Texas. His career is difficult to assess since his descendants control his records and have carefully censored them. Richard King amassed over 600,000 acres of land during his lifetime, and his widow increased the family holdings to over 1,000,000 acres.

The King Ranch Corporation commissioned a professional author and artist, Tom Lea, to eulogize Richard King in a two-volume work entitled *The King Ranch*. Lea portrayed King as a tough-minded, two-fisted Horatio Alger who brought prosperity to South Texas. In the process Richard King, according to Lea, never harmed anyone, except in self-defense. Lea denied charges against King and ignores the allegations that he unscrupulously drove out small Mexican ranchers to get their land and was brutal to those who opposed him. When referring to Mexican resentment toward Anglos like King, Lea writes it off as jealousy.[29]

Richard King was born in 1824 in New York City of poor Irish immigrant parents. As a youth he ran away to sea, eventually becoming a pilot on a steamboat that was mastered by Mifflin Kenedy. The two men became fast friends. The Mexican-American War took them to the Rio Grande, and after the war they remained to cash in on the boom. King ran a flophouse at Boca del Rio and later bought a vessel from the U.S. government and went into the freighting business. Much of his business consisted of smuggling goods to the Mexican ranchers and miners in northern Mexico.

Although at first the principal competitor of King and Kenedy was Charles Stillman, in 1850 they joined him. The association prospered, soon monopolizing the water-borne trade into northern Mexico. In 1852 King purchased the *Santa Gertrudis* Grant. Title to 15,500 acres cost him less than 2¢ an acre. King also entered into a land purchasing partnership with Gideon K. Lewis, later buying Lewis's shares.

During the Civil War King was pro-South and profited from the war trade by selling cattle, horses, and mules to the troops. He continued his freighting operations, running Union blockades by flying the Mexican flag. In 1866 Stillman left the border area, and King and Kenedy took over many of his operations.

In the 1870s, the Mexican Border Commission reported that much of the border friction was caused by Texas thieves. The report claimed that Mexicans raided the Nueces area to retrieve their stolen cattle and that Richard King branded calves "that belonged to his neighbor's cows."[30] The report indicted King, charging that he did not respect the law and that he employed known cattle rustlers such as Tomás Vásquez and Fernando López to steal cattle and horses from Mexicans. Other prominent Texans such as Thadeus Rhodes, a justice of the peace in Hidalgo County, were also accused of making huge profits from cattle rustling.[31]

During this period King became president of the Stock Raisers

Association of Western Texas formed by Texas ranchers to protect their "interests." They organized a private militia, called minute companies, to fight so-called Mexican bandits. Later they disbanded when Ranger Captain McNeely took over the fight for them.

King made his money as a smuggler; he associated with a band of cutthroats and, in fact, played a leading role in their operations; he was accused of cattle rustling and of murdering small land owners to get their land; and he paid bonuses to the Rangers.

THE REVOLT OF "CHENO" CORTINA

An oligarchy of Anglo-Americans controlled the wealth. Class was largely based on race. One result of this process was banditry. Denied the opportunity to acquire property, to exercise political control over their own lives, and to maintain their rights within the society, many took to the highway. Added to this were conditions of lawlessness that prevailed among all groups on the frontier, the disruptions of the Mexican and Civil wars, and the often corrupt nature of the administration of justice. These circumstances made attempts to survive outside the law inevitable.[32]

E. J. Hobsbawm, in his *Primitive Rebels: Studies in Archaic Forms of Social Movement in the 19th and 20th Centuries*, sheds light on the *bandidos'* motives. Taking Mexican banditry in the context of history, it represented "in one sense . . . a primitive form of organized social protest, perhaps the most primitive we know."[33]

For example, California outlaw Tiburcio Vásquez (see Chapter 5), having once broken an Anglo-American law, became an outcast who was forced to steal to survive. Like other Mexican *bandidos*, his activities were directed against Anglo-Americans and only in time of dire need did he steal from his own people. In this way he retained the support of the Mexican people, who considered him a hero, a Robin Hood of sorts (even though he never gave to the poor). "The tough man . . . unwilling to bear traditional burdens of the common man in a class society, poverty and meekness."[34] He revolted against the *gringo* and the people admired him for doing what they were unwilling to do.

Vásquez and other Mexican bandits easily fit the Hobsbawm model of the primitive rebel. However, Juan N. Cortina, who has been called the "Red Robber of the Rio Grande," goes beyond the *bandido* model. Unlike the social bandit, he had an organization with a definite ideology that led guerrilla warfare against the *gringo* establishment. As with so much of the Chicano's history, Mexican records must be examined, especially those of Tamaulipas, to understand the rise of Juan Cortina.[35]

As in the case of the social rebels, an attempt has been made to discredit Cortina's motives. Many Anglo-American historians have labeled him an outlaw. They portray him as an illiterate rogue who came from a good family but "turned bad." Lyman Woodman, a retired military officer, wrote a biography of Cortina, describing him as a "soldier, bandit, murderer, cattle thief, mail robber, civil and military governor of the State of Tamaulipas, and general in the Mexican army" who was, in short, a *gringo* hater.[36]

Juan "Cheno" Cortina, a product of Mexico's northern frontier, was born on May 16, 1822, in Camargo, located on the Mexican side of the river. His parents were from the upper class, and his mother owned a land grant in the vicinity of Brownsville. Cortina and his family moved to that grant while the War of 1846 raged. He did not return to Mexico, and, under the terms of the Treaty of Guadalupe Hidalgo, became a U.S. citizen.[37] Cortina was a regionalist who identified with northern Mexico and had fought to protect the land from the Anglo-Americans. He also resented the abuses, insults, and plundering that marked the Anglo-American occupation.

In the period after the war, however, Cortina gave little indication that he would emerge as the border's leading champion of Mexicans. He backed the filibustering expeditions led by José María Cabajal in 1851 which were financed by local Anglo merchants who wanted to separate the Rio Grande Valley from Texas to form the Republic of the Sierra Madre. The separatists were led by people like King and Kenedy who were hardly friends of Mexicans. He also engaged in rustling Mexican cattle in partnership with the nefarious German, Adolphus Glavecke. Glavecke gave evidence against Cortina in the spring of 1859 and Cortina was indicted for cattle stealing. Glavecke continued a personal vendetta against Cortina. He had political clout, serving at various times as alderman for the city of Brownsville, and played a major role in building the legend of Cortina as a notorious bandit.[38]

The betrayal, indictment, and prosecution embittered Cortina and proved to be the prelude to a complete change in his life. Cortina's revolutionary career began on a hot July morning in 1859. While returning to his mother's ranch, he saw Marshall Bob Spears pistol-whipping a Mexican who had had too much to drink. The victim had worked for Cheno's mother. Cheno offered to take responsibility for the offender, but Spears replied, "What is it to you, you damned Mexican?" Cortina fired a warning shot, and then shot the marshall in the shoulder. He then rode off with the victim.

With no possibility of a fair trail, Cheno prepared to leave for Tampico, Mexico. Before his departure with fifty to sixty followers, he rode into Brownsville and raised the Mexican flag. Cortina's detractors claim that he plundered the city; however, his partisans point out that he did not rob and steal when he had the city at his mercy as he certainly would have done had he been a bandit. He and his men attacked those who had blatantly persecuted Mexicans, killing the jailer and four other men, including William P.

Neal and George Morris, both of whom had murdered innocent Mexicans but continued to walk the streets.[39]

Cortina did not plan to lead a revolution when, from his mother's *Rancho del Carmen*, he issued a circular justifying his actions. The crux of his "declaration of grievances" was the injustice that Mexicans suffered at the hands of the occupiers. According to Cortina, he had gone to Brownsville solely to punish those guilty of terrorizing Mexicans, and he appealed to the Anglo-American government to bring the "oppressors of the Mexicans" to justice and not to protect them. Cortina, after issuing his statement, again prepared to emigrate to Mexico.

Seeking revenge, Brownsville citizens took Tomás Cabrera prisoner. Cabrera was a man of advanced age whose only crime was that he was Cortina's friend. When Cortina learned that his friend had been arrested, he recruited an army of about 1,200 men. He demanded the old man's release, threatening to burn Brownsville if the townspeople did not comply. The Brownsville Tigers (the local militia) and the Mexican army at Matamoros attacked him, but Cortina defeated them in battle, whereupon the *gringos* lynched Cabrera. Rangers were called in, but he defeated them as well. The merchants protested to Mexican authorities, but the Mexicans disclaimed responsibility since Cortina was a U.S. citizen.[40]

Flushed by his victories, he "envisioned raising an army powerful enough to force the Texas authorities to grant the Mexicans those rights . . . guaranteed them by the Treaty of Guadalupe Hidalgo."[41] He issued a proclamation that "reviewed the crimes against Mexicans" and suggested that the colonized form a secret society to achieve justice. He called for the liberation of Mexicans and the extermination of the "tyrants." He charged that the Mexicans' land had been stolen from them by "flocks of vampires, in guise of men." Cortina continued:

> It would appear that justice had fled from this world, leaving you to the caprice of your oppressors. . . . The race has never humbled itself before the conqueror. . . . Mexicans! My part is taken; the voice of revelation whispers to me that to me is entrusted the work of breaking the chains of your slavery, and that the Lord will enable me, with powerful arm to fight against our enemies.[42]

Not all Mexicans supported Cortina; the upper class often joined in the oppression of their own people.[43] Cortina's main appeal was among the poor, a fact that is admitted by Ranger "Rip" Ford:

> Sometimes Cortina would make a speech in the market place and the poor would listen intently to what he had to say. He would not harm the innocent, but would fight for the emancipation of the hungry *peons* along the border. . . . They must love the land for the land was all they had.[44]

The reaction of state authorities was violent. Many innocent people became victims. Federal troops poured into the valley, forcing Cortina across the border. A state commissioner wrote Governor Sam Houston:

> The Mexicans are arming everything that can carry a gun, and I anticipate much trouble here. I believe that a general war is inevitable. . . . New arms have been distributed to all the *rancheros,* so I apprehend trouble."[45]

Houston appealed to the federal government for assistance and wrote to the secretary of war for help.[46]

Newspapers echoed Houston. The *San Antonio Light* played up the Cortina threat, headlining "Brownsville Captured: 100 Americans Slain." New Orleans merchants petitioned for more U.S. troops to fight Cortina. Rumors circulated in the national press that Cortina had captured Corpus Christi. Ironically, this came at a time when the U.S. government was removing troops from Brownsville, Laredo, and Eagle Pass.[47]

Washington responded in February 1860 by sending Robert E. Lee to Texas to lead the expeditions against Cortina. Mexican authorities cooperated with Lee. However, throughout March Lee could not catch the elusive Cortina and began referring to "that myth Cortina."

Rumors raged that Cortina threatened all strategic points, but by May Lee believed that Cortina had left Texas. Cortina had not abandoned his war with the *gringo;* he had merely shifted his base of operations. He went to Tamaulipas where from 1861 to 1867 he was involved in defending the state against the French. He settled in Tamaulipas and became for a time its military governor as well as a general in the Mexican army. After the war with France, he allegedly controlled the politics of Tamaulipas, making and unmaking governors. He cleaned up banditry in Tamaulipas. Anglo-Americans claimed that he "told thieves in Mexico that he would hang them for stealing in that country, but that there was plenty for them to take in Texas." From his base in Mexico he allegedly led rustling operations against the Anglo-Americans and had a flourishing trade with Cuba, thus hitting at the heart of Anglo-American concerns—its economy. It was reported that King and Kenedy lost 200,000 head of cattle and 5300 horses from 1869 to 1872.[48] Rip Ford wrote: "Cortina hates Americans, particularly Texans. . . . He has an old and deep-seated grudge against Brownsville."[49]

A reign of terror began which is difficult to put into perspective because of the sensationalism and outright lies of the press. Robert Taylor, a commissioner sent by Houston to investigate matters on the border, filed a confidential report: "I am sorry to say a good many of the latter [Anglos] in fact some of them who have been

Burning and Hanging and shooting Mexicans without authority by law are more dreaded than Cortina."[50]

The 1870s saw an intensification of hostilities between North Americans and Mexicans. Vigilantes took the law into their hands spreading more terror. They effectively used Cortina as an excuse, stating in October 1871 that Cortina had formed a cavalry corps. Rangers had fourteen companies in 1870; when they were disbanded two years later, twenty-seven state militia minutemen companies took their places. Merchants, claiming that they were losing 5,000 cows a month, increased the tensions as they called for more federal troops and demanded that the United States take over northern Mexico to the Sierra Madres.[51]

The Frontier Protection Act of 1874 reestablished the Rangers and six mounted batallions of seventy-five men each roamed the region. During the spring and summer of that year a virtual race war raged. Anglo ranchers had more than adequate support in these wars: "After a group attacked Woakes' Store some fifteen miles from Corpus Christi in 1875, Anglos began general warfare against Mexicans in the region, killing wantonly many peaceful Mexican residents who had no connection with any bandit activity."[52] Naturally, they blamed Cortina for the invasion.[53]

The Anglo forces had no success against Cortina, but during the 1870s, as U.S. political influence with the Mexican government increased, pressure was brought to eliminate him. In 1875 he was taken to Mexico City and jailed on charges of cattle rustling. When Porfirio Díaz seized power, Cortina was exiled to Mexico City. He did not return to the border until the spring of 1890, when he visited the area for a brief time, receiving a hero's welcome.

THE PEOPLE'S REVOLT

The El Paso Salt War of 1877 is an example of a people's revolt. Mexicans in the country banded together along lines of race and class, taking direct action in response to the political chicanery of foreigners. The mob's action was not based on an abstract political ideology, but was an emotional response to the oppression. It was a class struggle against the rich, powerful *gringo* establishment. It became a people's revolt against the foreign occupier's domination.

Mexicans settled in the El Paso area in the early 1600s, and until the 1840s most of the population lived south of the Rio Grande. After the Mexican-American War settlements sprang up north of the river, capitalizing on the Chihuahua-Texas-New Mexico trade. Soon a handful of Anglo-Americans joined the overwhelmingly Mexican population in El Paso County. The Anglos took immediate control of the county's politics, managing the Mexican vote through agents whom the bosses rewarded through patronage. The Mexican population was dispersed in small hamlets around the present-day city of El Paso. The fact that Mexicans were not familiar with Anglo politics worked to the politicians' advantage. By 1870 El Paso, like Brownsville and San Antonio, was "dominated by a handful of leading merchants or financial men." Anglo-Americans held the majority of elected offices as well as the wealth of the county.[54]

Mexicans were almost all poor and Spanish-speaking. In 1862 lives of the marginally subsisting people were lightened by discovery of salt at a location about 100 miles from the area where most of the population was clustered. People traveled to the salt beds to obtain salt for their own use as well as for sale to Mexicans south of the river. It did not occur to them to claim the beds, for the Spanish crown had designated salt pits as community property. Sam Maverick from San Antonio soon staked out a substantial portion of the salt beds. Still, Mexicans continued to use the remaining portion, content to take out what they could use.

A group of Anglo politicians, who became known as the Salt Ring, conspired to gain control of the beds used by the Mexicans. In the election of 1870 A. J. Fountain, leader of the forces opposed to the ring, ran against the Salt Ring's leader, W. W. Mills, for a seat in the state senate. He ran with the support of Antonio Borajo, an Italian priest, and campaigned on the promise that the salt beds would be made public. Fountain defeated the ring.

Fountain attempted to keep his campaign promise, but Borajo wanted him to stake out the beds and share profits with him. The state senator's refusal led to the end of his political career in El Paso, and Borajo joined Louis Cardis, another Italian, to back Charles Howard in 1875 for county judge; Cardis, it was agreed, would run for state senator. Both men were elected. Borajo and Cardis's power rested in their ability to speak Spanish, allowing them to cultivate the Mexican majority. Borajo also used his powers as a priest. It appeared that the three men would control the county's politics, but Howard defected, staking out the salt beds for himself in his father-in-law's name.[55] His political career ended in 1877 when the two Italians opposed him, but he retained control of the beds.

Howard attempted to profit from the "legal" claim by charging Mexicans for the salt they removed and in June 1877 he warned them not to take any salt.[56] Borajo incited the people from the pulpit, and the bishop removed him for meddling in politics. The friction continued, and two Mexicans were arrested when local authorities learned that they intended to remove salt in violation of the law. Several hundred *paisanos* (countrymen) of one of the arrested men forcibly freed him and called mass meetings to demand their rights.

Soon afterwards, they seized Howard and held him prisoner

until he promised to leave the county and to post a bond to insure that he would not return. Although Howard left El Paso, he had every intention of returning and knew that the authorities would enforce his claim. Upon his return he shot Cardis down in cold blood, but the authorities did not prosecute him or forfeit his bond.[57]

Texas Governor Richard B. Hubbard had ordered Major John B. Jones of the Texas Rangers into the area. When he arrived, the Mexican people approached him. They produced the U.S. Constitution and showed him the amendments which gave them the right to assemble and bear arms. Jones guaranteed them that Howard would be arrested and charged with murder.[58] Howard was arrested, but Jones had a change of mind, and he actively cooperated with Howard. Howard wrote a friend that he "did not wish to see general punishment visited on the rioters, who were ignorant as mules and misled, but thought that the leaders should be punished and made to respect the law," concluding that, "If the governor don't help us, I am going to bushwhacking. . . ."[59]

Local authorities released Howard and supported his claim. Rangers set out with him to see to it that Mexicans did not take the salt. Francisco "Chico" Barela, an Ysleta farmer, organized a group of eighteen Chicanos to oppose the Rangers. At first they hesitated to take direct action, but when word arrived from Borajo, "Shoot the *gringo* and I will absolve you," they shot Howard on December 17, 1877.[60]

The Salt War had begun. Moves to punish the Mexicans touched off several days of rioting, which were finally suppressed by Rangers, posses, and other *gringos*. Governor Hubbard sent to Silver City for thirty hired gunmen who were put under the command of Sheriff Charles Kerner. Among them was John Kinney, the self-styled King of Cattle Rustlers. The revolt was put down brutally "with rapes, homicides, and other crimes."[61] Many Mexicans fled in terror to Mexico where during the winter they perished from exposure and starvation. The gang from New Mexico was finally dispersed. Since it was claimed that they were acting to suppress a revolt, no one was ever punished. In fact, the Texas Rangers even demanded that Mexico pay $31,000 in reparations.[62]

According to Professor Seymour Connor, "The denouement of the affair included a congressional investigation, a diplomatic exchange between the United States and Mexico, and reestablishment of Fort Bliss in El Paso. Thereafter, no open attempt was made to subvert private ownership of the salt deposits."[63] Denial of community ownership of the salt pits represented the removal of a remnant of rights to which Mexicans were entitled before the conquest. The fact of being in the majority might have afforded them some protection had they had access to the political power of the new system imposed on them. However, even the potential advantage of their numbers was soon lost as the commercial and industrial boom of the 1880s brought a flood of Anglos to the area.

THE NEW SOCIAL STRUCTURE

During the 1860s the size of the Mexican population declined in relation to Anglos. In 1860 about 12,000 Mexicans lived in the state; even in Mexican towns such as San Antonio Germans already outnumbered them and by 1877 Anglos outnumbered both Germans and Mexicans. In the mid-1860s the slave population, which performed much of the manual labor, numbered about 182,000, a third of the state's total population. After the Civil War, a number of economic developments took place. The emancipation of the slave changed the economy of Texas and unstabilized its captive labor force. Cattle boomed during the 1860s and 1870s, spurred by transportation improvements and demand for beef on the domestic and world markets. Demand for sheep increased and by the 1880s cotton production reached an all-time high. The expansion of the railroads facilitated the rush of Anglos to this booming area in such large numbers that soon even border counties had equal Mexican and Anglo populations.[64] Finally, by 1890 the open range for cattle declined as agriculture expanded through mechanization and irrigation. The changed production methods increased the demand for Mexican labor, and Mexicans started to return to Texas in large numbers.

The abolition of slavery changed the attitude of many planters. Mexican labor now became more attractive. It was used as surplus labor to beat down wages of the Black pickers who were now wage earners. Planters on the Colorado River, near Bastrop in San Marcos and Navidad, Lavaca County where Mexican labor had been expelled before the Civil War and threatened with extermination, were now desperate for Mexican labor.[65] By the 1880s Mexican migration to Texas from Mexico accelerated and internally it began to fan out. The Anglos, as always, were in power and now the majority, maintained attitudes and a social structure designed to control the increasing number of Mexicans.

Social relations between Mexicans and the dominant society became more rigid with the passage of time. Contact often depended upon class or sex. The latter involved a degree of sexual politics common to most colonized experiences. The conqueror intermarried with the native aristocracy both because of the lack of white women and for control of the native population. The colonial situation also led to sexual subjugation through prostitution.

Intermarriage between Anglos and Mexicans offers an interesting paradox. Although Mexicans were considered a mongrel and inferior race, intermarriage took place. Captain Mifflin Kenedy, for instance, married the wealthy widow Petra Vela de Vidal, who reportedly helped him court the support of a large number of Mexicans whose vote was essential to the maintenance of his power. It became popular to speak about the "dark-eyed *señoritas.*" Dr. Arnoldo De Leon in his superb work "White Racial Attitudes Toward Mexicanos in Texas, 1821–1920," writes: "There existed at least some indication that Mexican women could have been accepted by whites in Texas under certain circumstances without reservation." In some instances Mexican women were compared favorably to the ideal southern belle, and especially *Las Güeras* (the blonds) were singled out. These light-skinned Mexicans were described as of pure Spanish descent from northern Spain with "faultlessly white" flesh and blue eyes.[66] As more Anglos moved into the area, intermarriage declined and racially mixed couples became subject to social disapproval and eventually persecution.[67]

As in the case of the Black in the South, the dominant society fabricated sexual myths about Mexicans. According to De Leon "Texas history is replete with accounts (by white men) suggesting that, if Mexican women easily lapsed from propriety, they especially coveted company (and intimacy) of white men."[68] This attitude is natural to privileged classes who may use the sexual act not only to assert dominance, but also to seek reassurance of their self-concept of superiority.

Only a few serious studies have been made of the role of the Mexican woman on the frontier. Jane Dysart, in "Mexican Women in San Antonio, 1830–1860: The Assimilation Process," deals with the question of intermarriage and her conclusions reinforce De Leon. She describes the woman in an active role. For instance, she states that during the colonial period Mexican women played a much greater role in government than generally portrayed by historians. On the frontier women had much more freedom than in established areas where traditions and social constraints demanded a less visible profile. According to Professor Dysart, Josefa Becerra Seguín "drilled the troops stationed in San Antonio during her husband's frequent absences." In spite of the "liberating influences of the frontier, the role of the Mexican woman," was largely that of a pawn.[69]

Distinctions were made between the light-skinned Mexican women and those of the poorer classes, and skin color often determined social status. In a letter from R. W. Brahan, Jr., to his cousin John Donelson Coffee, Jr., dated January 20, 1855, he referred to contacts with women of Castilian blood whose "parents avowed their determination to have them wed to genuine Americans . . ."[70] Brahan dwelt on Mexican women's color. Of some he said, "Their complexion is very fair," but he described poorer Mexican women as "styled greasers." His conditional racism was evident: "many of these 'greasers,' of fine figures & good features, the color of a mulatto, are kept by votaries of sensuality."

Dysart underscored the class nature of intermarriage in Texas and more specifically San Antonio: For instance, between 1837 and 1860:

> 906 Mexican women wed Mexican men, while only 88 chose to marry Anglos. But of those Anglo-Mexican unions almost half, or 42, involved women from high status families. The significance of those interracial marriages goes far beyond their numbers, since at least one daughter from every *rico* family in San Antonio married an Anglo.[71]

Only five unions between Mexican males and Anglo females were verified.

Intermarriage with Anglos was based on "economic necessity" more than on any other single factor. The Mexican family received some legal protection and freedom from the stigma of disloyalty, while the Anglo got a wife and property, since daughters under the law inherited property on an equal basis with their brothers. Intermarriage accelerated "Americanization," and although children maintained strong Mexican influences "during their early childhood," they strongly identified with the father's ethnic group. For instance, the daughters of Antonio Navarro became Methodists, which is in itself an indication of assimilation, and affiliation with English-speaking Roman Catholic parishes by the mixed couples was common.[72]

This is not to say that the *ricos* escaped racial discrimination through intermarriage and assimilation, for even rich *tejanos* were victims of racism. The majority of San Antonio Mexicans, even if Americanized, were not treated as equals. "Only the women and children with Anglo surnames, light skins, and wealth had a reasonable chance to escape the stigma attached to their Mexican ancestry."[73] The chance offered by intermarriage was perhaps the only one available to Mexican women, but even that decision was made by the male head of the family based on class interests and material factors which operated in an Anglo dominant society.

The poor had fewer alternatives. The *ricos* rarely sided with the masses of Mexicans. They displayed attitudes and interests attendant to their class and even emphasized racial differences between themselves and the lower classes, stating that the poor did not belong to the white race. Many old families openly sympathized with the Ku Klux Klan. The stronghold of the Mexican elite centered in San Antonio where Alejo Ruiz, Vicente Martínez, John Barrera, Rafael Ytúrris, and José Antonio Navarro allied themselves with ultraconservative elements. After the Civil War they even campaigned on behalf of northern Democrats, advocating the supremacy of the white race.[74] They seemed oblivious to persecution of their fellow Mexicans.

The violence which had characterized earlier relations between the two groups did not let up. During the 1880s and 1890s lynchings continued to be commonplace. Mexicans resisted. In August 1883 Captain Juan Cardenas in San Antonio headed a protest march on San Pedro Park because Mexicans could not use the dance floor. Protestors attacked Fred Kerble, the lessee, because he had yielded to town racism in imposing the restriction. The next year Mexicans fled the Fort Davis area to escape daily lynchings; the townsfolk encouraged the exodus hoping that it would continue until the last Mexican left the district.[75] Many Mexicans were forced to seek the protection of some of the local Anglo powers, who treated them as serfs. For instance, in Cameron County in South Texas Colonel Stephen Powers built a powerful political machine which was later taken over by his partner Jim Wells.[76] They controlled several counties from 1882 to 1920. They always helped their Mexicans to vote, transporting them to the polls and marking their ballots for them. Professor De Leon states that in the border areas whites employed Mexicans to cross into Mexico to recruit people who would be paid to vote for selected candidates. Hundreds would be imported, marched to the county clerk's office, and naturalized for the modest sum of 25¢.[77]

This practice continued into the twentieth century in spite of a constitutional amendment passed in 1890 requiring foreigners "to file for citizenship six months before an election." In 1902 a state constitutional amendment adopting a poll tax was passed to deter poor Mexicans from voting.[78]

The political situation in Mexico added to tensions in borderlands. The border served as a haven for revolutionaries who actively campaigned against Mexican dictator Porfirio Díaz. One such revolutionary, Catarino Garza, touched off an incident which demonstrated the growing solidarity among the poor Mexicans in that area.[79] In Corpus Christi Garza accused a U.S. customs inspector, Victor Sebree, of assassinating Mexican prisoners who actively opposed Díaz. The two encountered one another during an election at Rio Grande City in 1888, and Sebree shot and wounded Garza. Mexicans were incensed because nothing happened to Sebree. They threatened to lynch him, but the local U.S. army post commander intervened. Garza recovered and continued his activities. Four years later he was ready to launch an invasion of Mexico, but U.S. officials intervened; the local post commander arrested Alejandro Gonzales, Garza's brother-in-law, abusing him without cause (see Chapter 10).

Racial confrontations took a different twist in August 1894 when Blacks attacked Mexicans at Beeville, Texas. Growers encouraged antagonism between different ethnic groups. They brought Mexicans into Beeville to beat down wages of Blacks and to threaten the Blacks' jobs by an oversupply of labor. Blacks blamed the Mexicans, rather than the growers for their depressed state and raided the Mexican quarter. Throughout this period considerable tension developed between Mexicans and Blacks. The Federal government added to the antagonism by stationing Black soldiers in Mexican areas, using them to control the Mexican population. At Fort McIntosh in Laredo, the 10th Cavalry, a Black unit, participated in suppressing Mexicans.[80]

By the late 1880s both Populists and Republicans were campaigning to disenfranchise all Mexicans. The Populist or People's party, while fighting the growth of agribusiness and demanding reforms in government, led attacks on Mexicans, blaming them for the decline of small farms and the demise of rural America. In San Antonio A. L. Montalvo vowed to fight for civil rights and denounced the Populists for attempting to reduce the Texas Mexican "to the category of pack animals, who may be good enough to work, but not good enough to exercise their civil rights."[81]

Many of the interests of the People's party paralleled the Mexicans', but the party regarded them as its enemy. In Texas Populists had made an effort to forge an alliance with Blacks, while attacking Mexicans and threatening to deport them. They viewed Mexicans as a threat because the Democratic party had almost complete control over their vote. Local Anglo leaders through their political machine corralled Mexicans and through fraud, corruption, and force kept this vote in line. Instead of organizing progressive elements within the Mexican community and attempting to destroy the machines, the Populists made Mexicans their scapegoats, using crass racist arguments.[82]

Mexicans not only had to resist the loss of control of their voting power through the practice of "vote their Mexicans," but now had to resist the complete loss of their vote. In 1896 Ricardo Rodríguez was denied his final naturalization papers. The authorities argued in court that Rodríguez was not of white or African descent and "therefore not capable of becoming an American citizen." They wanted to keep "Aztecs or aboriginal Mexicans" from naturalization. Rodríguez won his case based on the Treaty of Guadalupe Hidalgo.[83]

During 1896 tensions reached an all-time high. In January 1896 authorities found the mutilated body of Aureliano Castellón. Castellón had made the mistake of courting Emma Stanfield, a white girl, over the objections of her brothers. He had been shot eight times and his body burned. On June 30, 1896, the *San Antonio Express* published a note entitled "Slaughter the *Gringo*" signed by twenty-five Mexicans. The signers threatened to kill only *gringos* and Germans, exempting Blacks, Italians, and Cubans.

Two years later, with the advent of the Spanish-American War, general panic spread among Anglos who believed that Mexicans would ally themselves with Spain and begin border raids. In places such as San Diego, Texas, Anglos formed minutemen companies to "protect" themselves. The uprisings never took place and Anglos soon learned that Mexicans had little sympathy for Spain, but the situation gave racists an excuse to persecute all Mexicans.

The white cap movement of South Texas in the late 1890s aggravated conditions. (Texas white caps should not be confused with the Mexican white caps of New Mexico; see Chapter 3). Texas white caps were an Anglo-American vigilante group. They demanded that white planters refuse to rent to Blacks and Mexicans and fire Mexican field hands. White cap activity centered in Wilson, Gonzales, and DeWitt counties.[84]

According to Dr. De Leon, violence without guilt raged during this period: "Astonishing numbers of Mexicans in the nineteenth century fell victim to lynch law and cold-blooded deaths at the hands of whites who thought nothing of killing Mexicans."[85] Social attitudes reinforced by violence froze Mexicans into a caste system which would facilitate exploitation of their labor in the twentieth century.

NOTES

1. T. R. Fehrenbach, *Lone Star: A History of Texas and the Texans* (New York: Macmillan, 1968), p. 245.
2. Ronnie G. Tyler, "The Callahan Expedition of 1855: Indians or Negroes?" *Southwest Historical Quarterly* 70, no. 4 (April 1967): 575, 582; Arnoldo De Leon, "White Racial Attitudes Toward Mexicanos in Texas, 1821–1920" (Ph.D. dissertation, Texas Christian University, 1974), p. 141.
3. Jack C. Vowell, "Politics at El Paso: 1850–1920" (Master's thesis, Texas Western College, 1952), p. 145.
4. Larry McMurtry, *In a Narrow Grave* (Austin, Tex.: Encino Press, 1968), p. 40.
5. McMurtry, p. 40. Anglo-Americans in Texas generally applauded McNeely. According to Michael Gordon Webster, "Texan Manifest Destiny and Mexican Border Conflict, 1865–1880" (Ph.D. dissertation, Indiana University, 1972), pp. 149, 152, rancher Richard King gave the Rangers a $500 bonus in appreciation for services rendered. In Las Cuevas, however, McNeely encountered a superior force of Mexicans and it took U.S. troops to bail him out.
6. McMurtry, p. 41.
7. McMurtry, p. 43. The renowned historian W. E. Hollon, in a letter to the author written in October 1972, wrote that a few weeks before Webb was killed, he said "that he did not feel like writing any more, but that he regretted that he probably would not have time to re-write his *Texas Rangers* and correct his comments and prejudices about the Mexicans as reflected in that book. All of us who grew up in Texas on Texas history two generations ago, did not know any better in our attitudes toward the Negroes and Mexicans. It takes a long time to grow out of one's environment. So, don't be too harsh on Webb. He grew into the most tolerant, intellectual giant that Texas ever produced."
8. Llerena B. Friend, "W. P. Webb's Texas Rangers," *Southwestern Historical Quarterly* (January 1971): 321.
9. Friend, p. 321.
10. Américo Paredes, *With a Pistol in His Hand* (Austin: University of Texas Press, 1958).
11. Editorial by John Salmon Ford in the *Texas Democrat* (September 9, 1846), quoted in Fehrenbach, p. 465.
12. Fehrenbach, pp. 473–474.
13. Walter Prescott Webb, *The Texas Rangers: A Century of Frontier Defense* (Austin: University of Texas Press, 1965), p. xv.
14. Webb, p. xv.
15. Paredes, p. 31.

16. Paredes, p. 29.
17. Webb, p. 463
18. Webb, p. 464.
19. John Salmon Ford, *Rip Ford's Texas*, Stephen B. Oates, ed. (Austin: University of Texas Press, 1963), p. 467.
20. Clarence C. Clendenen, *Blood on the Border: The United States Army and the Mexican Irregulars* (New York: Macmillan, 1969), p. 18.
21. Charles W. Goldfinch, *Juan Cortina, 1824–1892: A Re-Appraisal* (Brownsville, Tex.: Bishop's Print Shop, 1950), p. 21, 31.
22. Ford, p. 467; Frank H. Dugan, "The 1850 Affair of the Brownsville Separatists," *Southwestern Historical Quarterly* 61, no. 2 (October 1957): 270–273; Edward H. Moseley, "The Texas Threat, 1855–1860," *Journal of Mexican History* 13, (1973): 89–90.
23. De Leon, pp. 7, 147; David J. Weber, ed., *Foreigners in Their Native Land* (Albuquerque: University of New Mexico Press, 1973), pp. 155–156.
24. *Report of the Mexican Commission on the Northern Frontier Question* (New York, 1875), in Carlos E. Cortes, ed., *The Mexican Experience in Texas* (New York: Arno Press, 1976), p. 129.
25. Webster, pp. 30, 75.
26. *Report of the Mexican Commission*, p. 209; Raúl Fernández, *The United States-Mexican Border: A Politico-Economic Profile* (Notre Dame: University of Notre Dame Press, 1977), p. 79.
27. Webster, p. 76; James LeRoy Evans, "The Indian Savage, the Mexican Bandit, the Chinese Heathen: Three Popular Stereotypes" (Ph.D. dissertation, University of Texas, 1967), p. vii.
28. Ralph Wooster, "Wealthy Texans," *Southwestern Historical Quarterly* (October 1967): 163, 173.
29. Tom Lea, *The King Ranch*, 2 vols. (Boston: Little Brown, 1957). The facts of King's life presented in the following discussion are based on Lea's work. (See vol. I, p. 457.)
30. Lea, vol. 1, p. 275.
31. *Report of the Mexican Commission*, pp. 29–30, 62, 105.
32. Paul S. Taylor, *An American-Mexican Frontier* (New York: Russell & Russell, 1971), p. 49.
33. E. J. Hobsbawm, *Primitive Rebels: Studies in Archaic Forms of Social Movement in the 19th and 20th Centuries* (New York: Norton, 1965), p. 13.
34. Hobsbawm, p. 13.
35. The best work on the Cortina years is Michael Gordon Webster, "Texan Manifest Destiny and the Mexican Border Conflict, 1865–1880" (Ph.D. dissertation, Indiana University, 1972). See also Pedro Castillo and Albert Camarillo, eds., *Furia y Muerte: Los Bandidos Chicanos* (Los Angeles: Aztlán, 1973).
36. Webb, p. 176; Lyman Woodman, *Cortina: Rogue of the Rio Grande* (San Antonio, Tex.: Naylor, 1950), p. 8.
37. Goldfinch, p. 17; José T. Canales, *Juan N. Cortina Presents His Motion for a New Trial* (San Antonio, Tex.: Artes Gráficas, 1951), p. 6.
38. Evans, pp. 107, 118; *Report of the Mexican Commission*, pp. 28–29.
39. Webb, p. 178; Goldfinch, p. 44; Webster, p. 18; Evans, pp. 107, 121.
40. Goldfinch, p. 45; *Report of the Mexican Commission*, pp. 137–139.
41. Goldfinch, p. 48.
42. Wayne Moquin et al., eds., *A Documentary History of the Mexican American* (New York: Praeger, 1971), pp. 207–209. For the complete text of the speech, delivered on November 23, 1859, see *Report of the Mexican Commission*, p. 133, n. 62.
43. Evans, p. 111.
44. Ford, pp. 308–309.
45. Woodman, p. 53.
46. Woodman, p. 55.
47. Evans, pp. 105, 113.
48. Woodman, pp. 59, 98–99.
49. Ford, *Rip Ford's Texas*, p. 371.
50. Evans, p. 127.
51. *Report of the Mexican Commission*, pp. 154–155, Webster, pp. 79–80.

52. Evans, p. 132.
53. Leonard Morris, "The Mexican Raid of 1875 on Corpus Christi," *Texas Historical Association Quarterly* 55, no. 2 (October 1900): 128.
54. Vowell, pp. 72–73; Fehrenbach, p. 289; Carey McWilliams, *North from Mexico* (New York: Greenwood Press, 1968), p. 110.
55. Webster, p. 234; Webb, p. 350; Vowell, pp. 65–66.
56. Vowell, p. 66. Leo Metz, "The Posse Stuns New Mexican Wagon Train. Opening Round of Magoffin's Salt War," *El Paso Times*, February 17, 1974. There had been a previous encounter over salt in December 1853 when James Wiley Magoffin who had claimed salt pits in the San Andrés Mountains, sought to prevent salt gatherers from New Mexico from taking salt from them. An armed conflict almost broke out between Texans supporting Magoffin and New Mexicans, but a New Mexican court found in favor of the salt gatherers.
57. Vowell, p. 69.
58. Leon Metz, "San Elizario Salt Gatherers Pursue Justice by the Gun," *El Paso Times*, March 10, 1974.
59. Webb, p. 356.
60. Webb, pp. 360–361; Vowell, pp. 69–70.
61. Leon Metz, "Atrocities, Plunder Mark End of El Paso Salt War," *El Paso Times*, March 17, 1974; Webster, p. 238.
62. Joe B. Frantz, "The Borderlands: Ideas on a Leafless Landscape," in Stanley R. Ross, ed., *Views Across the Border: The United States and Mexico* (Albuquerque: University of New Mexico, 1978), p. 89.
63. Seymour V. Connor, *Texas: A History* (New York: Crowell, 1971), p. 235.
64. Fehrenbach, pp. 678–679. Weber, p. 146, states that 11,212 Mexicans lived in Texas in 1850, constituting only 5 percent of the population. See also John R. Scotford, *Within These Borders* (New York: Friendship Press, 1953), p. 35.
65. De Leon, p. 140.
66. De Leon, pp. 112–113, 115, 116, 122.
67. E. Larry Dickens, "Mestizaje in 19th Century Texas," *Journal of Mexican American History* 2, no. 2 (Spring 1972): 63.
68. De Leon, p. 126.
69. Jane Dysart, "Mexican Women in San Antonio, 1830–1860: The Assimilation Process," *Western Historical Quarterly* (October 1976): 366.
70. Quoted in Aaron M. Boom, ed. "Texas in the 1850's as Viewed by a Recent Arrival," *Southwestern Historical Quarterly* (October 1966): 282–285.
71. Dysart, p. 370.
72. Dysart, pp. 370–374.
73. Dysart, p. 375.
74. De Leon, p. 161, 159–160.
75. De Leon, pp. 172, 239.
76. O. Douglas Weeks, "The Texas-Mexican and the Politics of South Texas," *American Political and Social Science Review* (August 1930): 611–613.
77. De Leon, 164.
78. Weber, p. 147.
79. De Leon, pp. 234–235, 263–264.
80. De Leon, pp. 238, 239.
81. De Leon, pp. 166, 168.
82. Fehrenbach, p. 627; Rupert N. Richardson, *Texas: The Lone Star State*, 2nd ed. (Englewood Cliffs, N.J.: Prentice-Hall, 1958), pp. 271, 274.
83. De Leon, pp. 232, 226–227, 186–187.
84. De Leon, pp. 267–268.
85. De Leon, pp. 192–193.

Chapter 3
Freedom in a Cage:
The Expansion into New Mexico

New Mexicans have historically found security in believing that they assimilated into Anglo-American culture and that they effectively participate in the democratic process. This myth has been articulated so often that they believe it. The reality that a small oligarchy of Anglo-Americans, aided by a small group of *ricos*, established their privilege at the expense of the Mexican masses has been conveniently ignored. Even the knowledgeable Fray Angelico Chávez, a prominent New Mexican Catholic priest, historian, and writer, stated as late as 1970:

> In short New Mexico quickly became a willing enclave of the United States, all of her citizens of whatever economic or social level deeming themselves true and loyal American citizens. And what they evidently liked best, the poor as well as the more affluent, was the game of politics within the framework of the Democratic and Republican parties. It has become New Mexico's chief indoor and outdoor sport with all the shenanigans connected with it.[1]

Although Fray Angelico's perspective ignores history, it is at the crux of New Mexican myths. In order to survive economically, many descendants of the original New Mexican settlers found it convenient to separate themselves from Mexicans who arrived at the turn of the twentieth century. Many New Mexicans called themselves *Hispanos* or Spanish-Americans, as distinguished from other Mexicans. They rationalized that they were the descendants of the original settlers, who were Spanish *conquistadores*. According to them, New Mexico was isolated from the rest of the Southwest and Mexico during the colonial era; thus, they remained racially pure and were Europeans, in contrast to the *mestizo* (half-breed) Mexicans.

Through this process, they separated themselves from intense discrimination toward Mexicans, allowing them to better their economic and, in some cases, their social status. George Sánchez, Arthur L. Campa, Carey McWilliams, and others have exploded this "fantasy heritage." Indeed, the *Hispanos* were Mexicans, for the majority of the original settlers from Mexico in 1598 were males who, over the years, mixed with the Pueblo Indians as well as with Mexican Indians who settled in the area. During the nineteenth century, although the label Spanish-American was used throughout the Southwest and Latin America, New Mexicans were commonly referred to by Anglo-Americans as Mexicans. Nancie González wrote that it was not until the twentieth century that New Mexicans denied their Mexican identity. During the 1910s and 1920s a large number of Mexican laborers entered New Mexico, and at the same time, many Texans, Oklahomans, and other southerners settled in the eastern plains, intensifying discrimination against Mexicans. More affluent New Mexicans, thinking of themselves as Caucasians, rationalized to the Anglos: "You don't like Mexicans, and we don't like them either, but we are Spanish-Americans, not Mexicans."[2] By this simple denial of their heritage, New Mexicans thought they could escape discrimination and become eligible for higher paying jobs.

THE MYTH OF THE BLOODLESS CONQUEST

Fray Angelico also expounded the myth that New Mexicans peacefully joined the Anglo nation and "became a willing enclave of the United States." The myth of the "bloodless conquest of New Mexico," has been repeated by a majority of historians and is believed by most people. By this sleight of hand New Mexicans are not seen as the victims and, consequently, the enemies of the Anglo-Americans, but rather as their willing friends. In fact, the majority of the 50,000 to 60,000 people who lived in New Mexico were not enthusiastic about the United States invasion of their land.[3] Considerable anti-American feeling existed before the United States occupation, and only a handful of merchants saw an advantage to be derived from it.[4]

Hostilities began many years before Stephen Kearny led the "Army of the West" through New Mexico during the Mexican war. Texans claimed that their boundary followed the Rio Grande and included a sizeable portion of New Mexico. A large enclave of United States citizens near Taos, led by Charles Bent, formed what was called the American party. The party, hated by the Mexicans, openly supported the Texas cause.[5]

In 1841 General Hugh McLeod led an expedition of about 300 Texans, divided into 6 military companies, into New Mexico. Governor Manuel Armijo sounded a general alarm. His militia was badly equipped, but he succeeded in tricking the Texans into believing he had a large army and the Texans *surrendered*. Although it was claimed that McLeod was leading simply a trading expedition, New Mexicans believed that they were being attacked. They blamed Bent and his party for the invasion and imprisoned him in Santa Fe. A mob invaded the house of United States Counsel Manuel Alvárez with the intention of killing him. New Mexicans accused the United States government of complicity and the government responded with open hostility.[6]

The fate of the expedition caused considerable controversy.

One source charged: "Many of the prisoners were shot down in cold blood, others cruelly tortured, and most of them forced into a death march southward apparently as dreadful as the march of Bataan."[7] However, historian Hubert Howe Bancroft's version differed. He gave little credence to accounts of atrocities, writing that to the New Mexicans "They [the Texans] were simply armed invaders, who might expect to be attacked, and if defeated, to be treated by the Mexicans as rebels, or at best—since Texan belligerency and independence had been recognized by several nations—as prisoners of war. . . . There can be no doubt that Governor Armijo was fully justified in seizing the Texan invaders, disarming them, confiscating their property, and sending them to Mexico as prisoners of war."[8]

Texans retaliated and a nasty guerrilla war with racial overtones followed. During 1842 and 1843 clashes between the two sides increased. For example, in 1843 the Texans under Colonel A. Warfield attacked the small town of Mora and plundered innocent Mexicans. Bent was accused of contraband and theft, collusion with the Texans, harboring thieves, and selling firearms to Indians. He fled to the Arkansas River in Colorado (he later moved in and out of the province and eventually became its governor). Bent's associate, Carlos Beaubien, wisely left the area temporarily. Colonel Jacob Snively raided a New Mexican caravan, shooting twenty-three Mexicans.[9] In 1843 Padre Antonio Martínez, a leader of the opposition to the American party, wrote to Antonio López de Santa Anna, warning him of Anglo encroachments and the construction of forts on the Arkansas and Platte rivers. He warned Santa Anna that Anglos were depleting buffalo herds and criticized Armijo's policy of allowing foreigners to colonize empty lands.[10]

By the time Zachary Taylor attacked northern Mexico, no love was lost between Anglo-Americans and the New Mexicans. Colonel Stephen Watts Kearny, in June 1846, prepared approximately 3,000 members of the Army of the West to occupy the Mexican lands from New Mexico to California. His instructions were to use peaceful persuasion whenever possible, force when necessary. By late June he was ready to march west from Fort Leavenworth along the Santa Fe Trail. As Kearny approached New Mexico, he sent James W. Magoffin, a merchant well known in New Mexico, with an ultimatum to Governor Armijo, stating that if the New Mexicans surrendered they would not be disturbed; otherwise, they would suffer the consequences.[11]

Armijo, despite the fact that he had a shortage of arms and trained men, had been prepared and could have defended the province. By August 1846, Kearny captured Las Vegas, New Mexico, and prepared to attack Santa Fe. He had to pass through Apache Canyon, a narrow passage southeast of Santa Fe, where Armijo could easily have ambushed him. Surprisingly, Kearney met no resistance at the canyon. Armijo had fled south without firing a shot, allowing the Army of the West to enter the capital. Some sources claim that negotiators bribed Armijo to sell out the province. In fact, Magoffin later submitted a $50,000 bill to Washington, D.C., for "expenses," of which he received $30,000. There is no proof that Armijo took the bribe, but there can be little doubt that his actions were highly suspicious, especially since Magoffin later boasted that he bribed Armijo.[12]

On August 22, Kearney issued a proclamation to the people of New Mexico, announcing the intention of retaining the province as a permanent possession of the United States. This was the first statement of the real purpose of the war—the acquisition of territory. Pretensions of defense of Texan boundaries, avenging Mexican insults, and indemnity were abandoned. Kearney's action clearly violated international law.[13]

The myth of a bloodless conquest stems largely from Armijo's inaction; however, resistance had gone underground and by the fall of 1846 a movement to expel the hated *gringo* was afoot. Kearny was lulled into thinking that there would be no further resistance, and on September 25, he left for California. In mid-December Colonel Alexander W. Doniphan was sent south to conquer Chihuahua. Colonel Doniphan observed: "A people conquered but yesterday could have no friendly feeling for their conquerors, who have taken possession of their country, changed its laws and appointed new officers, principally foreigners."[14]

Influential New Mexicans conspired to drive their oppressors out of the province. Patriots included Tomás Ortiz; Colonel Diego Archuleta, a military commander; the controversial Padre Antonio José Martínez; and the Reverend Juan Félipe Ortiz, vicar general of the diocese and brother of Tomás. Conspirators planned to attack the Anglo authorities during the Christmas season when many of them would be in Santa Fe and when Anglo-American soldiers could be expected to be drinking heavily. However, the plans were uncovered by Governor Bent, who "beginning to feel uneasy over the sullen reaction of the 'mongrels' to Anglo-American rule," had organized an elaborate spy system.[15]

After this, the original leadership did not take part in other plots, and Anglo-Americans believed that the spirit of New Mexicans had been broken. They were mistaken. Resentment smoldered among the masses. Pablo Montoya, a Mexican peasant, and Tomasito Romero, a Pueblo Indian, led the resistance. On January 19, 1847 they attacked, killing Governor Bent and five other important members of the American party. Rebels destroyed documents and deeds which exposed "the land schemes of the American party."[16] There were also widespread acts of resistance in Arroyo Hondo and other villages.

The role of Padre Martínez is uncertain in the revolt. He is accused of being the instigator, and his brother Pascual allegedly took part in the revolt.[17] However, he also apparently tried to restrain the rebels so Padre Martínez was a realist, and he knew that an unorganized revolt would be disastrous; he also knew the consequences of failure.

Under the leadership of Colonel Sterling Price, well-armed soldiers retaliated by attacking some 4,500 Mexican and Pueblo Indians armed with bows, arrows, and lances. The army slaughtered rebels on the snow-covered ground outside the insurgent capital of Taos. Offenders retreated into the pueblo's church, fighting bravely in face of intense artillery fire:

> About 150 Mexicans were killed; some twenty-five or thirty prisoners were shot down by firing squads; and many of those who surrendered were publicly flogged. Colonel Price's troops are said to have been so drunk at the time that the Taos engagement was more of a massacre than a battle.[18]

The trial of surviving rebels resembled those in other occupation situations: "One of the judges was a close friend of the slain governor and the other's son had been murdered by the rebels. The foreman of the grand jury was the slain governor's brother and one of the jurors a relative of the slain sheriff." The town was so emotionally charged that it was surprising that the defendants received any kind of trial at all. Fifteen rebels were sentenced to death—one for high treason. Most historians have condemned charges against rebels as illegal since a state of war existed and the defendants were still Mexican citizens.[19]

The failure of the rebellion made it evident that armed revolt on a limited scale could not succeed, but resistance continued, inflamed by the rule of Colonel Sterling Price, which was so despotic that even the Anglos objected. Guerilla warfare continued under the leadership of Manuel Cortes, a fugitive of the Taos rebellion, and as late as 1851 James S. Calhoun, who was soon to become governor, stated that "treason is rife."[20]

THE LAND GRAB IN NEW MEXICO

Land, New Mexico's basic resource, is at the heart of Mexican grievances against the United States. It is an emotional issue, involving traditions and aspirations of the people. A traditional belief holds that all people came into the world equal, their nudity being the symbol of their equality, and weakness, and that God gave them land without which they could not survive. When greedy men monopolize the land, they take the source of life from many and thus create inequality. The solution is to give all men equal access to the land in order that they may revert to the state of equality which God intended.[21]

An organized seizure of land followed the conquest. To understand how this took place, the Anglo-American and Mexican pioneering experiences must be contrasted. The Anglo-American experience was largely based on the movement of individuals into new areas with the accoutrements of civilization following; Mexicans moved into their northwest territory collectively. The land was arid and communal cooperation was necessary for survival. Settlement of New Mexico was planned in advance. The principal institution resembled those in other villages throughout the Spanish Americas. Government furnished new settlers with basic equipment to farm their lands. They became members of a village and, in return, acquired water rights, rights to farm a plot of land, and rights to use the communal pasturelands and forests. Necessity bound them together, relying on each other for assistance in building their homes, tending crops and animals, maintaining the village, entertainment, and caring for the sick and aged, as well as burying the dead.

Life in the pueblos was not idyllic, for the privilege of a few was established by tradition. Some exploited their fellow villagers as well as the surrounding native Indians. A definite class society developed with a small number of rich New Mexicans owning large tracts of land. They exploited those who worked for them and participated in enslavement of nonsedentary Indians.[22]

However, even with the faults of the Mexican system, a large number of families did share in communal grants and Pueblo Indians had specified rights. Many small farmers grazed their flocks on land that belonged to the state as needed. After the initial confrontations between Mexicans and sedentary native Indians, both groups lived in relative harmony, with miscegenation taking place.

The Anglo-American land grab in New Mexico resembled the one that took place in Texas. The difference was that in New Mexico the Mexican settlements were more extensive. The province had many villages and some cities. Santa Fe had grown into a trade center. Some mining took place and both Mexicans and Anglos knew the future mining potential of the territory. Extensive agriculture existed. Sheep raising gave the people their principal contact with the outside world. The life style which had taken root resisted concerted efforts by United States officials to change it.

After 1848 Anglo-Americans moved into New Mexico to enjoy the spoils of conquest. Victory meant the right to exploit the territory's resources. These opportunists formed an alliance with the rich Mexican class and established their privilege, controlling the territorial government and administering its laws to further their political, economic, and social dominance. They maintained their power through *political* influence in Washington, D.C., access to capital, and command of technological innovations. Systematically, these men used these advantages to gain total control. First, New Mexico was a territory and the United States President appointed executive and judicial posts. These and other state offices went to Anglo-Americans who were recommended by the territorial political machine.[23]

Second, control of the legislature by the political oligarchy was maintained through the influence of the *ricos*.

Third, the new economic order made access to capital imperative. Anglos owned banks, prime sources from which Mexicans could obtain capital. Bankers charged excessive interest rates, the New Mexicans used their land as collateral, and foreclosures followed the Mexicans' inability to meet payments.

Fourth, government allowed speculators to initiate exploitive land and timber policies which eroded the land, hastening the demise of the small farmer.

Fifth, reclamation projects in general did not help small farmers. After the Civil War it was the corporate agriculturalists, those who raised crops in large quantities, who were subsidized by water made available at government expense.

Reclamation projects changed the balance of nature, greatly affecting the Rio Grande; they reduced the supply of water in many areas and provided too much water in other places. The people had no say as to where the government would build dams. New Mexican farmers had to pay for "improvements" through taxes whether they wanted them or not, and when they could not pay the increased taxes, their land was forfeited.[24]

Large farm corporations were granted extensive land tracts. Using mechanization, they led in the production of cash crops, such as cotton. Small farmers could not compete, because they did not have the capital to mechanize.

Sixth, the federal government granted large concessions of land to railroad corporations and to some institutions of higher learning.

Seventh, at the turn of the century conservationists, concerned over industry's rape of timber and recreation land, moved to create national forests. Shepherds were not allowed to graze sheep on national forest lands without permits, which over the years went increasingly to the large operators.[25] In the process Mexicans in New Mexico lost 2,000,000 acres of private lands and 1,700,000 of communal lands.

Today, the federal government owns 34.9 percent of the land in New Mexico, the state government owns 12 percent, while federal Indian reservations own 6.8 percent. The state and federal governments together, therefore, own 53.7 percent of New Mexico, with the forestry service controlling one-third of the state's land.[26]

THE AMERICANIZATION OF THE CATHOLIC CHURCH

The Roman Catholic church was the most important institution to New Mexicans, directly touching their lives from cradle to grave. However, unlike the Irish clergy who provided unifying support for their congregations when Irish-Americans faced repression in the eastern United States, the New Mexican clergy became an active ally of the state, accelerating the assimilation process.

Soon after the occupation, the church limited its functions to tending strictly to the spiritual needs of the people. With few exceptions it did not champion the rights of the poor; instead, it worked to Americanize New Mexicans. Before the conquest the New Mexican clergy actively participated in the life of the people. After 1850 control of the church passed to an Anglo-American hierarchy. It became an alien clergy that related more to the power establishment and a few rich Anglo-American parishioners than to the masses. It became a pacifying agent, encouraging Mexicans to accept the occupation.

Undisputed leader of the Mexican clergy was Antonio José Martínez. His devotion to the Catholic church was deep and abiding, but he saw it as an institution for benefit, not enslavement, of mankind. Padre Antonio José Martínez was one of the most important figures in New Mexican history, as well as one of the most beloved.

The "priest of Taos," as he was known, was born in Abiquir in Rio Arriba County, on January 7, 1793. He married in 1812 and had a daughter, but when his wife died, he entered the priesthood and was ordained in 1822. His daughter, Luz, died in 1825. In 1824, Martínez took charge of a parish in Taos, where after two years he established a seminary. Graduates of the seminary were great advocates of his philosophy, thus spreading his influence throughout New Mexico. He taught grammar, rhetoric, and theology, as well as law. From 1830 to 1836 he was a member of the departmental assembly of the state under the Mexican government, and in 1835 he published a newspaper called *El Crepúsculo (The Dawn)*. He also wrote and printed books and pamphlets. Martínez took a progressive religious stand, refusing to collect tithes from the poor and opposing large land grants, claiming the land should go to the people. Even before the Anglo occupation Martínez had opposed Anglo encroachments. He was involved in the first liberation movement. He served in the legislature from 1851 to 1853. Known as a fighter against both church and state, he criticized the church for "its policy of allowing the clergy to exact excessive and oppressive tithes and fees for marriages, funerals, and like services."[27] He also advocated separation of church and state.

In 1851, however, Padre Martínez's liberal, people-oriented

philosophy of the role of the church was challenged with the arrival in New Mexico of a new vicar general Fray J. B. Lamy. French by birth, Lamy worked in the Baltimore diocese and in the mid-1850s became a bishop. His partisans claimed that he revitalized religion in New Mexico by founding schools, building churches, and increasing the number of priests in his diocese from 10 to 37. They also claimed that through his alliance with the government he was able to maintain control of education, which might otherwise have been lost to the Protestant churches. His critics contended that he did this at a tremendous cost, and they condemned him for his failure to speak out against the injustices suffered by the people.[28]

Even his admirers concede that Lamy was a "cultured" Frenchman who never fully understood the traditions of Mexicans and had little respect for their clergy. Lamy came out of postrevolutionary France and came into fullness of mind "after reign of libertarian principles, and during the restoration of the Church," when liberalism was looked upon as anti-Catholic.[29]

Lamy persecuted the Holy Brotherhood of Penitents. The brotherhood was most popular among the poor of northern New Mexico. Descended from the Third Order of St. Francis of Assisi, it practiced public flagellation and during Holy Week imitated the ordeals of Christ. A secret society, it was a strong force in local politics; prominent leaders like Antonio José Martínez belonged to it.[30] Establishment Mexicans like Miguel A. Otero looked down on the Penitents, stating, "At present they [the Penitents] are found among those classes of natives where ignorance predominates."[31] Lamy and his successors fought to abolish the brotherhood, slandering and libeling them, persecuting them, and even denying them the sacraments.[32]

Soon after Lamy's arrival, a power struggle erupted between him and the Mexican clergy, many of whom were Martínez's former students. Martínez was attacked on the grounds of not being celibate (charges that were not proved), but the real reason was the involvement of the Mexican clergy in temporal matters, especially their functioning as advocates for the people. The people wanted a native clergyman who knew their language, traditions, and problems. In contrast Anglo-American priests came from an alien culture.[33] They did not involve themselves with the material welfare of Mexicans, attempt to Americanize them.

At first, Martínez avoided an open rift with Lamy, keeping quiet even when close friends were excommunicated. Gradually, however, Lamy's edicts became more obtrusive. Finally, when he sent a letter to all the parishes insisting that priests collect tithes and first fruits and telling them to withhold the sacraments from those who did not comply, Martínez rebelled. When Lamy finally excommunicated Martínez, the padre defied the bishop by continuing his ministry until his death, on July 28, 1868.

THE SANTA FE RING

After the conquest the American party and its New Mexican associates expanded their operations. An influx of newcomers and capital formalized and extended the range of the group, with the creation of a network of speculators. The addition of a large number of lawyers made the group especially dangerous. In fact, "one out of every ten Anglos in New Mexico in the 1880s was a lawyer."[34]

During the occupation the network completely dominated the government, using its powers to steal the land from the people. To facilitate these thefts, they formed small political cliques, which resembled the political machines of the eastern United States. Most cliques were associated with, and subservient to, the Santa Fe Ring, which Carey McWilliams described as "a small compact group of Anglo-American bankers, lawyers, merchants, and politicians who dominated the territory through their ties with the *ricos* who in turn controlled the votes of the Spanish-speaking."[35] The network woven by the ring paled its eastern counterparts.

The leaders were Thomas B. Catron, Stephen B. Elkins, and Le Baron Bradford Prince, all of whom were prominent Republicans. A number of Democrats as well as rich Mexicans also belonged. The ring controlled the governor and most of the office holders in the territory and was supported by Max Frost, editor of the *New Mexican*, the territory's most influential newspaper. "Frost, who was at one time during his active career indicted in a land fraud prosecution, acted as the journalistic spokesman for the Ring, effectively using the press to discredit critics of the Ring and to place its activities in the best possible light."[36]

Thomas B. Catron, the ring's official leader, and mastermind of its New Mexico operation, arrived in New Mexico in the late 1860s, eventually becoming United States attorney general for the territory. "Throughout his life in New Mexico, Catron wielded more power than any other single individual in the territory. Through land grant litigation and by purchases he acquired more than one million acres of land."[37]

Stephen Elkins, a lawyer and close friend of Catron, came to New Mexico in 1863. In 1871 he was president of the First National Bank of Santa Fe. He represented the ring's interests in Washington, D.C., becoming a delegate to the United States Congress and later serving as secretary of war under President Benjamin Harrison.[38] In 1884 he became chairman of the executive committee of the National Republican Committee.

Le Baron Bradford Prince came from New York, where he had had experience in machine politics. Through the influence of powerful friends in Washington, D.C., he was offered the governorship of New Mexico, but he turned it down to become chief justice of New Mexico in 1879. Later, in the 1890s, he became governor.

Governor Edmund Ross, appointed by President Grover Cleveland, described the ring's network and influence:

> From the Land Grant Ring grew others, as the opportunities for specu-
> lation and plunder were developed. Cattle Rings, Public Land Steal-
> ing Rings, Mining Rings, Treasury Rings, and rings of almost every
> description grew up, till the affairs of the Territory came to be run
> almost exclusively in the interest and for the benefit of combinations
> organized and headed by a few longheaded, ambitious, and unscrupu-
> lous Americans.[39]

This maze of rings was further complicated by a proliferation of joint stock companies, private investment pools, and individual speculators, all active in the promotion of land, railroads, milling, farming, small-scale manufacturing, and shipping.[40]

One of the ring's most infamous capers was its takeover of the Maxwell Land Grant. The land was originally granted to Charles Beaubien and Guadalupe Miranda in 1841. When the grantees re-quested execution two years later, Fray Martínez objected on grounds that part of the land belonged to the people of Taos and because it was going to members of the American party. Over the next years, various other groups claimed parts of the Beaubien-Miranda Grant: Indians, Mexican tenant farmers, Mexican villages, and Anglo squatters.

Lucien Maxwell, the son-in-law of Beaubien, bought Miranda's share of the grant in 1858, as well as a tract from his father-in-law's share. Some years later, after the death of his father-in-law, Maxwell began to buy up other shares. His total outlay was not more than $50,000.

In 1869 Maxwell sold his grant to a British-Dutch combine which was also composed of members of the Santa Fe Ring. Miguel A. Otero was among the purchasers. After it took control of the Maxwell Land Grant, the combine ran into many obstacles. The sale created problems because a number of tenant farmers lived on the property. Another complication was that Maxwell did not know how much land was included in the grant. The discovery of gold on the property in 1866 brought in many prospectors. Finally, when it was learned that the federal government had laid claim to a portion of the Maxwell grant for reservation and park land, Mexican and Anglo squatters moved onto the land, believing it would become public domain and under United States law they would be entitled to it. The squatters each cultivated between 20 to 50 acres of irri-gated land.[41] Therefore, in order to get clear title to the grant, the combine had to eliminate each of these obstacles.

While Lucien Maxwell probably estimated the size of the grant at between 32,000 and 97,424 acres, when the ring gained control of the grant it was expanded to 1,714,765 acres. The residents of Col-fax County felt threatened as the boundaries of the grant moved outward engulfing those lands to which owners held legal title. Open conflict erupted. For example, on September 14, 1875, T. J. Tolby, a Methodist minister and a leading opponent of the ring, was killed. Cruz Vega, a Mexican and constable of the Cimarron precinct, was accused of the murder; although he denied any involvement, he was lynched. Vigilantes believed that he had been hired by the ring, but according to some sources, the lynching seems to have been racially motivated. The Tolby murder set the stage for a bloody war between the company and the squatters. *Mexicanos* generally remained aloof. Anglos resented Mexicans, not only on racial grounds, but because they believed Mexicans to be the source of the ring's power.[42]

During the 1880s Mexican *paisanos* continued to move onto the land; slowly they became more involved. When the squatters formed the Squatters Club to raise money for defense in 1881, only one Mexican was in the club; by 1887 both groups rode together. In that year the combine brought legal proceedings against the squatters. M. P. Pels, the company agent, attempted to divide squatters by promising cash settlements if they would leave. On July 23, 1888, seventy-five armed Mexicans and Anglos turned back the sheriff. Masked riders patrolled the area, frustrating company efforts to evict them. Jacinto Santistevan and his son Julian were among the leaders of the resistance. Like the other squatters, he was a small farmer, with 160 acres of fenced land of which he farmed 80. The total value of Santistevan's holding was estimated at $300.[43]

The period of unity was short-lived, however. In 1888, the same year in which the riders faced the sheriff successfully, a division arose. When Anglos refused to help Mexicans run company agent Charles Hunt out of Vermejo Park, the Mexicans were so angered that "many vowed never to aid Americans again."[44]

On February 21, 1891, a company business agent was killed and the company retaliated, mounting a twenty-three man posse to track down the men. Violence remained at a high level after this incident: Mexicans burned crops, cut fences, and destroyed buildings. They killed cattle and, as the spring wore on, armed skirmishes became more frequent. Cowhands were reluctant to risk their lives for the company; Mexican violence increased. The company, however, changed its tactics and began to single out *paisanos* for preferential treatment. During 1893 it continued its court battle and just plain wore Santistevan down. That year Jacinto left, marking the beginning of the end;[45] many farmers came to terms with the company. "Under Dutch leadership, the reorganized Maxwell Land and Railway Company," was more formally brought into the Santa Fe network and when the case finally went to the higher courts, the ring's agent protected its interest.

Throughout the violence, the Santa Fe group continued its

relentless drive to gain control of the land by manipulating the law. It influenced the territorial legislature to pass legislation that "authorized the courts to partition grants or put them up on the sale block, even when the smallest owner petitioned such action. Another territorial law, enacted in January 1876, annexed Colfax County to Taos County for political purposes for at least two court terms."[46] Thus, where the ring owned even a small portion of land, it could force a sale; and since the ring also controlled Taos judges, the annexation was a great boon to it. During this period the ring received the cooperation of the appointed governors, who refused to intervene even though there was considerable bloodshed. Moreover, when the government surveyed the Maxwell grant, John T. Elkins, a brother of Stephen B. Elkins, was appointed as one of the surveyors. Finally, on April 18, 1887, a decision was reached by the United States Supreme Court, which completely disregarded the rights of the Indians, Mexicans, and squatters. It found for the Maxwell Company (which the ring now owned), thus dispossessing the Indian and the Mexican tenant farmers (both of whom had lived on the land included in the grant until the land grabbers moved in), and marking the end of an era.[47]

THE LINCOLN COUNTY WAR

After the Civil War immense profits were made from the open range where land and water could be used free of charge. The causes of the Lincoln County War were similar to those in Colfax County. The controversy again involved the Santa Fe Ring, but centered on a smaller ring and a group of its challengers. The power blocs in this rivalry were led by Anglo-Americans—one a Republican and the other a Democrat. In this area small Anglo farmers were not involved as they had been in Colfax County. Losers, as always, were the poor—principally Mexican sheepherders and farmers.

Lincoln County is in the plains area of New Mexico. Contrary to Webb's statements in *The Great Plains,* Mexicans had moved into the area, and had established small villages and farms in the county prior to the 1870s, when Anglos began arriving in large numbers. In the 1870s demand for American beef and mutton in the United Kingdom as well as increased consumption in the eastern United States created a boom. New markets had been opened in February 1875 when a refrigerated ship with dressed beef left for Liverpool, England. With an opportunity to profit in cattle, the adventurers moved into Lincoln County. They clashed with the Mexicans, who herded sheep on the open range. The Anglos wanted not only the land for cattle grazing, but also dominance of the entire area.[48]

The Lincoln County War (1876–1878) often has been portrayed

as a personal feud or as a cattle or range war, with the conflict growing out of cattle rustling and range rights. Robert N. Mullin, editor of *Maurice Garland Fulton's History of the Lincoln County War,* has clarified this situation:

> The Lincoln County War was essentially a struggle for economic power. In a land where hard cash was scarce, federal contracts for the supply provisions, principally beef, for the military posts and for the Indian reservations, were the grand prize. Since the early 1870's Laurance Gustave Murphy had been the Lincoln County sub-contractor for William Rosenthal and the political clique at Sante Fe which enjoyed a near-monopoly in supplying the government with beef, even though neither Rosenthal nor Murphy himself then raised or owned any significant number of cattle. They were challenged by John H. Chisum, owner of the largest herds in the territory, who declined to do business through Rosenthal but instead bid direct on the beef contracts. Thus began Chisum's struggle with Murphy and his successors along with their backers at Santa Fe—a struggle out of which grew the Lincoln County War.[49]

By the 1870s, Lincoln County had become a haven for outlaws. The group led by Murphy encouraged lawlessness by hiring Anglo-American gangs as rustlers for their beef-supply business, thus bringing into the territory men who had little concern for law or life—especially Mexican life. The largest group migrating into Lincoln was Texans, who brought with them "a tradition of violence nurtured by the Civil War," blood feuds, and hatred for Mexicans. Relations between cattlemen and sheepmen were not good anywhere in the nation, but because of the racism of the Texans, they were especially bad in New Mexico.[50]

One outlaw band, the Harrell clan, rode into the town of Lincoln, formerly the Mexican pueblo La Placita, in 1873 and began to entertain themselves by abusing townspeople. When Constable Juan Martínez attempted to restrain them, a gun fight followed in which three of the marauders and Constable Martínez were killed. The outlaws retaliated by attacking the town and shooting indiscriminately into a crowd of people attending a dance. Four Mexicans were killed. Troops finally chased the Harrells out of the county, but en route they killed José Haskell because he had a Mexican wife. As they rode toward Texas, Ben Turner, a member of the gang, was shot from ambush, whereupon they went on another rampage, killing five Mexican freighters.

By January 27, 1874, the *New Mexican* in Sante Fe announced that Lincoln County had exploded into an "unfortunate war between the Texans and the Mexicans."[51] There is ample proof, however, that Santa Fe Ring partisans wanted to focus the public's attention on racial conflicts in order to conceal the economic struggle which was the basis of the hostilities. A major part of the war involved the power play between the Murphy group, who controlled Republican party politics in Lincoln, and John H. Chisum, who represented the Democrats.

Juan Patrón emerged as the Mexican leader in Lincoln. Born in 1855 in La Placita, he attended parochial schools in New Mexico, eventually graduating from the University of Notre Dame in Indiana. Friends described him as "honest, studious, and industrious."[52] His father was killed by the Harrell clan. In 1878 he was a delegate to the territorial House of Representatives, where deputies elected him speaker. He functioned, without pay, as the town's only school teacher.

In 1875, Patrón was employed as a clerk of the probate court. John Copeland, an Anglo rancher, and his neighbor John Riley, a member of the Murphy clan, accused two Mexican workers, of stealing property from their ranches. The workers ran because of threats by Copeland, but Copeland and Riley pursued them, killing one and capturing the other. Copeland and Riley decided to take their prisoner to Fort Stanton, seven miles away, and these "cowboys," who were accustomed to riding, set out on foot with the prisoner in front of them. When the unarmed Mexican allegedly attempted to escape, they shot him. They reported their version of the incident to Probate Judge Laurence Murphy, an associate of Riley and leader of the Murphy ring, who acquitted them.

Patrón investigated the incident and concluded that the men were shot at the ranch and not, as alleged, on the road. His demand for a grand jury investigation was denied. Determined not to allow this injustice to go unpunished, Patrón, as probate clerk, signed a warrant for the arrest of Copeland and Riley, enlisted a posse, and rode to the Copeland ranch. They eventually found both men, took them prisoner, and interrogated them. Concluding that the two Mexicans had been shot in cold blood, many in the posse wanted to shoot the accused murderers, but Patrón calmed them. When troops arrived from Fort Stanton (their aid had been sought by one of Riley's friends), the posse released the two *gringos*. Riley went into his house, got a gun and shot Patrón in the back. The army arrested the Mexicans.

Patrón was taken prisoner and held in the post hospital, where he remained in critical condition for some time. Although Patrón was indicted on the demand of John Riley, he did not go to trial. He recovered to lead the Mexicans during the Lincoln County War.

Juan Patrón and most Mexicans sided with Chisum against Murphy, probably because they considered the Murphy ring to be the principal and most immediate threat to them. Murphy viewed the rise of Patrón as a threat to his dominance. The Murphy group's involvement with the Harrell gang and the Riley-Copeland affair undoubtedly influenced the Mexicans' decision to support the opposition. In addition, James Dolan, a violent man who committed many atrocities, became the leader of the Murphy group.[53]

The Lincoln County War was set in motion in the spring of 1877 when an Englishman, John H. Tunstall, opened a mercantile store in competition with the Murphy establishment. Alexander McSween, a lawyer, and John Chisum, were Tunstall's associates. In addition, the Chisum-Tunstall group opened a bank that competed with the First National Bank, controlled by Elkins and Catron.

When Dolan threatened Tunstall, two armed camps formed. Most Mexicans joined Juan Patrón in backing the Tunstall group. Tensions mounted and bloodshed followed. Dolan employed the Jesse Evans gang to do the dirty work. Even though the gang had a few Mexican members, it viciously murdered and persecuted the Mexican community. Finally, Tunstall was murdered by Dolan's men, and revenge was immediately sought by the Englishman's supporters, among whom was the notorious William Bonnie, alias Billy the Kid. Dolan attacked Patrón in the *New Mexican,* charging that he was leader of the county's lawless Mexican element. As far as the Murphy group was concerned, all Mexicans were in the Tunstall camp.

Both groups recruited gunmen. Among the newcomers to the territory were John Selman and his so-called scouts. Selman, a well-known cattle rustler, was hired by Dolan. According to Maurice Fulton, "During the latter part of September, Selman's group moved to the vicinity of Lincoln and inaugurated a worse type of terrorism than heretofore known." With Dolan forces, they committed "apparently motiveless deeds of violence." Sam Corbet, in a letter to Tunstall's father, wrote: "They killed two men and two boys (Mexicans) only about 14 years old, unarmed and in the hay field at work. Rode right up to them and shot them down." These actions "roused the Lincoln County Mexicans, some even determined to visit retaliation on the first *Americanos,* in particular *Tejanos,* that came their way."[54]

Governor Samuel B. Axtell sided with the Dolan faction and maintained that the situation in the county did not require intervention. Many people believed he was a member of the Sante Fe Ring. However, the murders of Reverend Tolby in Colfax and of Tunstall, a British subject whose death attracted international attention, signaled Axtell's political demise. On September 4, 1878, over the protests of Catron, Elkins, and other prominent ring members, General Lew Wallace was appointed governor by President Rutherford B. Hayes. Wallace was a Republican, so New Mexicans waited nervously to see if he would prove to be another Axtell. President Hayes had given him a mandate to clean up the trouble in Lincoln County, and he took vigorous action to do so. He formed a local militia, led by Juan Patrón, and peace was restored in 1879.

Because of harassment, Patrón moved to Puerto de Luna, several hundred miles away. Misfortune hounded him. While in a saloon having a drink with a friend, a cowboy named Mitch Maney shot him. Many believed Dolan had hired Maney as an assassin and certainly the subsequent trial raises some questions. Although Maney was a penniless cowboy, one of the most expensive legal firms in the territory defended him. Moreover, the main prosecutor was Thomas Catron. The outcome was a hung jury, and Maney was never retried.[55] However, the fact that the ring was both defense and prosecution proved to many that a conspiracy existed. Juan Patrón, an effective and honest leader, had been a threat to the establishment. One can speculate that if his challenge had gone unpunished, other dissidents might have been encouraged to rebel. His violent death, therefore—whether there was evidence of design or not—served to intimidate incipient rebels.

Mexican shepherds and Texas cowboys continued to fight for land and water. But, by the 1880s, the cattlemen had eliminated the Mexican as a competitor. During the decade the conflict degenerated into a race war. Time favored the Anglos with railroads linking Lincoln County to markets. During the same period railroads spurred wool shipments and soon nearly three million head of sheep roamed the territory, but now the sheep belonged to the Anglo-Americans. A thousand ewes brought $15,000 a year, whereas a Mexican herder could be employed for less than $200 annually.[56] Thus, in the end, economics brought about a victory of sheep—without Mexicans.

THE RESISTANCE

The 1880s crystallized opposition to encroachments. Mexican enterprises suffered from the impact of the railroad; private contractors were stripping the timber from the land; competition with Anglo workers strained an already bad economic situation; and inequalities in the pay scale for Anglo and Mexican workers increased antagonisms. By the middle of the decade Mexicans organized the Association of the Brotherhood for the Protection of the Rights and Privileges of the People of New Mexico, whose stated purpose was to free New Mexico from corrupt politicians and monopolies.

One of the many resistance societies formed in New Mexico was *Las Gorras Blancas* (the White Caps), who operated in San Miguel County from 1889 to 1891. This group used offensive tactics to sabotage the efforts of the Anglos and the *ricos* to deprive them of their land. *Las Gorras* saw the central issue as a change in land tenure.[57]

San Miguel County is located in northern New Mexico, a mountainous land. Its principal town is Las Vegas. "The tract of land that came to be known as the Las Vegas Grant contained 500,000 acres of fine timber, agricultural and grazing lands, the meadows in the area of the future town of Las Vegas being espe-cially rich." As early as 1821, grants to portions of this region had been awarded to individuals; however, because of Indian attacks, most of the grantees failed to settle on their grants. Nevertheless, by 1841, 131 families were living in the area of Las Vegas. "On June 21, 1860, Congress confirmed 496,446 acres as the grant of land made to the town of Las Vegas."[58] Also confirmed was the grant which had been given to Luis María Cabeza de Baca in 1821. Much of the population of Las Vegas subsisted by grazing sheep and farming. The land, in accordance with Mexican law and traditions, was held in common by the people and could not be sold. After the Civil War this way of life was challenged by the arrival of Anglo-Americans who were accustomed to squatting on public domain land and had little knowledge or respect for village lands or the open range. In the 1880s they began to buy tracts from New Mexi-cans even though, according to Mexican law the settlers, as users of the land, did not have the right to sell it if such a sale conflicted with communal interests.

Land grabbers claimed an absolute right to lands and fenced their claims, enclosing as many as 10,000 acres. This action denied Mexicans access to timber, water, and grazing lands. Naturally the Mexicans resented the action, especially when Anglos brought a suit, *Milhiser v. Padilla,* in 1887 to test ownership of the land. The court found that "The Las Vegas Grant was a community grant and that the plaintiffs had no case. . . . However, the plaintiffs muted the finding by dropping their case on November 25, 1889, thus not allowing the judgement to be finalized."[59] The favorable court deci-sion did nothing to deter fencing and other encroachments. The attitude of territorial authorities was one of apathy and indifference. The rapid increase in the county's population intensified the strug-gle for its resources.[60]

On November 1, 1889, Mexicans moved to defend themselves. "Armed with rifles and pistols, draped in long black coats and slickers, their faces hidden behind white masks . . . ", sixty-six horsemen rode into Las Vegas. They converged on the jail, asking for Sheriff Lorenzo López, and then on the home of Miguel Salazar, the prosecuting attorney. No property was damaged at this time, but the action climaxed a year of fence-cutting by night riders. Offensive actions were blamed on *Las Gorras Blancas,* and indict-ments of Mexicans were issued. The secrecy of the organization was an advantage, making it difficult to identify and bring charges against the participants in raids. The White Caps enjoyed public support, and claimed a membership of 1,500. On December 16, 1889, there was a march through the town to demand the release of suspected White Caps. On March 11, 1890, *Las Gorras* made a tour of East Las Vegas, leaving copies of their platform, which in part read:

Nuestra Plataforma

Our purpose is to protect the rights and interests of the people in general and especially those of the helpless classes.

We want the Las Vegas Grant settled to the benefit of all concerned, and this we hold is the entire community within the Grant.

We want no "land grabbers" or obstructionists of any sort to interfere. We will watch them.

We are not down on lawyers as a class, but the usual knavery and unfair treatment of the people must be stopped.

Our judiciary hereafter must understand that we will sustain it only when "justice" *is* its watchword.[61]

Of course, many Anglos and establishment Mexicans condemned the platform as anti-American and revolutionary. Miguel A. Otero described the White Caps as "a criminal organization."[62] *The Optic*, the town newspaper, portrayed them as a destructive influence in the community.

Las Gorras continued fence-cutting and destruction of property. The railroad also became their target, since it appropriated land for rights-of-way and brought people and commerce that destroyed the old way of life. The government stepped up activities against them. Governor Le Baron Prince threatened to move troops into the area if local authorities did not stop *Las Gorras*. He proposed that one or two companies of federal troops be stationed in San Miguel to demonstrate power and protect railroad property and that detectives be employed to infiltrate *Las Gorras*. He was not able to carry his plans to fruition since the Secretary of the Interior did not cooperate and the territory did not have enough money for the spies.[63]

Prince went to the area to talk to *Las Gorras*. Félix Martínez, a leader among the poor Mexicans, confronted him, stating, "On one hand, you have the power of money—the rich land grabbers—on the other, the physical might of the people. True, the innocent with good titles are made wrongfully to suffer on account of the land thieves."[64] These remarks met with general approval of Mexicans of Las Vegas. Governor Prince responded that grievances of the people could not be righted until "law and order" was reestablished. Russell Kistler, editor of *The Optic*, was not totally insensitive, and he condemned land grabbers who bought small claims for $5 and expanded these holdings to 5000 acres.[65]

From 1889 to 1891 the White Caps mobilized the resistance and provided action when efforts at peaceful reform had failed. But the opposition of the authorities and other factors began to dilute their support. To many Mexicans they represented an extreme solution, for they operated outside the law.

Alternative solutions also defused the *Las Gorras* movement. The Knights of Labor, an early national trade union, moved to support the poor people's cause. They issued a declaration on August

25, 1890: "A cry of discontent has become general among the people of San Miguel County on account of party abuses against the sovereignty of the people, and public and private interests of the same, especially the interests of the working people."[66]

The principal signer of the declaration was Juan José Herrera, a district organizer for the Knights who had been suspected of being a leader of *Las Gorras*. In his tactics Herrera combined a knowledge of San Miguel county with other factors. He was a literate man who had published a newspaper; he had experience as an organizer; and he had traveled outside the local community, having been involved with the Knights in Colorado. Herrera played the role of agitator. He expanded the targets of *los pobres* to include the railroads and lumber operations as well as crystallizing labor grievances. He was an optimistic leader who employed labor tactics. Herrera was building a movement based on the ethnic and class identification of *Las Gorras*. He and other popular leaders of this movement, Félix Martínez and Nestor Montoya, launched a political party, the United People's Party (*El Partido*).[67]

The Knights of Labor began to disassociate themselves from Herrera because of his link with *Las Gorras*. They could not understand the violence and anti-Anglo sentiments of Mexicans. The Knights could understand class conflict, but not the issue of communal land and the desire to expel the *gringo* from the county. They had "little sympathy for the 'ignorant Mexicans' who were swelling the ranks of their order."[68] As in the case of many liberal and radical organizations they could not understand the need for building on ethnic identification in face of racial slurs and economic threats.

There is no question of the influence of the White Caps on Mexicans, and if allowed to evolve, they might have had a far-reaching impact on their condition. However, despite the United People's party's initial success and promise, its effectiveness was gradually diminished by the manipulation within the political system by its opponents. Some leading *Mexicanos* defected to the People's party when it nominated candidates for offices in 1890, and significantly, fence-cutting decreased.

The party won every race it entered by a margin of two to one, running on an anticapitalist, antimonopoly, antirailroad, antiland-grabber, anti-Santa Fe Ring, and anti-Republican platform. Throughout the conflict it based its power on *los pobres*.[69]

The voice of the poor was *La Voz del Pueblo*, a Spanish language newspaper, founded by Nestor Montoya, who vehemently opposed the ring. In 1890 he associated himself with Félix Martínez and moved the newspaper from Santa Fe to Las Vegas "to champion the cause of the people against the agents of corruption." And, while *La Voz* never condoned fence-cutting, it did explain the reasons for it.[70]

Meanwhile, the Republicans, who were controlled by the Santa Fe Ring, organized opposing political forces. They sponsored *Los Caballeros de Ley y Orden Protección Mutua*, who were the law-and-order Republicans. Since many Mexicans joined the group, its existence accentuated class divisions within the Mexican population. *Los Caballeros* were linked to Tom Catron and were led by Eugenio Romero, the Republican boss of San Miguel County. This organization attracted middle-class Mexicans whose limited prosperity had been disrupted by the violence. In May 1891, these Mexicans founded a newspaper, *El Sol de Mayo*, to counter the views expressed by *La Voz*.[71] The views of *El Sol* were reinforced by *La Revista Católica*. Published by Jesuits in Las Vegas, *La Revista* was generally considered to represent the views of the church and it consistently attacked *Las Gorras*.

Republicans played up the issue of the White Caps. A vote for the Democrats or for the People's party was said to be a vote for *Las Gorras Blancas*. The People's party swept the county elections of 1890 throughout the territory.[72] It won four seats in the Assembly.

Soon afterwards a People's party assemblyman, Pablo Herrera, announced his disillusionment. Speaking before the legislature in February 1891, he said:

> Gentlemen . . . I have served several years time in the penitentiary but only sixty days in the legislature . . . I have watched the proceedings here carefully. I would like to say that the time I spent in the penitentiary was more enjoyable than the time I spent here. There is more honesty in . . . prison than . . . [in] the legislature. I would prefer another term in prison than another election in the house.[73]

Pablo Herrera returned to San Miguel and attempted to revive *Las Gorras Blancas*, but he was expelled from the Knights of Labor and after this point he lost his effectiveness. He became a fugitive when he killed a man in Las Vegas. Herrera was eventually fatally shot by Félipe López, a deputy sheriff.[74]

Reforms at the county level were frustrated and attacks on the White Caps continued. Beset by factionalism *El Partido* faded away. In 1894 the United States Court of Private Land Claims ruled the San Miguel claim a community grant, but the court limited its decision to house lots and garden plots, excluding common pasturage.[75] And while *los hombres pobres* continued to cut fences as late as 1926, they failed to stop the influx of Anglos and capital which symbolized the changes that were taking place.

CONCLUSION

The furor over the Maxwell Grant coincided with the San Miguel County Wars and its conclusion came about the same time. By 1896 only Stonewall County remained in open rebellion with violence taking the form of burning 130 tons of hay in December 1898 north of Stonewall. Improved transportation cut into isolation, with the influx of more federal troops and company posses. By 1900 the company had absolute title to the land; the Rocky Mountain Timber Company acquired the Maxwell Land Grant Company.[76]

Toward the end of the century, many mines were developed in New Mexico, copper, coal, zinc, and other minerals were mined in substantial quantities. Again the owners were Anglo-Americans, and again Mexicans were the low-paid workers who generated large profits. Irrigation brought large-scale agriculture to New Mexico, changing the life style of the residents to the detriment of the *paisano*, who provided the bulk of the labor force in that industry as well.

The opportunity for wage labor "on the railroads, in the mines, in the timber industry, or as freighters—minimized the initial impact of the loss of grazing lands" and postponed the inevitable conflict until the depression of the 1930s.[77]

By 1900 the economic privilege of a handful of Anglo-Americans had become permanent: with few exceptions, Mexicans did not share in the control of production. Occasionally, some of *los ricos* and even some of the *patrones* (bosses) joined the poor, but these alliances were rare, and the rich usually used them to promote their own self-interest. They were opportunistic, using nationalism to gain the support of the masses. New Mexico was also plagued with tensions between north and south *Hispanos* who sided along sectional rather than ethnic lines. The poor in both regions were used by them.[78] More Texan cowboys entered New Mexico, reinforcing discrimination. By 1912, when New Mexico achieved statehood, Anglo-American mining, ranching, and transportation combines owned the state and the society was frozen.

NOTES

1. *Albuquerque Journal*, December 18, 1970.
2. Nancie González, *The Spanish-Americans of New Mexico: A Heritage of Pride* (Albuquerque: University of New Mexico Press, 1967), p. 205.
3. The population statistics are not exact. According to Hubert Howe Bancroft, *History of Arizona and New Mexico, 1530–1888* (Albuquerque: Horn & Wallace, 1963), p. 642, the U.S. Census of 1850 listed a population of 61,547, exclusive of the Indian population; in 1860 the figure was 80,853, of whom 73,859 were native to New Mexico. D. W. Meinig, *Southwest: Three Peoples in Geographical Change, 1600–1970* (New York: Oxford University Press, 1971), p. 31, writes that by the late 1840s there were about 70,000 *Hispanos* and about 10,000 Pueblo Indians.
4. Howard R. Lamar, *The Far Southwest, 1846–1912: A Territorial History* (New York: Norton, 1970), p. 30.
5. Ward Alan Minge, *Frontier Problems in New Mexico Preceding the Mexican War, 1840–1846* (Albuquerque: University of New Mexico Press, 1965), p. 9.
6. Minge, p. 41, 44, Lamar, p. 53.
7. Warren A. Beck, *New Mexico: A History of Four Centuries* (Norman: University of Oklahoma Press, 1962), pp. 126–127.

8. Bancroft, pp. 324, 327.

9. Lamar, p. 53.

10. Benjamin M. Read, *Illustrated History of New Mexico* (New York: Arno Press, 1976), pp. 407–408; Minge, pp. 304–306.

11. Magoffin had come to the region in 1828 and was married to María Gertrudes Valdez. He met with President Polk before the march, giving him a considerable amount of information about New Mexico. Stella M. Drumm, ed., *Down the Santa Fe Trail and into New Mexico* (New Haven, Conn.: Yale University Press, 1962), p. xxiv.

12. Lynn I. Perrigo, *The American Southwest* (New York: Holt, Rinehart and Winston, 1971), p. 164; Ralph Emerson Twitchell, *The Conquest of Santa Fe 1846* (Española, N.M.: Tate Gallery Publications, 1967), p. 52.

13. Carolyn Zeleny, "Relations Between the Spanish Americans and Anglo-Americans in New Mexico: A Study of Conflict and Accommodation in Dual Ethnic Situation" (Ph.D. dissertation, Yale University, 1944), p. 137.

14. Quoted in Beck, p. 134.

15. Alvin R. Sunseri, "New Mexico in the Aftermath of the Anglo-American Conquest" (Ph.D. dissertation, Louisiana State University and Agricultural and Mechanical College, History, 1973), p. 131.

16. Ralph Emerson Twitchell, *The History of the Military Occupation of the Territory of New Mexico* (New York: Arno Press, 1976), p. 125; Lamar, p. 70.

17. Twitchell, *Conquest of Santa Fe*, p. 133.

18. Carey McWilliams, *North from Mexico* (New York: Greenwood Press, 1968), p. 118.

19. Bancroft, p. 436; Zeleny, p. 118; (Sister Mary) Loyola, *The American Occupation of New Mexico, 1821–1852* (New York: Arno Press, 1976), p. 71.

20. Sunseri, p. 143; Larry Dagwood Ball, "The Office of the United States Marshall in Arizona and the New Mexico Territory, 1851–1912" (Ph.D. dissertation, University of Colorado, 1970), p. 23.

21. Based on conversations with Gilberto López y Rívas, May 4, 1977.

22. According to Daniel T. Valdes, *A Political History of New Mexico*, rev. ed. (privately printed, 1971), p. 5, in 1780 there were 110 *rico* families, 2,500 debtor *peones*, 12,000 farmer *peones*, 22,000 *paisanos*, and 400 military personnel.

23. Robert Johnson Rosenbaum, "Mexicano Versus Americano: A Study of Hispanic-American Resistance to Anglo-American Control in New Mexico Territory, 1870–1900" (Ph.D. dissertation, University of Texas, 1972), p. 5. Meinig, pp. 63–64.

24. González, p. 52.

25. Quoted in González, p. 53.

26. Stan Steiner, *La Raza: The Mexican Americans* (New York: Harper & Row, 1969), p. 8.

27. Pedro Sánchez, *Memorias Sobre la Vida del Presbitero Don Antonio José Antonio Martínez* (Santa Fe, N. Mex.: Compania Impresora del Nuevo Mexicano, 1903) reprinted in David Weber, ed., *Northern Mexico on the Eve of the North American Invasion* (New York: Arno Press, 1976), p. 11; William A. Keleher, *Turmoil in New Mexico, 1846–1868* (Santa Fe: Rydal Press, 1952), p. 132, n. 71; William A. Keleher, *The Maxwell Grant* (Santa Fe: Rydal Press, 1942), pp. 15, 133.

28. Zeleny, p. 257–258; Robert W. Larson, *New Mexico's Quest for Statehood, 1846–1912* (Albuquerque: University of New Mexico Press, 1968), p. 82; Perrigo, pp. 219–220. On April 7, 1974, the Santa Fe *New Mexican* published an article called "Was He Racist? Carson Debate Set," by Don Ross. It stated that the G.I. Forum was against the naming of a national forest after Kit Carson. Loyola, p. 35, Carson was very much tied to the establishment; he belonged to the American party prior to the war, and he was married to Josefa Jaramillo, the sister of Charles Bent's wife.

29. Paul Horgan, *Lamy of Santa Fe: His Life and Times* (New York: Farrar, Straus & Giroux, 1975).

30. Alex M. Darley, *The Passionist of the Southwest or the Holy Brotherhood* (1893), reprinted in Carlos E. Cortes, ed., *The Penitentes of New Mexico* (New York: Arno Press, 1974), p. 5; Francis Leon Swadesh, *Los Primeros Pobladores* (Notre Dame: University of Notre Dame Press, 1974), p. 78.

31. Miguel Antonio Otero, *Otero: An Autobiographical Trilogy*, vol. 2 (New York: Arno Press, 1974), p. 46.
32. Alice Corbin Henderson, *Brothers of Light: The Penitentes of the Southwest* (1937), reprinted in Cortes, *Penitentes of New Mexico*, p. 77; Swadesh, p. 75.
33. Horgan, p. 229, does not repeat the charge of Martínez' immorality and there is a question as to its truth; on p. 353 Horgan makes the point that Martínez died one of the richest men in New Mexico.
34. Armando Váldez, "Insurrection in New Mexico: The Land of Enchantment," *El Grito* (Fall 1967): 21.
35. McWilliams, p. 122.
36. Larson, p. 143.
37. Keleher, *The Maxwell Grant*, p. 152.
38. Larson, p. 143.
39. Quoted in Howard R. Lamar, *The Far Southwest, 1846–1919* (New Haven, Conn.: Yale University Press, 1966), p. 150.
40. Herbert O. Brayer, *William Blackmore: The Spanish-Mexican Land Grants of New Mexico and Colorado, 1863–1878* (1949), reprinted in Carlos E. Cortes, ed., *Spanish and Mexican Land Grants* (New York: Arno Press, 1974), p. 173.
41. Keleher, *The Maxwell Grant*, p. 150; Rosenbaum, p. 42; Lamar, p. 142; Rosenbaum, pp. 71, 75–79.
42. Keleher, *The Maxwell Grant*, p. 29; F. Stanley, *The Grant That Maxwell Bought* (Denver, Colo.: World Press, 1953), p. i; Rosenbaum, pp. 61, 64.
43. Rosenbaum, pp. 80, 86–91, 98.
44. Rosenbaum, pp. 92–93.
45. Rosenbaum, pp. 95–96, 99.
46. Larson, p. 138.
47. Keleher, *The Maxwell Grant*, pp. 109–110.
48. Charles L. Kenner, *A History of New Mexican-Plains Indian Relations* (Norman: University of Oklahoma Press, 1969), p. 41; Brayer, pp. 244–245; Beck, pp. 255, 260.
49. Maurice G. Fulton, *History of the Lincoln County War*, Robert N. Mullen, ed. (Tucson: University of Arizona Press, 1968), p. 8.
50. Rosenbaum, p. 115; Meinig, p. 34.
51. Rosenbaum, p. 116.
52. Fulton, pp. 406–407.
53. Rosenbaum, p. 119; Fulton, pp. 45–47.
54. Fulton, pp. 291–292.
55. Fulton, pp. 405–409.
56. Rosenbaum, p. 340; Perrigo, p. 279.
57. Rosenbaum, pp. 132–133, 139–140; Andrew Bancroft Schlesinger, "Las Gorras Blancas, 1889–1891," *Journal of Mexican American History* (Spring 1971): 87–143.
58. Schlesinger, pp. 93, 44.
59. Rosenbaum, p. 148.
60. Rosenbaum, p. 198.
61. *The Optic*, March 12, 1890, quoted in Schlesinger, pp. 107–108.
62. Otero, vol. 2, p. 166.
63. Rosenbaum, pp. 171, 200. Ironically, Judge James O'Brien, on July 30, 1890, wrote to Prince: "The so-called outrages are the protests of a simple pastoral people against the establishment of large landed estates, or baronial feudalism, in their native territory."
64. *The Optic*, August 18, 1890, quoted in Schlesinger, p. 115.
65. *The Optic*, August 7, 1890, quoted in Schlesinger, p. 116.
66. *The Optic*, August 25, 1890, quoted in Schlesinger, p. 117.
67. Rosenbaum, pp. 208, 216, 223.
68. Rosenbaum, p. 156.
69. Rosenbaum, pp. 225, 229, 235.
70. Rosenbaum, p. 201.
71. Rosenbaum, pp. 279, 270; Otero, vol. 2, p. 254.
72. Schlesinger, pp. 121, 122.
73. Schlesinger, p. 123.
74. Rosenbaum, p. 247.

75. Rosenbaum, pp. 324, 261. Between 1891 and 1904 the Court of Private Claims heard cases involving 235,491,020 acres, allowing 2,051,526 acres to remain intact. "Unfortunately for *Mexicanos,* the court reviewed most claims with suspicion, and worked to return land to the public domain." Weber, p. 157, writes, "In New Mexico, for example, more than 80 percent of the grant builders lost their land. There, since community grants and communal holdings were more common than individual grants, the slowness of litigation had its greatest impact on small farmers and herders."

76. William Taylor and Elliot West, "Patron Leadership at the Crossroads: Southern Colorado in the Late Nineteenth Century," in Norris Hundley, Jr., ed., *The Chicano* (Santa Barbara: Clio, 1975), p. 79.

77. Rosenbaum, p. 327; Zeleny, p. 145.

78. Rosenbaum, pp. 215–216, 102; Meinig, p. 63.

Chapter 4
Sonora Invaded:
The Occupation of Arizona

Many historians are captives of their sources, believing that the strip of territory in the Mesilla Valley, south of the Gila River, was purchased by the United States in 1854 solely for the purpose of building a southern railway route. Additionally, many allege that Mexico sold the territory, which included parts of southern New Mexico, because President Antonio López de Santa Anna needed money and believed that Mexico would lose the land anyway. These historians deny that a prime motive was the desire of the United States to obtain the area for its mineral wealth. They ask: How would the Anglo-Americans know of mineral wealth in an area far to the west and south—an area considered uninhabitable? These historians have not consulted newspapers and other sources in the Mexican state of Sonora.

Many Anglo-Americans who passed through the area after 1849 were interested in the mineral wealth of Mesilla. Historian Hubert Howe Bancroft commented that although many U.S. citizens criticized the government's purchase of worthless land for a railroad route, "the northern republic could afford to pay for a railroad route through a country said to be rich in mines."[1] Bancroft wrote: "Still the fame of hidden wealth remained and multiplied; and on the consummation of the Gadsden purchase in 1854, we have seen, Americans like Poston and Mowry began to open the mines. Eastern capital was enlisted. . . ."[2] Further, it was also no coincidence that Charles Poston and Herman Ehrenberg were surveying for gold and silver in the Santa Cruz Valley in 1854 the year that the treaty was ratified.[3]

Historian Howard Lamar also stated that those dubious about the value of the purchase were consoled by both public and private promoters who soon countered criticism with the rumor that rich mineral deposits existed in the Gadsden area.[4] Further, in spite of the fact that the U.S. military did not take possession until 1856, the Ajo copper mine in the Sonoita region, which had been discovered by Mexicans, was worked by a San Francisco company from 1855.[5] It is quite evident that the wealth of the newly purchased land was not a surprise.

Sonora was, in fact, a land renowned for its mineral wealth. Mexicans as well as foreigners in Sonora knew of the mineral potential of southern Arizona. For example, Juan A. Robinson, a merchant and at times the U.S. consul in Guaymas, was a long-time resident and knew the conditions in Sonora well. He lived in the state long before the signing of the Gadsden Treaty. Many other Anglo-Americans in Sonora were well versed concerning the potential of southern Arizona. Before Mexican Independence, extensive ranching and farming existed there. In 1736 *bolas de plata* (nuggets of silver) were found 10 miles southwest of Nogales, Arizona. The mine, which yielded large amounts of silver, significantly was called *Arizonac* or *La Mina Real de Arizona*.[6] As early as 1760 ore was also found in Cananea, just across today's U.S. border. In 1830 Don Francisco de Gamboa's work was translated into English which listed the mines in New Spain, including those in Upper Pimeria in Sonora, where "some large masses of virgin silver were found in the year 1736."[7] Southern Arizona's topography resembled that of the rest of Sonora, and citizens from that state never doubted its potential.

The French had shown considerable interest in Sonora. In January 1852, *Jecker-Torre y Cia*, a company with French connections, signed a contract with the local government to exploit northern Sonora. The exploring company was called *La Mineral de la Arizona*. An ill-fated expedition made up of Frenchmen was launched from San Francisco, California. The French, however, never abandoned their interest in the rest of the state, and it is said that this interest encouraged the intervention of Napoleon III in Mexican affairs in the 1860s.[8]

The economic motive for the seizure of southern Arizona makes further sense when the negotiations are reviewed. James Neff Garber wrote what has been called the definitive work on the Gadsden Treaty.[9] However, the weakness of the work is obvious. He deals with the political history of the negotiations and almost totally ignores the motivational factor. We concede that the United States wanted a southern railroad route, but in order to make this route economically feasible, the Sonoran port of Guaymas was essential. When Mexico proved unwilling to sell this area, Gadsden settled for the mineral potential of southern Arizona and New Mexico. He used heavy-handed methods in the negotiations, threatening Mexican ministers that, if they did not sell southern Arizona and parts of New Mexico, "we shall take it."[10] Mexico ceded over 45,000 square miles, of which some 35,000 were in southern Arizona, for $10 million.[11] That much money would have been too large an amount to pay for land through which a railroad route was no longer feasible, for without the port of Guaymas, the Mesilla was considered worthless and uninhabitable. Therefore, it is logical to conclude that a prime consideration was the potential mineral wealth of the area.

THE DRIVE ON SONORA

Arizona's geographical isolation presented a barrier to its economic development. In order to survive, it needed cheap labor and inexpensive transportation. Vast deserts separated the Arizona mines from California ports, and eastern routes were even more hazardous. Climate, lack of transportation, and frontier conditions made it virtually impossible to attract white labor in sufficient quantities to fill labor needs. Anglo-American capitalists who came to the territory knew of these liabilities and realized that Sonora, Mexico, was essential to their economic survival. The Mexican state had a good supply of experienced miners and manual laborers, and the Sonoran seaport of Guaymas was one of the finest on the Pacific Coast. From the beginning it was necessary to rely on Mexican labor; and to make the mines and other industries of the territory pay, the Mexican wage scales were kept below subsistence.

The stakes were high for the mines in the area were rich in bullion and Mexican labor made their exploitation possible. This economic dependence led to conspiracies to annex Sonora in order to gain Guaymas and to an active policy of gaining dominance over the Mexican state to insure a ready flow of labor.

Mexican sources charged that Anglos in Arizona encouraged Apaches to raid the Mexican state in order to weaken it and make it vulnerable for annexation. According to Sonoran historian, Laureano Calvo Berber, "The North American government permitted unscrupulous traders to trade with the Apaches at various crossings on the Colorado River, buying property that they stole [in Sonora] and supplying them with equipment, arms, and munitions."[12] On January 25, 1856, Joaquín Corella, head of Arizpe's *ayuntamiento*, wrote a letter to the Sonoran governor:

> The Gadsden Treaty, we repeat, has again brought misfortune to Sonora; it has deprived the state of its most valuable land, as well as resulting in the protection of the apache who launch their raids from these lands [Arizona] and to North Americans [bandits] who live among them, because in less than twenty-four hours they can cross the boundary; there the robbers and assassins remain beyond punishment; in our opinion it is vital as well as indispensable to garrison the border with sufficient troops that are always alert, since only in this way can their operation be successful and [only in this way] can they defend the integrity of a state threatened by filibusters.[13]

Private treaties were negotiated by Anglo-Americans with Apache bands. Arizona miners and ranchers made bargains with the Apaches, giving them sanctuary in Arizona in return for immunity from Apache raids, "providing economic ends [the Apache's] could be served by raiding elsewhere."[14] Charles D. Poston, owner of the Sonora Exploring and Mining Company and later called the

"Father of Arizona," made such a treaty with the Apaches. He negotiated the treaty through Dr. Michael Steck, Superintendent of Indian Affairs in New Mexico.[15]

Poston admitted that Steck instructed the Apaches "that they must not steal any of my stock nor kill any of my men. The chiefs said they wanted to be friends with the Americans, and would not molest us if we did not interfere with 'their trade with Mexico.'"[16] Steck made other treaties for Anglo-Americans during this period. This problem was compounded by the inactivity of the U.S. army, which ignored the Apache raids into Mexico. In fact, Captain R. S. Ewell, the commanding officer at Fort Buchanan, was more interested in exploiting the Patagonia Mine, of which he was part owner, than in tending to his duties as military and civil administrator.[17]

Cynical disregard by Anglo-Americans for Mexican life was demonstrated in the private treaty provisions of noninterference with "the Apache's trade with Mexico." A welcome side effect for Anglo-Americans was that this forced many Sonoran citizens to seek refuge in Arizona, making cheaper labor more available and depopulating the Mexican state. Annexationists knew that the population drain weakened Sonora so that it became difficult for it to defend itself. Thus, many Anglo-Americans publicly stated that they hoped Apaches and Mexicans would club one another to death. Sylvester Mowry, a prominent miner, expressed this hope in an address to the Geographical Society in New York on February 3, 1859:

> The Apache Indian is preparing Sonora for the rule of a higher civilization than the Mexican. In the past half century the Mexican element has disappeared from that which is now called Arizona, before the devastating career of the Apache. It is every day retreating further south, leaving to us (when the time is ripe for our own possession) the territory without the population.[18]

Not every Anglo-American agreed with the policy of genocide by proxy. The *Weekly Arizonian,* on April 28, 1859, strongly condemned the use of the Apache to annihilate Sonorans: "It is, in fact, nothing more nor less than legalized piracy upon a weak and defenseless state, encouraged and abetted by the United States government." Prominent miner and soldier Herman Ehrenberg echoed the *Arizonian:* "If we hate Mexicans, or if we want to take their country, we want no blood-thirsty savages to do the work for us, or to injure them."[19] Although Ehrenberg was a realist who knew that Mexican labor as well as trade with Sonora was essential to the growth of Arizona, he condemned the policy of making separate treaties with the Apache.

Two factors were at the crux of the annexationists' "Sonora-without-Mexicans" designs. They wanted title to all Sonoran mines without having to worry about the former owners; and they were racists, who looked upon Sonorans as half-breeds who were not assimilable into the superior Anglo-Saxon population.

Anglo-Americans were caught in a dilemma: while they did not want Mexicans as citizens, they needed them as laborers. This contradiction hit close to home during the Henry Crabb filibuster of 1857. Crabb led about a hundred Californians into Sonora on what he claimed was to be a peaceful colonizing expedition. The party marched into the state in military formation disregarding an order to leave by the Sonoran authorities. The Sonorans ambushed the Californians, executed Crabb, and cut off his head and preserved it in alcohol. Anglo-Americans retaliated against Mexicans in Arizona, and small-scale warfare broke out. President James Buchanan condemned the Mexican "brutality" and attempted to use it as an excuse to invade Mexico. Many Mexicans fled across the border, abandoning Arizona, and paralyzing the mines and Arizona's economy. Owners and supervisors of mines used their influence to cool emotions on both sides. "Crabb's ill fortune prevented later attempts of a similar nature, but the spirit of filibusterism was potent in Arizona, and the Sonoran authorities were always fearful and suspicious."[20]

Expansionist forces were active in Washington, D.C., where Senator Sam Houston sponsored a resolution to make Mexico a protectorate. Twenty-two years later Poston confirmed expansionist intentions:

> Among other secrets, it may now be told that President Buchanan and his cabinet, at the instigation of powerful capitalists in New York and New England, had agreed to occupy northern Sonora by the regular army and submit the matter to Congress afterwards. Ben McCullough was sent out as agent to select the military line, and Robert Rose was sent as consul to Guaymas with an American flag prepared expressly to hoist over that interesting seaport upon receiving proper orders.[21]

Although Poston's quote does not conclusively prove that there was official U.S. action toward acquisition, the evidence is strongly indicative. In 1859 Buchanan sent an armed vessel, the *St. Mary's*, to Guaymas to precipitate a fight, an action that resembled Commodore Stockton's adventure in Texas. His pretext was the refusal of Governor Ignacio Pesqueira to allow Charles P. Stone to survey public lands of Sonora. The Mexican government had entered into a contract with the Jecker-Torre Company and a group of Anglo-American capitalists, in which, in return for the survey, the foreigners would get one-third of the public lands and an option to buy another third. Pesqueira, resenting Stone's arrogant manner, as well as the prospect of foreigners—especially Anglo-Americans—owning two-thirds of Sonora's northern frontier, challenged the contract. Since Stone's party resembled a military operation more than a survey team, and with the Texas and Southwest experience still fresh in his mind, Pesqueira ordered him out of the state.

Stone made no secret of his desire to annex Sonora and encouraged Washington, D.C., to take action:

> I have carefully studied the country and people for eight months past, in which time I have had an excellent opportunity of gaining information from my position in the Survey of the Public Lands, and I feel confident that the only means of saving this state from a return to almost barbarism will be found to be its annexation to the United States. In this opinion I only agree with the most intelligent inhabitants of the State, both native and foreign.[22]

Captain William Porter of the *St. Mary's* demanded that Pesqueira allow Stone to continue his survey and in May protested Stone's expulsion. Anglo-American partners pressured Buchanan to intervene. Captain R. S. Ewell of Fort Buchanan, later a well-known general, entered Sonora and further increased tensions by his insolent manner. Finally, in November Captain Porter threatened to bombard Guaymas. Pesqueira replied that if one bomb fell on Guaymas he would not be responsible for Anglo-American property or lives in Sonora. The *St. Mary's* sailed away, but the incident did not end. On December 19, 1859, Buchanan complained that Mexicans had expelled peaceful Anglo-Americans, violating their personal and real property rights. He requested the U.S. Congress to approve occupation of Sonora as well as Chihuahua.[23]

Anglo-Americans did not annex Sonora, but their continuing attempts kept the state in constant disorder. In addition to the problems of Apache raids and the threats of occupation, Sonora was plagued by Anglo-Americans who bred dissatisfaction within the state in much the same way as had been done in Texas and New Mexico. Because of the internal chaos, caused in great part by Anglo-American actions, Mexicans fled from the disorder of the northern frontier to relatively safe conditions in Arizona. After 1876 the expansionist policy became unnecessary, since Anglo-American capitalists were given preferential treatment in Sonora.

THE POLARIZATION OF SOCIETY

From the time of their arrival in the territory Anglo-Americans in Arizona comprised a privileged class. Mining was the territory's leading industry and in most mining enterprises production required large capital investments. Access to large amounts of capital eluded most Mexicans. Two societies developed: masses of Mexicans who performed the manual labor and the Anglo entrepreneurs. There were, of course, some poor Anglos as well as poor Mexicans, but even at the lowest level in society racism played a major role in keeping the two groups apart. And there were, of course, some rich Sonorans who maintained their elite status. The situation resembled that in Texas and New Mexico, differing mainly in that border conflict in this area generated even more anti-Anglo-American sentiments.

Sonoran elites were well aware that the *gringos* coveted their land and that their privileged position would end if the territory were absorbed by the United States. Still considerable cooperation existed between the two groups of elites which in some cases was consummated by marriage. Southern Arizona in the 1850s was the epitomy of the wild frontier and few white women lived in the area during this time of turmoil. Many prominent Anglo-Americans, such as Governor Anson Stafford, married into Sonoran families. Between 1872 and 1899 intermarriages still remained high with 148 of 784, or 14 percent of all marriages, being between Anglo men and Mexican females; during the same period only 6 involved Mexican men and Anglo women. This situation changed drastically in the twentieth century; by 1946 only 3 percent of the marriages were between Anglo men and Mexican women, and only 1 percent between Mexican men and Anglo females.[24] Historian Kay Briegel indicates that the sparseness of the Anglo population of both women and men made intermarriage desirable for the Anglos in Arizona. First, there were few women who were not of Mexican descent. Second, the Anglos needed harmonious relationships with the Mexicans, which were encouraged by intermarriage, so that the Mexicans would help them defend themselves against the Apache threat. Once the railroad ended Arizona's isolation, bringing both Anglo women and men, and once the Indian threat was reduced, this special relation ended and intermarriage was taboo.[25]

Joseph Park, curator at the University of Arizona Library, criticizes the role of the historian in creating myths like that of the "Murderous Apache and the Mexican Outlaw, [who] rivalled each other in their deeds of pillage, robbery, and slaughter."[26] The portrayal of Mexicans as negative participants made them unworthy of leadership and justified their control by an orderly race. A further justification for the permanent caste system was racism.[27]

Peonage, the practice of legally binding a debtor or members of his family to a creditor until the debt was paid, was carried over from the Mexican period and practiced by Anglo-Americans in Arizona. For a number of reasons, it did not become a permanent institution. First, proximity of the border made it easy for a runaway to cross into Sonora. Second, it was cheaper to pay a man wages and cut him loose when there was no work. Third, soon after slavery was abolished, peonage was also made illegal. Nevertheless, the practice did continue de facto for many years in Arizona as well as in other places in the United States.

Many mines, ranches, and businesses practiced peonage during the 1850s and 1860s. In 1864 Sylvester Mowry praised the institution stating:

The lower class of Mexican, with the Opata and Yaqui Indians, are docile, faithful, good servants, capable of strong attachment when firmly and kindly treated. They have been "peons" (servants) for generations. They will always remain so, as it is their natural condition.[28]

Peonage was protected by law until it was abolished by the Fourteenth Amendment to the Constitution. If a peon ran away, the law would hunt him down, try him, and punish him. The punishment, in many instances, was inhumane. Witness, for example, the following cases. N. B. Appel owned a mercantile store in Tubac. His servant, who was indebted to him for $82.68, ran away and allegedly took a rifle and other articles of worth. The law returned the peon to Appel and prosecuted him. He was found guilty and publicly received fifteen lashes.[29] A similar episode occurred on the Riverton Ranch where seven peons escaped, but were returned and charged with debt and theft. The overseer, George Mercer, whipped them and cut off their hair as punishment. Mercer's shears got out of control and he took some skin with the hair. Stories of the "scalping" spread as far as San Francisco. Mercer publicly denied the charge, but readily admitted the whippings; nonetheless, the stories were widely believed.[30]

A double wage standard existed for Mexicans and Anglos. In the mines Mexicans' wages were 30¢ a day for wood choppers or ore sorters (this was called peon's wages); $12.50 to $15.00 a month for pick and crowbar men *(barrateros)* and ore carriers *(tantateros);* and $25.00 to $30.00 a month for skilled workers such as furnace tenders or smelters. In addition, they received 16 pounds of flour a week. They worked for twelve hours a day, six days a week. These wages prevailed through most of the 1800s and were slightly above those paid in Sonora. The mine operators' actual outlay for wages was even lower, because they recovered most of their capital from their company stores. Operators extended liberal credit to miners and charged them outrageous prices—stores made as much as 300 percent profit on their goods. The stores also provided a mechanism by which operators could maintain peonage and, by that means, a stable work force; indebted miners had to remain in order to pay off their debts.[31]

Anglo-American workers demanded wages that were double those received by Mexicans and received from $30.00 to $70.00 a month.[32] Mexicans were always assigned the dirtiest jobs—"Mexican work"—and were the first fired. When Anglo-Americans did not receive preferential treatment, they spread the word that "the managers . . . employed foreigners and greasers, and would not give a white man a chance."[33] Preferential treatment reinforced the ethnic division within what might have become a unified working class and so worked toward the operators' goal of maintaining depressed wages.

Some Mexicans, returning from the California diggings, realized that the wealth was not in the mines, but in services. Others started small mercantile businesses, and others freighted ores and other goods. Félipe Amabisca and Antonio Contreras arrived in Arizona City in 1858, and Amabisca opened a mercantile store. In partnership with Contreras, he also started a freighting business, making hauls from Tucson to Los Angeles. But these businesses were marginal, revolving around the mining and large-scale agriculture from which Mexicans were almost universally excluded. Mexicans were rarely found in industries requiring a large outlay of capital or in supervisory positions. They collectively remained at the bottom of the economic and social ladder and were stereotyped as "peons." Occasionally, Americanized Mexicans were referred to as "Spanish," but to the overwhelming majority of Anglo-Americans, they remained "greasers."

The boom in mining came in the 1880s spurred by railroads as well as by breakthroughs in technology and engineering. Telegraph and electrical wires created a demand for copper, and the copper mines of southern Arizona attracted capital from San Francisco, the eastern states, and foreign countries. In 1880 the Copper Queen Mining Company, financed by California capitalists and Louis Zeckendorf, was founded in Bisbee. Phelps Dodge Company, the largest copper producer in the territory, was owned by eastern capitalists.[34]

The mining boom stimulated activity throughout the whole territory. The presence of more miners created a demand for food, cattle and services. New industries demanded and received more government protection, which meant more army forts, which in turn meant more contracts. Indians were herded into reservations and again a bonanza in orders spurred the economy. The need for large quantities of wood for the mine shafts spread the boom to northern Arizona.

With the new activity bringing in more white settlers the territory's population increased from 40,000 in 1880 to 90,000 seven years later.[35] Anglos outnumbered Mexicans. The market value of property was an estimated $26 million.

Mexicans remained the essential element in economic expansion by providing cheap labor.

As the territory grew, polarization between the two societies increased. In agriculture Mexicans formed the work force, but the Anglo-American farmers, arriving in the area, brought with them antagonism to Mexicans. Discrimination increased as new settlers arrived from Utah, Colorado, and points east. The new settlers were mostly farmers who came to plow their own lands and so did not even have a labor relationship with the separate Mexican society. These were "peace-loving and God-fearing" settlers, but they were also bigoted toward Mexicans and considered them intruders.

In the late 1850s Mexicans began to move out of the Santa

Cruz-Sonoita region, pioneering new areas around the junction of the Gila and Colorado rivers. As placerers, men who panned for gold, they went into western Arizona and worked many new strikes, followed by an avalanche of Anglo adventurers. Even after the boom, Mexicans lingered on to rework abandoned Anglo diggings. Mining treasures of the Black Canyon mines, Bradshaw District, and Walnut Grove yielded to the Mexican's *batea* (a cone-shaped placering pan). In spite of harassments in mining areas during the 1860s Mexicans continued to push the frontier back.

Relations between Anglos and Mexicans at the mining sites were often strained. The course of events at the Walker diggings at Lynx Creek is representative of Anglo-Mexican confrontations.[36] A Mexican by the name of Bernardo Freyes discovered gold at the diggings near Prescott, Arizona. He was paid $3,000 and exiled to Sonora by Anglo-American miners. As they began to work the diggings, they feared that word of the strike might bring Mexican miners to the area. During 1863–1864 the town of Walker passed a law stating that "No Mexicans shall have the right to buy, take up, or preempt a claim on this river [the Hassayampa] or in this district for the term of six months." The only Mexican that was exempted was Lorenzo Parra, who had been among those who bought Freyes out. While the town would not allow Mexicans to own claims, it did allow them to work for wages. The town of Walker was nicknamed "Greaserville." Conflict broke out between the two groups when the expected flood of Mexicans arrived. At a meeting on July 12, 1863, the Walker miners banished Asiatics and Sonorans from even working in the district.

The 1870s brought changes that directly affected Mexicans. Machines began to replace Mexicans in mining and agriculture. No longer were as many Mexicans needed to perform the all-purpose skills. By the turn of the century not farm hands, but only seasonal farm workers were needed:

> Coincident with large scale mining, ranching and farming the economic position of the Mexican declined. Mexicans had been involved in small scale mining and ranching in Sonora and Arizona. The use of barbed wire by Anglos to fence huge Anglo farms and ranches brought about economic subordination of Mexicans.[37]

They lost what land they had and were forced into wage labor in cotton, cattle, and copper.

In the mines the *arrastra* and the *patio* processes* began to be phased out. Steam engines and the ten-stamp mills appeared, relieving the miners of much of the back-breaking work. Mexican miners, however, did not enjoy the benefits of the new well-paying

---

Arrastra refers to a burro- or horse-drawn mill where ore was pulverized; *patio* refers to a court or leveled yard where ore was spread out and then pulverized.

jobs (smelters, blacksmiths, carpenters, millwrights, etc.); the mine owners imported Anglo-Americans from places such as San Francisco to reap the harvest of the Mexicans' early labors. Adding to the Mexicans' plight was that during the 1870s the mines frequently shut down because of mechanization, a change of owners, the declining value of metals, and the fluctuation of the economic cycle. Mexicans were always the first affected during these periods—the last to be hired and the first fired. For a time placering offered a safety valve, with many Mexicans turning to prospecting when no other work was available. They would work exhausted ground, literally wringing ore from the land. Mexican ingenuity demonstrated itself in many ways and allowed many Mexicans to become more independent. Many started small smelting enterprises and subcontracted work from the mines.

Throughout Arizona, mining towns such as Clifton stood as tributes to the Mexicans' abilities. Although Mexicans had known about copper in the mountains north of the Gila, this area had not been worked. In 1864 Henry Clifton rediscovered the body of ore, but many Anglos believed that the area was too isolated to develop, and Clifton himself left the site. Several years later another Anglo-American filed a claim for the mine and, in turn, sold it to Charles and Henry Lesinsky, who incorporated the Longfellow Copper Company. They recognized the Mexicans' skill in smelting and hired an experienced Mexican crew. The owners then left the Mexicans alone, later returning to find the settlement of Clifton "built entirely by Mexican labor." Within a few years the mines at Clifton produced thousands of tons of ore. But in spite of the Mexicans' contributions, a double wage standard persisted and the Mexicans were paid their lower wages by the *boleta* system (scrip redeemable at the company store).[38]

In Arizona, as in other places in the Southwest, "acts of lawless violence, including murders, robberies, and lynching" were all too common and "too often . . . [there was] a clamor for the expulsion of all Mexicans."[39] During the Crabb filibuster of 1857 "there were public meetings held to urge the expulsion of the hated 'greasers' from the mines and from the country. A war of races at times seemed impending."[40] Mexicans were blamed for every crime imaginable.

Anglo-American conflicts often created international incidents. Mexican authorities, partly because they were aware of the biased administration of justice in border areas, often refused to extradite alleged criminals who had fled into Sonora. The Mission camp affair was typical. According to Arizona officials, on December 24, 1870, some Mexicans killed Charles Reed, James Little, and Thomas Oliver and wounded Reed's wife in a dispute over the Mexicans' alleged theft of some furniture and five horses. The culprits fled into Sonora, and Arizona authorities wanted them back.

According to the Mexicans' account, the employer abused them and when he severely beat one of them, they armed and protected themselves.[41] A group of Anglos did not wait to find out what had really happened and went to the ranch of Francisco Gándara, brother of the former governor of Sonora, to make reprisals. They accused him of stealing a mule, which he denied. A shoot-out between the Anglos and Gándara's men ensued. Gándara and one of the assailants, James Bodel, were killed. The Anglo gang then left the ranch and hunted down and killed a Mexican who had vowed to avenge Gándara.

The press of each state hurled accusations at the other. Naturally, the Sonoran press brought up the issue of discrimination in Arizona.[42] Governor Pesqueira refused to extradite the accused Mexicans, although he carried on lengthy negotiations with the Arizona governor, A. P. K. Safford. Similar occurrences continued throughout the 1870s. Anglo-Americans used the incidents to justify attacks on Mexicans, and Mexicans reacted to the violence by fighting back.

Antipathy toward Mexicans reached its highest pitch in places where there were "cowboys." In Tombstone, Arizona, famous for harboring the most corrosive outlaws of Texas, businessmen and mine owners would not hire Mexicans because they did not want to incur the wrath of cowboys who controlled the town. Cowboys formed gangs to raid defenseless Mexican villages. The shooting of Mexicans became commonplace, with cowboys showing little respect for women or children.[43]

As in other territories and states in the Southwest, Mexicans in Arizona had to fight the land-grant battle, although on a smaller scale. Grants in the Arizona territory were guaranteed by the Gadsden Purchase treaty, but in controversies characterized by fraud and delay, Mexicans lost their land. Congress in 1870 authorized the surveyor-general of Arizona "to ascertain and report" upon claims.[44] According to Bancroft:

> Most of the claims are doubtless equitably valid and will eventually be confirmed, though since 1879 the surveyor-general has investigated fourteen of them or more, and recommended them for approval or rejection. This delay on the part of the government has been entirely inexcusable, as the matter might have been easily settled fifteen years ago. Since that time lands have increased in value; conflicting interests have come into existence; probably fraudulent schemes have been concocted; and even a hope has been developed that all the Mexican titles might be defeated. Owners have no real protection against squatters, cannot sell or make improvements, and in fact have no other right than that of paying taxes; while on the other hand the rights of settlers are jeopardized by possibly invalid claims, and a generally unsettled and unsatisfactory system of land tenure is produced.[45]

In short, Mexicans played a major role in the development of territorial Arizona, but their status in the colonial society was minimized by physical and legal violence, by racism, and by economic exploitation.

THE QUEST FOR LABOR

Mining and agriculture boomed during the latter part of the nineteenth century. The railroad held the key to the development of the Southwest. By 1880 the Southern Pacific reached Tucson and by 1890 the territory had 1,000 miles of line. The rail lines, added to the 700 miles of canals, made a fairly complete transportation network.[46] The population in the territory increased rapidly. The number of those engaging in trade jumped from 591 in 1870 to 3,252 in 1880.[47] Dependence on Sonoran markets lessened. Until the 1870s pesos were used as the dominant currency and trade had been mainly through Sonora. Transportation was more convenient through Guaymas than hauling ores to the California coast. The railroad changed Arizona contact from north and south to east and west.[48] Capital investment in large-scale mining, ranching, and agriculture followed the railroad to the territory.

Although the population increased, the labor pool was not sufficient to meet the needs of railroad construction or the new industries, both of which depended upon a large supply of cheap labor. Mexicans from the territory and others who traveled north from Mexico to seek work provided this supply. Development of the territory had encouraged the importation of Mexican workers to such an extent that Sonora, the traditional supply depot, could not furnish them. El Paso then became a clearing house for Mexican labor.[49]

Although the immigration acts of the 1880s prohibited foreign contracted labor, the practice of contracting Mexican labor became widespread. Anglo-American agents in El Paso hired Mexican agents called *enganchadores* (hookers), who traveled into the interior of Mexico, usually to the cities, to recruit Mexicans. *Enganchadores* paid the workers' train fare, which was later deducted from wages. The agent acted as a subcontractor and sold his contracts to Anglo-American employers. Sometimes problems developed. Often Mexican workers signed up to get a free train ride, and just before the destination was reached, they would jump the train in order to avoid paying. They could also contract for better wages than the *enganchadores* had offered them. To prevent this, the *enganchadores* hired armed guards, who locked the workers in box cars.

The U.S. government did not protect Mexicans exploited by these practices. It ignored the fact that it was illegal to bring contract labor into the United States. The need for cheap labor and the demands of capitalists in the Southwest overrode the legal restraints.[50] Meanwhile, the influx of large numbers of poor and unorganized Mexicans, who had none of the rights of citizenship, cemented the master-servant relationship that already existed.

RESISTANCE THROUGH THE LABOR MOVEMENT

By the 1890s Mexican resistance to Anglo-American oppression began to find expression in a new form. Unorganized physical resistance became more difficult as the number of Anglo-Americans increased in the territory. Moreover, the attitude of the Mexican government changed. In the 1850s and 1860s, and even during the early 1870s, Mexicans could find refuge in Mexico, but as U.S. control over the Mexican government increased during the Díaz years, this safety valve was turned off.[51] Mexicans then turned to defensive measures such as labor organization. The promanagement attitude of the territorial government made this activity hazardous. The pecking order that separated Mexican, Anglo-American, and Asian workers prevented any effective unity in the laboring ranks.

The arrival of the railroad further depressed the Mexicans' status. This group was organized to defend white American hegemony by actively promoting anti-Mexican propaganda and the exclusion of the latter from government and power. It also promoted a limitation on Mexican immigration. Many Mexican enterprises were driven out of business by the railroads. For example, Estévan Ochoa and Pinckney Randolph Tully's freighting business, with $100,000 worth of equipment, became obsolete overnight. Texas cowboys migrated in large numbers into the territory, bringing with them a pattern of discrimination which did not distinguish between rich and poor.

The depression of 1893 increased friction between races, with many working-class and middle-class Anglos blaming the depression on the Mexicans. In 1894 nativists formed the American Protective Association in Tucson.[52]

A group of Mexican elite founded *La Alianza Hispanoamericana* on January 14, 1894, in response to this new threat to their power. "Through this organization they sought to maintain political representation as well as continue the contribution of Mexican-Americans to the development of Arizona and the greater Southwest."[53] Ignacio Calvillo, one of the founders of the organization, stated, "In those days the English and Spanish-speaking had a hard time getting along. The element opposed to the Spanish-American people in the Southwest had organized itself into the American Protective Association. . . ."[54] *La Alianza*, at first a local organization, expanded, and in 1879 it held its first national convention. By 1910 it had over 3,000 members in Arizona, Texas, New Mexico, California, and Mexico. In 1913, influenced by the women's suffrage movement, it voted to admit women to full membership in the society.[55]

The end of the nineteenth century saw considerable labor organization throughout the Southwest, especially among miners. The sphere of influence of the Arizona labor movement extended into the neighboring mines of eastern California. *La Alianza* became involved in trade union organizing. In 1897 Mexican railroad workers struck at Mammoth Tank, 40 miles west of Yuma. When the 200 strikers saw Undersheriff Wilder and a posse ride up, they mistakenly thought that he had come to interfere with the strike. Because he could not communicate in Spanish, the undersheriff could not make clear that he was in fact pursuing a man unconnected with the strike. Threatened by the workers, he fired his pistol in the air. This action infuriated the Mexicans who took the sheriff's gun away from him. A deputy with a shotgun dispersed the crowd. Reinforcements were imported and the strike leaders were shipped to prison in San Diego, California.[56]

In general, unions were more successful in mining than in other fields because the industry had a year-round, stable work force. Much of the work in mining was skilled labor. The hazardous nature of the work bound the workers together for survival. In contrast, the labor movement remained relatively weak in agriculture during the nineteenth century because farm workers were generally unskilled and migratory and easily replaceable.

Mexican aliens were often used as scabs. At first, union officials attempted to restrict Mexican immigration by using strikebreaking as an excuse, clearly differentiating between Mexican aliens and Chicanos. Later their arguments became racist. Traditionally the role of unions has been to obtain higher pay and better working conditions for its members. Instead of educating members, unions often have reflected some of the most base prejudices of their memberships. Increasingly, Anglo mine workers became anti-Mexican—not only on the strikebreaking issue, but also on the race question and even on the right of Mexicans to work in the mines. They jealously guarded the privileged double wage standard that they enjoyed. Anglos viewed the Mexicans as competitors and believed their own economic survival depended on the latter's exclusion, lumping Mexican labor into the category of "cheap labor." Mexicans, on the other hand, resented the higher wages paid to Anglos for the same work. Fights erupted between the two groups.

Two opposing camps developed. The Western Federation of Miners (WFM), a union led by radicals, actively recruited in Arizona. Although they recruited Mexicans in other parts of the Southwest, in Arizona the strategy at first was to concentrate on Anglo-Americans, a policy pursued because of the growing rivalry between the two groups. For a while the WFM was fairly successful. Arizona legislators feared the union's presence and passed special legislation in 1901 that created the Arizona Rangers, an organization that closely resembled the infamous Texas Rangers. The intended role of the Rangers was to assist cattlemen in ending rustling and to assist local law officers. In reality, the mine owners used them as strikebreakers and to help maintain their privilege.[57] Labor's power had, however, increased, forcing the legislature to pass prolabor legislation, which went into effect in 1903, making the eight-hour day in Arizona mandatory.

Mine owners sabotaged the law by cutting the workers' wages by 10 percent. On the morning of June 3, three days after the law had gone into effect, miners walked off the job, shutting down the smelters and mills; and beginning what Jeanne Parks Ringgold, granddaughter of then-sheriff Jim Parks of Clifton, called the "bloodiest battle in the history of mining in Arizona."[58]

The walkout at the mines in the town of Clifton was 80 to 90 percent effective. Between 1,200 and 1,500 strikers participated of whom 80 to 90 percent were Mexicans. Clifton was the center of the largest producing district in Arizona. During the strike armed miners took control of the mines and shut them down. The Arizona Copper Company, the Shannon Copper Company, and the smelters at Morenci were involved, but the main opponent was the Detroit Copper Company which refused to even talk to strikers.[59]

Mexicans were in control of the strike; many leaders came from the ranks of Mexican *mutualistas*. The *Bisbee Daily Review* of June 3, 1903, stated, "The Mexicans belong to numerous societies and through these they can exert some sort of organization stand together."[60] At first there was cooperation among the ethnic groups. The leaders were Abraham Salcido, the president of a Mexican society, Frank Colombo, an Italian, and W. H. Laustanau, a Rumanian, and A. C. Cruz, a Mexican.[61] Two days later the *Bisbee Daily Review* observed that "the strike is now composed almost entirely of Mexicans. Quite a number of Americans have left."[62] During the *huelga* (strike), tempers rose and racial animosities heightened.

Among the demands of members were free hospitalization, paid life insurance for miners, locker rooms, fair prices at the company store, hiring of only men who were members of the society, and protection against being fired without cause.

The governor called the Arizona Rangers into action in an effort to intimidate Mexican workers, and on June 9, 1903, workers responded by staging a demonstration of solidarity. In direct defiance of the Rangers, 2,000 Mexicans marched through the streets of Morenci in torrential rains. A clash seemed inevitable, but the increasing rainstorm broke up the demonstration. A flood threw the city into panic, killing almost 50 people and causing some $100,000 worth of damage.[63]

The local sheriff reported that Mexicans had armed themselves and requested additional assistance from the governor. The Mexican consul in Arizona, a tool of Porfirio Díaz, was sent "to talk some sense to the Mexicans." Federal troops, along with six companies of national guardsmen, were sent to the trouble area, and martial law was declared.[64] This action was not necessary, since the disastrous flood had hit the Mexican community hard and had ended the strike.

The strike leaders Salcido, Cruz, Colombo, and Laustanau were convicted for inciting a riot. (Laustanau died in the Yuma State Penitentiary as the result of prolonged confinements in solitary.) This ended Arizona's first major strike. Officials with an army larger than it had taken to fight the Indian wars insured that Mexicans did not challenge the mine owners' privileged status.[65] The *huelga,* while it failed, went a long way in politicizing miners throughout Arizona; the Clifton-Morenci strike became known as the "Mexican affair."

While the WFM took notice of Mexican tenacity and capitalized on the drama by issuing a statement of support, it actually had abandoned Mexicans. The violence of Arizona Rangers continued unchecked, and in 1906 Rangers even crossed the international border into Mexico to suppress Mexican strikers during the Cananea mine strike (see Chapter 8).

The labor difficulties continued in the Clifton-Morenci district, the major copper producer in Arizona.[66] Breakthroughs in technology by 1910 made possible mass production, making Arizona the nation's number one producer of copper.[67] World War I had increased the demand for copper. Production of copper increased from 23,274,965 pounds in 1883 to 719,035,514 pounds in 1917.[68] The size and importance of the industry gave added significance to the labor difficulties.

The WFM began to organize all workers in the area after the 1903 strike, and by 1915 conditions again forced workers to strike. Because the mining companies owned all the land, their company stores had a monopoly. Through the company stores the miners were constantly kept in debt.[69]

The workers' indebtedness to the company was further increased by the company's monopoly of the water supply. The owners deducted water fees from the workers' wages:

> The inarticulate Mexicans suffered silently the dishonest and often brutal yoke of many of these lesser officials. Often workers complained among themselves of being compelled by petty foremen to buy chances on worthless, or nearly worthless, items, but what they particularly resented was the bribery required by minor officials to get or keep a job. Shift bosses collected from $5 to $15 a month for such services.[70]

Foremen also made a profit by renting shacks to the workers for $10 a month. This was a high rate, considering that Mexican workers only earned $2.39 for a 7½-hour shift.

By August 1915 the union had gained sufficient power that it could make demands on mine owners. A $3.50-per-day minimum was demanded for all underground miners, regardless of their race. Once again, Mexican leadership was prominent. Many were veterans of Sonoran copper mines and had experience in strikes in the Mexican state. In September, when the owners rejected the WFM's demands, miners went on strike. The strike lasted five months, but involved no major violence. This time, Arizona had a governor who was not appointed by Washington, D.C., and who was beholden to labor.

The miners won a raise of $2.50 per day for surface workers and $3.00 for men working underground. Workers were forced to abandon the WFM for the milder Arizona State Federation of Labor, an affiliate of the American Federation of Labor (AFL).

The 1915 victory did not end miners' grievances and throughout the next three years strike activity continued in Miami, Globe, Ray, Ajo, Jerome, and Warren, as well as Clifton-Morenci. The war in Europe drove up demand and prices for copper; however, mine owners were determined to control wages. Capitalists effectively stirred nativist sentiments among Anglo-Americans. Unfounded fears of Pancho Villa allowed the firing of some 1,200 Mexican miners at Ajo in 1916, when they requested a raise and a grievance committee.[71] Vigilantism was rampant, colliding with the new influx of Mexican miners who entered the United States under wartime exemptions to immigration restrictions.

President Woodrow Wilson responded to the threat of work stoppages by appointing a mediation commission in 1917 to help resolve disorders in the industry. According to federal mediator Felix Frankfurter, efforts of mine owners to deepen the labor pool by bringing in miners from Mexico backfired since many of the new arrivals were Sonoran miners who had participated in strikes in that state and were radicalized. In 1917 strikers struggled for the right to organize unions and end extortion, fraud, graft, and racism prevalent in the mines of corporations such as Phelps Dodge, Jackling, and Guggenheim. The mines at Ray and Clifton were especially bad.[72] In that year mine owners locked out Clifton miners, forcing them to subsist on $1.25 a month while the mines were closed; the owners ended the lockout only when the price of copper was too high to keep the mines closed.

Mine union organizing was hampered during this period by internecine struggles. The WFM had become the International Union of Mine, Mill, and Smelter Workers. Its president, Charles Moyer, had moved to the right and different factions within the international challenged his leadership. The members divided into pro-Moyer, Wobbly, socialist, and Arizona State Federation of Labor camps.[73]

Throughout the state Anglos formed loyalty leagues which participated in mass deportations of Mexicans. The Bisbee Loyalty League helped local authorities deport over a thousand workers at gun point during July 1917 alone, holding some in concentration camps in Columbus, New Mexico.

Federal authorities backed mine owners. In their reports they blamed the Mexican element. The U.S. cavalry openly sided with local officials, and Ray troops were used to control miners. At the height of the strike Wilson broadened the exemptions which allowed large numbers of Mexicans to be imported to the strike area.[74] And, although the president's mediation commission noted flagrant violations of human rights, federal authorities ignored the violations.

At the state constitutional convention in Phoenix on October 10, 1910, labor organizers had exposed their true colors. While their reasons for wanting limitation of aliens are understandable—alien labor offers unfavorable competition, drives wages down, and stifles union organization—what cannot be understood is the racism that appeared. At the convention labor men introduced resolutions that would exclude non–English-speaking persons from hazardous occupations and would force mines to employ 80 percent U.S. citizens. These resolutions, if they had been passed, would have driven Mexicans from the mines and caused hardships among the Mexican population. As one mine owner pointed out, 50 percent of Mexican miners he employed would have to be fired, even though they had been with the company for as long as twenty-five years. Union leaders replied workers should have learned English or declared their intention to become citizens. Owners' representatives prevented these resolutions from becoming law—probably because they realized the importance of Mexican labor to continued growth of the state.

The Claypool-Kinney Bill was introduced in November 1914. "The provisions of the bill were that no firm could hire more than twenty percent aliens" and it prohibited anyone who was deaf, dumb or did not speak English to be employed in a hazardous occupation. The intent was evident: to exclude Mexicans from the mines.

In 1914 at Phoenix, Mexicans formed a *mutualista, La Liga Protectora Latina*, to oppose the discriminatory bill. Ignacio Espinosa, Pedro G. de la Loma, and Jesús Meléndez led the society.[75] By May 1915 the Tempe lodge had eighty members and had established a bureau to provide employment referral and financial assistance. *La Liga* stood in solidarity with striking miners at Ray and began to involve itself with the education and protection of Mexicans. By 1917 it had 30 lodges, focusing on political and legal action to protect the rights of Mexicans, increased financial mutual aid for *Liga* members, greater emphasis on education. It supported miners striking at Jerome, Globe, Miami, and Clifton-Morenci. It also had a series of meetings with Governor Thomas Campbell, calling for night classes, especially in mining areas.[76]

La Liga supported Campbell's candidacy, since his opponent was attempting to revive the 80 percent bill. At its third annual convention members established a commission headed by Amado Cota Robles to lobby the state legislature for bilingual education at the primary level. Under Cota Robles's leadership night classes were begun in Spanish, arithmetic, geometry, geography, and Mexican history. Emphasis was on learning English and on reading. By 1919 lodges had been established in Arizona, California, New Mexico, and Philadelphia with 3,752 members and it began publication of a journal, *La Justicia.*[77] However, by 1920 the organization began to decline. When the dues were raised to $3.00 initiation fee and $1.25 a month, poor members protested, and a division took place along class lines.

Meanwhile, the power of the mining corporations and agribusiness increased. The war intensified the demand for copper while the reclamation act put large amounts of land into production. Arizona mining and agriculture demanded the kind of capital investment which could only be furnished by rich capitalists from San Francisco and New England. Government protected the capitalists who kept the workers unorganized and divided along racial and class lines.

NOTES

1. Hubert Howe Bancroft, *History of Arizona and New Mexico* (Albuquerque, N. Mex.: Horn & Wallace, 1962), p. 493.
2. Bancroft, p. 579.
3. Howard R. Lamar, *The Far Southwest, 1846–1912: A Territorial History* (New York: Norton, 1970), p. 418.
4. Lamar, p. 417.
5. Bancroft, pp. 496, 498.
6. John B. Brebner, *Explorers of North America, 1492–1806* (Cleveland, Ohio: World Publishing, 1966), p. 407; Francisco R. Almada, *Diccionario de historia geografía y biografía sonorenses* (Chihuahua: n.p., 1952), pp. 140–144.
7. Don Francisco Xavier De Gamboa, *Commentaries on the Mining Ordinances of Spain*, vol. 2, trans. Richard Heathfield (London: Longman, Reese, Orme, Brown and Green, 1830), p. 333.
8. Jack A. Dabbs, *The French Army in Mexico, 1861–1867* (The Hague: Mouton, 1963), pp. 14, 65, 241, 283.
9. James Neff Garber, *The Gadsden Treaty* (Gloucester, Mass.: Peter Smith, Publisher, 1959).
10. J. Fred Rippy, "A Ray of Light on the Gadsden Treaty," *Southwestern Historical Quarterly* 24 (January 1921): 241.
11. Bancroft, p. 491; Edwin Corle, *The Gila: River of the Southwest* (Lincoln: University of Nebraska Press, 1967), p. 181. Michael C. Meyer and William L. Sherman, *The Course of Mexican History* (New York: Oxford University Press, 1979), p. 353, list the area as 30,000 square miles.

12. Laureano Calvo Berber, *Nociones de Historia de Sonora* (México, D.F.: Libería de Manuel Porrua, 1958), p. 50.
13. Fernando Pesqueira, "Documentos Para la Historia de Sonora," 2nd series, vol. 3 (Manuscript in the University of Sonora Library, Hermosillo, Sonora).
14. Joseph F. Park, *The History of Mexican Labor in Arizona During the Territorial Period* (Tucson: University of Arizona Press, 1961), pp. 15–16. Park's work is the best account of this subject.
15. Lamar, p. 419.
16. Charles D. Poston, "Building a State in Apache Land," *Overland Monthly* 24 (August 1894): 204.
17. See P. G. Hamlin, ed., *The Making of a Soldier: Letters of General B. S. Ewell* (Richmond, Va.: Whittel & Shepperson, 1935); and Clement W. Eaton, "Frontier Life in Southern Arizona, 1858–1861," *Southwestern Historical Quarterly* 36 (January 1933).
18. Sylvester Mowry, *Arizona and Sonora* (New York: Harper & Row, 1864), p. 35.
19. Quoted in Park, p. 20.
20. Bancroft, p. 503.
21. *Arizona Weekly Star*, quoted in Park, p. 29.
22. Stone to Lewis Cass, Guaymas, December 23, 1858, Dispatches from United States Consuls in Guaymas.
23. Edward Conner to Cass, Mazatlán, Mexico, May 26, 1859, Dispatches from United States Consuls in Mazatlán, Mexico, GRDS, RG 59; *La Estrella de Occidente*, November 18, 1859; Alden to Cass, Guaymas, November 18, 21, 1859; Thomas Robinson to Alden, Guaymas, November 20, 1859, Dispatches from U.S. Consuls in Guaymas; Rudolph F. Acuña, "Ignacio Pesqueira: Sonoran Caudillo," *Arizona and the West* 12, no. 2 (Summer 1970): 152–154; Rodolfo F. Acuña, *Sonoran Strongman: Ignacio Pesqueira and His Times* (Tucson: The University of Arizona Press, 1974), pp. 52–64.
24. Harry T. Getty, "Interethnic Relationships in the Community of Tucson" (Ph.D. dissertation, University of Chicago, 1950), pp. 208–209.
25. Kay Lysen Briegel, "Alianza Hispano-Americana, 1894–1965: A Mexican American Fraternal Insurance Society" (Ph.D. dissertation, University of Southern California, 1974) p. 27.
26. Thomas Farish, *History of Arizona* (San Francisco: Filmer Brothers, 1915), p. 346, quoted in Park, p. 40.
27. Rufus Wyllys, *Arizona: The History of a Frontier State* (Phoenix, Ariz.: Hobison & Herr, 1950), p. 81.
28. Mowry, p. 94.
29. *Weekly Arizonian*, June 30, 1859.
30. *Weekly Alta Californian*, May 28, 1859.
31. *Report of Frederick Brucknow to the Sonoran Exploring and Mining Company upon the History, Prospects and Resources of the Company in Arizona* (Cincinnati, Ohio: Railroad Record, 1859), pp. 17–18; *Fourth Annual Report of the Sonora Exploring and Mining Company, March 1860* (New York: Minns, 1860), pp. 12–14.
32. Raphael Pumpelly, *Across America and Asia*, 4th ed., rev. (New York: Leypodt & Holt, 1870), p. 32.
33. Park, p. 78.
34. Lamar, p. 466.
35. Lamar, p. 475.
36. The events at Lynx Creek are described by Robert L. Sprude in "The Walker-Weaver Diggings and the Mexican Placero, 1863–1864," *Journal of the West* (October 1975): 64–74.
37. Jacqueline Jo Ann Taylor, "Ethnic Identity and Upward Mobility of Mexican Americans in Tucson" (Ph.D. dissertation, University of Arizona, 1973), p. 16.
38. James Colquhoun, "The Early History of the Clifton-Morenci District," reprinted in Carlos E. Cortes, ed., *The Mexican Experience in Arizona* (New York: Arno Press, 1976).
39. Hubert Howe Bancroft, *History of Arizona and New Mexico* (San Francisco: The History Co., 1889), p. 575.
40. Bancroft, pp. 503, 575.
41. Editorial, *La Estrella de Occidente*, April 12, 1872.

42. "La Prensa de Arizona y los Horrores Perpetados en el Rio Gila," *La Estrella de Occidente*, March 22, 1872; "Asesinator en el Gila," *La Estrella de Occidente*, March 22, 1872; "Trouble Ahead," *Arizona Citizen*, June 24, 1871.
43. Douglas D. Martin, *Tombstone's Epitaph* (Albuquerque: University of New Mexico Press, 1951), pp. 139–165.
44. Jay J. Wagoner, *Arizona Territory, 1863–1912: A Political History* (Tucson: University of Arizona Press, 1970), p. 164.
45. Bancroft, pp. 599–600.
46. Lamar, p. 475.
47. Bancroft, p. 602.
48. David J. Weber, ed., *Foreigners in Their Native Land* (Albuquerque: University of New Mexico Press, 1973), p. 211.
49. Colquhoun, p. 49, reports that the Mexicans were recruited from El Paso for the Clifton area in the 1870s when many single men left the area because of Apache raids: "Mexicans began to leave in search of safer quarters, and it became necessary to fill the gaps by importing more Mexicans from El Paso, but at least it was realized that to have permanent laborers it was necessary to have married men who would settle down with their wives and families."
50. Park, p. 190. See Victor S. Clark, *Mexican Labor in the United States*, U.S. Department of Commerce Bulletin no. 78 (Washington, D.C.: U.S. Government Printing Office, 1908).
51. By the 1880s Mexicans, even in Sonora, began to change their attitude toward Anglos. The capitalist class there, which owned the resources but did not have sufficient capital to develop them, began to cooperate with Anglo-American and foreign investors. See Acuña, *Sonoran Strongmen* for background material.
52. Briegel, pp. 34–38; José Hernández, "Chicano Mutualistas" (Dissertation in progress, University of California at Riverside).
53. Manuel P. Servín, "The role of Mexican-Americans in the Development of Early Arizona," in Manuel P. Servín, ed., *An Awakening Minority: The Mexican-American*, 2nd ed. (Beverly Hills, Calif.: Glencoe Press, 1974), p. 28.
54. Hernández ms.
55. Briegel, pp. 51, 64.
56. Frank Love, *Mining Camps and Ghost Towns* (Los Angeles: Westernlore Press, 1974), pp. 141, 143.
57. Carl M. Rathbun, "Keeping the Peace Along the Mexican Border," *Harper's Weekly* 50 (November 17, 1906): 1632.
58. Park, p. 257.
59. Hernández ms.
60. Quoted in Park, p. 257.
61. Wagoner, p. 386.
62. *Bisbee Daily Review* June 5, 1903, quoted in Park, p. 257.
63. James H. McClintock, *Arizona: The Youngest State*, vol. 2 (Chicago: Clarke, 1916), p. 424.
64. Park, p. 258.
65. Wagoner, pp. 387–388.
66. James R. Kluger, *The Clifton-Morenci Strike: Labor Difficulty in Arizona, 1915–1916* (Tucson: University of Arizona Press, 1970), p. 9.
67. Michael E. Parrish, "Labor, Progressives, and Copper: The Failure of Industrial Democracy in Arizona During World War 2" (Unpublished paper, History Department, University of California at San Diego), p. 6.
68. Mario T. García, "Obreros: The Mexican Workers of El Paso, 1900–1920" (Ph.D. dissertation, University of California at San Diego, 1975), p. 24.
69. Kluger, p. 20.
70. Kluger, p. 23.
71. Parrish, p. 32.
72. Parrish, pp. 58, 15.
73. Parrish, p. 22.
74. Parrish, pp. 29, 56, 70, 45–46, 40.
75. James D. McBride, "The *Liga Protectora Latina:* A Mexican-American Benevolent Society in Arizona," *Journal of the West* (October 1975): 83.
76. McBride, p. 83.
77. McBride, pp. 85, 86, 87.

Chapter 5
California Lost: America
for Anglo-Americans

Before the conquest many *Californios* welcomed Anglo-Americans, often granting them large sections of land. When Spanish colonialism ended in 1821, California became part of the Mexican republic, and thereafter the number of foreigners entering the province increased. The first Anglos to arrive—often trappers and traders who were tired of wandering—intermarried with Mexicans and lived in peace. *Californios* did not view Anglos as enemies and were not prepared for the conflicts that ultimately arose.

Prior to 1841 foreigners had been ex-sailors, commercial agents, and businessmen who became assimilated with Mexicans; after this date newcomers brought their wives and families and the relationship between them and the native population changed markedly. About 1,500 Anglos reached California between 1843 and 1846. These people mixed less readily and there was less intermarriage. Not surprisingly, the Texas adventure had an effect on Mexican attitudes toward immigrating Anglos.

Anglo-American trade with Asia increased, and the ports of California became even more valuable. Moreover, the discovery of gold by Francisco López in 1842 at San Feliciano Canyon in southern California focused attention on a fact: there was gold in California.

In 1835 President Andrew Jackson authorized his diplomatic agent to Mexico to offer $500,000 for San Francisco Bay and the northern part of Alta California; the minister added to the insult of the offer by attempting to bribe Mexican authorities. Two years later Jackson urged Texas to claim California in order that Anglo-Americans could bypass negotiations. In 1842 the U.S. minister to Mexico praised California's potential proposing that efforts to acquire California be renewed.[1]

That same year Commodore Thomas Jones raised the stars and stripes over Monterey. He believed that the United States had already started the war with Mexico. The excuse made by many Anglo historians is that "the United States did not intend to be caught unprepared in any ruse between the great powers to acquire California."[2] John C. Frémont led three expeditions into the Southwest for the U.S. army's topographical engineers. Although these expeditions were supposedly scientific, they were heavily armed. On his second expedition in 1843–1844, Frémont "mapped, surveyed, and charted the trails" to and in California. Thomas Oliver Larkin, the U.S. consul at Monterey, California, served as an agent, reporting conditions in California and fomenting discontent among natives, while President James K. Polk conspired to pull off another Texas adventure in California.[3]

The last link in the United States' Bismarckian conspiracy was the third expedition of Frémont, who left St. Louis for California in May 1845. Part of the peaceful scientific expedition reached California in December 1845, whereupon Frémont went to Monterey to purchase supplies. There he met with Larkin. José Castro, the commander of the garrison in Monterey, was highly suspicious and watched Frémont closely. Frémont asked to be allowed to quarter in California for the winter, and permission was granted, with the stipulation that the expedition stay away from coastal settlements. By March 1846 the main body of Frémont's expedition entered California. Emboldened by additional soldiers, Frémont raised the U.S. flag at Hawk's Peak, about 25 miles from Monterey. His actions give credence to Leonard Pitt's conclusion: "The United States connived rather cynically to acquire California, provoked the native Californians into a dirty fight, and bungled a simple job of conquest."[4] Castro, understandably, ordered Frémont to leave California. Just as the expedition was about to leave, Lieutenant Archibald H. Gillespie, a marine, reached Frémont and gave him personal letters in addition to verbal instructions from Polk.[5] Frémont was told that the war with Mexico was near and to hold in readiness. Frémont returned to the Sacramento Valley. This was a hostile act intended to create an incident, since he blatantly ignored Castro's orders to leave.

Anglo-American immigrants in California joined Frémont and, adopting the symbol of the bear flag, rose in arms to attempt to Americanize California.[6] Many Mexican ranch owners were convinced that joining the invaders represented their self-interest; the poor on the other hand had the strongest feelings of patriotism and harbored anti-*gringo* sentiments.[7] The actions of Frémont's marauders soon antagonized their few friends.

In June 1846, they took Mexican General Mariano Vallejo prisoner at his ranch in Sonoma. Vallejo had been sympathetic to Anglo-Americans. They took Vallejo and his brother to Sutter's Fort and subjected them to indignities and harassments. Frémont further alienated rich merchants and landowners by initiating a policy of forced loans, confiscating land and property.[8]

Bear Flaggers terrorized the Mexicans and Indians, taking cattle and horses, looting homes, and wounding and murdering innocent people. On one occasion a scouting party under Kit Carson came upon José de los Reyes Berreyesa and his twin nephews,

Francisco and Ramón de Haro. The men were unarmed, but the Anglos shot at them anyway. They killed Ramón, whereupon Francisco "threw himself upon his brother's body." One of the assassins then shouted, "Kill the other son of a bitch!" Seeing his two nephews killed, the old man said to the Anglos: "Is it possible that you kill these young men for no reason at all? It is better that you kill me who am old too!" Bear Flaggers obliged by killing him.[9] It is of significance that the Berreyesa killings had no military value.

Mexicans resisted, but they were caught by surprise and had limited arms. Commodore John Drake Sloat arrived in July, landed 250 marines at Monterey, and raised the Anglo-American flag on the tenth.[10] He was replaced by Commodore Robert F. Stockton, a well-known expansionist (see Chapter 1). Frémont was promoted to the rank of major and placed in charge of the California Battalion of Volunteers. Naval forces entered Los Angeles harbor, and Captain Archibald Gillespie was placed in charge of occupying the area.

At Los Angeles a resistance movement was led by José María Flores. His band of guerrillas chased the *gringos* into the hills. Although the patriots were poorly armed, they defeated Gillespie and forced him to surrender. Six thousand Angelenos viewed and cheered Flores's men.

Kearny believed California had been conquered, so he left most of his soldiers in New Mexico, bringing only 125 men. Kit Carson advised him that Mexicans were "cowardly" and could be easily subdued. On December 5, 1846, the invaders were met by a force of sixty-five Mexicans at San Pasqual Pass, northeast of San Diego. Led by Andrés Pico, the Mexicans, armed with lances, attacked the Army of the West. Although outnumbered, they won the battle, killing eighteen Anglos and suffering no losses. Kearny and many of his men were wounded.[11] The conquerors, however, had warships, marines, and a well-armed cavalry.

Kearny's reinforcements soon arrived. The regrouped Anglos, led by Kearny, marched north to Los Angeles in late December. Frémont approached Los Angeles from the north. Flores led the Mexicans, but this time they were overwhelmed. Kearny's army entered Los Angeles on January 10, 1847. At the Cahuenga pass Andrés Pico surrendered to him and signed the Treaty of Cahuenga. After the conquest, U.S. troops poured into California, securing their occupation.

THE OCCUPATION OF CALIFORNIA

The newcomers depended almost totally on the marketplace and the transaction of capital. Its *continued* development depended on unremitted exploitation of resources which spurred growth of factories in its northeast. The Californian economy it replaced was based on the *rancho* and had just begun to enter the international marketplace. The province had been an underdeveloped region much like the United States' western states. The *rancho* system had depended on the whole on Indian labor with whom it maintained a paternalistic relationship. To bring California completely into the U.S. capitalist orbit, it became expedient to destroy that system. The new order created a large, poorly paid wage force.

The presence of the army of occupation insured that colonial administrators could proceed with Americanizing California. At first the process moved slowly because Mexicans so overwhelmingly outnumbered the encroachers. But on January 24, 1848, before the signing of the Treaty of Guadalupe Hidalgo, James Wilson Marshall found gold on John Sutter's property, and almost overnight thousands of outsiders flooded into California, overwhelming Mexicans and ending any hope they might have had of participating in the new government.

By 1849 almost 100,000 people lived in California, 13,000 of whom were Mexicans. This substantial population qualified the territory for statehood. A constitutional convention was held in August of that year at Monterey. Eight of forty-eight delegates to the convention were *Californios* who had the opportunity, if they had voted as a bloc, to champion the rights of the masses. However, like elites in other colonial situations, they attempted to ally themselves with colonizers to salvage the little power they had. At this point their relations with the colonizers were cordial. The possibility of prestigious positions within the new order and the desire to believe that they were different from the *cholo* masses (pejorative term for low-caste Mexicans) separated them from their base. Instead of voting as a bloc, *Californios* voted for what appeared to be their own immediate self-interests. Of the eight Spanish-speaking delegates, only José A. Carrillo voted for the admission of free Negroes into California, and he did this out of political expediency, since he believed that it would enhance California's chances for early admission as a state. *Californios* could also have voted as a bloc to split the territory into north and south. This would have given Mexicans control of the southern half. Again, they voted for their self-interests; many of the delegates were from the propertied class and believed that taxes would be placed on northern commerce rather than on land. Generally, the state constitution established laws favorable to Anglo-Americans. Mexicans won only token victories: suffrage was not limited to white males (the Mexicans were half-breeds), laws would be printed in Spanish and English, etc. On the other hand, they accepted even the California Bear, the symbol of the conquest, as the state seal. Tragically "the constitution was the only document of importance in whose drafting the Mexican Californians shared."[12]

THE CHANGING ELITES

Capitulation at Monterey set the stage for change in the ruling elite and exposed Mexican workers to a higher level of exploitation. California had experienced changes during the 1830s, with secularization of the missions which controlled agriculture and the hide and tallow trade. In 1827 the missions had 210,000 branded cattle, with an estimated 100,000 unbranded cows. They slaughtered 60,000 cows annually and sold 30,000 to 40,000 hides annually, bringing two pesos each. After secularization the land passed to private owners and the *rancho* system. Although under law Indians legally owned half of the secularized property, they did not receive the benefits. Secularization in fact reduced them to working for wages as *vaqueros* in the expanding *rancho* system or as laborers in pueblos. The lower-class *mestizos* and mulattoes joined the Indians in this labor pool.[13]

Conditions for Mexicans in California varied with location. In the northern part of the state the gold rush made them an instant minority, while in the southern part they remained the majority for the next twenty years. Los Angeles became the center for Mexicans, mirroring life in other pueblos. Population in Los Angeles had declined, with many of its citizens rushing north from 1849 to 1851 to find their fortune. The Mexicans were joined on the northern river banks by people from Chile, Peru, and other Latin American countries, but remained the majority of these so-called Latinos. Many Latinos were experienced placerers and their early successes infuriated Anglo-American miners. In 1848 there were about 1,300 Mexicans and 4,000 Yankees in the fields and not much friction existed, but by mid-1849 nearly 100,000 miners panned for gold. Food and other resources were scarce and competition increased. In short, there was not enough gold for the "80,000 Yankees, 8,000 Mexicans, 5,000 South Americans, and several thousand Europeans," seeking gold by the end of 1849.[14]

Mexicans were scapegoats for Anglo-American miners' failures, and Anglo-American merchants resented the success of Mexican peddlers and mule dealers.[15] A movement to exclude foreigners from the mines gained popular support. General Persifor F. Smith expressed the Anglos' feelings in a circular published in 1849:

> The laws of the United States inflict the penalty of fine and imprisonment on trespassers on the public lands. As nothing can be more unreasonable or unjust than the conduct pursued by persons, not citizens of the United States, who are flocking from all parts to search for and carry off gold from lands belonging to the United States in California, and as such in direct violation of law, it will become my duty, immediately upon my arrival there, to put those laws in force, and to prevent their infraction in future, by punishing by the penalties provided by law, all those who offend.
>
> As these laws are probably not known to many about to start to

California, it would be well to make it publicly known that there are such laws in existence, and that they will in future be enforced against all persons, not citizens of the United States, who shall commit any trespass over the land of the United States in California.[16]

Anglo miners approved of the Smith "doctrine" because if foreigners were allowed to mine, they would take all the gold out of the United States of America and strengthen some other nation at the expense of Anglo-America. They pressed politicians to exclude them and persecuted them. In fact, conditions were so bad by the autumn of 1849 that the Mexican minister in Washington, D.C., sent an official protest condemning violent treatment of Mexicans in California citing the Treaty of Guadalupe Hidalgo.[17]

Considerable support for exclusion existed in the California legislature. G. B. Tingley of Sacramento warned of a foreign invasion and described Mexicans and Latins:

Devoid of intelligence, sufficient to appreciate the true principles of free government; vicious, indolent, and dishonest, to an extent rendering them obnoxious to our citizens; with habits of life low and degraded; an intellect but one degree above the beast in the field, and not susceptible of elevation; all these things combined render such classes of human beings a curse to any enlightened community.[18]

Many legislators shared Tingley's views and would have voted for total exclusion. However, Thomas Jefferson Green, a Texan, hater of Mexicans, expansionist, and white supremacist, proposed a compromise bill. Green, responsible for seeking new sources of revenue for the state government, hit on the plan of taxing foreigners $20 per month. Legislators knew that if they placed a direct tax on all miners for the right to mine, there would be trouble. Foreigners, however, did not have a vote. Anglo legislators rationalized that the tax would prevent violence, since foreigners with licenses would have the right to mine and would be accepted. On April 13, 1850, the California state legislature passed its first foreign miner's tax. In reality, the tax was directed primarily at Mexicans and other Latins.[19] It affirmed the right of the Anglos to exclude Mexicans from the public domain and thus deny them access to capital necessary to upward mobility.

Although the courts upheld the constitutionality of the act in *People v. Naglee* in 1850, the act failed; neither the foreigners nor the Anglo-Americans reacted as expected. Foreigners, for the most part Mexicans, objected to the arbitrary tax. Rather than pay the exorbitant fee, they abandoned their diggings, and many former boom villages turned into ghost towns as one-half to three-fourths of the "foreigners" left the southern mines.[20] This crippled commerce in mining-related businesses. White miners did not accept the licensed foreigners, but drove Latinos off the sites (license or no license), beat them, and even lynched them. After a series of such events, so-called Mexican banditry flourished.

The tax itself was repealed less than a year after it had passed, not because the legislators cared about Mexicans or other foreigners, but because the merchants pressured Sacramento for repeal. During the period of lobbying for repeal even the *Daily Pacific News* wrote: "The Mexican is, so far as the development of the resources of the country is concerned, the most useful inhabitant of California."[21]

Money power had repealed the law, but discrimination continued in the mines. "As early as 1852 the state assembly committee on mines recommended in its report that a resolution be sent to Congress declaring the importation by foreign capitalists of large numbers of Asiatics, South Americans, and Mexicans (referred to as "peons" and "serfs")" be made illegal.[22]

A change in mining was already underway by the early 1850s as placers played out. Miners turned to quartz mining which entailed digging 50-foot holes. At first Mexicans enjoyed more success than *gringos*, apparently because they were more patient and skilled, but the arrival of new machinery limited Mexicans to wages and manual work as the Anglo-Americans claimed the privilege of running it.[23]

The gold rush almost over, the Yankees turned their interest to farmland. In 1851 a land law was passed that set in motion the mechanism through which Mexicans could be legally robbed of their land. Anglo-Americans entered California, as elsewhere in the Southwest, believing that they had special privileges by right of conquest. It seemed to them that it was "undemocratic" that 200 Mexican families owned 14 million acres of land.[24] Armed squatters kicked the Mexicans off their land, the legislature taxed them out of existence, and claimants insidiously bled them by the costs of litigation imposed by the land law of 1851. The Treaty of Guadalupe Hidalgo and its Statement of Protocol, which gave Mexicans specific guarantees, was completely ignored. William Gwinn, a notorious anti-Mexican who sponsored the land law, later admitted that his purpose was to force Mexicans off the land by encouraging squatters to invade them.[25]

A popular belief among historians is that the size of Spanish-Mexican land grants in great part determined the size of holdings in the Anglo period. However, considering the game of monopoly that capitalists played in California during the nineteenth and twentieth centuries, results would most likely have been the same whether or not there had been large *ranchos*. Given the fact that California was an undeveloped region which needed large amounts of capital to develop, it was inherent in the process of development that land holdings would become concentrated in the hands of the few Anglo corporate entities that controlled such capital. Just one Anglo corporation, the Southern Pacific, accumulated 11,588,000 acres, an area which is one-fifth of privately owned land today in California and is larger than the 8,850,000 acres which composed the combined grants of the *ricos*.[26]

The law gave Anglo-Americans an advantage, and in fact it encouraged them to homestead Mexican-owned land. Its ostensible purpose was to clear up land titles, but it placed the burden of proof on landowners, who had to pay exorbitant legal fees to defend titles to land that was already theirs. Judges, juries, and land commissioners were open to intrigue and were guided by their prejudices. Hearings were held in English, which put Spanish-speaking grantees at an additional disadvantage. The result was that the commission heard over 800 cases, approving 520 claims and rejecting 273.[27]

The Land Act, by implication, challenged the legality of Mexican land titles. It told land-hungry Anglo-Americans that there was a chance that *Californios* did not own the land. The squatters then treated the *ranchos* as public land on which they had a right to homestead. They knew that local authorities would not or could not do anything about it. They swarmed over the land, harassing and intimidating many landowners.

By standing by and doing nothing, law officers condoned the legal and physical abuse that followed. "José Suñol was killed somewhere on confirmed land, shortly after his family had acquired title."[28] In 1858 200 squatters and 1,000 "gun-carrying settlers" ambushed surveyors and held Domingo Peralta hostage. Salvador Vallejo, rather than lose everything, sold his Napa ranch for $160,000; he had paid $80,000 in legal fees to secure title.[29] José Joaquín Estudillo paid $200,000 in litigation fees for Rancho San Leandro; squatters burned his crops while they appealed the case.

Manipulators like Henry Miller, a former German butcher, used numerous schemes to steal land. One of his favorite devices was to buy into ranches held by several owners. Even though he was a minority owner, he could then graze as many head of cattle as he wished; also, according to California law, if one of the property owners, even one owning the smallest portion, called for a partition of the land, the property would be sold at auction. Miller could then buy cheap.

By 1853 squatters had moved onto every *rancho* around San Francisco:

> In 1856, when the [Land Act] board had concluded its deliberations, most of the great Mexican estates in the northern half of California had been preempted by squatters or sold off by their owners to pay the legal fees incurred in trying to have the titles validated.[30]

Mexicans had been frozen out of northern California and only in the southern half of the state did the former Mexican elite have any influence. The economy of southern California depended on cattle. The *rancheros* experienced a brief boom in the early 1850s when they were able to drive 55,000 head of cattle to San Francisco annually at $50 to $60 a head, but by 1855 the price of cattle fell and economic conditions of the southern Mexican ranchers began to crumble.[31] In 1850 the state legislature had initiated a tax on land. At the same time *rancheros* were obligated to pay county, road poll, and other special taxes. Between 1850 and 1856 the tax rate multiplied two-fold while mines were exempted; landowners felt the burden of the load.[32] *Rancheros* were unable to cope with the fluctuation in the economy and pay taxes. Inexperienced in the new economic order, they had speculated and mortgaged their property heavily during the early 1850s. Historian Mario T. García, in his study of San Diego, whose population although small mirrored events in other parts of southern California, writes:

> By 1860 the economic downturn of the "ricos" became evident. The total value of real estate in San Diego that year was $206,400 and of this figure, the total value of the land belonging to Mexicans had fallen to $82,700 while the value of the Anglos lands rose to $128,900. These are impressive figures, since in 1850 the Mexican had held the overwhelming amount of property.[33]

By 1860 the land base of the *ricos* in southern California had eroded.[34]

Loan sharks descended on California, hastening the ruin of the *ricos*, charging them 10 percent interest, compounded monthly.[35] The government did nothing to protect people against these excessive practices.

Intermarriage with daughters of the *ricos* was profitable. Horace Bell described the Anglo males in such marriages as "matrimonial sharks" marrying "unsophisticated pastoral provincials." He wrote "marrying a daughter of one of the big landowners was in some respects a quicker way to clean her family of its assets than to lend money to the 'old man.'" Stephen C. Foster married Don Antonio María Lugo's daughter, who was a widow and a wealthy woman in her own right with future interests in her father's holdings. Two granddaughters of Lugo who were also the daughters of Isaac Williams married Anglos. One of them, John Rains, inherited the Chino Ranch. All of the granddaughters of General Mariano Vallejo of Sonoma married Anglos; he had obviously forgotten that "his liberators" had once called him a greaser. According to Bell, "Mostly the native daughters married good looking and outwardly virile but really lazy, worthless, dissolute vagabond Americans whose object of marriage was to get rich without work." Many of them brought the women whom they married to ruin.

As in other southwestern states, there is little indication that any significant number of Mexican men, whether rich or poor, married Anglo women. There was a scarcity of Anglo women, and the old game of supply and demand operated with the conquerors monopolizing the available supply of women, who were reduced to the level of a commodity. Bell explained that the head of a family often "felt that the future was in the hands of the invading race" and that the marriage of the daughter to a *gringo* was a form of protection. Bell also thought that "the girls felt that they acquired prestige by marrying into the dominant race."[36] To marry a *gringo* was to be accepted as white; to marry a *gringo* was to associate oneself with privilege.

Racism cut across class lines and did not exclude *ricos* whether or not they were married to *gringos*. Section 394 of the Civil Practice Act of 1850 excluded Chinese and Indians from testifying against whites. In the *People v. Hall*, 1854, the court reversed the conviction of George Hall because he had been convicted on the testimony of the Chinese. In April 1857 Manuel Domínguez, one of the signers of the first California constitution and a wealthy landowner, was denied the right to testify. Domínguez, a Los Angeles supervisor, was declared incompetent as a witness because of his Indian blood.[37] Most *ricos* were not pure-blooded Castilians, but descendants of the frontier people, who were a mixture of Indian, Black, and Spanish. Another direct slap at the Spanish-speaking came in 1856 when the California assembly refused funds to translate laws into Spanish and further passed an antivagrancy act which was commonly referred to as the "greaser act" because section two of that act specified "all persons who are commonly known as 'Greasers' or the issue of Spanish or Indian blood."[38]

Natural disasters of the 1860s accelerated the decline of *Mexicanos*. In 1862 a flood devastated California ranches. Then two years of drought, followed by falling cattle prices, made it necessary for ranch owners to mortgage their property at outlandish interest rates, resulting in foreclosures. In Santa Barbara, by 1865 300,000 head of cattle had been reduced to 6,000 to 7,000 by the drought, with only a third of the sheep remaining.[39] In the 1860s epidemics broke out, and in 1868 entire families in poor *barrios* such as Sonoratown in Los Angeles were decimated.[40]

✱ Prior to 1860 *Californios* owned all the land valued at over $10,000; by the 1870s they owned only one-fourth of this land and most Mexican ranchers had been reduced to farming rented land.[41] By the 1880s Mexicans were relatively landless in California.

As Mexicans lost their land, they also lost their political power. Only in southern California, where Mexicans had an absolute majority, did they retain some local representation, but even there Anglos dominated political offices. The gigantic increase of Anglos statewide crowded Mexicans out of government. Mexicans were not experienced in competing in the game of Anglo politics, which was especially crooked in California. Proslavery Democrats and anti-Mexican politicians dominated the California legislature. By

1851 all native Mexicans had been excluded from the state senate; by the 1860s only a few Mexicans remained in the assembly; and by the 1880s people with Spanish surnames could no longer be found in public offices. Methodically, Mexicans became more dependent on the colonizers, and they lost whatever control over their lives that they may have had. A conqueror-conquered relationship existed, and by the 1850s even the elite publicly recognized their subjugated status and economic demise. And although many of the *ricos* became disenchanted with the Anglo rule, most of them continued to side with Anglo-Americans. In places like Los Angeles the Mexican population had grown with migration from outside of California. These were Mexicans for the most part from the laboring classes, and class differences between the *ricos* and *cholos* increased as the number of laborers increased.[42]

VIOLENCE IN OCCUPIED CALIFORNIA

Vigilante mobs set the tone for a kaleidoscopic series of violent experiences for Mexicans and Latin Americans. Following are some of the tragic incidents that were recorded. On June 15, 1849, a "benevolent, self-protective and relief society" called the Hounds attacked a Chilean *barrio* in San Francisco. The drunken mob of trespassers rioted, killed a woman, raped two, looted, and plundered. This action aroused the ire of many Anglo-Americans who condemned the Hounds and moved to control them.

In 1851, when the foreign miner's tax was passed, Antonio Coronel, a school teacher, came upon a mob that was about to lynch five foreigners accused of stealing 5 pounds of gold. Coronel offered to pay them that amount for the release of the prisoners. They refused, whipped three of the men and hanged two.[43]

One of the most distorted stories about violence at the mines occurred at Downieville in 1851.[44] It involved the kangaroo trial and lynching of a Mexican woman. Historians have called it the first lynching of a woman in California; they have written that her name was Juanita and that she was a prostitute (implying that it was lamentable but, after all, she was antisocial). Contemporary accounts make it clear that her name was Josefa, that she was not a prostitute, and that in fact "She was Sonorian [sic] and all agreed her character was good, that is she was above the average of camp women, of those days." (The attribution of bad character is part of the racist justification for abuse, but the nature of her character is irrelevant to the judgement that lynching of anyone is wrong.)

Josefa lived in a shack with a gambler, Manuel José. According to J. J. McClosky, an early resident of Downieville, she "was about 26 years old, slight in form, with large dark eyes that flashed at times . . . like a devil." On July 4, 1851, during a drunken rage, Fred Cannon, one of the miners, intentionally broke down Josefa's door.

The next morning José approached Cannon and asked him to pay for the door. Cannon became belligerent: "That door of yours would fall down if anyone coughed—show me the damage." As they went to inspect the door, Josefa stepped out of the house and became involved in an argument with Cannon who shouted, "I'm getting mighty tired of standing out here arguing with a lyin' son of a bitch about nothing." When Cannon threatened José, who did not want to fight, Josefa intervened: "Go on, why don't you hit me?" Cannon called Josefa a whore and the enraged Josefa went to the door of her home and said, "This is no place to call me bad names, come into my house and call me that." As Cannon entered the house, continuing to call Josefa vile names, she avenged her honor by killing him with a knife. Josefa had thus stood up to years of abuse in which Mexicans, especially women, were fair game for arrogant bullies.

Although the miners wanted to lynch Josefa and José on the spot, they held a trial of sorts. "Cannon was popular along the river and had many friends who were interested in vengeance and not justice. The hard feelings against Mexicans, engendered by the late war, were not likely to be put aside by a frenzied half-drunken mob of frontier miners" who put Cannon's body on display in a tent, dressed in a red flannel shirt, unbuttoned to display the wound. Throughout the trial Cannon was described as a calm and peaceful man. The defense brought out that Josefa was pregnant and that they would be killing two people. Josefa was condemned to hang while José was banished.

Senator John B. Weller was in town but he did nothing to stop the hanging. Weller was an ambitious politician who was later to become governor, and one voteless Mexican made no difference. Over 2,000 men lined the river to watch Josefa hang at the bridge. After this, lynching became commonplace and Mexicans came to know Anglo-American democracy as *"Linchocracia."*[45]

On July 10, 1850, four Sonorans were charged with the murder of four Anglos near Sonora, California. A group of Anglo-Americans had come upon the Mexicans while they were burning two of the Anglo corpses, which were already in a decomposed state. The Mexicans explained that it was their custom to burn the dead (three of the four belonged to the Yaqui tribe). Justice of the Peace R. C. Barry believed the men innocent and attempted to forestall violence, but the mob had its way. The four men were hanged.[46]

Public whippings and brandings were common. To the Anglo-Americans, "Whether from California, Chile, Peru, or Mexico, whether residents of 20 years' standing or immigrants of one week, all the Spanish-speaking were lumped together as 'interlopers' and 'greasers.' "[47]

Violence had to be justified. In the case of vigilante action the stance was that the mob championed the law and was attempting to

rectify conditions by demanding "an eye for an eye." Another justification was that Mexicans' criminal nature had to be controlled; to
Anglo-Americans every Mexican was a potential outlaw, and Anglos used the outlaw activity as an excuse to rob and murder peaceful Mexicans.

Racial tensions polarized the two communities, especially in
the Los Angeles area where although Mexican elites actively cooperated with the new order, they often became victims of mob violence. One such celebrated case involved the Lugo brothers, Francisco, 16, and Menito, 18, who were accused of killing a white man
and his Indian companion.[48] This case is interesting since the men
involved were the grandsons of Antonio María Lugo. The Anglo-
American populace was pitted against one of the richest and most
powerful California families. The Lugos were defended by Joseph
Lancaster Brent, a Los Angeles attorney and a native of Maryland,
who had strong southern sympathies and who related to the *ricos*
exceedingly well (one patriarch to another).

In January 1851 the Lugos, with fifteen or twenty ranch hands,
rode up the Cajon Pass from their San Bernardino ranch in pursuit
of Indians who had raided their stock. On their return they met
Patrick McSwiggin and a Creek Indian. Later the Irishman and the
Indian were found dead, and Francisco and Menito were charged
with murder.[49]

Only about seventy-five Anglo-Americans lived permanently
in Los Angeles. They lived in perpetual fear of a *Californio* revolt.
The McSwiggin murder inflamed the Anglos. The town mayor further polarized the situation: ". . . full of credulity and fright, rushed
around calling upon all the Americans to arm themselves and report to him for service."[50] The mayor so overreacted that he became
a joke.

At the inquest Ysidro Higuera testified that he had seen the
Lugos and another Mexican kill the deceased. The Higuera testimony was questioned because he had been previously convicted of
horse stealing and because he had been persuaded to testify, by the
jailer, George W. Robinson, who hated the Lugos. The *vaqueros*
who had ridden with the Lugos swore that the brothers had never
left the camp and that they had not killed the deceased.[51]

Meanwhile, a justice of the peace held the prisoners without
bail, an action applauded by the Anglo population. When the district court judge reversed this order and released the Lugos on a
$10,000 bond, he was immediately accused of taking a payoff.
Anglo-Americans threatened to take matters into their own hands.
Californios feared that the brothers would be lynched before they
were released on bail. Captain John "Red" Irving and about
twenty-five men approached Brent and demanded $10,000 to re-
lease the Lugos, threatening to lynch the boys if they were not paid.
The Lugos refused the offer and Irving vowed to kill the brothers

before they were released on bond. Brent became convinced that the only way to save the brothers was a show of force. Sixty armed *Californios* showed up, followed by U.S. troops whose presence prevented a confrontation. The Lugo boys were escorted by the *Californios* to the judge who released them on bail after which they were escorted to their ranch by the armed *Californios*.

A month later, Red, Irving and his men set out for the Lugo ranch to kill the brothers, but word of their plan got back to the Lugos. Their Cahuilla Indian friends set a trap for the gang, leading them into a ravine where all except one were killed. After additional turmoil the court finally dismissed the case on October 11, 1852. Brent had done a brilliant job of defending the Lugos; it was rumored that he collected a fee of $20,000, a measure of the price for justice.[52]

The fear of an uprising of *Californios* and racism established a pattern of indiscriminate attacks on Mexicans. Any incident became an excuse for a series of other violent incidents. For example, in 1856 Juan Flores (to be discussed later) escaped from San Quentin Prison and rallied fifty Mexicans to his cause. During the time Flores was chased, a group of *gringos* stopped two Mexicans near San Gabriel because they looked "suspicious" and began mistreating them. The Mexicans attempted to escape. The *gringos* killed one and then pursued the other, and a massive roundup of Mexicans followed.

The El Monte gang (a group of Anglos dominated by Texans from El Monte, California) arrested Diego Navarro, who was seen riding away from the gun battle. Navarro claimed that he was on his way to San Gabriel when he saw the gun fight; he rode away because he knew that all Mexicans became victims of the Anglo wrath. The gang threw hot tar on his family home and broke into the house, and dragged him out and executed him, along with two other Mexicans who were accused of being members of the Flores gang.

Shortly afterwards, Encarnación Berreyesa was lynched in San Buenaventura. The justification for the hanging was that Berreyesa was a member of the Flores gang; however, the truth was that the family had been victims of continual persecution. On March 28, 1857, a letter by José S. Berreyesa, reprinted in *El Clámor* from the *San Francisco Daily Herald,* reminded Californians of the terrible series of tragedies that had visited his family since the arrival of Anglo-Americans. Troubles started, the letter said, with Bear Flaggers' assassination of the elder Berreyesa and his two nephews. The family's sufferings were compounded when in July 1854 the body of an Anglo-American was found on the San Vicente ranch, which belonged to the Berreyesa family. A band of Anglos from Santa Clara, suspecting that the Berreyesas had murdered the man, invaded the house of Encarnación Berreyesa, dragged him out while his wife and children looked on, and suspended him from a tree. When he did not confess to the killings, vigilantes left him half dead and turned on his brother Nemesio. Nemesio's wife fled to San José to summon friends to help. When friends reached the ranch, they found him dead, dangling from a tree. Encarnación took his family to San Buenaventura to be with relatives and friends. However, at the time of the Flores affair a vigilance committee went into action. Though Berreyesa was not officially accused of being a follower of Flores, he was charged with the murder of an Anglo in Santa Clara. Under the cover of night Anglos lynched Encarnación. The writer then listed members of the Berreyesa family who had been assassinated: "Encarnación, José R. Berreyesa, Francisco de Haro, Ramón de Haro, Nemesio Berreyesa, José Sunol, José Galindo, Juan Berreyesa—fathers, brothers, cousins." Similar incidents occurred during the early 1850s when the legendary Joaquín Murietta was hunted down.

Throughout this time, considerable police brutality took place. A double standard of justice existed for Mexicans and Anglos. On July 26, 1856, Francisco Ramírez wrote in *El Clamor Público* that conditions had never been so bad. Six years of assassinations had created armed camps in California. "The criminals have always escaped. Justice is almost never administered." Ramírez attacked Anglo-Americans' indiscriminate murder of Chicanos, demanding an immediate cessation of violence. Ramírez was temperate, although his patience was strained by the Ruiz incident. William W. Jenkins, a deputy sheriff, alleged that Antonio Ruiz had interfered in an argument between the deputy and Ruiz's landlady. When Ruiz protested the deputy's mistreatment of the landlady, the armed Jenkins shot Ruiz in the chest. The defense, which had the support of the court, based its case on discrediting the witnesses to the Mexican's death. Police officials backed Jenkins. It took the jury only fifteen minutes to return a verdict of not guilty. Soon afterwards Jenkins returned to the task of maintaining "law and order" in Los Angeles.

CURRENTS OF RESISTANCE

From 1855 through 1859 *El Clamor Público* was published in Los Angeles by Francisco P. Ramírez, a 20-year-old Chicano, who had been a compositor for the Spanish page of the *Los Angeles Star*.[53] In 1859, because of lack of money, the newspaper went out of business. After this venture Ramírez returned to Sonora where he worked as a newspaper publisher. In the 1860s he appeared again in California where he worked as a printer, postmaster, and the official translator for the state. He tried a comeback in 1872 as editor of *La Crónica* in Los Angeles.

Ramírez's editorials reflected the *Mexicanos'* disappointments

with Anglo justice. On June 19, 1855, his newspaper editorials began on a moderate tone by calling for justice within the system and
recognizing that California was now part of the United States. He
asked the *Californios* for financial support, writing that a free press
was their best guarantee of liberty. He pledged his paper to an
independent course, promising that the newspaper would:

> Uphold the Constitution of the United States, convinced that only
> through it will we obtain liberty.... We shall combat all those op-
> posed to its magnanimous spirit and grand ideas.[54]

Ramírez's editorials changed, and his coverage became more
nationalistic. In an article on the filibuster William Walker,
Ramírez commented:

> World history tells us that the Anglo-Saxons were in the beginning
> thieves and pirates, the same as other nations in their infancy . . . [but]
> the pirate instinct of old Anglo-Saxons is still active.[55]

Throughout the paper's publication Walker remained the special target of the newspaper's editorials, as did the other "pirates"—
politicians and filibusters—who had designs on Mexico or Latin
America. In September 1855 Ramírez reprinted an article that
questioned:

> Who is the foreigner in California? He is what he is not in any other
> place in the world; he is what he is not in the most inhospitable land
> which can be imagined. . . . The North Americans pretend to give us
> lessons in humanity and to bring to our people the doctrine of salvation
> so we can govern ourselves, to respect the laws and conserve order.
> Are these the ones who treat us worse than slaves?[56]

The article condemned lynchings of Chicanos. By October he encouraged Mexicans and Chileans to join Jesús Isla's *Junta Coloni-
zadora de Sonora* and return to Mexico. He promoted this emigration society even when it was evident that it was not getting the
proper support from Mexico. Ramírez's loss of faith in the U.S.
government is beyond question.

On May 10, 1856, Ramírez protested Anglo-American nativism,
writing:

> California has fallen into the hands of the ambitious sons of North
> America who will not stop until they have satisfied their passions, by
> driving the first occupants of the land out of the country, villifying
> their religion and disfiguring their customs.[57]

Ramírez encouraged Mexicans to return to Sonora. One reader objected to Ramírez's "return-to-Mexico" stance, saying: "California
has always been the asylum of Sonorans, and the place where they
have found good wages, hospitality, and happiness." The writer
implied that Mexicans never had it so good. Ramírez caustically
replied that the letter did not merit comment and asked: "Are the
Californios as happy today as when they belonged to the Republic

of Mexico, in spite of all of its revolutions and changes in government?"[58]

Pages of *El Clamor Público* also reveal a schism between establishment Mexicans and *cholos*. Oppression and its attendant discrimination was obvious; however, many elites continued to work within the system and cooperated with Anglo-Americans to frustrate, not only resistance movements, but the Mexicans' justifiable demands.

Resistance often expressed itself in antisocial behavior. The best known case in California is that of Joaquín Murietta; lesser known is that of Juan Flores. Writers of the time freely labeled Flores's activities as the "Juan Flores Revolution."[59] However, it soon became more popular just to write him off as a bandit.

Flores, 21 years old, escaped from San Quentin Prison where he served a term for horse stealing. He returned to Los Angeles and formed a group of almost fifty Chicanos, including Pancho Daniel. There was widespread unrest. The murder of Antonio Ruiz had divided Mexicans across class lines, with the lower classes harboring deep-seated grievances against Anglos.[60] The Flores band operated around San Juan Capistrano. When Los Angeles Sheriff James Barton and a posse went to investigate, the band killed the sheriff. Rumors spread that they intended to kill all whites. A vigilante committee was organized and Anglos flooded into Los Angeles for protection.

The Flores revolt split Mexicans in two: the *ricos* backed the Anglo-Americans in suppressing the rebels and *los abajos* (the underdogs) supported Flores. Ramírez condemned the "bandits" in an editorial dated January 31, 1857, and called for *Californios* to join in the protection of their families and enforcement of laws. In doing so, Ramírez represented the class interests of his suscribers. Tomás Sánchez, a Democratic party *cacique* (boss), and Andrés Pico, the hero of the battle against Kearney at San Pasqual Pass, led the posse comprised of Anglos and *Mexicanos*. They joined with the El Monte gang to pursue Flores.

El Monte was the *gringo* stronghold—the only community in the Los Angeles area that was predominately Anglo-American. Many inhabitants were former Texans (some were even ex-Rangers). In almost every altercation between Mexicans and Anglos, the El Monte crowd posed as defenders of white supremacy. Many Mexicans considered them outlaws. The El Monte gang, which operated separately from the Los Angeles posse, captured Flores and Pancho Daniel, but the two escaped. Anglos then insured "justice" by hanging their next nine captives.

Meanwhile Andrés Pico set out with California Native-Americans to track down Flores. Pico emulated the *gringos* and hanged two of his countrymen whom he had captured. Martial law was imposed and the entire section of "Mexican Town" in Los Angeles was surrounded. The search for Flores was relentless, with houses broken into in the middle of the night and suspects herded to jail. During the hunt fifty-two men were crammed into the jails, many of whom had later to be discharged for lack of evidence. With the exception of Pancho Daniel, the entire gang was captured. Flores was hanged after being convicted by a kangaroo court on February 14, 1857.[61]

El Clamor Público praised Andrés Pico in an editorial published on February 7 and congratulated him for cooperating with the citizens of El Monte. Ramírez praised the spirit of unity and even wrote that *Californios* had vindicated their honor. The *ricos* denied a race war existed. Professor Pitt notes, "Sánchez and Pico, who gladly rode with Texans to track down 'their own kind,' thereby won the gringos' everlasting gratitude." They were rewarded; Sánchez became sheriff and Pico was made a brigadier in the California militia and was also elected to the state Assembly.[62] Many *Mexicanos* did not share the enthusiasm of *El Clamor* and the *ricos,* and condemned their participation in suppressing the Flores-Daniel rebellion. The poor could not forget the ethnic distinctions between "American" citizens.[63]

Why had Ramírez supported this action? The only explanation is that he believed the cooperation of Mexicans with the Anglos would improve relations between the two peoples, that is, the two peoples of the class that read his newspapers. These hopes were shattered by lynchings of Mexicans throughout the state, and Ramírez had a change of heart. He had applauded the hanging of Flores, but several months later when Pancho Daniel was captured and hanged, Ramírez called his execution "barbaric and diabolic" and lambasted the Chicano population, writing: "And you, imbecile Californios! You are to blame for the lamentations that we are witnessing. We are tired of saying: open your eyes, and it is time that we demand our rights and interests. It is with shame that we say, and difficult to confess it: you are the sarcasm of humanity!" He scolded readers for not voting and for putting up with indignities, calling them "cowards and stupids." He warned *Californios* that until they cared, they could never cast off the "yoke of slavery."[64] In less than four years, Ramírez had changed from an assimilationist to a nationalist. Regrettably, he could not understand the class conflict which divided the Mexican people.

Mexicans were not treated as individuals, and when some Mexicans took to the highway, all were collectively guilty in the eyes of most *gringos* in California. Voices of protest were gradually silenced as the Mexican population grew too poor to support newspapers. The California of Mexicans and Anglos grew further apart, with *Mexicanos* growing more resentful of *gringos.*

When people cannot earn a living within the system or when they are degraded, they strike out. Rebellion against the system can take the form of organizd resistance, as in the case of Juan Cortina in Texas, or it can express itself in bandit activity. An analysis of the life of Tiburcio Vásquez clearly demonstrates that, while the ruling society called him a criminal, his underlying motivation was self-defense. His actions fit into the mode of the primitive rebel and not the comical and oversexed Mexican bandit that some Anglo-American folklorists attempted to portray. In stereotyping Vásquez, Anglos have purposely or unconsciously attempted to use satire to dismiss legitimate grievances of *Mexicanos* during the nineteenth century. While it is true that Tiburcio Vásquez was an outlaw, many Mexicans supported him and many still consider him a hero.

Tiburcio Vásquez had been born in Monterey on August 11, 1835. His parents had a good reputation, and Vásquez had an above-average education for the times. Vásquez never married. In about 1852 he was involved in the shooting of a constable and fled to the hills.[65] At the end of his career Vásquez explained the incident and his reasons for turning *bandido:*

> My career grew out of the circumstances by which I was surrounded. As I grew to manhood I was in the habit of attending balls and parties given by the native Californians, into which the Americans, then beginning to become numerous, would force themselves and shove the native born men aside, monopolizing the dance and the women. This was about 1852. A spirit of hatred and revenge took possession of me. I had numerous fights in defense of my countrymen. The officers were continually in pursuit of me. I believed we were unjustly and wrongfully deprived of the social rights that belonged to us.[66]

To understand Vásquez's feelings the times must be kept in perspective: By the middle of the 1850s California "was experiencing an economic depression. Money was short, the great flood of gold was nearly played out, land and cattle prices were down, and banditry was rampant."[67] During this time Vásquez attracted a large following and his popularity grew since it was alleged that he gave goods to the poor. Also at the same time the "people" convicted Vásquez in Los Angeles for horse stealing and sentenced him to five years in San Quentin Prison. From this point until 1870 Vásquez was in and out of jail.

The *ricos* were afraid that he wanted to incite an uprising or revolution against the "Yankee invaders" of California, and from all indications the rural poor supported and shielded him.[68] The *Los Angeles Express* (date unknown) quoted Vásquez as claiming, "Given $60,000 I would be able to recruit enough arms and men to revolutionize Southern California."

In the fall of 1871 Vásquez and his men robbed the Visalia stage. His reputation as a *desperado* grew and he was soon being blamed for crimes that he did not commit. The magnitude of the manhunts increased. Authorities paid informers in an effort to locate Vásquez. Throughout 1871 Vásquez not only continued his activities, but also avoided arrest. The Chicano populace continued to aid him for "to some, Vásquez must have seemed a hero dealing out his own particular brand of justice. Certainly his reputation was growing fast."[69]

On August 16, 1873, he and his men converged on Snyder's store in Tres Pinos and robbed it of $1,200. It was this daring raid that brought Vásquez to statewide prominence. Newspapers sensationalized Vásquez's raids, and wanted posters circulated. Vásquez prudently decided to shift activities to Southern California.

During the next year he became bolder and newspapers played up his activities and Sheriff Harry Morse quickened the pace of the chase, covering 2,720 miles in 61 days searching for Vásquez. Authorities learned that Vásquez was hiding out at the ranch of George Allen, better known as Greek George, and surrounded the ranch. Vásquez was captured. An all-Anglo jury found him guilty, and he was sentenced to hang.

Beers offered a partial explanation of why Vásquez captured the imagination of the Mexican populace:

> Vásquez turned to the life of a bandido because of the bitter animosity then existing, and which still exists, between the white settlers and the native or Mexican portion of the population. The native Californians, especially the lower classes, never took kindly to the stars and stripes. Their youth were taught from the very cradle to look upon the American government as that of a foreign nation.
>
> This feeling was greatly intensified by the rough brutal conduct of the worst class of American settlers, who never missed an opportunity to openly exhibit their contempt for the native Californian or Mexican population—designating them as "d——d Greasers," and treating them like dogs. Add to this the fact that these helpless people were cheated out of their lands and possessions by every subterfuge—in many instances their property being actually wrested from them by force, and their women debauched whenever practicable—and we can understand very clearly some of the causes which have given to Joaquin (Murietta), Vásquez, and others of their stripe, the power to call around them at any time all the followers they required, and which secured to them aid and comfort from the Mexican settlers everywhere.[70]

Vásquez's execution deepened racial tensions. Two weeks after the hanging a man named Romo killed two Anglo-Americans who had participated in Vásquez's capture; he was caught and lynched. Groups of *Mexicanos* met secretly and the *ricos* grew anxious, fearing a race war which would include them.

The Catholic church played the same role in California as it did in New Mexico, that is, it cooperated with the elites, actively Americanizing and destroying any nationalist base that existed. In 1850 the Right Reverend Francisco Diego y Moreno was replaced by Fr. Joseph Sadoc Alemany, a non-Mexican, as the head of the church in the Los Angeles area. A Frenchman replaced Fr. Gonzales Rubio. "During this period the Catholic hierarchy was anxious to put into effect a program for Americanizing the foreign born members of the church."[71] In 1852 the Plenary Council of Bishops, meeting at Baltimore, laid out a master plan of stricter enforcement of tithes and increased effort to establish parochial schools. The impoverished state of the masses of Mexicans and Indians was not discussed, but it was decided to renew political pressure on the Mexican government to gain control of the Pious fund (a large fund collected during the Spanish colonial period for the benefit of the missions).[72]

Bishop Taddeus Amat summed up the priority of the church in 1870, stating that the church was "the main support of society and order, which imperatively demands respect for legitimate authority and subjugation to legitimate law."[73] Therefore, European and Spanish priests teamed to control the plaza in Los Angeles and to discourage Mexicans from rebelling against what the church considered legitimate authority.

THE FROZEN SOCIETY IN CALIFORNIA

No force did more to bring about change in social relations in California than the arrival of the railroad. Mexicans were affected in obvious ways. The isolation they enjoyed during the 1850s and 1860s abruptly ended. Over the next three decades Mexicans receded into the role of a small and politically insignificant minority. However, this same railroad also put into motion forces which set the stage for the mass migration of Mexicans to California in the first three decades of the twentieth century and continuing to this day. In short, railroads made possible the full development of California resources, and Mexican labor became essential to this process.

Tiburcio Vásquez's death ended the era of intense Mexican rebellion. Anglo-Americans in southern California, who in the first years had lived in fear of a Mexican uprising, soon numerically overwhelmed Mexicans. Railroads ended the dominance of the Mexican population in southern California just as the gold rush had in northern California. Los Angeles, where the Southern Pacific arrived in 1876, is typical of this change. The Mexican population increased only slightly from 1,331 in 1850 to 2,231 in 1880, whereas the Anglo population rose from under 300 to some 8,000 during this same period. By 1890 the city had grown to 50,395, with the Mexican population increasing slightly.[74]

Los Angeles underwent other changes. In 1850 it had 1 factory employing 2 men; in 1880 it had 172 factories and 700 workers. Property values in this same period increased from $2,282,949 to $20,916,835.

The 1880s transformed Los Angeles into a modern city. However, Mexicans did not participate in many of the improvements. Their status changed little from the Mexican period, with 65 percent employed as manual laborers as contrasted to the 26 percent of Anglo-Americans employed in laboring occupations. The economic order froze Mexicans into a set class and occupational mobility was limited among all workers; race and a historical tradition of oppression facilitated continued subjugation.

Although their status remained the same as in the Mexican era, subtle changes had taken place. For instance, not only were they set off from the upper levels of society by class, as they had been before, but now they were separated also from others in the lower levels by race. They became easy scapegoats for failures of the economic system. After 1848 land became less accessible. In 1850 60 percent of the Mexican families had property of one kind or another in Los Angeles, whereas in 1870 less than 24 percent owned property.

While the isolation of Los Angeles ended, segregation of Mexicans became more complete. By 1873 the participation of Mexicans on juries became rarer, as did their involvement in any other forms of government. The city fathers ignored problems of health and urbanization in the *barrios* (Sonoratown). Between 1877 and 1888 infant mortality was double that of Anglos; the death rate among Mexicans between ages 5 and 20 was also double, with smallpox a leading killer. Cost of medical care was prohibitive. Doctors charged for house calls according to how far the patient lived, and, since most doctors did not live close to the Mexican *colonia*, the usual fee was $10—a week's salary for most Mexicans.[75]

Mexicans attempted to deal with these problems within their own community. They formed self-help associations, such as in 1875 *La Sociedad Hispanoamericana de Beneficio Mutua,* to raise money for hospitals and charitable purposes, and the Sisters of Charity established a hospital for indigents in 1887.[76] Organizations in these years reflected the Mexicans' isolation and as a consequence became increasingly nationalistic, celebrating the Mexican patriotic holidays such as the 16th of September and the 5th of May and sponsoring parades, speeches, and other festivities.

Meanwhile, large corporations gained tighter control of California. The Southern Pacific Railroad alone owned more land than all of the *rancheros* combined. Most of Southern Pacific's holding were in the southern half of the state. During the land boom of the 1880s the Southern Pacific advertised throughout the East and Europe for buyers. It even established an employment agency for the new settlers.[77]

Industrial growth created a heavy demand for cheap labor. As in Arizona, Chinese workers filled the need in the preliminary stages. After their exclusion other groups filled the vacuum, but reclamation programs of the early 1900s caused a revolution in agriculture which forced California capitalists to look to the most logical and available source of labor—Mexico. Further changes were brought about by the discovery of oil and the opening of the Panama Canal in the 1900s. The isolation of California and Los Angeles had completely ended.

Discrimination toward Mexicans in the wage labor market increased; a dual wage system existed with Mexicans and Chinese paid less than Anglos. This arbitrary treatment of Mexicans often led to confrontations. For instance, on August 20, 1892, a mob in Santa Ana broke into the jail and hanged Francisco Torres, a native of Colima, Mexico.[78] Torres worked at the Modjeska ranch for a wage of $9.00 for a 6-day week. The foreman of the ranch, William McKelvey, withheld money from Torres's check for a road poll tax, but not from any of the other workers' pay. Torres refused the check, demanding full payment, and in an ensuing argument killed McKelvey. Torres stated that he did not have a gun, that he had taken a club away from the larger man, and that, in fear that the foreman would use his gun, he had killed McKelvey with a knife in self-defense.

A posse captured Torres and he was charged with murder. The press inflamed the populace, calling Torres a "brutal greaser." Before Torres could be tried, a mob broke into the jail and executed him, hanging a sign around his neck which read "Change of venue." The *Santa Ana Standard* wrote:

> Torres was a low type of Mexican race, and was evidently more Indian than white. True to his savage nature he had no more regard for human life than for the merest trifle. . . . He belongs to a class of outlaws in southern California and old Mexico. . . .[79]

In contrast, *Las Dos Repúblicas,* wrote:

> This time the victim has been a Mexican whose guilt perhaps consisted solely in his nationality. . . .A town which occupies so high a rank in world civilization ought not to let crime such as this go unpunished.[80]

The execution went unpunished. Prominent citizens of Santa Ana were known to have participated in the lynching, but no attempt was made to prosecute them. A year later Jesús Cuen was lynched in San Bernardino.[81] During these incidents, racial tensions remained high, but by this time it did not matter whether the *ricos* were embarrassed or not; California had been lost.

NOTES

1. John W. Caughey, *California: A Remarkable State's Life History,* 3rd ed. (Englewood Cliffs, N.J.: Prentice-Hall, 1970), pp. 142, 144, 156, 157.
2. Andrew F. Rolle, *California: A History* (New York: Crowell, 1963), p. 191.
3. Manuel Castanares, "Collección de documentos relativos al departamento de California" (1845) in David Weber, ed., *Northern Mexico on the Eve of the United States Invasion* (New York: Arno Press, 1976).

4. Leonard Pitt, *The Decline of the Californios* (Berkeley and Los Angeles: University of California Press, 1966), p. 26.
5. Whether Frémont received orders from Polk to incite the war cannot be proven. George Winston Smith and Charles Judah, *Chronicles of the Gringos* (Albuquerque: University of New Mexico Press, 1968), p. 141 and 149, do, however, make a good case for such a conclusion. See also Simeon Ide, *Biographical Sketch of the Life of William B. Ide* (Glorieta, N. Mex.: Rio Grande Press, 1967), p. 133; and *Who Conquered California?* (Glorieta, N. Mex.: Rio Grande Press, 1967).
6. Oscar Lewis, ed. "California in 1846," (San Francisco: Grabhorn Press, 1934) in Carlos E. Cortes, ed., *Mexicans in the U.S. Conquest of California* (New York: Arno Press, 1976), p. 31.
7. Richard Griswold del Castillo, "*La Raza Hispano-Americana:* The Emergence of an Urban Culture Among the Spanish Speaking of Los Angeles, 1850–1880" (Ph.D., dissertation, University of California at Los Angeles, 1974), p. 45.
8. Pitt, p. 27; Griswold del Castillo, p. 49
9. Pitt, p. 30.
10. Walter Colton, *Three Years in California* (New York: A. S. Barnes, 1850), p. 2.
11. Walton Bean, *California*, 2nd ed. (New York: McGraw-Hill, 1973), p. 104; Caughey, p. 168. Bean places the number of Americans killed at 22 with 16 wounded. Bill Mason of the Los Angeles County Museum stated in an interview that the number of Mexicans present was exaggerated. Mason said that they had been able to document the presence of only 65 Mexicans at San Pasqual; popular accounts place the number at approximately 150. Dewitt C. Peters, *Kit Carson's Life and Adventures, from Facts Narrated by Himself* (Hartford, Conn.: Dustin, Gilmain, 1875), pp. 282–283, confirms that word of the Mexican force was received by Kearny in late October.
12. Robert F. Heizer and Allan F. Almquist, *The Other Californians* (Berkeley: University of California Press, 1971), p. 149; Bean, pp. 132–134; Stephen Clark Foster, delegate to the Constitutional Convention of 1849, *El Quachero: How I Want to Help Make the Constitution of California—Stirring Historical Incidents*, in Carlos E. Cortes, ed., *Mexicans in California* (New York: Arno Press, 1976).
13. José Bandini, *A Description of California in 1828* (Berkeley: Friends of the Bancroft Library, 1951), reprinted in Carlos E. Cortes, ed., *Mexican California* (New York: Arno Press, 1976), pp. vi, 11; Don Thomas Coulter, *Notes on Upper California: A Journey from Monterey to the Colorado River in 1832* (Los Angeles: Glen Dawson, 1951), reprinted in Cortes, *Mexican California*, p. 23; Heizer and Almquist, p. 120.
14. Heizer and Almquist, p. 144.
15. Heizer and Almquist, pp. 143, 144.
16. Quoted in Leonard Pitt, "The Foreign Miner's Tax of 1850: A Study of Nativism and Anti-Nativism in Gold Rush California" (Master's thesis, University of California at Los Angeles, 1955), p. 9.
17. David J. Weber, ed., *Foreigners in Their Native Land* (Albuquerque: University of New Mexico Press, 1973), p. 151.
18. Pitt, "Foreign Miner's Tax," pp. 49–50.
19. Richard Morefield, "Mexicans in the California Mines, 1848–1853," *California Historical Quarterly* 24 (March 1956): 38.
20. Heizer and Almquist, pp. 121, 145.
21. *Daily Pacific News*, October 19, 1850.
22. Heizer and Almquist, p. 155.
23. Morefield, p. 43.
24. Charles Hughes, *The Decline of the Californios: The Case of San Diego, 1846–1856*, reprinted in Cortes, *Mexicans in California After the U.S. Conquest*, p. 17.
25. Mario T. García, *Merchants and Dons: San Diego's Attempt at Modernization, 1850–1860*, reprinted in Cortes, *Mexicans in California After the U.S. Conquest*, p. 70.
26. Bean, p. 224; Caughey, p. 344.
27. García, p. 70. Pitt, *Decline of the Californios*, p. 118, states that 813 titles were reviewed and 32 rejected. Bean, p. 157, says more than 800 cases were heard,

that 604 were confirmed and 209 rejected. We rely here on the García figures cited.

28. Pitt, *Decline of the Californios*, p. 119.
29. Hughes, p. 17.
30. Heizer and Almquist, p. 150.
31. Griswold del Castillo, p. 76; Albert Michael Camarillo, "The Making of a Chicano Community: A History of the Chicanos in Santa Barbara, California, 1850–1930," (Ph.D. dissertation, University of California at Los Angeles, 1975), p. 43.
32. Hughes, p. 18.
33. García, p. 70.
34. Griswold del Castillo, p. 78.
35. Horace Bell, *On the Old West Coast* (New York: Morrow, 1930), pp. 5–6.
36. Bell, pp. 255–257.
37. Heizer and Almquist, pp. 128–129, 131.
38. Heizer and Almquist, p. 151.
39. Camarillo, p. 65.
40. Richard Griswold del Castillo, "Health and the Mexican Americans in Los Angeles, 1850–1867," *Journal of Mexican History* 4 (1974): 21; Richard Romo, "Mexican Workers in the City: Los Angeles, 1915–1930" (Ph.D., dissertation, University of California at Los Angeles, 1975), p. 80.
41. Camarillo, p. 68.
42. Griswold del Castillo, "La Raza," p. 29.
43. Pitt, *Decline of the Californios*, pp. 50–51.
44. William B. Secrest, *Juanita: The Only Woman Lynched in the Gold Rush Days* (Fresno, Calif.: Saga-West, 1967), pp. 8–29.
45. Secrest, p. 23, *El Clamor Público*, April 4 and 16, 1857.
46. Pitt, *Decline of the Californios*, pp. 61–63.
47. Pitt, *Decline of the Californios*, p. 53.
48. W. W. Robinson, *People Versus Lugo: Story of a Famous Los Angeles Murder Case and Its Aftermath* (Los Angeles: Dawson's Book Shop, 1962), reprinted in Cortes, *Mexicans in California After the U.S. Conquest*, p. 6.
49. Joseph Lancaster Brent, *The Lugo Case: A Personal Experience*, reprinted in Cortes, *Mexicans in California After the U.S. Conquest*, pp. 12–13; Robinson, pp. 1–5.
50. Robinson, p. 14; Brent, p. 4.
51. Robinson, pp. 10–11, 17–18, 40; Brent, pp. 17–19.
52. Robinson, pp. 21–22, 26–27, 33–37, 40; Brent, pp. 20–33.
53. See Pitt, *Decline of the Californios*, chap. 17, for a biography of Ramírez.
54. *El Clamor Público*, June 19, 1855.
55. *El Clamor Público*, August 20, 1855.
56. *El Clamor Público*, September 18, 1855.
57. *El Clamor Público*, May 10, 1856.
58. *El Clamor Público*, May 17, 1856.
59. Bell, p. 72.
60. Griswold del Castillo, "*La Raza*," pp. 195–196.
61. Hubert Howe Bancroft, *Popular Tribunals*, vol. 1 (San Francisco: History Company, 1887), pp. 501–503; Griswold del Castillo, "*La Raza*," pp. 195–196.
62. Pitt, *Decline of the Californios*, p. 174.
63. Griswold del Castillo, "*La Raza*," p. 197.
64. *El Clamor Público*, December 18, 1858.
65. Ernest May "Tiburcio Vásquez," *Historical Society of Southern California Quarterly* 24 (1947): 123–124, places the time in spring of 1851. His article is unsympathetic. He writes that Vásquez was in the company of Anastacio García, whom May calls an outlaw, and José Guerra. May admits that Constable Hardimount had been rude to Mexicans. Guerra was caught and hanged. Griswold del Castillo, "*La Raza*," p. 198, states that Vásquez began his career by escaping from a lynch mob.
66. Robert Greenwood, *The California Outlaw: Tiburcio Vásquez* (Los Gatos, Calif.: Talisman Press, 1960), p. 12.
67. Heizer and Almquist, pp. 150–151.
68. May, p. 124; Greenwood, p. 13; Griswold del Castillo, "*La Raza*," p. 199.
69. Greenwood, pp. 23–24.

70. Greenwood, p. 75.
71. Griswold del Castillo, *"La Raza,"* pp. 270, 271.
72. Griswold del Castillo, *"La Raza,"* p. 272.
73. Quoted in Griswold, *"La Raza,"* p. 271.
74. Griswold del Castillo, *"La Raza,"* p. 66; Caughey, pp. 349–350.
75. Griswold del Castillo, *"La Raza,"* pp. 156, 202; Griswold del Castillo, "Health," p. 22.
76. Griswold del Castillo, *"La Raza,"* p. 227; Griswold, "Health," p. 22.
77. Caughey, pp. 344–345.
78. Jean F. Riss,"The Lynching of Francisco Torres," *Journal of Mexican American History* (Spring 1972): 90–111.
79. Riss, p. 109.
80. Riss, p. 111.
81. Griswold del Castillo, *"La Raza,"* p. 193. Also see Richard Griswold del Castillo, "Myth and Reality: Chicano Economic Mobility in Los Angeles, 1850–1890," *Aztlán* 6, no. 2 (Summer 1975): 151–171.

Part II
A RADICAL VIEW
OF THE
TWENTIETH-CENTURY
CHICANO

During the nineteenth century Mexicans had been frozen into caste through a process of political and economic exclusion in addition to sanctioned violence. Deeply rooted racist stereotypes developed about Mexicans during the conquest—for after all they were enemies. Generally Mexicans lived apart from the Anglo-American population and during the early colonial period constituted a majority in whole sections of the Southwest. However, the arrival of the railroad ended this isolation. A dramatic increase in Anglo-Americans threatened to swallow up the Mexican population and for a time it seemed as if Mexicans would disappear. Around the turn of the century private industry and governmental authorities began to encourage a revival of Mexican migration to the Southwest. Capitalist interests wanted the Mexicans for only one reason: not because they would make good neighbors nor because brown was beautiful, but to work as cheaply as the labor market would permit. The more Mexicans, the lower wages could be kept and the more profit capitalists developing the Southwest could make. At the same time strong measures were taken to keep this group in its place.

Part II deals with three topics—immigration, labor, and the political experiences of Mexican people in the United States. The position of Mexicans in America was to a large extent determined by their position in the marketplace. The commodity known as Mexican labor was purposely relegated to the lowest value and kept there. Unlike European immigrants, most Mexicans did not pass into the middle class. And as the United States entered the twentieth century, society became more rigid, and economic opportunity and resources became scarcer.

Chapter 6
"Greasers Go Home"

The reaction of Anglo-Americans to Mexican migration to the United States has been one of "Greasers go home!"—an attitude fomented by the proximity of the border and the anxious feeling that millions of Mexicans are poised just across the border. Near panic was produced between 1910 and 1930 as Anglo-American nativists witnessed one of the largest mass movements of people in history with approximately one-eighth of Mexico's population shifting "north from Mexico." This movement occurred in a period of tremendous change which saw the demise of small farmers, a world war, the rise of radicalism, and recessions and depressions. As changes took place, Anglo-Americans grew more puzzled and frustrated and, not understanding what was happening, they blamed the destruction of their old ways on Mexicans.

BACKGROUND OF THE MIGRATION
NORTH OF THE RIO BRAVO

The first U.S. industrial revolution spread to agriculture in the Southwest by the 1850s, with McCormick's machine reaping grain in fields that had once belonged to the Mexicans. Mining bonanzas attracted large numbers of Anglos. Railroad interests laid track linking East and West, greatly accelerating the development of the Southwest. The Southwest supplied raw materials for the East, which in turn provided the "colony" with manufactured goods and capital. Fuel and minerals were needed, as well as food to feed European immigrants who manned new factories. The refrigerated car went into service one year before transcontinental railroads were completed in 1869. Both railroads and refrigerated cars proved to be revolutionary in the last quarter of the nineteenth century. Eastern and foreign capital gushed into the Southwest, monopolizing all sectors of the economy.

Large-scale development depended on large numbers of workers; to maximize profits, wages were kept as low as possible. What Anglo-American society wanted were workers who would do work white men would not, who would accept below-subsistence wages, and who would return home to their native lands when they finished their work. It was believed that Mexicans could supply this kind of labor at minimum expense and inconvenience.

Prior to 1880 contact between the United States and Mexico had been limited to the sparsely settled borderlands of northern

Mexico. Although this area did not have sufficient manpower to supply the Southwest's growing labor demands, conditions in Mexico soon changed this situation and encouraged large numbers to migrate north of the Rio Bravo.[1]

The roots of these conditions can be traced back through the history of Mexico. By the sixteenth century Mexico, one of the cradles of civilization, had reached a stage of advanced and complex social organization. Several cities reached populations of 100,000 or more and with such a large and increasing population technological changes and a more complex society with increased centralization, bureaucratic organization, division of labor, and widespread commerce promised to develop. By the 1520s 25 million inhabited central Mexico, and it can only be speculated as to what changes would have taken place if the Spanish invasion had not stopped the upward spiral of Mexico's growth.[2]

The northward movement was a natural process which began before the arrival of the Spaniards. Mesoamerica was continuously extending its sphere northward into the "Great Chichimeca." By the tenth century the Mesoamerican area of cultural influence included the southern half of Sinaloa, the rest of Jalisco, large western sections of present-day Aguascalientes and Zacatecas, and into Durango.[3] In the Toltec Period (900–1200) the northern line extended from the Río del Fuerte in Sinaloa to the Soto la Marina region in the Gulf of Mexico. Considering the growth of population in Mexico's interior, there is little doubt that the process of cultural, political, and economic integration would have continued if the Spaniards had not invaded the region. Population created a push both to the south and north.

The story of capitalism in Mexico begins with Spanish imperialism. However, the conquest retarded economic development, for by 1605 the Indian population of central Mexico dropped to 1,075,000, a condition which literally bled Mexico dry.[4] The economic system imposed on what was then New Spain was not solely feudal, but mixed with the beginnings of capitalism. Feudal institutions were established in the southern part, while in other sectors mines, ranches, artisan workshops, small factories, and *haciendas* developed. Early in the colonial period the system of labor grants or allotments was phased out in industries like mining, with salaried workers dominating the work force.[5] By the end of the colonial period it became evident that the Mexican economy had begun to stabilize, and by independence in 1821 there was a nucleus of merchants, mine owners, and professionals who wanted to follow the example of the United States and industrialize the country. A power struggle followed between these capitalists and the old elite—large landowners, the military, and the Catholic church. Capitalists won by the mid-1850s when Benito Juárez's liberal party finally took what proved to be full control of government.

However, Mexico's economic growth had been severely destabilized by its extensive land losses to the United States, the Wars of Reform (1858–1861), and French intervention (1861–1867).

Porfirio Díaz (1876–1910) implemented a program of industrialization which accelerated the decline of feudalism in Mexico. Mexico's population increased slowly. In the 1840s the population was about 7,000,000. In 1875 it reached 9,495,000, in 1880 10,448,000, 1895 12,632,000, in 1900 13,607,000.[6] By 1910 it had reached 15,160,000, still far below the 25,000,000 of the preconquest period. Meanwhile, the push north was revived, following the river bed rutted before the Spanish invasion.

The Díaz years produced tremendous changes in Mexico. "Economically, railroad building and industrialization were the most important innovative processes generating social change in Mexico during the Porfiriato."[7] Both processes were financed to a large degree by foreign capital from the United States and European countries. Between 1880 and 1910 15,000 miles of railroad were built, most lines running north and south, with short lines providing better access to mineral deposits and making growing of specialized crops such as sugar cane more profitable.[8]

Industrialization uprooted many *peones* either because mechanization displaced them from *haciendas* or because they were attracted to better paying jobs on railroad construction crews, in the booming mines of northern Mexico, or in the nascent urban industries. Before the twentieth century Mexican laborers had begun their northward migration to the mines of Coahuila and the smelters of Monterey. Pay in the north was 75¢ a day versus 25¢ a day in the interior.[9] Peonage did not disappear since the new capitalist agriculturalists protected the institution to ensure a generous supply of cheap labor and resisted the loss of labor to other sectors.

New capitalists subverted the laws of the reform, especially *La Ley Lerdo*, which provided for the breakup of church holdings by specifying that corporations must sell excess lands. They distorted the law to give *hacendados* the right to encroach on *ejidos*, communal lands of Indian villages. As in the United States, the Mexican farm family was doomed:

> Private property holders like the Zapata family lost their lands, as did the communal land holders (*ejidatarios*), to big commercial farmers interested in expanding the sugar industry in Morelos by developing large plantations with cheap labor and by constructing sugar mills on the plantations themselves. . . . Between 1876 and 1910, maize prices increased 108 percent, bean prices 163 percent, and chile prices 147 percent; since wages increased only 60 percent during the same period, real income for the masses declined an estimated 57 percent.[10]

Decline in purchasing power cannot altogether be blamed on the Díaz regime. Marked increase in population played a role. It increased the surplus labor pool which in part explains the static wages and rising food prices.[11] Not only railroads flowed south to north, but capital, which could have stabilized the Mexican economy, also went in that direction. Victor Alba, a Mexican historian, states that U.S. corporations owned three-quarters of mineral holdings in Mexico and that by 1910 "U.S. investment amounted to more than $2 billion, more than all the capital in the hands of Mexicans."[12] According to Alba the Díaz government gave foreign investors preferential treatment. For example, Edward L. Doheny bought oil-yielding tracts in Tampico for $1 an acre and companies exporting oil did not pay taxes.[13] Furthermore, during labor disputes the Mexican government intervened on the side of management.

The interference of U.S. capitalists kept Mexico's economy destabilized, thus ensuring a constant supply of raw materials as well as cheap labor for their parent corporations in the Southwest. Monopolies, such as United States Steel, the Guggenheim, Anaconda, Standard Oil, and others were active in both countries, and the United States controlled the flow of migration. U.S. business interests built railroads that facilitated movement of Mexicans to the border areas, and in many instances they paid workers' fares to the United States, even when contract labor was in violation of U.S. law. Well before 1900 over 22,000 railroad cars transporting an estimated 77,000 Mexicans entered the United States.[14]

U.S. business policies also encouraged millions of others to flock to border cities, which became labor pools for both legal and illegal recruitment by agribusiness and large corporations. At the turn of the century most border cities numbered about a thousand inhabitants. Since then, growth of these cities has been phenomenal. For example, the population of Juárez was 10,621 in 1910, 48,881 in 1940, and 252,119 in 1960.[15]

Foreign domination of the Mexican economy cannot be attributed solely to the U.S. or the British and French investors who were also active. It took the collusion of Mexican capitalists to make foreign control possible. However, once the railroads were constructed, the United States outstripped all other interests:

> Rail connections to seven land ports of entry into the United States and heavy U.S. investments in Mexico, all tended to divert the exports from Europe, which in 1877 took nearly 60 percent. . . . In 1877 the United States took 42 percent of the Mexican goods, and Great Britain, 35; by 1901 the northern neighbor absorbed 82 percent, and Great Britain, a meager 6.[16]

By 1910 foreign investors controlled 76 percent of all corporations, 95 percent of mining, 89 percent of industry, 100 percent of oil, and 96 percent of agriculture. The United States owned 38 percent of this investment, Britain 29 percent, and France 27 percent.[17] Trade with the United States had jumped from $7 million in 1860 to $63 million in 1900.[18] Anglo-Americans alone owned over $100 million in the state of Chihuahua. In contrast, 97.1 percent of the families in Guanajuato were without land, 96.2 percent in Jalisco, 99.5 percent in Mexico (state), and 99.3 percent in Pueblo.[19]

Given the population boom in Mexico and the flight of capital Mexicans did what people have always done—they followed the resources. Migration in search of food, clothing, and shelter is a basic behavior pattern which certainly predates the relatively recent concept of national borders. The policy of President Díaz toward the large exodus of Mexican citizens was one of indifference, for he placed little value on the *peon* and *campesino*. This was not the case with the Catholic church or *hacendados* in Jalisco, Guanajuato, and Michoacán, both of whom complained that the country was being depopulated. In 1906 the *Partido Liberal Mexicano* (PLM) urged Díaz to repatriate Mexicans, to pay for their transportation and give them land. Three years later Francisco Madero called the flight of Mexicans to the United States a "serious national disease," but little could be done to stop the process.[20]

The flight was encouraged by a series of economic developments in the United States, all of which increased the market for labor. Mining booms of the 1880s and 1890s, expansion of railroads, exclusion of the Chinese in 1882, the Dingley tariff on foreign sugar imports, growth of specialized farming requiring seasonal labor, and the Reclamation Act of 1902, which allowed the irrigation of large tracts of farm lands, all contributed to the pull of Mexicans northward. Mexican labor was the commodity essential to making large profits in a system in which surplus labor became surplus capital. Officially 103,000 entered the United States by 1900, but that number may have been much higher. Officially 222,000 entered by 1910, but experts estimate that that number may have been as high as 500,000.[21]

In the first decade of the twentieth century Mexicans departed from their traditional areas of settlement. In 1908 Victor Clark stated: "As recently as 1900, immigrant Mexicans were seldom found more than one hundred miles from the border. Now they are working as unskilled laborers and as section hands as far east as Chicago and as far north as Iowa, Wyoming, and San Francisco."[22] Incoming Mexicans settled permanently only in Texas; Clark estimated that prior to 1908 about 60,000 entered the United States annually, with most Mexicans remaining for only a brief period in the United States.[23]

Lastly, the role of the railroads cannot be underestimated in this northward movement. It allowed the movement of large numbers of Mexicans from Mexico's interior across thousands of miles of desert and rugged terrain in northern Mexico.

NATIVIST REACTION TO MEXICAN MIGRATION

Victor S. Clark's *Mexican Labor in the United States,* a 1908 study by the U.S. government, dramatically documented the plight of Mexicans transported thousands of miles to the Southwest: "One is told of locked car doors and armed guards on the platform of trains to prevent desertion on route."[24] It records the exploitation of Mexicans in the United States and sets the tone for later stereotypes of the Mexicans, describing them as physically weak, irregular and indolent, their only virtues being that they were docile and worked for low wages.[25]

Two years later the 1910 *Report of the Immigration Commission* continued Clark's view of Mexicans. It reported that they were the lowest paid of any laborers and that the majority worked as transient and migratory labor, did not settle, and returned to Mexico after only a few months.

The 1910 *Report* however warned that: "The assimilative qualities of the Mexicans are slight because of the backward educational facilities in their native land and a constitutional prejudice on the part of the peons toward school attendance. . . ." The report concluded that Mexicans regarded public relief as a "pension."[26]

By 1909 Mexicans comprised 98 percent of the crews employed by the Atchison, Topeka, and Santa Fe Railways west of Albuquerque; the Southern Pacific Railroad employed a similar percentage.[27] As conditions in Mexico worsened as a result of the revolution, many middle- and upper-class Mexicans entered the United States. In 1913, primarily due to an economic depression, the commissioner sounded the alarm, indicating that Mexicans might become a public charge.[28] Newspapers created an anti-Mexican environment by making Mexicans scapegoats during times of depression. This is a pattern of repression that would be repeated throughout the twentieth century.

Capitalists welcomed Mexicans as temporary laborers, but not as residents. Only Mexicans who would do the work that white men would not were wanted, and then only when there was general prosperity. Nativists responded to events in Mexico and the activities of the *Partido Liberal Mexicano* in the United States. On November 18, 1913 the Los Angeles police assigned several officers to investigate a plot by Mexican "reds" and *cholos.*[29] According to the *Los Angeles Times* at least 10 percent of Los Angeles's 35,000 Mexicans were "known to the police to be rabid sympathizers with the outlaw Villa."[30] With the advent of war in Europe business interests called for more Mexican labor and the "brown scare" intensified, with nativists now accusing all Mexicans of disloyalty. The Justice Department suspected German agents in Los Angeles of recruiting Mexicans as spies and saboteurs and they hired a former *Porfirista* to spy on the Mexican community. The degree of the hysteria was such that U.S. troops crossed the border into Mexico to attempt to capture Pancho Villa. Los Angeles officials talked about placing Mexicans in a "workhouse" or "isolation camp." Two days after Villa's raid on Columbus, New Mexico, the supervisors requested federal action in deporting *cholos* likely to become public charges.[31] However, if conditions were bad in Los Angeles, they were worse in other sections of the country, especially in Texas (to be discussed in Chapter 10).

To a large extent the United States's entry into World War I relaxed efforts to control immigration. In 1916 the commissioner general of immigration commented that "The volume of refugees of a nonpolitical stripe has greatly increased. Fortunately for this, a general revival of industrial activity throughout the Southwest, and even in regions more remote from the border, has created a demand for unskilled labor."[32]

In 1917 a substantial number of Mexicans returned to Mexico. The reasons varied. On May 18, 1917, draft laws had been passed and Mexicans were reluctant to be drafted into a foreign army. The cost of living had increased in the United States. Conditions had improved in Mexico and by the end of June nearly 10,000 Mexicans had returned to Mexico voluntarily. Moreover, the Mexican government feared the effects of the exodus of so many productive workers and began a campaign to entice them back.

Meanwhile, the war caused a labor shortage and the U.S. government actively worked to reverse this trend and Secretary of State Robert Lansing enlisted Catholic bishops to assure Mexicans that they would not be drafted.[33] This was not an easy task since, although the Immigration Act of 1917 was aimed primarily at Eastern Europeans, Mexicans were included in its literacy provision and were made subject to a head tax. Previous acts had excluded "contract laborers" and "persons likely to become a public charge." However, the wording was so broad and vague that employers and contractors who made large profits from importing labor ignored the laws. After 1917 the $8 head tax was a major obstacle to poor Mexicans, who had no recourse but to remain in Mexico or enter the United States without documents. But, because a labor shortage threatened to cripple the war effort, industrialists and growers pressured the federal authorities to waive those sections of the immigration act that limited the free flow of Mexican labor. The commissioner of immigration affirmed that U.S. employers feared they might have to pay higher wages if Mexicans were excluded. Soon afterwards exemptions allowed illiterate contract workers from Mexico to enter the United States and the head tax was waived because of pressure from U.S. farmers who were in the "habit of relying to a considerable extent upon seasonal labor from Mexico."[34]

Even though the United States was at war, border control by

the military was conspicuously absent during this period. And while public policy encouraged Mexican labor to flow into the United States, local authorities and the public at large continued to discriminate against Mexicans. In 1917 the Los Angeles Police Department closely monitored the Fifth of May celebration after it heard rumors that radicals would be there. Three suspected members of the PLM were arrested and booked on the charge of attempting to incite a riot.[35] When war was declared on Germany, Los Angeles sheriffs spread hysteria by stating that Mexicans were preparing to join Germany in the conflict.

The Labor Department assured Congress that the exemptions and the open border were only "stop-gap" measures; they continued until the end of the 1921 fiscal year, when a surplus of labor developed in the United States. In the four years the exemptions were in force (1917 to 1921), 72,862 Mexicans entered the United States with documents, whereas hundreds of thousands crossed the border without documents.[36] The influx of undocumented workers continued as long as jobs in the United States were plentiful, and as long as the U.S. government looked the other way. By the 1920s Mexican migration was no longer limited to the Southwest, but began to spread into the Midwest.

THE RESTRICTIONIST MOVEMENT OF THE 1920s

Opposition to Mexican immigration crystallized in the 1920s. Reaction toward Mexicans intensified as their numbers became larger. In Mexico road and rail transportation was no longer disrupted by the intense fighting of the revolution. Moreover, prices in Mexico rose 300 percent faster than wages. In 1920, a labor shortage in Colorado, Wyoming, Utah, Iowa, and Nebraska resulted in the heavy importation of Mexicans into those states. Industrialists imported Mexicans to work in the mills of Chicago—first as an army of reserve labor and then as strikebreakers. During the 1919–1920 and 1920–1921 seasons the Arizona Growers Association spent $325,000 recruiting and transporting Mexicans to cotton areas.[37]

Suddenly in early 1921 the bottom fell out of the economy and a depression caused heavy unemployment. If in times of prosperity their numbers had generated hostility, in time of crisis Mexicans became the scapegoats for the failure of the U.S. economy. The corporate interests which had recruited Mexicans felt little responsibility to them and thousands of Mexicans throughout the country were left stranded and destitute. In Arizona, although transportation fees had been deducted from the pay of Mexican workers, growers did not give them return passage. *El Universal* of Mexico City on March 5, 1921, reported: "When they arrived at Phoenix a party of Mexican workers were taken to Tempe and introduced to a concentration camp that looks like a dung-heap." According to this source the men were chained and put into work parties.[38] The situation was repeated in Kansas City, Chicago, and Colorado. In Fort Worth, Texas, 90 percent of 12,000 Mexicans were unemployed; whites threatened to burn out Mexicans and rid the city of "cheap Mexican Labor." Truckloads of Mexicans were escorted to Texas chain gangs. In Ranger, Texas, terrorists dragged a hundred Mexican men, women, and children from their tents and make-shift homes, beat them, and ordered them to clear out of town.[39] In Chicago employment of Mexicans shrank by two-thirds between 1920–1921. Police raids became frequent and vagrancy laws were strictly enforced. Conditions grew so bad that Mayor William Hall Thompson allocated funds to ship several hundred families back to the border. The *Denver Post* headlined "Denver Safety Is Menaced by 3,500 Starving Mexicans."[40] Mexican workers from the Denver area were shipped to the border. Although these workers had been recruited to the United States, the U.S. government did little to ameliorate their sufferings. The Mexican government in contrast spent $2.5 million to aid stranded Mexicans.[41] Many workers would have starved if it had not been for Mexican President Alvaro Obregon.

Nativist* efforts to restrict the entry of southern and eastern Europeans bore fruit with the passage of the Immigration Act of 1921. Many wanted to include Mexicans in the provisions of the act, but Congress felt that the opposition of agribusiness to their inclusion might block passage of the bill. The 1921 act was generally considered too lenient. Nativists replaced it three years later with a permanent quota act that excluded most Asians and drastically cut the flow from southern and eastern Europe, identified as "racially inferior Europe." The act started a battle between the restrictionists, who wanted to keep the country "Anglo-American" and felt too many foreigners would subvert the "American way of life," and the capitalists, who set aside prejudices for low-cost labor, remembering that the 1917 act had hurt them financially. They opposed any restrictions on the free flow of Mexicans to the United States, especially since the supply of European labor was cut.

In 1923 the commissioner of immigration turned his attention more fully to Mexicans: "It is difficult, in fact impossible, to measure the illegal influx of Mexicans crossing the border."[42] During

---

*Nativism in the historical sense should not be confused with its anthropological use. Historically speaking it refers to anti-immigrant sentiments whereas in the anthropological sense it refers to a "revival of indigenous culture, especially in opposition to acculturation." Native American party in this text refers to an ultranationalist group of Anglo-Americans who considered themselves the true Americans, excluding even the Indian. Moreover, in this text we loosely use the word Anglo to refer to white Americans which include Italians, Jews, and Slavs. As in the case of any rule, it has its exceptions.

the previous two years, there had been an economic depression in the United States, but by 1923, the economy had sufficiently recovered to entice Mexican workers again.[43] The increase continued into 1924, as the statistics on legal migration show:

1920	52,361	1923	63,768
1921	30,758	1924	89,336
1922	19,551		

SOURCE: Lawrence Anthony Cardoso, "Mexican Emigration to the United States, 1900–1930: An Analysis of Socio-Economic Causes" (Ph.D. dissertation, University of Connecticut, 1974), p. 60.

This *"legal"* migration was accompanied by an avalanche of undocumented workers who were encouraged to avoid the head tax as well as visa charges by U.S. employers and government authorities. The new migration differed from that of earlier years, becoming more permanent. Permanency and large numbers of Mexicans alarmed nativists, who deplored the fact that the Johnson Bill, which later became the Immigration Act of 1924, did not limit Mexicans. Debate over the issue of Mexican immigration was heated in both houses of Congress. The decision to exclude Mexicans from the quota was a matter of political opportunism. Albert Johnson of Washington, chairman of the House Immigration and Naturalization Committee and sponsor of the bill, bluntly stated that the Committee did not restrict the Mexicans because it did not want to hinder the passage of the 1924 Immigration Act.[44] Johnson promised that the committee would sponsor another bill to create a border patrol to enforce existing laws, and he claimed that a quota alone would not be effective. Representative John E. Raker of California seconded Johnson, and he saw no need for further legislation to restrict Mexicans. Raker felt that enforcement of existing laws would cut their numbers to 1,000 annually, by ending the employers' practice of paying the head tax for them and by excluding illiterates (according to Raker, "from 75 to 90 percent of all Mexicans in Mexico are illiterate").[45]

Nativists were not convinced. Secretary of Labor James J. Davis called for a quota for the Western Hemisphere. He was alarmed that Mexican labor had infiltrated into U.S. industries such as iron and steel and arranged meetings with Samuel Gompers to plan a strategy to remove this "menace." Representative Martin Madden of Chicago, chairman of the House Appropriations Committee, stated, "The bill opens the doors for perhaps the worst element that comes into the United States—the Mexican *peon.* . . . [It] opens the door wide and unrestricted to the most undesirable people who come under the flag."[46] Representative John O. Box of Jacksonville, Texas, a former Cherokee county judge and ordained Methodist minister, seconded Madden and demanded a 2 percent quota for Mexicans based on the 1890 population as well as additional funds for its enforcement. Box supported an amendment to put only Mexico on a quota basis, exempting the rest of the nations in the Western Hemisphere.[47] The Johnson bill, however, passed the House without the proposed amendment.

In the U.S. Senate, Frank B. Willis of Ohio echoed restrictionist sentiment: "Many of [them] . . . now coming in are, unfortunately, practically without education, and largely without experience in self-government, and in most cases not at all qualified for present citizenship or for assimilation into this country."[48] Senator Matthew M. Neeley of West Virginia charged: "On the basis of merit, Mexico is the last country we should grant a special favor or extend a peculiar privilege. . . . The immigrants from many of the countries of Europe have more in common with us than the Mexicanos have."[49]

Antirestrictionists continued to argue that it would be difficult to enforce such a quota, that Mexicans stayed only temporarily anyway, that they did work white men would not, and that an economic burden would result. However, the argument of Pan-Americanism proved to be the most effective. Many senators wanted to use the Pan-American union as a vehicle for establishing the political and economic dominance of the United States over Latin America. Senator Holm Bursum of New Mexico summed up the feeling of most senators, stating that he did not favor disrupting Pan-Americanism, that Mexico was sparsely populated anyway, and "So far as absorbing the Mexican population. . . . that is the merest rot. . . ."[50] In the end the economic interests supporting the Mexicans' entry won out.

In 1924 hostility to Mexican immigration continued across the country and restrictionists lobbied for the exclusion of Mexicans throughout the 1920s and into the 1930s. Although border officials strictly applied the $8 head tax, plus the $10 visa fee, Mexicans still entered with and without documents. Johnson's committee, true to its promise, began hearings on the Mexican problem. Reports of the commissioner of immigration devoted more space to Mexicans. They stated that *peons* benefited from the reduction of European immigrants. In 1926 the commissioner wrote that 855,898 Mexicans entered with documents and predicted, "It is safe to say that over a million Mexicans are in the United States at the present time [including undocumented], and under present laws this number may be added to practically without limit."[51]

Discussion turned to the question of the Mexicans' race. The United States government listed incoming Mexicans as "white" in order to exempt them from race stipulations of the 1921 and 1924 quota acts. The public at large did not accept this classification. In Los Angeles a special census classified the Mexican as "red" and stated that 17 percent of Los Angeles school children belonged to the "red race" in 1927.[52] Similar attitudes were common throughout the Southwest and Midwest.

An open fight broke out in Congress in 1926. Restrictionists introduced two bills. The bill proposed by John Box simply sought to apply quota provisions to the whole Western Hemisphere; the other bill, sponsored by Robert L. Bacon of New York, sought to apply them only to Mexico. The Box bill emerged as the main bill before the House. Western representatives opposed any attempt to restrict Mexicans. S. Parker Frieselle of California stated:

> We, gentlemen, are just as anxious as you are not to build the civiliza-
> tion of California or any other western district upon a Mexican founda-
> tion. We take him because there is nothing else available to us.[53]

Representative John Nance Garner of Texas emphasized that Mexicans returned home after the picking seasons:

> All they want is a month's labor in the United States, and that is
> enough to support them in Mexico for six months. . . . In our country
> they do not cause any trouble, unless they stay there a long time and
> become Americanized; but they are a docile people. They can be
> imposed on; the sheriff can go out and make them do anything.[54]

Garner praised the contributions of Mexicans to his state. Both the restrictionists and the antirestrictionists displayed nativist and racist attitudes. The antirestrictionists wanted an open border because they wanted to exploit Mexicans for labor. Box candidly accused opponents of his bill of attempting to attract only the "floating Mexican *peons*" for the purpose of exploiting them, charging that "they are to be imported in trainloads and delivered to farmers who have contracted to grow beets for the sugar companies." Box stated, "They are objectionable as citizens and as residents."[55] During committee hearings, Box questioned a farmer as to whether what the farmer really wanted was a subservient class of Mexican workers "who do not want to own land, who can be directed by men in the upper stratum of society." The farmer answered, "I believe that is about it." Box then asked, "Now, do you believe that is good Americanism?" The farmer replied, "I think it is necessary Americanism to preserve Americanism."[56]

Restrictionists could not muster sufficient power to push either the Box or the Bacon bill through Congress. The power of agribusiness and other industrial giants employing Mexicans blocked them. The role of these combines in fighting restrictionists is similar to the one they played in the debates over restricting Europeans. They warded off public opinion, which in both cases was anti-immigrant, but in this case their opposition was weaker. The restrictionist movement against Mexicans centered in the Southwest, which at that time had relatively little influence on national politics, whereas the nativist opposition to European immigration centered in the powerful eastern seaboard. Southwestern nativists attempted to ally with eastern restrictionist groups, but Mexicans were not as visible a threat in the nation's most populated centers.

Without widespread national support southwestern restrictionists could not muster sufficient power to defeat agribusiness and the industrial giants.

In 1928 a congressional fight again loomed. The commissioner general of immigration recommended "that natives of countries of the Western Hemisphere be brought within the quota provisions of existing law." The commissioner specifically recommended restriction of Mexicans, stating, "The unlimited flow of immigrants from the Western Hemisphere cannot be reconciled with the sharp curtailment of immigration from Europe."[57] A definite split developed between the Department of Labor, which favored putting Mexicans on a quota system, and the Department of State, which opposed it. The State Department opposed placing Mexicans on the quota because it knew that such action would seriously weaken its negotiations with Latin America concerning economic trade treaties and privileges for Anglo-American interests. Anglo-American racism was a sensitive area. Placing Mexicans on a quota would be a legal affirmation of discrimination toward all Latin Americans. State Department officials were involved in sensitive negotiations with Mexican officials, who threatened to expropriate Anglo-American oil. The State Department, representing Anglo-American foreign investors and exporters, joined southwestern industrialists to kill restrictionist measures. They attempted to sidetrack debates, and for a time congressional debate centered around enforcement of existing immigration laws. Many congressmen were not satisfied and pushed for quantitative restrictions. Anglo-American labor supported the restrictionists, and questioned, "Do you want a mongrel population, consisting largely of Mexicans?"[58]

The *Saturday Evening Post* ran a series of articles by Kenneth L. Roberts advocating that Mexicans be restricted. The author flatly prophesied that Mexicans would become public charges if their immigration were allowed to continue.[59] J. S. Stowell wrote in the *Journal of Current History*, "While certain interests have pleaded for the United States to invade Mexico, that country has unostentatiously accomplished an invasion of the United States, which is bound to have its effect on our future."[60]

Growers and other industrialists joined forces with the Departments of State, Agriculture, and Interior and formed a solid front to overwhelm restrictionists, and immigration continued. Immigration statistics for the second part of the decade were:

1926	43,316
1927	67,721
1928	59,016
1929	40,154

SOURCE: Lawrence Anthony Cardoso, "Mexican Emigration to the United States, 1900–1930; An Analysis of Socio-Economic Causes" (Ph.D. dissertation, University of Connecticut, 1974), p. 60.

The decrease in immigration in 1929 was partially due to negotiations by the State Department in which Mexican officials agreed to limit the number of visas they would grant in return for an end to the agitation for restrictive legislation. The Department of Labor ignored this diplomatic coup. In 1929 the Commissioner General once more called for a quota. Congress made it a felony for an alien to enter the country illegally. The restrictionists would not compromise.

THE NATIVIST FEVER OF THE 1930s

The year 1929 began the Great Depression. Whereas the number of Mexicans entering the United States from 1925 to 1929 was 238,527, from 1930 to 1934 it fell to only 19,200. From 1935 to 1939 the number dropped even further to 8,737. The decline in Mexican immigration did not quiet restrictionists; they became more vocal. The House Committee on Immigration and Naturalization again held hearings in 1930. Debates were a replay of previous sessions. Agricultural and industrial interests again defended the Mexicans' "special standing" and again nativists opposed them. The Harris bill, one of the several bills introduced in 1930, advanced three new arguments for restriction: widespread unemployment, racial undesirability, and un-Americanism.[61]

The best example of overt racism can be found in a report prepared for John Box by Dr. Roy I. Garis of Vanderbilt University. Garis reported to the congressional committee as an authority on eugenics that "the following statement made to the author by an American who lives on the border seems to reflect the general sentiment of those who are deeply concerned with the future welfare of this country:

> 'Their [the Mexicans'] minds run to nothing higher than animal functions—eat, sleep, and sexual debauchery. In every huddle of Mexican shacks one meets the same idleness, hordes of hungry dogs, and filthy children with faces plastered with flies, disease, lice, human filth, stench, promiscuous fornication, bastardy, lounging, apathetic peons and lazy squaws, beans and dried chili, liquor, general squalor, and envy and hatred of the gringo. These people sleep by day and prowl by night like coyotes, stealing anything they can get their hands on, no matter how useless to them it may be. Nothing left outside is safe unless padlocked or chained down. Yet there are Americans clamoring for more of this human swine to be brought over from Mexico.' "[62]

Garis's American said that the only difference between Mexican women of the lower and higher classes was that high class Mexican women were just more "sneaky in adultery."[63]

The Immigration Restriction League of New York asserted that Mexicans could not be assimilated into Anglo-American institutions. It charged, "It is ridiculous for us to limit European immigration and continue to admit Mexican *peon* labor."[64] It stated that Mexicans were not naturalizing and becoming citizens like other immigrants.

In the Senate the Harris bill was placed on the calendar without scheduled hearings. If applied it would have reduced the number of Mexicans entering the country from 58,000 to 1,900.[65] It obviously discriminated against Mexicans, because it singled them out as the only group to be withdrawn from special status. Harris complained that Mexican immigration was especially offensive, since Mexico sent the largest number of undesirables to the United States. He cited unemployment among Anglo-Americans and made unsubstantiated statements to alarm listeners about the number of Mexicans entering the United States. For example, he claimed that "thousands and thousands" of Mexicans were "subject to charity" in the southwestern states, that a third of the children born in California were Mexicans, and that in a few years Mexicans would take over.[66] The Harris bill passed the Senate by voice vote of 51 to 16. On May 15 senators referred the bill to the House, where it was placed on the calendar.

Proponents of the bill maintained that Mexican migration had slowed only temporarily and that as soon as the economic situation bettered here or there was trouble in Mexico, Mexicans would return. Again, agricultural and industrial factions dwelt on the assertion that Mexican laborers were temporary residents:

> The Mexican "peon" is an intense nationalist, but he is an individual nationalist. He has no real conception of a unified national consciousness. Nevertheless, the love of his native land is so strong that practically no Mexican "peon" enters the United States without expecting to return.[67]

They also argued that, after all, the Mexican was preferable to the "Filipino or Puerto Rican."[68] By August of 1930 the House had still not taken action on the bill, but by that time the depression had cut the number of Mexicans entering the United States to a few hundred and the House saw no reason to pursue the issue.

If Mexican immigration had continued at the 1920 rate, restrictionist legislation probably would have passed, since even the champions of no quota would have grown nervous at having so many Mexicans living "next door." As it was, the Harris bill failed to pass the House, and for a time longer an immigration quota for Mexicans was averted.

THE DEPORTATION OF THE CHICANOS

As long as business interests needed Mexicans as laborers, they defended their coming and employment. But in 1929 prosperity suddenly became a thing of the past, and white Americans, desperate for work, took jobs that once they had scorned. They displaced many Chicano laborers, and it was no longer necessary for business to defend their presence. Many *Mexicanos* displaced from farms migrated to the cities hoping to find work or to obtain money through relief programs. Anglo-Americans, concerned about unemployment and the growing cost of welfare, adopted a "take care of our own" attitude. They resented using funds to aid the "brown men" in their midst who, after all, did not qualify to be "Americans"; they blamed foreigners for the unemployment and felt that they should return to their homeland. Local authorities decided that money could be saved by shipping Mexicans home, a plan that appealed to many Anglo-American taxpayers. Between the years 1931 and 1934 thousands of Chicanos, many of them U.S. citizens, were sent back to Mexico. Official U.S. records put the number at around 300,000, but the figure may well have reached a half million.[69] In all about one-third of those counted in the 1930 census were repatriated, about 60 percent of whom were children who had been born in the United States and thus were citizens. Meanwhile, the Mexican government viewed the return of Chicanos favorably.[70] Most Anglo-American officials attempted to emphasize the "voluntary" nature of repatriation in contrast to deportation, or forcible expulsion from the country. To Chicanos, however, the term *repatriation* became synonymous with deportation and most Chicano experts agree that the line differentiating the two is very thin.

President Herbert Hoover encouraged the "send-the-Mexican-back-to-Mexico" movement when after three years of depression he settled on the so-called foreigner as one of many excuses for failure of the U.S. economy. The foreign worker became a favorite scapegoat, especially the "illegal" aliens, which to most meant Mexicans. All the ingredients were operative for a major outbreak of nativism: crisis, fear, racial antipathy, and a group highly visible because of its large numbers on which to blame the breakdown of the system.

U.S. consuls restricted the number of visas issued and strictly enforced the terms of the Immigration Act of 1924 which excluded those "likely to become a public charge." Secretary of Labor William N. Doak stated, "My conviction is that by strict limitation and a wise selection of immigration, we can make America stronger in every way, hastening the day when our population shall be more homogeneous."[71]

On January 6, 1931, Doak requested that Congress appropriate funds for the deportation of illegals from the United States. He alleged that an investigation revealed that 400,000 aliens had evaded immigration laws and that at least a fourth of these illegals were readily deportable. "Doak's immigration agents raided both public and private places seeking aliens who were deportable, and they did so in a search which extended from New York to Los

Angeles."[72] The California senate considered a bill to prohibit "illegal aliens from engaging in business or seeking employment, and making it a misdemeanor to have such an alien as a partner."[73] Antiforeign sentiment reached its zenith during this period of insecurity.

Local authorities throughout the Southwest and the Midwest emulated the actions of the chief executive; they went one step further and devised a program to encourage even documented immigrants to return to Mexico. They seized on Doak's statements, newspapers drummed the "take care of our own" theme, and they manufactured an enemy. Los Angeles papers ran articles with titles such as "U.S. and City Join in Drive on L.A. Aliens." They played up alleged Mexican crime, sensationalizing themes of shootings, fights, and rapes. They also applied the label "alien" to all Mexicans.[74]

On January 6, 1931, C. P. Visel, the Los Angeles local coordinator for unemployment relief, urgently requested guidance in a wire to Washington, D.C.:

> We note press notices this morning, figure four hundred thousand deportable aliens United States. Stop. Estimate five percent in this district. Stop. We can pick them all up through police and sheriff channels. Stop. United States Department of Emigration incapacitated to handle. Stop. You advise please as to method of getting rid. Stop. We need their jobs for needy citizens.[75]

Visel circulated leaflets in the Chicano community stating that deportations would include all Mexicans, legal or illegal. He admitted that he wanted to intimidate illegals and force them to abandon the Los Angeles areas. Concerned over loss of Mexican labor, the Los Angeles Chamber of Commerce criticized his actions and warned him that the Mexican community would misunderstand the "wholesale raids"; Visel did not moderate his attacks and issued press releases advertising arrests of Mexicans. Visel advertised that "20,000 deportable aliens were in the Los Angeles area." So blatant were the raids that the normally apathetic Chicano businessmen protested the treatment of nationals to authorities both in Washington, D.C., and Mexico City.[76] The protests did not dissuade immigration authorities. On the 26th of February at 3 P.M., aided by a dozen police, they surrounded the Los Angeles plaza, detained over four hundred people for over an hour, and arrested eleven Mexicans and five Chinese. They released nine of the Mexicans the next day. In the next months authorities rounded up 3,000 to 4,000 Mexicans and held them without benefit of counsel. The effect of the raids on the Mexican community were traumatic and they often resulted in the separation of entire families. In this hostile environment authorities asked Mexicans if they wanted to return to Mexico. "Faced with poverty, discrimination, and uncertainty as to their

status, many Mexican families seriously considered the idea of repatriation."[77]

City officials, along with national and state officials, planned its
strategy. The Mexican government approved and cooperated with
the repatriation and guaranteed transportation from the border to
the repatriate's colony. Mexican authorities encouraged Mexican
governors and labor unions to welcome repatriates, and the government promised land and other benefits. Mexican officials cooperated with the program not because they approved of the motives of
the U.S. officials, but because Mexico had lost an estimated one-
eighth of its population to the United States.[78] Mexican revolutionaries, such as the artist Diego Rivera, urged Mexicans to return
home. In Detroit Rivera helped found the League of Workers and
Peasants of Mexico. The Mexican government, however, did not
have the resources to provide for mass repatriation or to absorb
such large numbers of workers and their families. Economically,
Mexico still suffered from the chaos of the Revolution of 1910, and
it had difficulty providing for citizens in Mexico, let alone for those
who lived in the United States. As a consequence, the repatriates
became disillusioned with the program.

Local officials continued to devise programs to encourage Mexicans to return home. In California charity organizations and the
California Department of Unemployment cooperated. When a Chicano approached these agencies for assistance, a case worker called
on the family and attempted to persuade them they would be hap-
pier in Mexico. If a Chicano agreed to return, fare and subsistence
to the border were paid for the entire family. In many instances
local authorities used the Mexican consul to help "persuade" the
welfare recipient to return.

Generally, fathers wanted to leave, since they had never intended to stay permanently, but the children had roots here, were
U.S. citizens, and desired to remain. Some teen-age children bitterly resented being uprooted. The mother was caught between her
husband and her children. When the client hesitated, the welfare or
case worker became more persuasive.[79]

Just how persuasive officials were is open to conjecture, since
local authorities always maintained that returns were voluntary.
However, two leading authorities on the Chicano in the 1930s contradict local authorities' interpretation of "voluntary." Professor
Norman D. Humphreys of Detroit wrote:

> Even the families of naturalized citizens were urged to repatriate, and
> the rights of American-born children to citizenship in their native land
> were explicitly denied or not taken into account. The case workers
> themselves brought pressures to bear in the form of threats of deporta-
> tion, stoppage of relief (wholly or in part, e.g., in matters of rent, or by
> means of trampling on customary procedures).[80]

Repatriation was severe in the Midwest where thousands of Mexicans had been recruited to work in the railroads, packinghouses, and steel mills. A disproportionate number of Mexicans were deported from Illinois, Michigan, Indiana, and Ohio. The number of Mexicans had increased in the Gary-Chicago area to over 20,000 by 1930. Newspapers there began a campaign to discredit the Mexicans and by the mid-1930s job discrimination and exclusion from federal projects convinced many Mexicans to return to *la tierra del sol* (the land of the sun).[81]

Michigan officials admitted that some Mexicans left involuntarily with some even jumping the train to evade "repatriation." A medical doctor was put on the train because some of the repatriates had been removed from the hospitals to be shipped south. Tales of hardships are told of programs in Detroit, Grand Rapids, Fort Huron, Saginaw, Flint, Blissfield, and Mt. Pleasant.[82]

Lorraine Esterly Pierce states that in St. Paul, Minnesota, over 300 out of a population of some 1,500 were deported. In Chicago the 1930 census had reported 20,000 Mexicans, but the number declined to 16,000 by 1940.[83]

Social workers used subtle measures to persuade the prospective repatriates. In Detroit they placed Mexican families on a "cafeteria list," forcing them to eat at a local mess hall. There they were fed unfamiliar foods such as sauerkraut instead of traditional beans. Case workers continually harped that Mexicans would be much healthier in Mexico. In some cases officials made overt threats that rent would not be paid or that welfare payments would be cut. Deceit surrounded the whole affair. Authorities in most cases promised that those who chose to leave could return to the United States when they wanted; however, exit cards were stamped charity cases, which automatically excluded them from reentry. "The average Mexican family repatriated had four children, all or most of whom were American citizens by birthright."[84] Most experts agree that the authorities violated the Mexicans' rights.

The repatriation program was basically a "money-saving device." Enthusiasm for the program lessened as local authorities learned that funds from the Reconstruction Finance Corporation (RFC) could no longer be used for the transportation of repatriates. For example, in the first three years of the Los Angeles program, 1931 to 1934, the county shipped 12,668 Chicanos back to Mexico at a cost of $181,228, whereas from 1935 to 1938 it shipped only 3,560 at a cost of $160,781.[85]

Officials kept accounts to be sure their programs continued to yield a savings. Carey McWilliams underscored the dollars-and-cents approach: "It cost the County of Los Angeles $77,249.29 to repatriate one train load, but the savings in relief amounted to $347,468.41"—a net savings of $270,219.12.[86] In the last analysis

President Coolidge's maxim—"the business of America is business"—was applicable, and repatriation proved profitable, at least in dollars and cents.

HUMAN RIGHTS FOR WHOM?

Besides forced repatriations, mass roundups, and newspaper hysteria, Mexicans became victims of government and public violence. Labor became the primary targets of vicious assaults and red-baiting (to be discussed in the following chapter) and denial of civil liberties to individual members of the oppressed class was also common.

The case of Jesús Pallares is typical.[87] Pallares was deported on June 29, 1936, as an undesirable alien. He had emigrated from Mexico as a teenager and was 39 years old at the time of deportation. He had fought in the revolutionary ranks and was a skilled miner and a talented musician. In the United States Jesús had been a dedicated union man. In 1923 he opposed the anarchist faction at Dawson, New Mexico. In 1930 at the Gallup-American Coal Company, a subsidiary of the Guggenheim interests, he was fired for complaining about working conditions.

Jesús, his wife, and their three children moved to Madrid, New Mexico, a company town. The company paid workers in scrip that could be used only at its store. It owned all the houses and charged workers $3 a month for coal, for which they had to pay whether they needed it or not. Workers had to contribute to an employee's fund that the company managed, yet they were not given an accounting of funds. In the summer of 1933 the company made wholesale layoffs. Pressure mounted for management to comply with provisions of the National Industrial Relations Act (NIRA), which specified in section 7(a) that employees had the right to unionize. The company circumvented the requirement and established its own company union. Jesús joined the union, but when he realized that it did not represent the workers, he resigned.

Dissident workers established their own union and smuggled an organizer into town. Elected local union representative, Jesús attempted to open negotiations. He failed, so the union appealed to the federal government for hearings conducted under the NIRA code. The hearings were a farce; the chairman of the hearings was promanagement. Paid cronies of the company attended and interrupted the workers' testimony. Hearings did not advance the cause of workers, and the union had no alternative but to strike—a maneuver that failed.

The NIRA code specified that a man could not be fired for union activities. Nevertheless, the company harassed Jesús until he left. They transferred him to a mine that had been exhausted. An experienced miner, he knew that he could not earn a living wage there, since he was paid for piecework. Company officials red-baited Jesús, calling him a communist agitator. When he could not pay his rent, the company evicted him, even though his wife was expecting a baby at any time. Jesús tried to enter his home and was charged with "forcible entry." He then appealed to federal officials, but they ignored him. Blacklisted and unable to find employment as a miner, Jesús and his family moved to Santa Fe where, for the first time, he went on relief.

In 1934 Jesús became an organizer for *La Liga Obrera de Habla Española,* which concerned itself with the problems of the poor Chicanos. Membership was small at first, but by February 1935 it had grown to 8,000. To deal with organizations like *La Liga,* the Democratic state legislature made syndicalism a felony, punishable by fourteen years' imprisonment. The law specified that it was illegal to be seen with an issue of *The Nation* magazine or any other printed material that advocated "any change in industrial ownership." *La Liga* assembled 700 pickets and entered the senate galleries protesting the law. Members of the senate changed their votes, infuriating big business interests.

Jesús was the best recognized leader and local authorities pressured immigration officers to deport him. On April 23, 1935, he was jailed. After three weeks N. D. Collear, a federal immigration inspector, who served as initiator, investigator, prosecutor, judge, jury, and even interpreter, conducted a secret hearing. Governor Clyde Tingley asked Secretary of Labor Frances Perkins to expedite Jesús's deportation on the grounds that *La Liga* was a communist organization. After the hearings Jesús was released on $1,000 bond. Esther Cohen, of the Emergency Relief Appropriation Program in New Mexico, stated that there were repeated attempts to intimidate Jesús; officials threatened to take his relief away and "starve his family." The outcome of the hearing was predictable. Although the administration of President Franklin D. Roosevelt was considered progressive, big business, especially mining, still ruled the state of New Mexico and had considerable influence on the U.S. government. Jesús Pallares was deported.[88]

The Bureau of Immigration was involved in numerous labor conflicts during the 1930s, constantly arresting and deporting strike leaders, and acted in concert with "patriotic groups" such as the American Legion to root out un-Americans. The nation's press continued their antialien policy (particularly the *Chicago Tribune,* the Hearst chain, and the *Saturday Evening Post*).[89] Not until the war effort of the 1940s bettered economic conditions and created a shortage of labor did public policy toward *Mexicanos* change.

THE PHARAOHS RENT THEIR BRACEROS

World War II created a labor shortage in the United States. Many Chicanos volunteered for the armed forces and the government drafted them in large numbers. Chicano farm workers joined many other migrants to the cities where they obtained jobs that had previously been closed to them and where employers paid them much higher wages.[90] The farm labor shortage became more acute when federal authorities placed Japanese-Americans in concentration camps. Japanese included small farmers as well as farm workers. With the United States requiring food not only for domestic consumption, but for its allies as well, maximum farm production was vital to the war effort. Once more, U.S. growers turned to Mexico. They had two alternatives: simply open the border and allow Mexican workers to come into the United States unencumbered or enter into an agreement with Mexico for an agreed upon number of Mexican *braceros* (helping arms). Growers preferred the first alternative, since they could hire the unencumbered Mexicans at the lowest possible wage. The Mexican government, however, would not permit this and insisted on a contract that protected the rights of its workers.[91]

Mexico was not enthusiastic about sending large numbers of workers to the United States, but U.S. authorities pressured it to consent. The two governments entered into a preliminary agreement in 1942, called the Emergency Labor Program, under which both would supervise the recruitment of *braceros*.[92]

They agreed to a contract guaranteeing the workers' rights. The contract provided, among other things, that Mexican workers would not displace domestic workers, they would be exempted from military service, and discrimination would not be tolerated. It also regulated transportation, housing, and wages of the *braceros*. Under this agreement about 220,000 *braceros* were imported into the United States from 1942 to 1947. The first were admitted into El Paso, Texas, on September 27, 1942.[93]

At first many farmers opposed the *bracero* agreement, preferring the World War I arrangement when they recruited directly in Mexico with no government interference. They resented any form of government regulation. Texas growers in particular wanted the government to open the border. Only a handful of U.S. growers participated during the first year. States like Texas had always had all the "illegals" they needed, and wanted to continue to control their "free market." They did not want the federal government to regulate the Mexicans' wages and housing. Growers especially disliked the 30¢ an hour minimum wage, charging that this was the first step in federal farm-labor legislation. Texas growers, thus boycotted the program in 1942 and moved to circumvent the agreement.[94]

The executive branch of the U.S. government did not receive congressional approval for the *bracero* program until 1943, when Congress passed Public Law 45. This act put the government in the role of labor contractor and began the "administered migration" of Mexicans into the United States.[95] The initial contract placed administration of the program under the Farm Security Administration. "The growers' primary concern was crops; the FSA was concerned about those who worked the crops."[96] One year later, because of grower pressure, the *bracero* program was transferred to the War Food Administration.[97]

As a result of lobbying by the powerful American Farm Bureau Federation, an escape clause had been written into the act. Under this clause, found in section 5(g), the commissioner of immigration was empowered to lift the statutory limitations of the act on the condition that such an action was vital to the war effort. Almost immediately farmers pressured the commissioner to use the escape clause; he acceded, and the border was unilaterally left open and unregulated (an amazing action considering that the United States was at total war).

Mexicans flooded into border areas where farmers employed them without worrying about federal regulations. The United States had breached its agreement, and the Mexican government objected. In Washington some officials bluntly advocated disregarding Mexico's complaints. In the face of pressure, Mexican authorities agreed to allow workers who had entered outside the contract agreement to remain for one year, but made it clear that they would not tolerate uncontrolled migration in the future and that if farmers wanted a steady supply of labor, they would have to adhere to the bilateral agreement.

In the summer of 1943 Texas growers finally asked for *braceros,* but the Mexican government refused to issue permits for Texas-bound temporary workers. They considered intolerable the Anglo-Texans' extreme racism and brutal transgressions against Mexican workers. Governor Coke Stevensen in an attempt to placate the Mexican government induced the Texas legislature to pass the so-called Caucasian Race Resolution, which affirmed the rights of all Caucasians to equal treatment within Texas. Since most Texans did not consider Mexicans Caucasians, the law had no relevance. Governor Stevenson attempted to ameliorate tensions by publicly condemning racism. The Mexican government seemed on the verge of relenting when further racist incidents were reported from Texas. On September 4, 1943, Stevenson established the Good Neighbor Commission of Texas, financed by federal funds, supposedly to end discrimination toward Chicanos through better understanding. The Mexican government did not change its position forcing Texas growers to finish the season without Mexican labor.[98]

Not all *braceros* worked on farms; by August 1945, 67,704 *braceros* were working on U.S. railroads. The work was in general physically oppressive and often hazardous. There are several recorded cases of death resulting from accidents on the railroads, sunstroke, heat prostration, and the like. Abuses of the contract agreement were frequent. Many *braceros* were not paid and many had to make involuntary payments from their wages to employers, as in the case of workers for the New York Central who had to pay $1.50 per day for food whether they ate or not.[99] *Braceros* had other complaints such as unsafe transportation, unsanitary toilets, substandard living quarters, and lack of heat in winter months. Some growers worked the *braceros* for 12 hours while paying them only for 8. *Braceros* did not take it lying down. For example, in December 1943 they struck the Southern Pacific at Live Oaks, California, over the dismissals of Anastacio B. Cortes and Manuel M. Rivas.[100]

From 1943 to 1947 the Mexican government refused Texas's requests since there was no evidence of any decline in its racist actions. Nevertheless, Texas growers continued to press for *braceros*. In October 1947 the Mexican government finally agreed to issue permits to Texas.

Although labor shortages ceased after the war, the *bracero* program continued. The U.S. government functioned as a labor contractor at taxpayers' expense, assuring nativists that workers would return to Mexico after they finished picking the crops. Growers did not have to worry about labor disputes. The *braceros* were used to glut the labor market to depress wages and were also used as strikebreakers. The U.S. government fully cooperated with growers, allocating insufficient funds to the border patrol, insuring a constant supply of undocumented laborers.

When negotiations to renew the contract began, Mexico did not have the leverage it had during the war. It had become dependent on the money brought back by the workers. The United States, now in a stronger negotiating position because it was no longer limited by the critical wartime labor shortage, could pressure Mexico to continue the program on U.S. terms. The 1947 agreement allowed U.S. growers to recruit their own workers and did not require direct U.S. government involvement. The Mexican government had wanted recruitment in the interior and more guarantees for its citizens, but it got few of its demands.[101] Growers were permitted to hire undocumented workers and certify them on the spot. This procedure along with recruitment at the border produced a magnetlike effect.

In October 1948 Mexican officials finally took a hard line, refusing to sign *bracero* contracts if workers were not paid $3.00 per hundred pounds for picked cotton rather than the $2.00 offered by Anglo-Americans. The Mexican government was also still concerned about racism in Texas and still wanted recruitment from the interior rather than at the border as was then the case. Border recruitment created hardships on border towns with workers frequently traveling thousands of miles only to be left there unselected. (Border towns have grown over 1000 percent since 1920 and unemployment remains extremely high; they serve as employment centers for Anglo-American industry.) The surge of workers to the area gave an advantage to the United States, for Mexico might be forced into signing *bracero* contracts to relieve the problems it created.

As the 1948 harvest approached, Anglo-American growers grew concerned and in response to their pressure Grover C. Willmoth, district director of the Immigration and Naturalization Service (INS) at El Paso, Texas, instructed his inspectors to open the border.[102] When U.S. officials removed the physical barriers, the thousands of desperate Mexican workers at Juárez naturally crossed over to U.S. territory. Immediately the INS placed them under technical arrest (for illegal entry) and then paroled them to the U.S. Employment Service, which distributed them to employers and labor agents. Willmoth defended his actions by alleging that Mexican officials had broken the *bracero* agreement and were blackmailing the United States by demanding a wage guarantee of $3.00 a hundred before the workers would be allowed to cross. Another U.S. official complained that "These Mexicans were pointing a pistol at the American farmer's head. It was an outright breach of the labor agreement."[103] Willmoth felt he summed up the situation when he said, "they need the work, our farmers need them and the crops were going to waste."[104]

The act of opening the border effectively destroyed Mexico's negotiating position. It could only accept official "regrets" and continue negotiations.[105] A new agreement was reached which reaffirmed the growers' right to recruit *braceros* directly on either side of the border. The agreement failed to provide any substantial protection for the workers. Between 1947 and 1949 alone 142,000 undocumented workers were certified, whereas only 74,600 *braceros* were hired by contract from Mexico.

The Truman administration supported the farmers. On a whistle-stop tour in October 1948, Truman was told by El Paso farm agents, sugar company officials, and immigration agents of their problem with Mexico. Shortly after he left, Mexican workers were allowed to pour across the bridge into the United States with or without Mexico's approval. Farmers waited with trucks and the Great Western Sugar Company representative had a special train waiting. "Though there were some exceptions, the 'wetbacks'*

---

*"Wetback" is a pejorative name applied to undocumented workers, referring to the act of swimming across the Rio Grande to avoid the border patrol.

were employed mainly by small growers. It was from these United States farmers that President Truman received support in his upset election in 1948."[106]

Under the Republican administration of the 1950s farmers had increasingly more to say about the administration of programs, while the Mexican government had fewer choices. In 1951 Public Law 78 renewed the *bracero* agreement putting the federal government back into the employment business. PL 78 went a long way in institutionalizing the *bracero* program.[107]

In 1953 negotiations began anew for a renewal of the *bracero* program. An impasse resulted when U.S. negotiators refused to make any concession to Mexico's demands for better wages. To force Mexico's hand the departments of State, Justice, and Labor agreed to open the border until the wage issue was resolved. They issued a press release on January 15, 1954, that as of the 18th the U.S. would act unilaterally.[108]

According to another source, "From January 23 to February 5, a series of bloody clashes and riots between Mexican guards and aspiring *braceros* erupted at several cities along the border."[109] Short of shooting its own citizens, Mexico could not prevent the workers from crossing the line. Mexico, had no other choice but to sign a contract favorable to the United States.

An administration spokesman displayed the arrogance of power: "They [the Mexican Government] want to set the wages. We [the U.S.] are going to set them. We'll give them the right of appeal if they think they are too low."[110] This arrogance was underscored when Congress passed legislation authorizing unilateral recruitment at the border.

Actions of Anglo-American authorities were a flagrant violation of international law which caused bitter resentment in Latin America at the United States' use of the "big stick" and Mexico's obvious humiliation.[111] Opening the border ended the labor shortage, and thereby served notice to Mexico that it had better negotiate because the United States had the power to get all the workers from Mexico it wanted—agreement or no agreement. It was evident that the United States would act unilaterally and that it completely controlled the *bracero* program. In fact many congressmen suggested that they abandon the *bracero* program and just open the border.[112] Growers protected the *bracero* program because of its stability. At government expense they could have all the workers they wanted without having to worry about collective bargaining. In California *braceros* were used for "tomatoes, lettuce, strawberries, sugar beets, lemons, melons, asparagus, miscellaneous vegetables, grapes, and cotton in that order."[113] In other crops domestic labor supplemented *braceros*. Increased dependence of Anglo-American growers on the *bracero* is reflected in the figures on *braceros* entering the United States under contract:

1942	4,203	1950	67,500	1958	432,857
1943	52,098	1951	192,000	1959	437,643
1944	62,170	1952	197,100	1960	315,846
1945	49,454	1953	201,388	1961	291,429
1946	32,043	1954	309,033	1962	194,978
1947	19,632	1955	398,650	1963	186,865
1948	35,345	1956	445,197	1964	177,736
1949	107,000	1957	436,049		

SOURCE: Leo Grebler et al., *Mexican-Mexican People: Nation's Second Largest Minority* (New York: Free Press, 1970), p. 68.

The decline in the 1960s marks a convergence of several factors working against the program: resentment of the Mexican government, grievances of the *braceros,* increased opposition by domestic labor, and, probably most important, changes in agricultural labor-saving techniques and the U.S. economy.

The *bracero* program "proved nationalistically humiliating" to Mexico; "The [Mexican government] did not have the power to end racial and religious discrimination; Mexicans performed the most menial work; and even many of Mexico's skilled workers bribed officials for the 'privilege' of becoming a temporary migrant."[114]

Through the work of Dr. Ernesto Galarza, both Mexican authorities and U.S. politicians became aware that the status of the *bracero* resembled that of a prisoner of war, herded to and from work. Workers had many grievances; they especially resented paying $1.75 (in 1955) for meals consisting of mainly beans and tortillas when they earned $3.00 for a 10-hour day. Growers recovered a good part of their wage outlay through the company store and in some camps by acting as pimps. According to a physician, the *bracero,* after he was used, was just dumped across the border to fend for himself.[115]

The 1950s saw a tremendous change in agriculture. From 1949 to 1965 the total U.S. population increased some 45 million, while the farm population dropped almost 12 million; in 1949 the farm population was 16.3 percent of the total, but in 1963 it dropped to 6.4 percent. The number of farms declined from 9,640,000 to 5,610,000. During the same period the number of migrants rose from 422,000 to 466,000.[116] This increase, however, did not occur in areas of agriculture heavily dependent on *braceros.* Mechanization of large farm operations in crops in which *braceros* were used actually lessened demand:

> In 1950, approximately 8 percent of United States cotton was machine harvested. By 1964, the final year of the bracero contracting, the figure had risen to 78 percent. In Arizona and California, two principal bracero-using states, 97 percent of the 1964 cotton crop was machine harvested.[117]

The principal justification for the *bracero* program was that farmers could not find sufficient domestic labor and that without the *braceros* their crops would rot. However, the *bracero* users gradually were deprived "of one of their principal arguments in behalf of *bracero* importation."[118] The unemployment caused by the 1958 recession intensified domestic labor's opposition to the *bracero* program.[119] Moreover, the executive branch and Congress moved towards a prolabor position. Politicians slowly extended many of the guarantees that the *braceros* enjoyed to domestic farm workers and began to monitor programs making sure that prevailing wages, housing, and working conditions were adhered to. All these factors contributed to the demise of the *bracero* program on December 31, 1964.[120]

NOTES

1. Max Sylvius Handman, "The Economic Reasons for Mexican Immigration," *American Journal of Sociology* 35 (January 1930): 601–611.
2. Enríque Semo, *Historia del Capitalismo en México: Los Origenes, 1521–1763,* 5th ed. (México, D.F.: Ediciones ERA, 1976), p. 28; Michael C. Meyer and William L. Sherman, *The Course of Mexican History* (New York: Oxford University Press, 1979), pp. 87–89. In 1521 Mexico's population approached 30 million, making it larger than that of any European nation.
3. Ignacio Bernal, "The Cultural Roots of the Border: An Archaeologist's View," in Stanley R. Ross, ed., *Views Across the Border* (Albuquerque: University of New Mexico Press, 1978), pp. 26–27.
4. Semo, pp. 15, 30.
5. Semo, p. 146.
6. Lawrence Anthony Cardoso, "Mexican Emigration to the United States, 1900–1930: An Analysis of Socio-Economic Causes" (Ph.D. dissertation, University of Connecticut, 1974), p. 23.
7. James D. Cockcroft, *Intellectual Precursors of the Mexican Revolution, 1900–1913* (Austin: University of Texas Press, 1968), p. 14.
8. Charles C. Cumberland, *Mexico: The Struggle for Modernity* (New York: Oxford University Press, 1968), p. 216.
9. Cardoso, pp. 34–35.
10. Cockcroft, pp. 32, 46.
11. Cockcroft, p. 46.
12. Victor Alba, *The Mexicans* (New York: Praeger, 1967), p. 106.
13. Alba, p. 106.
14. Cardoso, pp. 57, 54; Alba, p. 106.
15. Oscar J. Martínez, *Border Boom Town: Ciudad Juárez Since 1848* (Austin: University of Texas Press, 1978), p. 158. Also see Julian Samora, *Los Mojados* (Notre Dame, Ind.: University of Notre Dame Press, 1971), p. 10.
16. Cumberland, p. 228.
17. Peter Baird and Ed McCaughan, "Labor and Imperialism in Mexico's Electrical Industry," *NACLA Report on the Americas* 6, no. 6 (September-October 1977):5.
18. Tomás Almaguer, "Historical Notes on Chicano Oppression: The Dialectics of Racial and Class Domination in North America," *Aztlán* (Spring & Fall, 1974): 40.
19. Cardoso, pp. 18, 57; Ed McCaughan and Peter Baird, "Harvest of Anger: Agro-Imperialism in Mexico's Northwest," *NACLA Latin America and Empire Report* 10, no. 6 (July-August 1976): 5.
20. Cardoso, p. 59.
21. Jorge A. Bustamante, "Mexican Immigration and the Social Relations of Capitalism" (Ph.D. dissertation, University of Notre Dame, 1975), p. 50; Cardoso, p. 60.
22. Victor S. Clark, *Mexican Labor in the United States,* U.S. Department of Com-

merce Bulletin No. 78 (Washington, D.C.: U.S. Government Printing Office, 1908).

23. Gilbert Cardenas, "Public Data on Mexican Immigration into the United States: A Critical Evaluation," in W. Boyd Littrell and Gideon Sjoberg, eds., *Current Issues in Social Policy Research* (New York: Russell Sage, 1976), p. 2, states that data for 1820–1874 was collected by the Department of State from incoming ships; 1867–1895 statistics were gathered by Bureau of Statistics of the Treasury Department; 1899–1933 data by the Immigration Service of the Department of Labor; 1933–1941 figures by the Bureau of Immigration, and data for 1942 to the present by the Immigration and Naturalization Service of the Department of Justice. Also see Larry García y Griego, "*Los Primeros Pasos al Norte: Mexican Migration* to the United States" (Bachelor's thesis, Princeton University, 1973).

24. Clark, p. 471.

25. Clark, p. 496. Other recent works of interest have been compiled by Antonio José Ríos-Bustamante, ed., *Immigration and Public Policy: Human Rights for Undocumented Workers and Their Families* (Los Angeles: Chicano Studies Center Publications, University of California, 1977). Gilbert Cardenas of the University of Texas at Austin has also done solid research in the area of migration. His works include: "A Theoretical approach to the Sociology of Mexican Labor Migration" (Ph.D. dissertation, University of Notre Dame, 1977); "Public Data on Mexican Immigration into the United States: A Critical Evaluation," in Littrell and Sjoberg, *Current Issues in Social Policy Research*, which deals with the limitations and abuses of data research by the INS; and "United States Immigration Policy Toward Mexico: A Historical Perspective," *Chicano Law Review* 2 (Summer 1975). Also see Gilbert Cardenas and Estebán Flores, "Political Economy of International Migration," prepared for the Joint Annual Meeting of the Latin American Studies Association and African Studies Association, Houston, Texas, November 1977.

26. U.S. Congress, *Report of the Immigration Commission*, 61st Cong., 3rd sess. (1910–1911), I:682–691, quoted in Job West Neal, "The Policy of the United States Toward Immigration from Mexico" (Master's thesis, University of Texas at Austin, 1941), pp. 58–59.

27. Paul Shuster Taylor, "Some Aspects of Mexican Immigration," *Journal of Political Economy* 38 (October 1930): 610.

28. U.S. Department of Labor, "Report of the Commissioner General of Immigration," *Report of the Department of Labor* (Washington, D.C.: U.S. Government Printing Office, 1913), p. 337.

29. Ricardo Romo, "Mexican Workers in the City: Los Angeles, 1915–1930" (Ph.D. dissertation, University of California at Los Angeles, 1975), p. 109.

30. Romo, p. 116.

31. Romo, pp. 122, 117–118.

32. U.S. Department of Labor, "Report of the Commissioner General of Immigration," *Report of the Department of Labor* (Washington, D.C., U.S. Government Printing Office, 1916), p. 397.

33. Cardoso, pp. 83–87.

34. Quoted in Neal, p. 81.

35. Romo, p. 119.

36. Neal, p. 100. Mark Reisler, *By the Sweat of Their Brows: Mexican Immigration in the United States, 1900–1940* (Westport, Conn.: Greenwood Press, 1976), p. 38, states that 34,922 Mexicans had returned to Mexico, 15,632 were still employed in 1921, 414 had died, and 21,400 had deserted and found other employment.

37. Cardoso, p. 97; Paul Morgan and Vince Mayer, "The Spanish Speaking Population of Utah: From 1900–to 1935" (Working Papers Toward a History of the Spanish-Speaking People of Utah, American West Center, Mexican-American Documentation Project, University of Utah, 1973), p. 39; Reisler, p. 39.

38. Quoted in Herbert B. Peterson, "Twentieth-Century Search for Cibola: Post-World War I Mexican Labor Exploitation in Arizona," in Manuel P. Servín, ed., *An Awakening Minority: The Mexican-American*, 2nd ed. (Beverly Hills, Calif.: Glencoe Press, 1974), pp. 127–128.

39. Reisler, pp. 50–51, 53.

40. Mark Reisler, "Passing Through Our Egypt: Mexican Labor in the United States, 1900–1940 (Ph.D. dissertation, Cornell University, 1973), pp. 84–85; Reisler, *By the Sweat of Their Brows*, p. 53.
41. Morgan and Meyer, p. 8.
42. U.S. Department of Labor, *Annual Report of the Commissioner General of Immigration* (Washington, D.C.: U.S. Government Printing Office, 1923), p. 16.
43. Reisler, *By the Sweat of Their Brows*, p. 55.
44. Quoted in Neal, p. 106.
45. Neal, pp. 107–108.
46. Reisler, *By the Sweat of Their Brows*, pp. 66–69; quoted in Neal, p. 108.
47. Reisler, *By the Sweat of Their Brows*, p. 66.
48. Quoted in Neal, p. 112.
49. Quoted in Neal, p. 113.
50. Quoted in Neal, p. 117.
51. U.S. Department of Labor, *Annual Report of the Commissioner General of Immigration* (Washington, D.C.: U.S. Government Printing Office, 1926), p. 10.
52. Robin Fitzgerald Scott, "The Mexican-American in the Los Angeles Area, 1920–1950: From Acquiescence to Activity" (Ph.D. dissertation, University of Southern California, 1971), p. 84.
53. U.S. Congress, House, Committee on Immigration and Naturalization, *Seasonal Agricultural Laborers from Mexico: Hearing No. 69.1.7 on H.R. 6741, H.R. 7559, H.R. 9036*, 69th Cong., 1st sess. (1926), p. 24.
54. U.S. Congress, *Seasonal Agricultural Laborers*, p. 190.
55. U.S. Congress, *Seasonal Agricultural Laborers*, p. 325.
56. U.S. Congress, *Seasonal Agricultural Laborers*, p. 112.
57. U.S. Department of Labor, *Annual Report of the Commissioner General of Immigration* (Washington, D.C.: U.S. Government Printing Office, 1928), p. 29.
58. Quoted in Robert J. Lipshultz, "American Attitudes Toward Mexican Immigration, 1924–1952 (Master's thesis, University of Chicago, 1962), p. 61.
59. Kenneth L. Roberts, "West and Other Mexicans," *Saturday Evening Post* (February 4, 1928): 146.
60. J. S. Stowell, "Danger of Unrestrained Mexican Immigration," *Journal of Current History* (August 1928): 763.
61. Neal, p. 172.
62. U.S. Congress, House, Committee on Immigration and Naturalization, *Western Hemisphere Immigration, H.R. 8523, H.R. 8530, H.R. 8702*, 71st Cong., 2nd sess. (1930), p. 436.
63. U.S. Congress, *Western Hemisphere Immigration*, p. 436.
64. U.S. Congress, *Western Hemisphere Immigration*, p. 394.
65. Arnoldo de Leon, "The Rape of Tio Taco: Mexican Americans in Texas, 1930–1935," *Journal of Mexican American Studies* I (Fall 1970):5.
66. Neal, p. 194.
67. James Hoffman Batten, "New Features of Mexican Immigration" (Address before the National Conference of Social Work, Boston, June 9, 1930), p. 960. The author was the executive director of the Inter-American Federation of Claremont, California.
68. Batten, p. 960.
69. Materials on the Mexican repatriation of the 1930s are still scarce. Works that have been useful include Ronald W. López, *"Los Repatriados"* (Seminar paper, History Department, University of California at Los Angeles, 1968); Gregory Ochoa, "Some Aspects of the Repatriation of Mexican Aliens in Los Angeles County, 1931–1938" (seminar paper, History Department, San Fernando Valley State College, 1966); the Clements Collection, Special Collections Library, University of California at Los Angeles; and Abraham Hoffman, *Unwanted Mexican Americans in the Great Depression* (Tucson: University of Arizona Press, 1974). Peter Neal Kirstein, "Anglo over Bracero: A History of the Mexican Worker in the United States from Roosevelt to Nixon" (Ph.D. dissertation, Saint Louis University, 1973), states that the repatriation retarded the urbanization of Mexicans in the United States. Kirstein also discusses agribusiness's active campaign to protect its Mexican labor pool.

70. Neil Betten and Raymond A. Mohl, "From Discrimination to Repatriation: Mexican Life in Gary, Indiana, During the Great Depression," in Norris Hundley, ed., *The Chicano* (Santa Barbara, Calif.: Clio, 1975); Hoffman, p. 95; Emory S. Bogardus, "Repatriation and Readjustment," in Manual P. Servín, ed., *The Mexican-Americans: An Awakening Minority* (Beverly Hills, Calif.: Glencoe Press, 1970), p. 89.

71. Quoted in López, p. 51.

72. Abraham Hoffman, "Stimulus to Repatriation: The 1931 Federal Deportation Drive and the Los Angeles Mexican Community," in Norris Hundley, ed., *The Chicano* (Santa Barbara, Calif.: Clio, 1975), p. 110.

73. López, p. 63.

74. Quoted in Hoffman, *Unwanted Mexican Americans*, pp. 52, 55.

75. López, p. 55.

76. López, p. 58; Hoffman, "Stimulus to Repatriation," pp. 113, 116, 118.

77. Hoffman, "Stimulus to Repatriation," pp. 120, 122; Hoffman, *Unwanted Mexican Americans*, p. 84. A more detailed commentary on Visel's plan, entitled "DEPARABLE (sic) Aliens: Visel's Plan," is found in the Clement Papers. It was hoped that an army of aliens would walk out after the first publicity out of fright, that aliens in Los Angeles would become "deportable conscious," that actual deportations would follow, and that jobs would become available.

78. López, p. 43.

79. Bogardus, pp. 92–93.

80. Norman D. Humphrey, "Mexican Repatriation from Michigan: Public Assistance in Historical Perspective," *Social Service Review* (September 1941): 505.

81. Hoffman, *Unwanted Mexican Americans*, p. 120; Betten and Mohl, pp. 125, 138, 139.

82. George Kiser and David Silverman, "The Mexican Repatriation During the Great Depression," *Journal of Mexican American History* 3 (1973): 153.

83. Lorrain Esterly Pierce, "Mexican Americans on St. Paul's Lower West Side," *Journal of Mexican American History* 4, no. 4 (1974): 3; Louise Año Nuevo Kerr, "The Chicano Experience in Chicago: 1920–1970: (Ph.D. dissertation, University of Illinois at Chicago Circle, 1976), pp. i–ii, 69–77.

84. Ochoa, p. 66.

85. Ochoa, pp. 65–66.

86. Carey McWilliams, *North from Mexico* (New York: Greenwood Press, 1968), p. 193; Robert N. McLean, "Good-bye Vincente," *Survey* (May 1931). McLean p. 195, states that the Southern Pacific fixed "charity Mexican fares" in repatriation. Arnoll to Matson, June 4, 1931, in the Clements Papers, indicates that the Chamber of Commerce feared that repatriation would cause problems in Mexico, driving trade and services to the British.

87. This section draws heavily on Philip Stevenson, "Deporting Jesus," *The Nation* 143 (July 18, 1936): 67–69.

88. D. H. Dinwoodie, "Deportation: The Immigration Service and the Chicano Labor Movement in the 1930s," in Antonio José Ríos Bustamante, ed., *Immigration and Public Policy: Human Rights for Undocumented Workers and Their Families* (Los Angeles: Chicano Studies Center Publications, 1977), p. 165, states that Palleres' fellow organizer in *La Liga*, Julio Herrera, had been deported the previous year, charged with illegal entry in 1908.

89. Dinwoodie, pp. 163–174.

90. George O. Coalson, *The Development of the Migratory Farm Labor System in Texas: 1900–1954* (San Francisco: R & E Research Assoc., 1977), p. 67, states that in March 1943 the Bureau of Agricultural Economics reported a loss of 2.8 million agricultural workers since 1939, 40 percent to the armed forces and 60 percent to war industries, and that between April 1940 and January 1942 an estimated 280,000 workers left the farms for the armed forces.

91. Juan Ramón García, "Operation Wetback: 1954" (Ph.D. dissertation, University of Notre Dame, 1977), pp. 16–17.

92. Cardenas, "United States Immigration Policy," p. 75.

93. Ernesto Galarza, *Merchants of Labor* (Santa Barbara, Calif.: McNally & Loftin, 1964), p. 47; García, p. 23.

94. Richard B. Craig, *The Bracero Program* (Austin. University of Texas Press, 1971), p. 198; O. M. Scruggs, "Texas and The Bracero Program," *Pacific Historical Review* (August 1962): 251–252.

95. Cardenas and Flores, p. 14.
96. Kirstein, p. 39.
97. Coalson, p. 94.
98. Scruggs, pp. 253–254.
99. Kirstein, pp. 83–84, 90–91.
100. Henry P. Anderson, *The Bracero Program in California* (Berkeley: School of Public Health, University of California, July 1961), p. 146; Kirstein, pp. 94–95.
101. Craig, p. 54. Mexico, during the 1940s, asked for the protection of *braceros* since it vividly remembered the repatriation of the 1930s when the United States literally dumped and stranded thousands of Mexicans at the border, García, p. 92.
102. Coalson, p. 82; J. B. Jones, "Mexican-American Labor Problems in Texas" (Ph.D. dissertation, University of Texas, 1965), p. 23.
103. Hart Stillwell, "The Wetback Tide," *Common Ground* (Summer 1949): 3–4.
104. Kirstein, p. 147.
105. Craig, pp. 58–59.
106. Nelson Gage Copp, "Wetbacks and Braceros: Mexican Migrant Laborers and American Immigration Policy, 1930–1960" (Ph.D. dissertation, Boston University, 1963), pp. 156, 189.
107. Craig, p. 36.
108. Galarza, p. 66.
109. Quoted in Craig, p. 112; also covered in Howard Lloyd Campbell, "Bracero Migration and the Mexican Economy, 1951–1964" (Ph.D. dissertation, The American University, 1972), pp. 69–71.
110. Patricia Morgan, *Shame of a Nation* (Los Angeles Committee for Protection of Foreign Born, September 1954), p. 28.
111. Craig, p. 119.
112. Craig, pp. 104, 107, 109. Craig, p. 107, states that Mexico did not believe that the United States would be so arrogant and its national pride had not permitted it to back down during the negotiations.
113. Ray Gilmore and Gladys W. Gilmore, "Braceros in California," *Pacific Historical Review* (August 1962): 272.
114. Garcia, p. 29, states that opponents of the bracero program were amazed that "foreigners" were repeatedly guaranteed fringe benefits that had been repeatedly denied U.S. citizens in the migrant stream. Craig, p. 68, makes the point that Mexico had not been happy during the 1948-1951 period. See also Craig, pp. 22–23.
115. Copp, pp. 107, 109; Anderson, p. 39.
116. Craig, p. 10.
117. Quoted in Craig, p. 11.
118. Quoted in Craig, p. 182. Campbell, pp. 5–6, 101, is an interesting study of the decline of the dependence on the *bracero* in the 1960s as the result of mechanization, particularly in cotton.
119. Copp, p. 102.
120. Ernesto Galarza, *Tragedy at Chualar: El Crucero de las Treinta y dos Cruces* (Santa Barbara, Calif.: McNally & Loftin, 1977). The book describes the death of 32 *braceros* while being transported in a hazardous bus on September 18, 1963. The American Committee for the Protection of the Foreign Born, *Our Badge of Infamy*, A Petition to the United Nations on the Treatment of the Mexican Immigrant (April 1959), reviews the excesses of the program. On page 24 it tells of the decapitation of a *bracero* driving a tractor by a low-flying airplane on May 28, 1958. The Justice Department investigation took 24 hours. Ralph Guzmán's editorial in the *Eastside Sun*, March 4, 1954, is a good review of the literature up to that time and the exploitation of braceros. Guzmán states that Truman's Committee on Migratory Labor confirmed the influence of agribusiness on the INS.

Chapter 7
The Scapegoats: The Mexicans Are Coming

The 1950s was a decade of apathy and reaction. Disillusionment over the lack of victory in the Korean War, followed by economic recessions, unnerved the Anglo-American public, encouraging a renewal of nativism. During this time, government authorities, public and private institutions, as well as the Anglo-American public, looked for scapegoats. The Mexicans, both with and without documents, became special targets for nativists.

The migration of Mexicans to the United States was neither accidental nor spontaneous. As has been mentioned, it was part of a process. Several factors contributed to the migration north. Improved transportation in Mexico facilitated flow from the interior. In 1940 all-weather roads numbered 9,929 kilometers; by 1950 the figure increased to 23,925 kilometers. Moreover there were 23,672 kilometers of railroad lines.[1]

Mexico's population increased between 1940 and 1950 by 16.5 million or 30 percent. Cotton production on the Mexican side of the border, especially around Matamoros, provided employment for workers from the interior. As in the United States, Mexican growers advertised for more workers than needed, so many continued northward across the border to find work in the expanding cotton fields of the Rio Grande Valley of Texas.[2]

Collusion between the Immigration and Naturalization Service and the growers was a fact. For instance, rarely were undocumented workers rounded up during harvest time. In 1949 the Idaho State Employment Service wrote:

> The United States Immigration and Naturalization Service recognizes the need for farm workers in Idaho, and, through cooperation with the state employment service, withholds its search and deportation until such times as there is not a shortage of farm workers.[3]

In Portland, Oregon, an INS officer said:

> I might state that in 1949 representatives of the Federal Employment Service asked us not to send our inspectors into the field to apprehend "wet" Mexicans, for the purpose of deporting them, until after the emergency of harvesting the crops had been met.[4]

In other words, when sufficient numbers of *braceros* or domestic labor worked cheaply enough, the laws were enforced; when a labor shortage occurred the doors were open, regardless of international or moral law.

OPERATION WETBACK

Undocumented workers have always been most vulnerable in times of economic crisis. Massive roundups beginning in 1949 extended into *barrios* all over the country.

Earlier depressions or recessions had discouraged Mexican migration; but with the impetus of the *bracero* program this was no longer true during the 1953–1955 recession. Official U.S. policy excluded "illegals," but during the 1950s hundreds of thousands of Mexicans crossed the border in search of work. Newspapers reacted by calling for their exclusion, and arousing antialien sentiments: undocumented workers were portrayed as dangerous, malicious, and subversive.[5] The contradictions were that while the press condemned the migration from Mexico, the *bracero* program magnetized the border and the border patrol looked the other way when growers asked.

Liberal Democrats supported the border patrol, calling for fines on employers who hired undocumented workers. Hubert Humphrey, Paul Douglas, Herbert Lehman, and others supported the traditional trade union position. The Mexican government as did most Chicano organizations called for fining U.S. employers who hired undocumented workers.

Both labor and community activists were under attack by the same interests that encouraged the free flow of labor across the border. The National Labor Relations Act guaranteed wage workers the right to collective bargaining and the right to strike, but failure to extend its protection to agriculture left farm labor defenseless and seemingly unorganizable. Consequently through manipulation of *braceros* and undocumented workers, growers broke strike after strike, forcing many Chicano migrants to move to the Midwest or other sections. The frustrated Chicanos pecked down and joined the attack on the "wetbacks." In contrast "growers and their powerful lobbies were convinced that they had vested rights in cheap Mexican labor and that any interference with its influx was un-American."[6]

In 1953 Lieutenant General Joseph M. Swing, who was sometimes called a "professional, long-time Mexican hater," was appointed commissioner of the INS.[7] Swing had been a classmate of President Dwight Eisenhower at West Point in 1911, and had been on General Pershing's punitive expedition against Pancho Villa in 1916. He conducted his operations in a military manner and regarded his objective to be to flush out Mexicans. He even requested $10 million to build a 150-mile-long fence to keep Mexicans out, and set a quota to be deported for each target area.[8]

In the fiscal year 1953 the INS deported 875,000 Mexicans; 20,174 Mexicans were airlifted into the interior from Spokane, Chicago, Kansas City, St. Louis, and other cities.[9] In 1954 it deported 1,035,282, in 1955 256,290, and in 1956 90,122. The accuracy of the figures is questionable since the INS added estimates of the number it assumed were scared out of the country to the number it actually apprehended and deported. Moreover, the INS stood to gain by inflating the figures, since success of the operation might be used as grounds for an increase in budget. And, in fact, in 1957 the border patrol budget doubled.[10]

Local police actively supported the INS. Swing hired two other generals—Frank Partridge and Frank Howard. Operations reached extreme proportions with John P. Swanson, chief patrol inspector, even contracting with Native Americans north of Yuma, Arizona, to hunt down undocumented workers who crossed their reservation for a bounty of $2.50 to $3.00 per person.

During the raids U.S.-born citizens became entangled in the web. It was a victory for the INS, and a blow to the human rights of Mexicans. Every brown person was suspect. Homes were searched illegally and U.S. citizens were seized and detained illegally. To this day, immigration authorities periodically conduct similar roundups that spread terror in the *barrios*. One such raid occurred in Los Angeles when the 1970 census was being conducted, compromising the legitimacy of the statistics regarding the Chicano population.[11]

A sometimes forgotten aspect of "Operation Wetback" was the role of Attorney General Herbert Brownell. Professor Juan García at the University of Michigan at Flint illuminates this dark passage of history.[12] Brownell had testified before the House Appropriations Committee soon after the Senate confirmed him in 1953 that he opposed additional appropriations for the border patrol. Four months later at the request of President Eisenhower he made a tour of the border after which he suddenly called for increased appropriations for the patrol as well as tougher laws. It was on this tour that Brownell met Swing, who had commanded the Sixth Army. Brownell had wanted to use the army to stem the "tide" by sending them to the border, but army brass was cool to the idea. When Swing retired from the army, Brownell offered him the job as Commissioner. Brownell seems to have reached a state of near paranoia.

On October 15, 1953 Ralph Guzmán, a Chicano activist, wrote "A few weeks ago Herbert Brownell, the U.S. Attorney General, wanted to shoot wetbacks crossing into the U.S., but farmers fearing the loss of a cheap labor market because of G.I. bullets, complained bitterly and Brownell changes [sic] his mind."[13] Guzmán's charge was not unfounded. In May 1954 William P. Allen, publisher of the *Laredo Times*, had written Eisenhower that Brownell had asked for the support of labor leaders at a May 11 dinner if he shot the "wet-backs" down in cold blood.[14]

Ultraconservatives intimidated progressives. In 1947 Congress moved to check many of the gains made by labor, in great part neutralizing the National Labor Relations Act by passing the Taft-Hartley Act of 1947. The whip of Joseph McCarthy's U.S. Senate Special Investigative Committee was felt by Chicano leaders. Many leaders were ordered to testify at the committee hearings and as a result many were blacklisted; other Chicanos were denaturalized and deported. So strong was the red baiting that most Chicano organizations were intimidated. Chicano educators and professional groups abandoned the Chicano movement in the face of accusations and threats of voices of reaction. An exception was *La Asociación Nacional México-Americana* which was closely affiliated with progressive trade unions such as the Mine, Mill and Smelter Workers and actively cooperated with the Independent Progressive Party and the National Committee for the Protection of the Foreign Born. The leaders who did fight back were harassed, imprisoned, and deported. The most undemocratic obstacle to the Chicano movement in the 1950s was the McCarran-Walter Act.[15]

Francis E. Walter, chairman of the House Un-American Activities Committee, and Senator Pat McCarran from Nevada sponsored the McCarran Act to tighten immigration legislation to exclude subversive elements. By the late 1940s the problems of the refugees and displaced persons created by World War II encouraged many liberals to think about scrapping the system of immigration quotas based on national origins. However, McCarran, the chief guardian of the nation's racial mix, saw the admission of any number of foreigners as a threat. "To forestall the impending breakdown in American culture, Senator McCarran had been busy since 1947 with hearings and drafting of legislation; his aim: the codification of all the scattered immigration and naturalization acts in the federal statute books." In 1951, McCarran testified: "The times, Mr. President, are too perilous for us to tinker blindly with our basic institutions. . . . If we scrap the national origin formula we will, in the course of a generation or so, change the ethnic and cultural composition of this nation."[16] Chicanos, along with many other immigrants, became victims of McCarran's crusade.

Elaboration on the substance of McCarran's crusade and the several acts he sponsored is beyond the scope of this book. We shall concentrate on Titles I and II of the McCarran Internal Security Act of 1950 and the denaturalization aspect of the Immigration and Nationality Act of 1952.[17] The legislature he proposed was not the first case in the history of the United States in which deportation was used to intimidate dissenters and the unwanted. Robert K. Murray wrote in his book *Red Scare* that:

from the Alien and Sedition Acts of 1798 to the McCarran-Walter legislation of 1954, we have most often assumed the existence of an innate affinity between alien and radical. If every alien was not necessarily a radical, certainly every radical was in some way alien, that is, un-American. . . .[18]

Title I established a Subversive Activities Control Board (still in existence) that would label and investigate subversion in the United States. Title II authorized construction of concentration camps in which to intern suspected subversives without a trial or hearing if either the president or Congress declared a national emergency. Two years later, the government built six camps. Largely through efforts of Japanese-American Citizens League, Title II has recently been abolished after over twenty years of controversy. Briefly, the 1952 Act provided for: (1) the codification of previous immigration acts, relating to national origins; (2) the abolishment of racial bars to entry and citizenship; (3) the establishment of a complicated procedure for admitting Asians; (4) the inclusion of a long list of grounds on which aliens could be deported or excluded; (5) the inclusion of conditions whereby naturalized citizens could be denaturalized; and (6) the granting of power to the INS "to interrogate aliens suspected of being illegally in the country, to search boats, trains, cars, trucks, or planes, to enter and search private lands within 25 miles of the border, and to arrest so-called 'illegals' and also those committing felonies under immigration laws."[19]

The McCarran-Walter Act passed in 1952 over President Harry S. Truman's veto. The president stated it created a group of second-class citizens by distinguishing between native and naturalized citizens. The naturalized citizens' citizenship could be revoked and they could be deported for political reasons.

The President's Commission on Immigration and Naturalization, appointed by Truman in 1952, criticized denaturalization clauses of the act, charging that provisions were too vague and gave administrators too much latitude. Visits to the United States for political reasons could be banned. The commission complained that "a substantial proportion of deportations are based on technical violations of the laws. . . ."[20] Additionally, while a statute of limitations under federal law protected criminals, the 1952 act eliminated protection for foreigners "and therefore, an alien now is subject to deportation at any time for even minor technical violations."[21] In fact, the 1952 act "retroactively rescinded the limited statute of limitations fixed by previous law."[22] The commission stated it violated the *ex post facto* provisions of the Constitution, and concluded that "the new act actually restores the threat of cruel and inhuman punishment for offenses long since forgiven."[23] The commission criticized the shotgun approach, because it forbade entry or could denaturalize and deport members or affiliates of "subversive organizations." The law further did not spell out the term "affiliation" but left it to the arbitrary determination of the U.S. attorney general.

These two laws led to gross violations of human rights. The law intimidated many activists who feared being placed in a concentration camp, being labeled a subversive, or being deported.[24] The Los Angeles Committee for the Protection of the Foreign Born, an affiliate of the American Committee for the Protection of the Foreign Born, was placed on the subversive list by the Subversive Activities Control Board because it challenged the two acts. The committee, as well as many of its members, was cleared after extensive litigation.

Union busting under the McCarran-Walter Act was common. A popular case was that of Humberto Silex who had organized Local 509 of the Mine, Mill and Smelters Union of El Paso. He had entered the United States legally in 1921, had served in the armed forces, was married, and had two children. Silex was employed by American Smelting and Refining Company, helped organize the local, and served as its president. In 1945 he got into a fistfight, was arrested and fined $35, and was discharged from his job. Shortly afterwards, his union called a strike; Silex was labeled a potential trouble maker and a warrant was issued for his deportation on grounds of "moral turpitude," citing the fist fight. The union helped contest the case and eventually the order was set aside.[25]

The 1950 and 1952 McCarran acts thwarted the development of effective organization both in the *barrios* and among working-class Chicanos by deporting some of its most effective leaders and intimidating others with the threat of deportation. The Los Angeles Committee for the Protection of the Foreign Born reported in 1954 that of Chicanos defended by the committee on deportation charges, seven had been in the country for over seven years, three for more than twenty years, three for over thirty years, seventeen had U.S.-born children and grandchildren, and twenty-two were trade unionists.

Justo S. Cruz, 66, had come to the United States when he was 19. He was a machinist who had joined the Workers' Alliance during the depression and championed the workers' rights for relief and freedom from harassment. Although there had been no restrictions on Alliance membership in the 1930s, when the Alliance was placed on the attorney general's list of subversive organizations, past membership became punishable by deportation if one was either a noncitizen or a naturalized one. Immigration authorities attempted to have Cruz fired, but his employer refused. An order for his deportation was issued. Cruz fought back and was finally absolved. Supported by *La Asociación Nacional México-Americana* (ANMA), he began to address groups of Chicanos as part of the association's protest against the acts. María Cruz, 51, the widow of Jesús Cruz, who died after deportation to Mexico, had entered the United States legally at the age of 5 and was the mother of two U.S.-born children, one of whom was a war hero. When her purse was stolen, she applied for a new registration card. Immigration authorities attempted to force her to inform on her husband's associates, who were suspected of being communists. When María refused, she was arrested and charged with illegal entry. Later the charge was altered to membership in the Communist party. She had once been a member of the CIO Cannery Workers Union.[26]

Agapito Gómez, 46, had lived legally in the United States since the age of 21 and had a U.S.-born wife and two children. During the war he joined the United Steelworkers of America (CIO). After the passage of the McCarran Act of 1950, immigration service agents called on him and demanded that he account for past activities and provide them with a list of fellow workers and union members. When he refused, the agents took away his alien card. He had joined a depression relief organization in the 1930s and had been a member of the CIO.[27]

José Noriega, 67, came to the United States legally at the age of 25. He worked in the construction industry in Texas and became a longshoreman when he moved to California. He joined the International Longshoremen's Association. He took part in the longshoremen's strike of 1923 and was arrested. José was blacklisted and he moved to San Bernardino. He later returned to the docks and joined the International Longshoremen's and Warehousemen's Union, working at the docks in Wilmington, a port section of Los Angeles. In 1952 immigration agents called. They wanted information, names, dates, and places of organizational meetings and participants. When he refused to cooperate, deportation proceedings were initiated.[28]

The INS's abuse of power is underscored in the manner that it conducted its deportation proceedings. Tobias Navarrette went before the U.S. Board of Immigration Appeals on May 17, 1957. He was represented by the American Civil Liberties' Union. Navarrette, 55, had entered the United States in 1927, was married, had eight U.S.-born children, and had served in the armed forces. From 1936 to 1938 he had been a member of the Workers' Alliance. The INS alleged that he was also a member of the Communist party. The witnesses against him were questionable. Hernández (no first name listed) had been deported in 1951 for membership in the Communist party. He admitted that he wanted to return and that he hoped his testimony would help him in this endeavor. Hernández was paid $25.00 a day and was placed on parole during the numerous trials at which he testified for the state. He alleged that he saw Navarrette at two Communist party meetings in 1938 and at a rally.[29]

Another state witness, Gonzales (no first name), had been a member of the party from 1934 to 1942. He testified that Navarrette had been a member of the Belvedere unit and had been active in the Spanish-Speaking People's Congress (to be discussed later). He further stated that he had seen Navarrette pay dues. Gonzales like Hernández was a professional witness for the INS and was paid $37.00 a day. He stated that he wanted to return to the United States and work against the communists. The testimony of the two state witnesses contained inconsistencies and contradictions. After a long struggle Navarrette won his case and continued to work in Boyle Heights as a jeweler and watch repairman, dying in April 1964.[30]

Bernardo Díaz was a U.S.-born Mexican, with a wife and six children. In 1945 at the age of 19 he had gone AWOL from Camp Roberts, was tried for desertion and convicted, and spent eighteen months in Ft. Leavenworth. Díaz thought that he had paid his debt and was never further trouble, working as a grounds keeper at the La Habra Golf Course. He made frequent visits to Mexico. In January 1955 he was not allowed to return to the United States and he was later declared an inadmissible alien.

Díaz was separated from his family and forced to work in Tijuana for $2.00 a day. His wife Inez kept the family together by picking strawberries at 90¢ an hour, refusing to apply for state aid because this required her to sign a statement that her husband had abandoned her and she did not want to prejudice his case.[31]

Many of the victims of McCarran-Walter had to wait for years for final disposition of their cases. José Gastelum was finally freed of deportation charges after seven years by the U.S. Supreme Court on a 5–4 decision. He was defended by the Los Angeles Committee for the Protection of the Foreign Born.[32]

The American Civil Liberties Union committed resources to fighting those violations of human rights and the Community Service Organization in Los Angeles extended free legal services to anyone whose human rights were violated due to immigration policies.[33]

MAGNETIZING THE BORDER

The INS successfully intimidated labor as well as the Mexican community. Empowered by the McCarran-Walter Act, agents indiscriminately searched and rounded up Mexican-looking people, focused on union leaders as special targets, and in some cases forced undocumented workers to act as strikebreakers.[34] "Operation Wetback" accomplished its purpose; the massive roundups spread fear which for a time ended the flow of undocumented workers. At the end of 1956, according to Mexican sociologist, Dr. Jorge Bustamante, some people considered Mexican workers without documents to be a closed episode. However, conditions in Mexico and the United States revived push-pull factors of migration—poverty in Mexico pushed the undocumented north and the need for cheap labor pulled workers north.

Concerned Americans joined the protest against blatant violations of Mexicans' Human Rights. On April 17, 1959, a petition was presented to the United Nations, charging mistreatment of Mexican immigrants in the United States under a provision of Universal Declaration of Human Rights adopted by that tribunal in 1948. The petition indicted INS practices as well as those of the Justice Department in treatment of Mexicans. The preface quoted Archbishop Robert E. Lucey of San Antonio: "And so the poor bracero, compelled by force and fear, will endure any kind of injustice and exploitation to gain a few dollars that he needs so desperately." The INS's militarylike sweeps of the mid-1950s came under special scrutiny with the report stating that they subjected the Mexican to "a state of permanent insecurity," subjected to continual "raids, arrests, and deportation drives."[35]

According to Dr. Louise Kerr, Loyola University historian, the *bracero* program, while purporting to ameliorate the push-pull factors, actually abetted immigration by introducing potential immigrants to the United States and encouraging border recruitment. When *braceros* returned home, their "success" encouraged others to follow.[36] The new wave of undocumented workers began not long after termination of the *bracero* program in the mid-1960s. Reasons for the renewed migration are complex and must be analyzed systematically.

According to Dr. Julian Samora, "The most compelling reasons for illegal immigration are the insatiable demands for cheap labor in the United States and the tremendous population increase occurring in Mexico." He attributed migration to the success of agriculture which depended on cheap labor and U.S. government subsidies and the growers' realization that the "Wetback labor . . . [was] even cheaper" than Chicano labor. To this end "the recruitment process [of U.S. growers and government officials] served to create a large labor pool on both sides of the border."[37] As mentioned, mechanization of cotton had decreased growers' dependency on this administered labor pool, but many people realized that growers wanted a continuance to break attempts to unionize migrants.

Mexico had increasingly been drawn into the capitalist orbit in the north and activity there magnetized the border. Multinational corporations such as Del Monte, Campbell, and General Foods steadily tightened their control over processing and marketing. Del

Monte by 1967 had international sales in twenty Latin American countries and ranked as the largest canning corporation in the world.[38]

U.S. companies had controlled the winter vegetable market in key Mexican states such as Sinaloa since the 1920s, entering into partnership with Mexican *latifundistas* who monopolized the land there. In 1962, 334 million pounds of vegetables were exported; these exports climbed to 1,108 million pounds in 1975.[39] The produce, rather than being used to feed or bring profits to Mexicans, went to U.S. food monopolies which shared large profits with a small oligarchy of Mexican capitalists. Mexico at certain seasons of the year supplies 60 percent of the fresh vegetables of the United States, with some 300 trucks passing through Nogales daily.[40] Export on this scale is important in a nation with limited arable land.[41]

U.S. economic penetration in Mexico during the 1960s totaled $1.1 billion, while total profits (and payments abroad on interest, royalties, and patents) drained $1.8 billion out of the country. Thus $700 million more was sucked out of the country by foreign companies than was invested.[42] In its September-October 1977 issue, *The North American Congress on Latin America* summarized the process: "The penetration of foreign monopoly capital into Mexico has greatly advanced the process of monopolization. By 1965, 1.5 percent of the industrial corporations in Mexico controlled 77 percent of all industrial capital."[43]

Foreign investment did little to solve Mexico's unemployment problem and in fact made it worse. During the 1960s over 60 percent of the new foreign investment went to purchase already existing companies and thus did not substantially increase employment. Figures advanced by U.S. investors showing that they generated employment are deceiving. For instance, between 1963 and 1970 workers employed by foreign companies in Mexico increased by 180,000; however, 105,000 of these jobs were in already existing firms. At the same time labor-saving devices reduced availability of jobs. Foreign companies controlled 31 percent of the total value of Mexico's industrial production, but they employed only 16 percent of the industrial work force. Farm work was also reduced by mechanization. In addition many peasant farmers who could not afford the new machinery had to abandon their farms.[44]

In 1960 3 percent (79,000) of the 2.5 million farms produced 55 percent of all agriculture. These farmers did not sell the bulk of the products to domestic markets but continued to export heavily. Combines, such as Anderson-Clayton, controlled cotton in Mexico through credit and marketing. According to Professor Raúl Fernández of the University of California at Irvine, Anderson-Clayton extended more credit to Mexican growers than did the National Edijal Bank; it manipulated prices through its control of the world cotton market and kept Mexico in line by dumping cotton on the world market to depress prices.[45]

Mexico struggled to control its own public utility companies and, like many third world countries, paid a high price. The only countries that have had some success have been nations that have nationalized these foreign-owned companies. Mexico did not have this option since it depended on world markets and banks controlled by the very corporations that owned the utility companies; 1960 was not 1938, when President Lazaro Cardenas had seized foreign oil interests. The North American Congress on Latin America's report on labor and imperialism in Mexico's electrical industry, documents effects of monopoly capital on utilities.[46] General Electric and Westinghouse had been active in Mexico since the turn of the century; the Mexican Revolution did little to lessen their power. In the late 1950s the World Bank pressured the Mexican government to allow increases in electricity rates. Mexicans could not accept these increases since they were inflationary and U.S. pressure represented an affront to their national dignity. Forced to choose, they offered to purchase companies for an inflated price of $122 million (for outdated machinery and installations). Former owners then reinvested in manufacturing companies which proved more profitable.

From 1961 to 1970 "foreign investments in the electrical equipment industry in Mexico more than tripled—from $62 million to $215 million—with the most rapid growth being in the late '60s."[47] "Monopoly in technology" practiced by the United States and other industrial nations became evident with Mexico forced to buy machinery, transistors, wires, generators, and other equipment from foreign-owned companies at the latter's terms.

U.S. economic penetration and growing monopolization within Mexico greatly destabilized the labor picture within Mexico. Flight of capital drained the capital necessary to stimulate growth and thus encouraged the flight of labor. Mechanization of agriculture accelerated urbanization while the introduction of more sophisticated machines speeded urbanization and industrialization. The population boom during the 1960s threw millions into the labor pool. In 1950 Mexico had a population of 25.8 million, jumping to 34.9 million ten years later, and rushing toward 50 million by the end of the 1960s. Mexico's annual population growth had dramatically increased from an average of 1.75 percent (1922–1939) to 2.25 percent (1939–1946) to 2.8 percent (1947–1953) to well over 3 percent after 1954.[48] The abrupt end of the *bracero* program further destabilized the Mexican economy; it had served as a crutch during the postwar period, increasing Mexican dependence on the United States and discouraging Mexico from reaching internal solutions. The end of the program did not end the pull toward the United States.

Two other programs magnetized the border accelerating migration north, the commuter program and the Border Industrial Program. The commuter program had its origin in the loose interpretation of statutes regulating the flow of labor across the border. Authorities allowed growers to circumvent the Alien Contract Law of the 1880s by granting special status to Mexican and Canadian workers, allowing them the option of living outside the United States while admitting them for work purposes on a daily seasonal basis. Labor leaders challenged the fictional status of commuters, especially during the hearings on immigration quotas during the 1920s. In a 1928 Canadian case, *Karnuth* v. *United States,* the court found "by admitting aliens temporarily for business, to permit their coming to labor for hire in competition with American workmen" immigration authorities contradicted the intention of Congress.[49]

The INS ignored this court decision. In 1952 the Immigration and Nationality Act removed "the contract labor clauses from the law and introduced in their place, a system of selective immigration giving special preference to skilled aliens urgently needed in this country." Contract labor provisions were replaced by selective allocation of "quota numbers or permits [green cards] for temporary residence on the basis of need for labor and services of aliens."[50] The Secretary of Labor was empowered to issue the permits only when and if the "green carders" did not compete with domestic workers and if they did not adversely affect wages or working conditions. These restrictions were included as safeguards for domestic workers but were not enforced.

While opposing the influx of undocumented workers, the INS had defended the commuter program on the grounds that it involved only a comparatively small number of workers. It has even allowed commuters to be used as strikebreakers. In the Payton Packing Company strike of 1960 in El Paso "overnight the management of the plant replaced the strikers, for the most part Mexican-Americans, with Mexican commuter labor."[51] Although the INS reported that in 1972 there were about 48,000 commuters, 39,500 of whom were from Mexico, there is some question about these figures and the exact dimensions of the commuter program during the 1960s and 1970s are not known.[52] However, whatever the number issued, the availability of green cards contributes to the build-up of Mexican workers at the border.

Another program which increased the pull toward the border began in the mid-1960s. The Border Industrial Program (BIP) accelerated the entry of the multinational corporation into the economic development of the border area. The purpose of the BIP was to create jobs, to attract capital, to introduce modern methods of manufacturing in assembling, processing, and exporting, and to increase consumption of Mexican raw materials. The Mexican government waived duties and regulations on the import of raw materials and waived restrictions on foreign capital within 12.5 miles of the border (this area has continuously been expanded); 100 percent of the finished products are exported out of the country with 90 percent of the labor force being Mexican citizens.[53] In 1966 20 plants functioned under BIP; this number increased to 120 in 1970 and to 476 in 1976.[54]

These plants encouraged the already rapid urbanization of northern Mexico. In quest of cheap labor by the early 1970s thousands of U.S. companies went south. These U.S. owned companies generated 20,327 jobs in 1970; that number increased by 164 percent to 53,680 in early 1974. The jobs are mostly held by women with a high percentage of positions classified as "seasonal employment" consequently not paying fringe benefits.[55] Although twin plants often exist on the U.S. side, they are small in relation to their Mexican counterparts. Dependence on the border industries increased.

The world recession of the late 1960s hit Mexico hard, stagnating economic growth and increasing its already high trade deficit, foreign debt, and inflation. Internal discontent increased as unemployment affected a large sector of the Mexican labor market. Emigration consequently skyrocketed. Conditions were aggravated by the 1965 immigration act. Liberal congressmen sponsored this new legislation to correct the injustices of the past in relation to Asians. However, in the process they allowed nativist legislators to launch an attack on immigration from Latin America and especially from Mexico. For the first time a quota was placed on immigrants for the Western Hemisphere. The new law allowed 170,000 to enter annually from the Eastern Hemisphere and set a ceiling of 120,000 for the Western Hemisphere. No more than 40,000 could enter from any one nation (a direct slap at Mexico which received the bulk of the visas).[56]

Lastly, the very nature of the border served to magnetize it. The Pan-American Highway facilitated the northward movement. In fact, travel south to north was often easier than east to west between the border states. Heavy outlays of capital came into the region through tourism from a richer country. A heavy concentration of Mexicans north of the border attracted paying customers from that sector for familiar products and services.

Most Mexican manufacturing centered around food and drinks which together made up 50 percent of the manufacturing on the border. And while there had been considerable mechanization of agriculture in the border states, agricultural production declined during the 1960s, falling from 31 percent of the national agricultural output in 1960 to 17 percent in 1970.[57] As a consequence by the start of the 1970s many more of the migrants who were attracted to the border had very little choice but to cross that arbitrary line in search of food, shelter, and clothing.

HUMAN RIGHTS—AN AMERICAN FICTION

The number of deportees gradually increasd during the second half of the 1960s:

1964	222,222
1965	48,948
1966	89,683
1967	107,695
1968	142,520
1969	189,572
1970	265,539

SOURCE: Refugio I. Rochin, "Economic Deprivation of Chicanos—Continuing Neglect in the Seventies," *Aztlán* (Spring, 1973): 96.

This substantial increase went for the most part unnoticed by the general public and newspapers. The mid-1960s, spurred by a wartime economy, saw a high level of prosperity and near full employment. Also, the United States was preoccupied with war protests and the Black movement. When the United States entered an economic recession in the 1970s and economic squeezes occurred, the undocumented workers again became scapegoats for the nation's failures.

While mainstream Chicano organizations, labor leaders, and activists had supported the INS in the 1950s, actually encouraging apprehension of undocumented workers, their attitude took a 180 degree turn in the late 1960s. This change was in part due to the higher level of political consciousness; it represented a break with trade unionist tradition which simplistically blamed the victims. The person most responsible for changing the antiundocumented worker position was Bert Corona, who organized the *Centro de Acción Social Autonoma–Hermandad General de Trabajadores* (CASA-HGT; The Autonomous Center for Social Action–the General Brotherhood of Workers, at first known as CASA-MAPA) in 1968. Corona began to organize this sector of the community during a time when most other activists were concerned with the Vietnam war and the civil rights struggle. It was a difficult task since there was not much public consciousness about the struggle of the undocumented.

Bert Corona's activist career spanned three decades in both the mainstream and radical sectors of the Chicano movement; he had the uncanny ability to feel at home and be accepted by both groups. Corona, born in El Paso in 1918, moved to Los Angeles in 1936. There he dropped out of college and joined Harry Bridge's longshoremen's union; he participated in the Spanish-Speaking People's Congress in the late 1930s and 1940s. In the 1940s he became president of his local, working with labor and community activists. Corona joined *La Asociación Nacional México-Americana* (ANMA) which was one of the few organizations which protested not only McCarthy hysteria and the McCarran-Walter Act, but also the Korean War. Corona had a firsthand knowledge of the work of the Community Service Organization which helped undocumented workers with papers and counseling. He took a leading role in the Mexican-American Political Association, leading the fight to end the *bracero* program. Through years of struggle, he correctly anticipated the awakening of nativism and organized CASA-HGT.

Corona recognized that the heavy migration of undocumented workers from Mexico was not a legal problem, but part of the labor process and that solutions required organizing undocumented workers as well as educating the community to real reasons why Mexicans were migrating to the United States. In excellent trade union fashion Corona set out to make CASA self-sufficient, charging the members at first $15.00 to process their papers. The dues gave members an active voice in the management of the organization. Corona convinced progressive elements to volunteer their time and money. Popularity of the organization grew with deescalation of the Vietnam War when the issue of immigration became a priority cause for most Chicano activists. Through Corona's efforts militant Anglo-American organizations adopted the human rights struggle of undocumented workers.

Chapters spread to San Diego, San Jose, San Antonio, Colorado, and Chicago. The organization had over 2,000 members; although the different chapters were affiliated, their structure was decentralized. CASA's degree of self-sufficiency gave mobility to Corona and his associates (most important being Soledad "Chole" Alatorre, a charismatic woman, who was especially effective with the rank and file itself) to attend meetings and conferences, to conduct fund-raisers and rallies, to lobby politicians, and so forth. The leadership and character of CASA-HGT changed in 1973 when CASA Carnalismo, the Committee to Free *Los Tres*, and the *Comité Estudiantil del Pueblo* (CEP) combined to play a more active role in the direction of CASA-HGT. These sectors were under the leadership of Antonio Rodríguez, a lawyer and *barrio* activist.

By 1975 Corona left CASA over complex internal struggles. CASA changed from a service organization to a vanguard organization with a smaller and more disciplined cadre. After Corona left CASA-HGT, the membership spent more time in Marxist study and developed an existing newspaper, *Sin Fronteras*, into a first-class newspaper. The group also became more involved in other activist issues and mass rallies. It went out of the business of servicing workers in obtaining their documents. Its leadership spent additional time and energy lobbying progressive professions and organizations such as the National Lawyers Guild to deal with constitutional issues.

Corona moved the center of his activity from Central Los Angeles to the San Fernando Valley and continued to work with undocumented workers. He has since organized the National Immigration Coalition which is comprised of numerous community organizations. Corona is also very active in labor coalitions, working closely with the United Auto Workers. CASA put together its National Coalition For Fair Immigration Laws and Practices and Rosalio Muñoz (to be discussed) who later organized the Los Angeles Immigration Coalition. Churches and poverty agencies such as one called Stop Immigration in Los Angeles established undocumented worker centers to assist workers with their papers. This pattern was followed throughout the Southwest and Midwest. A cadre of Chicano and Anglo scholars specializing in Mexican migration formed, creating a body of research and analysis which exposed most of the contradictions of the 1950s.

Meanwhile, in 1971, the INS apprehended 348,178 undocumented workers, 430,213 in 1972, and 609,673 in 1973. By 1976 the number climbed to 870,000 (approximately 90 percent of whom were Mexican). The economic recessions and rising unemployment increased interest in the undocumented worker. According to F. Ray Marshall, formerly a professor of economics at the University of Texas and now Secretary of Labor under President James Carter, prior to 1970 undocumented workers worked primarily in agriculture, but during the 1970s went into other occupations. This assumption is not entirely correct. The undocumented after World War II moved into marginal jobs such as restaurants, sweat shops, and domestics, which were abandoned by Chicanos and other minorities as their aspirations increased. The Chicanos themselves shifted to the cities. In the 1950 and 1960 censuses Chicanos were the least urbanized of the racial groups in the Southwest; the 1970 census showed they were the most urbanized. As the Chicano shifted to the cities so did undocumented workers.[58]

Nativist reaction to undocumented workers escalated about 1971. Trade unions and politicians led the assault. State legislators proposed restricting migration by fining employers who hired undocumented workers. The prototype passed in California in 1971—the Dixon-Arnett Act. It was declared unconstitutional in 1974 because the State Supreme Court found California was infringing on the powers of the federal government.

Migration from Mexico, while still comprised principally of single men, changed and a growing number of families and even single women became visible. Often the women were more adaptive to the urban industries such as clothing and food processing and were even more exploitable than Mexican men. Without the *Mexicanas'* labor the expansion or even maintenance of the garment industry would have been retarded and the process of moving the industry to other nations would have been accelerated.

According to Lamar Barington Jones' study of border cities such as Laredo, there is evidence "that citizens do suffer from active competition of alien workers. . . . Because of the pressure of *surplus labor* highly qualified workers can be secured for low wages."[59] This surplus labor led to surplus production which in turn yielded surplus capital, and in the quest for large profits growers played Mexicans off against Chicanos. Profit through employing Mexican labor—undocumented, commuter, or *bracero* led to protection of this commodity (labor) by industry and its manipulation through its brokers in government. However, the absence of Mexican labor would not insure automatic unionization or higher wages. Rather, it would accelerate mechanization. It is not Mexican labor that limits the number of jobs for domestic labor or depresses wages, but the owners of production, who profit from playing them off against each other. It would do very little good to fine employers since losses could be recovered by other means. It would also allow employers to discriminate further against Chicanos since they could use the excuse that they did not know whether they were documented or not.

Professor Vernon M. Briggs, Jr., University of Texas economist, is one of the principal proponents of fining employers. He says, "The massive flow of illegal immigrants has had, is having, and will continue to cause a serious disruption of the normal labor force adjustment processes throughout the Southwest and, increasingly, in a number of northern cities."[60] Although Brigg's research is solid, he has so narrowed his focus that he misses the total picture. If the objective is to raise the standard of living of Chicanos and other exploited workers, it would be better to focus on the historical exclusion of farm labor from the protections of the Wagner Act and on the limitations of the Taft-Hartley Law (1947) on the unionization of marginal industries. (Before passage of the Wagner Act industrial-based unions were small compared to what they are today and wages and conditions have improved considerably.)

Protection of the open shop by Taft-Hartley thwarted labor organization more than any other single act, and it is a matter of fact that workers in right-to-work states earn considerably less than closed-shop states. The passage of the California Agricultural Labor Relations Act has given agricultural workers a fighting chance. The best answer to depressed wages is to pass laws protecting unionization and minimum wages rather than to blame Mexicans.

An antipathy toward undocumented workers has in great part been manufactured by the INS and newspapers. Both have treated Mexicans as social problems rather than as part of the process of labor migration. Both have dwelt on "illegal aliens and the law," "illegal aliens and welfare," "illegal aliens and poverty," and in the process they have conditioned the public at large to perceive any one of Mexican extraction as a criminal, free loader, and loser. The INS released selective data which the newspapers only too enthusiastically and uncritically sensationalized. They have definitely followed patterns set in 1913, 1920–1921, the 1930s, and the 1950s: "The co-mingling [sic] of strategy and methodology is further revealed when the INS, as a matter of policy, seeks to intimidate aliens through the creation of public fear."[61] Newspapers did not bother to check the validity of INS research, but exploited its sensationalism. Professor Vernon Briggs accurately described the prevailing attitude: "As one government official, who has decried the widespread abuses and exploitations of aliens, has stated, 'nobody gives a damn since aliens are nobody's constituents.' "[62]

Current attacks began about the time "Operation Clean Sweep" started in May of 1972; the Justice Department investigated allegations of corruption within the INS. Critics charged that the investigations were biased since the INS is part of the Justice Department, and in fact the initial investigations were cursory and were in effect abandoned by September 1973. Further findings by investigative reporters and some persistent congressmen of a department coverup reopened a Pandora's box. The investigations were at the same time as the Watergate hearings which overshadowed charges of perjury, fraud, smuggling of drugs, abuses of undocumented aliens, and bribery. By June 1974, 54 persons had been indicted out of some 228 possible cases, with some involving high-ranking officers.[63]

Two Chicano investigative reporters, Frank Cruz, who at that time worked at KABC-TV in Los Angeles, and Frank Del Olmo, a reporter with the *Los Angeles Times,* uncovered many abuses, some of which were reported and others not. For instance, they found that Mexican bus companies that transported laborers paid kickbacks to INS officials; former INS officers set up offices and charged undocumented workers exorbitant fees; and INS officers sold immigration papers at four border cities for $100 to $200. On July 19, 1974 Del Olmo wrote that evidence existed as to corruption which implicated key members of the House Judiciary Committee charged with the investigation, including Congressman Peter Rodino (D-NJ). The allegations were especially embarrassing since that committee was currently embroiled in the impeachment proceedings. Del Olmo uncovered taped evidence that INS officials sought to compromise Rodino and other top-ranking officials by supplying them with Mexican prostitutes. INS officer Norman Summers of Yuma, Arizona, who was under indictment, told the subcommittee investigators that in 1971 he arranged entertainment in Mexico designed to compromise Rodino and that at another time entertainment was arranged for Gardiner J. Cline, associate counsel for the House Judiciary Committee. Summers further testified that it was common practice to compromise officials. Summers, a twenty-year veteran of the INS, was not taken seriously by investigators since he was under indictment and had tried to plea bargain in return for more information. The Justice Department in fact turned down an offer by Summers to tell all after pressure from the Judiciary Committee. Former Assistant Attorney General Leo M. Pellerzi corroborated this testimony. He testified that on three different occasions he had been offered prostitutes while making an investigation in June 1969, and one night after he had gone to his room a young Mexican girl was shoved into his room.[64]

On September 18 Robert L. Jackson charged in the *Los Angeles Times* that the "clean sweep," probe was "incompetent." He disclosed that Saúl Rodríguez, a Mexican attorney and undercover agent for "Clean Sweep," stated that he had given names of at least six border officers from whom he bought documents to the U.S. attorney in San Diego. Nothing was done and the officers were still working at the time of the testimony.[65]

Despite the explosive nature of the disclosures and the fact that they were never disputed, reporters did not follow up the story. Del Olmo was pulled off the story. Outside the *Los Angeles Times* scant attention was paid to the scandal. More and more the newspaper coverage focused on the "illegal alien," and on statements of General Leonard F. Chapman, Jr., the newly appointed INS commissioner. The uncritical reporting of INS data diverted public attention from INS corruption.

Dr. Gilbert Cardenas, a sociologist at the University of Texas, condemned the lax research methods of INS, Chapman's "roll your own" statistics based on "estimates," and the lack of an index of available data. He states that the INS gives no account of how data is obtained in concluding undocumented workers are a "menace" or that they have an "adverse effect" on the economy. Dr. Cardenas charged that the INS manipulated statistics and through a calculated campaign sought to intimidate aliens through fear. "The selective reporting of data by INS during these periodic campaigns serves to distract attention away from the harshness and illegal manner in which many aliens have been treated by the agency."[66]

In 1975 a *Washington Post* investigative reporter exposed Leonard Chapman's contradictions. He reported that Chapman's figures varied from 1.5 million to 12 million, depending on the audience that he addressed.[67] Chapman consistently sounded the themes that it was a national crisis, "illegals" displaced American workers, thus costing the taxpayers millions of dollars.[68] Naturally Chapman wanted more money for the INS to save America.

Human rights abuses of undocumented workers by the INS have just begun to surface. The *American G.I. Forum* in its October 1972 newsletter reported that a border patrol officer, Kenneth Cook, had picked up three Mexican women at the home of Mrs. Vera De León—Martha López, María Sándoval and Teresa Castellano. He took them to San Ysidro and ordered Sándoval and Castellano across the border. When they would not leave he threatened to harm López, 26, who had two children; he later raped her. In January 1973 in testimony before a Congressional committee it was reported that border inspectors conducted "vaginal and rectal searches."[69] In 1973 Santos Castellon De Jesús, while awaiting a hearing, was forced to leave his wife without protection and without funds. His requests for due process and an attorney were refused.[70] In December 1976 Hector Moreno, age 4, was taking a walk with a friend José Gonzales, 19, of the city of Commerce in California. INS made a sweep and the two found themselves in Tijuana.[71] In March 1974 border inspectors beat José and Virginia Gamboa of Arizona, Susan Gamboa of California, and Ramón and Romano Toriqueros of Arizona while crossing the border at Columbus, New Mexico. The concentration center at El Centro, California was severely criticized. Some 80,000 passed through the facility in 1972 alone. Jammed with as many as 1,000 prisoners it only had a capacity of 576. Detainees were forced to buy tickets to the interior. President Luis Echeverría finally complained: "There are flagrant violations of human rights of Mexicans who are in the United States as illegal aliens."[72]

Special interests exerted considerable pressure both in Mexico and the United States to renew the *bracero* program. Mexico's Foreign Minister Emilio O. Rabasa was reported to be strongly in favor of the program. At one point he said, "Americans don't like hard work." Rabasa pushed the *bracero* program as a solution to the current Mexican economic depression and entered into talks with Henry Kissinger. It was generally conceded that when presidents Gerald Ford and Luis Echeverría met in October that a new pact would be signed, but an unexpected change took place in Mexico. A growing number of intellectuals led by Dr. Jorge A. Bustamante of the *Colegio de México* convinced the Mexican President to meet with Dr. Ernesto Galarza. After these briefings, Echeverría reversed his position and decided the *bracero* program was not in the best interests of Mexico.[73]

The treaty would have allowed 300,000 *braceros* to work in the United States. Echeverría stated, "We cannot compromise ourselves in order to have a quota of workers every year. . . . The problem must resolve itself in Mexico. . . . It is the lack of land and water that has created the problem of *braceros*."[74] The change in policy neutralized the influence of Rabasa who was very pro-United States.

Legislators continued to concentrate on the presence of aliens rather than on abuses of them or on the real reasons for their presence. President Ford, addressing representatives of the Texas Mass Media Network, said on April 22, 1976; "The main problem is how to get rid of those 6 to 8 million aliens who are interfering with our economic prosperity."[75] Proposed legislative remedies followed the same pattern. The Rodino Bill, proposed in 1972, would have made it a felony to "knowingly employ undocumented workers and placed penalties which ranged from warnings to first-time offenders to fines and jail terms for repeated offenders."[76] The bill got through the House but died in the Senate. Senator Edward Kennedy proposed a similar bill which in addition granted amnesty to all aliens who had been in the country for at least three years. These bills did not pass partly because of the efforts of Chicano and progressive organizations and leaders. However, the principal reason that it did not pass was because Senator James O. Eastland, (Mississippi-D), a large grower and proponent of the *bracero* program, as chairman of the Senate Judiciary Committee, allowed the bills to die in committee.[77]

Congressman Joshua Eilberg (D-Pa) led the fight of imposing employer sanctions which to date have been unsuccessful. During the closing days of Congress in August 1976 Eilberg was successful in sneaking through a bill which reduced the quota of Mexican immigrants from 40,000 to 20,000. This law added a new bias in that it reinforces preference of professionals and scientists whereby the quota had previously been on a first-come first-served basis encouraging brain drain from Latin America.[78] It also eliminated the equity of U.S.-born children, who could now be deported and could return legally when they were of legal age.

Antagonism toward undocumented workers has increased in the Anglo and Mexican communities. In October 1977 George Gallup released a survey on attitudes toward workers without visas.[79] The response to the question of whether it should be illegal to hire aliens without visas was:

	SHOULD BE	SHOULD NOT	NO OPINION
National	72%	23%	5%
Whites	72	23	5
Nonwhites	70	23	7
College	73	24	3
High school	71	23	6
Graduate school	70	23	7
East	69	20	5
Midwest	74	23	3
South	72	19	9
West	74	23	3

SOURCE: George Gallup, "Majority: Deny Illegal Aliens Jobs," *Denver Post*, October 3, 1977.

Amazing is the uniformity of the responses: there is little variation among regions, levels of educational achievement, or racial groupings, all categories are within three points of the national average of 72 percent, and only a small percentage expressed "No Opinion."

Constant emphasis in the press on the "illegal" Mexicans and the threats they pose has generated anti-Mexican sentiment among Chicanos and Anglos alike. Consider the following sample of headlines which appeared in newspapers during 1976 and 1977:

Illegal Entrants Flock to U.S.—A New Poverty Class[80]
Can We Stop the Invasion of Illegal Aliens[81]
New Breed of Aliens Turn to Crime[82]
3.5 Million Jobs Lost to Silent Invasion of U.S.[83]
Police Study Calls Peaceful Image False[84]
200,000 at Tijuana Wait To Be Smuggled into U.S. by Deadline.[85]

Similar articles in national magazines and coverage on television reinforced these negative images. For example, on May 2, 1977 *Time* Magazine ran two articles; "Getting Their Slice of Paradise" and "On the Track of the Invader."[86] The first begins, "The U.S. is being invaded so silently and surreptitiously that most Americans are not even aware of it. The invaders come by land, sea, and air." It rehashed statistics supplied by the INS—that $13 billion a year was being spent on the "illegal alien" in social services with another $13 billion or more being sent out of the country. In the second article an immigration officer states that he can spot the illegals because "Most aliens are hungry, dirty, and walk with a nervous gait." The article then describes electronic sensing devices called "people sniffers." The same stories were given television coverage. The source for statistics was again the INS. The effect of the stories was again to create the feeling of invasion of criminals, free loaders, losers, and job thieves.

Although ignored by the press, studies have challenged the INS statistics. For example, David North and Marion Houston conducted the Linton Company study for the Department of Labor in 1975.[87] Their research covered 19 cities for the fiscal year 1974. The study is the most thorough that has been done and it dispels most of the myths manufactured by the INS. North and Houston found that 788,145 aliens were apprehended, 90 percent of whom were Mexican. The following table shows the occupational breakdown of the apprehended:

	WHITE COLLAR	CRAFT	OPERATIVE	SERVICE AND LABOR TOTAL	AGRICULTURE
Eastern Hemisphere illegals	48%	13%	27%	13%	1.2%
Western Hemisphere illegals	34	15	27	24	13
Mexican illegals	7	15	13	63	50
Total	18	15	18	80	39
U.S. Labor Force	49	13	16	27	4

SOURCE: David S. North and Marion Houston, "Illegal Aliens: The Characteristics and Role in the U.S. Labor Market." Study conducted for the U.S. Department of Labor by Linton and Co., Inc., November 17, 1975, p. 6.

The wage breakdown contradicts the INS data that Mexicans without visas displaced U.S. citizens in high paying jobs:

Eastern Hemisphere illegals	$4.08 an hour
Western Hemisphere illegals	$3.04 an hour
Mexicans	$2.33 an hour

SOURCE: David S. North and Marion Houston, "Illegal Aliens: The Characteristics and Role in the U.S. Labor Market." Study conducted for the U.S. Department of Labor by Linton and Co., Inc., November 17, 1975, p. 6.

The study also broke down the hourly wage by regions:

Southwest	$1.98
California	$2.60
Midwest and Northwest	$3.18
East Coast	$3.29

SOURCE: David S. North and Marion Houston, "Illegal Aliens: The Characteristics and Role in the U.S. Labor Market." Study conducted for the U.S. Department of Labor by Linton and Co., Inc., November 17, 1975, p. 7.

The study also found that only 4 percent of those interviewed had collected one or more weeks of unemployment insurance; 1.3 percent had gotten food stamps; 5 percent had collected welfare, and 7.6 percent had children in U.S. schools.[88]

In fact, every major study on the undocumented worker that employed scientific methodology reached the conclusion that the undocumented worker was not a drain on the economy. For example, Vic Villalpando's 1975 study for the San Diego County Board of Supervisors revealed that out of the 9,132 WR-6 welfare cases reviewed by the San Diego County Welfare Department, March 12 to September 16, 1975, only 10 involved people without visas; the yearly cost of providing welfare for the undocumented was $13,608. The county hospital paid $513,063 for medical care for the undocumented; out of a total of 107,563 bookings, 601 were classified as undocumented and "576 noted Mexico as their country of origin." Undocumented workers in San Diego County were estimated to earn a total of $34,560,000 in a year; they spent $20,736,000 in San Diego and sent $13,824,000 out of the country. These workers were estimated to have paid $6,768,000 in federal and state income taxes. They also paid state and local taxes and renter tax credits in property taxes (the county benefiting by $643,500). They paid social security taxes which were never collected.[89]

The hysteria generated by the media caused many incidents that are not narrated in studies. One such incident was the Hannigan case which happened near Douglas, Arizona. In the summer of 1976 George Hannigan, a local rancher and owner of Dairy Queens of Southern Arizona, and his two sons Patrick, 22, and Thomas, 17, kidnapped three Mexicans without visas who looked for work. They "stripped, stabbed, burned [them] with hot pokers and dragged [them] across the desert." They pretended to hang one of the Mexicans and even shot another with buck shot. Judge Anthony Deddens, a long-time friend of the Hannigans, declined to issue arrest warrants and disqualified himself from the case. The Hannigans, prominent in Cochise County Republican politics, had their trial postponed three times. In October 1976 a Bisbee jury acquitted the Hannigan brothers (the father had died in the interim) and although a large Mexican population lived in the area, not one Chicano sat on the jury. Mexicans on both sides of the border protested this violation of human rights, holding mass demonstrations in Agua Prieta, Nogales, and Tucson and boycotting U.S. merchants along the border. Chicano activists demanded federal intervention and justice.[90]

City and county agencies throughout the Southwest often use the undocumented workers as justification for asking for increased budgets. For example, Chief Ed Davis of the Los Angeles Police Department consistently said that undocumented workers were not a problem, but in a 1977 report he portrayed the undocumented aliens as a menace and claimed his department was understaffed. The report estimated the illegal population of the city at 650,000 and suggested that by 1981 it would be up to 1,110,000. These projections are ridiculous since the major portion of the Chicano population would be Mexican born which contradicts the U.S. census data as well as school statistics. The report underscored that "This alarming rate of increase in illegal alien population has a direct impact on police resources" and calculated that based on 2.65 officers per 1,000 citizens the department should have 1,703 more officers (the actual ratio was 2.14). According to these calculations taxpayers were cheated out of $37,050,000 annually by undocumented workers. The report claimed 36.3 percent of all felony arrests in Ramparts Division in one month were committed by the undocumented. The report emphasized that the peaceful image was not accurate, estimating that the undocumented worker committed 16 percent of all crime in the city.[91]

On May 24, 1977, Captain Rudy De León, Commander of the Hollenbeck Division of the LAPD, was interviewed by Frank Cruz on KNBC-TV. De León has a reputation as a firm, but honest man. He contradicted the police report and Chief Davis, and when asked whether the "undocumented aliens" had changed and if they were now more prone to crime, De León responded, "Absolutely not!"

Federal policies toward the undocumented have become more complex with the election of Jimmy Carter. Carter, while preaching human rights to the world, has not moved to cope with labor migration. In June 1977 his administration approved the certification of 809 undocumented workers to pick onions and cantaloupes for U.S. growers near Presidio, Texas. The Labor Department had been opposed to importation of workers, since it was not satisfied that growers paid the prevailing wage of $2.89 an hour or that proper housing was available. The INS was also reluctant. In allowing certification, the Justice Department violated regulations set up by the Labor Department. The action was called necessary in order to save a $6 to $12 million dollar crop. Carter ignored the fact that farmers had been paying $2.30 an hour instead of $2.89. The reaction of the press was interesting: "Presidio Farmers Watch Life Rot Away" and "Mexicans Stream Across Rio Hoping Their Names on List."[92]

Carter, caught in the middle between the nativist and Chicano and humanitarian groups, decided to continue past policies, that is, to continue what was basically a police action. On May 13, 1977 he replaced Leonard Chapman as INS commissioner with Leonel Castillo, a well-known and respected Chicano politician from Texas. Castillo, 37, had been comptroller of the city of Houston. From all reports, he was a good party man, and worked actively for the welfare of the Mexican community in the U.S. He had been active in the *Viva Kennedy* Campaign of 1960 and had served in the Peace Corps. Castillo walked into an impossible situation. He inherited a staff that was used to following established procedures for "tracking down" Mexicans. Moreover, since he held an appointed position (which brought with it a salary increase from $14,500 to $50,000 a year), his continuance in the political arena depended on satisfying Jimmy Carter. Also, the INS had established excellent ties with the House Judiciary subcommittee and especially its head Representative Joshua Eilberg, who had consistently voted for higher appropriations for INS and was a leading proponent in Congress to limit immigration from Mexico.[93]

Castillo, who had a sympathy for the plight of Mexicans (his grandfather had been an undocumented worker), soon learned that his humanitarian interests came into conflict with his new role as a policeman; being a party man he was conditioned to compromise. One of Castillo's first acts was to send 100 INS reinforcements to California, according to him, to help stem the tide and reduce violence. He stated "I hope to have within the next several months upwards of 1,000 additional workers." The *New York Times* reported, "Mr. Castillo said that he had other plans to strengthen border enforcement to curb illegal Mexican immigration." Castillo was sensitive to the Chicano community's concern over past INS sweeps, explaining that "he [was] considering the establishment of a countrywide force to crack down on persons who smuggle aliens into the country for pay."[94]

Chicano activists split over Castillo's appointments. Many stated that they should not criticize another Mexican and should give him a chance; others stated that the issue was not Castillo, but the policies of the Carter administration that he enforced. While Castillo's dilemma can be appreciated, the change in him must be noted. In a *U.S. News and World Report* interview on February 20,

1978, he continued his theme of concentrating on the coyote [smuggler], but added, "Last year we exceeded a million apprehensions. That's the highest since 'Operation Wetback', when the service carried out a major roundup of undocumented aliens in 1954." And while Chapman justified a larger budget for the INS based on the "silent invasion," Castillo justified it by pointing to organized crime (a large network of smugglers). Castillo stated that by 1979 he planned to have $300 million more and an additional 11,000 men.[95]

In the summer of 1977 Castillo* learned the limitations of his job when Carter finally unveiled his plan to deal with undocumented workers.* Essentially it was a watered down and expanded version of the Kennedy and Rodino bills, designed to satisfy everyone: (1) undocumented workers who had entered the United States before January 1970 and who had *continual* residence would be granted amnesty and would qualify for permanent status; (2) those who had entered after January 1970 would become temporary workers with a nondeportable status, but would be barred as permanent immigrants; (3) any employer "who engaged in a 'pattern or practice' of hiring undocumented workers became subject to civil penalties in the form of injunctions and fines of $1000 per hire"; any employer who defied the injunction would be subject to criminal prosecution; (4) after December 31, 1977, Mexican migration would not be tolerated, and to control the flow, 2000 or more border policemen would be hired; and (5) Mexico would receive a package of aid and loans to create jobs.[96]

The Carter plan came under immediate attack from Chicanos and human rights groups. They charged that the provision to grant amnesty for those in continual residence before January 1, 1970 was a sham. They had to prove length of residence by employer's payroll stubs, receipts, or similar documents and how many people keep these kinds of receipts for over eight years? Also, considering the proximity of the border, how many would not have gone to Mexico for a visit? Under the second provision of the plan those who entered after January 1970 had to rely on faith or trust alone and would be subject to deportation at the whim of U.S. authorities.[97] As to the sanctions against employers, it would be almost impossible to prove a pattern of noncompliance, and if the pattern were proved and a fine imposed the employers would pass the cost on to undocumented workers, and it would give employers an excuse to further reduce the workers' salaries and to discriminate against any brown person.[98] The plan to "control the flow" simply opened the way to more repressive police actions and massive roundups of undocumented workers. Finally, aid to Mexico would

---

*Castillo resigned his position in 1979 after considerable dissension within the INS. After his resignation, raids increased.

represent further U.S. economic penetration into Mexico which would actually accelerate the flow to the U.S. instead of stemming it.[99]

Agencies and individuals who assisted or supported the rights of the undocumented were subject to official harassment. They were likely to be charged with harboring aliens by the INS and the Justice Department. Prime targets were agencies which provided undocumented workers with free counseling and legal assistance. For example, in Spring 1976 INS officers broke into the office of *El Concilio Manzo*, a social service center in Tucson, Arizona. They confiscated files and arrested Marge Cowan, the director Sister Ann Gabriel Marcaisq, Margarita Ramírez, and Cathy Montaño. All four were charged with violating immigration laws for not reporting "aliens" to the INS.[100] The case was later dismissed.

On May 19, 1977, in Ontario, California, Dr. Armando Navarro called together selected leaders from California, New Mexico, and Texas to map out a national campaign and, although they broke up into essentially three groups with different programs, the thrust in all was the same: oppose the Carter plan. Navarro held his mobilization in December 1977, involving about 1,200 community people from the San Bernardino-Riverside area. He worked closely with church groups. José Angel Gutiérrez, who attended the Ontario meeting, issued a nationwide "Call to Action" which was directed mainly at the student and activist sector. He organized the National Chicano/Latino Conference on Immigration and Public Policies held in San Antonio, Texas, on October 28–30. Upwards of 2,600 people from throughout the United States attended. The significance of this mass demonstration is that poor people from every sector of the nation made considerable financial sacrifice to attend and to demonstrate their commitment. Chicanos from Milwaukee, Detroit, Chicago, and Los Angeles joined with Latinos from New York, Florida, Baltimore, and other places in an attempt to reach some sort of counter strategy. In terms of solidarity and the establishment of a communication network involving various groups within the Latino community from Marxists to conservatives, the conference was successful.

The Ku Klux Klan provided still another threat to activists. The Klan in Texas announced that it would patrol the border to stop the "rising flow of color washing over our border, [that is] washing away our culture, our racial fabric and changing America as we know it." In Texas Chicano activists patrolled the KKK, while the Mexican government threatened to send troops to patrol the border to make sure that the KKK did not violate its territory. In San Diego, California, 1,000 persons led by Herman Baca, Rodolfo "Corky" Gonzales, and Bert Corona marched on October 29, 1977 to rouse solidarity against the Klan. In contrast, the Justice Department, in spite of letters from leading politicians, did nothing.[101]

A SOLUTION TO THE PROBLEM

Foundations and public sources today have a new revived interest in the border and are currently heavily financing research projects. Ironically, the overwhelming majority of grants are not allotted to Chicano scholars who did much to stimulate research in this neglected area, but to U.S. historians who specialize in Mexican history and who have close ties with the U.S. government. The National Endowment for the Humanities heavily funded Arthur Corwin in the early 1970s to conduct a border study. These funds established Corwin as an expert on border history, and soon afterwards he began to attack the research of Chicano social scientists. In August 1973 he wrote "An Assessment" of works on Chicano history in which he crassly divided Chicano scholars into the good guys and the bad guys.[102]

On July 16, 1975 Corwin continued his assault on the Mexican community; in a letter from his Milford, Iowa, home he wrote to Henry Kissinger warning him about the third world menace. Corwin blamed the Mexican migration on social welfare and alleged that 40 to 50 percent of Mexicans in the United States received some form of public assistance. He prophesied that the United States would become a "welfare reservation" and that the Southwest would turn into a Chicano Quebec. Corwin proposed that INS be appropriated a billion dollars and that it hire 50,000 more officers to stop Mexicans. Fortunately, a Chicano scholar received a copy of the letter and passed it on to a Mexican social scientist who released it to the Mexican press. The contents caused an uproar, with Corwin becoming *persona non grata* in Mexico. Ironically, Corwin had been a favorite of the Mexican Office of Exterior Relations; he had been introduced to them by the U.S. State Department as an expert on Chicanos.[103]

Currently several academic networks specializing in border studies are operating; none are controlled by Chicano scholars. The most prominent is headed by Dr. Stanley Ross of the University of Texas at Austin. This group has the potential of monopolizing borderlands research since Ross has excellent private and public funding contacts. U.S. Secretary of Labor F. Ray Marshall is closely associated with this network and Chicano scholars have adopted a wait and see attitude.

Some scholars have taken a middle position on reduction of labor from Mexico, favoring a gradual leveling off. Their reasons are not the same as Carter's, since control of the flow is and always has been in the hands of U.S. authorities. The massive roundups of the 1930s and 1950s created untold hardships in Mexico.[104] The scholars are aware that an escalation of deportations and dumping of large numbers of undocumented workers into the Mexican interior would worsen the economic depression there, forcing Mexico into further concessions of its natural resources to the United States, while at the same time increasing the push northward. A sudden reduction in undocumented workers would cause a crisis in some sectors of agriculture since growers have intentionally depressed wages by forcing domestic labor out of the market. A labor shortage would pressure Washington, D.C. to pressure Mexico into a renewal of the *bracero* program, which is what growers have always wanted. Therefore, Mexico must be *eventually* freed of this dependency.

Mexican President José López Portillo stated that "They [the undocumented] aren't fleeing, they are looking for jobs" and advised that the United States should forget about police methods.[105] He recognized that the causes are economic; Mexico has more than 65 million people with a per capita income of $1,190—one-seventh that in the United States; half of the population is under 17; a 30 percent inflation and a trade deficit of $25 billion are worsening unemployment.[106]

Many experts feel that much of Mexico's plight can be attributed to U.S. economic policies. Along with the World Bank and the International Monetary Fund in 1974 it pressured Mexico to freeze wages, devalue the *peso*, and to develop its oil reserves for export. All these measures hit the working person hardest. Recently López Portillo received a $1.2 billion loan from the International Monetary Fund on the condition that (1) wage increases be held under 10 percent, (2) social service spending be cut in favor of increased subsidies to the business sector, and (3) employment in the public sector be held at 2 percent annually.[107]

Discovery of oil reserves in southern Mexico exposed more contradictions in U.S. policy, bringing out the fact that the United States does not want to curtail the flow of undocumented workers if it means lessening its control over Mexico. In 1974 the Mexican government announced that it had found reserves totaling 6.3 billion barrels of crude oil in Chiapas and Tabasco and estimated that the number might be as high as 75 billion. If the estimate proves true, Mexico would be second only to Saudi Arabia which has reserves of 170 billion barrels.

Mexicans looked to oil to save them from bankruptcy. The government made moves to join the Organization of Petroleum Exporting Countries (OPEC) which helps member nations get the maximum price. The United States was already importing two thirds of Mexico's daily export of 115,000 barrels and its stake increased. At a meeting of international bankers U.S. representatives told Mexico that it would frown on Mexico's membership in OPEC and would retaliate by eliminating Mexico's preferential trade position.[108]

In 1977 U.S. oil companies entered into an agreement with PEMEX whereby Mexico would build a 48-inch gas line from the oil fields to Texas, a distance of just over 800 miles. Tentatively they agreed to pay Mexico between $2.60 to $2.80 per 1000 cubic feet of natural gas. In his first state of the union address President Portillo boasted; "In today's world, countries can be divided into those who have oil and those who do not. . . . We have it."[109] He made the mistake of believing the United States; energy Czar James Schlesinger nullified the agreement.[110]

Mexico had counted too much on the fact that the United States had an insatiable lust for natural oil, consuming 42 percent of the world's natural gas.[111] The United States could wait since many of Mexico's debts matured in 1978. By December Mexico had built its gas line to within 100 miles of the Texas border and was stuck with a white elephant. Mexico rejected the U.S. offer of $2.16. Reynosa Mayor Romeo Flores Salinas summed up Mexican frustration: "The gas is not a renewable resource. When it's gone, there won't be anything else. For the good of the country, Mexico must hold out for its price."[112]

According to Dr. Wayne Cornelius, "The flow of illegals is likely to continue as long as reasonably attractive *alternatives* to migrating to the U.S. do not exist."[113] This means that the flow will continue as long as high unemployment exists in Mexico and wage disparities between the two nations push the Mexican workers north. A solution to these problems cannot be found until the United States stops manipulating the labor market to its advantage and discontinues draining both food and capital out of Mexico. The flow of undocumented workers will continue as long as the United States does not allow Mexico to evolve into a more efficient economic system, allowing it to make more efficient use of its resources and capital. In order to give Mexican workers alternatives, the Mexican government must redistribute land and not allow a small oligarchy of capitalists to control production; it must stop flow of profits and recycle them into the Mexican economy to create jobs and quicken industrialization. To accomplish this, many foreign companies must be nationalized. Mexico cannot continue to subsidize the private corporations by providing cheap electricity, fuel, and transportation. The people must derive the benefit of its oil profits. Those who expect to end the flow by increasing policing along the border or fining U.S. employers are unrealistic. The only way the labor flow from Mexico will stop is to create jobs there as well as eliminate the gap in wages between the rich and the poor. Capitalism cannot achieve these ends.

NOTES

1. John Phillip Carney, p. 20, "Postwar Mexican Migration: 1945–1955, with Particular Reference to the Policies and Practices of the United States Concerning Its Control" (Ph.D. dissertation, University of Southern California, 1957). Carney, p. 48, states that in 1950 an estimated 86 percent of the working population in Mexico made less than 300 pesos ($35) per month. In 1947 farm workers in

the interior of Mexico earned 38¢ a day; on the border they earned $1.10 a day.
2. Lyle Saunders and Olen E. Leonard, *The Wetback in the Lower Rio Grande Valley of Texas*, reprinted in Carlos E. Cortes, ed., *Mexican Migration to the United States* (New York: Arno Press, 1976), p. 165; Art Liebson, "The Wetback Invasion," *Common Ground* 10 (Autumn 1949): 11–19. Liebson, pp. 11–13, explores the reasons for the migration, the effect of cotton on the migration, and how weak labor unions affected the lack of regulation.
3. Nelson Gage Copp, "'Wetbacks' and Braceros: Mexican Migrant Laborers and American Immigration Policy" (Ph.D. dissertation, Boston University, 1963), pp. 79–80.
4. Carney, p. 122.
5. E. Idar, Jr., and Andrew C. McLellan, *What Price Wetbacks* (American G.I. Forum of Texas, Texas State Federation of Labor [AFL], Austin, Texas), reprinted in Carlos E. Cortes, ed., *Mexican Migration to the United States* (New York: Arno Press, 1976), pp. 28–29; Juan Ramón García, "Operation Wetback: 1954" (Ph.D. dissertation, University of Notre Dame, 1977), p. 194.
6. For the different perspectives of Mexican migration during this time, see Saunders and Leonard, p. 16; see Idar and McLellan for the AFL perspective on the undocumented worker; and see Copp, pp. 80–90, for a further statement of the liberal position. Also see García, p. 64.
7. Patricia Morgan, *Shame of a Nation* (Los Angeles: Los Angeles Committee for the Protection of the Foreign Born, 1954), p. 3; García, p. 76, 215.
8. García, pp. 215, 213.
9. Lamar Babington Jones, "Mexican American Labor Problems in Texas" (Ph.D. dissertation, University of Texas, 1965), pp. 25–26.
10. García, p. 317; Carney, p. 127.
11. García, pp. 216, 265–268, 275. See also the following works by Gilbert Cardenas: "United States Immigration Policy Toward Mexico: An Historical Perspective," *Chicano Law Review* 2 (Summer 1975); "A Theoretical Approach to the Sociology of Mexican Labor Migration" (Ph.D. dissertation, University of Notre Dame, 1977); "Public Data on Mexican Immigration into the United States: A Critical Evaluation," in W. Boyd Littrell and Gideon Sjoberg, eds., *Current Issues in Social Policy Research* (New York: Sage, 1976); and, with Esteban Flores, "Political Economy of International Labor Migration" (Prepared for the Joint Annual Meeting of the Latin American Studies Association and African Studies Association, Houston, Texas, November 1977).
12. García, pp. 189–190, 191–192, 209–210.
13. Ralph Guzmán, "Hunger Drives Wetbacks into U.S.," *Eastside Sun*, September 3, 1953.
14. García, pp. 214–215.
15. *Eastside Sun*, August 16, 1951, March 13, 1952, June 26, 1952. Morgan, p. 4, states that "the McCarran-Walter Law passed in the midst of the war in Korea and at the end of a five-year 'anti-alien' drive in which the U.S. Justice Department had suffered numerous court set-backs in seeking to deprive noncitizens of their constitutional rights."
16. Jethro K. Lieberman, *Are Americans Extinct?* (New York: Walter, 1968), 106, 109.
17. *Whom We Shall Welcome* (New York: Da Capo Press, 1970) includes an excellent analysis of the McCarran acts, published by the President's Commission on Immigration and Naturalization in January 1953.
18. Robert K. Murray, *Red Scare* (Minneapolis: University of Minnesota Press, 1955), p. 65.
19. Leo Grebler et al., *The Mexican-American People: Nation's Second Largest Minority* (New York: Free Press, 1970), p. 519. Grebler et al. state that "although the job-certification procedure was authorized in the 1952 Immigration and Naturalization Act for broad classes of immigrants from any country, it was implemented against Mexicans only."
20. *Whom We Shall Welcome*, p. 196.
21. *Whom We Shall Welcome*, p. 197.
22. *Whom We Shall Welcome*, p. 198.
23. *Whom We Shall Welcome*, p. 198.
24. "Hope Mendoza Gets Immigration Job Appointment," *Eastside Sun*, June 4,

1953. Ralph Guzmán, "Front Line G.I. Faces Deportation," *Eastside Sun*, June 30, 1953.

25. *Our Badge of Infamy*, A Petition to the United Nations on the Treatment of the Mexican Immigrant, American Committee for the Protection of the Foreign Born, April 1959, pp. 13–14.

26. Morgan, pp. 39–43; "Nacional-Mexico Americano [sic] Fights Deportation Move," *Eastside Sun*, March 13, 1952.

27. Morgan, pp. 44–45.

28. Morgan, pp. 45–47.

29. Joseph Eli Kovner, "The Tobias Navarrette Case," *Eastside Sun*, July 25, 1957.

30. *Eastside Sun*, August 8, 1957; *Eastside Sun*, August 29, 1957; George Mount, "Tobias Navarrette [sic], E.L.A. Humanitarian, Is Dead," *Eastside Sun*, September 6, 1964.

31. *Our Badge of Infamy*, pp. 36–38. One of the best studies is Ralph Guzmán, *Roots Without Rights* (Los Angeles: American Civil Liberties Union, Los Angeles Chapter, 1958).

32. "Jose Gastelum Free of Mexico Deportation," *Eastside Sun*, June 20, 1963.

33. "Deportation Is Meeting Topic," *Eastside Sun*, March 28, 1957, John F. Mendez, *Eastside Sun*, May 2, 1957.

34. Helen Taylor, "Wage at Stake," *People's World*, June 3, 1954.

35. *Our Badge of Infamy*, pp. iii–v.

36. Louise Año Nuevo Kerr, "The Chicano Experience in Chicago: 1920–1970" (Ph.D. dissertation, University of Illinois at Chicago Circle, 1976), pp. 157, 172. Dr. Kerr states that she conducted an extensive search to see what happened to Martínez. She believes he was deported.

37. Julian Samora, *Los Mojados: The Wetback Story* (Notre Dame, Ind.: University of Notre Dame Press, 1971), pp. 9, 39.

38. "Del Monte: Bitter Fruits," NACLA's *Latin America and Empire Report* 4, no. 7 (September 1976): 3–9.

39. Ed McCaughan and Peter Baird, "Harvest of Anger: Agro-Imperialism in Mexico's Northwest," NACLA's *Latin America and Empire Report* 10, no. 6 (July-August 1976): 10–11.

40. Carey McWilliams, "The Borderlands Let Justice Make Us Friends," *Fronteras 1976: A View of the Border from Mexico*, Proceedings of a Conference on Border Studies, San Diego, Calif., May 7–8, 1976, p. 3.

41. Copp, p. 16., states that Mexico has 494 million acres of land, of which 58 million are arable. In 1956, 22 million were actually harvested.

42. Ed McCaughan and Peter Baird, "Immigration Plan for People or Profit," *Immigration: Facts and Fallacies* (New York: North American Congress on Latin America, 1977), p. 12.

43. McCaughan and Baird, "Immigration Plan," p. 18.

44. Ed McCaughan and Peter Baird, *Carter's Immigration Policy: Attack on Immigrant Labor* (New York: North American Congress on Latin America, 1978), pp. 3–4.

45. Raúl A. Fernández, *The United States-Mexico Border* (Notre Dame, Ind.: University of Notre Dame Press, 1977), pp. 102, 108.

46. Peter Baird and Ed McCaughan, "Labor and Imperialism in Mexico's Electrical Industry," *NACLA Report on the Americas* 6, no. 6 (September-October 1977): 8.

47. Baird and McCaughan, "Labor and Imperialism," p. 8.

48. Morris Singer, *Growth, Equality and the Mexican Experience* (Austin: University of Texas Press, 1969), p. 31.

49. Cardenas, "United States Immigration Policy," pp. 81–82; quoted in Jones, p. 33.

50. Jones, pp. 35–36.

51. Jones, p. 37.

52. F. Ray Marshall, "Economic Factors Influencing the International Migration of Workers," in Stanley R. Ross, ed., *Views Across the Border* (Albuquerque: University of New Mexico Press, 1978), p. 169.

53. Fernández, pp. 132, 134; Victor Urquidi and Sofia Méndez Villareal, "Economic Importance of Mexico's Northern Border Region," in Ross, ed., *Views Across the Border*, pp. 147, 135.

54. Urquidi and Villareal, p. 148.
55. Urquidi and Villareal, p. 149; Fernández, p. 141.
56. Kerr, p. 177.
57. Urquidi and Villareal, pp. 144, 145.
58. Jorge A. Bustamante, "Commodity-Migrants: Structural Analysis of Mexican Immigration to the United States," in Ross, *Views Across the Border*, p. 129; Marshall, p. 165; Vernon M. Briggs, "Labor Market Aspects of Mexican Migration to the United States," in Ross, *Views Across the Border*, p. 216.
59. Jones, pp. 32, 70.
60. Briggs, pp. 215–216.
61. Cardenas, "A Theoretical Approach," pp. 97, 109, 119.
62. Briggs, p. 216.
63. Cardenas, "United States Immigration Policy," p. 86; Frank Del Olmo, "Probe of Possible Corruption Coverup Sought," *Los Angeles Times*, June 13, 1974; Frank Del Olmo, "Probe of Immigration Service Will Reopen," *Los Angeles Times*, June 18, 1974.
64. *Los Angeles Times*, September 13, 1974; Frank Del Olmo, "Rodino Reportedly Tied to Border Probe," *Los Angeles Times*, July 19, 1974; Robert L. Jackson, "Witness Says Border Agents Offered Him Girls," *Los Angeles Times*, August 14, 1974.
65. Robert L. Jackson, "Clean Sweep Probe Criticized as "Incompetent," *Los Angeles Times*, September 18, 1974.
66. Cardenas, "Public Data," pp. 3–5, 61.
67. *Washington Post* article quoted in Cardenas, "Public Data," p. 3 (no date noted). The *Congressional Digest* (January 1975): 8, states that in November 1974 Chapman estimated 10 to 12 million.
68. Marshall, p. 165.
69. *The Forumeer*, June 1972, reported a woman stripped and examined at the U.S.-Mexico border.
70. John Mosqueda and Frank Del Olmo, "Roundup of Illegal Aliens Stirs Angry Charges," *Los Angeles Times*, June 27, 1973.
71. "Kidnapped Boy, 4, Had Been Deported," *San Francisco Chronicle*, December 10, 1976.
72. Frank Del Olmo, "Alien Detention Center at El Centro Stirs Up Criticism," *Los Angeles Times*, February 24, 1974; "Blast at U.S. Over Illegal Aliens Rights," *San Francisco Chronicle*, September 2, 1976. *Albuquerque Journal*, March 1, 1977.
73. "Mexico Seeking to Allow Farm Workers to Enter U.S. Legally," *El Paso Times*, August 30, 1974; Stanley Meisler, "Echeverria Expected to Press Ford today on Bracero Issue," *Los Angeles Times*, October 21, 1974; Stanley Meisler, "Mexico Drops Goal of Migrant Pact with U.S.," *Los Angeles Times*, October 24, 1974.
74. *Los Angeles Times*, October 24, 1974.
75. Jorge Bustamante, "The Silent Invasion Issue," in *Fronteras 1976*, p. 17.
76. Briggs, p. 211.
77. Cardenas, "United States Immigration Policy," p. 84; Ronald Bonaparte, "The Rodino Bill: An Example of Prejudice Toward Mexican Immigration to the United States," *Chicano Law Review* (Summer 1975):40; Briggs, p. 221; Frank Del Olmo, "Softer Penalties in Alien Cases Urged," *Los Angeles Times*, April 20, 1977.
78. *U.S. News and World Report* (December 31, 1976); *Chicano Times* (San Antonio) October 29-November 11, 1976; Tirso Saenz and Emilio García Capote, "The Brain Drain in Latin America," *Granma* (Havana), June 5, 1977.
79. George Gallup, "Majority: Deny Illegal Aliens Job," *Denver Post*, October 3, 1977.
80. *Washington Post*, February 2, 1975.
81. *El Paso Times*, February 29, 1976.
82. *San Antonio Express*, May 30, 1976.
83. *Los Angeles Herald Examiner*, June 28, 1976.
84. *Los Angeles Times*, January 30, 1977.
85. *New York Times*, August 8, 1977.

86. *Time* Magazine (May 2, 1977): 26, 30.
87. David S. North and Marion Houston, "Illegal Aliens: Their Characteristics and Role in the U.S. Labor Market," study conducted for the U.S. Department of Labor by Linton and Co. (November 17, 1975), p. 6.
88. North and Houston, pp. 11, 15.
89. Vic Villalpando, "Abstract: A Study of the Impact of Illegal Aliens in the County of San Diego on Specific Socioeconomic Areas," in Antonio José Ríos-Bustamante, ed., *Immigration and Public Policy: Human Rights for Undocumented Workers and Their Families*, Chicano Studies Center Document no. 5 (Los Angeles: Chicano Studies Center Publications, University of California at Los Angeles, 1977), pp. 223–231; Also see Orange County Board of Supervisors (Task Force on Medical Care for Illegal Aliens), *The Economic Impact of Undocumented Immigrants on Public Health Services in Orange County*, March 1978. Jorge Bustamante, "The Impact of the Undocumented Immigration from Mexico on the U.S.-Mexican Economics: Preliminary Findings and Suggestions for Bilateral Cooperation," Forty-sixth Annual Meeting of the Southern Economic Association, Atlanta, Georgia, November 1976; and Wayne A. Cornelius, "When the Door Is Closed to Illegal Aliens, Who Pays?" *New York Times*, June 1, 1977.
90. *El Paso Times*, August 22, 1976; Patricia Bell Blawes, *People's World*, October 29, 1977; *Sin Fronteras*, October 1976; *Arizona Republic*, August 31, 1976; *People's World*, October 29, 1977; *Arizona Republic*, October 11, October 19, 1977.
91. John Kendall, "L.A. May Have 1 Million Aliens By 1981: Police Study Calls Peaceful Image False," *Los Angeles Times*, January 30, 1977, Illegal Alien Committee, "The Illegal Alien Problem and Its Impact on Los Angeles Police Department Resources," Los Angeles Police Department report, January 1977; Illegal Alien Committee, pp. 5, 9, 10.
92. Ralph Guzmán, "Ojinaga, Chihuahua Wetbacks," *Eastside Sun*, October 15, 1953. Neil Paulson, "Few Farmers, Rangers Favor Tightened Alien Jobs Plan," *Denver Post*, June 3, 1977, estimated that 90 to 98 percent of the apple crop at Hotchkins, Colorado, was picked by undocumented workers and that in sugar beet fields the going rate for domestic workers was $15.50 an acre, while undocumented workers were paid $10 to $12 an acre. It is evident that wages were manipulated, and if there had not been an abundant supply of undocumented workers there would have been overwhelming pressure on Carter from the growers to save the crops, not taking into consideration that the growers had intentionally depressed the wages. Guy Cook, in "Apple Growers May Seek Alien Okay," *Denver Post*, October 6, 1977, wrote that the apple growers around Grand Junction, Colorado sought an injunction preventing INS enforcement of laws against the use of illegal aliens. See also Tom Butler, *El Paso Times*, June 19, June 20, 1977.
93. James P. Sterba, "Tackling the Immigration Mess," *New York Times*, May 14, 1977; Castillo was the INS commissioner when Carter decided to allow the importation of Mexican labor at Presidio, Texas, in June 1977. See also James Reston, "The Silent Invasion," *New York Times*, May 4, 1977 and Marjorie Hunter, "Immigration Agency Engulfed in Trouble," *New York Times*, May 13, 1977.
94. James P. Sterba, "100 Border Patrolmen Rushed to California," *New York Times*, May 24, 1977.
95. "Why the Tide of Illegal Aliens Keeps Rising: Interview with Leonel J. Castillo, Commissioner INS," *U.S. News & World Report* (February 20, 1978): 33–35.
96. Jimmy Carter, "Undocumented Aliens: Message to Congress, August 4, 1977," in San Antonio José Rios-Bustamante, ed., *Immigration and Public Policy: Human Rights for Undocumented Workers and Their Families*, Document no. 5 (Los Angeles: Chicano Studies Center Publications, University of California at Los Angeles, 1977), pp. 52–57.
97. Wayne A. Cornelius, "A Critique of the Carter Administration's Policy Proposals on Illegal Immigration," Presentation to the Carnegie Endowment for International Peace, "Face to Face" Seminar, Washington, D.C., August 10, in

Ríos-Bustamante, *Immigration and Public Policy: Human Rights for Undocumented Workers and Their Families*, p. 85.

98. Cornelius, pp. 77–78.
99. The Illinois Migrant Legal Action program brought a class action suit in November 1976 for undocumented workers who had applied before January 11, 1977 and had been put on a waiting list. From July 1, 1968, to December 31, 1976, the INS had arbitrarily admitted Cuban "refugees" under the 120,000 quota. U.S. District Judge John F. Grady of Chicago found in favor of the undocumented workers and issued a restraining order prohibiting this deportation. See Ron Dusek, "Aliens Given Deportation Reprieve by Chicago Judge," *El Paso Times*, March 25, 1977; *Los Desarraigados*, Notre Dame University, (Winter 1976–1977): 9; and James P. Sterba, "Alien Ruling Snarls Migrant Job Inquiry," *New York Times*, August 14, 1977.
100. *Tucson Daily Citizen*, April 17, 1976; *The Arizona Daily Star*, April 4 and 22, 1976; *Sin Fronteras*, December 1976. In the spring of 1977, due to a public outcry, charges were dropped.
101. Robert Kistler, "No Effort to Block KKK 'Patrol' of Border Planned," *Los Angeles Times*, October 10, 1977; *CCR Newsletter* (San Diego), October 29, 1977.
102. See Arthur F. Corwin, "Mexican-American History: An Assessment," and Rodolfo Acuña, "Mexican-American History: A Reply," in Norris Hundley, Jr., ed., *The Chicano*, Santa Barbara: Clio Books, 1975).
103. Arthur F. Corwin, Letter to Kissinger, July 16, 1975, pp. 2–3, 20, 21, 39.
104. Cornelius, p. 75.
105. *U.S. News & World Report* (July 4, 1977): 28–29.
106. Harold K. Milks, "32 Million People Foreseen for Mexico City in 25 Years," *Arizona Republic*, February 9, 1977; Jorge A. Bustamante, "The Illegals: Americans Talk of Fences," *Los Angeles Times*, October 9, 1977; Richard Critchfield " . . . While Mexico's Villagers Look North With Hope . . . " *Los Angeles Times*, October 9, 1977.
107. McCaughan and Baird, "Carter's Immigration Policy," pp. 4–5.
108. *Rubio's Mexican Financial Journal* (August 5, 1976): 7–8.
109. Leonard Greenwood, "Mexican President Foresees Gains Through Oil Sales," *Los Angeles Times*, September 2, 1977.
110. Leonard Greenwood, "Mexico Says It Will Not Cut Gas Price for U.S.," *Los Angeles Times*, December 1, 1977.
111. Linda Gillam, " 'Subsidy' of Mexican Gas Hit by Texas Producers," *Los Angeles Times*, September 9, 1977.
112. "Mexicans Hold Out for Top Gas Price," *Los Angeles Times*, December 22, 1977.
113. Cornelius, pp. 7–8.

Chapter 8
Mexican Labor in
the United States

Some historians have generalized about the roots of the Chicano labor movement in the United States. They have assumed that Mexico was a feudal country which did not have a developed labor movement and that the Mexican *peons* came to the United States without a tradition of organized labor struggle. A white chauvinist perspective is that the Mexican peasant was politicized by the more progressive U.S. labor movement. While it is true that Mexico was a rural nation and that many Mexicans who migrated to the United States were from rural areas, they did not come to the north without a tradition of labor struggle. The roots of the Chicano labor movement are in Mexico. The Mexican Revolution was not solely a rural phenomenon; the proletarianization of Mexican workers in Mexico provided the spark for the revolutionary fires that swept Mexico after 1910. The ideas of Mexican radical intellectuals and activists were brought to the United States by many of these early migrants who influenced the struggle of Mexican workers in the United States through the 1930s.

THE ROOTS OF MEXICAN LABOR:
BACKGROUND AND COLLECTIVE ACTION

As early as 1823 Mexico had 44,800 miners and 2,800 textile workers.[1] In that year seven mills operated around Mexico City and by 1845 seventy-four textile factories functioned in the nation. Modernization with the use of mechanized cotton looms, accompanied this growth. By the latter part of the nineteenth century, many *hacendados* had become agribusinessmen; mechanization and improved transportation allowed them to put larger tracts of land into production and to ship the surplus to domestic and foreign markets. This encouraged further encroachment on Indian communal land as well as on small subsistence farmers. The Constitution of 1857 and the rise of the Liberal party greatly accelerated this so-called modernization. Thus, by the end of the nineteenth century, according to Professor Rodney Anderson, "Mexican land holders became less feudal lords and more landed capitalist."[2]

The Mexican proletariat class, still small, numbered only an estimated 365,000 workers; the middle class can be estimated at 213,000 rural and 776,000 urban members. By far the largest class was the agrarian workers with 7,853,000 *peones* living on *haciendas*. By 1910 68 percent of the Mexican labor force worked in agriculture and 16.3 percent in industry. Urbanization also increased and there were twenty-two cities of between 20,000 to 50,000, five of 50,000 to 100,000, and two of over 100,000.[3] The full force of urbanization and industrialization reached Mexico in the late nineteenth century. A network of rail lines and telegraph wires interconnected a once divided nation; rail lines increased from 400 to 15,000 miles and telegraph wires from 4,500 to 20,000 miles. New iron works, factories, smelters, meat packing companies, paper mills, and breweries were evident, with the number of textile mills increasing to 146. Mining of gold and silver jumped to a gross of $160 million by 1910.[4]

Exploitation of workers was brutal, and the state protected the industrialist class. Mexican workers reacted collectively and by the 1850s formed self-help groups in the form of mutual aid societies (*mutualistas*). These associations were popular among artisans of Mexico City and cotton textile workers. During the 1870s *mutualistas* often evolved into cooperatives and worker collectives. For artisans mutual aid societies became a means of protecting their economic and social status, whereas for workers they provided some sort of security through burial funds, savings, medical expenses, unemployment compensation, and pensions. Early workers' groups emphasized education, sponsoring night classes and libraries.[5]

The ideological perspective of the members was often mixed. The early efforts to motivate workers to act collectively were heavily influenced by the anarchist philosophy of Joseph Proudhon and Mikhail Bakunin. They were also influenced by the work of the Greek immigrant Plotino C. Rhodakanaty, who in the 1860s headed *El Grupo de Estudiantes Socialistas* (The Socialist Student Group), a group whose ideological approach could be called anarchist or libertarian socialist. Francisco Zalacosta, Santiago Villanueva, and Hermengildo Villavicencio, prominent members of the group, soon formed a secret cell (including women) called *La Social*, dedicated to organizing the proletariat. In 1865 they led the first industrial strike at the San Ildefonso and La Colmena cotton mills. Three years later, still under the leadership of Santiago Villanueva, anarchists led the first successful strike at La Fama Montanesa in Mexico City. Workers at other mills, inspired by this victory also struck when employers reduced their wages. The Juárez government backed management and abrogated progressive labor laws passed under Maximilian. The Juárez administration attempted to infiltrate the *mutualistas* by granting them annual stipends, but the anarchist faction opposed any government support or sponsorship.[6]

In the mid-1860s Rhodakanaty and Zalacosta founded a workers' school, *La Escuela Moderna y Libre*, at Chalco, working primarily with the peasantry. Julio Chávez López, a student, formed the Socialist Club (as the anarchists called themselves) and called for a revolution to overthrow the Juárez government. He led an uprising in 1869, but was caught and executed. Meanwhile, Villanueva incorporated *mutualistas* of the Valley of México into *El Gran Círculo de Obreros de México* (The Great Center of the Workers of Mexico) with the purpose of eventually establishing a national labor central. Thirty-two thousand textile workers belonged to the *Gran Círculo* in 1873; two years later it had twenty-eight branches in twelve states including the Federal District. Within the *Gran Círculo* the anarchists and the moderates disagreed over the issue of government subsidies. The anarchists held that "the total emancipation of the working class" was to be achieved only through revolution and not through any dealings with the government. The moderates wanted "to reform through legislative action."[7]

The *Gran Círculo* called the first Mexican workers' congress in 1876. Anarchists through *La Social* participated in this congress, sending women delegates. The next year farm workers formed *El Primer Congreso Campesino de la Ciudad de México* (The First Congress of Farm Workers of Mexico City). The second workers' congress was held in 1879; Carmen Huerta, a *Mexicana*, served as its president. Meanwhile, the Mexican government made numerous efforts to curtail organizing activities among workers. When a faction of the *Gran Círculo* backed the opponent of President Porfirio Díaz's puppet, General Manuel González, the organization was physically crushed.[8]

Strikes occurred chiefly in mining, railroad, and tobacco industries. Textile manufacturing had escalated Orizaba into a metropolitan area of nearly 100,000. A group of French capitalists owned the majority of the textile mills. For self-protection workers had formed two *mutualistas—La Sociedad de Soccoros Mutuos* and *El Círculo Liberal Mutualista*. As conditions worsened in 1906 workers met to discuss deteriorating relations at the mills, and took the name *El Gran Círculo de Obreros Libres* (GCOL).[9] Much of the leadership enjoyed contacts with the *Partido Liberal Mexicano* (PLM).

Organization included women and children employed in the mills. In Mexico City and Puebla the majority of workers were male, but in northern Mexico, where a scarcity of labor existed, women and children were in the majority.[10] Conditions at all the factories were oppressive with children of 8 years of age often working 16-hour shifts. Many children joined union activity at an early age. For example, María Díaz started working in the mills around Guadalajara at the age of 8 in 1904. After being dismissed at age 12 for union organizing, she moved to another factory to organize workers there. During the Mexican Revolution she continued to support progressive elements.[11]

Throughout 1906 union organizers recruited textile workers; by June the Mexican government arrested *Gran Círculo* (GCOL) leaders. During the fall of that year a series of small strikes were called which the GCOL strike fund supported. Díaz's policies hardened; mill owners also became more militant and in December they reduced the workers' wages. The owners formed an employers' association, and severely restricted the workers' freedoms by forbidding them to read the newspaper or to have house guests without permission. When workers protested mill owners locked them out. Thirty thousand workers were involved at Orizaba alone. Finally, Díaz intervened and on January 4, 1907, he ordered employees to return to the mills.[12]

At the Rio Blanco mill workers refused to return to work. On the morning of January 7 they congregated in front of the mill, blocking entrances. The men marched on the company store. The reason for the march is clear: The company store at the foreign-owned mills had become the "most hated symbol of capitalist exploitation and foreign domination."[13] The incident that set off the march is unknown, but a popular account is that women led by Margarita Martínez and Isabel Díaz de Pensamiento had been insulted that morning by clerks at the store. They went to the strikers and harangued them into action.[14] When the clerks panicked, fired on the marchers, and killed a number of them, the angry workers looted and burned the store. Authorities arrested many workers and pursued and killed others.

Federal troops arrived on January 8. As workers prepared to return to work the next day, federal authorities marched six prisoners to the burned company stores and shot them as their comrades watched. Soldiers shot a seventh worker at Río Blanco when he defiantly cursed the executioners, "unable to contain his rage at what he had seen." In total about 150 workers and 25 soldiers were killed.[15]

In Cananea, Sonora, a group of thirty miners formed *La Unión Liberal Humanidad* in January 1906. Its charter members belonged to the Liberal Club of Cananea, an affiliate of the PLM. Workers had grievances against the Consolidated Copper Company (a subsidiary of Anaconda) including the fact that Anglos worked eight hours while Mexicans labored for ten to twelve hours at half the Anglo wage. On the evening of May 31 Mexican workers walked off the Oversight mine, demanding 5 pesos for an 8 hour day. Two thousand miners joined the strike. Sonoran governor Rafael Izábal sent state militia to support mine owner Colonel William C. Greene. Mexican miners were unarmed while Greene's men were heavily armed. Tempers rose and when William Metcalf, a company lumber yard employee, killed three demonstrators, workers burned the lumber yard. Arizona Rangers crossed the international line to help Greene. Díaz ordered his henchman General Luis Torres into the area. He immediately issued an ultimatum to miners—go back to work or get drafted into the army. Torres arrested a hundred men and sent dozens to prison.[16]

In July of that year mechanics on the Mexican Central Railroad in Chihuahua struck the line. Workers shut down repair shops from the border to Mexico City, and by mid-August the strike involved 1,500 mechanics and 3,000 other railroad employees. As expected, Díaz ordered workers to return to work, charging that they had violated the Constitution of 1857.

Injustices at the mills, mines, and railroads were mirrored in other industries and in the countryside. Another facet of the modernization was improved communication, through an increase in newspapers, easier transportation, and concentration of workers in urban areas and company towns. The improved communication network facilitated the spread of knowledge of injustices throughout urban centers and rural areas.[17]

PRECURSORS TO THE CHICANO LABOR MOVEMENT

Mexican *mutualistas* influenced the founding of similar organizations throughout the Southwest, serving as the springboard to collective action. By the late 1880s Mexicans in the United States worked on railroads for as little as 50¢ a day; they tended sheep for $6.00 to $8.00 a month. They worked in the mines of Arizona and Colorado and gradually followed the cotton harvest in Texas and other southwestern states. In most cases they did work that white men would not, and were paid half of what the white man earned.[18]

One of the first national labor figures of Mexican extraction was Lucy Eldine Gonzales from Johnson County, Texas. Most historians list her as Mexican-Indian; a current biographer raises the possibility that she may also have been part black. Lucy Gonzales married Albert Parsons, who was executed as a conspirator in the Haymarket Riot of 1886. Lucy was an avowed anarchist who published newspapers, pamphlets, and books, traveled and lectured extensively, and led many demonstrations. In the 1870s she was a charter member of the Chicago Working Women's Union, and in 1905 she was a founding member of the Industrial Workers of the World (IWW). Twenty-two years later she was elected to the National Committee of the International Labor Defense. Lucy believed that "the abolition of capitalism would automatically produce racial and sexual equality." Despite her involvement in national and international issues, she did not directly participate in the organization of Mexican workers.[19]

An early labor organizer in the Southwest was Ricardo Flores Magón, born in Oaxaca in 1873. He crossed into the United States on January 4, 1904 with the intention of agitating for the overthrow of Díaz, but treatment of *Mexicanos* in the United States so embittered him that for eighteen years he worked in their behalf. Flores Magón and his followers in the United States published the PLM's newspaper *Regeneración* which by 1906 had a circulation of 30,000 in Mexico and the United States.[20]

In Arizona Rangers confiscated letters linking Flores Magón with strike activity there. He and two comrades spent eighteen months in a Los Angeles jail, awaiting extradition. In March 1910 Flores Magón and his cohorts resumed publication of *Regeneración,* reporting bad working conditions, discrimination, police brutality, and lynchings. In 1911 the courts sentenced Flores Magón to three years. After his release he continued to agitate and in March 1918 issued a manifesto calling for a world anarchist revolution. The courts sentenced him to twenty years and his comrade Librado Rivera to fifteen years for violation of U.S. neutrality acts. "True to their anarchist principles, Rivera and Flores Magón refused all such support. When [Alvaro] Obregon finally gained U.S. approval of their return to Mexico in November 1922, Ricardo Flores Magón mysteriously died in his cell—murdered, according to Rivera."[21]

Many PLM leaders organized among Mexican workers in the United States. Práxedis G. Guerrero stood out; born in León, Guanajuato, in 1882, he dedicated his life to organizing the oppressed. Guerrero worked as a miner in Colorado and as a woodcutter in San Francisco. In 1905 he joined the PLM, and in 1906 he organized *Obreros Libres* in Morenci, Arizona. Guerrero took special interest in Mexicans in the United States and contributed articles to *Regeneración.* On December 30, 1910, Guerrero was killed in a clash between federal and PLM troops at Janos, Chihuahua.[22]

In the tradition of *La Social,* women enjoyed equality within the PLM and *Regeneración* carried countless articles about their participation in the movement. For instance, in Laredo, Texas, Sara Estela Ramírez was a staunch supporter of Flores Magón and participated in union activity. A socialist, she worked for the Federal Labor Union and *La Sociedad de Obreros, Igualdad y Progreso,* a mutual aid society formed in the mid-1880s.[23] In San Marcos, Texas, in 1913 Elisa Alemán of San Antonio gave a speech urging women to participate in the PLM.[24] In the 1911 invasion of Baja California Margarita Ortega acted as a messenger and gun runner and crossed enemy lines to care for the wounded. She and her daughter, Rosaura Gotari, were exiled to the United States where authorities hounded the two women. Rosaura died, and Margarita, with her comrade Natividad Cruz, returned to struggle; both were captured and executed.[25]

THE BEGINNINGS OF THE MEXICAN
LABOR MOVEMENT IN THE UNITED STATES

The Southwest during the early twentieth century was still relatively undeveloped. Southwesterners worked principally at occupations involving the soil and subsoil. Except in California Mexicans remained the core of workers involved in manual labor.[26]

Arizona miners traveled to El Paso as early as 1872 to recruit Mexican labor. Mexicans took jobs in coal and copper mining operations which others refused, chopping timber, doing general clean-up work, and performing pick and shovel work. Mines in northern Mexico attracted workers from the interior. These mines, most of which were owned by U.S. capital, served as a stepping-stone into the United States and kept mines there supplied with experienced labor.[27]

Mexicans in Texas had been employed as *vaqueros* during the nineteenth century, but the agricultural revolution was underway. The open range disappeared by the 1870s and wire fencing during the next decade raised the price of land. In the Rio Grande Valley Mexican workers cleared brush and planted cotton and winter vegetables. In Nueces in 1900, 107,860 head of cattle roamed the land, whereas twenty-five years later the number of cattle had dwindled to 10,514; in Dimmit County cattle declined from 74,641 to 7,334 during the same period. Migrant farm laborers thus displaced *vaqueros.* Tenant farmers became common during the first two decades of the twentieth century in Texas with one-third of the land worked by sharecroppers.[28]

Cattle ranches had dominated much of the area in the 1880s; this changed with the arrival of railroads (see Chapter 2). At the turn of the century extensive irrigation projects and commercial farming radically changed south Texas.[29] Commercial farming introduced a paternalistic system of open racism, social segregation, and sharecropping. Commercialized farms began around 1904 with the arrival of large land companies which brought in small farmers. Many larger ranches were subdivided and sold to these new settlers. The digging of artesian wells and utilization of Mexicans with flamethrowers to clear the land of mesquite converted the valley into cash-producing farm areas, with fast profits made on cotton and vegetables.[30]

Many farmers owned plots of between 80 and 160 acres; one man could cultivate 40 to 50 acres and rent the remaining land to a tenant or two. White tenants got land and contracts superior to those offered to Mexicans. Whites received two-thirds of the profits from vegetables and three-quarters of the profits from cotton. Mexicans generally received only half the profits, an arrangement which greatly favored the owner. Farmers offered Anglos larger sections than *Mexicanos,* and often the Anglo tenant would sublease to Mexicans or other whites. Many white landlords did little work with Mexicans performing most of the manual labor. The system had many abuses. Many growers forced Mexican sharecroppers to leave when it appeared that they had a good crop by withholding credit, harassing them, or calling the border patrol. White tenants averaged $3,750 compared to $500 a year for Mexicans during the 1920s.[31]

On farms over 500 acres, contractors furnished Mexican crews from border towns. Few Mexicans owned farms during the early 1900s, but some acquired 40 to 50 acres in the 1930s. Up to the late 1920s cotton was the area's main crop but after this spinach and other vegetables took a great share of the market. By the mid-1920s Mexicans began to move off *ranchos* to *colonias* which served as a base for their migrant way of life. Such a life style took Mexicans to California, Colorado, and Michigan.[32]

The Dingley Tariff of 1897 caused the sugar beet boom in the United States by placing a high duty on imported sugar. Sugar beet companies in Colorado, Kansas, and California quadrupled between 1900 and 1907. To ensure a large supply of produce sugar beet refineries made contracts with farmers, promising them an ample supply of cheap labor. Companies such as the Holly Sugar Company and the American Sugar Beet Company recruited and transported large numbers of Mexicans to farms throughout the Southwest, Northwest, and Midwest.[33] The Mexicans increasingly displaced Germans, Russians, and Belgians in sugar beets. The Minnesota Sugar Company (now the American Crystal Sugar Company) provided transportation, housing, and credit and moved Mexican workers to the Chaska and Savage areas of the state. By the winter of 1912 a Mexican *colonia* formed on the west side of St. Paul where Mexican beet workers found refuge from the harsh winters.[34] In 1909 the Great Western Company in Colorado alone employed 2,600 Mexican beet workers.

The growth of agriculture was further encouraged by the Newlands Reclamation Act of 1902 which authorized construction of large dams and furnished a reliable and inexpensive supply of water. This act was originally intended to ensure the Jeffersonian dream of a nation of small farmers. It limited the number of acres that could be subsidized and after ten years those possessing acreage in excess of 160 acres had to sell at pre-dam prices, with no family able to possess more than 480 acres. The owner of the property had to reside on the farm. In practice the law was never properly enforced. As the supply of water allowed new land to be cultivated, new towns sprang up.

Agriculture grew in other areas; for example, in 1904 Kingsville, Texas, did not exist; ten years later it was a town of 3,000 residents. Life centered around a machine shop and a railroad roundhouse. Nearby in Corpus Christi sheep and cattle gave way to cotton, vegetables, and pecans. In Nueces County growers produced 498 bales of cotton in 1899; eleven years later 8,566 bales were grown. Changes generated a demand for more Mexicans.[35]

In 1907 the *California Fruit Grower* magazine advised its readers that Mexicans were "plentiful, generally peaceable, and are satisfied with very low social conditions." The next year the first commercial cotton was harvested in the Imperial Valley of California. Improved refrigerated railway cars, more sophisticated canning and food preservation techniques also contributed to the agricultural revolution in the Southwest. From 1907 to 1920 orange and lemon production in California quadrupled; between 1917 and 1922 cantaloupes doubled, grapes tripled, and lettuce quadrupled. Such unprecedented production intensified the need for Mexican labor in California agriculture.[36]

Although agriculture was overtaking sheep raising, the wool industry was also expanding. In 1850 the Southwest produced 32,000 pounds of wool; thirty years later it increased to 4 million pounds. Again the demand for Mexican shearers and shepherds increased as production zoomed.[37] Mexican labor also worked in the lumber industry.

During this period there was limited mobility for Mexican workers. An Anglo-American mechanic conceded, "They will never pay a Mexican what he's really worth compared with a white man. I know a Mexican that's the best blacksmith I ever knew. He has made some of the best tools I ever used. But they pay him $1.50 a day as a helper, working under an American blacksmith who gets $7 a day." Woman and child labor was confined to agriculture. Most Mexicans worked in farming, mining, and on the railroad, but they began to migrate to the cities with places like Los Angeles becoming urban centers.[38]

Industrial expansion in the East created a demand for natural resources while the railroad provided linkage to centers of distribution. As the railroads spread from Mexico City to Chicago, it played a key role in the dispersion of Mexicans, with Los Angeles, San Antonio, El Paso and Kansas City becoming distribution centers. Colonies set up by railroad crews where they worked later were raided by farmers and ranchers for labor. For example, the first Mexican colony was established in Fort Madison, Iowa, by 1885. In Kansas City in 1907 30 percent of the laborers had left the railroad for the wheatfields. The same process occurred with desertions to cotton.[39]

Unions often perceived Mexicans as enemies and made little effort to organize them. Generally Mexicans earned lower wages and in addition they were often used as strikebreakers. The American Federation of Labor openly discriminated against Mexicans and many of its affiliates, such as the Texas Federation of Labor, proposed a limitation on Mexican immigration. Even at this time

American labor took great pains to separate itself from anything that might appear radical. In fact "often the Texas Federation of Labor belligerently joined management in efforts to defeat Chicano strikes." Most Anglo miners condemned Mexicans as scabs and refused to work with them, much less admit them into their unions. They claimed Mexicans were careless and exercised bad judgment.[40]

As Mexican workers settled, they protested poor working conditions and low wages. In 1903 Japanese and Mexican workers in Oxnard, California, protested the practices of the Western Agricultural Contracting Company. The company withheld a percentage of the worker's salary until the end of the contract. Workers were charged for unnecessary services. They were paid in scrip and thus were forced to buy at the company store at inflated prices. The beet workers formed the Japanese-Mexican Labor Association and after a series of meetings struck on February 28, 1903. From the beginning "the growers, the major contractors, major businessmen, the judges, juries, sheriffs, and officials," all of whom were Anglo, united to oppose workers.[41] On March 23 an armed conflict broke out and Luis Vásquez died of shotgun wounds.

Workers won a limited victory with the concession that union members be employed on the majority of the contracting companies' farms. After the strike they formed the Sugar Beet and Farm Laborers Union of Oxnard and petitioned the American Federation of Labor for affiliation. Samuel Gompers, president of the AFL, turned down the request unless the membership guaranteed that Chinese and Japanese would not be admitted, but the Mexican workers refused to abandon their Japanese comrades.[42]

In 1903 Mexican workers at the Johnston Fruit Company in Santa Barbara, California, struck for higher wages and shorter hours. Lemon pickers and graders demanded the lowering of the 10 hour day to 9 hours. When demands were not met, they walked off the job, paralyzing operations. It was at the height of the season and workers got their 9 hour day and overtime. It was the first time that Mexican workers had stopped production in the area.[43]

Mexican workers in the spring of 1903 struck Henry E. Huntington's Pacific Electric railway. Mexican track workers had formed *La Unión Federal Mexicana* (the Mexican Federal Union). A. N. Nieto served as executive secretary and it had 900 track workers, a bank account of $600, and headquarters in Sonoratown (as the Mexico *barrio* was called). They demanded a raise from 17.5¢ an hour to 20¢ an hour, 30¢ an hour for evenings, and 40¢ an hour for Sundays. While company officials at first acceded to demands, Huntington countermanded the agreement, and 700 Mexican workers walked off the job, leaving only 60 "Irishmen, negroes and whites." The Los Angeles Merchants and Manufacturers Association and the Citizens Alliance joined with Huntington to fight trade unions and to keep Los Angeles as an open shop city. They recruited Mexicans from El Paso to replace strikers. Huntington raised salaries of scabs to 22¢ an hour—2¢ more than the union demanded. And even though the union gained the support of Samuel Gompers and Eugene Schmitz, the San Francisco Union Labor party mayor, as well as contributions from the Los Angeles Council of Labor and the local chapter of the Socialist party, it lost. Anglo car men belonging to the Amalgamated Association of Street Car Employees planned a walkout on April 29, but only 12 of 764 walked out. Failure of Anglo-American workers to support the Mexican strike doomed it.[44]

A year later *La Unión Federal* protested a reduction in pay from $1.75 a day to $1.00. Pacific Electric claimed that the cut represented what workers owed the company for housing. The rents were double the going rate and the housing was in a deplorable state. Dr. J. Powers of the Los Angeles County Health Department called it a "menace to public health and a disgrace to civilized communities." Another unsuccessful strike against the railway company was in 1910.[45]

In 1901 200 Mexican construction workers struck the El Paso Electric Street Car Company for higher wages. The company hired Juárez residents to replace strikers. After negotiations the company agreed not to hire outsiders, but refused to increase wages. El Paso police helped the company to break the strike by protecting strikebreakers. Workers struck again in 1905.

Two years later 150 smelter workers in El Paso walked off the job demanding a raise from $1.20 to $1.50 a day. They won a 20¢ a day pay increase, but the company had hired nonunion workers in the interim and refused to fire them. Disgusted, about half the strikers left for Colorado.[46]

In 1907 1,600 Chicano workers struck the Texas and Pacific Company in Thurber, Texas, for better working conditions including an 8 hour day, "the removal of company fences around the town and the removal of armed guards." The United Mine Workers supported strikers who won an increase in wages, an 8 hour day, and bi-monthly pay periods.[47]

In Laredo, Texas, in 1905 Chicano workers formed the Federal Labor Union representing various skilled and nonskilled workers in the Mexican Railway Company shops located in that city. It served cooperative and trade union functions. The union published a newspaper, *El Defensor del Obrero*, to educate workers and the public. In November 1906 it called its first general strike, demanding an increase from 75¢ to $1.00 per 10 hour day. When Mexican workers pointed out that Anglo workers had received similar concessions, the railway responded that there was a difference between the two races. After a hard fight, the company finally acceded on February 8, 1907, to a 25¢ a day raise, but reserved the right to retain strikebreakers. Some of the union members refused to return to work.

The Federal Labor Union of Laredo then organized miners, chartering Mine Worker's Union Local 12340. A month after settlement of the railway strike, Chicano smelter workers walked off the job. When the Mexican Railway Union threatened to call a general strike in support of the strikers, the mining company settled. Conditions on the railway deteriorated and in March members voted a general strike. The Federal Labor Union failed to organize a wide enough base and the general strike failed. When the Mexican Railway Company moved across the line to Nuevo León, Tamaulipas, the Federal Labor Union died.[48]

STABILIZATION OF THE MEXICAN WORKER POPULATION

Heavy Mexican migration to the United States continued during the second decade of the twentieth century, with Mexican workers finding employment in iron, auto factories, packinghouses, and agriculture. El Paso continued as the principal distribution center with six employment agencies.[49] Although this new wave destabilized the Mexican community, sufficient numbers had entered the United States during the previous decades to allow substantial numbers to root and settle into industries that required year-round employment. It was in those sectors of the economy that the pattern of resistance was the most intense.

Mexicans migrated to Los Angeles in great numbers and as the population settled, strike activity increased. In August 1910 workers, 90 percent of whom were Mexicans, struck the Los Angeles Gas Works for higher wages. They were influenced by the IWW. After two weeks the company settled for $2.25 a day and agreed to hire union members. *Magonistas* (followers of Flores Magón) actively participated in Los Angeles Mexican politics and labor circles. For instance, *La Liga Pan-Americana de Trabajo* was led by Julio Mancillas (secretary), Francisco B. Velarde (organizer), and Lazaro Gutiérrez de Lara (treasurer). *La Liga* operated a socialist library and center for study and discussed the role of the Mexican proletariat at its meetings.[50]

In 1911 California State Federation of Labor organizer Juan Ramírez helped form *La Unión de Jornaleros Unidos* Local 13097 with *Magonista* Amelio B. Velarde as its secretary. It affiliated with the AFL and actively organized migrants and unskilled workers in the Long Beach and San Pedro areas. In San Antonio, Texas, in that same year *La Agrupación Protectiva Mexicana* (the Mexican Protective Association) was organized. Its goals were to protect Mexicans from increasing racism and violence and to organize farm workers. It functioned as a *mutualista* and its membership included property owners, shopkeepers, and tenants. Differences between moderates and radicals eventually contributed to the association's demise in 1914.[51]

In Texas land monopolization and large-scale agriculture by 1910 eliminated tenant farming, leaving many homeless. The Socialist party organized renters and assigned J. A. Hernández to work with Mexicans. His organizational efforts were compromised by limited funds, the size of Texas, and the harshness of police reprisals. Texas authorities arrested union members on charges of sedition and deported others. They justified repression by falsely linking the Socialist party to Ancieto Pizaña (see Chapter 10) and successionist aspirations of many Chicanos. Moreover, Socialist party influence declined because of white chauvinism and racism of some of its members and the inconsistency of many of its programs.[52]

Important to Mexican workers was the IWW whose agitation was primarily among the casual workers. It had been organized in Chicago in 1905. The International grouped trade unionists of all political stripes under its umbrella, but by far anarchists were the most energetic. The anarchists had close ties with the PLM. The most dramatic strike involving the Wobblies was the "Wheatland Riot," of August 3, 1913, at the Ralph Durst Ranch in Wheatland, California.

Durst needed between 1,000 and 1,500 workers, but advertised for double the number, intentionally creating a large excess labor pool to depress wages below subsistence level. It was a recession year and hungry people of all nationalities were there; Mexicans were in the minority. Conditions in the fields were horrible. Durst's relatives even sold the hop pickers lemonade. A third of the workers were women and children; the 12 hour day began at 4 A.M. and wages were $1.50 a day; 78¢ to $1.00 a day was withheld from the workers' pay and if they did not complete the season, they lost the withheld portion. Durst intentionally attempted to make workers leave the fields and constantly cheated and insulted them. Police authorities and the Burns Detective Agency harassed the workers.

The workers organized and presented demands to Durst: "water twice a day, separate toilets for women and men and a $1.25 a hundred [pounds]." Richard "Blackie" Ford, a member of the IWW, emerged as a strike leader. While he addressed the workers, the local sheriff and a group of a hundred or more vigilantes attempted to arrest Ford; when the sheriff fired into the crowd of workers and wounded one, the crowd exploded. During the ensuing riot two workers, the district attorney, and a deputy were killed. Governor Hiram Johnson ordered four national guard companies into the area to support Durst. Over a hundred workers were arrested and eight months later Ford and Herman Suhr, who had not been at Wheatland, were convicted and sentenced to 12 and 13 years, respectively.[53]

Miners struggled against the corporate giants of that industry. In Colorado mine owners suppressed strikes in 1883, 1893, and 1903 by expelling organizers and importing strikebreakers. In the 1910s northern Colorado was in a state of upheaval with mine operators calling for and receiving the aid of the governor. Organizers and workers were arrested. In 1913 agitation shifted to southern Colorado, centering in Huerfano and Las Animas counties, an area of 120 miles. In September a fifteen-month strike commenced which involved Greeks, Italians, Slavs, and Mexicans. The United Mine Workers represented miners; owners were led by the Colorado Fuel and Iron Company in which the Rockefellers, John D. Sr. and Jr., owned 40 percent of the stock. As soon as the strike was called, miners moved from company housing into tent colonies. As winter approached conditions worsened.[54]

The governor ordered the National Guard into the area in October 1913. The Baldwin-Feltz Detective Agency harassed workers and even hunted down and killed strike leaders. Running gun battles raged. Strikers accused guard members of pressuring strikebreakers to remain on the job, holding them in virtual peonage. A congressional investigation restored calm for a time. In April 1914 the National Guard withdrew, leaving 35 men in the Ludlow area; 1,200 men, women, and children remained in the Ludlow tent colony. On April 20 the guardsmen occupied a hill overlooking the camp, mounted a machine gun, and exploded two bombs. The miners armed themselves and the guardsmen attacked.[55] "The Chicano tents and dugouts were among the first hit; of the eighteen victims nine were Chicanos, five of them children."[56] Ten days of bitter fighting followed, with at least 50 persons killed. When it was all over, a grand jury indicted 124 strikers, not charging a single deputy. Guardsmen who were court-marshaled were acquitted. Mine owners refused to negotiate forcing the union to call off the strike.[57]

In 1917 in Arizona mine locals 80, 84, and 86 had a membership of some 5,000 Mexican miners. The AFL resolved at its state convention to organize 14,000 Mexican miners in the state. However, this unity was short-lived, and the AFL leadership soon forgot their commitment. With the advent of the war organized labor, influenced by Gompers, increasingly looked upon Mexicans as competitors. Gompers feared that Mexicans would not remain in the rural areas, but would filter into the urban factories. He vehemently criticized the federal government for using Mexican labor on a construction project at Fort Bliss near El Paso because he wanted these jobs solely for "Americans."[58]

On June 24, 1917, Mexican miners struck at Bisbee and

Jerome. The Cochise County sheriff immediately labeled the strike as subversive and announced intentions of deporting any member of the IWW. With the aid of a vigilante committee he deported 67 Mexicans in Jerome and some 1,200 in Bisbee. In Bisbee every Mexican male who could not prove that he was employed was herded into the local ballpark. The sheriff seized the telegraph and telephone office and did not permit news dispatches. Local authorities and nativists loaded Mexicans into box cars and shipped them outside of Columbus, New Mexico, where they dumped them in the open desert without food or water.[59]

In April 1917 in Colton, California, Mexican workers protested the 50 percent reduction in wages by the Portland Cement Company. Management responded that the pay was high for Mexicans. When workers protested, the company fired 50 workers triggering a walkout by 150 employees. They formed a union called *Trabajadores Unidos* and won a 56¢ an hour raise, union recognition, and removal of strikebreakers. After the victory, however, the organization deteriorated into a fraternal lodge.[60]

The war intensified demand for Mexican labor especially in farming, railroads, and mines. Between 1918 and 1921 the Arizona Cotton Growers Association imported over 30,000 Mexican workers.[61] Conditions during this time were harsh and the arrival of such a large number of *Mexicanos* triggered nativist reactions. In many places any labor agitation by Mexicans was viewed as a sign of disloyalty. In Los Angeles a strike by 200 Mexicans against the Pacific Sewer Pipe Company in 1918 was branded as German made. A deputy by the name of Reyes told workers to return to work because they "had no grievance."[62]

Establishment of the *Confederación Regional Obrera Mexicana* (CROM) in Mexico in 1918 encouraged Mexican labor organization in the United States, but on the whole, it proceeded slowly. Growers stymied organizational efforts by massive importations of labor. Anglo-American labor leaders simplistically called for immigration quotas instead of organizing the exploited workers. Mexican workers were at a premium and growers protected their supply. Some went so far as to handcuff workers at night so that they would not escape.[63]

The utility of Mexican workers as well as their abundance did not go unnoticed by the steel industry in the Midwest. During the 1919 steel strike in the Chicago-Calumet area the steel companies imported large numbers of Mexicans who they worked under guard. Throughout the history of the U.S. labor movement the role of strikebreaker has always fallen not to any particular ethnic group, but rather to the latest arrival, whether it be Mexican, Polish, Italian, or any other nationality. Mexicans employed in the steel industry before the strike supported collective bargaining efforts. In any event, Mexicans were in the minority among the strikebreakers during the steel strike. During the strike, which lasted from September 22, 1919, to January 7, 1920, steel mills employed some fifty different nationalities, about a third of whom were U.S. citizens of northern European extraction. This group controlled the craft trades, were better paid, had shorter hours, and were better treated than the other ethnic groups who were played off against each other by management for jobs and promotions. A nationality report by Homestead Steel Works, Howard Axle Works, and Carrie Furnaces on October 8, 1919, showed that out of the 14,687 employed by these mills, only 130 were Mexican, that is, Mexicans comprised less than 1 percent of the work force.[64]

Sugar beet companies continued their relentless search for Mexican labor. By 1919 ninety-eight U.S. factories produced upwards of a million tons of sugar annually. Leading producers of sugar beets were Michigan, Ohio, and Wisconsin in the Midwest, Colorado, Utah, and Idaho in the mountain region, and California in the Far West. Continuing increased production and the heavy reliance on Mexican labor led farm journals in 1920 to refer to the sugar crop as a "Mexican Harvest."[65]

Little has been written on the occupational distribution of Mexicans during the period from 1910 to 1920. Professor Mario T. García of the University of California at Santa Barbara has made significant contributions to this area of study. In his article "Racial Dualism in the El Paso Labor Market, 1880–1920," García notes, that racial dualism meant "the second-class subordination of the Mexican at every level of activity: occupational distribution, residential patterns, political representation, participation, and social–cultural relationships."[66]

In El Paso Mexicans generally received lower pay than Anglo-Americans, producing an almost static occupational pattern. In 1900 71.51 percent of the Mexican workers worked as laborers, service workers, or operatives. Twenty years later the percentage had declined slightly to 67.54 percent, and by 1940 it showed little change, declining to 66.36 percent. The number of professionals remained insignificant (1900, 3.03 percent; 1920, 3.31; 1940, 2.42).[67]

Professor García also analyzes the position of Mexican women in the situation of racial dualism. Hearings conducted in El Paso in November 1919 by the Texas Industrial Welfare Commission found Mexican women were "the lowest-paid and most vulnerable workers in the city."[68] El Paso laundries employed large numbers of *Mexicanas* to work at unskilled jobs, whereas Anglo women received the skilled jobs. Mexicanas earned $8.00 a week compared to $16.55 for Anglo women. The hearings revealed that some *Mexicanas* actually earned only $4.00 to $5.00 a week. In the department stores Anglo women generally worked on the main floor, whereas *Mexicanas* worked in the rear or basement. Anglos earned as high as $40.00 a week compared to Mexican clerks who were paid from $10.00 to $20.00. *Mexicana* workers constituted the overwhelming majority of workers in the El Paso garment industry. Workers in a union shop were reported to average between $18.00 and $20.00 a week for piece work, although the owner of one factory conceded that they averaged $9.50. *Mexicanas* who testified before the commission stated that they earned from $6.00 to $9.00. Employers attempted to explain away this difference by claiming that Anglo women outworked *Mexicanas,* that they hired *Mexicanas* only because they could not employ a sufficient number of "white" women, and that, after all, the standard of living among Mexicans was much lower than that of whites and so they required less money.[69] The García article in short documented how capitalists institutionalized a large reserve labor pool comprised of Mexicans, using race to justify the dual wage system.

THE EXPANSION OF AGRICULTURE AND DISPERSAL OF MEXICAN WORKERS

The 1920s was a decade of "normalcy" marked by political apathy and devoid of militancy. For the majority of society it represented a period of prosperity; for Mexicans and other poor people it was a period during which capitalist interests continued to buy their labor at depressed levels. Farming became the leading area of employment for Mexicans. The immigration acts of 1921 and 1924 had been passed at a time when demand for fresh fruits and vegetables was high.[70] In California cultivation of truck garden products increased by more than 50 percent, fruits and nuts by 30 percent, and cotton by 400 percent. Cotton production increased in the Southwest and sugar beet production expanded throughout most of the western section of the country. This process of expansion and dispersal was accelerated by the mechanization of agriculture.

Although many small farmers experienced a postwar economic slump, the large growers of the Southwest maintained a high level of production and profit because of their ability to control production, prices, and the flow of labor. In 1921 California growers formed the Valley Fruit Growers of San Joaquin County, the Sun-Maid Raisin Growers' Association (which included 75 to 90 percent of the raisin farmers), the Western Growers Protective Association, the California Growers' Exchange, to name just a few. The Arizona Cotton Growers' Association served as the model for the San Joaquin Valley Agriculture Labor Bureau, founded in 1925. The bureau consisted of six county farm bureaus, six county chambers of commerce, and raisin, fresh fruit, and cotton producers.[71] Its job was to maximize profit by developing a pool of surplus labor that could be hired at the lowest possible rate; "migratory farm labor was as peculiar to California as slavery was to the old South."[72]

Even when farm profits rose, growers were reluctant to increase workers' wages or improve living conditions. California was the ideal location for these "farm factories" for its climate allowed year-round production. The federal government furnished water at below cost levels, making the irrigation of vast areas possible. By the 1920s California had 118 distinct types of farms producing 214 different agricultural products.[73]

The Southern Pacific Railroad alone owned 2,598,295 acres in southern California. The Kern County Land Company controlled some million acres in Kern County. Farm monopolization in California reached high levels by the end of the 1920s with 37 percent of all large-scale farms in the United States operating in that state and 2.1 percent of California farms producing 28.5 percent of all U.S. agricultural products.[74] Technological advances made many workers in preharvest operations unnecessary. They also required large capital outlays. Mechanization displaced many year-round farm workers and increased dependence on migrant labor since increased production required larger labor pools at harvest time.[75] U.S. farms mechanized at an unprecedented rate. After 1920 the harvest combine displaced many Mexicans in the wheat fields of northern Texas and the Midwest. Even so from 1920 to 1930, the number of Mexicans in agriculture tripled, increasing from 121,176 to 368,013.[76] The reason was that mechanization made it possible to cultivate more land and also as animals were displaced by machines, land which had been used for feed could be turned to cash crops.

Increasingly Mexicans organized collective bargaining units. *La Liga Protectora* of Arizona (discussed in Chapters 4 and 6) championed farm worker causes. In the late 1910s, it filed charges against Rafael Estrada, a bully and agent for cotton growers. On May 15, 1919, it submitted a long list of complaints to Governor Thomas E. Campbell and among other things charged that Mexican workers were paid less than what they had been promised by the Arizona Cotton Growers' Association (ACGA). The Arizona Federation of Labor began an organizational drive among cotton pickers in the Salt River Valley. The ACGA countered by having Mexican leaders deported. Six Mexicans were arrested on a farm near Glendale, Arizona, in June 1920 when they complained of low wages and breach of contract. When one of the deportees, Apolino Cruz, was picked up for deportation, his 8-year-old son was left on a ditch bank; friends later took the boy to Tempe and the ACGA shipped him to Mexico unescorted. Deportations were common. The Arizona Federation of Labor hired R. M. Sánchez and E. M. Flores. They met with Mexican President Adolfo de la Huerta, calling his attention to gross violations of human rights in an effort to enlist his support. The Mexican president attempted to stop Mexican migration to the United States, an action which enraged growers.[77]

A joint Arizona-Sonora commission investigated work conditions. It found 12,000 to 15,000 Mexicans housed in tents in the Salt River Valley, where temperatures reached well over 100 degrees. The investigation uncovered gross violations—poor and inadequate housing, poor transportation, abusive treatment by ACGA foremen, cases of illegal deportations in response to workers' complaints about mistreatment (200 Mexican workers had been cut adrift without pay). The ACGA arrogantly ignored charges and offered pickers 4¢ a pound more (when the market fell later in the year, the pay raise was rescinded).[78] Governor Campbell distorted findings and assured the Sonora governor that grievances had been corrected. The union prepared to fight.

The U.S. Justice Department sided with the ACGA. Its agents raided the AFL Hall in Phoenix, arrested Sánchez without a warrant, and eventually turned him over to military authorities who held him for another two weeks before charging him with desertion on November 19, the day before the ACGA was to meet. The *Arizona Republican* had labeled Sánchez an alien and a radical. Sánchez was released on February 3, 1921—after the harvest season ended. The AFL struggled for strong union representation under the leadership of Lester Doane and C. N. Idar who had been recruited from Texas for this organizational drive. In 1921 they formed fourteen federal unions, averaging 300 to 400 per local, mostly in Maricopa County. Success was short-lived and within a year the locals dwindled.[79]

Mexicans continued to migrate to cotton fields. Differentials in pay rate often influenced geographic dispersion. For instance, in Texas a cotton picker averaged $1.75 a day, in Arizona $2.75, in California $3.25, and, ironically, in Arkansas, Louisiana, and Mississippi $4.00 a day. Better pay in other regions encouraged migration from Texas into the Midwest, but Texas cotton growers kept their labor reservoir full by recruiting heavily from Mexico. In Texas counties such as Nueces 97 percent of the cotton workers were Mexicans and 3 percent were Black. Mexicans comprised 65 percent of the Southwest's seasonal labor with 20 percent Blacks and 15 percent whites.[80] In 1921 the Rural Land Owner's Association spent $1,000 advertising for cotton pickers. One of the reasons growers kept wages low was that they believed that higher wages would provide labor with the necessary resources to leave.

Many Texas-Mexicans talked about leaving for Pennsylvania or the auto factories of Michigan where they received better wages and treatment. A movement to the city among Mexican workers was evident. Many who migrated north ended up in Chicago which to this day houses the bulk of the million Mexicans in the Midwest. Most came from Guanajuato, Michoacan, and Jalisco via Texas. Many had worked on midwestern farms, the packing houses of Kansas, or the railroads. They centered in railroad, steel, and meat packing industries; 82 percent of Mexicans migrating to Chicago were unskilled workers.[81]

Railroads paid Mexicans the lowest industrial salaries, ranging from 35¢ to 39¢ an hour. In packinghouses they earned between 45¢ to 47¢ an hour, while in steel they earned 45¢ to 50¢ for 8 hours or 44¢ for 10 hours. Salaries were much higher than those in the Southwest; most important was that they worked year-round. However, even with higher pay, two-thirds of Mexicans in Chicago earned less than $100 a month which was below the poverty line. Competing for limited housing, they paid $27.00 a month compared to $21.00 for an Irish family with the same conveniences. Families relied heavily on the women to supplement their incomes (65 percent of the males were unmarried). The majority of working wives labored outside the home, although a large number kept lodgers. The cold winters added extra burdens; warm clothing and heating were expensive and respiratory diseases were common. *Mexicanos* seldom received adequate medical attention.[82]

In the plants management played Blacks and Mexicans against each other. Not one of the steel plants employed a single foreman of Mexican extraction. Rank and file Anglo workers practiced open racism toward Mexican workers.[83] Chicanos were excluded from building trades by unions who generally required citizenship for membership. The American Federation of Railroad Workers did not have a single Mexican tradesman. They continued to be stereotyped as wage cutters. Other ethnics were antagonistic toward them. Factory tensions carried over into the streets; many neighborhoods would not rent to them. In 1922 a series of small riots broke out.

The Mexican population in the Midwest (Ohio, Indiana, Michigan, Wisconsin and Illinois) grew from 7,583 in 1920 to 58,317 ten years later. By the end of the decade, Midwest Mexicans had become increasingly urbanized (from just under 70 percent to some 88 percent). Nationwide by 1930 40.5 percent of the Mexican males were in agriculture, 26 percent in manufacturing, and 16.3 percent in transportation.[84]

An important factor in geographical dispersal during the 1920s was the continued impact of reclamation projects on the growth of sugar beet and cotton production. These crops, valued at $28,043,322 in 1928, represented 34.6 percent of all crops produced on the four reclamation projects in the Southwest and Mexicans constituted 65 percent of common labor in these areas. Most of the beet workers came via Texas and from there spread out to the rest of the southwestern fields and then throughout the Midwest. The seasonal nature of the work also encouraged dispersion and urbanization as many workers migrated to cities in search of work or shelter during the winter months.[85]

In 1922 Mexicans comprised 24 percent of the sugar beet contract labor in Michigan, Ohio, Iowa, Kansas, and Minnesota; in 1926 50 percent. In 1922 they comprised 16 percent of the work force in Nebraska, Colorado, Idaho, and Montana; in 1926 42 percent. In nineteen states some 800,000 acres produced 7,500,000 tons with an estimated value of $60 to $65 million a year. Of the estimated 58,000 hired hands about 30,000 were Mexicans.[86]

Beet workers formed small societies of the *mutualista* variety. Best known was *La Sociedad de Obreros Libres* (Free Workers Society) of Gilcrest, Colorado. Also, the *Alianza Hispano-Americana* organized in the beet fields around Brighton, Colorado, and Cheyenne, Wyoming. Wages remained low; for instance, in 1924 an entire family, including children as young as 6, would average $782.00 for six months' work. Growers continuously depressed wages; in 1920 workers averaged $33.71 per acre, in 1924, $23.72, and in 1933, $12.37. Labor contractors further depressed wages by oversupplying growers with workers.[87]

Whites planted, irrigated, and cultivated, while Mexicans did heavier work of weeding, hoeing, thinning, and topping. Growers encouraged workers' indebtedness to company stores. The IWW formed the Agricultural Workers Industrial Union Local 110 but had limited success. Colorado authorities intimidated workers and state troopers went into the fields to discourage strike activity. Beet workers demanded improved housing, clean drinking water, sanitary facilities, and payment of wages at a guaranteed rate. Management responded that demands were reasonable, but did nothing. The local Knights of Columbus subverted workers' efforts by labeling actions a "red socialist menace."[88]

In 1927 the American Federation of Labor again recruited C. N. Idar, this time to organize beet workers. In the next two and a half years Idar traveled Colorado, Nebraska, and Wyoming. He was able in 1929 to put together a labor front comprised of the AFL, IWW, the communists, and the various Mexican unions. The loosely knit group, called the Beet Workers' Association, was held together by the force of Idar's leadership. When he took ill and had to leave, the association fell apart. During the 1930s union organizing was frustrated when large numbers of unemployed Anglos broke the Mexican efforts.[89]

Although Texas growers continually renewed their labor supply from Mexico, they became concerned about the constant drain as the Mexicans dispersed across the country. By the 1920s not only was their labor in demand as far away as Pennsylvania and Montana, but they had acquired a new mechanism of mobility—the automobile. Many Texas growers blamed autos for ruining "their Mexicans" and began to hire those who did not have transportation. Mexicans travelled and worked in family groups; autos and trucks made them more independent, for they were not solely dependent on the contractors. The growers did not counter this labor drain by paying their workers to encourage them to remain, but found ways to restrict travel. Basically, Texas-Mexicans were landless and depended on wages. They were vulnerable to exploitation. A form of debt peonage existed; local sheriffs arrested Mexicans by enforcing vagrancy laws and contracted workers to local farmers. Law enforcement officials deceived Mexicans into believing that they faced imprisonment if they left without paying commissary debts. Growers also tried to restrain recruitment drives by northern sugar beet companies. Labor contractors from Michigan and northern Ohio alone hired about 10,000 Texas-Mexicans each year.[90] In May 1929 the first session of the 41st Texas Legislature passed the Emigrant Labor Agency law which levied a $7,500 occupation tax on out-of-state labor contractors; this act was enjoined, but the Texas legislature passed another law which stood (and was in effect to the 1940s). The law gave local authorities a means to harass out-of-state labor contractors. Mexicans had to leave Texas by night.[91]

In California labor agitation increased in agriculture. In 1922 Mexican workers in Fresno formed the Grape Pickers' Union of the San Joaquin Valley; that same year Mexican cantaloupe workers organized in Brawley, California.[92] Undoubtedly, many such small unions existed, but large-scale organization efforts were limited by the Mexicans' vulnerability to deportation and by restraints on the activities of national labor groups such as the IWW. The Mexicans were subject to deportation sweeps not only because they were a highly visible group, easily identified by color and language, but also because some 80 percent had no documents. During World War I, Wobblies were treated as subversives and tried under the Federal Espionage Act. The California Criminal Syndicalism Act of 1919 made it a felony to "teach, advocate, aid or abet acts of violence to effect political change."[93] Judge Busick, on August 23, 1923, extended the law when he issued an injunction against the IWW, its various committees, officers, and members. In short, "anyone who belonged to a group which advocated criminal syndicalism was guilty of a felony punishable by imprisonment from one to fourteen years." In California 504 Wobblies and communists were arrested. Their bail was usually set at $15,000 and 264 were actually tried, 164 convicted, and 128 sentenced to San Quentin. These penalties limited IWW organizing in the Mexican community.[94]

Farm workers in California faced overwhelming opposition by agribusinessmen. The most powerful grower association, the American Farm Bureau Federation, united farmers nationally. Today it is a $4 billion empire as large as Du Pont or General Motors and has organizations in 2,800 out of 3,000 counties in 49 states and Puerto Rico.[95] Government workers at taxpayers' expense organized farmers into county farm bureaus which federated into state bureaus which consolidated into a national farm bureau. The AFBF was the creation of the Agricultural Extension Service at various state colleges of agriculture whose county agents promoted the idea. In the 1920s and 1930s, U.S. and state chambers of commerce and the National Association of Manufacturers supported the AFBF. Over the years it separated from the extension service officially but protected the service from government cuts. Large growers controlled the AFBF and through it lobbied to exclude farm workers from regulatory legislation. It won congressional support for its programs. President Warren G. Harding called in the president of the Farm Bureau for advice, setting a precedent for future presidents.

Many U.S. labor leaders did not believe Mexicans were educated to the level that trade-unionism required. *Mutualistas*, brotherhoods, and protective associations, however, laid groundwork for the development of the "job conscious labor movement." In November 1927 the Federation of Mexican Societies, mostly *mutualistas*, met in Los Angeles with the express purpose of encouraging members to support trade unionism by financing organizational efforts. Shortly afterwards, on March 23, 1928, they formed *La Confederación de Uniones Obreras Mexicanas* (Federation of Mexican Workers Unions). This organization had communist and IWW sympathizers. In their by-laws members recognized the principle of class struggle and that they belonged to an exploited class.[96]

CUOM held its first convention in May 1928. Many delegates came from the *mutualistas;* eventually it encompassed twenty-one locals with approximately 2,000 to 3,000 members. CUOM called for the restriction of immigration and solidarity with the AFL, highlighted unemployment and labor exploitation, and emphasized the importance of establishing Mexican schools.[97] In spite of an optimistic start, by 1929 CUOM dwindled to a handful of members.

In 1928 another Mexican union was formed in the Imperial Valley of California. Again local *mutualistas* led the struggle. That year farmers expressed optimism; crops flourished and an abundant supply of Mexican workers was available to harvest them. Indeed, at harvest time Mexicans comprised 90 percent of field workers. In recent years the Mexican population had stabilized. More and more Mexicans lived and worked year-round as field hands.[98]

The Valley produced two main crops—lettuce and cantaloupes. Both required highly specialized harvesting methods in picking and packing. Labor contractors managed work crews. Growers paid contractors, who in turn paid workers after subtracting their fee from each man's earnings. Contractors withheld the first week's wages until the end of the harvest. Many workers complained that contractors often absconded with their money.

The steady growth and relative stability of a community of year-round workers contributed to unifying the Mexicans. They formed two *mutualistas–La Sociedad Mutualista Benito Juárez* of El Centro in 1919 and *La Sociedad Mutualista Hidalgo* of Brawley in 1921. *La Liga Protectora* had also been active in El Centro and *La Alianza Hispano-Americana* had lodges in the area.[99] Mexican consul Carlos Ariza worked with leadership of the two *mutualistas* and formed *La Unión de Trabajadores del Valle Imperial*. On May 3, 1928, the union sent letters to cantaloupe growers and the chambers of commerce at Brawley and El Centro. They requested: wages be increased to 15¢ per standard crate of cantaloupes or 75¢ an hour; that growers supply free picking sacks and ice; that growers deposit workers' withheld wages in the bank instead of allowing contractors to hold them; and that growers take over from the contractors the responsibility for paying workmen's compensation, because contractors did not pay it.[100] Although demands were moderate and reasonable, the growers refused. The union threatened to strike. On May 7 workers at the Sears Brothers Ranch presented a set of demands. When managers refused to consider their grievances, half the crew walked out. Sears called the county sheriff, Charles L. Gillett, who arrested four Mexicans for disturbing the peace. Soon, two to three thousand workers joined the strike. Officials of *La Unión de Trabajadores del Valle Imperial* confused growers and local authorities by denouncing the strike publicly, but supporting it before Spanish-speaking audiences.

Newspapers, public opinion, and local authorities openly supported growers. On May 10 Sheriff Gillett shut down the union's offices and outlawed all future strikes. He branded workers and their leadership "agitators," and intimidated the union into changing its name to the Mexican Mutual Aid Society. Growers could not believe that "their Mexicans" had caused trouble; they blamed "reds and radicals" instead of working conditions. The district attorney stated that he supported the growers because "they had millions invested in crops." Sheriff Gillett stated that if Mexicans did not like it there, they could return to Mexico. He continued mass arrests and the courts set bail from $250 to $1000. Charges were dropped if workers pleaded guilty and promised to return to work. Workers who did not return to work were deported. The tactics broke the strike.[101]

POLITICIZATION OF CHICANO LABOR

The 1930s saw intense labor and political activity by Chicanos in the United States. For the first time in the twentieth century large numbers of Mexicans did not enter the country and, in fact, local authorities deported some 500,000 Chicanos to Mexico (see Chapter 6). Employers for thirty years had built a vast labor pool made up chiefly of Mexicans.[102]

According to Professor Mark Reisler, "Regardless of whether they [Mexicans] labored in the fruit, vegetable, and cotton fields of the Southwest, on the beet farms of Colorado and Michigan, or in the factories of Chicago, the depression was disastrous for Mexican workers."[103] During the Great Depression thousands of Anglo farmers and urban workers sought agricultural employment—work that they had once shunned.

Conditions in California

California farms were the most specialized and industrialized in the United States.[104] According to Carey McWilliams, "farming [in California] has always resembled mining. . . . The soil is really mined, not farmed."[105] Capital investment ownership was narrowly concentrated: 10 percent of California farms received 53.2 percent of the gross income; 9.4 percent of the farms spent 65 percent of the labor costs; and 7 percent employed 66 percent of all workers. Joseph Di Giorgio owned twenty-seven farm properties and leased eleven others; in addition to growing operations he purchased enormous quantities of fruit for distribution; he owned a major share of Klamath Lumber and Box Co. which produced 25 million feet of lumber annually; he also owned 37½ percent of Italian Swiss Colony Wine and the Baltimore Fruit Exchange.[106]

Often profits were so high that growers could pay off low-term debts on mortgages in one year. The huge profits of the large growers guaranteed the large amounts of capital necessary to dig wells, to purchase machinery, to pay for electricity for water pumps, and to employ large numbers of seasonal workers. Small farmers remained more dependent upon banks.[107]

In 1927 California agriculture consumed nearly one-third of all electricity used on U.S. farms and one-half of all rural electricity. In the San Joaquin Valley farms were 96 percent electrified, housing 37,000 electric pumps. In 1930 California vied with Iowa for first place in total value of commodity farm products. Four counties—Los Angeles, Tulare, Fresno, and San Joaquin—led the nation in farm production. Fourteen counties placed in the top 25 agricultural counties and 33 in the first 100.[108]

Large farming in California had escalated during the 1920s with rapid expansion in labor-intensive crops like cotton, fruit, nuts, and vegetables, so that to the farmer a large supply of labor meant economic progress. Relations between employers and employees became more distant resembling urban industrial relations. "The attitudes of seasonal wage laborers to their employers on large farms were no longer like those of the farm hand."[109]

The federal government initiated large-scale reclamation projects in the San Joaquin Valley and throughout California to alleviate the crisis caused by the falling levels of wells. State revenue bonds totaling $170 million initially funded the Central Valley Project; "In constant sunshine and several inches of water, crop after crop is produced with factory-like precision."[110] In 1930 less than 10 percent of irrigated acreage was developed through federal financing, but by 1939 California had 4 million acres of irrigated land, watered by the federally and state funded California aqueduct and the Central Valley Project canals. This created heavy reliance on the export market which was served by processing, handling, and transportation networks. These networks intensified the need for more labor, and an increased labor force generated enterprises to service the growing population. Industrialization of agriculture forged a class system resembling that in the urban areas with a definite stratification between growers at the top and migrant labor at the bottom.[111]

Factors Affecting Chicano Labor

New techniques in production developed by federal and state extension services hastened farm industrialization—a process which benefited the farmer but not the farm workers. The Farm Bureau controlled many activities which federal, state, and county agencies financed. Agriculture was big business. Growers saw themselves as equivalent to urban industrialists and regarded farm workers as equivalent to factory workers. The growers achieved economic rewards and social status equivalent to their industrial counterparts, but the rural proletariat was denied advantages that the urban proletariat had achieved.[112] In fact the unstructured labor market that existed in California agriculture would have been envied by most urban capitalists. There were no unions to protect workers' rights such as seniority; the relationship between employer and employee was completely impersonal; the majority of productive employees were unskilled and available in large numbers; workers were paid by the piece not by the hour; and harvesting prior to 1920 was largely unmechanized. An interrelationship between marketing and production existed. Ten percent of the farmers controlled more than 75 percent of the state's agricultural land and the upper 10 percent of growers produced 50 percent of the annual agricultural product. Specialization simplified the collective approach to many problems from pest control to marketing. According to Carey McWilliams, California growers are "producers," not farmers.[113]

The depression hit California workers and farmers hard. The migrant pool in California expanded from 119,800 in 1920 to 190,000 in 1930 to nearly 350,000 in 1939. Nationally 3,216,000 Anglos were unemployed in January 1930; 7,160,000 in January 1931, and 10,197,000 in January 1932. By the mid-1930s, Anglos outnumbered Mexicans in the California fields. Some 275 agriculture strikes took place in the United States, involving 177,788 workers in 28 states; 140 of these strikes took place in California with 127,176 workers participating. Prices declined over 50 percent, while mortgage, electricity, water, fertilizer, and transportation expenses decreased little; surpluses piled up. The easiest solution for growers was to lower workers' wages over 50 percent. The situation eventually improved, but wages remained low.[114] Organizations like the California Farm Bureau Federation became more aggressive. In the 1930s, it took the leadership in controlling labor: "Farm groups worked to shift the tax burden from ownership of real property by imposition of a personal income tax and a general retail sales tax,"[115] which in most cases worked to shift the tax burden to the middle and lower classes.

Conditions In Texas and the Midwest

Up to most recent times Texas housed the largest Mexican population in the United States. In 1930 Mexicans numbered 685,681 out of 5,824,715 Texans (12 percent of the population); 536,875 of the Mexicans were born in Mexico.[116] Of the 685,681, 236,201 were ten years or older and were gainfully employed and 47 percent of those gainfully employed worked in agriculture. In 1916, 75 percent of all Mexicans entering the United States settled in Texas,[117] but by 1930 a shift to California was underway.

While agriculture was not as industrialized in Texas as in California, throughout the 1930s Texas farmers went through a period of rapid transition accelerating the demise of small farmers and the displacement of sharecroppers. In 1930 the number of sharecroppers was 205,122; it declined to 76,468 in 1935 and reached a low of 39,821 in 1940. After 1930 farmers turned increasingly to mechanization which lessened the demand for year-round labor, but in crops such as cotton and sugar beets increased the demand for migrants. Mechanization was slow at first since the cost of machinery was often higher than the cost of employing Mexicans. Growers always threatened to use machines to depress wages. Moving of produce sheds into the fields revolutionized harvesting of small vegetable crops and reduced labor costs in that sector. Machines, however, could not inspect, tie, and package vegetables or pick more sensitive varieties.[118]

Mexicans became less attractive to growers as the pool of white workers increased. Growers especially resented increased militancy among Mexicans. In 1930 Mexicans attempted to form a labor organization in Minnesota; this resulted in a decision in 1933 by the Minnesota Sugar Company to stop recruiting in Texas and to hire workers on the open market.[119] Increasingly, companies followed the practice of only white labor employed.

Labor contractors operated in agriculture and many other industries including the railroads, construction companies, and the garment trade. They were usually Mexicans who spoke English and thus could deal with both the growers and the labor supply.

Mexican labor worked with the contractors because the contractors were familiar with their language and customs, gave them steady employment, and served as brokers to find jobs and arrange transportation to the farms. A sizeable number of the 66,100 Mexicans who left Texas annually worked through contractors. A majority of the some 3,000 to 4,000 who went each year to sugar beet fields in Minnesota, Kansas, and Missouri were recruited by contractors. Another 10,000 left for the sugar beet fields of Michigan and northern Ohio where contractors handled 85 percent of recruiting and 57 percent of the workers were from Texas.[120]

Labor contractors made sizeable profits. They received 5¢ to 10¢ for every 100 pounds of cotton picked plus a daily allowance of $1.50 for transportation and $1.50 for supervising work and weighing. For example, Frank Cortez of San Antonio accumulated several stores, cafes, and a funeral parlor. He had contracts to ship 6,000 workers to Michigan at $1.00 a head. This fee was advanced to Cortez but it was later taken out of the workers' pay. He did not have overhead cost and recruited right outside his funeral parlor. Cortez sent workers to the Midwest by railroad, truck, and passenger cars. Frequently 60 to 65 Mexicans were packed into a truck. Growers paid Cortez's agent $10 for each worker upon delivery. Passengers often stood all the way, stopping "a few times for bowel evacuation and eating" or for gas and oil.[121]

Most labor contractors did not do the volume that Cortez did and traveled with their crews, acting as straw bosses. Some Mexican workers would work for as many as three employers a day. Employers and contractors charged workers for everything from cigarettes to transportation. Contractors were often paid directly by employers, and they, in turn, paid workers. In the beet industry contractors recruited workers, handled their wages and ran camps. Pickers often received pay in tickets which could be redeemed at local stores for a discount.[122] To employers, contractors were indispensable since they delivered a crew on the day promised.

Proponents of the contract system claimed that it was not the cause of exploitation but merely a symptom; they claimed that child exploitation, substandard wages, and other abuses would have existed even without the system. However, even proponents admitted that contractors contributed to the exploitation with excessive fees, overcharged for transportation, housing, and food, and frequently short-weighed pickers. Unscrupulous contractors often absconded with pay or worked in collusion with employers to depress wages. Employers were not liable for injuries and poor conditions and used contractors as insurance against unionization of workers. Understandably, contractors became the main grievance of workers.[123]

Strikes and Organizations

Given the industrialization of agriculture, the exploitation of Chicano labor, and the abuses of the contract labor system, conflict would have occurred without the depression, but the events of 1929 intensified the struggle. Farm industrialists were determined to make up their losses by fixing wages of the rural proletariat as low as possible. Wages plummeted from 35¢ to 50¢ an hour in 1931 to 15¢ to 16¢ an hour by mid-1933.[124]

Conditions forced Mexicans whom growers had considered docile into angry strikers. An all-out war broke out in which growers used the Immigration Service to deport leaders, pressured state and federal agencies to deny Mexicans relief, used local and state authorities to terrorize workers, killed and imprisoned strikers, and made a sham of any semblance of human rights.

Many Mexican workers had been politicized by the Mexican Revolution itself. In 1930 the *Confederación de Uniones Obreros Mexicanas* (CUOM) still existed, and although a skeleton of what it had been two years before, the flame still flickered. The Mexican Mutual Aid Association of the Imperial Valley still functioned. The Communist party at the Sixth World Congress of the Communist International announed its intention to organize farm workers. Delegates abandoned their "boring from within" strategy and actively competed with other unions. It organized the Trade Union Unity League (TUUL) to accomplish this end. According to Stuart Jamieson, the TUUL's "aggressive campaign of organizing casual farm workers in openly revolutionary unions" led to intense confrontations with other trade union organizations.[125]

In January 1930 5,000 Imperial Valley workers walked off the fields.[126] They were led by the Mexican Mutual Aid Association which had few resources and knew that a large percentage of its members were vulnerable to deportation. The TUUL jumped into the fray, going into competition with the *mutualista* by forming the Agricultural Workers Industrial League (AWIL). Its action caused confusion, contributing to the eventual collapse of the January strike. Many Mexican leaders resented the TUUL and accused it of raiding cadres. This confrontation between communist-led unions and nationalist Mexican unions was repeated throughout the 1930s. Generally, labor historians have glossed over this aspect of the farm worker struggle and generalized that the TUUL was more radical, more class conscious and more militant than the Mexican labor union.[127] Radical historians have glorified the role of communist organizers and vilified Mexicans as nationalistic and reformist.

Lately, however, a more balanced picture has emerged in which the pluses and minuses of both Mexican and communist are acknowledged. For instance, many of the TUUL's cadre were members of the Young Communist League who were young, altruistic, and often extreme. They pushed the movement to the left, but unfortunately, they did not understand and had little tolerance for Mexican nationalism and dedicated themselves more to leading than organizing. On the other hand many Mexican leaders were too nationalistic and resented what they considered Anglo chauvinism. This basic lack of understanding between the two groups caused damaging divisions.

Imperial Valley farm workers struck again in February 1930. The strike involved native white packers and trimmers and was settled quickly. Workers looked to the spring cantaloupe harvest. The Mexican Union was weakened not only by a power struggle with the AWIL, but also by an internecine struggle between radicals and moderates. Local authorities took advantage of the division. Sheriff Charles L. Gillett conducted wholesale raids, making 103 arrests in April 1930; 8 union leaders were charged with criminal syndicalism; Braulio Orosco and Eduardo Herrera were among those convicted, and were sentenced to San Quentin from 2 to 28 years.[128]

On November 30 in Crystal City, Texas, 450 Mexican spinach workers met at the Sacred Heart Catholic Church and elected the Reverend Charles Taylor, president of the union. Workers demanded that no outside labor be brought in, that children under 12 not be used in the fields, that a minimum wage of $2.00 a day be paid, and that workers be paid directly instead of through labor contractors. Workers struck and within a week all their demands except the minimum wage were met.[129]

In California Mexicans participated in strikes throughout 1930, 1931, and 1932. In July 1931 the AWIL changed its name to the Cannery and Agricultural Workers Industrial Union (CAWIU). Failure of Mexican unions to gain concessions from employers opened the field for the communist union. In the first years the CAWIU generally joined the strikes after they had started and it was not until November 1932 at Vacaville, California, that it initiated strike activity. In 1933 37 strikes took place, involving some 47,575 farm workers in California. The CAWIU participated in 25 of these strikes which involved 32,800 workers. Most of the strikes resulted in partial victory.[130] In describing the communist organizers, Caroline Decker, an activist in the CAWIU, said:

> Actually, most of the young people in the CAWIU were starry-eyed, dedicated idealists with a mission to save the agricultural workers. They were poorly paid and overworked. If someone had asked them if they were Communists, they would have replied "Yes." They were ideological communists. Communism was the thing to believe in if one were a radical with a social conscience.[131]

New Deal legislation passed in 1932 and 1933 helped urban workers, but no relief trickled down to farm laborers. In fact, conditions worsened and strike activities increased during 1933. The berry strike in El Monte and the cotton strike of the San Joaquin Valley stood out. El Monte, California, was a citadel of white supremacy, the place where the "Monte Boys" (mentioned in Chapter 5) struck terror in the nearby Mexican *colonias*. Gradually, some whites moved out of El Monte and nonwhites moved in. The town became an agricultural center. Although El Monte itself had only 4,000 inhabitants, it served a trade area for 12,000 local residents, 75 percent of whom were Anglos, 20 percent Mexicans, and 5 percent Japanese. The Chicano *barrio*, known as Hicks' Camp, was a shack village located across a dry river gulch from El Monte proper. Many of the 1,100 Mexicans were migratory workers. They constituted the bulk of the town's cheap labor force and earned an average 15¢ to 20¢ an hour.[132] Whole families worked just to subsist.

In May 1933 Chicanos, Japanese and Anglo workers went to the secretary of the growers association and demanded higher wages. When he refused their request, they held general meetings, voted to strike, and formed a strike committee of sixty workers, which included Chicanos, Japanese, and Filipinos.[133] Most Chicano leaders belonged to the newly formed Mexican Farm Labor Union; however, the CAWIU joined the strike and, at first, cooperated with the Mexican union. The strike began on June 1.

Growers played workers against each other. If Mexicans struck, Japanese laborers were brought in and vice versa. Japanese farmers were caught in the middle; they had to pay owners high rents for their land and owners gave them no relief.[134]

Strikers lowered their initial demand of 25¢ an hour or 65¢ a crate for berries to 25¢ an hour or 50¢ a crate. Growers knew that they had to act quickly, since the berries were highly perishable. Workers rejected a grower offer of 20¢ an hour or 45¢ a crate. The sheriff at first left strikers alone, but as the harvest season began, he arrested a number of picketers for disturbing the peace.

At the request of Armando Flores, the chair of the strike committee, the Mexican consul, Alejandro Martínez, supported them. A power struggle between the leadership of the CAWIU and the Mexican consul developed. Martínez denounced organizers as "Reds." At first the CAWIU gained control of the rank and file, but the Mexican farm labor union gained momentum when it affiliated with *La Confederación de Uniones de Campesinos y Obreros del Estado de California* (CUCOM) which had been recently formed by many of the leaders of CUOM.[135] The berry strike encouraged other strike activities and by the middle of June, strikes spread to the onion and celery fields of Venice, Culver City, and Santa Monica. On July 15, 1933, CUCOM held its organizing convention, which gave Mexican leaders more visibility, and CUCOM leaders by then had taken control of the berry strike.

The Los Angeles Chamber of Commerce became concerned

about the strike's duration. Ross H. Gast of the chamber, U.S. Labor Commissioner Marsh, and U.S. Department of Labor conciliator G. H. Fitzgerald urged the growers to compromise and to offer strikers a package that would make it possible for them to earn between 20¢ and 25¢ an hour for a 10-hour day. They pressured strikers to accept the offer, but strikers believed their bargaining position had improved and rejected the offer. Mediators charged that outside agitators were involved. Gast was convinced that Armando Flores was a Communist. The chamber of commerce was anxious to settle the strike; it feared that immigration restrictionists would exploit the strike in their efforts to limit Mexican migration, and it also feared that strike activity would spread even more. The Japanese consul worked behind the scenes with the Mexican consul to bring about a settlement. The Japanese wanted to compromise because they feared public opinion would turn against them.[136]

On July 6 a settlement was reached. Time favored growers, since the peak of the harvest season had passed. As a consequence, terms of the agreement were lower than those previously rejected by the union. They called for $1.50 for a 9-hour day or, where the work was not steady, 20¢ an hour. Some activists nevertheless, considered it a victory, because the growers recognized the union, and union members received preferential hiring with scabs fired.[137]

After the El Monte berry strike, militancy further intensified, with veterans of that strike exporting their fervor to other parts of California. In this charged climate the CAWIU became more attractive to the rank and file. The August 1933 strikes infused the "workers with a tremendous unifying spirit." The most important of the August strikes was that at the Taugus Ranch. CAWIU organizer Pat Chambers led the strike which was directed primarily at the California Packing Corporation. The strike involved seven counties.[138] Deputies and ranch guards made the strike a war, arming themselves and conducting raids on union headquarters and making mass arrests and deportations. Growers asked for the national guard to be sent in.

During the strike union organizers noticed the vulnerability of strikers who resided on company property and devised new strategies such as roving pickets. Union organizers, moreover, increasingly concentrating their struggle on the large orchards, attempting to win over the smaller farmers. Strikers won a 25¢ an hour settlement. This partial victory spread worker militancy, but left growers bitter and more resolute to break the worker movement.[139] These strikes set the stage for the San Joaquin cotton strike of October 1933.

The San Joaquin cotton strike was one of the largest strikes in agricultural history. It is an example of the confrontation between farm industrialists and the rural proletariat. In this struggle the cotton farmers were for the most part agents of larger interests.

In Spring 1933 San Joaquin cotton growers had signed contracts with ginning and banking companies, the Bank of America, the San Joaquin Ginning Company, and the local ginning operations of the Anderson Clayton Company. According to the terms of the contracts farmers assigned their crops to the companies in return for cash advances for labor costs, seeds, electricity, and other expenses. Anderson Clayton ginned an estimated 35 percent of the total California and Arizona production, and the Bank of America held mortgages on many farms in the area and leased land to smaller operators.[140] In 1929 over 30 percent of the large-scale U.S. cotton farmers operated in California with practically all of them producing in the San Joaquin Valley. These powerful interests set wages throughout the valley through the San Joaquin Labor Bureau.[141]

Pat Chambers, a CAWIU organizer, realized that the ginners and bankers determined wages and he knew that an industrywide contract would have to be negotiated. He therefore attempted to dissuade the workers from striking, but, according to Chambers, they would have walked out with or without the CAWIU. The San Joaquin growers at first set the price at 40¢ per hundred pounds, but as the harvest approached and it was evident that the workers would strike, 60¢ per hundred was offered. The strike committee demanded $1.00 per hundred, the abolition of the labor contract system, and the hiring of union members. When growers refused to negotiate, the strike began on October 2. The counties most involved were in the southern San Joaquin Valley (Kern, Kings, and Tulare); 10,000 to 12,000 workers, 80 percent of whom were Mexican, organized to stop production.[142]

Growers closed ranks. On October 10, 1933, in *The Visalia Times Delta,* the Farmer's Protective Association of Tulare published the following manifesto:

> We the farmers of your community, whom you depend upon for support, feel that you have nursed too long the Viper that is at our door. These Communist agitators must be driven from town by you, and your harboring them further will prove to us your non-cooperation with us, and will make it necessary for us to give our support and trade to another town that will support and cooperate with us.

In the same issue the association promised "armed aid" to ranchers. Local sheriffs dutifully deputized growers. Anthony Sola, a dairy farmer who was 30 at the time, sympathized with Mexicans since wages were just too low. Growers, according to Sola, were caught in the middle and their cotton had dried out. He admitted that some growers regarded Mexicans as slaves and that hotheads acted like driven men, but he blamed the ginning and finance companies who squeezed the farmers.[143]

Growers mobilized for an all-out war. Businessmen, newspapers, chambers of commerce, farm bureaus, elected officials, and local city and county police authorities all supported growers. District Attorney Clarence E. Wilson of Kings County stated that Mexicans should take 60¢ since they were better off than in Mexico. They arrested strikers, putting them in bullpens. Cotton growers pressured authorities to cut relief payments of Los Angeles residents and even mobilized school children. They labeled strikers as "reds" and agitators. Federal authorities backed the growers and ordered the deportation of L. S. Hill and Rubén Rodríguez.[144] A local sheriff later testified:

> We protect our farmers here in Kern County. They are our best people. They are always with us. They keep the county going. They put us in here and they can always put us out again, so we serve them. But the Mexicans are trash. They have no standard of living. We herd them like pigs.[145]

The strikers had few resources. Many were veterans of other strikes, earning just enough to get by between strikes. Others had arrived in the San Joaquin Valley with no surplus capital. The California Emergency Relief Administration, which was administered by federal authorities, broke precedent and, for a brief period made small relief payments to strikers. However, these payments were soon ended. The Workers International Relief of the Communist party raised food and money. Some local townspeople also helped. Moreover, the situation of the strikers worsened as the strike progressed. Growers fanned emotions by playing on the racial fears of Anglo-Americans. According to CAWIU organizer Caroline Decker it was fortunate that whites had begun to enter the fields that year since the strike could very easily have deteriorated into a race war.[146]

As expected on October 4, growers began evicting strikers, who had prepared for this contingency. Union organizers had rented five camp sites at Corcoran, McFarland, Porterville, Tulare, and Wasco. Strikers and their families moved into the camps. Each camp was given complete autonomy, and this autonomy contributed to a spirit of unity and consciousness among Mexicans. Union organizers made it clear that if any one of the camp committees voted to break the strike, strike activities would be terminated. The success of the strike depended on the camps. Therefore, top security was maintained, and grower propaganda entering the camps was filtered.[147]

Alejandro Rodríguez, 30 at the time, remembered that the first ranch struck in the Corcoran area was the Peterson Ranch. He worked for the Boswells and his father-in-law Mateo Castro was foreman. When the strike began, Mateo and his family were evicted; he protested since he was not a member of the union, but Boswell did not make distinctions and kicked everyone off. They were thus forced to join the strike and moved to the tent camp. Some 20 acres had been lent to them by a local farmer. Rodríguez took part in the caravan picketing and stood guard.[148]

If Rodríguez reluctantly joined the strike, this was not the case with Lilly Cuellar, 17 at the time. She had come to Corcoran with her first husband Arnulfo Cardenas, who was always participating in strikes for better pay. She remembers the camp was heavily guarded and feared vigilantes would break in. They survived with money saved during the grape harvest, but she remembers there was little to eat. She and her husband "slept under the sky."[149] Other pickers described their belongings being hauled to the highway and dumped. The Corcoran camp in retrospect symbolized the struggle and, according to Chambers, remains a tribute to the leadership and courage of the Mexican family. The Corcoran camp was occupied by 3,780 strikers, who outnumbered the some 2,000 townspeople. A committee to run the camp was elected. It laid out streets, had toilet facilities dug, maintained sanitation and clean drinking water, settled disputes, and guarded the camp.[150] A contemporary described the camps as follows:

> The camp was located on a vacant field, perhaps four acres in extent, across the tracks on the eastern outskirts of Corcoran. When the camp began to attain greater proportions, union leaders laid out rows of tents separated by dusty streets, named after towns or heroes of Mexico. Each family provided its own habitation—an old tent or burlap bags stretched between two poles and a car. These make-shift tents, in addition to family cars, cooking utensils, bedding and the ever-present dog, represented the total possessions of the evicted pickers—with perhaps a goat or several chickens for the more fortunate. Later wooden toilets and a water-pipe system, extending through the middle of the "city" with frequent spigots were added. An irrigative ditch served as the collective wash tub for the children. Garbage was burned in open pits.[151]

Barbed wire surrounded the camp and guards were posted at the entrance and exit. There was a tent school for about seventy children and an assembly space for meetings, generally presided over by the mayor of the camp Lino Sánchez, and for nightly performances dubbed an "Aztec Circus."[152]

Campers were continuously harassed by authorities such as Corcoran Sheriff W. V. Buckner. Chambers, the main organizer, feared another Ludlow massacre, since he believed that the governor would yield to grower pressure to send the National Guard; in that eventuality Chambers was prepared to call off the strike. How many fatalities actually took place is not known for sure. At the Corcoran camp one woman died of pneumonia and two infants died of malnutrition.[153]

According to Robert R. Lee, a male nurse, hospital officials refused to admit a Mexican woman from the Tulare County camp to the hospital because her husband was a striker. Without medical care she died. At the 1933 hearings Pauline Domínguez testified that she knew of two children who died of undernourishment. Domínguez stated that many Mexicans would not sign aid forms because they were afraid that if they accepted relief, they could be deported. At the hearings eyewitnesses testified that nine people died in the camps. Many mothers reportedly refused milk for their children rather than sign waivers.[154]

Strike leaders attempted to ameliorate tensions in the field. Instead of mass picketing they devised guerrilla-style pickets, that is, roving caravans would stop at several big farms a day, picket for a while and drive off. The area covered by these guerrilla bands was extensive, over 100 miles of battle front.

Newspaper headlines inflamed growers who formed the Agricultural Protective Association to hound labor organizers and strikers. Club wielding growers broke up worker rallies. Finally, on October 11 the ranchers gunned down three strikers; two were murdered at a rally in Pixley and another on a picket line near Arvin. Most sources believed that these murders were planned and a small grower later testified that the violence against the strikers had been planned at a growers' meeting four days before Pixley.[155]

At Pixley, as unarmed strikers listened to Pat Chambers speak, a dozen cars surrounded the group.[156] The strikers, wanting to avoid a confrontation, returned to the union hall. Farmers fired on them, killing two strikers and wounding eleven. During the attack growers murdered Dolores Hernández, 52, and Delfino D'Avila, 55. D'Avila was shot as he grabbed the grower's gun. Another farmer hit D'Avila with a gun, while still another shot him as he crawled away. When the strikers at Pixley rushed into the hall and attempted to leave through the rear, patrolmen prevented them from leaving. Eight ranchers were tried for the murders, but they were acquitted.[157] The California Highway Patrol (CHP) played a suspect role. B. H. Olivas of Madera, stated that "ranchers told our patrolmen that beginning today they would beat to hell every striker who so much as laid a hand on the fences on their properties."[158]

The killing at Arvin occurred that same afternoon. Tension had mounted that morning when the growers and picketers exchanged words—30 armed guards and about 200 picketers faced each other. At about three o'clock, fighting broke out. A prominent grower shot into the crowd, killing Pedro Subia, age 57, and wounding several strikers.[159] Witnesses testified that all the shots came from the growers' side and that the strikers did not have guns. Eyewitnesses also identified the man who shot Subia. Although authorities knew this, seven picketers were tried for Subia's murder.[160] Growers became even more aggressive. The Kern County growers were particularly active. The Ku Klux Klan there became more overt.[161] Wofford B. Camp, the leader of the growers, was the prototype of the Kern grower. According to Camp, who was originally from South Carolina, growers had launched a crusade during the early 1930s to save America and rid the valley of communists. Camp said that growers' protective organizations were like the Ku Klux Klan during reconstruction. Both fought the "carpetbaggers." In the process law enforcement authorities deputized growers, issuing 600 gun permits to ranchers to protect their way of life.[162]

The governor of California appointed a fact finding committee which made its report public on October 23. It recommended a compromise, raising the rate to 75¢ per hundred pounds. Although the committee found gross violations of human rights, it did not offer much relief to strikers. Growers agreed to the terms but workers held out for 80¢. The governor ordered relief payments stopped and supported the growers, forcing strikers to return to work.[163]

As a result of the cotton strike, the CAWIU gained credibility among Mexican workers. The leadership moved to capitalize on this new popularity. The *Western Worker* (a Communist party newspaper) criticized organizers for not infusing more propaganda into union meetings and being too concerned with immediate strike problems. The *Western Worker*, however, recognized the problem of overemphasizing political objectives since, according to it, workers quickly lost interest and joined the more opportunistic conciliatory affiliates of the AFL and independent unions.[164]

In October 1933 the Union of Mexican Field Workers in the Imperial Valley resumed strike activity. By November it had a contract with lettuce growers, but on the 17th of that month it called a one day strike to protest growers not living up to the agreed terms. In December the CAWIU entered the Imperial Valley calling for more militant tactics.[165] Many Mexicans joined the CAWIU but retained their membership in the Mexican union. In January the CAWIU brought to the Valley two well-known communist organizers, Dorothy Ray Healy and Stanley Hancock.[166] While the entrance of Healy and Hancock generated excitement, according to Pat Chambers, too much time was spent hiding them from police, time which could have been spent organizing.[167]

Police authorities in the Imperial Valley again supported the growers. On January 12, 1934, gun-wielding police attacked a union meeting, killing two, one of whom was a child. The CHP also sided with the growers, and eighty-six strikers were arrested in two weeks in August alone.[168] Vigilantes attacked and teargassed the strikers at will, and on January 23, they kidnapped American Civil Liberties Union (ACLU) lawyer H. L. Wirin. On February 19, they literally crushed the strike by burning the workers' shacks and evicting 2,000.[169] Meanwhile, even state authorities grew concerned over the blatant disregard for the rights of the strikers and forced growers to arbitrate the pea strike in the northern end of the Imperial Valley.

Divisions among the workers widened. Mexican consul Joaquín Terrazas helped form *La Asociación Mexicana del Valle Imperial* (The Mexican Association of the Imperial Valley). The CAWIU immediately branded the *Asociación* a company union. Nevertheless, the Mexican union seized leadership from the CA-WIU during the cantaloupe strike of April when its membership reached 1,806.[170] Although both groups won limited victories, the growers remained in control of the Imperial Valley.

On March 28, 1934, California growers led by the California Chamber of Commerce and the Farm Bureau formed the Associated Farmers of California.[171] The Associated Farmers established an espionage service and employed the Pinkerton Detective Agency. Photos of labor agitators were sent to Frank J. Palomares of the San Joaquin Labor Bureau (SJLB), an organization supported by the industrialist interests in California including growers, sugar companies, oil companies, railroads, and utilities. Many small farmers refused to join the Associated Farmers because they did not identify with it nor did they want to be controlled by the "bunch of big fellows who ran things." In a short time the group controlled local police, "influenced" the state legislature to pass laws that barred picketing, and finally, secured the arrest and later conviction of labor leaders.[172]

The mood of the farmers during 1934 can be summed up by a speech by Simon L. Lubin before the Commonwealth Club of San Francisco on March 23, 1934:

> The employers, victims of a totally inadequate economic system, are hardly in position, or in the mood, to work upon their problems calmly and with due consideration of others. . . . Having little or no control over market prices, freight-rates, and incidental costs, the employers seem to feel that their only resource is to take it out of labor. They are paying less than starvation wages. In the process they forbid free speech, free assembly and brutally break up meetings, blaming it all on agitators instead of realizing that discontent springs primarily out of poor wages and unhappy working and living conditions."[173]

On July 20, 1934, police raided Communist headquarters in Sacramento and confiscated numerous pamphlets and papers. This drive on the CAWIU was prompted by the highly publicized general strike of San Francisco in the summer of 1934. Pat Chambers in a radio interview had hinted that the CAWIU would join that strike. Within two hours the Sacramento headquarters was raided. The Associated Farmers contributed financially to the prosecution of the CAWIU leadership paying for secretarial assistance and hiring

Captain William Hynes of the Los Angeles Police Department's "red squad" to do intelligence work. It spent some $13,780.59, of which $6,700 went to Captain Hynes.[174]

Seventeen communists were indicted and fifteen prosecuted on charges of criminal syndicalism. Eight of the fifteen were convicted, among them Pat Chambers and Caroline Decker. They spent two years in jail before a higher court overturned the sentences. These arrests and convictions ended the four year career of the CAWIU.[175]

The loss of the CAWIU no doubt hurt the efforts of farm workers to organize. It had some excellent organizers such as Chambers. It also had national contacts which called attention to the plight of the workers. Its open declaration of being a communist organization, on the other hand, invited political repression. The CAWIU leadership can be criticized for promoting unnecessary fights with Mexican unions which they attempted to discredit by describing them as nationlist or reactionary. Much too often CAWIU organizers did not understand the history of the people they were attempting to lead. According to historian Douglas Guy Monroy, communist organizers failed to recognize the influence of the Mexican Revolution and the anarcho-syndicalist traditions of the PLM and the IWW on Mexican workers. When they did they "vilified this living tradition."[176] Consequently, too much time and energy was spent fighting the Mexican- and Filipino-led unions.[177]

In spite of criticisms, the communists must be commended for doing something about conditions. Their extremes were products of the times and the youth of the party's cadre. Many believed in the impending collapse of capitalism and adopted a mechanical interpretation of conditions.

AGRICULTURAL ORGANIZING
CONTINUES: CUCOM AND UCAPAWA

After the 1935 convictions the communists reverted to tactics of boring from within, joining the AFL and independent unions. According to Jamieson, "The most effective agricultural-labor unions during 1935 and 1936 were those organized among Mexicans." The CUCOM continued to organize and by 1934 had 10,000 members. Among the Mexican leaders were Guillermo Velarde, José Espinosa, and Bernard Lucero. CUCOM participated in the 1934 orange pickers strike in Riverside and San Bernardino and Velardi and Espinosa appeared in strikes in 1935 at Chula Vista and 1936 in Compton. CUCOM's leadership often clashed with the *Comisión Honorífica* which Mexican consuls controlled.[178]

Factionalism within the CUCOM occurred between radical and moderate members. After the collapse of the CAWIU, Chicanos formed several independent unions. The Mexican Agricultural

Workers Union in Santa Barbara led a vegetable workers strike in August 1934. It was a communist front as was the American Mexican Union in San Joaquin County which led a cherry strike near Lodi in June 1935.[179] The Mexican Labor Union of the Santa María Valley (an independent) united with Filipinos to strike local growers.

With the demise of the CAWIU most left-wing organizers worked through the CUCOM union which assumed leadership in six of the eighteen strikes called during 1935. Most of this activity centered in Orange and San Diego Counties. These strikes were small in relation to the massive 1933 strikes. Nevertheless, a positive aspect was cooperation between CUCOM and Filipino unions.[180]

In January 1936 the CUCOM led in forming the Federation of Agricultural Workers of America which was joined by eleven locals of Filipino, Japanese, and other nationalities.[181] During the spring of 1936 in Los Angeles County, CUCOM led a walkout of 2,600 celery workers: The Los Angeles "red squads" teargassed parades and picket lines, beating and arresting union members.[182] A favorite grower weapon was to withdraw relief. They had a statewide network and Los Angeles County served as its main labor reserve pool.

For the remainder of 1936 the CUCOM continued as the vanguard in farm labor organizing. In Orange County between 2,500 and 3,000 citrus-fruit pickers and packers went on strike on June 15. They averaged 22¢ an hour; workers demanded 27.5¢ an hour, transportation, and union recognition. Growers recruited 400 special guards, the California Highway Patrol harassed parades and picketers along roads, and police authorities arrested some 200, herding them into stockades. Local newspapers described the situation as a civil war and blamed the communists. The Associated Farmers coordinated assaults. Guillermo Velarde led much of the strike activity.[183]

In 1935 farm workers suffered the further injustice of being excluded from provisions of the National Labor Relations Act (the Wagner Act) which guaranteed other workers the right to organize, to engage in collective bargaining, and to strike. During 1937 and 1938 conditions in California verged on class warfare. In 1937 50,000 workers were needed to harvest crops; however, growers attracted 125,000 people and drove wages down to 75¢ to $1.25 a day, paying as low as $3.00 a week.[184]

By this time urban unions paid more attention to their rural counterparts, since they feared that oppression might endanger their rights. Mexican and Filipino unions realized that they must affiliate with the AFL since they were too small and isolated. The CUCOM during 1936 and 1937 entered into negotiations with other cultural labor unions to form an alliance. In July 1937 they sent delegates to Denver and joined the newly formed United Cannery, Agricultural, Packing, and Allied Workers of America (UCA-PAWA. Although Mexican locals and independent unions continued to agitate throughout the 1930s, more and more growers used "Okies" and "Arkies"* to break their strikes, and most of the independents affiliated with larger organizations. Charismatic leaders such as Luisa Moreno worked with UCAPAWA (see Chapter 10). She was the first woman of Mexican descent to serve on the executive committee of UCAPAWA.[185]

The pattern of organization and strikebreaking was similar in Arizona where ownership and control of land was even more concentrated than in California. During the depression Arizona became a highway for dust bowl refugees en route to California with 105,105 crossing the Arizona border in 1937 alone. During the 1920s and 1930s the AFL organized there, making early gains among cotton pickers. These organizations met the same fate as their California counterparts, eventually consolidating into the UCAPAWA.[186] Participation of Mexicans in the agricultural history of Arizona must be further researched.

In the Pacific Northwest areas like the Yakima Valley required 25,000 to 30,000 workers during the hop harvest in September. During the 1920s and the 1930s the work force was racially mixed. Mexicans were in the minority, brought in by the large growers of Oregon and Washington. Farms in the Northwest were not as industrialized as in California and Arizona. Therefore workers were not as concentrated and consequently were more difficult to organize.[187]

Mexicans organized within the ranks of the western sheep shearers. Spurred by the National Industrial Recovery Act (1933), organizational drives intensified in Texas and Arizona and the mountain states during 1934 and 1935. Conditions in Texas were markedly worse than in other areas with shearers earning 5¢ to 6¢ a sheep versus 12¢ to 15¢ in Wyoming, Montana, and California. In 1934 in the West Texas area about 750 members of the Sheep Shearers's Union (SSU) demanded better wages—12¢ per head for sheep and 8¢ for goats (compared to 8¢ and 5¢ then currently paid). The Sheep and Goat Raisers Association refused to negotiate and workers went on strike in February. The employers pressured state relief officials to refuse shearers relief and discussed bringing in the Texas Rangers. The usual arrests and harassment followed; 42 SSU members were arrested and jailed as vigilance committees were organized. Ranchers hired white crews to break the Mexican strike. By March they broke the strike. In October 1934 a Mexican crew leader by the name of Ramón attempted once more to orga-

*Pejorative terms used by growers.

nize sheepherders, but authorities in Sonora, Texas, arrested Ramón and his men for disturbing the peace.[188]

Mexican workers struggled to improve conditions within the beet industry. In Colorado Mexican beet laborers occupied the lowest caste in society and were denied admission to public places and were segregated from the mainstream of society.[189] When wages declined drastically in 1932, falling to $12.00 to $14.00 an acre, the Mountain States Beet Growers' Association blamed conditions on the sugar-refining companies which, in turn, claimed that they were losing money. Communists formed the Agricultural Workers Industrial Union, establishing locals in Greeley, Fort Lupton, Fort Collins, and Denver. Mexican workers participated in these and other unions. Various factions in February 1932 formed the United Front Committee of Agricultural Workers Unions. The United Front Committee demanded $23.00 an acre and union recognition. The committee concentrated its efforts in Colorado, Nebraska, and Wyoming. On May 10, 1932, it called a strike which was easily broken by the Great Western Sugar Company. Left-wing workers blamed their failure on "conservative" or "reformist organizations" such as the Spanish-American Citizens Association of Fort Collins, but, in fact, the strike was poorly planned. Refining companies had more than enough labor. Public agencies and law enforcement officials joined to frustrate beet workers. Mass arrests followed with the deportation of militant Mexican members of the United Front. This marked the end of the United Front. Mexican workers formed the Spanish-Speaking Workers League as a vehicle to hold more radical workers in Denver after the 1932 strike.[190]

Nativism intensified and Mexicans were laid off WPA projects on the assumption that they should work as beet laborers. Beet companies, although prices for sugar increased, kept wages depressed. The TUUL was active during the early 1930s attempting to form "unemployed councils" of beet workers for the purpose of agitating for adequate relief. In Colorado the State Federation of Labor took part in the organization of the unemployed and appears to have been more progressive than in other states. Membership in the council was free, but cards were forfeited when members found a job. Members were nonvoting members of the AFL. The Colorado Federation of Labor (CFL) reportedly had 25,000 unemployed members. A few of the councils struck work relief projects to improve conditions and took part in small agricultural strikes.

The Jones-Costigan Act of 1934 encouraged beet growers not to employ child labor. Growers received benefit payments averaging $17.15 per acre. Stimulated by the ability of growers to pay higher wages, during the next two years labor organization increased. Active was the Beet Workers' Association, which claimed

35,000 members in Colorado, Wyoming, Nebraska, and Montana. The workers received $23.00 an acre but the United States Department of Agriculture in Colorado set a rate of $19.50 per acre in northern Colorado and $17.50 for the southern section. The previous year beet laborers received $13.00 to $14.00 an acre. The Colorado State Federation of Labor in 1935 paid the expenses of Mexican organizers in the Beet Workers' Association. In 1936 the latter held a convention in Denver attended by fifty delegates representing thirty-nine local organizations in five states. Workers especially condemned the practice of closing relief agencies to swell the ranks of the unemployed and thus increase the size of the labor pool. Shortly afterwards the CFL held its official convention and it ratified demands of the association and the wage demand of $23.00 per acre. As a result, the Colorado Federation of Agricultural Workers Unions was established which included diverse groups, such as the *Comisión Honorífica Mexicana* (a protective association under the Mexican Consul). Union leaders condemned discrimination against Mexican beet workers on relief. The bargaining position of the union had been weakened since the year before the U.S. Supreme Court invalidated the Jones-Costigan Act and large numbers of children returned to the fields. The situation worsened when large numbers of workers were dropped from relief rolls. Companies threatened to import large numbers of workers from New Mexico.[191]

The Sugar Act of 1937 helped farmers as well as allowing the secretary of agriculture to set a minimum wage for beet workers. It was the only act which directly benefited Mexican labor. However, these gains were offset by the flood of Anglo labor to the fields. Many workers complained that the AFL gave them insufficient financial and organizational support. Fourteen federal unions surrendered their AFL charters and joined UCAPAWA. During 1937 and 1938 conditions worsened but the union could do little; growers were squeezed by refining companies. Surpluses shrank available acreage and while small strikes broke out, strategically a general strike was out of question. Migrating dust bowl refugees further weakened the union's position. Attempts to form alliances with the Farmers' Union did not help much and little progress was made during the rest of the decade.[192]

Texas housed the majority of Mexican workers and 85 percent of the state's migrant farm labor force was Mexican. Although growers claimed a worker shortage, a farm labor surplus existed. The sheer size of the state formed an obstacle to farm union organizing and the hub of the migratory stream, the lower Rio Grande Valley, was particularly difficult to organize since it was not heavily industrialized and most Mexicans did not work locally. Although in the early 1930s many farmers were smaller proprietors and much more diversified than in California, agriculture was in a state of transition and the farm hand and sharecropper relationships that still existed were gradually being displaced.[193]

In 1933, in Laredo, Texas, an independent union, *La Asociación de Jornaleros,* was formed. Like so many unions, it was a response to the National Recovery Administration. *Jornaleros* included hat makers, painters, carpenters, construction workers, miners, and farm laborers. During 1934 agents provocateurs disrupted union activity. In the spring of 1935 new life was breathed into the union as it assumed leadership over 1,200 union workers on strike, even though the strike failed, partly because of the inexperience of the organizers and harassment by Texas Rangers who arrested fifty-six strikers. The union had refused to sign with individual growers and had held out for an industrywide contract. Although the strike was settled by mediation, growers broke the agreement as soon as the mediators left.[194]

In the spring of 1936 workers gave new life to the *Jornaleros.* The union exchanged delegates with the Farm Workers Union of Mexico and cooperated with communist-led unemployed councils of San Antonio. Relief was a major problem for farm workers throughout the depression. Federal relief agencies excluded migrants and a residence of one year was often required by state agencies. When the *Asociación* attempted to organize workers on relief, local authorities, immigration officials, Texas Rangers, and the U.S. army harassed the *Jornaleros* and its sympathizers and members of relief organizations. The *Jornaleros* received a charter from the American Federation of Labor and became the Agriculture Workers Labor Union Local 20212.[195]

In January 1937, the Texas Federation of Labor endorsed a statewide conference in Corpus Christi. The Texas Agriculture Organizing Committee was formed which took part in a series of small strikes in late June and early July. However, its efforts were frustrated by the power of growers and state authorities to control the flow of migrant labor. The Texas State Employment Service, formed in 1935, recruited workers for the different crops and in 1939 alone placed 550,047 farm workers. The Texas labor pool was just too abundant to allow for effective organization.[196] In the summer of 1937 the committee was absorbed by UCAPAWA which eventually enlisted 5,000 paid members.[197]

Efforts to organize skilled Mexicans and Anglo packing-shed workers in the lower Rio Grande Valley received attention. Fruit and Vegetable Workers Local 20363, an AFL affiliate, claimed 500 to 600 members. In February 1938 it led a fifty car caravan across the lower Rio Grande Valley protesting antiunion activity in the valley. Economic conditions worsened so that by 1938 all organizing efforts had disappeared.[198]

CHICANO FACTORY WORKERS

UCAPAWA's best work was in the urban centers. Its most spectacular strike was the pecan shellers strike in San Antonio. The pecan industry used primarily nonskilled labor and employed between 5,000 and 12,000 Mexicans. Gustave Duerler, a Swiss candy manufacturer, recognizing potential profits in the numerous pecan trees of the area, began the industry during the Civil War when he bought pecans from the native Americans and hired Mexicans to crack them open and extract the meat. By the 1880s Duerler shipped pecans east. In 1914 he mechanized the cracking phase of his operation, but still used Mexican women to extract meats by hand. Duerler remained the "Pecan King" until 1926, when the Southern Pecan Shelling Company, with an investment of $50,000, was formed. Ten years later the shelling company's gross business had climbed to $3 million. The company demechanized because it was cheaper to hire Chicanos than to maintain machines and factories. The depression insured a surplus of cheap labor.[199]

The pecan industry used agribusiness employment practices. Contractors furnished crackers and pickers. On many occasions, contractors employed shellers to pick pecans in their own homes. They also worked in sweatshops packed with as many as 100 pickers packed in an unventilated room without toilets and running water.[200]

The shellers averaged less than $2.00 per week in 1934. This rate increased only slightly by 1936, when shellers could earn from 5¢ to 6¢ a pound for pecan halves. A pecan workers' union claimed that the pay was even lower. Management rationalized its admittedly low wages: Chicanos ate pecans while working; shellers would not work the necessary hours if they were paid more—they would earn 75¢ and go home, whether it was 3:00 PM or 6:00 PM; Chicanos were satisfied; shellers had a nice warm place in which to work and could visit friends as they did so; if Mexicans earned more, they would just spend it "on tequila and on worthless trinkets in the dime stores."[201]

Conditions forced workers to organize. El Nogal, the largest of the pecan workers' unions, claimed 4,000 members between 1933 and 1936. Another union, the Pecan Shelling Workers Union of San Antonio, was a company union led by Mageleno Rodríguez. When management declared a 1¢ a pound reduction in rates, thousands of shellers walked off their jobs on February 1, 1938, at the peak of the pecan shelling season.[202] Workers abandoned 130 plants throughout the west side of San Antonio. Local law authorities backed management and arrested over 1,000 pickets on a variety of charges included blocking sidewalks, disturbing the peace, and unlawful assemblies. "Within the first two weeks tear gas was used at least a half-dozen times to disperse throngs that milled about the shelle-

ries."[203] City officials even enforced an obscure city ordinance aimed at sign-carrying picketers, which made it "unlawful for any person to carry . . . through any public street . . . any advertising" until a permit had been obtained from the city marshall.[204] The office of city marshall had been abolished some years before. Since the picketers did not have the necessary permit, they were arrested and fined $10. In contrast to the chief of police, the county sheriff did allow picketing.

Police Chief Owen Kilday was determined to break the strike.[205] When CIO organizer J. Austin Beasley arrived in San Antonio, Kilday promptly arrested and detained him, alleging that Beasley was wanted in El Paso. Strikers attempted to obtain a court injunction to restrain Kilday from harassing the pickets, but the judge refused.

Chief Kilday labeled UCAPAWA organizers "disturbers of the peace." In spite of Kilday's opposition 6,000 of the 12,000 shellers joined the union. A special target of city officials was Mrs. Emma Tenayuca Brooks, "a fiery little Mexican woman about twenty years old," who was a leader among strikers and allegedly an admitted Communist.[206] Although the union leadership arbitrarily replaced her, attacks continued. The police, assisted by firemen, used tear gas and clubs to disperse the pickets.[207] Kilday issued inflammatory press releases: "[It's a] Communist revolution. . . . I branded the leadership as communistic and I still think so. . . . It is my duty to interfere with revolution, and Communism is revolution." The chief stated that if he did not act and if the strike were won, "25,000 workers on the West Side would fall into the Communist party." His definition of a communist was "a person who believes in living in a community on the government and tearing down all religion."[208]

The Mexican Chamber of Commerce and the League of United Latin American Citizens, as well as the Catholic church, refused to support the strike under its current leadership. These groups rarely opposed the Kilday machine and tacitly supported its running of the city. The archbishop went so far as to commend the police for acting against "Communistic influences." In all fairness to the archbishop, he did urge pecan owners to pay higher wages, even though he did so because in his view lower wages bred communism. A Reverend John López, a Roman Catholic priest, urged workers to return to the true friend of the working masses—the church. The San Antonio Ministers' Association called for a settlement and for a purge of "all Communistic, Fascist, or any un-American elements."[209] Many observers considered the CIO an arm of Moscow and any protest by Mexicans as communist inspired.

Federal and state officials disapproved of Kilday's methods. The National Labor Relations Board stated that "there has been a misuse of authority in handling the strike." The governor of Texas condemned Kilday's refusal to allow picketing. He censured the beatings and forcing Mexicans to become scabs under the threat of deportation. However, Chief Kilday continued his repression and even closed a soup kitchen, which provided free food to strikers, alleging a violation of city health ordinances.[210]

After thirty-seven days of Kilday, the parties submitted to arbitration. Pecan shellers had stopped production, calling national attention to conditions. The arbitration board recognized Local 172 as the sole bargaining agent and required owners to comply with the Fair Labor Standards Act which had been passed on June 25, 1938, and pay the minimum wage of 25¢ an hour. The victory was short lived; owners replaced workers with machinery. In 1938 the total annual income of 521 San Antonio pecan shellers' families, averaging 4.6 persons, was $251. This included all income, from relief work to the value of relief commodities.[211]

By the 1930s Mexican women made up a significant portion of the labor pool of the garment factories of the Southwest. Los Angeles had an estimated 150 dress factories, employing about 2,000 workers, 75 percent of whom were Mexicans (the rest were Italians, Russians, Jews, and Anglo-Americans).

Manufacturers preferred to hire Mexican women, not because they were inherently docile, but, as in the case of most new immigrants, they were the most vulnerable. They were forced to work in sweatshops for substandard wages.

Garment workers were sometimes paid as low as 50¢ a week; 40 percent of the women were paid less than $5 a week although the NRA code stipulated $15 a week. If they protested, they stood to lose their jobs and, being Mexicans, it was very difficult to get public relief or support from local institutions. Further, many were subject to deportation. The mass repatriations of the day were held over their heads, and if they persisted in protesting, the immigration authorities or local police were alerted. The industry employed a vicious kickback system whereby workers had to pay back a portion of their salary for the privilege of working.[212]

During depression years the labor market was even larger, with many former migrants settling in Los Angeles. Rose Pesotta, an organizer for the International Ladies Garment Workers Union (ILGWU), stated:

> Poorly paid and hard driven, many of these agricultural workers, seeking to leave their thankless labors, naturally gravitated to the principal California cities, where compatriots had preceded them. Thus hundreds of Mexican women and girls, traditionally skillful with needle and eager to get away from family domination, had found their way into the garment industry in Los Angeles.[213]

Many workers in fact were the sole support of a family with an unemployed husband at home. They, for the most part, lived in the outskirts of town "at the end of the car-lines, in rickety old shacks, unpainted, unheated, usually without baths and with outside toilets."[214]

The ILGWU in 1933 began to develop trade union leadership among Mexican women in Los Angeles. Although the workers had everything to lose and had no surplus income, they joined. Pesotta stated, "We get them . . . because we are the only *Americanos* who take them in as equals. They may well become the backbone of our union on the West Coast."[215]

On October 12, 1933, the ILGWU closed down the Los Angeles dress industry, with much of its success attributed to Mexican strikers. Mexican women were told the progress of the strike through the radio. When the local radio station was pressured to terminate broadcasting this news, "Some of the Mexican girls solved our problem. At their suggestion, we bought time from another station, *El Eco de México,* in Tijuana, just across the border." Broadcasts at seven each morning transmitted progress of the strike to the Los Angeles Mexican community. The workers stood firm even when manufacturers countered by closing the factories for two months. They responded to a court injunction against them by assembling a thousand people in front of the Paramount Dress Company. Captain William Hynes and the "red squad" were powerless to disperse such a large force. They could only harass the picketers, make them march two abreast, and forbid them to holler "Scab!" Five strikers were arrested for disorderly conduct.[216]

The NRA state board held hearings on October 13, 1933. The press distorted the testimony. Los Angeles employers put pressure on Washington, claiming their employees were "subnormal" and not entitled to minimum wages. The decision of the board was meaningless in terms of actual conditions. It found only that "working conditions should be those established under Section 7(a) of the National Industrial Recovery Act; the wages of the employees to be those provided in the Code for the dress industry. Without a signed agreement between employers and the union, workers had to rely on the NRA to enforce the order, and from the past record of the NRA union officials knew this was worthless. Union organizers, however, recommended that workers return and fight to enforce the order from within since they feared factionalism would confuse the workers. A struggle ensued with the communist-led faction issuing leaflets "Smash The Sellout!" and accusing the ILGWU of collaborating with the bosses. It urged the rank and file to join the Needle Trades Workers Industrial Union.[217]

The full particulars of the struggle must be researched. What should be remembered is that the real enemy was the employer who exploited the workers. The struggle between the two unions, on the other hand, cannot even be classed as ideological. Pesotta states that Lilly Tillie, a communist, had attempted to keep Mexicans out of the union. The Needle Trades Industrial Union had been liquidated in 1933 and its members ordered to join the IL-GWU.

There was little work and employers intimidated workers. They used devious methods to get around the wage minimums. Manufacturers used the Bureau of County Welfare and the Los Angeles County Charities against workers, sending out notices through these auspices with the intent of intimidating the strikers to return to work.[218]

The union continued its activities. Local 96 of the ILGWU had the following Chicana charter members; Anita Andrade, Jessie Cervantes, Emma Delmonte, Ramona Gonzales, Lola Patino, Carmen and Marie Rodríguez. Throughout the 1930s Mexican women supported organizing efforts but grew dissatisfied with union leadership because they wanted more independence within the International.[219]

In Texas, San Antonio, Dallas, Laredo, and Houston stood out as major garment manufacturing centers. During the mid-1930s, San Antonio had some 550 garment workers who worked 45 hours a week for $3.00 to $5.00 a week (6¢ to 11¢ an hour).[220] In March 1934 the ILGWU chartered two locals in the city: the Infants and Children's Wear Workers' Union Local 180 and the Ladies Garment Workers' Union Local 123. The ILGWU struck the A. B. Frank plant in 1936; this plant closed down when it was 100 percent organized. After six months of being picketed by Local 123 the Dorothy Frocks Company moved to Dallas where a Dallas local continued the strike until the company signed a contract in November 1936. However, Local 123 in San Antonio ceased to exist.

Although the strike activity against Dorothy Frocks lasted only six months in San Antonio, it was bitter. During a car caravan through the city by President Franklin Delano Roosevelt some fifty strikers publicly disrobed scabs from the company. Throughout these strikes Chief Kilday conducted mass arrests for unlawful assembly or obstructing the sidewalk. City authorities even denied that a strike existed.[221]

In the spring of 1937 Local 180 called a strike against the Shirlee Frock Company. Fifty pickets were arrested and picketing was limited to three persons by a local judge who also prohibited the use of banners. The strike was successful: the ILGWU was recognized with workers receiving the minimum wage of 20¢ an hour. The union conducted several more strikes. Chicanas were at the forefront of organizing and strike activity; in 1939 of the 1,400 San Antonio women who belonged to the ILGWU 80 percent were Mexican.[222]

The Houston garment industry employed about 600 women dressmakers. They toiled 48 to 54 hours weekly for $6.00 to $8.00. Workers at the five Houston plants organized Local 214 and won contracts with these plants, calling for a $12.00 minimum and a 40 hour week.

Laredo workers organized Local 350 which had several hundred Chicanas during the 1930s. The principal organizer was Sara Lizarde.

Dallas had 1,800 garment workers who worked from 35 to 40 hours a week. Cotton dress operators earned $12.00, cutters earned $27, and as a whole most of the garment workers earned less than $18. Owners refused to recognize the union. On March 6, 1935, union members voted for a strike when the Morten-Davis Company fired four union women. In August tempers flared so high that union groups stripped women strikebreakers naked in downtown Dallas. Local authorities arrested and harassed union members. Owners held firm and the strike collapsed.[223]

As in California, the ILGWU in Texas won only limited victories. Texas had special problems, being an open shop state, but a major portion of the blame for the failure to organize must be assigned to the ILGWU itself. Meyer Perlstein, who led union activities in the Southwest during the 1930s and 1940s, while a dedicated individual, never really seemed to make an effort to recruit Mexican organizers. He hired Rebecca Taylor, an Anglo, as the educational director for its San Antonio office. Miss Taylor, a school teacher, admittedly took the job because it paid more than teaching. Her sole qualifications were that she spoke Spanish and had received a BA from Curry College in Boston. Taylor was born in Mexico in a middle-class Arkansas-Oklahoma-Texas religious colony which had been established in the 1890s. The colony came to an abrupt end when revolutionaries disbanded it. Throughout her tenure with the union, she opposed anything involving radicals and any militancy that smacked of the Mexican revolution in which people like herself lost their privilege.[224] She opposed radical Chicano leadership during the pecan shellers' strike. During the 1950s, she quit the union and went to work for Tex-son, one of the ILGWU's principal adversaries, and during the 1970s she opposed *La Raza Unida*.

Another major center of urban organizing was Chicago, which remained the hub of the midwestern Chicano population, although repatriation reduced the Mexican population from 20,000 to 16,000.[225]

The impact of the depression fell hardest on the unskilled and semiskilled; 83 percent of the Chicagoans on relief were unskilled workers in 1935. Generally, unemployment corresponded with skill and race. The Mexican population of Chicago was 66 percent unskilled in the 1930s versus 53 percent for Blacks, 35 percent for foreign-born white, and 33 percent for native whites. It was not unusual for 35 percent of all Mexicans to be on relief versus 11 percent of the foreign-born whites, 15 percent of the native whites, and 47 percent of the Blacks. Chicanos had a lower median of education than other groups, 3.2 years versus a median of 4.7 for Blacks and 5.3 for European whites.[226]

In 1935 30 percent of Chicago's Mexican workers were unemployed. Mexicans suffered higher unemployment than any group in the city, with the possible exception of Blacks. Increasingly, from 1933 to 1937, employment and relief depended on citizenship. Employers and government authorities pressured Mexicans to prove legal residence or a willingness to become naturalized citizens. Government relief, in the form of work and aid, often required applicants to be citizens. Mexicans had a lower naturalization rate than any other group; therefore, many remained unemployed and ineligible for aid. In certain areas Chicanos fared better than in others; for example in South Chicago Chicano steelworkers fared better than in Back of the Yards where all groups shared high unemployment.[227]

By the mid-1930s conditions somewhat improved and a new wave of Chicanos from Texas and other sectors of the Midwest began arriving. During this period Mexicans actively joined a variety of labor clubs, unions, and workers' organizations for the employed and unemployed to counter the effects of the economic depression.

Mexicans in Chicago were greatly influenced by the *Confederación de Trabajadores Mexicanos* (CTM) and during 1935 they formed a Chicago chapter of *El Frente Popular Mexicano* which sponsored "a series of meetings, discussions, and lectures regularly attended by more than 200 people." Refugio Martínez, a leading activist during this period, was allegedly later deported during the McCarran-Walter witch-hunts of the 1950s. The organization was housed in the University of Chicago Settlement House in Back of the Yards. The *Frente* actively protected Mexican workers but its interests extended beyond labor issues to protests against Franco's despotism during the Spanish Civil War and to expression of anticlerical attitudes. These interests alienated many Catholic organizations and the church began to publish *El Ideal Católico Mexicano* in 1935, specifically to counter the radical appeal of the *Frente* and to crusade against Marxist tendencies and communism. It was supported by the *Sociedad de Obreros Católicos* (Society of Catholic Workers) which represented the conservative sector of the community.[228] However, neither the *Frente* or the *Sociedad* had wide followings. The most numerous of the Mexican workers' organizations remained the *mutualistas*.

Mexicans favored groups that were predominately Mexican and local in character such as the *Sociedad de Obreros Libres Mexicanos de Sud Chicago* (Society of Free Mexican Workers of South Chicago) which was made up of steel and foundry workers. Better known was the Illinois Workers' Alliance which had seventy-two locals throughout the state. It attracted a multiethnic membership of both employed and unemployed workers. It had a neighborhood orientation and three locals operated in Mexican neighborhoods. As early as 1933 it advertised in Mexican newspapers for recruits. This organization successfully pressured for more equitable relief and employment laws. Chicanos participated in Locals 32 and 36, each of which claimed fifty Mexican members.[229]

Unions such as the Brotherhood of Railroad and Maintenance Workers discriminated against Mexicans. However, after the Wagner Act steel and meat packing industrial unions increasingly solicited Mexican membership. During the early 1920s many unions stereotyped Mexicans as docile workers. This stereotype was proven false. In 1927 Basil Pacheco led a walk-out at the Youngstown Sheet and Tube plant in East Chicago in a protest over unfair calculation of work hours. The company fired Pacheco and the protest ended.[230]

In four months during 1936 the Steel Workers' Organizing Committee (SWOC) recruited between 150 and 200 Mexican workers.[231] Mexican workers were particularly active in Local 65 at United States Steel South Works in Chicago. Alfredo Avila played a major role. He and his wife worked closely with the local's president George Patterson. Manuel García also worked with the union and along with Avila sponsored meetings in Spanish and prepared union literature in that language. They enlisted the support of the Mexican consul and a priest at Our Lady of Guadalupe Church. By 1936, although only 5 percent of the South Works employees were Mexicans, they comprised 11 percent of the union; 54 percent of the general membership voted versus 88 percent of the Chicano membership. Following United States Steel's recognition of the union, workers elected Avila to the first executive board.

In East Chicago, Indiana Juan Dávila, Basil Pacheco, Max Luna, and Miguel Arredondo actively recruited Mexican steelworkers. On May 26, 1937, a strike was called against the "Little Steel" firms, Bethlehem, Republic, Inland, and Youngstown, when they refused to sign a contract. The Youngstown and Inland plants in East Chicago were completely shut down, with Mexicans playing a major role on the picket lines. At Inland, for example, Chicanos comprised 75 percent of the pickets.

The union was unable to close down the Republic plant in South Chicago. The union brothers from the other plants converged on Republic, holding meetings and demonstrations. During one of these demonstrations, on May 30, 1937, Chicago police fired at the strikers, killing ten and injuring sixty-eight. Although the crowd had a wide racial mix, one of the policemen said it resembled the "Mexican army." In reality, Mexicans made up about 15 percent of the demonstrators. According to most sources, Max Guzmán, a Republic employee, was one of the two flag bearers. Mexicans such as

Lupe Marshall, a Chicana social worker, marched at the front of the line; she played a leading role in caring for the wounded. At least eleven of the injured were Chicanos. Violence ended the strike and it was not until 1941 that the union was recognized. Chicanos remained active in union politics. Basil Pacheco, for example, an organizer at Youngstown, chaired Labor's Non-Partisan League in East Chicago in 1938.[232] Mexicans increasingly joined urban unions, but, unlike in agriculture, Midwest Mexican workers more and more joined mixed ethnic and racial industrial unions.

The influence of the CIO on Chicano participation in the labor movement can be seen in its work in California. According to historian Luis L. Arroyo "the C.I.O. was extremely successful in organizing workers and had 15,000 Mexicans in the Los Angeles area by 1942."[233] Chicanos participated in various locals in the county as well as the Los Angeles Industrial Council (later the Los Angeles CIO Council). Luisa Moreno of UCAPAWA served as vice-president of the council and vice-president of the California CIO Executive Board. Moreno, like other Chicano trade unionists, remained active in the Chicano community, representing its interests within the CIO. In 1941 the Los Angeles CIO Council established the Committee to Aid Mexican workers. The committee was chaired by Bert Corona, president of Warehouse Local 1–26 of the longshoremen's union.[234] The committee acted to implement President Franklin D. Roosevelt's 1941 Executive Order 8802 which prohibited race discrimination by firms having war defense contracts. It cooperated closely with the Black ministers and the Spanish-Speaking People's Congress in pressuring the Los Angeles Board of Education to set up job training programs for Mexicans. Chicano labor leaders such as Bert Corona and Frank López also joined the Sleepy Lagoon Defense Committee (to be discussed in Chapter 10), both as members of the Spanish-Speaking People's Congress and as official union representatives. Luisa Moreno also became active in the committee by working through the CIO Council. In 1942 the Committee to Aid Mexicans incorporated into the California CIO Anti-Discrimination Committee. In 1943 this committee gave way to the California CIO Committee on Minorities, which functioned until 1946. This integration led to a deemphasis of Mexican issues.[235] By the mid-1940s the Los Angeles CIO Council was apparently unwilling to establish Mexican committees.

The International Longshoremen's and Warehousemen's Union (ILWU) was founded on August 11, 1937, when it joined the CIO. Local 1–26 broke away from the AFL and affiliated with the ILWU. The local had about 600 members at that time. A year after the affiliation with the CIO, membership increased to 1,300 members. Bert Corona, William Trujillo, and other Chicanos served as volunteer recruiters. Drives were conducted to enlist workers in the drug warehouse industry as well as milling, paper, and hardware. By 1939 Local 1–26 had about 1,500 members.[236]

Between 1939 and 1941 organizers recruited warehousemen in the waste material industry in which about 50 percent of the workers were Mexicans. The union successfully organized some 1,000 workers in that industry, half of whom were Mexicans. Charles "Chili" Duarte led ILWU organization drives in Los Angeles, engaging in bitter jurisdictional fights with the Teamsters. By the end of 1941 the local had 3,400 members in the drug, milling, paper, metal trades, and waste material industries. In 1941 Bert Corona was elected president of Local 1–26, serving in that capacity until he entered the U.S. army in 1943. After this time the local continued organizing and by 1945 it held sixty contracts covering seventy-three shops. It had a multinational membership, one-third of whom were women. William Trujillo and Isidro Armenta occupied leadership capacities. In 1950 Local 1–26 broke with the CIO when the CIO National Executive Board charged that the ILWU was dominated by communists. Chicanos remained in the ILWU and supported the break with the CIO.[237]

In 1937 Local 576 of the United Furniture Workers of America (UFWA) also broke with the AFL after a bitter battle between those who wanted to maintain a craft orientation and members who wanted to organize on an industrywide basis, including all those who worked with wood. Those favoring an industrial union broke with upholsterers Local 15 (AFL) and formed Local 576 of Los Angeles (UFWA). Local 576 entered into a prolonged fight for membership with Local 15. Meanwhile, this same dispute broke out in Furniture Workers Local 1561 (AFL) which had some 1,000 members; the dissidents joined Local 576 (CIO). Armando Dávila was the business agent for the local and the union was heavily Chicano. Dávila along with Oscar Castro continued to organize during hard times brought about by World War II when domestic production was heavily curtailed. Ben Cruz became president of Local 576 in 1944, and Oscar Castro became a full-time organizer in 1946. By early 1946 Local 576 had 2,007 members; by 1947 it increased to 3,000 members, about half of whom were Chicanos. During this period Local 576 was attacked for its left-wing leadership by the UFWA executive board who labeled them communist sympathizers because they supported Henry Wallace for president in 1948. After a bitter quarrel over the local's autonomy, the leadership seceded from the CIO in August 1950; at the time it had 2,055 members, 950 of whom were Chicanos. The UFWA chartered Local 1010 to compete with Local 576. By the end of the year, Local 1010 had 1,738 members, 860 of whom were Mexicans. The full details of the battle are not known, but in the early 1950s Armando Dávila was deported, presumably under the authority of the McCarran Act.[238]

During World War II Mexicans continued to be victimized by discrimination in the war industries. Few rose to supervisory positions. Alonso S. Perales stated before the Senate Fair Employment Practices Act hearings in San Antonio in 1944 that at Kelley Field in Texas the federal government employed 10,000 people, and not one Mexican held a position above that of a laborer or mechanic's helper. Moreover, there were 150 towns and cities in that state which had public places that refused to serve Mexicans—many of whom were servicemen.[239]

At the same hearings Frank Paz, president of the Spanish-Speaking People's Council of Chicago, stated that 45,000 Chicanos lived in the area of that city, mostly employed in railroads, steel mills, and packinghouses. The overwhelming majority worked as railroad section hands. The railroad companies refused to promote them, and in fact were importing 150 temporary workers from Mexico to do skilled work as electricians, pipe fitters, steam fitters, millwrights, and so forth.[240] The Railroad Brotherhood refused membership to Mexicans or Blacks. Mexicans worked in track repair and maintenance, supervised by an Anglo foreman.

Paz told of the case of steelworker Ramón Martínez, a twenty year veteran, who was placed in charge of a gang of workers because they spoke only Spanish. He learned that he was paid $50.00 a month less than the other foremen. He was told that the reasons for the wage difference were that he was not a citizen and he did not have a high school education, but when he went to night school and received a diploma, he was still refused foremen's wages. Dr. Carlos E. Castañeda testified that in Arizona although Mexicans numbered 8,000 to 10,000 out of the 15,000 to 16,000 of the state's miners, they were restricted to common labor categories; the war had not broken down barriers.[241] California had about 457,900 Mexicans out of a population of 6,907,387; 315,000 Chicanos lived in Los Angeles. As of the summer of 1942 only 5,000 Chicanos worked in basic industries in that city. Further, only 19,500 Mexicans were employed in the defense plants of southern California. Lastly, Los Angeles County employed about 16,000 workers, 400 of whom were Mexican.[242] Mexicans, were better represented in combat troops, enlisted to fight in a war presumably to insure human rights.[243]

NOTES

1. Manuel Díaz Ramírez, *Apuntes sobre el movimiento obrero y campesino de México* (México, D.F.: Ediciones de Cultura Popular, 1974), p. 12.
2. Rodney D. Anderson, *Outcasts in Their Own Land: Mexican Workers, 1906–1911* (De Kalb: Northern Illinois University Press, 1976), pp. 12, 18, 26–27, 37.

3. Eric Wolf, *Sons of the Shaking Earth* (Chicago: University of Chicago Press, 1959), p. 247; Anderson, pp. 38, 43.
4. Hudson Stroude, *Timeless Mexico* (New York: Harcourt Brace Jovanovich, 1944) p. 210.
5. Alberto Trueba Urbina, *Evolución de La Huelga* (México, D.F. Ediciones Botas, 1950), pp. 60, 63; Anderson, pp. 79, 86; Díaz Ramírez, p. 52; John M. Hart, *Anarchism and the Mexican Working Class, 1860–1931* (Austin: University of Texas Press, 1978), pp. 50–51.
6. Hart, pp. 20–21, 23–24, 55, 45; Anderson, pp. 80, 45; Díaz Ramírez, p. 62.
7. Díaz Ramírez, pp. 66, 67–68, 70, 83; Hart, pp. 32–41; Anderson, p. 81.
8. Díaz Ramírez, p. 115; Hart, pp. 54–73; Anderson, p. 85.
9. Anderson, pp. 88, 92; Juan Gómez-Quiñones, "The First Steps: Chicano Labor Conflict and Organizing, 1900–1920, *Aztlán* 3, no. 1 (1973): 20; Charles C. Cumberland, *Mexican Revolution: Genesis Under Madero* (Austin: University of Texas Press, 1952), p. 16.
10. Dawn Keremitsis, *La Industria Textil Mexicana en el Siglo XIX* (México, D.F.: SepSetentas, 1973), pp. 208, 209, 210. Fewer women were employed in the interior of Mexico than in northern Mexican mills. It can be assumed that there was a surplus of male workers in the interior, whereas in the north a labor shortage existed at this time. For example, at *La Estrella* in Coahuila, out of 600 workers, 200 were women and 100 were children. In 1897 La Buena Fe employed 63 men, 74 women, and 33 children. *La Aura* employed 28 men and 40 women, and at El Labrador there were 19 men, 20 women, and 20 children working. In Coahuila men and women received the same wages, whereas children were paid less.
11. Octavio A. Hernández, *Esquena de la economia mexicana hasta antes de la Revolución*, quoted in Keremitsis, p. 210.
12. Anderson, pp. 133–134; Hart, pp. 83–103, 139–141; Ward Sloan Albro III, "Ricardo Flores Magón and the Liberal Party: An Inquiry into the Origins of the Mexican Revolution of 1910" (Ph.D. dissertation, University of Arizona, 1967), pp. 114–115. Albro places the date as the 22nd; the mills at Puebla, Vera Cruz, Tlaxcala, Jalisco, Queretaro, and Mexico City were also involved.
13. Anderson, p. 159.
14. Anderson, p. 157.
15. Anderson, pp. 163–164, 167; Albro, p. 115, places the number at between 200 and 800; the bodies were taken to Vera Cruz and dumped in the sea.
16. Laureano Clavo Berber, *Nociones de Historia de Sonora* (México, D.F.: Publicaciones del Gobierno del Estado de Sonora, 1958), p. 277; Antonio G. Rivera, *La Revolución en Sonora* (México, D.F.: n.p., 1969), pp. 139, 159.
17. Anderson, pp. 117–119; Gómez-Quiñones, p. 18.
18. Kaye Lyson Briegel, "Alianza Hispano-Americana, 1894–1965: A Mexican Fraternal Insurance Society" (Ph.D. dissertation, University of Southern California, 1974); José Amado Hernández, "The Development of Mutual Aid Societies in the Chicano Community," *La Raza* 3, no. 7 (Summer 1977); Paul Taylor, *An American-Mexican Frontier: Nueces County, Texas* (New York: Russell and Russell, 1971), p. 173; Carey McWilliams, *Ill Fares the Land; Migrants and Migratory Labor in the United States* (New York: Arno Press, 1976), pp. 208–209; D. W. Meinig, *Southwest: The Peoples in Geographical Change* (New York: Oxford University Press, 1971), p. 74; Meinig, p. 42; Gómez-Quiñones, p. 23.
19. Carolyn Asbaugh, *Lucy Parsons: American Revolutionary* (Chicago: Herr, 1976), pp. 267–268; Richard O. Boyer and Herbert M. Morais, *Labor's Untold Story*, 3rd. ed. (New York: United Electrical Radio and Machine Workers of America, 1970).
20. Juan Gómez-Quiñones, *Semradores: Ricardo Flores Magón y el Partido Liberal Mexicano: A Eulogy and Critique* (Los Angeles: Aztlán, 1973), p. 23; James D. Cockcroft, *Intellectual Precursors of the Mexican Revolution, 1900–1913* (Austin: University of Texas Press, 1968), p. 124. Also see Robert E. Ireland, "The Radical Community, Mexican and American Radicalism," *Journal of Mexican-American History* (Fall 1971): 22–29.
21. *Regeneración*, September 3, 1910, quoted in Ward Sloan Albro III, "Ma-

gonismo: Precursor to Chicanismo?" (Manuscript, Texas Arts and Industries University at Kingsville, n.d.), p. 5; Cockcroft, p. 231.

22. Albro, "Flores Magón," pp. 79–81, 85; Gómez-Quiñones, *Sembradores*, p. 46; *Regeneración*, January 14, 1911.
23. Emilio Zamora, "Chicano Socialist Labor Activity in Texas, 1900–1920," *Aztlán* 6, no. 2 (Summer 1975): 235.
24. *Regeneración*, October 25, 1913.
25. Numerous feminist groups such as *El grupo feminino* "Luz y vida" of Los Angeles, *Regeneración*, April 15, 1916, and *El grupo feminino* "Grupo Práxedis G. Guerrero" de San Antonio, *Regeneración*, March 25, 1916, participated in the struggle.
26. Meinig, pp. 62–63.
27. Larry García y Griego, "*Los Primeros Pasos al Norte*: Mexican Migration to the United States," (Bachelor's thesis, Princeton University, 1973), p. 33; Lawrence Anthony Cardoso, "Mexican Emigration to the United States, 1900–1930: An Analysis of Socio-Economic Causes" (Ph.D. dissertation, University of Connecticut, 1974), pp. 39, 50, 65. Cardoso, p. 38, summarizes the new technology—the steam shovel, dynamite, surveying devices, etc.
28. Paul S. Taylor, *Mexican Labor in the United States*, vol. I (New York: Arno, 1970), p. 320; García y Griego, pp. 19, 20. See George O. Coalson, *The Development of the Migratory Farm Labor System in Texas: 1900–1954* (San Francisco: R & E Research Assc., 1977), an excellent work on the expansion of the cotton industry in Texas; David Montejano, "Race, Labor Repression and Capitalist Agriculture: Notes from Texas, 1920–1930," (Berkeley, Calif.: Institute for the Study of Social Change, 1977), p. 2; Mark Reisler, "Passing Through Our Egypt: Mexican Labor in the United States, 1900–1940" (Ph.D. dissertation, Cornell University, 1973), p. 10; and Pauline R. Kibbe, *Latin Americans in Texas* (New York: Arno Press, 1974), p. 168.
29. Victor B. Nelson Cisneros, "*La Clase Trabajadora en Tejas, 1920–1940*," *Aztlán* 6, no. 2 (1975): 242–243; Taylor, *American-Mexican Frontier*, p. 84; Douglas E. Foley, Clarice Mora, Donald E. Post, and Ignacio Lozano, *From Peones to Politicos: Ethnic Relations in a South Texas Town, 1900–1977* (Austin: University of Texas Press, Center for Mexican American Studies, 1977), p. 14; Coalson, p. 47; Edgar Greer Shelton, Jr., "Political Conditions Among Texas Mexicans Along the Rio Grande" (Master's thesis, University of Texas, 1946), p. 9.
30. Foley et al., pp. 3–4, 12–13.
31. Taylor, *American-Mexican Frontier*, pp. 85–89, 131; Montejano, pp. 20, 24.
32. Foley et al., pp. 6–7, 70–71, 85; Montejano, p. 31.
33. Robert N. McLean and Charles A. Thomson, *Spanish and Mexicans in Colorado: A Survey of the Spanish Americans and Mexicans in the State of Colorado* (New York: 1924), reprinted in Carlos E. Cortes, ed., *Church Views of the Mexican American* (New York: Arno Press, 1974), p. 34.
34. *Gopher Historian* (Fall 1971) : 5.
35. Cardoso, pp. 40–44; 49; Manuel Gamio, *Mexican Immigration to the United States* (New York: Dover, 1971), p. 37.
36. Reisler, pp. 13, 15, 8–9.
37. García y Griego, p. 16; Winifred Kupper, ed., *Texas Sheepman* (Austin: University of Texas Press, 1951), pp. 37, 62, 63, 118; Edward N. Wentworth, *American Sheep Trails* (Ames, Iowa: Iowa College Press, 1948), p. 522; Cardoso, p. 33.
38. Victor Clark, *Mexican Labor in the United States*, U.S. Department of Commerce Bulletin No. 79 (Washington, D.C.: U.S. Government Printing Office, 1908), pp. 494, 507, 511.
39. George C. Kiser, "Mexican American Labor Before World War II," *Journal of Mexican American History* (Spring 1972): 123; Official Report of the Governor's Spanish Speaking Task Force, Submitted to Governor Robert D. Ray and the 66th General Assembly, *Conoceme en Iowa* (Des Moines, Iowa: 1976), p. 4.
40. Clark, p. 485; Kiser, p. 125; Zamora, p. 221; Clark, pp. 492–493.
41. Ernesto Galarza, *Farm Workers and Agribusiness in California, 1947–1960* (Notre Dame, Ind.: University of Notre Dame Press, 1977), p. 3; Stuart Jamieson, *Labor Unionism in American Agriculture* (New York: Arno Press, 1976),

pp. 53–54; Porter Chaffee, "Organizational Efforts of Mexican Agricultural Workers" (Unpublished ms., Oakland, Calif.: Works Progress Administration Federal Writers Project, 1938), pp. 6–7; Norman Lowenstein, "Strikes and Strike Tactics in California Agriculture: A History" (Master's thesis, University of California at Berkeley, 1940), pp. 22–24; Gómez-Quiñones, "The First Steps," 24–26.

42. Gómez-Quiñones, "The First Steps," p. 26; Sam Kushner, *Long Road to Delano* (New York: International Publishers, 1975), p. 20; Chaffee, pp. 6–7.

43. Alberto M. Camarillo, "Chicano Urban History: A Study of Compton's Barrio, 1936–1970," *Aztlán* (Fall 1971): 25.

44. Charles Wollenberg, "Working on *El Traque*," in Norris Hundley, Jr., ed., *The Chicano* (Santa Barbara: Clio Books, 1975), pp. 96–98, 102–105; Louis B. Perry and Richard S. Perry, *A History of the Los Angeles Labor Movement, 1911–1941* (Los Angeles: University of California Press, 1963), p. 71.

45. Wollenberg, p. 105.

46. Mario T. García, "Racial Dualism in the El Paso Labor Market, 1880–1920," *Aztlán* 6, no. 2 (Summer 1975): 213.

47. Gómez-Quiñones, "The First Steps," p. 22.

48. Zamora, pp. 223–226.

49. Barbara Jane Macklin, *Structural Stability and Cultural Change in a Mexican American Community* (New York: Arno Press, 1976), p. 23; Reisler, p. 92; McWilliams, p. 249.

50. Gómez-Quiñones, "The First Steps," p. 28; *Regeneración*, October 15, 1910.

51. Gómez-Quiñones, "The First Steps," pp. 28–29.

52. Zamora, pp. 227–230. Hernández himself was arrested in 1915 and acquitted. Hernández is quoted as saying, "I am a Socialist through reading Mexican Socialist papers."

53. Jamieson, p. 59; Hyman Weintraub, "The I.W.W. in California, 1905–1931" (Master's thesis, University of California at Los Angeles, 1947), pp. 5, 9, 16, 18, 49, 50, 68–69, 71–72. See James Weinstein, *The Decline of Socialism in America, 1912–1925* (New York: Knopf, 1967). The best source of information on California criminal syndicalist law is a document in the Paul S. Taylor Collection in the Bancroft Library entitled "Criminal Syndicalism Law Weapon Against Workers." See also Kushner, pp. 49–50, and Gómez-Quiñones, "The First Steps," p. 30.

54. Samuel Yellen, *American Labor Struggles* (New York: Russell, 1936) pp. 205–206; Colorado Adjutant General's Office, *The Military Occupation of the Coal Strike Zone of Colorado by the National Guard, 1913–1914*; Walter Fink, *The Ludlow Massacre, 1914*; George P. West, *Report on the Colorado Strike*, U.S. Commission on Industrial Relations, 1915; reprinted in Leon Stein and Philip Taft, eds., *Massacre at Ludlow. Four Reports* (New York: Arno Press, 1971), esp. pp. 15–16, 31.

55. Fink, p. 75; Colorado Adjutant General's office, pp. 60–61; Fink, p. 6; West, p. 124; Yellen, pp. 234–235.

56. Gómez-Quiñones, "The First Steps," p. 30.

57. West, p. 135; Yellen, pp. 240–241; McLean and Thomson, p. 7.

58. Ricardo Romo, "Response to Mexican Immigration, 1910-1930," *Aztlán* 6, no. 2 (Summer 1975) 186–187.

59. Ralph Guzmán, *The Political Socialization of the Mexican American People* (New York: Arno Press, 1976), pp. 65–66, Gómez-Quiñones, "The First Steps," p. 34; Andrés Jiménez Montoya, *Political Domination in the Labor Market: Racial Division in the Arizona Copper Industry*, Working Papers Series, (Berkeley, Calif.: 1977, Institute for the Study of Social Change), p. 12.

60. Gómez-Quiñones, "The First Steps," p. 35.

61. Reisler, p. 69.

62. Ricardo Romo, "Mexican Workers in the City: Los Angeles, 1915–1930" (Ph.D. dissertation, University of California at Los Angeles, 1975), p. 123.

63. Debra Anne Weber, "The Organizing of Mexicano Agricultural Workers: Imperial Valley and Los Angeles, 1928–1934: An Oral History Approach," *Aztlán* 3, no. 2 (1972): 313; Jamieson, p. 63; Kushner, p. 53.

64. Taylor, *Mexican Labor*, vol. 2, pp. 114–117; Romo, "Responses to Mexican Immigration," pp. 187–190; "The Commission of Inquiry, Interchurch World

Movement, *Report on the Steel Strike of 1919* (New York: Harcourt Brace Jovanovich, 1920), pp. 3, 132–133.

65. McLean and Thomson, pp. 29–30, 34.

66. García, "Racial Dualism," pp. 197–218.

67. Mario T. García, "Obreros: The Mexican Workers of El Paso, 1900–1920" (Ph.D. dissertation, University of California at San Diego, 1975), p. 199.

68. García, "Obreros: Mexican Workers," p. 201.

69. García, "Obreros: Mexican Workers," pp. 202–205.

70. Mark Reisler, *By the Sweat of Their Brow: Mexican Immigrant Labor in the United States, 1900–1940* (Westport, Conn.: Greenwood Press, 1976), pp. 77–78. In California during this decade the cultivation of truck garden products increased by more than 50 percent, that of fruits and nuts by 30 percent, and that of cotton by 400 percent.

71. Royce D. Delmatier, Clarence F. McIntosh, and Earl G. Waters, eds., *The Rumble of California Politics, 1848–1970* (New York: Wiley, 1970), p. 212; Carey McWilliams, *Factories in Fields: The Story of Migratory Labor In California* (Santa Barbara and Salt Lake City: Peregrine Publishers, 1971) pp. 185, 188; Jamieson, pp. 71–72.

72. Delmatier et al., p. 216.

73. Delmatier et al., pp. 212, 216–217.

74. Carey McWilliams, *California: The Great Exception* (Westport, Conn.: Greenwood Press, 1949), p. 95; McWilliams, *Factories in Fields*, p. 117; Galarza, *Farm Workers*, p. 98; Reisler, "Passing Through Our Egypt," pp. 138–139; Jamieson, p. 70. A *large-scale farm* was defined as a farm grossing over $30,000 per annum.

75. John Phillip Carney, "Postwar Mexican Migration: 1945–1955, with Particular Reference to the Policies and Practices of the United States Concerning Its Control" (Ph.D. dissertation, University of Southern California, 1957), p. 19.

76. Jamieson, p. 72; Reisler, in *By the Sweat of Their Brow*, p. 82, estimated that there were up to 200,000 farm workers in California in the 1920s. Mexicans constituted 75 percent of the *enganchistas* or labor contractors, who were used extensively. They charged fees of 50¢ to $1 for each laborer plus a percentage of their earnings.

77. Herbert B. Peterson, "Twentieth-Century Search for Cibola: Post World War I Mexican Labor Exploitation in Arizona," in Manuel Servín, ed., *An Awakening Minority: The Mexican American*, 2nd ed. (Beverly Hills, Calif.: Glencoe Press, 1974) pp. 117, 119–121.

78. Peterson, p. 122.

79. Peterson, p. 123; Jamieson, p. 195.

80. Montejano, p. 18; Taylor, *American-Mexican Frontier*, pp. 101, 103.

81. Taylor, *American-Mexican Frontier*, pp. 115, 156; *Report of Governor C. C. Young's Fact Finding Committee in California, October 1930* (Reprint, San Francisco: R & E Research Assc., 1970), p. 59; Cardoso, p. 111. Also see Louise Año Nuevo Kerr, "The Chicano Experience in Chicago: 1920–1970" (Ph.D. dissertation, University of Illinois at Chicago Circle, 1976; George Hinman, *Report of the Commission on International and Interracial Factors in the Problems of Mexicans in the United States*, National Conference concerning Mexican and Spanish Americans in the United States (Austin: University of Texas, 1926).

82. Kerr, p. 26; Reisler, *By the Sweat of Their Brow*, p. 102; Kerr, pp. 25–26, 33–36.

83. Taylor, *Mexican Labor*, vol. 2, pp. 111–112; Hinman, pp. 14, 27, 29.

84. Taylor, *Mexican Labor*, vol. 2, pp. 119–120, 222, 229; Immigration Committee, "Mexican Immigration," Chamber of Commerce of the United States, Washington, D.C., July 1930 (draft in the Bancroft Library), p. 21; Reisler, "Passing Through Our Egypt," pp. 102–103.

85. Immigration Committee, p. 27. Selden C. Menefee, *Mexican Migratory Workers of South Texas* (Washington, D.C.: Works Progress Administration, 1941), reprinted in Carlos E. Cortes, ed., *Mexican Labor in the United States* (New York: Arno Press, 1974), pp. 17–26, 41.

86. Coalson, p. 36; Reisler, *By the Sweat of Their Brow*, p. 88; Mark Erenberg, "A Study of the Political Relocation of Texas-Mexican Migratory Farm Workers to

Wisconsin" (Ph.D. dissertation, University of Wisconsin, 1969), p. 11; Immigration Committee, p. 11; McWilliams, *Factories in Fields*, p. 89.

87. Briegel, p. 94; Taylor, *Mexican Labor*, p. 184; Gamio, p. 86.
88. Jamieson, pp. 236–237.
89. Jamieson, pp. 237–239.
90. Montejano, pp. 22, 7, 8, 24, 27, 35; Taylor, *American-Mexican Frontier*, p. 150.
91. Coalson, p. 26; Montejano, pp. 35–37; McWilliams, *Ill Fares the Land*, p. 264.
92. Lowenstein, p. 25; Chaffee, p. 7; Jamieson, p. 76.
93. Hinman, p. 80; Joan London and Henry Anderson, *So Shall Ye Reap* (New York: Crowell, 1971), p. 25.
94. Weintraub, p. 164; McWilliams, *California*, p. 148.
95. Orville Merton Kile, *The Farm Bureau Through Three Decades* (Baltimore: Waverly Press, 1948); William J. Block, *The Separation of the Farm Bureau and the Extension Service* (Urbana: University of Illinois Press, 1960); Samuel R. Berger, *Dollar Harvest: The Story of the Farm Bureau* (Lexington, Mass.: Heath, 1971); Clark A. Chambers, *California Farm Organizations* (Berkeley: University of California Press, 1952), p. 22. Grant McConnell, *The Decline of Agrarian Democracy* (Berkeley: University of California Press, 1957), p. 160. Berger, p. 34, states that in 1968 its magazine, *Nation's Agriculture*, had a monthly circulation of 2 million copies, slightly less than *Newsweek*.
96. Jamieson, p. 75; *Report of C. C. Young*, p. 123; George T. Edson, "Mexicans in the Beet Fields of Northern Colorado," August 27, 1924, in the Bancroft Library, p. 5; Lowenstein, p. 25; Jamieson, p. 76; Edson, pp. 5–10; Jamieson, p. 76; *Report of C. C. Young*, p. 123; Robin Fitzgerald Scott, "The Mexican-American in the Los Angeles Area, 1920–1950. From Acquiescence to Activity" (Ph.D. dissertation, University of Southern California, 1971), pp. 25–26.
97. *Report of C. C. Young*, p. 126; Lowenstein, p. 25.
98. Charles Wollenberg, "Huelga, 1928 Style: The Imperial Valley Cantaloupe Worker's Strike," *Pacific Historical Review* (February 1969): 48.
99. Taylor, *Mexican Labor*, vol. 1, pp. 45, 64; Weber, p. 313.
100. Wollenberg, "Huelga," p. 50.
101. Wollenberg, "Huelga," pp. 53–56; Weber, p. 313. The valley was controlled by 74 huge growers, many of them absentee owners who also had a monopoly on shipping.
102. Varden Fuller, testimony, Hearings Before a Subcommittee on Education and Labor, U.S. Senate, 76th Cong., part 47 (Washington, D.C.: U.S. Government Printing Office, 1940), p. 17315. These hearings will hereafter be referred to as the *La Follette Hearings*. Hon. Culbert Olson, Governor of California, testimony, *La Follette Hearings*, part 47, p. 17257; Samuel E. Wood, "The California State Commission on Immigration and Function," (Ph.D. dissertation, University of California, at Berkeley, 1942), p. 9.
103. Reisler, *By the Sweat of Their Brow*, p. 228.
104. McWilliams, *California*, p. 108; Chambers, pp. 1–2. Walter Goldschmidt, *As You Sow* (New York: Harcourt Brace Jovanovich, 1947), pp. 187, 262–263, for an excellent definition of an industrial farm. Lloyd Horace Fisher, *The Harvest Labor Market in California* (Cambridge: Harvard University Press, 1953), p. 113; Goldschmidt, pp. 262–263; Varden Fuller, "The Supply of Agricultural Labor as a Factor in the Evolution of Farm Organization in California," in *La Follette Hearings*, part 54, p. 19782; Margaret Greenfield, *Migratory Farm Labor Problems: Summary of Findings and Recommendations Made by Principal Investigative Committees, with Special Reference to California, 1915 to 1950* (Berkeley: University of California, Bureau of Administration, 1950), p. 326.
105. McWilliams, *California*, p. 101. He points out that California differed from the other western states in that it skipped the frontier phase of land settlement.
106. McWilliams, *Ill Fares the Land*, pp. 16–17; London and Anderson, p. 2.
107. Wood, p. 3; McWilliams, *California*, p. 108, and Goldschmidt, pp. 84–85, make the point that farms of 160 to 200 acres required professional management with a full complement of power equipment. A farmer could work 40 acres himself except at harvest time; 1,000 or more acres required a professional manager.
108. McWilliams, *California*, pp. 121, 164; Chambers, p. 2.

109. Jamieson, p. 7.
110. Walker R. Young, Supervising Engineer for the Central Valley Project, testimony in the U.S. House of Representatives, Interstate Migration Hearings Before the Select Committee to Investigate the Interstate Migration of Destitute Citizens, 77th Cong., 3rd sess., Pursuant to H. Res. 63 and H. Res. 491, Resolution to Inquire into the Interstate Migration of Destitute Citizens, Survey and Investigate the Social and Economic Needs and the Movement of Indigent Persons Across State Lines (Washington, D.C.: U.S. Government Printing Office, 1940), pp. 2624–2625. (These hearings will hereafter be referred to as the *Tolan Hearings*.) McWilliams, *California*, p. 317, states that all the water in the Central Valley Project originated in the state. See also Wood, p. 10; Goldschmidt, p. 32; Truman E. Moore, *The Slaves We Rent* (New York: Random House, 1965), p. 15; and Chambers, pp. 155–160, 163.
111. Galarza, p. 25; Ronald B. Taylor, *Chavez and the Farm Workers* (Boston: Beacon Press, 1975), p. 39; McWilliams, *California* p. 136; Ellen L. Halcomb, "Efforts to Organize the Migrant Workers by the Cannery and Agricultural Workers" (Master's thesis, Chico State College, pp. 1–2; Goldschmidt, p. 248; Dale Wright, *The Harvest of Despair: The Migrant Farm Worker* (Boston: Beacon Press, 1965), preface.
112. Goldschmidt, p. 260; McWilliams, *California*, p. 102; Jamieson, p. 15; Berger, p. 100.
113. Fisher, p. 9; Laurence Hewes, "Some Migratory Labor Problems in California's Specialized Agriculture." (Ph.D. dissertation, George Washington University, 1945), p. 14; McWilliams, *California*, p. 112.
114. Cardoso, p. 121; p. 228, McWilliams, *California*, p. 161; McWilliams, *Ill Fares the Land*, p. 37; Walter J. Stein, *California and the Dust Bowl Migration* (Westport, Conn.: pp. 37–40; Jamieson, p. 17; Jerold S. Auerbach, *Labor and Liberty: The La Follette Committee and the New Deal* (Indianapolis: Bobbs-Merrill, 1966) p. 177; Reisler, *By the Sweat of Their Brow*, p. 228; Robert D. Tomasek, "The Political and Economic Implications of Mexican Labor in the United States Under the Non Quota System, Contract Labor Program and Wetback Movement" (Ph.D. dissertation, University of Michigan, 1957), p. 48.
115. Chambers, p. 33.
116. Lamar Babington Jones, "Mexican American Labor Problems in Texas" (Ph.D. dissertation, University of Texas, 1965), p. 262.
117. Montejano, p. 11; Wood, p. 46; Shelton, p. 5; Richard Wayne Ferguson, "Mexican American: An Economically Significant Market Segment" (Ph. D. dissertation, North Texas State University, 1972), p 29; Shelton, p. 9.
118. Kibbe, p. 170; Taylor, *American-Mexican Frontier*, pp. 109–113; Nelson Gage Copp, "Wetbacks and Braceros, Mexican Migrant Laborers and American Immigration Policy, 1930–1960" (Ph.D. dissertation, Boston University, 1963), pp. 63–64, writes that the technological displacement began after 1920, when the harvest combine displaced many Mexicans in the fields of northern Texas and the Midwest. After 1930 new machinery and methods, such as cross plowing, began to reduce the need for Mexican labor in the harvesting of cotton and sugar beets. However, the cost of equipment made the process of displacement slow. Growers found hiring Mexicans as cheap and sometimes cheaper than, buying and maintaining expensive machinery. See also Moore, p. 110, on the subject of mechanization; Robert A. Cuellar, *A Social and Political History of the Mexican American Population of Texas, 1929–1969* (San Francisco: R & E Research Assc., 1974), p. 3.
119. Lorraine Esterly Pierce, "Mexican Americans in St. Paul's Lower West Side," *Journal of Mexican American History* 4 (1974): 203.
120. Fisher, p. 42; Hewes, pp. 55–56; McWilliams, *Ill Fares the Land*, p. 257.
121. Coalson, p. 28; McWilliams, *Ill Fares the Land*, pp. 141, 259–260, 264–266; Moore, pp. 33–36.
122. Montejano, p. 9; Mary G. Luck, "Labor Contractors," in Emily H. Huntington, ed., *Doors to Jobs* (Berkeley: University of California Press, 1942), pp. 314, 342.
123. Luck, pp. 317, 338–341; Tomasek, pp. 21–23; Fisher, p. 22.
124. Halcomb, p. 2.
125. Kushner, p. 58; Jamieson, pp. 80–81.

126. Lina E. Brissette, *Mexicans in the United States* (Washington, D.C., 1929), reprinted in Cortes, *Church Views*, p. 10; Hinman, pp. 11–16, reviews some of the oppressive conditions Mexicans suffered.
127. Jamieson, pp. 81–82; Kushner, p. 59; Weber, pp. 313–321.
128. Pat Chambers, interview, California State University at Northridge, April 14, 1978; Jamieson, p. 83; Kushner, pp. 28, 63. Weber, p. 321, puts the number at nine. Also see "Syndicalism and 'Sedition' Laws in 35 States and in Philippine Islands Must Be Smashed!" in the Paul S. Taylor Collection of the Bancroft Library. This article refers to eight workers serving time in San Quentin and Folsom and discusses the Los Angeles Police Department's red squad's raids.
129. Jamieson, pp. 271–272; Nelson, p. 247; Coalson, p. 61.
130. Jamieson, pp. 84–85; London and Anderson, pp. 28, 29.
131. Interview with Caroline Decker, San Raphael, July 6, 1963, quoted in Halcomb, p. 110; confirmed by the author in an interview with Decker, August 8, 1973, and with Pat Chambers, August 24, 1973.
132. Charles B. Spaulding, "The Mexican Strike at El Monte, California," *Sociology and Social Research* (July-August 1934): 571–572; Jamieson, p. 90.
133. Actually, the workers were in a no-win situation. In an interview on April 14, 1973, Pat Chambers, a CAWIU organizer, stated that it was a strike that should have never taken place.
134. Weber, p. 328.
135. Ronald W. López, "The El Monte Berry Strike of 1933," *Aztlán* 1, no. 1 (Spring 1970): 105; Weber, pp. 326, 329. Flores was one of the original participants in the CUOM. The CUOM was formed in 1927 and was the forerunner of Mexican union. Emory Bogardus, *The Mexican in the United States* (Los Angeles: University of Southern California Press, 1934), pp. 41–42.
136. López, p. 107; Weber, p. 330.
137. López, p. 109; Jamieson, p. 92.
138. Halcomb, p. 9; Jamieson, p. 94.
139. Jamieson, pp. 95–96; Pat Chambers interview, April 13, 1978. Chambers stated that the people at the Taugus Ranch were so bitter over the loss that they destroyed prime orchard land. See also Jamieson, pp. 95–96.
140. Chambers, pp. 18, 66; In the San Joaquin Valley there was a split between the Grange and the Farm Bureau. The former represented the smaller farmer and the latter the large growers. *La Follette Hearings*, part 51, p. 18579; Mark Day, *Forty Acres: Cesar Chavez and the Farm Workers* (New York: Praeger, 1971), p. 27.
141. Sharecropping was virtually nonexistent in California. There had been a shift to irrigated crops, and this had increased the need for labor. Farming in this region was large scale. See Paul S. Taylor and Clark Kerr, *San Joaquin Valley Strike, 1933. Violations of Free Speech and Rights of Labor*, Hearings Before a Subcommittee on Education and Labor, U.S. Senate, 77th Cong. 3rd sess., pursuant to S. Res. 266, 74th Cong., part 54, *Agricultural Labor in California*. (Washington, D.C.: U.S. Government Printing Office, 1940), p. 19947. Halcomb, p. 69, states that growers admitted that if they could break the power of finance companies, and the San Joaquin Light and Power Company in particular, they would have no problem paying the workers living wages. Goldschmidt, p. 36, summarizes the allocations for the different phases of cotton production. *The Bakersfield Californian*, on October 25, 1933, stated that the Southern California Edison Company registered a profit of $8,498,703 in the first nine months of 1933. See also Porter Chaffee, *A History of the Cannery and Agricultural Workers Industrial Workers Union* (Unpublished, Oakland, Calif.: Works Progress Administration, Federal Writers Project, 1938), p. 8.
142. Pat Chambers, interview, April 13, 1978; Jamieson, p. 101; Taylor and Kerr, p. 19949; on p. 19947 Taylor and Kerr put the number at 15,000, 75 percent of whom were Mexican. In an interview given December 21, 1933, records of which are found in the Taylor Collection of the Bancroft Library, Sheriff Hill of Tulare County stated: "You know how the Mexicans are. You take off your hat and holler and they'll follow you any place. The strike was 95 percent Mexican with a few white leaders."
143. Anthony Sola interview, July 10, 1973.

144. Interview with Clarence H. Wilson, District Attorney, Hanford, Kings County, December 22, 1933, Paul S. Taylor Collection, Bancroft Library; *Visalia Times Delta*, September 19, 1933.

145. Quoted in Taylor and Kerr, p. 19992.

146. Jamieson, pp. 103–104; John W. Webb, *Transient Unemployed*, Monograph III. (Washington, D.C.: Works Progress Administration, Division of Social Research, 1935), pp. 1–5; Caroline Decker, interview, August 8, 1973.

147. Jamieson, p. 102; Halcomb, p. 5. On p. 101 Jamieson states that tactics had been developed in the Arizona cotton strike involving several thousand cotton pickers a few weeks before. On August 24, 1973, Pat Chambers stated that the Taugus Ranch strike had had the greatest influence on the San Joaquin cotton strike tactics; he emphasized the fact that the strikers were experienced.

148. Alejandro Rodríguez interview, July 12, 1973, Corcoran, California. Issues of the Corcoran newspaper covering the strike dates are missing from the paper's back files. In an interview with Paul Taylor on December 20, 1933, Frank J. Palomares stated that the only reason that the strikers went on strike was for free food. The field notes for December 20–24, 1933, from the Taylor Collection of the Bancroft Library state that Mr. Morgan, a Corcoran farmer, rented some land to the union. He ran camp facilities next to his gas station and installed a water tank and toilets. Sixteen families were in the camp when the strike began. The strikers in the camp were armed, and many were veterans of the Mexican Revolution. They cleaned the camp and picked Morgan's cotton.

149. Lilly Cuellar, interview July 11, 1973. According to Alejandro Rodríguez there was plenty of food in the camp.

150. Taylor and Kerr, p. 19975.

151. Taylor and Kerr, p. 19981.

152. Taylor and Kerr, pp. 19958, 19975, 19981.

153. Taylor and Kerr, pp. 19984, 19976; Pat Chambers, interviews, August 24, 1973, October 4, 1973, November 6, 1973. Chambers repeatedly affirmed that the strike would have happened in spite of the union. The guts of the strike, he said, were the strikers and their families. Halcomb, pp. 75–76, reports 12 dead, 4 hurt, 113 jailed, and 9 children dead of malnutrition in the cotton camps.

154. Robert R. Lee, "To Whom It May Concern, October 19, 1933," in the Paul S. Taylor Collection of the Bancroft Library, University of California, Berkeley. According to a "Report on Cotton Strikers, Kings County," in the Taylor Collection, relief did not start until October 14, 1933. See also Chaffee, "Organizational Efforts," pp. 35, 49.

155. *The Bakersfield Californian*, October 9, 1933; Taylor and Kerr, p. 19963; Chaffee, "Cannery and Agricultural Workers," p. 49.

156. O. W. Bryan, a local hardware store owner at the time of the strike, was interviewed on June 22, 1973. Ronald Taylor, *Chavez and the Farm Workers* (Boston: Beacon Press, 1975), p. 54.

157. Dr. Ira Cross to Raymond Cato, head of the CHP, February 20, 1934, Taylor Collection, Bancroft Library; *Pixley Enterprise*, January 12, 1934, February 2, 1934.

158. *Visalia Times-Delta*, October 11, 1933.

159. In an interview with Paul Taylor on November 17, 1933, Kern County Undersheriff Tom Carter stated that he knew that the strike was coming and that the growers were well prepared. They had two machine guns and had bought $1,000 of tear gas (Taylor Collection, Bancroft Library).

160. *The Bakersfield Californian*, October 11, 1933. Also see Pedro Subia, #4717, Coroner's Inquest, County of Kern, State of California, October 14, 1933.

161. Taylor and Kerr, p. 19949.

162. Wofford B. Camp, *Cotton, Irrigation and the AAA: An Interview Conducted by Willa Lug Baum* (Berkeley, Calif.: Regional Oral History Office, University of California, Bancroft Library, 1971), p. 21; Chaffee, "Organizational Efforts," p. 16.

163. Halcomb, pp. 72–74; Taylor and Kerr, p. 2000; Louis Block, California State Emergency Relief Administration, C-R, f.4, Taylor Collection, Bancroft Library, states that only $9,822.90 was paid in direct relief in Kern, Kings, and Tulare counties, with some $7,500 paid in December—after the strike had ended. These funds were spread over 1933. Local authorities called for the

state to send 1,000 CHP officers to Corcoran because of the militancy and alleged rioting. The local sheriffs moved in and the camps were disbanded. Corcoran was the last camp to disband. The growers burned the camp after they left. *The Bakersfield Californian*, October 28, 1933, blared "Growers To Import 1000 L.A. Workers." On July 20, 1932, the price of cotton was 5.8¢ a pound; a year later it rose to 10.5¢, an 81-percent increase (Taylor Collection, "Cotton Prices in California"). After government supports, the ginners made even higher profits. On January 13, 1934, *The Bakersfield Californian* reported "Cotton Men's Income Twice That of 1932." On February 6, it reported that the Agricultural Adjustment Agency paid Kern County growers $1,015,000 for plowing under 20 to 40 percent of their crop. According to the paper, the growers received 3.5¢ per pound for not harvesting the cotton. (See "Average Cost of Producing Cotton in the San Joaquin Valley," an unpublished manuscript in the Taylor Collection.) The February 20, 1934 issue of the *Agricultural Worker*, published by the Cannery and Agricultural Workers Industrial Union, a copy of which is also in the Taylor Collection, analyzes the cotton strike and admits that preparations were inadequate.

164. Jamieson, pp. 106–107.
165. *La Follette Hearings*, part 55, p. 20140; Jamieson, pp. 107–108; Weber, p. 321; Lowenstein, p. 94. Halcomb, p. 79, states that the Mexican union was in control until early January but that the CAWIU assumed leadership about the 7th or 8th of that month.
166. Guillermo Martínez, interview, Los Angeles, June 23, 1978; *La Follette Hearings*, part 55, p. 20180.
167. Pat Chambers, interview, June 26, 1978.
168. Weber, p. 323; Halcomb, p. 23.
169. In February 1934, David Martínez, R. Salazar, and F. Bustamante were sentenced to eight months for disturbing the peace (Chaffee, "Cannery and Agricultural Workers," section entitled "Imperial Valley in 1934," p. 34). See also Jamieson, p. 108, and Weber, p. 323. Halcomb, pp. 104–106, sets the date at January 24. See C. B. Hutchison, W. C. Jacobson, and John Phillips, *Imperial Valley Farm Situation*, Report of the Special Investigating Committee Appointed at the Request of the California State Board of Agricultue, the California Farm Bureau Federation and the Agricultural Department of the California State Chamber of Commerce, April 16, 1934, p. 19.
170. Jamieson, p. 109; Hutchison et al., p. 24.
171. Among the other founders of the Associated Farmers of California were the Pacific Gas and Electric Company, the Southern Pacific Gas and Electric Company, the Southern Pacific Railroad, the Bank of America, the Canners League of California, the five largest banks in San Francisco, and Standard Oil. See Tomasek, p. 95; McWilliams, *California*, p. 162; Chambers, p. 69. The formation of the Associated Farmers was the result of the Contra Costa county strike in the spring of 1934 (*La Follette Hearings*, part 67, p. 24459, exhibit 11327-A, Articles of Incorporation of Associated Farmers of California). Among the signers were S. Parker Frisselle of Fresno and Floyd W. Frick of Kern County. See Jamieson, p. 40; Auerbach, p. 186; Lowenstein, p. 95; Halcomb, p. 5; Richard S. Kirkendall, *Social Scientists and Farm Politics in the Age of Roosevelt* (Columbus: University of Missouri Press, 1966), pp. 118–119; London and Anderson, p. 4; Delmatier, p. 72; and Chambers, p. 33.
172. Bryan Theodore Johns, "Field Workers in California Cotton," (Master's thesis, University of California, at Berkeley, 1948), pp. 79–80; McWilliams, *Ill Fares the Land*, p. 16; Lowenstein, p. 120; Chambers, p. 53; *La Follette Hearings*, part 49, pp. 17911–17945; Block, p. 36.
173. "Can the Radicals Capture the Farms of California," *La Follette Hearings*, part 68, pp. 24967–24971.
174. Pat Chambers, interview, August 24, 1973; Chambers, p. 108; Johns, p. 81.
175. Chambers, p. 108; Johns, p. 81; Chaffee, "Cannery and Agricultural Workers," section on "The Drive Against the Cannery and Agricultural Workers," pp. 6–7; Jamieson, pp. 114–115.
176. Douglas Guy Monroy, "Mexicanos in Los Angeles, 1930–1941: An Ethnic Group in Relation to Class Forces (Ph.D. dissertation, University of California, Los Angeles, 1978), p. 165.

177. London and Anderson, p. 3.

178. Jamieson, pp. 119, 122, 123; Weber, pp. 330–331. Lucas Lucio was the leader of the *Comisión*.

179. Jamieson, p. 123.

180. Jamieson, pp. 128–134.

181. Jamieson, p. 124. Most Mexican unions could not afford to affiliate with the American Federation of Labor in this period.

182. Jamieson, p. 125; Lowenstein, p. 29; Johns, pp. 86–92.

183. Jamieson, pp. 126–127.

184. Ronald Taylor, *Sweatshops in the Sun: Child Labor on the Farms* (Boston: Beacon Press, 1973), pp. 6–7; Mattiessen, p. 9; Auerbach, p. 177; McWilliams, *Factories in Fields*, p. 196.

185. Jamieson, p. 191; Kushner, p. 92.

186. McWilliams, *Ill Fares the Land*, pp. 50, 71; Jamieson, pp. 193–199.

187. Jamieson, pp. 210–211.

188. Jamieson, pp. 224–228.

189. Coalson, pp. 40–42, reviews labor conditions in Michigan, Ohio, and Wisconsin in the sugar beet industry. McWilliams, *Ill Fares the Land*, pp. 257–258, states that 66,100 Mexicans left Texas annually for seasonal work. Many went to the beet fields. See also Jamieson, pp. 233–235.

190. Jamieson, pp. 238–241.

191. Jamieson, pp. 242–248. Menefee, p. 24, states that an experienced man could work 10 acres per week, a woman 7 acres and children smaller amounts.

192. Reisler, *By the Sweat of Their Brow*, pp. 248–249; McWilliams, *Ill Fares the Land*, p. 125; Kibbe, *Latin Americans*, p. 201; Jamieson, pp. 248–255.

193. Jamieson, pp. 270–273.

194. Coalson, p. 62; Nelson, p. 248; Jamieson, p. 273.

195. Coalson, pp. 51, 58.

196. Jamieson, pp. 275–276. Menefee, p. 52.

197. Jamieson, p. 277.

198. According to Jamieson, pp. 57, 277, several union organizers thought that it was more difficult to organize Texas Mexicans than Mexican nationals because the former "were brought up in a situation of greater dependence, and less freedom of expression, because of their political impotence imposed by the State poll tax and their inferior social status." See Coalson, p. 63; Jamieson, pp. 277–278; Nelson, pp. 249–250; and McWilliams, *Ill Fares the Land*, pp. 230–233.

199. Harold Arthur Shapiro, "Workers of San Antonio, Texas, 1900–1940" (Ph.D. dissertation, University of Texas, 1952); Kenneth Walker, "The Pecan Shellers of San Antonio and Mechanization," *Southwestern Historical Quarterly* (July 1965); Selden C. Menefee and Orin C. Cassmore, *The Pecan Shellers of San Antonio. The Problem of Underpaid and Unemployed Mexican Labor* (Works Progress Administration), reprinted in Cortes, *Mexican Labor*, pp. 7–8.

200. Shapiro, p. 117.

201. Shapiro, p. 119. Most of the San Antonion pecan shellers were long-time residents of San Antonio (Menefee and Cassmore, pp. 3, 50).

202. Menefee and Cassmore, pp. 4–5.

203. Shapiro, p. 125.

204. Shapiro, p. 126.

205. Shelton, p. 92, states that Owen W. Kilday, sheriff of Bexar, and his brother, Paul Kilday, a San Antonio congressman from the 20th district, were the political bosses of the city. Larry Dickens, "The Political Role of Mexican Americans in San Antonio, Texas" (Ph.D. dissertation, Texas Tech University, 1969), pp. 47–48, states that the Kilday brothers controlled a large section of the Black and Chicano electorate. Their chief support came from Catholic churches, Catholic agencies, the American Legion, and the Mexican vote. Hershel Bernard, an observer of San Antonio politics, is quoted as saying: "Sheriff Kilday could put fifty pistols on the west side on the election and fear did the rest. When you have a sheriff's deputy at every polling place wearing his pistol, Mexican-Americans vote 'right.'"

206. Walker, p. 51; Landolt, p. 231. Emma Tenayuca headed the San Antonio chapter of the Workers Alliance of America. She became the standard bearer of the pecan workers struggle. Emma was a schoolgirl at the time of the strikes. She

was a brilliant public speaker "who bitterly resented discrimination against her and her fellow students of Mexican extraction. She quit school when she was denied membership on the school debate team because she was a Mexican. She became a communist and married a communist organizer." Landolt, p. 232, states that UCAPAWA took the leadership from Emma in the pecan strike. She had been the leader in the "spontaneous" strike, but did not have an office in the union.

207. Walker, p. 51.
208. Shapiro, pp. 128–129.
209. Landolt, p. 233; Shapiro, p. 130.
210. Shapiro, pp. 131–132.
211. Menefee and Cassmore, p. 24.
212. Rosa Pesotta, *Bread upon the Water* (New York: Dodd, Mead, 1944), pp. 19, 40, 23; Manuel Gamio, *The Life Story of the Mexican Immigrant* (New York: Dover, 1971), pp. 249–251.
213. Pesotta, p. 27.
214. Pesotta, p. 28.
215. Pesotta, pp. 22, 32.
216. Leo Grebler, Joan Moore, and Ralph Guzmán, *The Mexican-American People* (New York: Free Press, 1970), p. 91; Pesotta, pp. 22, 40, 43, 50.
217. Pesotta, p. 54–59.
218. Pesotta, p. 50.
219. Pesotta, p. 75, states that Mary Gonzales and Beatrice López were union organizers in the sweatshops of San Francisco's Chinatown.
220. George N. Green, 'The ILGWU in Texas, 1930–1970," *Journal of Mexican American History* 1, no. 2 (Spring 1971): 144–145.
221. According to Green, p. 145, another factor that made organizing difficult was the subcontracting of a lot of hand embroidery to women who worked at home.
222. Nelson, pp. 254–256; Menefee and Cassmore, p. 16; Martha Cotera, *Profile of the Mexican American Woman* (Austin: National Educational Laboratory Publishers, 1976), pp. 86–87.
223. Green, p. 154.
224. Green, p. 158.
225. Kerr, p. 75. The Chicago Mexican population had fallen from 20,000 in 1930 to 14,000 in 1933 and to 12,500 in 1934.
226. Kerr, pp. 78–79.
227. Kerr, pp. 69–70, 72–75, 75–78; Francisco A. Rosales and Daniel T. Simon, "Chicano Steelworkers and Unionism in the Midwest, 1919–1945," *Aztlán* (Summer 1975): 267. By 1926 Chicago steel mills employed over 6,000 Mexicans, 14 percent of the total work force.
228. Kerr, pp. 83–89.
229. Kerr, pp. 90–91.
230. Rosales, p. 269.
231. Kerr, pp. 91–92.
232. Rosales, pp. 267–272.
233. Luis Leobardo Arroyo, "Chicano Participation in Organized Labor: CIO in Los Angeles, 1938–1950. An Extended Research Note," *Aztlán* 6, no. 2 (Summer 1975): 277. Arroyo's article relied heavily on newspapers and oral interviews.
234. Arroyo, pp. 290–291.
235. Arroyo, pp. 277–295.
236. Arroyo, pp. 280–281.
237. Arroyo, pp. 281–284.
238. Arroyo, pp. 284–290.
239. Alonzo S. Perales, *Are We Good Neighbors?* (San Antonio: Artes Gráficas, 1948); pp. 117, 121. Also see Landolt, pp. 76–77, 88–117.
240. Kibbe, pp. 161–162.
241. Perales, pp. 93, 112–113.
242. Perales, p. 94.
243. Charles Loomis and Nellie Loomis, "Skilled Spanish-American War Industry Workers from New Mexico," *Applied Anthropology* (October, November, December 1942): 33.

Chapter 9
The Chicano Labor Struggle Continues

By 1945 the Chicano labor movement had rooted itself within the U.S. labor movement. Mexican unions became less common and the center stage of the Chicanos' labor activities was no longer dominated by farm struggles. The *mutualistas* which had been a popular vehicle for labor organization among Mexicans during the first quarter of the century continued to function; however, their involvement in labor strikes became almost nonexistent. Entering the 1950s Chicano workers were primarily urban; they were no longer a people on the move. With the geographical stabilization of the Chicano population, they were better able to organize themselves. Slowly Chicano workers became part of the national labor movement. In the third quarter of the twentieth century, while Chicano workers still suffered racism, nativism, and class discrimination, there was a realization both on their part and on the part of national labor leaders that Chicanos were here to stay.

MAJOR ORGANIZATIONAL EFFORTS

World War II made California a major industrial state. The change was reflected in the Chicanos' way of life and their struggle increasingly moved to the cities. By 1949 the California Mexican population was 75.8 percent urban, the highest of any of the five southwestern states. In that year the Mexican population in California was reported to be 760,453.[1] The struggle in agriculture continued. Distinctions between rich and poor, employer and worker, Anglo and Mexican remained clearest in this area.

Carey McWilliams described California farms as "farm factories." The "green giants" of agriculture in many cases were larger than the urban industries and more successful in getting substantial government support in the form of subsidies and exemptions from regulations such as the immigration quota, guarantees to workers under the National Labor Relations Act, and the 160 acre unit in the 1902 Reclamation Act.[2] California farms were as industrialized as their urban counterparts, but with the difference that they had more privileges.

In the San Joaquin Valley John G. Boswell of Corcoran netted $3,027,384 in 1968 for not growing cotton and other designated crops. The Russell Giffen Corporation of Huron earned $2,275,274 in subsidies that year. South Lake Farms in Corcoran received $1,194,022, the Saylor Land Company $786,459, and the Kern County Land Company $780,073. In the Valley the Southern Pacific owned about 201,852 acres, Kern County Land 348,460 acres, Standard Oil 218,485 acres, the Tejon Ranch (the Times-Mirror Corporation or, better still, the *Los Angeles Times*) 168,537, and the Boston Ranch Company 37,556 acres. The agricultural yield of the San Joaquin Valley ranked above forty-one states in the union.[3]

In 1902 the Newlands Reclamation Act put the federal government into the business of building dams and providing water for farmers. The intent of the U.S. Congress was to create an abundance of small farms. Each owner was limited to 160 acres, with an additional 160 acres for the farmer's spouse and another 160 acres for one child—a 480 acres limit per farm. If the owner had more than 480 acres, the excess would be sold off to a person who would reside and operate the farm at preirrigated prices. The intent of the law was subverted by the farm lobby; this pressure group alleged that if the law were enforced, it would hurt the public and work an injustice on the small self-made farmers. In the San Joaquin Valley, as a consequence, large farmers illegally received large subsidies. During the 1950s the water subsidy from the Central Valley Project amounted to $577 per acre annually or $92,320 for 160 acres.[4] In California 1,090,394 acres were classified as excess acreage, in Arizona 25,490, in New Mexico 9,498, in Texas 62,128, and in Colorado 16,371. In the Imperial Valley of California farmers have received over $100 million in water subsidies.[5]

The National Farm Labor Union

The *bracero* program was effectively used to break strikes. An example of grower abuse can be seen in the strike against the Di Giorgio Fruit Corporation at Arvin, California. On October 1, 1947, workers picketed the Di Giorgio farm. Local 218 of the National Farm Labor Union (NFLU) led the strike. It demanded: a 10¢ an hour increase in wages, seniority rights, a grievance procedure, and recognition of the union as the sole bargaining agent. Joseph Di Giorgio, founder of the corporation, refused the union's demands. *Fortune* magazine dubbed him the "Kublai Khan of Kern County"; in 1946 he had sales of $18 million.[6] When the demands were refused, efforts to stop production began.

The NFLU had definite liabilities: The AFL contributed only $6,000 a year to its support; it had a limited war chest; and Di Giorgio actively kept the different ethnic groups separated, preventing a history of multiracial cooperation. Bob Whately, a veteran organizer, did much of the preliminary work. In 1947 H. L. Mitchell, president of the NFLU, sent Henry Hasiwar and Ernesto Galarza to Arvin.[7]

Di Giorgio's position was strong. The press and local authorities unconditionally supported him, and he could move without restraints. He evicted strikers, his goons and the police attacked picketers, and vandalism of any kind was blamed on the strikers. Di Giorgio used undocumented workers at will. In turn the union was weak. It could not stop production, and when it attempted a boycott, the growers merely relabeled their products.[8]

Joseph Di Giorgio became obsessed with winning at any cost. He used the press and politicians effectively. Hugh M. Burns, California state senator and member of the Senate Committee on Un-American Activities, announced that his committee would investigate charges. Jack Tenney, co-chair of the committee, led the investigation, but did not uncover any evidence of communist involvement.[9]

Di Giorgio mobilized friends in Washington, D.C. Congressman Alfred J. Elliot took the fight to the House of Representatives. On March 22, 1948, he read a document, allegedly signed by 1,160 Di Giorgio employees, stating that workers did not want Local 218 to represent them; Congressman Elliot demanded a federal investigation.[10]

In November 1949 a subcommittee of the House Committee on Education and Labor held hearings at Bakersfield, California. Representative Cleveland M. Bailey (West Virginia) presided and Representatives Richard M. Nixon (California) and Tom Steed (Oklahoma) joined him. The two other members of the subcommittee, Thruston B. Morton (Kentucky) and Leonard Irving (Missouri), did not attend the hearings. The proceedings took two days, hardly enough time to conduct an in-depth investigation. The hearings were nonetheless dramatic, for the Di Giorgio Corporation had filed a $2 million suit against the union and the Hollywood Film Council, claiming that *Poverty in the Land of Plenty*, produced in the spring of 1948, libeled the corporation. The Di Giorgios wanted the subcommittee to substantiate their charge.[11]

The hearings followed standard House committee procedure. A committee chair charged a subcommittee to investigate a special matter. The subcommittee chairperson then drafted a report of hearings, submitted it to subcommittee members, and sent it to the committee of the whole. If findings and recommendations of the subcommittee were accepted, an official report was submitted to the House, with recommendations for specific action. In the case of the subcommittee investigating the Arvin strike, Congressman Bailey pigeonholed the findings; the subcommittee found nothing, so Bailey made no move to file an official report on the strike. Nor did he mention the controversy between the union and Di Giorgio in the report that the subcommittee eventually made to the committee of the whole.[12] (A partial explanation is that Bailey realized that the union had lost the strike.)

Joseph Di Giorgio, still intent on an official condemnation of the union, on March 9, 1949, commissioned Representative Thomas H. Werdel from Kern County to file a report, signed by Tom Steed, Thruston B. Morton, and Richard M. Nixon, in the appendix of the *Congressional Record*.[13] The appendix serves no official function other than to provide congressmen a forum in which to publish material sent them by constituents.

The report, a very clever piece of deceptive literature entitled "Agricultural Labor at Di Giorgio Farms, California," stated that *Poverty in the Land of Plenty* was libelous and it contained a favorable biography of Joseph Di Giorgio. The report claimed that the strike was "solely one for the purpose of organization" and that workers had no grievances, for "wages, hours, working conditions, and living conditions have never been a real issue in the Di Giorgio strike." The report further charged that taxpayers' money had been misused by holding hearings, since they publicized "the leadership of a labor organization which has no contracts, no grievances, no strike, no pickets, and only a handful of members." It concluded that it would be against the public interest to introduce new laws or to extend present laws to protect farm workers.

The report delivered a death blow to the NFLU. It panicked the California Federation of Labor leadership who ordered Local 218 to settle the libel suit (the CFL would not pay defense costs) and demanded that the strike be ended. Big labor had been scared off by a phony report that purported to be an official record, one that had been published in the "wastebasket" of the *Congressional Record*. The report had been issued on March 9 and by May the strike ended. The Di Giorgios agreed to settle the suit for $1 on the conditions that the NFLU plead guilty to the judgement, thus admitting libel; that they remove the film from circulation and recall all prints; that they reimburse the corporation for attorney fees; and that they call off the strike.[14]

For the next eighteen years Di Giorgio sued every time the film was shown or negative public commentary was made on Di Giorgio's role in the strike. Slowly Galarza gathered data which proved that the Werdel report had no official standing, that the report had been in fact written by the Di Giorgio attorneys, and that the signers, according to them, did not know who drafted it or, for that matter, remembered signing it. Werdel, Steed, Morton, and Nixon all knew that the report had no official status and was, at best, an opinion. In other words, they knowingly deceived the public to break the strike. Agribusiness had enough power to induce four congressmen to endorse a blank check in order to satisfy the whim of a very powerful man. Farm workers did not have countervailing power.[15]

The story of the NFLU during the 1950s is one of frustration for farm workers in California. Every time workers were able to mount an offensive effective enough to stop production, growers broke the drive by using *braceros* and undocumented workers. Growers used the departments of Labor, Agriculture, Justice, and State as their personal agents. The so-called liberal Democratic administrations favored growers. Little difference existed between the Republican Goodwin Knight and Democratic governor Edmund G. Brown, Sr., both of whom served the growers.

The control of farm workers was based on the labor contractor who furnished growers with an abundance of domestic scabs and undocumented workers once a strike was called. These contractors, usually of Mexican descent, were indispensable in keeping the exploitive system functioning. This reality forced the NFLU to change its response from conducting militant strikes to thoroughly documenting working conditions and the misuse of the *bracero* program and exposing them to the public. By the end of the decade the NFLU died an unnatural death; in June 1960 it surrendered its charter. The Agricultural Workers Organizing Committee (AWOC) took its place.[16]

Farm workers courageously fought back. In 1950 Ignacio Guerrero, his wife, and thirteen children lived in a makeshift home on the outskirts of Tracy, California. He read leaflets about the Di Giorgio and the potato strikes in Kern County. In Tracy twenty contractors, mostly Mexicans, managed several thousand tomato pickers. Conditions were miserable. Growers paid 18¢ a bag for first pickings, withholding 2¢ per box as a "bonus." The workers would lose the "bonus" if they left before the harvest ended. Guerrero took the initiative and held meetings in his home. Local 300 was chartered.

The Tomato Growers Association had substantial resources, while Local 300 had "no treasury, no strike fund, no regular staff, and only a token membership base." In spite of the handicaps the workers stopped production for a time. However, the strike was doomed when Teamster officials directed their drivers to cross the tomato workers' picket and the growers imported massive numbers of *braceros*.[17] The union won a limited victory; it signed some contracts and eliminated the bonus.

The next year the Federal Wage Stabilization Board wiped out whatever gains were made by fixing a ceiling of 20¢ for all pickings (second and third pickings had gone as high as 28¢). Many growers restored the bonus. Workers again turned to Local 300. It was powerless; the NFLU had financial problems and the California Federation of Labor ignored appeals. Ignacio Guerrero had to move his family in search of work.[18]

The Guerrero story was repeated in the Imperial Valley. The Imperial Valley Farmers Association was comprised of 480 members who controlled 90 percent of the acreage. The local labor force struggled to improve its working and living conditions which had deteriorated because of the heavy use of *braceros* which allowed growers to introduce back-breaking methods such as the short-handled hoe. They also substituted piecework for hourly wages. In 1950 about 5,000 undocumented workers worked in the valley, earning between 40¢ and 50¢ an hour, and sometimes as low as 35¢ an hour. *Braceros* earned 70¢ an hour.

Workers organized Local 280. They attempted to convince the Mexican government to stop the flow of *braceros* into the valley. However, U.S. Ambassador William O'Dwyer, whose brother was a partner of the president of the Imperial Valley Farmers Association, represented the growers' interests in Mexico City. After three years of struggle the results were the same as at Tracy; over 150 families moved north in search of work.[19]

By 1953 the NFLU changed its tactics, and concentrated its efforts on informing the public about the abuses in the *bracero* program and treatment of workers. During the next seven years an attack was launched against the *bracero* program which exposed its contradictions. Galarza and NFLU leaders realized that unionization was futile while the *bracero* program remained. During the late 1950s it seemed like the *bracero* program had become an institution. Edward R. Murrow's *Harvest of Shame* was shown on national television on Thanksgiving Day, 1960. This documentary rekindled interest in the plight of farm workers.[20]

THE TEXAS GARMENT WORKERS' STRIKES

In Texas, despite a growing anti-labor climate, the AFL-CIO unions increased their collective membership from roughly 200,000 in 1940 to 450,000 in 1970. In spite of the success of labor in general, industries which had a heavy concentration of Mexicans, such as agriculture and the garment industry, remained unorganized. The number of garment workers increased from about 6,500 in 1940 to about 25,000 in 1970, but the number of ILGWU members dropped from about 2,750 in 1940 to 1,375 in 1953 and 1,000 in 1956. In 1962 it fell to about 500 dues-paying members.[21] Considering the wealth (assets of $174 million in 1969) and growth in membership (340,000 in 1940 to 450,000 in 1970) of the national organization, the situation in Texas has to be blamed on the national office's unwillingness to commit funds or effort toward building a cadre of Chicano organizers.

During the late 1940s and the early 1950s San Antonio had about 800 union members in the garment industry. Half of them worked for the Juvenile Manufacturing Company, represented by Local 347. When ILGWU lost the certification election at that plant, this local died. Meyer Perlstein retired in 1956 and was replaced by another easterner, Sol Chaikin, who had little experience in the Southwest and less with Mexicans. He chose a staff, none of whom spoke Spanish. Rebecca Taylor and Elizabeth Kimmel (see Chapter 8) were told that they would be transferred; however, to everyone's surprise Taylor took a managerial position with the Tex-Son Company which manufactured boys' clothing.

A confrontation between Tex-Son and the union began in December 1958. Tex-Son had laid off large numbers of workers, subcontracting more and more work to another factory in Tupelo, Mississippi. The union was desperate and had to negotiate a good contract with Tex-Son or abandon its efforts in San Antonio. Tex-Son had the support of the Southern Garment Manufacturing Association and the other garment shops in the city. Local 180 did not even send a representative to the San Antonio Central Labor Council. When negotiations slowed down, René Sándoval gave an impassioned speech and the workers walked out on February 24, 1959.

The strike was one of the roughest in San Antonio history. The picketers threw eggs at owner Harold Franzel, and the police responded by beating the strikers. An unknown person shot into the homes of two strikebreakers. Sophie Gonzales and Georgia Montalbe emerged as strike leaders. Even scabs attempted to put a hex on Sophie Gonzales through the use of a voodoo doll; the strikers then paid the local *bruja* (witchdoctor) to endorse the strike. The ILGWU collected over $10,000 and began paying strike benefits of $20 a week. The strikers picketed stores carrying Tex-Son goods, solicited the support of the churches, marched in a parade, and improved relations with other unions.

The strikers could not stop production; there were too many workers ready to take their jobs. In the fall of 1959 the Landrum-Griffin Act stripped the strikers of the right to carry banners and signs outside of stores; the strikers were limited to leafleting the stores. The strike died of attrition in the spring of 1962, after costing the ILGWU $500,000.[22] The failure of the Tex-Son strike and the trend in the 1960s of moving plants to Mexico, Taiwan, Hong Kong, and Korea put an end to any effective efforts to organize in the garment trades.

GENERAL WORK CONDITIONS FOR CHICANO LABOR

Texas-Mexicans moved in increasing numbers to the Midwest. Housing and medical care remained primitive, and entire families, including children, worked.[23] Michigan Field Crops, Inc., organized during World War II, in 1950 recruited 8,767 beet growers, 6,800 pickle growers, and an estimated 3,300 growers of miscellaneous crops as members. In 1950 they imported 5,300 Texas-Mexican farm workers.[24] Before the war they had been taken north by contractors: now larger numbers went on their own. The war did little to improve opportunity for Texas-Mexicans in the Midwest where many depended on seasonal work in cherries, cucumbers, tomatoes, and the familiar sugar beet.[25]

Texas-Mexicans also migrated in larger numbers to the Pacific Northwest where after the war they made a "rapid transition from transient migrant farm worker to state resident employed in non-agricultural areas." By the 1940s Chicanos were firmly established in the Yakima Valley, and by the end of the decade this region supported a Spanish-language radio.[26]

Displacement of Texas-Mexicans accelerated in 1949 when Mexico removed Texas from the *bracero* "blacklist" (see Chapter 7). That year California received 8 percent of the *bracero* contract labor and raised cotton wages 15 percent; Texas received 56 percent of all *bracero* contract labor and lowered cotton wages 11 percent. As conditions worsened in Texas, Chicano migration to the Midwest increased.[27]

In the early 1940s contractors hauled workers throughout Texas. They followed the migrant stream, picking cotton along the Texas coast throughout central Texas and into western Texas. Many migrants, whether they went north or remained in Texas, returned for the winter to their base town where many owned small shacks. They would work at casual jobs until the trek began again.[28] These south Texas towns by the postwar era were interwoven by a network of contractors which furnished cheap labor to growers.

Many Mexican contractors amassed sizeable equities. By the late 1940s many had bought farms or leased land. In the postwar period a trend back to tenancy and lease-operation emerged. The leasers were predominantly second and third generation south Texas Anglos, but this group also included a dozen or so Mexican farmers, most of whom had originally been *contratistas* and truckers. One *Mexicano* family became one of the world's largest watermelon shippers, leasing several thousand acres of land.[29]

Chicano migrants became increasingly independent of the contractor and the local *patrones*. Although they still worked for exploitive wages as migrants, they no longer totally depended on the south Texas economy. They had options as to where they went and could find sources of wages on their own.[30]

Mexicans in Texas became increasingly urbanized. They worked in industries outside agriculture, such as oil, where they did the low-paying, back-breaking work. In 1945 the Fair Employment Practices Commission (FEPC) ordered Shell Oil to upgrade Mexican labor at the Deer Park refinery. The local Anglo union staged a wildcat strike in protest. In 1946 Gulf Oil's coast refinery hired twenty Chicanos; they were paid 91¢ an hour, while their Anglo counterparts earned $1.06 an hour.[31]

The war had opened some occupations to Mexicans. For instance, in the Fort Worth area they moved into service jobs such as bus boys, elevator operators, and the like. However, the better paying industries, such as Consolidated Fort Worth and North American Aircraft of Dallas, hired a limited number of Chicano workers. Unionization of industries helped Chicano workers little since unions relied on the seniority system and few Mexicans held membership in trade unions. In short, Texas industries followed the practice of discriminating against Mexican workers in terms of employment, wage scales, and opportunities for promotion.[32]

Mexicans earned low wages in Texas agriculture with cotton farmers in 1948 in the El Paso area paying pickers $1.50 per hundredweight of cotton picked. In 1950 farmers in the Rio Grande Valley paid $1.25 per hundred pounds with many farmers along the river paying as low as 50¢ to 75¢. The nationwide average was $2.45 per hundred pounds.[33]

The heavy use of contract and undocumented labor in agriculture made it difficult to organize and encouraged migration to other states. Organized labor in Texas frantically attempted to stop the manipulation of the *bracero* and undocumented worker by grower interests.[34] The number of *braceros* contracted in Texas increased from 42,218 in 1949 to 158,704 five years later, while emigration out of Texas jumped from just over 5,000 in 1939, to 22,460 in 1945, to 71,353 in 1949.

Factors Reinforcing the Unchanging Status

Organized labor suffered setbacks during the 1950s. The McCarthy era encouraged attacks on progrssive labor leaders and many CIO locals were purged because they allegedly had communist leadership. Chicanos were heavily concentrated in these industrial unions. Increasingly, the Taft-Hartley Act was used to break strikes. State and local authorities also cooperated in suppressing labor. Major efforts of the NFLU and the ILGWU failed to have any noticeable effect. In this atmosphere progressive movements slowed down and retreated into nonvisible activities.

As the reaction and apathy of the 1950s suffocated the progressive labor movement, many Chicanos compromised their commitment. The old locals of the Mine, Mill and Smelters Workers Union were absorbed by the United Mine Workers and the United Steel Workers of America. Progressive labor leaders such as Alfredo Montoya turned inward, limiting their activity to trade union business. In the early 1950s the Greater Los Angeles CIO Council had supported the Community Service Organization,[35] but by the 1960s leadership had grown more conservative with mergers of the AFL-CIO. Much of the leadership maintained their "Mexicanism" and participated in more traditional organizations such as the Mexican-American Political Association (MAPA) and the Political Association of Spanish-Speaking Organizations (PASSO). However, while unions have been important to Mexicans, they have traditionally served only a minority of the total work force. In 1968, a zenith year for union membership, only 26.3 percent of all the nation's workers belonged to a union, one out of four workers.[36]

The Southwest itself has had a history of antiunionism and in states like Arizona and Texas right-to-work laws have frustrated the entrance of Chicanos into the ranks of labor. Effective campaigns to unionize Chicanos were infrequent, and even rich unions refused to make a long term commitment. Many international central offices were in the East and Midwest where Mexicans were unknown. Moreover, the unions themselves restricted the entry of Chicanos.[37]

The record of Chicano employment in government service was as dismal as in the private sector. In California in 1960 Chicanos comprised 4.7 percent of the total public employees; in Texas, 13.4 percent of the total of whom almost 40 percent were laborers. In New Mexico they comprised 29.8 percent, but 60.6 percent of this group were laborers.[38]

Unemployment among Chicanos remained high throughout most of the early 1960s. In Los Angeles, which has been traditionally more progressive than other Southwestern cities, in 1964 Chicanos filed 12 percent of all unemployment claims.[39] In Tucson, Arizona, 54 percent of the Mexican workers were unskilled and much more prone to unemployment.[40] In Texas unemployment was 8.7 percent for Mexicans, 7.3 percent for nonwhites, and only 3.3 percent for Anglo-Americans.[41]

Social scientists have blamed the lack of unionization among Mexicans in Texas on the high proportion of undocumented workers entering the state. However, a more reasonable explanation is that the lobbying of employer groups resulted in an absence of federal and state legislation protecting the rights of farm and urban workers to organize. For Texans right-to-work laws meant use of the Texas Rangers to discourage union organizing. As in California, the Chicano in Texas became increasingly urban with some 80 percent living in urban communities. Unemployment remained high because these workers often came to the city not because of increased opportunities, but because of dwindling opportunities in permanent farm work caused by increased mechanization. They were not able to find employment in the city or the farms. A high percentage of even urban workers have been forced to join the migrant stream. Local, state, and federal authorities did nothing to stabilize this situation and, in fact, passed laws giving employers additional advantages over workers. They did absolutely nothing to support workers in collective bargaining situation.[42]

Precise figures as to the number of Texas Chicano farm workers are unavailable. In 1960 an estimated 261,000 Chicanos worked as farm wage laborers. Nationally, 9 percent of all farm wage laborers could be classified as migrants, whereas 40 percent of all Chicano farm workers fell into the migrant category. Migrants occupied the bottom rung of the ladder earning $600 less than nonmigrant farm workers. In 1963 Texas farm workers averaged 81¢ an hour versus $2.46 an hour for factory workers, $2.75 for miners, and $3.42 for construction workers.[43]

San Antonio in 1960 was unquestionably the most important Texas city for Chicanos both in terms of history and population. San Antonio had a Mexican population of 243,627; 17.2 percent of the 1,417,810 *Mexicanos* in the state. It had a permanent Mexican population; 30,299 were first generation, 75,950 second generation, and 137,738 third or later generations. As in the case of El Paso and Corpus Christi, a substantial number worked as migrants. The total unemployment in San Antonio for males of all races was 5.1 percent in 1960 versus 7.7 percent for Spanish surname; the unemployment of Chicanas was 7.9 percent versus 4.7 percent for all other females.[44] These figures did not include migrant workers.

Chicanos and Chicanas in the major Texas cities were predominantly nonskilled workers and were heavily concentrated in manufacturing industries. Blatant discrimination in transportation, communications, and other public utilities kept employment of Mexicans low, especially in San Antonio where only 4.9 percent were employed in those sectors.[45] A dual wage structure also existed with Mexicans generally averaging some $2,000 a year less than whites. For example, in San Antonio the median income for a Spanish-surname family was $3,446 versus $5,828 for whites; 21,458 out of 50,579 (42 percent) Spanish-surname families earned under $3,000, which was the poverty line, versus 16.2 percent of the Anglo-American families.[46] The difference between the figures was even greater in terms of per capita income since Mexican families were larger than those of Anglos. Mexicans earned 59 percent of what Anglo families earned and even at Kelly Air Force Base, which employed a great percentage of the better paid Chicanos, in 1962 the average wage for Anglo-Americans was $6,700 versus $4,500 for Chicanos. Mexicans comprised 23.5 percent of the base's employees.[47]

Adding to the Chicanos' economic plight in San Antonio was the fact that it was the least unionized Texas city. Less than 10 percent of the total population belonged to unions and only 25 percent of the building and construction trades of the city were under union contracts. As of 1963 few Mexicans had participated in the city's craft unions' apprenticeship programs. The pattern was clear; the higher paying and more prestigious trades like electricians had the lowest number of Mexicans (6 percent), whereas the back-breaking occupations such as cement finishers had the highest (62.5 percent). Chicanos fared even worse in union membership. A survey of membership in selected construction trades showed that only the hod carriers and cement workers were predominantly Chicano (85.4 percent and 90 percent, respectively). The hod carriers who were not Mexicans were Blacks. Chicanos made up 90 percent of the cement masons, but comprised only 10 percent of the higher paid plasterers.[48]

In the manufacturing and nonmanufacturing sectors Mexicans fared as badly as in the construction trades. Out of eighteen manufacturing firms there were no Chicano administrators and only three first-line supervisors. By the mid-1960s changes occurred and organized labor slowly began to look to Chicano and Black organizations for support against San Antonio's reactionary leaders.[49]

The migration of Chicanos to the Midwest continued in the 1960s.[50] In agriculture in the 1960s the amount of capital needed to replace manpower decreased, with the result that capital was substituted for labor. Government support cut the cost of the machinery, and the cost of food production decreased while profits increased. Midwestern employers rushed to modernize operations. For example, by 1970 in Wisconsin three-quarters of the cucumber and over half of the cherry crop were machine harvested. Anglo-Americans who once shunned stoop labor were more willing to take jobs operating machines. Therefore, Chicanos benefited little from mechanization. The situation in the Midwest reflected national trends. The agricultural work force declined from 9 percent of the U.S. total in 1960 to 6 percent in 1965 to 5 percent in 1970.[51]

The reason for the pull to Midwestern cities is obvious. Dr. Louise Kerr, in her excellent study on Mexicans in Chicago, compiled the accompanying chart on income and education of Chicanos in the United States.

INCOME AND EDUCATION: CHICANOS IN THE UNITED STATES, 1950

	INCOME	EDUCATION
Los Angeles		
Mexican-born	$1,931	6.1
Mexican-American	1,731	9.5
Texas urban		
Mexican-born	1,164	3.1
Mexican-American	1,096	6.0
Texas rural		
Mexican-born	748	1.4
Mexican-American	803	3.8
Chicago		
Mexican-born	2,566	5.6
Mexican-American	2,066	9.0

SOURCE: Louise Año Nuevo Kerr, "The Chicano Experience in Chicago: 1920–1970," (Ph.D. Dissertation, University of Illinois at Chicago Circle, 1976), p. 138.

Economically, life in Chicago was an improvement for both Texas-Mexicans and Mexican nationals. The U.S. census in 1960 (in its usual undercount) stated that the Mexican population had grown to 45,000. While Chicanos were still clustered in less desirable employment, some Mexicans working in steel averaged $12,500 a year by the late 1960s with some earning as high as $25,000 a year. Second generation steelworkers in 1966 integrated into the Chicago political milieu and formed the Tenth Ward Spanish-speaking Democratic Organization which functioned within the Democratic machine.[52]

THE ROAD TO DELANO: THE FARM LABOR STRUGGLE CONTINUES

The road to Delano has been forged through the struggles and sacrifices of farm workers regionally and nationally. Not to minimize the importance of César Chávez and the United Farm Workers (UFW), the successes of his union in the 1960s and 1970s were linked to the labor movement and confrontations of the nineteenth century led by Native Americans, Mexicans, Chinese, Japanese, as well as other ethnic and racial groups. In the twentieth century these groups confronted growers in vegetable, fruit, cotton, sugar beet, and other farm operations. California's battleground was the most dramatic and best documented because of the size of the factory farms; however, similar struggles took place elsewhere. The importance of Delano is that after a period of what appeared to be continual defeat, that is, the unsuccessful NFLU efforts of the 1950s, the UFW regained impetus, not only for the farm workers' struggle, but for the Chicano movement. The gains made by the UFW represented tangible progress for the toilers of the soil everywhere in the United States who realized that if it could be done in California where the power of the "green giants" was the strongest, there was hope for them. The change in attitude brought about by César Chávez and the United Farm Workers cannot be underestimated.

César Chávez and the United Farm Workers

On September 8, 1965, the Filipinos in the Agricultural Workers Organizing Committee (AWOC) struck the grape growers of the Delano area in the San Joaquin Valley. Militancy among the Filipino workers had been heightened by a victory in the spring of 1965 in the Coachella Valley, where the U.S. Labor Department had decreed that *braceros* would be paid $1.40 an hour. The domestic pickers received 20¢ to 30¢ an hour less. Joined by Mexicans, the Filipinos walked out, and ten days later they received a guarantee of equivalent pay with *braceros*. When the Filipinos requested the same guarantee in the San Joaquin Valley, growers refused, and led by Larry Itlong, they voted to strike. The strike demands were simple: $1.40 an hour or 25¢ a box. The Di Giorgio Corporation again became the major target. The rank and file of the National Farm Workers Association (NFWA) voted on September 16 to join the Filipinos. In December 1964 Public Law 78 expired, which significantly strengthened the union's position.[53]

Chávez emerged as the central figure in the strike. He was born in Yuma, Arizona, in 1927. He spent his childhood as a migrant worker. His father had belonged to farm labor unions and Chávez himself had been a member of the NFLU. In the 1940s he moved to San Jose, California, where he married Helen Fávila. In San Jose he met Father Donald McDonnell, who tutored him in *Rerum Novarum,* Pope Leo XIII's encyclical which supported labor unions and social justice. Through Father McDonnell Chávez met Fred Ross of the Community Service Organization (CSO). He became an organizer for the CSO and learned grass-roots organizing. Chávez rose to the position of general director of the national CSO, but in 1962 he resigned. He then moved his family to Delano and began to organize his union with no outside support. Chávez picked Delano because his brother Richard, a carpenter and head of the local CSO, lived there.[54] He built his union by going from door to door in the *barrios* where the farm workers lived. Delano was an important choice because of its substantial all-year farm worker population; in 1968 32 percent of the 7,000 harvest workers lived and worked in the Delano area year-round.

Chávez concentrated his efforts on the Mexican field hands, for he knew the importance of nationalism in solidifying an organization. He carefully selected a loyal cadre of proven organizers, such as Dolores Huerta and Gil Padilla, whom he had met in the CSO. He avoided quixotic fights, and by the middle of 1964 the NFWA was self-supporting.[55]

By 1965 the NFWA had some 1,700 members. Volunteers, fresh from civil rights activities in the South, joined the NFWA at Delano. Protestant groups, who had been evangelized by the civil rights movement, championed the cause of the workers. A minority of Catholic priests, inspired by inner revival, began to take seriously the *Rerum Novarum.*[56] With a possibility of victory and nationwide publicity and perhaps with some shame for its many years of neglect, Anglo-American labor jumped on the bandwagon. In Chávez's favor was the growing number of Chicano workers living in the United States. Over 80 percent lived in cities, and many belonged to unions. Many in fact belonged to big labor such as the United Auto Workers (UAW).

Many leaders before him had attempted to organize Chicano workers, but they had failed. Chávez was the right man to get the nationalistic Mexicans together with other workers and supporters.

Chávez put them all under a red flag with the thunderbird symbol and a banner of *La Virgen de Guadalupe*. His approach gave him a national forum and media publicity; publications such as the *Wall Street Journal* and *Life* wrote about him and even *Time* magazine featured him in a cover story.

The most effective strategy was the boycott. Supporters were urged not to buy Schenley products or Di Giorgio grapes. The first breakthrough came when the Schenley Corporation signed a contract in 1966. The Teamsters unexpectedly refused to cross picket lines in San Francisco. Rumors of a bartenders' boycott reached 75-year-old Lewis Solon Rosenstiel, Schenley's president, who decided that a settlement was advisable.[57] Soon afterwards Gallo, Christian Brothers, Paul Masson, Almaden, Franzia Brothers, and Novitiate signed contracts.

The next opponent was the Di Giorgio Corporation, one of the largest grape growers in the central valley. The ruthless, tough patriarch and founder of this corporation, Joseph Di Giorgio, had died. The corporation was in the process of diversifying its operations; it had become a modern-day trust with processing and canning operations as well as stocks in other companies. Executives realized that the times had changed and they were concerned about the corporation's public image. Robert Di Giorgio, the new president, was more concerned about public relations than his uncle Joseph had been.[58]

In April 1966 Di Giorgio unexpectedly announced he would allow his workers at Sierra Vista to vote on whether they wanted a union and who would represent them. However, this move was a ploy. While awaiting the election Di Giorgio agents openly intimidated picketers, with a security guard beating a woman striker.[59] In collusion with Di Giorgio the Teamsters opposed the farm workers and bid to represent the workers. Di Giorgio, without consulting the NFWA, set the date for the election. The NFWA urged its followers not to vote, since it did not have time to campaign or to participate in establishing the ground rules. Furthermore, it had to have enough time to return eligible voters to the Delano area. Out of 732 eligible voters only 385 voted; 281 voters specified that they wanted the Teamsters as their union agent. The NFWA immediately branded the election as fraudulent and pressured Governor Edmund G. Brown, Sr., a friend of Robert Di Giorgio, to investigate the election. Brown needed the Chicano vote as well as that of the liberals who were committed to the farm workers. The governor's investigator recommended a new election, and the date was set for August 30, 1966.[60]

That summer an intense campaign took place between the Teamsters and the NFWA. A state senate committee investigated charges of communist infiltration of the NFWA; the committee found nothing to substantiate charges. As the election neared,

Chávez became more somber. He had to keep the eligible voters in Delano, and he had the responsibility of feeding them and their families as well as the army of strikers and volunteers. The Di Giorgio campaign drained the union's financial resources. Chávez had to keep the organization alive if Delano were not to become another page in the annals of unsuccessful strikes. Therefore, some weeks before the strike vote, he reluctantly merged the NFWA and AWOC into the United Farm Workers Organizing Committee (UFWOC).[61]

Teamsters red-baited the UFWOC and circulated free copies of Gary Allen's John Birch Society pamphlet. The UFWOC passed out excerpts from *The Enemy Within*, in which Robert Kennedy indicted Hoffa and the Teamsters in scathing terms; association with the Kennedy name helped. Finally the vote was taken. The UFWOC won the election, receiving 573 votes to the Teamsters' 425. Field workers voted 530 to 331 in favor of Chávez and his followers. The Teamsters' vote came from the skilled workers. Soon afterwards the Di Giorgio Corporation and the UFWOC signed a contract.[62]

Other growers proved to be more difficult. In 1967 the first target was Giumarra Vineyards Corporation, the largest producer of table grapes in the United States. When Guimarra used other companies' labels to circumvent the boycott, in violation of the Food and Drug Administration rules, the union extended its boycott to all California table grapes.[63] Boycott activities spread into Canada and Europe. Grape sales decreased significantly. Some of the slack was taken up by the U.S. Defense Department. In 1966 U.S. troops in Vietnam were shipped 468,000 pounds of grapes, in 1967 555,000 pounds, in 1968 2 million pounds, and by 1969 more than 4 million pounds. Many private citizens protested Defense Department interference with the boycott at the taxpayer's expense, but the practice continued. In fact, the Defense Department extended this practice to buying lettuce when that industry was the object of a strike by Chávez and the UFWOC.[64]

In the summer of 1970 the strike approached its fifth year. That summer Chávez intensified picketing in the Coachella Valley. In June 1970 a group of growers agreed to sign contracts, followed by a majority of Coachella growers. Crates containing union grapes displayed the UFWOC flag with its eagle; sales of union grapes jumped as many markets requested the "thunderbird." Growers of the San Joaquin Valley wanted the "bird," and also signed with Chávez, and soon most of the California table grape industry signed contracts. The price of victory came high; the five-year battle cost 95 percent of the farm workers involved their homes and their cars.[65]

After this victory the union turned to the lettuce fields of the Salinas Valley. Salinas growers were among the most powerful in the state. During July 1970 the Growers-Shippers Association and twenty-nine of the largest growers in the valley entered into negotiations with the Teamsters.[66] Contracts signed with the truckers' union in Salinas were worse than sweetheart contracts: they provided no job security, no seniority rights, no hiring hall, and no protection against pesticides.

Many growers, like the Bud Antle Company (a partner of Dow Chemical), had dealt with the Teamsters since the 1950s. In 1961, in return for a $1 million loan, Antle signed a contract with the truckers.

By August 1970 many workers refused to abide by the Teamster contracts and 5,000 walked off the lettuce fields.[67] The growers initiated a campaign of violence. Jerry Cohen, farm worker lawyer, was beaten unconscious. On December 4, 1970, Judge Gordon Campbell of Monterey County jailed Chávez for refusing to obey an injunction and held him without bail. This arbitrary action gave the boycott considerable impetus. Dignitaries visited Chávez in jail; he was released on December 24, 1970.[68]

By the spring of 1971 Chávez and the Teamsters signed an agreement that gave the UFWOC sole jurisdiction in the lettuce fields and that allowed Meany and Fitzsimmons to arbitrate the situation. The Teamsters were supposed to pull back. Throughout the summer and into the fall, however, growers refused to disqualify Teamster contracts and gradually the situation became stalemated.

The fight with the Teamsters had hurt the UFWOC since it turned its attention from servicing contracts. Chávez refused help from the AFL for professional administrators, for he believed that farm workers had to learn from their own mistakes. According to *Fresno Bee* reporter Ron Taylor, although Chávez was a patient teacher, he did not delegate authority and involved himself with too much detail. The basic problem was, however, that farm workers had never had the opportunity to govern themselves and Chávez had to build "ranch committees." This took time and the corporate ranchers who ran agribusiness had little tolerance for democracy.[69]

During 1971 and 1972 the UFW built on its gains, coordinating its administration of contracts and its boycott activities. Its success brought a change in social relations which was of great concern to the growers who changed their strategy (1) to drop their traditional opposition to the inclusion of farm workers under the National Labor Relations Act; (2) to organize the small farmers and to use them as a front to battle Chávez; and (3) to cooperate with the Nixon administration to encourage the Teamsters to bust the UFW. The fight at the national level was led by Nixon who obligingly opposed the grape boycott and sponsored a farm bill that outlawed secondary boycotts for farm workers, while giving them nothing. It required that farm workers give ten days' notice before striking and then gave growers a thirty-day cooling-off period before going to binding arbitration. The bill thus ended the possibility of a strike during the harvest period.[70]

The American Farm Bureau sponsored similar bills at the state level. Growers's strategy to put Chávez in the position of opposing secret elections for workers. Chávez's position was clear: he did not want to come under jurisdiction of the dreaded Taft-Hartley amendment which outlawed the secondary boycott and opened the way for the open shop and right-to-work laws. Moreover, the grower bills both at the federal and state levels were blatantly anti-worker. The American Farm Bureau put a similar bill through the Oregon legislature, but in response to UFW pressure Governor Tom McCall vetoed the law. However, in Arizona Governor Jack Williams signed a farm bureau bill in May 1972.[71] The UFW initiated a recall election of Williams. In spite of the fact that 176,000 signatures were secured on recall petitions, the recall never went to the people.[72]

In California growers paid professional petition gatherers to put Proposition 22 on the November 1972 ballot.[73] Their campaign represented the proposition as giving workers the right to vote by secret ballot and protecting the public from the secondary boycott, but its intent was clearly to destroy the power of the workers' union. The UFW enlisted church and liberal support, sending farm workers throughout the state with gigantic "No on 22" signs and placing them as human billboards at key corners and events. The UFW uncovered fraud in the collection of petition signatures by growers and pressured the reluctant secretary of state, Jerry Brown, to file a suit to take Proposition 22 off the ballot. A Los Angeles grand jury investigated the charges and indicted sponsors of "22." On November 7, 1972, the UFW and the voters of California won.

In the summer of 1972 Schenley again forced the UFW to strike. The Schenley Corporation employed scabs to harvest its $3 million wine-grape crop. The battleground was White River Farms in the San Joaquin Valley. Schenley effectively used small farmers to confront the union. On Sunday mornings 600 farmers and their families harvested Schenley's grapes. The small farmers ignored the fact that Schenley was part of a conglomerate owned by Buttes Gas and Oil; they believed that their enemy was Chávez and that if he went away, their problems would go away. Agribusinessmen also used small farmer associations such as the Nisei Farmers League. At White River Farms authorities arrested 269 strikers, including Chávez and Huerta. Both sides lost: Schenley lost about a million dollars, while the UFW lost a key contract.[74]

During the White River Farms strike U.S. Secretary of Agriculture Earl Butz traveled to California to campaign for a local congressman. He publicly condemned the strike: "Such actions should be outlawed. It is not fair for a farmer to work all year to produce a crop and then be wiped out by a two-week strike."[75] The NLRA then brought a suit to block the UFW's boycott against wineries. The federal court nullified the action.

The Teamster leadership drew closer to Nixon and openly campaigned to reelect him. Behind the scenes Charles Colson, special counsel to Nixon, had the American Farm Bureau Federation schedule Teamster president Frank Fitzsimmons as its principal speaker at its Los Angeles convention on December 17, 1972.[76] Fitzsimmons attacked everyone connected with the UFW, especially Chávez, proposing legislation that would put the farm workers under the NLRA. Two days after the convention the Western Conference of Teamsters created the Agriculture Workers Organizing Committee and in the spring of 1973 declared war on the UFW in the Imperial Valley.[77]

Many UFW contracts expired in the spring of 1973. Imperial Valley growers realized that the UFW was changing the social relations of the past. The hiring hall destroyed labor contractors. Growers negotiated with the Teamsters and truckers moved into the vineyards. Encouraged by the silence of the AFL-CIO, the Teamsters prepared for an all-out fight. Meany was angry at Chávez for the union's unconventional behavior, especially the UFW's boycott of entire supermarket chains. It embarrassed the AFL-CIO when its affiliates crossed the farm worker picket lines. But when the AFL-CIO saw the Teamsters move its army of goons into Coachella, Meany finally committed $1.6 million to the fight.[78]

The Teamsters' goons were paid $67.50 a day; armed with chains they assaulted picketers and badly beat a Catholic priest. Paul Hall, president of the Seafarers' Union, offered to send his sailors into Coachella to clean up the Teamsters (as he had done in Chicago and Puerto Rico), but Chávez refused the aid and used the sailors only as guards. Head-on fights between the two unions nevertheless took place. On June 21 Riverside deputies arrested two Teamsters on charges of assault, kidnapping, and attempted murder (Teamsters had abducted a worker and stabbed him six times with an ice pick).[79]

The war between the two unions shifted to the San Joaquin Valley. Between March and September California authorities arrested 3,500 men, women, and children.[80] Gallo had signed with Teamsters and picketing followed. Again, Teamsters and Meany met and a settlement was agreed upon, but Fitzsimmons repudiated his agreement. This did not surprise anyone since the Teamsters have a long history of opportunism. The UFW unleashed 2,000 pickets by August 1 at 29 ranches. In early August a shotgun blast hit a picketer, and on August 14 a UFW striker from Yemen, Dagi Daifullah, 24, died from massive head injuries inflicted by Kern County deputy sheriff Gilbert Cooper in Arvin.[81] The next day the UFW set up a silent picket. On August 16, on the weedpatch highway near Arvin a young man in a pick-up shot four times into the pickets, killing Juan de la Cruz, 60, who had been with the union from the beginning. Five thousand farm workers turned up for the Daifullah funeral and three days later for Juan de la Cruz. Chávez called off the pickets and stepped up boycott activities.[82]

Fitzsimmons, worried about his tarnished image, once more entered into negotiations with the AFL-CIO. *Again,* an agreement was reached. And, *again,* Fitzsimmons backed out of the agreement. Charles Colson, acting for Nixon, pressured Teamsters to cancel the agreement with the AFL.[83] At this point it looked as if the UFW was finished.[84]

On January 15, 1974, tragedy again struck. Nineteen strikebreakers were killed near Blythe in the Imperial Valley when their bus plunged into a drainage ditch filled with water. An investigation revealed that the bus had flimsy seats which contributed to the high death toll. Chávez charged that the "inhuman treatment of farm workers must end," and blamed the fatal crash on greed. Not long afterwards another bus crashed killing twelve undocumented workers and injuring six. The vehicle was being driven from El Centro to San Ysidro when the driver had a heart attack, hitting a parked truck.[85]

In April 1974 the UFW called off the Safeway boycott in return for AFL-CIO backing on the lettuce and grape boycott, an act which improved relations between the UFW and the international. In May of that year 600 farm workers struck the strawberry harvest in Ventura County. Eight were arrested.[86]

In September 1974 twenty-six union members were arrested for disturbing the peace in Yuma, Arizona.[87] The successes in Arizona were limited. Arizona growers were large; due to the limited industry in the state, agriculture was just that much more powerful. Grower interests united to oppose Chávez and even elements which were considered liberal supported the state's right-to-work law. Raúl Castro, a Chicano Democratic candidate for governor who was later elected, backed the right-to-work laws. State authorities turned the other way when on September 25, growers forced farm workers to remain at the groves at gun point.[88]

UFW membership plunged from 55,000 in 1972 to some 6,000 members in 1975.[89] The press predicted a doomsday for the union. Growers moved to finish the UFW by placing farm workers under the NLRA. Senator John Tunney proposed a bill to delete the words that excluded farm workers from the original 1935 Wagner Act. Chávez's position remained consistent: the NLRA was ineffective. The National Labor Relations Board handled 42,000 cases a year and had a backlog of 13,000 cases. Chávez realized that he needed a law that was based on 1975 realities and would be enforced.

Farm workers in California earned $1.20 an hour in 1965; by 1975 the minimum had been raised to $2.50 and in some cases $4.00 to $5.00 an hour. A few farm workers earned $7,000 a year and through the collective bargaining process had impressive fringe benefits. Still Chávez at his zenith represented less than 10 percent of the nation's farm workers, limited to the states of California, Arizona, and Florida. Nationwide, a farm worker employed over 300 days a year averaged $1.84 an hour or $4,358 a year and migrants averaged $2,434 a year. According to Chávez, "By keeping the farm workers from organizing and bargaining collectively, agribusiness has managed to hold labor costs far below the industrial averages ($10,000 to $11,000 a year). Agribusiness is saving $3 billion a year by keeping farm labor unorganized and powerless."[90]

Chávez worked behind the scenes to get a bill before the state legislature which would protect the rights of farm workers. He received the support of Governor Edmund G. Brown, Jr., who got growers and the UFW together to pound out a compromise bill.[91] By late May 1975 the California state legislature passed a bill which included the following provisions: (1) An Agriculture Labor Relations Board (ALRB) would be established to supervise elections. Both seasonal and permanent farm workers would vote at the peak of the harvest season. Said election would occur within one week of the workers' petition of an election. (2) Secondary boycotts would be restricted to employers refusing to negotiate after the UFW had won the election. (3) The board would recognize only "one industrial bargaining unit per farm." (4) Workers under Teamster or UFW contract could petition for an election which "could result in decertification of a union as bargaining agent and nullification" of existing contracts. (5) The board would establish the eligibility of 1973 strikers to vote in the new election.[92] Although the bill was not totally acceptable to either side, both agreed to abide by it. Teamsters did not participate in the discussion since they disliked the industrial base aspect of the act and the close scrutiny of the election process.

Enforcement of the act began on August 28, 1975. It pitted the small UFW against the 2.2 million member Teamsters. Within the first month the UFW won 17 farms, employing 3,800 workers; the Teamsters won 11 locations which employed 2,100 persons.[93] The UFW lost the E. J. Gallo vote where from the start employer favoritism of the Teamsters was evident. The growers harassed the UFW. The Elmco Vineyards of northeast Delano surrounded their property with a wire fence and would not allow the UFW to see the workers; Bud Antle drove his workers to the polls not allowing them to speak to anyone. In spite of this by November 1975 the UFW had won 167 elections, representing 24,334 workers or 49.1 percent of the 49,529 ballots cast. The Teamsters had won 95 elections, covering 11,802 workers. Throughout September and October the growers attempted to intimidate workers by firing UFW supporters.

Facing overwhelming defeat, growers began to rethink their agreement. They claimed that the ALRB was pro-farm worker and complained about the access rule which allowed UFW organizers to enter their factory farms to talk to workers during nonworking intervals.[94] Electoral violations were so flagrant that the ALRB was overworked and was running out of funds by January 1976. A coalition of Republicans and rural Democrats in the senate defeated a bill for $3.8 million in emergency appropriations; the vote was 20 to 15 in favor of the bill, but two-thirds of the senate or 27 votes were needed.[95] Growers did not limit their attacks to legal channels. In January 1976 Jerry Ducote, a 46-year-old ex-sheriff's deputy and former young Republican leader who had been associated with former Lieutenant Governor John Harmer, admitted to seventeen burglaries and break-ins of UFW offices. Salinas grower Stephen D'Arrigo and Delano grape grower Jack Pandal financed a campaign to discredit Chávez. Harmer had formed a public relations institute in Los Angeles as a vehicle to get grower money to publish an anti-Chávez pamphlet called *We Dare Not Fail*. Ducote gave files of his burglaries to Larry Cott of the FBI's San Francisco office. Also involved was the Santa Clara Farm Bureau.[96] The story did not get widespread coverage.

Chávez began an initiative drive for Proposition 14 which would take the enforcement of the ALRB out of the hands of the legislators and insure consistent application of the law. In less than a month farm worker supporters collected 719,589 signatures, 303,807 in the Los Angeles area alone. The California Farm Bureau allocated $2.5 million for the "No on 14" drive.[97] The campaign portrayed Chávez as the enemy of private property. The bureau poured millions into a mass media campaign. It made a special appeal to the small farmer, especially Japanese-Americans, by asserting that a vote for 14 would allow the invasion of small farms. California voters, according to a Mervin D. Field poll, lacked awareness of the issues behind 14. The UFW attempted to reach the people, but the courts supported the growers and limited the right of UFW supporters to leaflet shopping centers.[98]

The state senate meanwhile funded the ALRB. They argued that 14 would seriously compromise the powers of the legislature. The *Los Angeles Times* on October 29, 1976 stated in an editorial that ". . . public issues should not be removed from the give-and-take of the legislative process and frozen into law by initiative." The *Los Angeles Times* ignored how easily "the give-and-take of the legislative process" had been frustrated by agricultural and oil interests. Oil companies such as Getty Oil, Standard Oil, and Superior were heavily involved in defeating 14.[99]

Voters believed the growers' arguments that the initiative

would destroy property rights. The fact that "less than 10 percent of California growers employed about 75 percent of the state's farm workers" was ignored. Public opinion also ignored the fact that the California Supreme Court had found the access rule constitutional. Californians overwhelmingly voted against Proposition 14 which would have taken protection of farm workers out of the arena of political blackmail; property rights for the rich were more important to Californians than human rights.[100]

After the defeat Chávez struggled to get contracts. Operations continued in Arizona where its Agricultural Employment Relations Board was an obstacle. In Arizona it took three to six weeks to organize an election.[101] Throughout 1977 the UFW struggled in California to get certification and then win the election. By March 1977 the Teamsters again left the fields, signing an accord with Chávez.[102]

Growers acquired more influence over the ALRB. Several members of the ALRB resigned and Brown, after the defeat of 14, became more "pragmatic" and appointed pro-grower members. The general counsel Harry Deligonna increasingly dragged his feet.[103] Growers pressed for a renewal of the *bracero* program, and the UFW won elections. In the Imperial Valley they won 750 to 19. By April 1977 wages had been standardized and farm workers in California earned $3.53 an hour with fringe benefits.[104]

By February 1978 Chávez had called off the boycotts on grapes and lettuce. He stated that he took this action because of the effectiveness of the California Agricultural Labor Relations Act. People close to Chávez said that he and others wanted to concentrate all their forces on winning elections. The boycott spread them too thin. In April 1978 Chávez had high hopes of extending his organizational efforts into Texas and Florida.[105]

Other Delanos in the Midwest

Inspired by the *campesino* (farm worker) movement in California, farm worker activism in the Midwest increased during the second half of the 1960s. Texas-Mexican cucumber workers in Wisconsin were led by Jesús Salas, 22, from Crystal City, Texas, on a 90-mile march to Madison in 1966 carrying the symbolic thunderbird flag of the farm worker. Workers demanded a migrant representative on the Governor's Committee on Migratory Labor, enforcement of the state minimum wage of $1.25 an hour, and state housing camps. Salas organized an independent farm workers union called *Obreros Unidos* (United Workers) of Wisconsin in January 1967 and it remained active throughout that year.[106]

In Michigan, which used more migrant workers than any northern state, farm workers organized in the summer of 1966. In March 1967 migrants took part in a 70-mile "March for Migrants" from

Saginaw to Lansing. They reached the state capitol on Easter Sunday.[107] These marchers spoke for the thousands of workers who would arrive in Michigan starting in May.

That same year in Ohio Mexican farm workers demanded better wages and enforcement of health and housing codes. They had been influenced by the Chávez movement and the actions of Jesús Salas. Eighteen thousand to 20,000 Mexicans worked in Wallace County, Ohio, and throughout the tomato belt which circled northwest Ohio, southern Michigan, and northern Indiana. Most of the crops in this area were contracted by Hunt, Campbell Soup, Libby, McNeil, Vlasic, and Heinz. Baldemar Velásquez, 21, and his father emerged as the leaders of this movement. They organized a march in 1968 from Leipsic to the Libby tomato plant and later a march to the Campbell Soup plant. They established a newspaper, *Nuestra Lucha,* and a weekly radio program. By this time many of the former migrants had settled in urban industries and were members of associations such as the Meat Cutters Union in Toledo. They supported organizing efforts and helped form the Farm Labor Organizing Committee (FLOC). As the result of a series of strikes against individual farmers in 1968, FLOC signed twenty-two contracts. FLOC soon realized that the food processors throughout northwest Ohio and Indiana determined wages since they controlled the prices and paid farmers for their crops. They knew that signing contracts with individual farmers was good for morale, but it did not touch the source of power. Further, the small farmer could get around a contract by merely switching crops the following year.[108]

By 1973 FLOC had developed into more than a union. It was part of the Chicano movement of the region, supporting many of the local urban grievances such as police brutality, better education for Chicanos, and the struggle of the undocumented worker. For instance, on March 26, 1977, FLOC and the Ohio Council of Churches sponsored a conference in Findlay, Ohio, which drew about 200 people. They protested raids like those at the Morgan Packing Company in Warren, Indiana, where INS agents made forty-six arrests. They also condemned the abduction of a worker in Ottawa, Ohio, by INS officers.[109]

After 1973 FLOC actively sought outside funds and support. From the beginning many Protestant churches supported it. It was not until recently that the Indiana Catholic bishops endorsed FLOC. The union was also active in attempting to get the Ohio and Indiana state governments to respond to Chicanos in general. The Ohio legislature in 1976 passed a bill to establish a Mexican affairs department, but the bill was vetoed by Governor James Rhodes who excluded Mexicans from the Committee on Migrant Labor.[110]

Velásquez realized that mechanization was rapidly displacing many union members so he moved to keep contact with them as they moved to the city. FLOC continued to service them in their adjustment to urban life.

FLOC did not abandon the immediate struggle of the farm workers. A 1976 study by the American Friends Service Committee (AFSC) found that a large number of the northwest Ohio farm workers were not paid the federal minimum wage, with most families averaging $1.89 an hour. The AFSC study also found gross violations of child labor laws.[111]

In 1977 FLOC fought its battle with tomato processors asking for 34¢ a hamper (33 pounds) of tomatoes. The growers were paying 20¢ to 24¢ a hamper.[112] The problem was how to stop production. FLOC's leverage was weakened by rapid mechanization of tomato picking and the hundreds of growers it had to deal through. It did not have the money and the army of volunteers necessary to sustain a national boycott.

In 1977 it supported workers fired by Walter Krueger from the Lakewood Greenhouse, Inc. The workers, led by Jane Hernández, had protested that the florist was selling flowers treated by a chemical, TEMIK, developed by Union Carbide. Flowers remained toxic until four weeks after treatment, but the florist sold the poisoned flowers before the toxic effects wore off and thus forced workers to prematurely handle the flowers. Amelia Arribe, who had worked there for five years, complained to the Occupational Safety and Health Administration and she was laid off. When the other women protested, Krueger fired eight of them (most of them Chicanas). They asked the Teamsters for help, but they were refused. FLOC then sponsored a secondary boycott and as of May 1977 had pledges from six florists not to buy the flowers. May Rodríguez, who was six months pregnant, and Jane Hernández became ill as the result of TEMIK poisoning. Velásquez and Rodríguez were arrested and others were abused on the picket line.[113]

The struggle of the florist workers represents FLOC's battles. Most are small in comparison to those in California, and for that reason FLOC has not received national support or attention.

Chicanos struggled to organize in other regions. On February 15, 1969, at the Kitayam Brothers' flower farm outside Brighton, Colorado, five Chicanas chained themselves to the main gate of the farm. They belonged to the National Florist Workers Organization and wanted to prevent scabs from entering the farm. They had called a strike to force management to meet their demands for higher wages and for better working conditions. Chicanas laid on the frozen ground as county sheriff deputies moved in wearing gas masks and carrying acetylene torches. Mary Padilla, Martha Del Real, Lupe Biseño, president of the NFWO, Rachel Sándoval, and Mary Salas held out to the last.

ISSUES CONFRONTING THE CHICANO WORKER IN THE 1970s

Significant breakthroughs for Chicanos have been made in the craft, operative, and service categories. Although the status of Chicanos has improved as a result of the move to the cities and economic growth during three major wars, their opportunities for upward mobility remain collectively restricted. Since the 1930s the occupational distribution of Chicanos in the professional classes has changed relatively little.

OCCUPATIONAL DISTRIBUTION OF MEXICAN-AMERICAN MALES IN THE SOUTHWEST

OCCUPATION	1930	1950	1960	1970
Professionals and Technical	0.9%	2.2%	4.1%	6.4%
Managers	2.8	4.4	4.6	5.2
Sales	2.4	6.5	3.6	3.9
Clerical	1.0		4.8	6.6
Crafts	6.8	13.1	16.7	20.8
Operative	9.1	19.0	24.1	25.4
Service	4.0	6.3	7.5	10.5
Laborer	28.2	18.7	15.2	12.1
Farmers	9.8	5.1	2.4	0.9
Farm labor	35.1	24.7	16.8	8.1

SOURCE: Vernon M. Briggs, Jr., Walter Fogel, and Fred Schmidt, *The Chicano Worker* (Austin: University of Texas Press, 1977), p. 76.

Mobility was more restricted in the 1960s than in the previous decades even though the 1960s were growth years. It was a decade spurred by a thriving civil rights movement and a "war on poverty" which supposedly created jobs for the so-called disadvantaged. The gap between Chicano and Anglo males in the Southwest and nationally remained wide, with the majority of white Americans employed in white-collar occupations (46.8 percent in 1960 and 53.3 percent in 1970) and the overwhelming majority of Chicanos remaining in blue-collar occupations (80.9 percent in 1960 and 78.4 percent in 1970).[114]

This differential, according to Professor Vernon Briggs, Jr., contributed to a "social caste" system accentuating class differences between Mexicans and Anglos.[115] By the 1970s a rise in automation, the decline in population among the majority society, growing internationalization of capital and labor, and spiraling inflation all contributed to shrinking opportunities for Chicanos and further restricted upward mobility. By the 1970s there was a surplus of professionals; there were too many teachers, lawyers, university professors, etc. Chicanos were thus again restricted in their vertical mobility.

Social scientists and economists often advanced simplistic solutions: "The Mexican-American workers could on their own initiative, increase their income and standard of living in several ways. Limiting the size of the family would increase the standard of living by increasing per capita income."[116] U.S. social scientists have been reluctant to blame the Chicanos' plight on the system and its maldistribution of resources; instead they blame the size of the Chicanos' family.

By the mid-1970s nearly 40 percent of Chicanas 16 and over, were members of the work force.[117] A decline in real wages and purchasing power drove them and their Anglo and Black counterparts into the labor force in larger numbers. Chicanas trailed their White and Black counterparts in almost every category. There were fewer Chicanas in professional occupations (7.6 percent versus 18.4 percent for Anglo women and 11.6 Black women) and twice as many in the operative occupations (23.3 percent versus 7.6 percent Anglo and 12.2 percent Black).[118] The median income of Spanish-surname females in the Southwest relative to all white females in 1969 was 76 percent. The poverty level in 1970 was $4,200; the median income for Latin women over the age of 16 nationally was $2,313.[119] Chicanas in short earned three-quarters of what both Black and Anglo female workers earned.[120]

Both male and female Chicanos consistently had higher unemployment than Anglos. In 1969, although the Vietnam war stimulated heavy employment, unemployment among Mexicans in the Southwest was high (6.2 percent among males and 8.7 percent among females). Professor Briggs pointed out that the percentage would have been higher if it had not been for manpower program enrollees.[121]

In California Chicanos comprised less than 6 percent of the government employees versus 9 percent of all employment. In Texas they were 15 percent of the government employees compared to 11.5 percent of all employment. The reason given for the high percentage in Texas was that much government employment was in agencies in South Texas which the federal government funded. Even in this situation Chicanos did not share equally since they were concentrated in maintenance and service jobs.[122]

By the 1970s large numbers of the Chicano labor pool had been condemned to a life of unemployment or poverty program migrancy.[123] The government funded a labyrinth of federal programs to train a small number of Chicanos but in the end they remained frozen in place, with most too frustrated to meander through the labyrinth again. This situation was especially depressing among Chicanas who were entering the labor force in increasing numbers as heads of households. An example of a program that institutionalized poverty was the Aid to Families with Dependent Children (AFDC). Seventy percent of the aid was to female household heads. In San Antonio the figure is 80 percent. Nationally 17 percent of the

Chicano families were headed by women with 51 percent of these female headed households living in poverty. The overwhelming proportion of these women were young, with one or two children, locked out of improving themselves because of rigid and arbitrary AFDC regulations.

Supposedly to improve mobility for women on AFDC the work incentives (WIN) program was initiated to encourage employees to hire poor women. The government paid from 50 to 100 percent of the WIN employee's salary. There was no guarantee that that employment was permanent and critics saw it as a further way to get cheap labor for employers rather than as a way to help the poor. In contrast, a woman with dependents who wanted to pursue a college education was discouraged. Many were forced to quit college in their senior year because their child reached the arbitrary age of six.[124]

In 1969 86 percent of all Chicanos in the Southwest lived in urban areas. As in 1959 their median income per family still lagged behind the majority society. The income level for Chicanos in the Midwest was generally higher than other regions—$9,300 in Illinois and $9,400 in Michigan.[125]

MEDIAN INCOME PER FAMILY, 1970

STATE	MEDIAN INCOME	SPANISH SURNAME PERCENTAGE OF ANGLO	SPANISH SURNAME PERCENTAGE OF BLACK
Arizona	$7,350	74	129
California	8,430	73	113
Colorado	6,930	69	97
New Mexico	5,890	67	113
Texas	5,600	58	105

SOURCE: Adapted from Vernon M. Briggs, Jr., Walter Fogel, and Fred Schmidt, *The Chicano Worker* (Austin: University of Texas Press, 1979), p. 47.

The figures for family income do not take into account the size of the families, which was larger among Mexicans than either Anglos or Blacks. If per capita income were considered, the gap between Chicano and Anglo would increase and the Chicano and Black incomes would become approximately equal. In 1970 the average Mexican family consisted of 4.5 persons, Black and Puerto Rican 4.1 persons, and Anglo 3.6 persons.

In 1969 the poverty line for a nonfarm family was $3,743, and 24 percent of all Spanish-surname families fell below this line. By the mid-1970s 27 percent of the Latino families had fallen below the poverty line versus 9.7 percent of Anglos and 31.3 percent of Blacks. More significant was that in the Southwest between 1959 and 1969 the income of Mexicans in relation to Anglos had not increased more than 1 percent.[126] Chicano income was 65 percent of Anglo income in 1959, 66 percent in 1969. During this same period in California Chicano family earning power dropped from

79 percent to 73 percent. These statistics dampened any optimism "about the rapid attainment of equality of Mexican-American income with that of Anglos."[127] In fact, many predicted that due to a constricting economy and a white backlash, the inequality would widen during the 1970s.

THE TEXAS FARM WORKER MOVEMENT

Texas in the 1970s remained a union organizer's nightmare. Its long border insured growers access to a constant and abundant supply of cheap labor. Efforts to organize farm workers had been literally stomped to death by the overt misuse of the Texas Rangers, the local courts, and the right-to-work laws. Texas farm workers have courageously struggled to organize, but their road to Delano was littered with broken strikes. The present Texas farm worker organizing effort has its roots in the 1966–1967 strikes which, like Mexican farm worker struggles in the Midwest, were influenced by the Chávez movement in California.

The 1966–1967 drive to organize Mexican farm workers in the Rio Grande Valley was brief, fiery, and tumultuous. Eugene Nelson, 36, who had been with Chávez in California, but who did not have his approval to organize in Texas, joined with Margil Sánchez and Lucio Galván to found the Independent Workers Association (IWA) in May of 1966. The need for a union was evident. Workers' per capita income was $1,568; most earned less than $1.00 per hour. The IWA called a strike and demanded $1.75 an hour.[128] Farm workers saw hope and they enthusiastically joined pickets and rallies, supporting the IWA's demands. The success of the strike depended on whether the union could persuade Mexican nationals from strikebreaking. Several attempts were made to block entrance of undocumented workers into Texas at the international bridge at Roma, Texas.

In June 1966 IWA members voted to affiliate with the National Farm Workers Association (NFWA) and became Local 2. This move was not popular among all the Texans. Galván and Sánchez resented California's control and moved to take over the local.[129] Although Sánchez and Galván may have had legitimate grievances, they resorted to red-baiting, citing an article in the *American Opinion,* a John Birch Society publication, as positive proof that the NFWA leaders in California were communists. On July 18 a new vote was taken and the members voted 101 to 3 to maintain NFWA affiliation. Sánchez and Galván bolted and they formed the Texas Independent Workers Association.

On August 16, Local 2 voted 99 to 0 to affiliate with the AFL-CIO and became the United Farm Workers Organizing Committee (UFWOC). In the last days of June strikers marched from Rio Grande City to Austin. In their trek through the Rio Grande Valley the marchers were greeted by the LULAC, G.I. Forum, and PASSO. Al Ramírez, the mayor of Edinburg, on July 7 left his hospital bed to welcome the 120 marchers. On July 8 a thousand people gathered to hear mass at San Juan Catholic Shrine. Union people along the route warmly greeted the strikers. By July 30 they reached Corpus Christi. The small band wound up Highway 181, and in spite of heavy rain, over a thousand partisans waited for them in San Antonio where a two-hour parade followed. Archbishop Lucey said mass. The march to Austin continued.[130]

Outside the capital Governor John Connally met the marchers. He was accompanied by Ben Barnes, the speaker of the House, and Waggoner Carr, Texas attorney general. They chatted with the leadership and left. The strikers attempted to pressure Connally to call a special session to pass a minimum wage bill, but he refused and told the marchers he would not be in Austin on Labor Day.

Ten thousand converged on the Texas state capital. César Chávez and U.S. Senator Ralph Yarborough participated. Reyes Alaniz, 62, who had marched all the way, was also there. After the rally Chávez visited Rio Grande City with Bill Kircher, national organizing director of the AFL-CIO. Two hundred and fifteen attended a rally in that city.[131]

Demonstrations continued, mainly in Starr and Hidalgo counties. On October 25 a group of strikers locked arms and laid down on the Mexican side of the Roma bridge. Starr County Sheriff Rene Solis crossed to the Mexican side, grabbed a demonstrator by the foot, and dragged him across the bridge into the United States. Mexican authorities then forced the demonstrators onto the U.S. side where authorities arrested them. On October 31 Mexican authorities arrested Marshall Méndez of the Bishop's Committee for the Spanish Speaking and Antonio Orendain, national treasurer for the UFWOC, for locking the gate at the center crossing. On November 16 a report issued by a Starr County grand jury called the strike "unlawful and un-American" and "abusive of the rights and freedom granted them as citizens." Texas Rangers made mass arrests and guarded the undocumented workers bussed to the fields by growers to break the strike. Meanwhile, Gil Padilla had assumed leadership of the strike.[132]

An organizing rally was held in Rio Grande City on June 10. Hidalgo County officials demanded a $250,000 bond to insure a peaceful demonstration and would not accept anything but cash. César Chávez attended the rally and, although the event was successful, the union could not stop production. On September 30, 1967 a hurricane destroyed the citrus crop, depressing labor conditions and ending all hope.[133]

A postscript to the strike was that in June of 1972 a three judge federal panel ruled that the Texas Rangers used selective enforcement of Texas laws during the 1966–1969 strikes in Starr County.

The court criticized the Rangers for taking sides, declared that the anti-mass picketing statute, the law against secondary boycotts, and the statute on breach of peace were all illegal. As to the statutes on abusive language and unlawful assembly, the court stated: "The police authorities were openly hostile to the strike and individual strikers, and used their law enforcement powers to suppress the farm workers strike."[134] A small victory for the farm workers, considering it *only* took five years to find out that they were right.

After 1967 Chávez pulled back, realizing that the strike was premature. He realized that his California base was far from secure and that in Texas he did not have the liberal support that he had in California. The right-to-work laws also retarded a strong trade union movement that could support him. Lastly, Texas growers were not as vulnerable to a secondary boycott. He left Antonio Orendain, 37, in charge of member and placement services.

The union leadership realized that it needed federal legislation to protect the NFWA in order "to either overthrow or diminish the power of the Valley economic and political structure." Orendain worked to gain support. He had a radio program, "Voice of the Farm Worker," and a farm worker newspaper, *El Cuhamil*.[135] For a short time he left Texas to head the boycott in Chicago, but returned in response to letters from farm workers and pledged that he would not leave until they won the struggle.

Even at this time, a break between Chávez and Orendain was near. According to Dolores Huerta, Orendain was very critical of the church and did not approve of Chávez's frequent fasts and church orientation; he was not at the time as committed to non-violence.[136] Time and distance contributed further to the alienation between Chávez and Orendain. In all probability, partisans added to the new breach between the two men by spreading rumors and muddying the waters. Surely personalities played a role in the break.

In May 1975, the passage of the California Agriculture Labor Relations Act absorbed the UFW. Orendain was told to call off strike activities because resources were needed in California. The Texas venture was criticized as too violent and adventuristic. Texans questioned the channeling of money through California. Bad feelings developed and, on August 14, 1975, Orendain formally founded the Texas Farm Workers (TFW).[137]

Since May 26, 1975, organizers had leafleted green carders crossing the International Bridge at Hidalgo. Orendain had called strikes against El Texano and Miller Ranches. Texas farm workers wanted to persuade the green carders not to break the strike and to join the union. This bitter strike lasted throughout the year. The goal of the TFW became to get a law like the California ALRA.[138]

The strike continued into the summer of 1976. Deputy Sheriff Harry Colwell harassed the TFW; a grower's wife challenged pick-

eters to cross the line so she could shoot them; and the field foreman of the Miller Ranch declared "open season" on farm
workers.[139] Realizing that the growers in Texas would not be controlled by local authorities, Orendain launched a drive to collect a
half-million signatures demanding rights for workers such as the
right to collective bargaining, fair and reasonable procedures so
that workers could choose their representatives, and a vehicle to
guarantee agreements.[140]

During the summer of 1977 Orendain led the TFW on a 1,500
mile march to Washington, D.C. In Washington 800 members gathered at the Lincoln Memorial calling for rights for undocumented
workers, the right to organize, the elimination of section 14B of the
Taft-Hartley Act. They wanted to meet with President Carter, but
he refused to meet with the workers.[141] The future of the TFW
largely depends on its staying power as well as the support it can
generate from Texas's large Chicano population. The question also
arises whether the TFW can maintain its struggle without the support of the powerful national trade union movement which this
time remains committed to the UFW.

THE SPREAD OF STRIKE ACTIVITY

During the 1970s strike activity spread among farm workers
throughout the United States. Most of these efforts have not been
recorded and are isolated. For example, in the summer of 1972
4,000 beet workers struggled in northern Utah for better housing.[142]
That same summer the Colorado migrant council brought proceedings against Mike Tashiro, owner of farm labor camps near Brighton
for the dilapidated housing facilities he provided.[143] The *Michigan
Free Press* on August 15, 1976 found the camps of the Blissfield
Canning Company overcrowded and with inadequate sanitation
facilities: "Morrin's Camp has no inside running water or toilet
facilities." Victor Morrin responded, "We are not obligated to house
these people [his workers]. The federal government should provide
low-cost housing for them. If society demands good housing then
society should provide the housing."[144] The next year United Farm
Workers struck the Mel Finerman Company (a lettuce producer) in
Center, Colorado. Authorities teargassed lettuce workers when
they did not disperse.[145] Three months later Chicano pecan shellers
walked out of the McCrea and Son Plant on the Tehuaucana Farms
in Yancey, Texas. Spokespersons Dahlia F. Tara, Janie Moncada,
and Rosa Jasso said that they walked out because they were paid
less than the men. Many women were coerced into buying Avon
products from the employer's wife.[146]

In October 1977 citrus workers struck the Goldmar Farm in
Glendale, Arizona, operated by Robert Goldwater, brother of Senator Barry Goldwater. Maricopa County Organizing Project led the

strike. The Organizing Project had found workers sleeping in the groves. Strikers demanded $3.00 an hour and accused the Goldmar Farm of inaccurate bookkeeping, of withholding social security payments from the workers' salary but providing no social security benefits, of withholding a week's pay from the workers which was forfeited if workers were picked up by the INS, and of providing drinking water from a canal where the workers also bathed.[147]

The Farah Strike

Chicanos played the major role in the Farah strike of the early 1970s. Although Farah had numerous factories throughout Texas, the eye of the storm was in El Paso. The abundance of cheap labor in the area encouraged many garment factories to settle in that city. About 25,000 workers, almost all of whom were Mexican, were employed in men's and boys' apparel. The largest company was the Levi-Strauss Company which did over a billion dollars in annual sales. The largest employer was Willie Farah who owned four factories.[148] Eighty-five percent of the employees were women.[149] On May 2, 1972, Farah workers at the San Antonio plant struck, seven days later three-quarters of the shipping department at Farah's giant Gateway plant in El Paso walked out. Three thousand workers from eight plants took part.

Several weeks before the walkout workers from San Antonio and El Paso paraded to protest conditions at Farah. They had no job security, no maternity leave, an inadequate insurance program, and an average take home pay of $69.00 while workers at Levi-Strauss and Tex-Toggs netted $102.00 a week.[150]

The union, the Amalgamated Clothing Workers Union of America (ACWUA) had been organizing at Farah since the late 1960s. Many workers had heard about César Chávez and were inspired to take some kind of action. The ACWUA had problems recruiting the women because Farah intentionally segregated the men and women, starting the latter earlier and staggering the breaks. In October 1970 the cutting department voted in an NLRB election to affiliate with the ACWUA. Farah refused to honor the vote. Meanwhile, the union sent organizers to San Antonio where many workers resented their lack of protection and their dependence on the whims of Farah officials. Organizing went slowly.[151]

The May walkouts were premature. Strategically, May was a bad month to strike since shipping was slow, but the union had no choice but to back the workers. It needed victories in the South and Southwest. It knew that Willie Farah would be a tough adversary. He had built his parents' small shop into the largest employer in El Paso. Farah employed 9,500 workers by 1971 (14 percent of the work force of El Paso employed in the private sector), had a payroll of $40 million, and grossed $164.6 million with a net profit of $4 million.

Farah knew that he had a giant pool of workers in El Paso and across the border in Juárez. Moreover, he knew how to play the role of the *patrón*, offering his workers free coffee and sweet rolls while he ran his factory with an iron hand. Everyone got along as long as they played by Willie's rules; dissenters were ruthlessly purged.

Farah hated unions, calling them communist-inspired and filled with agitators. He publicly announced he would fire trouble-makers. He set out to intimidate strikers. Farah used police dogs, over 1,000 were arrested, and he flagrantly broke rules of the NLRB. He closed two plants and had his sympathizers picket Bishop Sidney Metzger for supporting the strike. The union retaliated by picketing Farah's home.[152]

The union knew that it could not stop production, so in July 1972 it called a nationwide boycott of Farah pants. A National Committee for Justice for Farah Workers was formed which included many national figures. Fr. Jesse Muñoz of Our Lady of the Light loaned the use of his church to strikers and church members who formed a support committee. The strike politicized many of the workers. The boycott proved to be a strong weapon and by April 1973 Farah sales for that quarter fell $9.1 million from the previous year.[153]

Still, Farah refused to give an inch. He recruited heavily in Juárez and took out a huge ad featuring a petition signed by his "8000 happy Farah workers" (actually there were only 2,310 names). Farah denied the union the opportunity to talk with "happy workers." Farah was further infuriated when he lost a court suit and was ordered to pay eighteen workers who walked out of the NW Gateway Plant in March 1972 $9,994 in back wages.[154]

Some strikers criticized the boycott strategy and favored the raising of broader social issues and conducting more militant picketing. They alleged that the boycott left too much to the leadership and did not raise the consciousness of workers themselves. They all realized that the strike had done a lot to break down the dependency created by people like Farah who exploited them by controlling basic needs. They criticized the union for concentrating too much on the economic struggle instead of the social struggle. Most conceded that the boycott did make Anglo-Americans outside El Paso aware of the exploitation of Chicanos.[155]

Farah stock plummeted from $39.5 to below $7 a share.[156] Willie stonewalled it until February 24, 1974, when he reached an agreement with Amalgamated. In March the Farah workers ratified the agreement in San Antonio. Farah was jubilant and forecast a goal of $200 million in sales in 1975.[157] Farah workers received an 80¢ an hour increase with skilled workers paid up to $4.75 an hour and double time on Sunday. The company paid major medical insurance, approved seniority rights, and recognized the ACWUA.[158]

Some bad feelings remained since some workers protested allowing workers who had not walked out to vote. Amalgamated felt that many "happies" had remained loyal and it knew that the fight had just begun. After twenty-two months of battle, however, many strikers were not in a mood to be liberal.[159] Willie Farah attempted to subvert the union by building an inside core of people loyal to him and by encouraging company officials to harass union partisans. The union struggled with Farah who sent an increasing volume of work to be done in Mexico. Moreover, Farah made the mistake of changing production during the recession of 1974–1975 which caused severe marketing problems, resulting in a 40 percent decline in sales. Large lay-offs were made during 1976 and 1977, and in 1977 the San Antonio plant was closed down.[160]

On the plus side Amalgamated had built its El Paso operation from a cadre of Farah strikers. Practically the entire staff was Chicano. They extended their organizing to the Levi-Strauss plant and some twenty nonunion shops from Corpus Christi to Albuquerque.[161] The future is questionable, especially since these manufacturers can simply move across the border and exploit nonunion workers there.

CONCLUSION

The histories of long forgotten organizational efforts and strikes are today being researched. Each discovery adds to the analysis of Chicano labor history. Current research is becoming more difficult since Chicanos have been increasingly integrated within established labor internationals such as the United Auto Workers and the U.S. Steelworkers. Chicanos have struggled within these unions to democratize them.

NOTES

1. Leo Grebler, Joan Moore, and Ralph Guzmán, *The Mexican American People* (New York: Free Press, 1970), pp. 51, 83, 106, 113. The actual population probably approached 1 million; there is traditionally an undercount in census data dealing with Chicanos. The population in the five southwestern states was as follows: Arizona, 128,310; California, 760,453; Colorado, 118,131; New Mexico, 248,880; and Texas, 1,033,768.
2. Carey McWilliams, *California: The Great Exception* (New York: Current Books, 1949), p. 48.
3. *La Causa: The California Grape Strike* (New York: Collier, 1970), p. 56; Ernesto Galarza, *Farm Workers and Agribusiness in California, 1947–1960* (Notre Dame, Ind.: University of Notre Dame Press, 1977), pp. 23, 98–99; Paul S. Taylor, "Water, Land and People in Great Valley," *American West* (March 1968): 27. The net income of the Kern County Land Company in 1956 from oil, cotton, cattle, and crops was $11,745,000. See also David Nesmith, *National Land for People* (November 2, 1977).

4. See Paul S. Taylor, "The Excess Land Law: Pressure vs. Principle," *California Law Review* 47, no. 3 (August 1959): 499–541; Joan London and Henry Anderson, *So Shall Ye Reap* (New York: Crowell, 1971), p. 4. Growers pay $3.50 per acre foot for water; it costs the government $14 an acre foot. Galarza, p. 26, states that as of December 1959 the projected cost was $2 billion. Growers also received interest-free loans.

5. McWilliams, p. 306. The Imperial Valley was once a desert; it bloomed because of water made available by U.S. taxpayers. In the 1940s unirrigated land sold for $75 an acre; in 1978 irrigated land sold for an average of $1,000 an acre. For an excellent background on the question of government water projects see David Nesmith, "Discover America," *National Land For People* (October 1977).

6. Ernesto Galarza, *Spiders in the House and Workers in the Field* (Notre Dame, Ind.: University of Notre Dame Press, 1970); John Phillip Carney, "Postwar Mexican Migration: 1945–1955, with Particular Reference to the Policies and Practices of the United States Concerning Its Control" (Ph.D. dissertation, University of Southern California, 1957) p. 150; Galarza, *Farm Workers*, pp. 100, 103, 99.

7. Galarza, *Farm Workers*, pp. 107–108; *Spiders in the House*, pp. 21–22.

8. Galarza, *Spiders in the House*, pp. 23–24, 27, 77; National Advisory Committee on Farm Labor, *Farm Labor Organizing, 1905–1967: A Brief History* (New York: National Advisory Committee on Farm Labor, 1967), p. 37.

9. Galarza, *Spiders in the House*, pp. 25–26, 153.

10. Galarza, *Spiders in the House*, pp. 26, 35.

11. Galarza, *Spiders in the House*, pp. 40–48.

12. Galarza, *Spiders in the House*, p. 48.

13. Galarza, *Spiders in the House*, pp. 288–297.

14. Galarza, *Spiders in the House*, pp. 64–66, 88.

15. Galarza, *Spiders in the House*, pp. 231–247; Sam Kushner, *Long Road to Delano* (New York: International Publishers, 1975), p. 82.

16. Galarza, *Farm Workers*, pp. 204–205, 259–260; London and Anderson, pp. 46–47.

17. Galarza, *Farm Workers*, pp. 137, 289–297.

18. Galarza, *Farm Workers*, pp. 145–146; London and Anderson, pp. 118–119.

19. Galarza, *Farm Workers*, pp. 148–149, 171, 174, 186.

20. Galarza, *Farm Workers*, p. 315.

21. George N. Green, "The ILGWU in Texas, 1930–1970," *Journal of Mexican American History* 1, no. 2 (Spring 1971): 144–145.

22. Green, pp. 146–156.

23. Gregory W. Hill, *Texas-Mexican Migratory Agricultural Workers in Wisconsin*, Agricultural Experimental Station Stencil Bulletin 6 (Madison: University of Wisconsin, 1948), pp. 15–16, 18–20.

24. George O. Coalson, *The Development of the Migratory Farm Labor System in Texas: 1900–1954* (San Francisco: R & E Research Assc., 1977), p. 110.

25. Hill, pp. 5–6; Pauline R. Kibbe, *Latin Americans in Texas* (Los Angeles: Arno Press, 1974), pp. 199–200.

26. Richard W. Slatta, "Chicanos in the Pacific Northwest: An Historical Overview of Chicanos," *Aztlán* 6, no. 3 (Fall 1975): 327; Erasmo Gamboa, "Chicanos in the Northwest: An Historical Perspective," *El Grito* 7, no. 4 (Summer 1973): 61–63.

27. Everett Ross Clinchy, Jr., *Equality of Opportunity for Latin-Americans in Texas:* (New York: Arno Press, 1974), p. 87; Alonso S. Perales, *Are We Good Neighbors* (San Antonio: Artes Gráficas, 1948).

28. Douglas E. Foley, Clarice Mota, Donald E. Post, and Ignacio Lozano, *From Peones to Politicos: Ethnic Relations in a South Texas Town, 1900–1977* (Austin: University of Texas, Center for Mexican American Studies, 1977), p. 85.

29. Foley et al., 75, pp. 85–86; Kibbe, p. 169.

30. Foley et al., p. 89.

31. Kibbe, pp. 160–161.

32. Kibbe, pp. 153, 162–163; Robert Garland Landolt, *The Mexican-American Workers of San Antonio, Texas* (New York: Arno Press, 1976), p. 117.

33. Coalson, pp. 87–88.

34. Coalson, pp. 100–101, 102, 107.
35. *Eastside Sun,* April 13, 1950.
36. Ellwyn R. Stoddard, *Mexican Americans* (New York: Random House, 1973), p. 191; "Unions' Muscle Flexes Far Beyond Numbers," *U.S. News & World Report* (May 1, 1978): 57.
37. Grebler et al., pp. 90, 220
38. Grebler et al., p. 223.
39. *Eastside Sun,* January 16, 1964. It is reasonable to assume that the number of unemployed Mexicans was even higher. Also see "Unemployment Residents of East L.A. To Be Part of Gigantic Survey, Says McDowell of Local SDE," *Eastside Sun,* May 11, 1961.
40. Jacqueline Joann Taylor, "Ethnic Identity and Upward Mobility of Mexican Americans in Tucson" (Ph.D. dissertation, University of Arizona, 1973), p. 35.
41. Lamar Babington Jones, "Mexican American Labor Problems in Texas," (Ph.D. dissertation, University of Texas, 1965), pp. 2, 41.
42. Landolt, p. 1; Jones, pp. 102–103.
43. Jones, pp. 153, 154, 164–165, 166–184.
44. Landolt, pp. 29, 44, 53. El Paso had 125,745, Houston, 63,372, Corpus Christi, 59,859, and Laredo, 49,819.
45. Landolt, pp. 56–57. See Jones, p. 56, for occupation charts comparing San Antonio, Dallas, El Paso, and Houston.
46. Landolt, pp. 69, 71, 353.
47. Landolt, pp. 87, 89.
48. Landolt, pp. 111, 120, 124, 127, 130. In July 1963, 13 out of 55 carpenters' apprentices (23.6 percent) were Mexican; 6 of 71 electricians (8.4 percent), 6 of 39 plumbers (15.4 percent), and 2 of 25 sheet metal workers' apprentices (8 percent) were also Mexican.
49. Landolt, pp. 219, 144. On p. 263, Landolt makes the point that the $1.75 poll tax severely restricted Mexican voting power, delaying a political solution. Also see Sam Frank Parigi, *A Case Study of Latin American Unionization in Austin Texas* (New York: Arno Press, 1976).
50. Barbara Jane Macklin, *Structural Stability and Cultural Change in a Mexican American Community* (New York: Arno Press, 1976), pp. 13–15.
51. Mark Edward Erenberg, "A Study of the Political Relocation of Texas-Mexican Migratory Farm Workers to Wisconsin" (Ph.D. dissertation, University of Wisconsin, 1969), pp. 39, 40.
52. Louise Año Nuevo Kerr, "The Chicano Experience in Chicago: 1920–1970" (Chicago: University of Illinois at Chicago Circle, 1976), pp. 173, 178, 183–184.
53. Howard Lloyd Campbell, "Bracero Migration and the Mexican Economy, 1951–1964" (Ph.D. dissertation, American University, 1972), p. 101. Mechanization in California was the chief reason for the decreased use of *braceros* in the last five years of this program. It reduced the need for them up to 73 percent.
54. Peter Matthiessen, *Sal Si Puedes; Cesar Chavez and the New American Revolution* (New York: Random House, 1969), pp. 41, 50–51.
55. London and Anderson, pp. 146–148, 149.
56. Mark Day, *Forty Acres: Cesar Chavez and the Farm Workers* (New York: Praeger, 1971), pp. 54, 55.
57. Samuel R. Berger, *Dollar Harvest: The Story of the Farm Bureau* (Lexington, Mass.: Heath, 1971), pp. 161–163, *Forumeer,* May 1966. Schenley had also been influenced by the march to Sacramento, which covered 300 miles and ultimately drew 8,000 marchers in that city.
58. Gregory Dunne, *Delano* (New York: Farrar, Straus & Giroux, 1967), pp. 51, 144; Ronald B. Taylor, *Chavez and the Farm Workers* (Boston: Beacon Press, 1975), p. 157.
59. Ronald Taylor, *Chavez,* p. 287.
60. Day, p. 42; Dunne, pp. 145, 147–148.
61. Day, p. 43; Dunne, p. 156.
62. Matthiessen, p. 122; Dunne, p. 166.
63. Paul Wallace Gates, "Corporate Farming in California," in Ray Allen Billington, ed., *People of the Plains and Mountains* (Westport, Conn.: n.d.) in the Taylor collection of the Bancroft Library.

64. Armando Rendon, *Chicano Manifesto* (New York: Collier, 1971), p. 149. The growers' most powerful friend at the federal level was Senator James Eastland, who received $146,000 in farm subsidies in 1969 and consistently vetoed a $55,000 ceiling on subsidies. The headline in the *California Farmer* on July 6, 1968, was "Boycott Jeopardizes Entire Grape Crop," (quoted in Matthiessen, p. 40).

65. Kushner, p. 173.

66. Taylor, *Chavez*, p. 251. Campbell, p. 7, Salinas growers had been heavy users of *braceros*. In 1963, 85 percent of the workers used in the tomato fields, 70 percent of the workers in the strawberry fields, and 80 percent of the workers in the lettuce fields were *braceros*.

67. Matthiessen, pp. 333–334.

68. Ronald Taylor, *Chavez*, pp. 259, 261; *Los Angeles Times*, December 5, 6, 24, 1970. Two years later, the Supreme Court struck down the law that had imprisoned Chávez.

69. Ronald Taylor, *Chavez*, pp. 262–269.

70. Ronald Taylor, *Chavez*, p. 278.

71. "Chavez Plans Farm Bureau Picketing in 34 States," *Arizona Republic*, May 9, 1972. See also "Workers Continue to Protest Against Farm Labor Measure," *Arizona Republic*, May 10, 1972; Charles Kelley, "Churchmen Support Chavez-Led Boycott, Denounced Williams," *Arizona Republic*, May 26, 1972; Athia Harde, "Chavez Ends 24-Day Fast; Heart May Be Damaged," *Arizona Republic*, June 5, 1972. The *Arizona Republic* ran articles condemning Chavez throughout June and July.

72. Ronald Taylor, *Chavez*, pp. 280–281; *Arizona Republic*, June 12, 1972. See "The UFW Has Shown Its Hand," *Arizona Republic*, July 21, 1972, for the grower perspective. Bill King, in "William Foes Get Setback on Recall Lists," *Arizona Republic*, July 28, 1978, questioned signatures on the petitions.

73. *Arizona Republic*, July 1, 1972.

74. Ronald Taylor, *Chavez*, pp. 279–288; Matthiessen, p. 229. Giumarra Vineyards, Inc., is often portrayed as a small grower. Giumarra is actually a $25-million corporation that owns 12,000 acres, or 19 square miles, in Kern and Tulare counties. See Frank Del Olmo, "Farm Union Opens Massive Picketing Drive at Vineyards," *Los Angeles Times*, July 31, 1973. John Giumarra, Jr., was the official leader of the growers. In 1953 the Di Giorgio Corporation derived 100 percent of its revenue from agriculture; by 1972 it had diversified so that only 2 percent of its $459.8 million in revenues was from agriculture. (See "Corporations Finding They're Poor Farmers," *Arizona Republic*, December 30, 1973.)

75. Quoted in Ronald Taylor, *Chavez*, p. 289.

76. "Watergate Figure Accused of Helping Anti-Chavez Campaign," *Los Angeles Times*, April 17, 1975. George Meany charged Colson and the Teamsters with collusion. Colson had joined Fitzsimmons in blaming the violence in Coachella on Chavez. When Colson left the White House, he was given a $100,000-a-year retainer as a lawyer for the Teamsters. Many of these facts were pieced together through conversations with investigative reporters and corroborated by the sources cited. See for example, Harry Bernstein, "Teamsters President Proposes Alliance with Growers Group," *Los Angeles Times*, December 12, 1972. Bernstein covered the AFBF convention. He stated that Fitzsimmons called for an alliance between the AFBF and the Teamsters. Fitzsimmons accused the UFW of being a revolutionary group. Bernstein, in an article headlined "Role of Farm Workers in Teamsters Stalled" in the *Los Angeles Times*, April 28, 1973, quotes Einar Mohn, head of the Western Conference of Teamsters, as saying: "[A] Shortage of jobs is the problem. If there weren't such a shortage of jobs, Mexican-Americans could get jobs! I don't know what will happen to Mexican-Americans. After all, you can't expect whites (who often operate machines now) to step aside and let Mexican-Americans and Negros have the (machine) jobs they have had for years."

77. Ronald Taylor, *Chavez*, pp. 290–292. Sources close to the study state that Fitzsimmons was reluctant to repudiate his agreement with Meany, but that the Nixon people reminded him of past favors, especially the terms of Jimmy Hoffa's parole. At the Republican National Convention Reagan and Butz

lauded the Teamsters' support of Nixon. See Tony Castro, *Chicano Power* (New York: Sutton, 1974), p. 94.

78. Ronald Taylor, *Chavez*, pp. 292–294; Frank Del Olmo and Harry Bernstein, "Coachella Grape Harvest May Trigger Violence," *Los Angeles Times*, June 11, 1973.

79. Harry Bernstein and Frank Del Olmo, "Picketing Resumed at Vineyards as Harvest Speeds Up," *Los Angeles Times*, June 5, 1973 and "Teamsters Hit Use of Guards by Farm Workers," *Los Angeles Times*, June 12, 1973; Ronald Taylor, *Chavez*, pp. 296–302; *Los Angeles Times*, June 24, 1973.

80. Frank Del Olmo, "30 Teamsters Arrested After Battle at Ranch, Four UFW Members Hospitalized," *Los Angeles Times*, June 24, 1973; "Jails Loaded in Farm Picket War," *Arizona Republic*, July 22, 1973. Also see *Arizona Republic*, July 21, 1973; Frank Del Olmo, "450 Arrested in Kern County Farm Dispute," *Los Angeles Times*, July 19, 1973.

81. *Arizona Republic*, August 2, 1973; "Chavez Calls for 3-Day Fast to Protest Violence in Fields," *Arizona Republic*, August 17, 1973.

82. Frank Del Olmo and Tom Paegel, "Chavez Picket Shot to Death in Violence near Bakersfield," *Los Angeles Times*, August 17, 1973; Ronald Taylor, *Chavez*, pp. 302–303; Frank Del Olmo, "Chavez Charges Deputies Broke Grape Strike," *Arizona Republic*, August 19, 1973; Frank Del Olmo, "Farm Union Halt? Picketing; Rites held for Striker," *Los Angeles Times*, August 18, 1973.

83. Ronald Taylor, *Chavez*, pp. 314–315; Harry Bernstein, "Peace Talks Collapse in Grape Strike Dispute," *Los Angeles Times*, August 11, 1973; Harry Bernstein, "Will Resume Peace Talks Under Certain Conditions, Chavez," *Los Angeles Times*, August 12, 1973. The following series of articles document a pattern of Teamster duplicity: Harry Bernstein, "Teamsters-Farm Union Partial Cease-Fire Seen," *Los Angeles Times*, August 9, 1973; "Progress Made at Farm Labor Peace Meeting," *Los Angeles Times*, August 4, 1973; Frank Del Olmo, "Teamsters Void Contracts with Delano Growers," *Los Angeles Times*, August 22, 1973; "Teamsters Allow Chavez Free Hand with Farm Labor," *Arizona Republic*, September 29, 1973; Harry Bernstein and Frank Del Olmo, "Chavez Union, Teamsters End Long Fight, Agree on Treaty," *Los Angeles Times*, September 28, 1973; "U.S. Threatens to Sue Teamsters, Truckers," *Los Angeles Times* October 31, 1973; Harry Bernstein, "Hoped for Teamsters-Chavez Union Peace Pact Hits Snag," *Los Angeles Times*, October 16, 1973; Harry Bernstein, "Chavez Calls for Wine, Grape, Lettuce Boycott," *Los Angeles Times*, November 8, 1973; and Harry Bernstein, "Teamsters Break Chavez Peace Promise—Meany," *Los Angeles Times*, November 17, 1973.

84. "Table-Grape Fields Picketed by UFW," *Arizona Republic*, July 31, 1973, quotes Chávez as saying, "We're fighting to keep what we got after five years of struggle." At one time he had 180 contracts and 40,000 workers. The union at this point had only 40 contracts and 15,500 workers; 28 contracts were due to expire and if they were not renewed he would be down to 700 workers. See Harry Bernstein, "Chavez' Farm Workers Facing Severest Crises," *Los Angeles Times*, July 26, 1973; Jim Wood, "Is Chavez' Union Near the End?" *San Francisco Chronicle*, July 29, 1973; and Harry Bernstein and Frank Del Olmo, "Doubt, Uncertainty Shroud Future of Chavez Farm Union," *Los Angeles Times*, September 27, 1973.

85. Frank Del Olmo, "Pablo Torres: Farm Work Gave Him a Life—and Took It," *Los Angeles Times*, January 26, 1974; Paul Houston, "Flimsy Seats on Bus Blamed for High Death Toll," *Los Angeles Times*, February 8, 1974; Cesar Chavez, "Chavez Blames Fatal Bus on Greed," *Los Angeles Times*, February 11, 1974; *Los Angeles Times*, March 9, 1974.

86. Harry Bernstein, "Farm Workers Will End Safeway Stores Boycott," *Los Angeles Times*, April 9, 1974; *Los Angeles Times*, May 30, 1974.

87. *Arizona Republic*, September 17, 1974.

88. Bernie Wynn, "State's Right to Work Law Backed by Raul Castro," *Arizona Republic*, October 9, 1974; John J. Hannigan, "Farm Workers Testify They Were Forced to Stay at Groves," *Arizona Republic*, October 24, 1974.

89. *Time Magazine*, May 19, 1975.

90. Ronald B. Taylor, "Chavez and the NLRA: Something Is in the Wind," *The*

Nation (February 22, 1975): 206–209, is an excellent article that clearly states the farm workers dilemma at the beginning of 1975.

91. "A Boost for Chavez," *Newsweek* (May 26, 1975); "California Compromise," *Time* Magazine (May 19, 1975).

92. See Ronald B. Taylor, "Farm Union Peace Is Seen on Coast," *New York Times*, May 1, 1975.

93. "Chavez vs. the Teamsters: Farm Workers' Historic Vote," *U.S. News & World Report* (September 22, 1975): 82–83; *U.S. News & World Report* (September 22, 1975): 82.

94. See Cesar Chavez, 'Why the Farm Labor Act Isn't Working," *Los Angeles Times*, November 17, 1975, for Chavez's side. See Lloyd Evenland, "Why the Farm Labor Act Isn't Working," *Los Angeles Times*, November 17, 1975, for the growers' side.

95. Bob Barber, "Farm Labor Elections Stop Cold," reprinted in *La Gente*, March 6, 1976,; "Strengthening the Farm Board," *Los Angeles Times*, January 18, 1976; Larry Liebert, "Farm Board Funds Refused by Senate," *San Francisco Chronicle*, January 28, 1976.

96. Rick Carroll, "Political Burglar Says Harmer Knew of the Chavez Break-ins," *San Francisco Chronicle*, January 15, 1976. This story was not reported in Los Angeles until Daryl Tembke, "Farmer Deputy Tells of Burglarizing UFW Office," *Los Angeles Times*, June 25, 1976.

97. Cesar Chavez, "Chavez, Farm Worker Initiative Is Needed to Guard Against Abuses," *Los Angeles Times*, April 18, 1976; News release, Office of the President, United Farm Workers of America, AFL-CIO, La Paz, Keene, Calif., April 20, 1976; Harry Bernstein, "Chavez Supporters Cap Drive: Farm Initiative Petitions Turned in Around State," *Los Angeles Times*, May 1, 1976; "Farm Bureau Giants to Battle Chavez," *Los Angeles Times*, June 27, 1976.

98. Even the small farmers in California owned more than 200 acres, the value of which generally ran between $600,000 and $1 million. See "Chavez Asks FCC to Halt Radio, TV Ads by Prop. 14 Opponents," *Los Angeles Times*, October 19, 1967; Mervin D. Field, "Majority Swings to No on 14," *San Francisco Chronicle*, October 15, 1976; "Farm Workers Ordered off 2 More Centers," *Los Angeles Times*, October 15, 1976 and Harry Bernstein, "State to Investigate 'No on 14' Charges," *San Francisco Chronicle*, October, 24, 1976.

99. Harry Bernstein, "Brown Assails Oil Firm on Farm Law: Charges Alliance with Growers & Sabotage State," *Los Angeles Times*, October 29, 1976; Harry Bernstein, "Prop. 14 Foes Attack Statements by Brown," *Los Angeles Times*, October 30, 1976.

100. Harry Bernstein, "Arguments Obscure Prop. 14's Basic Points," *Los Angeles Times*, October 31, 1976; Narda Zachino, "At Prop. 14 Headquarters Farm Workers Cheer Chavez—Even in Defeat," *Los Angeles Times*, November 4, 1976.

101. Brent Whiting, "Two Inhibits Farm Unions, Chavez Says," *Arizona Republic*, January 19, 1977.

102. Harry Bernstein, "Teamsters to Withdraw; Leave Field to Chavez," *Los Angeles Times*, March 11, 1977; Jackson Rannells, "UFW, Teamsters Sign Accord," *San Francisco Chronicle*, March 11, 1977; "How Farm Foes Made Up," *San Francisco Chronicle*, March 13, 1977.

103. *People's World*, March 19, 1977.

104. Robert McGwen, "Cesar Chavez Looks Back on Long Struggle," *Imperial Valley Press*, April 25, 1977.

105. Larry Pryor, "Grape, Lettuce Boycott Ended by Farm Union," *Los Angeles Times*, February 1, 1978; William P. Coleman, "Farm Workers' Union Undergoes Changes," *Fresno Bee*, April 2, 1978.

106. Mark Erenberg, "*Obreros Unidos* in Wisconsin," U.S. Bureau of Labor Statistics, *Monthly Labor Review* 91 (June 1968): 20–23; National Advisory Committee on Farm Labor, p. 59.

107. National Advisory Committee on Farm Labor, p. 60.

108. Macklin, p. vi.

109. For a background on the development of FLOC, the following material was relied upon, Baldemar Velásquez, interview, Toledo, Ohio, August 8, 1977; "Statement of Problem," Farm Labor Organizing Committee Newsletter Janu-

ary 1977; "FLOC: Both a Union and a Movement," *Worker's Power*, May 9, 1977; Thomas Ruge, "Indiana Farm Workers, Legislative Coalition Fights H.B. 1306," OLA, April 1977; Jim Wasserman, "FLOC Goal Is Power Base for Migrants," *Fort Wayne Journal-Gazette*, September 14, 1976; "FLOC Hearing—Abuses of Undocumented Workers," *Los Desarriagados* (Winter 1976–1977). Eventually FLOC won the Morgan strike. (See "FLOC Wins Morgan Strike," *El Cuhamil*, October 22, 1976.)

110. Baldemar Velásquez, interview, Toledo, Ohio, August 8, 1977; "Gov. Rhodes Having Hard Time Finding Chicanos," *Nuestra Lucha*, January 1977.

111. American Friends Service Committee, "A Report of Research on the Wages of Migrant Farm Workers in Northwest Ohio," July, August 1976, pp. 1–9.

112. "Farm News," *Putnam County Sentinel*, April 27, 1977.

113. "We've Been Spit at, Sworn at," *Nuestra Lucha* (June 1977); Linda Cunningham, "Fired Employees and Supporters Picket Lakewood Greenhouse and Local Florist," *Community News*, Toledo, Ohio, May 21–31, 1977; *The Blade*, Toledo, Ohio, May 14, 1977; Dan La Botz, "It's All in a Day's Profit: Farm Workers Poisoned," *Worker's Power*, May 9, 1977.

114. Moore, p. 64; Vernon M. Briggs, Jr., Walter Fogel, and Fred Schmidt, *The Chicano Worker* (Austin: University of Texas Press, 1977), p. 5.

115. Briggs et al., p. 74

116. John Mills Thompson, "Mobility, Income and Utilization of Mexican American Manpower in Lubbock, Texas, 1960–1970," (Ph.D. Dissertation, Texas Tech University, 1972), p. 292.

117. Rosaura Sánchez, "The Chicana Labor Force," in Rosaura Sánchez and Rosa Martínez Cruz, eds., *Essays on La Mujer*, Anthology no. 1 (Los Angeles: Chicano Studies Center Publications, University of California at Los Angeles, 1977), p. 6.

118. Briggs et al., p. 64

119. U.S. Bureau of Census, *1970 Census of Population: Subject Reports, Persons of Spanish Origin* (Washington, D.C.: U.S. Department of Commerce, 1973), p. 67; Yolanda Nava, "The Chicana and Employment: Needs Analysis and Recommendation for Legislation," *Regeneración* 2, no. 3 (1973): 7.

120. "Some statistics; Chicanas and Non-Chicanas," MALDEF 6, no. 4 (Fall, 1977).

121. Briggs et al., pp. 34, 36–38.

122. Castro, pp. 210–211, stated that nationally Latinos comprised 7 percent of the population, but only 2.9 percent of federal employees. See also Briggs et al., p. 68.

123. Sue Mullin, "Hispanic in the U.S. Called the Sleeping Giant," *SER News* (Winter 1978): 26.

124. Lupe Anguiano, "Employment and Welfare Issues as They Affect Low Income Women," *Southwest Regional Office for the Spanish Speaking*, February 19, 1976. Also see "Chicano Rights: A Major MALDEF Issue," MALDEF 6, no. 4 (Fall 1977): 5; "Some Statistics; Chicanas; Non-Chicanas," MALDEF 6, no. 4 (Fall 1977); Alexis M. Herman, "Hispanic Women in the Labor Market," *SER News* 7, no. 11 (Winter 1978). Patricia Vásquez, an attorney for MALDEF, heads the Chicana Rights Project, which addresses these problems.

125. Briggs et al., pp. 47–48. The pull to the midwest is because of the wage differentials between there and the southwest. For example, the following is a breakdown of median income for Latinos in key cities: Detroit $8,000; Los Angeles $6,150; San Francisco, $6,580; Denver $5,410.

126. Briggs et al., pp. 44, 53–54; Moore, p. 60; *Los Desarriagados* (Winter 1976–1977): 6.

127. Briggs et al., pp. 59–60.

128. Charles Winn Carr, "Mexican Americans in Texas Labor Movement" (Ph.D. dissertation, Texas Christian University, 1972), pp. 98–100, 101; National Advisory Committee on Farm Labor, pp. 53–54.

129. Carr, pp. 106, 114.

130. Carr, pp. 114–122; *Forumeer*, October 1966.

131. Carr, pp. 122–124; National Advisory Committee on Farm Labor, p. 55.

132. Carr, pp. 125–128, 132–133; National Advisory Committee on Farm Labor, p. 56.

133. Carr, pp. 139–140, 144.

134. "U.S. Judges Rap Ranger Acts in Valley," *San Antonio Express*, June 27, 1972.
135. Carr, pp. 145–148. One pro-Orendain article published recently is Ignacio M. García, "The Many Battles of Antonio Orendain," *Nuestro* Magazine (November 1979): 25–29; Ronald B. Taylor, *Sweatshops in the Sun: Child Labor on the Farm* (Boston: Beacon Press, 1973), p. 87. The Spanish-language radio station was intended to penetrate into Mexico to counter recruiting efforts by growers.
136. Jacques Levy, *Cesar Chavez: Autobiography of La Causa* (New York: Norton, 1975), pp. 227, 282.
137. *The Struggle of the Texas Farm Workers' Union* (Chicago: Vanguard, 1977), pp. 4, 14–15.
138. *Sin Fronteras*, November 1975.
139. *El Cuhamil*, San Juan, Texas, June 4, 1976.
140. Cecil Clift, "Farm Workers Seek Signatures," *San Antonio Express*, October 12, 1976; *El Cuhamil*, October 22, 1976; *Chicano Times*, October 29 – November 11, 1976.
141. *Chicano Times*, July 1–15, 1977; *El Sol de Texas*, September 9, 1977.
142. "Weber County Threatens Sanctions on Migrants' Tent City," *Salt Lake Tribune*, June 13, 1972.
143. Judith Brimbers, "36 Migrants Found Living in 'Unfit' Barn," *Denver Post*, August 2, 1972.
144. *Michigan Free Press*, August 15, 1976.
145. "UFW Strikers Tear Gassed," *Denver Post*, July 18, 1973. In August of 1973 twenty-five UFW members marched to Denver, *Denver Post*, August 26, 1973.
146. Martha Cotera, *Pofile of the Mexican American Woman* (Austin, Tex.; National Educational Laboratory, 1976), p. 179.
147. Tom Kuhn, "Citrus Grove Field Hands Go on Strike," *Arizona Republic*, October 4, 1977.
148. "Farah Workers on Strike—Do Not Buy Any Pants," *Texas Observer*, December 29, 1972, reprinted in *Regeneración* 2, no. 3 (1973): 10. A recently published work on the subject is Laurie Coyle, Gail Hershatter, and Emily Honig's *Women at Farah: An Unfinished Story* (El Paso: Reforma, 1979).
149. Bill Finger, "Victoria Sobre Farah," *Southern Exposure* 4, no. 1–2 (1976): 5.
150. Castro, p. 193.
151. Finger, p. 46; "Farah Workers on Strike," p. 10; "Farah Has Troubled Times," *San Antonio Express*, November 24, 1972.
152. "Farah Workers on Strike," p. 10; "Clothing Workers Union Blasts Farah Vote Request as 'Gimmick,'" *El Paso Times*, August 10, 1973; "Strikers Told of NCRB Complaint Against Firm," *San Antonio Express*, August 16, 1973; Workers at Farah Protest Metzger's Union Support," *El Paso Times*, November 4, 1973; "Retaliatory Pickets 'Visit' Farah Home," *El Paso Times*, November 5, 1973.
153. "Why the Union Lost the Strike Against Farah," *San Antonio Express*, August 8, 1973; "Farah Turns Down Pastor's Request to Tour Plants," *El Paso Times*, July 20, 1973; Robert Ewegen, "Pickets at Joslins Urge Farah Boycott," *Denver Post*, August 10, 1972.
154. "Farah Stance Rapped," *San Antonio Express*, December 31, 1973; Finger, pp. 47–48; *El Paso Times*, November 28, 1973.
155. Castro, p. 194; Finger, pp. 47–48.
156. Farah blamed the work cutbacks and the closing of the Victoria and Los Cruces plants on the union. See Nell Fenner Grover, "Union Tells of Farah Plants' Work Cutbacks," *San Antonio Express*, August 15, 1973; "Farah Closes Two Plants," *San Antonio Express*, November 2, 1973 and "Editorial: Union Boycott Costs 900 San Antonians Jobs," *San Antonio Express*, December 8, 1973.) (See Sylvia Thomas, "Fury Faces Farah Fury," *San Antonio Express* December 8, 1973. Nell Fenner Grover, "Fury Stands Pat on Farah," *San Antonio Express*, December 14, 1973, is a solid article that lays out reasons for the bishop's support of boycott.
157. Fritz Wirt, "Willie Farah More Than Just a President of Company," *El Paso Times*, March 26, 1974.
158. "Farah Workers OK Three-Year Pact," *El Paso Times*, March 8, 1974.
159. Finger, pp. 47–48; Castro, p. 19.
160. "Import of Foreign Textiles Hit by Farah Workers," *Chicano Times*, April 15–

April 29, 1977; Sara Martinez, "Employees Were Not Told of the Plant Closing Until It Was All Over," *San Antonio Express*, April 1, 1977; Sara Martinez, "800 Lose Jobs as Farah Closes Down," *San Antonio Express*, April 6, 1977. Coyle et al., p. 55.

161. Finger, pp. 48–49; Laura E. Arroyo, "Industrial and Occupational Distribution of Chicana Workers," *Aztlán 4*, no. 2 (1973): 358–359.

Chapter 10
Forging a Community:
Repression and Resistance

The past four chapters dealt with Chicanos as workers. The next chapters deal more directly with the struggle to form organizations which defended their human dignity. The sections on immigration and labor have laid a foundation for this political history, for to understand the political repression of the Chicanos it is essential to know why they came or were brought here. It is also important to understand how they resisted repression.

THE LONG BORDER FOSTERS NATIONALISM

Texas in many ways symbolizes the Chicanos' struggle. It shares the longest border with Mexico. Its southeastern tip dips into the interior of Mexico so that it is closer to Mexico City than to Washington, D.C. This long border serves as a magnet attracting Mexicans on both sides, constantly revitalizing the Mexican culture on the northern side, and providing a point of entry from which Mexicans fan out through the United States. Years of border warfare have produced a history of resistance.

In the 1890s Anglo-American authorities supported the dictatorship of Porfirio Díaz and cooperated with his regime to suppress any Mexican revolutionary movement originating on the U.S. side of the border. One such revolt, known as the Garza Movement, was centered in Starr and Duvall counties, 100 miles from the Rio Grande and Fort Ringgold. Caterino E. Garza, born on the Mexican frontier and raised in Texas, led revolutionary activities. On three different occasions in 1891 he crossed into Mexico and attempted to liberate it from Díaz. Twice his small bands reached Nuevo León where Mexican troops turned them back. Garza had about 1,000 followers and was reported to have widespread support. Garza was pursued by the U.S. cavalry, sheriffs, and marshals.[1]

His activities caused intense denunciations by Mexican authorities who in the spring of 1891 called Mexican inhabitants of the valley "ignorant" and "unscrupulous." Military authorities spread hysteria by asking for an additional 10,000 troops. The hysteria resembled that of the 1860s and 1870s when military authorities and Rio Grande Valley merchants used the Cortina rebellion to justify an expansion of fort installations. U.S. authorities claimed that Garza had cost them $2 million.[2]

Newspaper accounts inflamed residents, spread rumors that citizens had armed themselves and that the customs house would be attacked, and stirred again the fears that had been raised by Cortina.[3] The *New York Times* reported:

> A great sensation has been created by the telegraphic announcement from the City of Mexico that General Juan Cortina, one of the greatest revolutionary leaders of Mexico, has been arrested and imprisoned in the San Juan Ulloa Prison by order of President Diaz for attempting to incite another revolutionary uprising against the Government. The City of Matamoras [sic] is General Cortina's old home. He was, twenty-five years ago, a desperate and greatly-feared man in Mexico. He ruled the Rio Grande border country from Laredo to the mouth of the river. . . . His influence was so great that he could inaugurate a powerful revolutionary movement against the Mexican Government by a single pronunciamiento with his signature attached. His exploits at the time of the Civil War caused the United States Government to lose many thousands of dollars. When President Diaz's revolution ended in success, General Cortina was summoned to the City of Mexico . . . [Cortina] has been kept in constant surveillance by President Diaz ever since to prevent him from inciting further revolutions.[4]

The Garza revolution ended, but the occurrence of similar incidents was used by Texans to put constant pressure on Federal authorities to station large numbers of armed troops at the border.

Mexicans in Texas were politically voiceless. The Democratic party remained in power by herding Mexicans to the polls and then voting them in blocs.[5] Political bosses paid the poll tax for the "faithful," but uncontrolled Mexicans could not afford to vote. The stronghold of this controlled Mexican vote was Starr, Zapata, Hidalgo, Cameron, and Willacy counties. The political bosses were not exclusively Anglos, but also wealthy Mexican landowners (for example, the Guerra family of Starr County). Reformers blamed Mexicans for political corruption; counties attempting to correct the abuse of voting Mexicans in mass prohibited Mexicans from voting. They disenfranchised them through covers such as the White Man's Union Association of Wharton County.[6]

Stephen Powers founded the political machine which controlled the Mexican vote in the valley. He arrived there during the invasion of Mexico, from New York where he had participated in Tammany Hall politics. His partner Jim Wells took over the machine in 1882 when Powers died.[7]

Wells based his political power on his ability to deliver the Mexican vote. Wells went to baptisms, marriages, and funerals and played godfather to the Mexican people. By the early 1920s he lost control, but the machine stayed intact, with power divided among his lieutenants. He died in 1922. Wells had shared his power with the Klebergs, who owned the King Ranch. Ed Vela from Hidalgo and the Guerra family, which controlled Starr, were among his Chicano lieutenants.[8]

The Guerras had one of the best organizations in the valley. They and the Yzaguirre and Ramírez families owned most of Starr County. The founder of the line was José Alejandro Guerra, a surveyor for the Spanish crown in 1767. He had received *porciones* in the valley which his heir Manuel Guerra inherited. Manuel started a mercantile house in Roma, Texas, in 1856. He married Virginia Cox, daughter of a Kentuckian and a Mexican mother. Guerra, a banker and rancher, became Jim Wells's right arm. For political favors he exchanged credit and teacher certificates. Guerra became the Democratic party of Starr. The Republican party, which was nationally the more progressive of the two parties, opposed him.

The machine was ruthless in its pursuits. In 1888 W. W. Shelby, leader of the Reds (the Democrats) and boss of Duval County, lost an election to Lino Hinojosa, leader of the Blues (the Republicans), by a two to one margin; however, Hinojosa was not allowed to take office because he did not speak English. Domingo Garza ran against Shelby in 1900, but just before the election Garza was thrown into jail on suspicion of murder; later charges were dropped, but he lost the election. In 1906 Shelby resigned and the machine appointed Deodora Guerra.[9]

The Guerras controlled the two counties into the 1940s. Politics in the valley were untouched by state authorities. It was common knowledge that up to the 1940s if someone raised the ire of the bosses, an assassin was employed from the interior of Mexico.[10]

Judge J. T. Canales of Brownsville led the opposition to the machine politicians. He served in the state legislature from 1909 to 1911, in 1917, and in 1919 and served as a county judge in 1914. Along with Alonso Perales, Manuel González, Ben Garza, Andrés de Luna, and Dr. George I. Sánchez, he led the progressive Chicano movement of the times.

Canales opposed the Guerras in Starr County. In 1933 he organized a new party to oppose them. While he addressed a crowd in Rio Grande City, a shooting broke up the rally. Two of Guerra's men were arrested, tried in Corpus Christi, and sentenced to twenty-five years. They were returned to Starr pending an appeal. The Guerras allowed them to escape. Five members of Canales's new party were deputized, tracked them down, and killed the escapees. The Guerras had them arrested. They were tried in Austin where the Guerras aided the prosecution and Canales the defense. "After an eloquent plea of self-defense, in which Canales wept in the court room, the five men were acquitted."[11]

POLITICS OF ACCOMMODATION

In New Mexico the land question was settled by the courts in 1891; the decision favored capitalist interests. A year later Anglo entrepreneurs were granted grazing privileges to U.S. forest lands. Thus New Mexicans were deprived of their traditional economic base— the land. Unconditional control of the land allowed an Anglo-American minority to subjugate the Mexican majority.[12]

The politics of the Santa Fe Ring during the 1800s determined the tone of state politics after 1912. "Hostility and conflict" gave way to accommodation by New Mexican politicians. By the turn of the century the 5 percent of the Chicano population in New Mexico that was better educated generally worked with Anglo-Americans in commercial enterprises. For instance, the Otero-Sellar Company made a proverbial killing in railroad construction.[13]

After the turn of the century the federal government encouraged large farming operations by the construction of dams. Small farmers could not compete with large commercial farmers. Although the agribusinessmen represented a small portion of the population, they controlled more than half of the grazing land. These large-scale enterprises worsened the status of many New Mexicans.[14]

Commercial farming attracted a large army of migrant workers from Mexico. As land resources became scarcer, a migration from the small villages to the cities was accelerated. In the cities New Mexicans sold their labor. Occupational and social segregation was common, and Mexicans suffered increasingly from racial and cultural discrimination.

Machine politics until the 1930s mediated conflicts between Anglos and Mexicans; the Catholic church served the same function. The machine gave the illusion of self-government to Chicanos, while it insured that key appointive positions went to Anglos. Appointments like that of Miguel A. Otero as territorial governor proved meaningless to the power of Chicanos since he strengthened machine politics in New Mexico to the degree that even an appointment as a notary public became a political favor; under Otero the spoils system sank to new depths. Otero promoted the politics of accommodation.[15]

Statehood in 1912 brought the issue of New Mexican civil rights into focus. Octaviano A. Larrazolo, a Mexican-born leader, raised the issue of equality of Mexicans at the constitutional convention. Some Anglo-Americans protested raising the race issue, but a coalition of Mexicans and Anglo sympathizers put a measure through assuring that the Chicanos' rights to vote, to hold office, and to sit on juries could not be denied on account of "religion, race, language or Spanish languages" and assuring the use of Spanish in public documents.[16] On paper it was a victory for the New Mexicans.

Larrazolo, a separatist, represented a break with the politics of accommodation. He made full use of the race issue. The first governor of the state was an Anglo, William C. MacDonald, who served from 1912 to 1917. Larrazolo organized a "native-son" movement, and although he was a Republican, in 1916 he backed Ezequiel Cabeza de Baca against the Anglo-Republican candidate. Cabeza de Baca won, but he died after a month in office and his Anglo lieutenant governor succeeded him. In 1918 both parties nominated New Mexicans to office; Larrazolo won and served from 1919 to 1921; he proved a capable and liberal executive, but the party never nominated him again. After 1921 the politics of accommodation resumed, with Mexicans occupying token positions in selected numbers and the political machines "neatly arranging the rival tickets of major parties in such a manner that Anglo runs against Anglo, and native competes with one of his group."[17]

EARLY MEXICAN RESISTANCE IN THE UNITED STATES

During these years one of the popular vehicles for organizing among Mexicans was the *mutualista* (mutual aid society).[18] Anywhere Mexicans moved, they established *mutualistas*. They varied greatly in their political direction from apolitical to reformist to radical, but all met needs for "fellowship, security, and recreation" and were basically a form of collective and voluntary self-help and self-defense.[19] Their motto *Patria, Unión y Beneficencia* became a common unifying symbol throughout the Southwest and eventually throughout the Midwest as well.

By 1900 Mexicans turned to the arena of education which next to labor has been their most intense battleground. In most places school authorities segregated them into "Mexican" schools.[20] The Chicano community fought segregation, inferior schools and education, the discrimination of IQ exams, poor teaching, the lack of Mexican teachers, and the socialization process which condemned them to failure and then conditioned them to accept it. Education, an important vehicle in the maintenance of class, was in the hands of local business leaders, ranchers, and bankers. They were supported by lower-class voters who needed to defend their own status by maintaining the myth of Mexican inferiority. The reasons given for excluding Mexicans from Anglo-American schools followed a pattern: Mexicans were ill-clad, unclean, and immoral; interracial contact would lead to other relationships; they were not white and learned more slowly; and so forth.[21]

In West Texas Mexicans were a small minority and generally heavily segregated. San Angelo had a population of about 10,000 inhabitants with not more than 1,000 to 1,500 Mexicans.[22] About 200 Mexican children attended segregated schools staffed by ill-prepared Anglo teachers. The townspeople generally viewed Mexicans as "foreign." In 1910 when new buildings for the white children were completed, the school board assigned the old buildings to the Mexicans. The Mexican community quietly protested by withholding their children from the school census, thus denying state aid to the school district. They stated that the reason that they would not cooperate was that they did not receive full benefit of state funds. On June 4 they confronted the board stating that they wanted to share the buildings with the Anglo children or at least have their buildings on the same grounds. They also complained that their furnishings were inferior, the Mexican children were not learning, and they needed a male teacher. The board refused to meet the parents' demands.

Mexican parents pressed for integration. Mexicans were assigned to segregated schools. On September 19, 1910, only two Chicanos appeared at the refurbished school, while seven showed up at the North Ward white school. Their entrance was blocked; the board stated that "to admit the Mexicans into white schools would be to demoralize the entire system and they will not under any pressure consider such a thing."[23]

Many parents sent their children to the Immaculate Conception Academy, a Catholic school which segregated Mexican students into a "Mexican room." Reverend B. A. Hodges, a Protestant minister, stated that "The Roman Catholic Church, with the increase of the American membership, more and more discriminated against the Mexicans."[24] The Catholic school refused a request to integrate.

The Presbyterian Church improved conditions somewhat. In 1912 it set up a mission school, teaching the writing of English and Spanish, mathematics, geography, and physiology. Mrs. Jennie Suter, who was described as having "Spanish" blood (which probably meant she was part Mexican), worked among the Mexicans and was influential in converting many to the church. Mrs. Suter's salary was often unpaid due to a lack of funds. By 1913 the school was "booming" with thirty-four Mexican children attending. The Catholic church vehemently opposed the school. "The priests and the sisters have made a house-to-house canvass, using persuasion, offer of rewards, threats, etc. to change the children back to their school." They then tried to buy Mrs. Suter away.[25]

The tension of maintaining the boycott split the Mexican group. The second year, 1911, again only seven Chicano students attended the segregated schools. The boycott continued to some degree for several years, but by 1915 attrition brought it to an end.

THE "BROWN SCARE" AND CHICANO RESISTANCE

During the 1910s the arrival of large numbers of Mexicans triggered what Dr. Ricardo Romo has labeled a "brown scare" which
raged from 1915 to 1917 throughout the Southwest. In Los Angeles
the rapid expansion of industry caused social problems which Anglos blamed on the Mexicans. In placing the blame the Anglos
focused on the arrival of 50,000 Mexicans, while ignoring the flood
of 500,000 new Anglos.[26]

The binding forces within the Mexican community were language and culture. Social and racial integration was slow with discrimination depending greatly on how dark the Mexican was. Mexicans had few choices as to where they could live; aside from social
discrimination, transportation costs were high and they were consequently forced to pay inflated rents for inadequate housing just to
be near work. For example, in Los Angeles the largest concentration of Mexicans was in the Central Plaza district. Near the plaza
40.1 percent of the Mexican workers surveyed worked for the
Southern Pacific Railroad. In an area of less than 5,000 square feet
of living space, 20 needy families lived in dilapidated house
courts.[27]

The *Partido Liberal Mexicano* threatened many Anglo-Ameri-
cans who believed that Mexicans were on the verge of revolt. In
Los Angeles the *magonistas* encouraged labor organization among
Mexicans and they supported the AFL's appointment of Juan
Ramírez as an organizer in 1910–1911 as well as the formation of
Jornaleros Unidos (later chartered by the AFL).[28]

The intense propaganda which accompanied U.S. intervention
in Mexico's internal affairs contributed to widespread fear among
Anglo-Americans. Law enforcement officials viewed Mexicans as
subversive reds and *cholos* who threatened the "American fabric."
The bombardment of Vera Cruz cost over 300 lives. The authorities
justified their actions by alleging that they were stopping a possible
shipment of German arms to the *Huertistas*. This rationalization
affected the treatment of Chicanos. For the next three years, Los
Angeles officials ignored all legitimate complaints on the pretext
that Mexicans were pro-German. When 200 Mexican laborers for
the Pacific Sewer Pipe Company went on strike in 1918, authorities
labeled the strike German-made.[29]

World War I intensified industrialization and urbanization in
California. The war industries attracted many Chicanos and Blacks.
The large numbers of Mexicans settling in Los Angeles created
new social and economic pressures. An already overcrowded housing situation worsened. Anglo-Americans blamed the blight on the
Mexicans and charged that these foreigners contributed to a rapid
disintegration of traditional "American values."[30] Mexicans by 1919

comprised 5 percent of Los Angeles's population of over a million. Twenty-eight percent of Mexicans lived in houses with no sinks, 32 percent had no lavatories, and 79 percent had no baths. The infant mortality for Anglos was 54 out of 1,000, while the rate for Mexicans was 152 out of 1,000. In 1914, 11.1 percent of the deaths in Los Angeles were Mexicans, although they comprised 5 percent of the population.[31] Angelenos ignored these facts since, according to them, the Germans or the reds created the problems.

The brown scare was most intense in Texas and the number of Chicanos killed by rangers, local authorities, and vigilantes climbed into the thousands.[32] There local groups, individuals, and the *mutualistas* began to express their protests against such outrages more actively. For example, when Gregorio Cortez was finally captured and convicted in 1901, "Free Cortez" committees were established.[33] On June 19, 1911, Antonio Gómez, 14, was asked to leave a place of business in Thorndale, Texas. He refused and had a fight with a Texas-German who died from a wound inflicted by Gómez's knife. Gómez was taken from jail by a mob and beaten and his body dragged around town tied to the back of a buggy. The *Orden Caballeros de Honor* protested the Thorndale assassination.[34]

León Cardenas Martínez, age 15, was arrested for the murder of Emma Brown in July 1911 in Saragosa, Texas. He signed a confession after a carbine was held to his head. Cardenas was sentenced to death; later the sentence was reduced to thirty years.[35]

The townspeople denied Cardenas due process by breaking up support meetings and running his lawyer out of town. Cardenas's family was also literally run out of town by a mob.[36]

Nicasio Idar, publisher of *La Crónica*, protested the Cardenas murder. He played an important role in convening *El Primer Congreso Mexicanista* on September 11, 1911 to discuss (1) deteriorating Texas-Mexican economic condition; (2) loss of Mexican culture and the Spanish language; (3) widespread social discrimination; (4) educational discrimination; and (5) lynchings. Men and women attended workshops and discussed issues still relevant today. Delegates also condemned recent lynchings, as well as the insult to the respected state representative J. T. Canales who had been called "the greaser from Brownsville."[37]

Various lodges of the *Orden* attended in addition to other community groups such as *La Agrupación Protectora Mexicana* (Mexican Protective Association) of San Antonio. The *Agrupación* was represented by Doneciano Dávila and Emilio Flores. The *Congreso* created *La Liga Femenil Mexicanista* whose first president was Jovita Idar. The women's contingent was comprised in large part of schoolteachers and was therefore prominent in the discussions on education. It also created *La Gran Liga Mexicanista de*

Beneficencia y Protección. Its motto was *"Por la Raza y Para la Raza."*[38]

The *Agrupación Protectora Mexicana,* founded in 1910 in San Antonio, actively defended human rights for Mexicans. It engaged in union organizing, but focused mainly on fighting against police brutality and lynchings. The *Agrupación* worked to release Gregorio Cortez and it was supported by individual contributions.[39]

The *Agrupación* functioned until 1914, when internecine strife split the organization. Like most organizations of the time, it divided into moderate and radical factions. The people at the *Congreso* accepted the *Agrupación,* but it received unrelenting criticism from the *magonistas.* The *magonistas* had asked the *Agrupació*n for help when its partisans in Marfa, Texas, were prosecuted for violation of the neutrality laws. The *Agrupación* did not help. Magón attacked the *Agrupación* as being inept and the laughing stock of the state, as not being fit to carry the fight against the bourgeoisie, and for not doing anything in the case of León Cardenas Martínez. He alleged that the *Agrupación* misappropriated funds.[40]

Intra- and intergroup fights plagued both Mexican and Anglo activist organizations. For instance, Magón criticized Eugene Debs for dragging his feet on the Mexican revolution, alleging that Debs believed that Mexican peons were too ignorant to retain their liberties if they should be successful in recovering them.[41] The division on ethnic grounds was intensified by an ideological difference. A fight between anarchists and socialists existed within the IWW, and the socialist Debs strongly opposed Magón's anarchist principles.

Within the Chicano community similar struggles often tore organizations apart. The PLM represented the more radical position, although its priority was always the struggle in Mexico. However, its impressive network of groups throughout the nation did organize many Mexicans and prepared the way for focusing on issues confronting the Chicano community here. Issues of *Regeneración* listed contributions from throughout the United States.[42]

The Mexican revolution escalated, and relatively minor border disturbances were distorted out of proportion. After 1913 reactionaries pressured the United States to intervene in Mexican affairs. The Texas governor sent almost a thousand Rangers to the Rio Grande Valley where all Mexicans were automatically suspect.

Anglo-American authorities took an obscure document called *El Plan de San Diego* and used it to persecute thousands of innocent people. The *Plan* was discovered in January 1915 when authorities arrested Basilio Ramos and found a copy of it on him. Essentially, the *Plan* called for a general uprising on February 20, 1915. All white males over 16 would be killed; the *Plan* exempted Blacks, Asians, and Native Americans from execution.[43] The Southwest would be declared an independent Mexican republic and the states of Oklahoma, Kansas, Nebraska, South Dakota, Wyoming, and Utah would be given to the Blacks.

The *Plan* was signed by Ramos and seven other *Huertistas.* The *Huertistas* were antirevolutionist with direct roots in the Porfirio Díaz regime. Nothing connected Ramos and the signers directly to any organizations or movements in the Rio Grande Valley, other than they shared the view that the United States was "tyrannical." Further, the signers did not have much influence with the forces of Carranza who dominated northern Mexico.[44]

In July 1915 Mexicans made a series of raids on several ranches; their estimated strength was forty armed men. They were led by Ancieto Pizaña and Luis de la Rosa, both of whom were reported to be *Carranzistas* and not *Huertistas.* Two Anglos were killed in one of the raids. Raids continued into October and at no time was the combined strength of Pizaña and de la Rosa estimated at more than fifty. The raids provided an excuse for reprisals by Rangers and Anglo authorities. They claimed the raids were part of the *Plan* and linked the *Plan* to the Germans or Flores Magón. This in turn justified further terror and buildup of troops along the border.[45]

Pizaña's or de la Rosa's involvement with the *Plan de San Diego* was questionable. Many Chicano activists at that time found it adventuristic and outright racist. Flores Magón in *Regeneración* never acknowledged or abetted the *Plan.* He stated: "They [the Anglo authorities] want to make it appear as if the Mexican uprising in that section of the United States is part of the Plan of San Diego."[46] Flores Magón called the Pizaña rebellion self-defense. According to him, *El Presente,* a San Antonio newspaper, stated that the uprising began in Brownsville when an Anglo killed a Mexican and his friends avenged him. Mexicans then banded together for self-defense and survival.[47]

In 1917 the atrocities peaked with 35,000 U.S. soldiers on the border. George Marvin wrote in *World's Work* magazine in January 1917:

> The killing of Mexicans. . . along the border in these last four years is almost incredible. . . . Some Rangers have degenerated into common mankillers. There is no penalty for killing, no jury along the border would ever convict a white man for shooting a Mexican. . . . Reading over Secret Service records makes you feel as though there was an open gun season on Mexicans along the border.[48]

Walter Prescott Webb excused the "Reign of Terror" by stating that the revolution created border incidents. Webb alleged that Germany had agents scattered throughout Mexico, that German officers trained Mexican soldiers, and that Germany supposedly had a powerful wireless station in Mexico City. According to Webb, prohibition also contributed to lawlessness and paranoia. According to Webb, when U.S. citizens heard that Germans supplied Mexicans with guns, that the IWW was passing out incendiary literature, and that the Japanese were supplying Mexicans, all in an effort to take over the Southwest, "their anger was lashed into fury. . . . In the orgy of bloodshed that followed the Texas Rangers played a prominent part, and one of which many members of the force have been heartily ashamed."[49] Most experts state that German involvement along the Rio Grande was unproved and that the involvement of the IWW and the Japanese was just not true.

In essence, the press exaggerated the *Plan* in order to discredit Mexican nationalism and to justify the wholesale murders of Mexicans. Many Anglos feared that Chicanos would extend the Mexican Revolution to the United States to end glaring racist injustices.[50]

ACCOMMODATION AND NATIONALISM

In the 1920s the growing numbers of second generation Chicanos drifted away from the nationalistic *mutualistas* to accommodationist organizations which resembled U.S. institutions. Although the majority of Mexican organizations were still *mutualistas,* the second generation became more Americanized (or assimilated).

Many of the newer organization were middle-class integrationist societies. For example, *El Orden de los Hijos de América,* established in San Antonio in 1921, was limited to either native-born or naturalized U.S. citizens. The stated purpose of the *Orden* was "to use their influence in all fields of social, economic, and political action in order to realize the greatest enjoyment possible of all the rights and privileges and prerogatives extended by the American Constitution."[51] The *Orden* fought for the constitutional rights of Chicanos and especially criticized the inequities of the jury system. By the late 1920s it had seven councils. In 1927 the League of United Latin American Citizens (LULAC) was formed in Texas to incorporate the councils of the *Orden* into one central organization with lodges.[52] However, the older councils refused to subordinate themselves to the new league.

LULAC, unlike most earlier organizations, used an English, instead of a Spanish name. Its members were middle-class Chicanos who were citizens of the United States. Its purpose was "to develop within the members of our race the best, purest and most perfect type of a true and loyal citizen of the United States."[53] It emphasized the learning of English and established preschools to teach Chicano children a basic English vocabulary, to help them function in the school system, as well as to aid in their eventual Americanization. LULAC councils spread to twenty-one states, but the organization's main strength remained in Texas, where it served both social and political functions. In general, members identified very closely with LULAC. It survived in the most hostile of environments and kept Chicano issues at the forefront.

Although it has become popular to criticize LULAC's middle-class, integrationist approach it should not be evaluated by present standards. Men like Alonso Perales and J. T. Canales courageously defended the rights of Mexicans in the United States. For years LULAC was the only organization with a nationwide network. It also cut reliance on the Mexican consuls and concentrated on U.S. issues.[54]

In Los Angeles in 1921 Edwardo Ruiz, the Mexican consul, founded *La Comisión Honorífica Mexicana* and soon other consuls formed hundreds of chapters of the *Comisión*. The chapters assisted nationals until the consular office could deal with their problems and then the *Comisión* acted as an ombudsman for the needy. The chapters were popular among middle-class Mexican immigrants.[55] The *Comisión* also participated in strikes during the 1920s encouraging its members to support the union.

The *Brigadas de Cruz Azul* (Blue Cross Brigades) were also organized by the Mexican consuls. They were comprised of Mexican women who volunteered their time, providing needed welfare services. The *Brigadas* established libraries and, like the *Comisión,* fostered Mexican nationalism.[56]

THE STRUGGLE TO ACHIEVE EQUAL EDUCATION

Education preoccupied Mexican organizations. In Texas, according to Paul S. Taylor, although segregation of school children on the basis of race was not legal, de facto segregation was the rule. School authorities openly defended it on the grounds that it allowed them to isolate the problem of shielding "the Mexican from the social prejudice of Americans."[57]

Segregation of Mexican students was widespread and the battle to desegregate schools was fought in the courts and before the state superintendent of instruction. In the 1928 case of *Vela v. Board of Trustees of Charlotte Independent School District,* Félipe Vela claimed that the school district had not allowed his adopted daughter to attend the white school because she was Mexican. He contended that she was not Mexican and therefore could not be excluded. The superintendent found that whether the girl was Mexican or not was irrelevant since the district did not have the legal authority to segregate Mexican children on a racial basis.[58] Since she spoke English she was entitled to go to the white school. The state board of education affirmed this decision, but Texas-Mexicans remained segregated in many places until the 1970s. In 1928 Dr. Hershel Manuel estimated that in Texas while 40,000 to 45,000 whites attended college fewer than 250 Mexicans and about 2,000 to 2,500 Blacks were enrolled in higher education.[59]

Programs in the schools existed mainly for Americanizing students. When Mexicans occasionally transferred to the "American" school in order to complete their education, Anglo-American children subjected them to severe hazing. The other students called them names, "sometimes provoking fights and ostracizing them from games and would not let them sit next to them."[60]

The fact of segregation and the inferior education available to Mexicans reinforced and contributed to their frozen social and economic status, for, according to Paul Taylor, "Education is not merely a means of acquiring literacy and culture; it may also be a stepping-stone to social and economic advancement."[61]

SOCIAL CONDITIONS IN LOS ANGELES IN THE 1920s

In California there was a proliferation of *mutualistas* and social clubs like *El Club Sonrense, El Club Automovilista Mexicano,* and *El Club Independiente* which lobbied against U.S. intervention in Mexico. *La Liga Cultural Mexicana* established a library in Belvedere in 1926.[62] Chicano organizations often were divided across class lines; for instance, *El Centro Hispano de Los Angeles* in January 1920 was limited to leading Mexican families, professionals, and intellectuals who supported the preservation of the Spanish language and Mexican folklore, music, dances, and culture in general. The upper-class Mexicans tended to extol the virtues of culture and heritage, thinking if the Anglos appreciated their culture, they would more readily accept them. Mexican workers, who were victims of segregation and discrimination in housing, education, and employment, struggled for their human rights.[63]

Exactly how many Mexicans resided in Los Angeles was not known. In 1929 Hazel Santiago, a social worker, estimated 189,850. Linna Bresette, another social worker, believed it perhaps approached 250,000.[64]

Housing for Mexicans in Los Angeles worsened in the 1920s. Wages were low, only about $8.00 to $15.00 a week. Elizabeth Fuller in a 1920 study found that 92 percent of the homes she visited did not have gas and 72 percent did not have electricity. Civic development in the west side of the center of the city, that is, demolition of areas that housed many Mexicans to make room for civic buildings, created invariable overcrowding and in 1924 and 1925 a plague of rats invaded the Mexican section. Some 140,000 rats were eventually exterminated. Five people died of bubonic plague with thirty more dying of pneumonia.[65]

The Mexican expansion to the east side continued: Thirty thousand lived in the Belvedere section alone; Los Angeles had the largest concentration of Mexicans in the United States by 1930.[66]

Residents found jobs in the newly established industries in Vernon, Maywood, Commerce, Bell, and Cudahy. According to the

1930 census only 13 Blacks lived in Belvedere; therefore, the two groups did not compete for the same blue-collar jobs. Homes were shacks constructed of scrap lumber, old boxes or other salvage.[67]

Other sections of the city excluded Mexicans. A 1930 report boasted, "Lynwood, being restricted to the white race, can furnish ample labor of the better class." In 1927, El Segundo reported no Blacks or Mexicans lived in that city. Long Beach had between 10,000 and 14,000 Mexicans, but advertised "Long Beach has a population of 140,000 people—98 percent of whom are of the Anglo-Saxon race."[68]

Mexicans did not fare much better in education. Dr. Merton Hill of the Chaffey School District wrote that they were: "the greatest problem confronting Southern California." Mexicans, according to Hill, did not learn as quickly as whites.[69]

In the 1920s relations between Chicanos and the police deteriorated. One of the more sensational cases was that of Aurelio Pompa, a Mexican immigrant, convicted in 1923 for killing an Anglo. Pompa committed the act in self-defense. The defense committee hired Los Angeles Chicano attorney Frank Domínguez to defend Pompa. Many *mutualistas,* such as *La Sociedad Melchor Ocampo,* and other civic groups supported him. They pressured the Mexican consul for support. Juan de Heras, editor of *El Heraldo,* led the movement to free Pompa. Supporters presented a petition with 12,915 signatures to Governor F. W. Richardson. Even Mexican President Alvaro Obregón petitioned Richardson to save Pompa's life. In spite of the pressure Pompa was executed.[70]

MEXICAN NATIONALISM IN THE MIDWEST IN THE 1920s

The lack of criminal justice for Mexicans was not limited to the Southwest. A persistent pattern of discrimination could be found in any city in the Midwest or Southwest. Paul S. Taylor reported that on April 11, 1924:

> ... the mutualistic societies established in Chicago have turned to the Mexican consul of the city, informing him that more than seven Mexicans are being tried for murder in the first degree in various cities, including Chicago, and probably they will be given the death sentence.[71]

A Davenport, Iowa, newspaper, *El Trabajo,* documented the network and unity among Midwestern Chicanos. *El Trabajo* reported support for José Ortiz Esquivel of Illinois who had been sentenced to death on June 12, 1925, for the murder of his sweetheart. The Mexican community sent donations and were successful in moving back the execution date to June 24. The Chicano community was offended since Ortiz would be the first man in Illinois in fifteen years to be executed. *El Trabajo* implored its readers to fight against this double standard of justice. The newspaper equated the Ortiz case with Mexican deaths throughout the Southwest. Apparently, efforts of the Midwest community were successful, since the Illinois supreme court granted Ortiz a new trial.[72]

When Anglo-Americans complained about the rights of citizens being violated in Mexico, *El Correo Mexicano,* a Chicano Chicago newspaper, on September 30, 1926, replied:

> The Chicago Tribune and other North American papers, like the Boston Transcript, should not be scandalized when an American citizen in Mexico is attacked, not by the authorities, as here, but by bandits and highwaymen.[73]

The *Correo* attacked the contradiction of North Americans calling for immediate justice in Mexico when *bandits* killed a U.S. citizen, pointing out that Mexicans in Chicago and other U.S. cities were victims of the *police.*

In Chicago Mexicans were regularly arrested for disorderly conduct; in 1928–1929 this charge constituted almost 79 percent of their misdemeanor offenses. Another common charge in Chicago and in the rural Southwest was vagrancy. In Chicago Polish police officers were especially brutal toward Chicanos. They looked upon Mexicans as competitors. A desk sergeant in 1925 readily admitted that he hated Mexicans and that he had told officers at another station not to take chances with Mexicans: "They are quick on the knife and are hot tempered. . . ."[74]

Many arrests were made using "dragnet" methods, that is, police would make sweeps of streets and places like pool halls, arresting Mexicans for carrying a jackknife or on the usual charge of disorderly conduct. This unconstitutional method was heavily relied upon by Chicago police. Once in custody the methods used to extract confessions in Chicago jails were (1) not giving the prisoner anything to eat for three days; (2) physical beatings; (3) sticking a revolver in the prisoner's mouth; and (4) beatings with a rubber hose.[75]

In Gary, Indiana, in 1924 police rounded up 400 Chicanos after a Mexican shot an officer. The police authorities wanted to run them out of the city. Mexicans in Gary formed *La Sociedad Protectora Mexicana* to protect their legal rights, providing funds for bail and an attorney.[76]

Poverty among Mexicans made justice difficult since they did not have the financial resources to defend themselves or appeal their cases. A contemporary study found that over three-quarters "did not have the money to hire a lawyer to defend them when they found themselves in trouble." The quality of the defense attorney was generally poor, and the inability to speak English worked against the defendant.[77]

Mutualistas were strong in Chicago and the Calumet area. According to Dr. Louise Kerr, "Like many earlier immigrants, the Mexicans were primarily concerned with daily physical survival and had little time to indulge in the luxury of defining long-term ambitions."[78] The *mutualistas* met these needs. The consul also became important because he was accessible.

Women in this hostile environment relied heavily on their own institutions, such as using midwives to deliver children. Socially Mexicans were segregated. In East Chicago two theatre owners limited Mexicans to the Black section and in Gary a section of the municipal cemetery was reserved for Mexicans.[79]

Nationalism was strong among Mexicans. "A widow with three small children, told that she would have to apply for citizenship before she could be given a mother's pension, chose rather to relinquish her right to the pension." The rest of the Mexican community helped her.[80] They followed Mexican politics closely and took sides on elections and other issues there.

Mexicans working for the Rock Island Railroad near Back of the Yards formed the *Juárez* Club which disbanded in 1921. *La Cruz Azul* helped for a time, but, as mentioned, gossip destroyed that organization. The *Sociedad Mutualista Obreros Libres Mexicanos* (Mutual Society of Independent Mexican Workers) funded a Mexican band in South Chicago.

Settlement houses such as Hull House became popular outlets for Mexican families, providing needed educational services, as well as recreation. These houses intervened with police and public health and welfare agencies.[81]

Protestant missionary work made heavy inroads among Chicago Chicanos, and by the early 1930s 23 percent of the active church-going Mexicans in the city were Protestants. Protestants were successful because they offered social services, legal aid, medical assistance, classes in English, and other aid. The Masons also sponsored three lodges among Chicanos.

The Catholic church combated militant unionism. The center for Mexican Catholics was Our Lady of Guadalupe Chapel built by the Inland Steel Company for Mexican workers in South Chicago. They were excluded from Polish and Slavic Catholic parishes. In the near westside, by 1928, Mexicans took over the Italian parish of St. Francis. The Catholic church assigned the first Spanish-speaking priest to serve the growing Mexican population. The Back of the Yards Poles and Irish were adamantly anti-Mexican and discouraged them from attending their churches. Active church attendance among Catholic Mexicans was low.[82]

The 1920s were important to Chicanos in the Midwest as settlements stabilized. After 1924 migration patterns changed, with greater numbers of Mexicans arriving directly from Mexico daily. Increasingly, single men left and more married couples rooted themselves in Chicago. In 1924 Chicanas were less than a third of the Chicano population; eleven years later they were over 50 percent. In 1924 U.S.-born children were less than 1 percent of the population; fourteen years later 53 percent of all Chicano children were U.S. born and 54 percent of these were Chicago born.[83] They moved into Flint, Saginaw, and other Michigan cities.

In 1923, 948 Mexicans were imported to Pennsylvania by Bethlehem Steel to work in the mills. They forged a community through considerable struggle, often surviving through self-help. In order to help the impoverished and the ill, Chicanos formed three beneficial associations in this small colony. In 1927 they formed *La Unión Protectora* which was disbanded because Mexicans believed that aliens could not organize a union. They formed *La Sociedad Azteca Mexicana* the next year; by 1930 it had 130 members (that organization still exists today and owns a social hall).[84]

Ohio had 952 Mexicans in 1920, but ten years later that population had grown to over 4,000. Most Chicanos were located in northwestern Ohio, with 554 living in Toledo, setting the foundation for future growth.[85]

By the 1920s the Mexican population of St. Paul, Minnesota, was settled. In 1924 Luis Garzán and friends formed the Anahuac Society which was a men's society formed to sponsor dances to raise money for the needy. They held parties at the Neighborhood House, a community center. In the fall of 1930 the Mexican women formed the Guild of Catholic Women at the Mission of Our Lady of Guadalupe.[86]

The Mexican community also grew in Utah where Chicanos worked in the railroads, in mines, and on farms. At the beginning of the decade 1,200 Mexicans lived in Utah; ten years later the number grew to over 4,000. Juan Ramón Martínez, a native of New Mexico, formed the Provisional Lamanite Branch in 1921. The usual *mutualistas*, Mexican protective associations and *La Cruz Azul* were formed by the mid-1920s. They regularly celebrated the *Cinco de Mayo* and other Mexican holidays. By 1930 Our Lady of Guadalupe Church had been established as a mission.[87]

In the Northwest the center of Chicano migration became the Yakima Valley. By the 1920s small numbers of Mexicans established a beachhead. Oregon had Mexicans working as muleteers and *vaqueros* since the mid-nineteeth century. Small numbers worked in the hop and bean fields in the 1920s, but they did not arrive in large numbers until after World War II. By the end of the decade Mexicans had small colonies throughout the Southwest and Midwest and began to move into the Northwest. They forged a community which depended on the unity of its members. In the face of extreme hostility they continued their hope to return to their native land. Excluded from Anglo-American organizations, they increasingly turned to their own self-help organizations.[88]

SECOND GENERATION RESISTANCE

By the 1930s a substantial portion of the Mexican population in the United States was second generation. The new generation of Chicanos was not as preoccupied with returning to Mexico as earlier generations of Mexicans had been. As the number of urban residents with full-time employment increased and as Mexican communities throughout the United States became more settled, Chicanos began to form more multi-issue organizations which not only functioned for the sake of self-defense but which advocated rights for its constituents. Although nationalistic ties with Mexico remained, they were less intense than in the 1920s. Organizations, individual activists, and academicians focused more on issues of segregation, discrimination, and denial of basic human rights and not as much on solving immediate problems of survival.

During the 1930s the Catholic church involved itself more with Mexican youth. Spanish-speaking priests organized religious seminars among many Chicanos; however, the Catholic hierarchy became alarmed about fostering of nationalism among Chicanos. Church authorities moved to defuse this movement and conducted intensive drives to recruit Chicano youth to programs sponsored by the Catholic Youth Organization and the Catholic settlement houses.

Another influence was that of the Communist party, which worked actively in the Chicano community during the 1930s. The communists formed clubs which were few in number but active. Finally, local unions, especially CIO locals, conducted organizational drives during this decade.

The Young Men's Christian Association (YMCA) expanded its services in the *barrios*. Clubs were formed within the YMCA which gave Chicanos the opportunity to function in a clublike atmosphere. Many early members were encouraged to attend college, and a civic attitude developed among the young.

The Mexican American Movement (MAM) was an outgrowth of the YMCA's Older Boys' Conference held in San Pedro in 1934. Annual boy's conferences held there were later renamed the Mexican Youth Congress. Through the years the functions of the Youth Conference broadened and it established a steering committee. This group evolved into the Mexican American Movement. In 1938 MAM published a newspaper, *The Mexican Voice.* In 1939 it established a leadership institute; in that same year it held its first regional conference at Santa Barbara, and by 1940 it sponsored a Mexican American Girls' Conference and a Mexican American Teachers' Association and established contacts with similar organizations in Arizona and Texas.[89]

The stated philosophy of MAM was to create Chicano leadership in education, social work, business and other professions.[90]

MAM struggled continuously toward its goal of "Progress Through Education"; it fought for better education and better family relations as it fought against discrimination and juvenile delinquency. World War II curtailed some of its activities, but it survived until about 1949. *The Mexican Voice* became the *Forward* in 1945 and reported on its members' progress in the armed forces. Among those who participated were Félix Gutiérrez, Sr., Richard Ibañez, a civil rights attorney and later a judge, Manuel Ceja, Mary Escudero of Claremont, and Mary Anne Chavolla of Placentia. Records of the organization indicate that many members were later absorbed into the Community Service Organization.[91]

MAM members participated with other organizations. In 1938 *El Congreso de los Pueblos de Habla Español* held the first national Conference of Spanish-Speaking Peoples. The principal organizer was Luisa Moreno, a leader and national organizer for the United Cannery, Agricultural, and Packing Workers of America, which was involved in the pecan workers' strike in San Antonio.[92] Moreno traveled throughout the United States and generated considerable interest in the conference later held in Los Angeles. Representatives came from all over the United States: Spanish and Cuban cigar makers from Tampa, Florida; Puerto Ricans from Harlem; steelworkers from Pennsylvania, Illinois, and Indiana; meat packers, miners, and farm workers from all over the country; and elected officials from New Mexico. The congress was broadly based: workers, politicians, youth, educators—people from all walks of life. Its stated purpose was "the economic and social and cultural betterment of the Mexican people, to have an understanding between Anglo-Americans and Mexicans, to promote organization of working people by aiding trade unions and to fight discrimination actively."[93]

Newspapers and local elected officials labeled it a "subversive gathering." Delegates pushed through a radical and progressive platform. Workers were to be organized, and a newspaper and newsletter were to be published. Delegates set legislative priorities and took stands against oppressive laws, immigration officials, vigilantes, and police brutality. They demanded the right of farm workers to organize as well as the extension of the benefits of the National Labor Relations Act to farm workers.

The Congress was very successful from 1938 to 1940, claiming over 6,000 members.[94] However, it had committed a strategic blunder in making its aims too sectarian and too specific. Neither the *Congreso* nor the Chicano community had many friends in the media or in positions of power. Because of its radical stands, the *Congreso* exposed itself to intense red-baiting and the FBI harassed its members. After 1940 its effectiveness waned rapidly, even though it continued to function in the postwar period.

The *Congreso* was important because it provided a forum for activists like Luisa Moreno. On March 3, 1940, she addressed a Panel on Deportation and Right of Asylum of the Fourth Annual Conference of the American Committee for the Protection of Foreign Born in Washington, D.C. She entitled her speech "Caravan of Sorrow":

> Long before the "Grapes of Wrath" had ripened in California's vineyards a people lived on highways, under trees or tents, in shacks or railroad sections, picking crops—cotton, fruits, vegetables, cultivating sugar beets, building railroads and dams, making barren land fertile for new crops and greater riches.[95]

Moreno continued that they had been brought "by the fruit exchanges, railroad companies and cotton interests in great need of underpaid labor during the early post-war period." She condemned the repatriations and the sufferings caused by it, charging that "Today the Latin Americans of the United States are alarmed by an 'antialien' drive." Citizenship became increasingly a requirement for continued employment and nativists conducted a drive to get federal legislation passed making it mandatory. Moreno explained that there were many reasons for not becoming a naturalized citizen: (1) lack of documentary proof because Mexicans were brought over *en masse* and many of the companies transporting Mexicans to the United States mishandled the paper work; (2) many did not learn English; and (3) many did not have money for the fee. Whatever the reason, Moreno added:

> These people are not aliens. They have contributed their endurance, sacrifices, youth and labor to the Southwest. Indirectly, they have paid more taxes than all the stockholders of California's industrialized agriculture, the sugar companies and the large cotton interests, that operate or have operated with the labor of Mexican workers.[96]

Moreno put the Spanish-Speaking Congress on record as opposing antialien legislation.

Local groups and individuals crusaded against other injustices. For example, in 1931 at Lemon Grove, California, near San Diego, the parents of seventy-five Chicano children protested an order by school authorities to assign Mexicans to a separate school in order to facilitate learning English. Parents and children boycotted the school and sued. The judge decided in favor of the Chicanos stating, "I believe that this separation deprives the Mexican children of the presence of American children which is so necessary for them in order to learn English."[97]

A few newspaper editors condemned discrimination and segregation in schools and public facilities. Ignacio López, editor of *El Espectador* carried the fight through his community newspaper. In the 1940s he established unity leagues in the area surrounding Pomona, and in the 1960s he took a leadership role in the Mexican American Political Association (MAPA).

In February a Chicano youth and a companion entered the movie theatre in Upland, California. They paid, entered the theatre, and looked for seats near the center. The assistant manager approached them and told them the first fifteen rows were reserved for Chicanos. The Chicanos asked if their tickets were not, in fact, general admission, entitling them to sit anywhere. The answer was that Chicanos sat in the first fifteen rows. The youths went to López who wrote a stinging editorial condemning the policy of the theatre house and calling for a mass meeting in Upland. Hundreds of Chicanos attended the meeting, which the Mexican consul from San Bernardino addressed. Chicanos boycotted the theatre and shortly afterward the theatre changed its segregationist policy.[98]

In another case the swimming pool at Chaffey Junior College during the academic year was used on an integrated basis, but when it was open to the general public during the summer, Chicanos were told they could use it only on Mondays.[99] In 1939, joined by Reverend R. N. Nuñez of Guadalupe Parish in San Bernardino, he brought suit against San Bernardino and got the courts to enjoin that city from excluding Mexicans from the pools.[100]

In 1930 the Federation of Spanish-Speaking Voters attempted to unite all Mexican societies. It was "perhaps the first political group to organize in Los Angeles." It ran candidates for state and local offices in 1930, but they all lost. In the 1930s the Council for Inter-American Affairs was formed in the Southwest. It spread to Los Angeles in the 1940s. Its goal was to get the United States to live up to the terms of the Treaty of Guadalupe Hidalgo. It held conferences and leadership training workshops.[101]

Isabel Malagram Gonzales worked in New Mexico and Colorado. In the late 1920s she led a strike of pea workers, and in 1930 she moved to Denver, where she worked for the Colorado Tuberculosis Society. In the 1940s she worked for *Challenge,* a progressive newspaper and was active in politics and ran for the city council. Isabel served as national president of the Friends of Wallace and was a delegate to the Independent Progressive party's national convention in Philadelphia. Later she was a founding member of *La Asociación Nacional México-Americana.* In 1946 she was refused the right to testify before the War Food Administration. In the late 40s she worked as a political activist in northern New Mexico. On May 31, 1949 she died in Denver.[102]

During the 1930s Drs. George I. Sánchez and H. T. Manuel analyzed the reasons for the Mexicans' position at the bottom of the social structure, reexamined the nature of IQ tests, studied the influence of environment on education, and vigorously criticized educational policy as it pertained to Chicanos.[103] Sánchez also raised the issue of biased historical interpretation. His statements that Mexicans often did not know their own history "because Anglo-American scholars control the analysis of the history of the region,"[104] initiated a struggle for control of history which has lasted to the present.

In Texas Chicanos had the potential to gain some political parity since they comprised 50 percent or more of the valley vote and about 40 percent of the San Antonio vote, but the poll tax and political machines prevented any effective suffrage.[105] A poll tax of $1.75 was equivalent to a day's pay, and Texas was a one-party state with all power centered in the Democrats; therefore, Mexicans had only one way to go. In spite of the work of J. T. Canales and others the "Mexican vote" remained solidly under the control of the machine. The "basic problem of enough to eat and of decent shelter" preoccupied most Mexicans.[106]

Many New Mexicans held to the myth that they fared better than Mexicans elsewhere. The 1930s further exposed that contradiction between the myth and their reality. Even after World War II, out of 1,093 listings in *Who's Who in New Mexico*, only 57 were Mexican. In eastern New Mexico Chicanos were barred from "better" barber shops, cafes, hotels, and recreation centers. In Anglo towns such as Rosewell Mexicans could not use the public pool. In the late 1930s, the illiteracy rate in Mexican counties, those in which they were the majority, was 16.6 percent versus 3.1 percent in Anglo counties. During the 1930s the public schools were widely segregated. It was obvious that Mexican schools were inferior. For instance, the percent of teachers in public schools in Anglo counties with degrees was 82.2 versus 46.6 percent in Mexican counties.[107]

The 1930s saw the complete control of New Mexico by the Democratic party.[108] In those years the Democrats controlled the presidency, the U.S. Congress, and the U.S. Supreme Court, and through the enormous patronage power it built a federal machine and a cadre of civil service and appointive office holders at the state level. In New Mexico 5,000 state jobs were available which when family members were counted meant a bloc of 25,000 votes; add this to the federal bureaucracy and quite a bloc of votes existed. In a state without much industry and high unemployment, jobs were a powerful weapon. In January 1935 more than 135,000 people or almost a third of the population were on relief. The Democrats controlled relief groups. In New Mexico Chicanos traditionally turned out to vote in larger numbers than Anglos.

Bronson Cutting was considered the head of the machine and he based his power on the "Mexican vote" and the American Legion. In 1934 U.S. Congressman Dennis Chávez challenged Cutting for the U.S. Senate seat. Chávez ran as a Democrat; Cutting was a Republican, but he had vast resources at his disposal. Cutting had acquired chips from the Roosevelt administration for his support of New Deal legislation. Nevertheless, the administration supported Chávez who lost 75,759 to 74,498—a difference of 1,261 votes.

Chávez charged fraud. Not getting satisfaction, Chávez petitioned the Senate to unseat Cutting. Before a decision could be made Cutting was killed in an air crash. The New Mexican governor, after pressure from the national Democratic machine, appointed Chávez Senator, and a new *patrón* was born. Chávez championed the interest of the Chicano population, working for jobs and antidiscrimination legislation. Ironically Chávez was a Democrat and the majority of Chicanos were Republicans.[109]

By the end of the decade Anglos were reaching numerical superiority. The decline of the Republican party hurt their political influence. Deals at the top were more prevalent and more aggressive Mexicans migrated out of the state in larger numbers. At the same time more Anglos migrated to New Mexico, so that by the end of World War II they became the majority. The bulk of the Anglo migration came from Texas and Oklahoma. New Mexico became a one-party state, with the Democrats totally dominating state politics, and the New Mexican strategy of splitting the Anglo vote was no longer effective.

Even at the height of their influence Chicanos in New Mexico, could not win the big offices—governor or land commissioner. By the Democratic primary of 1950 Anglos captured eight of the nine state offices. New Mexicans had some power within the old convention style of nominating candidates which functioned from 1912 to 1938. They made deals with party leadership to balance the ticket and not pit Mexicans against Anglos. This so-called gentleman's agreement was set up by O. A. Larrazolo. While two parties functioned New Mexicans had the swing vote in the Republican party. However, when all the Anglos concentrated in the Democratic party, they had the majority. When the procedure changed from nomination at conventions to nomination through primaries, the parties had an excuse for not balancing the ticket. Also, even under the gentleman's agreement New Mexicans did not fare well. To 1944 not one state supreme court justice was Chicano, while twenty-three were Anglo; Mexicans won only two gubernatorial elections and only one served out his tenure of office. New Mexicans occasionally got to be lieutenant governor, and without interruption they filled the office of secretary of state, while Anglos were state treasurers. Generally, Mexicans held the office of state auditor, while all other state offices, executive and judicial, were the province of Anglos.[110]

Chicago remained the center for Chicanos in the Midwest. Because of repatriation and decreased opportunities, Chicago's Chicano population declined from 20,000 to 16,000. The arbitrary nature of the repatriation angered many Chicanos, and although

Europeans and Asians were also repatriated, the program had singled out Mexicans. As in other U.S. cities by the mid-1930s employment increasingly depended on naturalization. Chicanos in that city had the lowest naturalization rate of any of the immigrant groups.

While in the 1920s the Mexican community had been largely single males, in the 1930s the *barrios* were more defined. The Chicano community in Chicago became more family oriented. Chicano families were not sharing apartments as in the previous decade, and the "boarding house" was disappearing. Official attitudes were slow to change and state relief agencies still counted Chicano as foreign born. Chicanos concentrated in South Chicago, the Near West Side, and Back of the Yards, with each community evolving its individual character.[111]

Interest in Mexico was still high, but the mere fact of having had to make a choice whether to return to Mexico or remain did cut ties. Many were, therefore, forced to accept the fight in Chicago, for there would be no escape and local needs had to be met. According to Dr. Kerr, the Chicano Chicagoans were "less concerned with politics than with jobs, relief, education, and accommodation to the urban environment."[112] They joined a variety of clubs, unions, and workers' associations to meet these needs. Local Spanish-language newspapers such as *La Defensa del Ideal Católico Mexicano, La Voz de México,* and *La Alianza* delineated community issues and divisions.

The pool hall was no longer the center of activity. U.S. sports such as basketball became more accepted. Mexican club teams, such as *Los Aztecas, Los Mexicanos,* and *Los Reyes,* played in leagues. As in the case of other immigrant groups, Chicano youth gangs emerged. According to Dr. Kerr, "social workers felt that participation in youth gangs was a form of adaption to the local community," a form of assimilation "learned" by Mexican youths "from the Italians and Poles who preceded them." More Mexican-run small businesses emerged and school attendance by Mexican youth increased. Adult English classes also became more popular.

Hull House in the Near West Side served the needs of Chicanos. However, as Hull House devoted more time to research, its advocacy role declined. During the late 1930s Frank Pax organized the Mexican youth party and the group met at Hull House. Some Mexicans preferred the Mexican Social Center, established in the early 1930s. This center was small. In South Chicago some Chicanos attended the Byrd Memorial Center which was staffed by the Congregational church whose staff looked upon Mexicans as backward and undependable. Chicanos still were prohibited from attending many of the Catholic parishes.

The University of Chicago Settlement House, located in Back of the Yards, had more personal involvement with Mexicans due to the work of its long-time director Mary McDowell. She worked toward interethnic cooperation and actively trained women to take leadership roles under the auspices of the Mexican Mothers' Club. The groups encouraged by McDowell continued after her death; in 1937 the Mexican Mothers' Club sponsored a series of discussions on local Chicago issues and interethnic cooperation remained better in this area than in other sections of the city.[113]

FIGHTING FOR WHOSE DEMOCRACY?

World War II interrupted the progress of the reform movements of the 1930s. The momentum of the Chicano movement was lost when many of its leaders entered the armed forces; many were killed and others, when they returned, had frankly tired of crusades. Chicanos were the most decorated ethnic group of World War II, yet they were also the least recognized. Raúl Morín, in his book *Among the Valiant*, documented the Chicanos' contribution to the war effort. When the war began, there were about 2,690,000 Chicanos in the United States, approximately one-third of whom were of draft age. According to Dr. Robin R. Scott, between 375,000 and 500,000 Chicanos served in the armed forces. In Los Angeles Mexicans comprised one-tenth of the population and one-fifth of the casualties.[114]

In spite of their contribution Mexicans were still treated as second-class citizens. For example, Sergeant Macario García, from Sugarland, Texas, a recipient of the Congressional Medal of Honor, could not buy a cup of coffee in a restaurant in Richmond, California; "An Anglo-American chased him out with a baseball bat."[115]

In December 1941 the median income for Mexicans in Los Angeles was $792 a year, $520 less than the government recommended minimum for a family of five. Segregated swimming pools were common with Chicanos and Blacks allowed to swim only on Wednesday—the day the pool was drained and cleaned. Schools were segregated. Population statistics for Chicanos are unreliable, but it is estimated that in 1945, they comprised roughly 10 percent of the population of Los Angeles County. Fifty-six percent of the people who dwelt in substandard houses were Chicanos, and Mexican Town was located in the unincorporated section of the county. Streets of Mexican Town were unpaved, and many of the services, taken for granted in the city of Los Angeles, were denied to the Chicano community. Suffice it to say that social and economic discrimination against Chicanos was severe, since many Anglo-Americans believed that these foreigners were a burden to them.[116]

Many Chicano youth between the ages of 13 and 17 belonged to *barrio* clubs that carried the name of their *barrio* or neighborhoods—the White Fence Gang, Alpine Street, El Hoyo, Happy Valley. The fad among gang members, or *pachucos* as they were called, was to tattoo on the left hand just above the thumb a small cross with three dots or dashes above it. Many *pachucos*, when they dressed up, wore the so-called zoot suit that was so popular among low-income youths at that time. *Pachucos* spoke Spanish, but more frequently they used *Chuco* among their companions. *Chuco* was the *barrio* language, a mixture of Spanish, English, old Spanish, and words adapted by the border Mexicans. Many experts say that it originated among Chicanos around El Paso who brought it to Los Angeles in the 1930s. Many of these so-called gangs even affiliated with the YMCA.

Similar gangs existed among Anglo youths, but as the state of war intensified nativistic feelings, Anglos singled out the *pachucos*. Racial xenophobia heightened in what, at that time, was a racially and culturally homogeneous Los Angeles community. Very few Blacks lived in Los Angeles County. Los Angeles did not have the large ghettoes of European immigrants peculiar to eastern cities. Japanese-Americans had just been rounded up and sent to internment camps.[117] Chicanos became obvious scapegoats for nativists and racists. Angelenos read with interest accounts of the activities of the "foreign" gangs, the so-called Chicano hoodlums.

The Sleepy Lagoon case exemplified the attitudes of the early 1940s. Chicanos used to swim in a dirty gravel pit which they called "Sleepy Lagoon," named after a popular melody played by bandleader Harry James. Unable to go to the public pool, they romanticized the gravel pit. On the evening of August 1, 1942, members of the 38th Street Club were jumped by another gang. When they returned with their home boys, the rival gang was not there. Later they witnessed a party in progress at the Williams Ranch which was nearby. They crashed the party and a fight followed.[118]

The next morning José Díaz, an invited guest at the party, was found dead on a dirt road near the house. Díaz had no wounds and could have been killed by a hit-and-run driver, but authorities suspected that some members of the 38th Street Club had beaten him and the police immediately jailed the entire gang. Newspapers sensationalized the story. Police flagrantly violated the rights of the accused and authorities charged twenty-two of the 38th Street boys of criminal conspiracy. "According to the prosecution, every defendant, even if he had nothing whatsoever to do with the killing of Díaz, was chargeable with the death of Díaz, which according to the prosecution, occurred during the fight at the Williams Ranch."[119]

The Sleepy Lagoon defendants became the prototype of the Mexican hoodlum as portrayed in the press. A special committee of the grand jury, shortly after the death of José Díaz, accepted a report by Captain Ed Durán Ayres, head of the Foreign Relations Bureau of the Los Angeles Police Department which validated the gross violation of human rights suffered by the defendants. Although the report admitted that discrimination against Chicanos in employment, education, schooling, recreation, and labor unions existed, it concluded that Chicanos were inherently criminal and violent.[120] Ayres stated that Chicanos were Indians, that Indians were Orientals, and that Orientals had an utter disregard for life. Therefore, since Chicanos had this inborn characteristic they were violent. Furthermore, the Chicanos were cruel, for they descended from the Aztecs who allegedly sacrificed 30,000 victims a day! Ayres wrote that Indians considered leniency a sign of weakness, pointing to the Mexican government's treatment of the Indians, which he maintained was quick and severe. He advocated that all gang members be imprisoned and that all Chicano youths over the age of 18 be given the option of obtaining work or enlisting in the armed forces. Chicanos, according to Ayres, could not change their spots; they had an innate desire to use a knife and let blood, and this inborn cruelty was aggravated by liquor and jealousy.[121] The Ayres report represented official law enforcement views and it goes a long way in explaining the events around Sleepy Lagoon.

The Honorable Charles W. Fricke permitted numerous irregularities in the courtroom during the trial. Assistant District Attorney Clyde C. Shoemaker instructed jailers not to allow the defendants to cut their hair or change their clothes and marshalls herded them into the courtroom, so that they made a bad impression on the jury. The prosecution failed to prove that the 38th Street Club was a gang, that any criminal agreement or conspiracy existed, or that the accused had killed Díaz. In fact, witnesses testified that there had been considerable drinking at the party before the 38th Street people arrived. If the theory of conspiracy to commit a crime had been strictly pressed, logically the defendants would have received equal verdicts. However, on January 12, 1943, the court passed sentences which ranged from assault to first-degree murder.[122]

The Sleepy Lagoon Defense Committee was formed to protect the defendants' rights. It was chaired by Carey McWilliams, a noted journalist and lawyer. McWilliams and other members were harassed and red-baited by the press and by government agencies. The California Committee on Un-American Activities, headed by State Senator Jack Tenney, investigated the committee. The Tenney investigation charged that it was a Communist-front organization and that Carey McWilliams had "Communist leanings" because he opposed segregation and espoused the principle of miscegenation statutes.[123] Authorities, including the FBI, conducted heavy surveillance of the committee and support groups such as *El Congreso Nacional de los Pueblos de Habla Español* (the Spanish-Speaking Congress). The FBI considered it a Communist front, stating that it "opposed all types of discrimination against Mexicans."[124]

On October 4, 1944, the Second District Court of Appeals reversed the lower court in a unanimous decision stating that Judge

Fricke had conducted the trial in a biased manner, that he had violated the constitutional rights of the defendants, and that no evidence existed that linked the Chicanos with the death of José Díaz.

After the Sleepy Lagoon arrests Los Angeles police and the sheriff's office intensified their harassment of Chicano youths. They set up roadblocks and indiscriminately arrested large numbers of Chicanos on countless charges, most popular being suspicion of burglary. These arrests naturally made headlines, inflaming the public to the point that the Office of War Information became concerned over the media's sensationalism as well as its racism.

Large numbers of servicemen on furlough or on short-duration passes visited Los Angeles. Numerous training centers were located in the vicinity, and the glitter of Hollywood and its famous canteen attracted many servicemen. Sailors on shore leave from ships docked in San Pedro and San Diego came to Los Angeles looking for a good time. Most were young and anxious to prove their manhood. A visible "foe" was the "alien" Chicano, dressed in the outlandish zoot suit that everyone ridiculed. The sailors also looked for Mexican girls to pick up, associating the Chicanas with the prostitutes they had encountered in Tijuana. The sailors were loud, boisterous, and rude to the females in the Chicano community. This attitude was bound to cause problems. The sailors' conduct had caused animosity in San Diego as well, where Anglo-American townspeople were openly hostile to them.[125]

In the spring of 1943 several small altercations occurred in Los Angeles. In April marines and sailors in Oakland invaded the Chicano *barrio* and Black ghetto, assaulted the people, and "depantsed" zoot-suiters.

On May 8 a fight between sailors and Chicanos, many of whom belonged to the Alpine, broke out at the Aragon Ballroom in Venice, California, when some high school students told the sailors that *pachucos* had stabbed a sailor. Joined by other servicemen, sailors indiscriminately attacked Chicanos. The battle cry was; "Let's get 'em! Let's get the chili-eating bastards!" Twenty-five hundred spectators watched the assault on innocent Chicano youths; the police did virtually nothing to restrain the servicemen and they arrested the victims. They charged Chicanos with disturbing the peace. Although Judge Arthur Guerin dismissed the charges for want of sufficient evidence, he warned the youths "that their antics might get them into serious difficulties unless they changed their attitudes." The press continued to sensationalize the theme of "zoot-suit equals hoodlum."[126]

The sparks that ignited the "sailors riots" against the Chicano community were lit on June 3, 1943. Allegedly, a group of sailors had been attacked by Chicanos when they attempted to pick up some Chicanas. The details are vague; the police allegedly did not attempt to get the Chicano side of the story, but took the sailors' report at face value. Fourteen off-duty policemen, led by a detective lieutenant, went looking for the "criminals." They found nothing, but they did get considerable publicity.

That same night, sailors went on a rampage; they broke into the Carmen Theatre, tore zoot suits off Chicanos, and beat the youths. As a result, many Chicanos were arrested, while sailors were not charged. Word spread that *Pachucos* were fair game and that they could be attacked without fear of arrest.[127]

Sailors returned the next evening with some 200 allies. In twenty hired cabs they cruised Whittier Boulevard in the heart of the East Los Angeles *barrio*, jumping out of the cars to gang up on neighborhood youths. Police and sheriff maintained that they could not establish contact with the sailors. They finally did arrest nine sailors, but released them immediately without filing charges. The press portrayed the sailors as heroes. Articles and headlines were designed to exploit racial hatred.[128]

Sailors, encouraged by the press and the applause of the "responsible" elements of Los Angeles, gathered on the night of June 5 and marched four abreast down the streets, warning Chicanos to shed their zoot suits or they would take them off for them. On that night and the next servicemen invaded bars and other establishments and victimized Chicanos, and police continued to abet the lawlessness. Police arrived only after damage had been done and the servicemen had escaped. Even though sailors had destroyed private property, law enforcement officials still refused to act. When the Chicano community prepared to defend itself, police arrested them.[129]

Events climaxed on the evening of June 7, when thousands of servicemen and civilians surged down Main Street and Broadway in search of *pachucos*. The mob crashed into bars and broke the legs off stools using them as clubs. The press inflamed the *gringo* mob with reports that 500 "zoot suiters" assembled for battle. By this time Filipinos and Blacks also became targets. Chicanos had their clothes ripped off, and the youths were left bleeding in the streets. The mob surged into movie theatres, where they turned on the lights, marched down the aisles, and pulled zoot-suit-clad youngsters out of their seats. Seventeen-year-old Enrico Herrera, after he was beaten and arrested, spent three hours at a police station, where he was found by his mother, still naked and bleeding. A 12-year-old boy's jaw was broken. Police arrested over 600 Chicano youths without cause and labeled the arrests "preventive" action. Angelenos cheered on the servicemen and their civilian allies.[130]

Panic gripped the Chicano community. At the height of the turmoil servicemen pulled a Black off a streetcar and gouged out his eye with a knife. Military authorities, realizing that the Los

Angeles law enforcement agencies would not do anything to curtail the lawlessness, intervened and declared downtown Los Angeles off limits for military personnel. Classified naval documents confirm that the navy believed it had a mutiny on its hands. Documents leave no doubt that military shore patrols quelled the riot, accomplishing what the Los Angeles police could or would not do.[131]

For the next few days police harassed Chicano youth and ordered mass arrests, even raiding a Catholic welfare center to arrest some of its occupants.[132] The press and city officials inflamed the mob. An editorial by Manchester Boddy on June 9 in the *Los Angeles Daily News* (supposedly the city's liberal newspaper) stated:

> The time for temporizing is past. . . . The time has come to serve notice that the City of Los Angeles will no longer be terrorized by a relatively small handful of morons parading as zoot-suit hoodlums. To delay action now means to court disaster later on.[133]

Boddy's statement taken alone would not mean much; it could be considered to be just one man's opinion. But consider that before the naval invasion of East Los Angeles the following headlines had appeared in the *Times:*

> November 2, 1942: "Ten Seized in Drive on Zoot-Suit Gangsters"
> February 23, 1943: "One Slain and Another Knifed in 'Zoot' Fracas"
> March 7, 1943: "Magistrate 'Unfrocks' Pair of Zoot-Suiters"
> May 25, 1943: "Four Zoot-Suit Gangs Beat Up Their Victims"
> June 1, 1943: "Attacks by Orange County Zoot-Suiters Injure Five"

During the assault marauders were encouraged by headlines in the *Los Angeles Daily News,* such as "Zoot Suit Chiefs Girding for War on Navy," and in the *Los Angeles Times,* such as "Zoot Suiters Learn Lesson in Fight with Servicemen." Three other major newspapers featured similar headlines which created an atmosphere of zoot-suit violence. The radio also contributed to the hysteria.

Rear Admiral D. W. Bagley, commanding officer of the naval district, took the public position that the sailors acted in "self-defense against the rowdy element." Privately Bagley ordered his commanders to order their men to stop the raids and then conducted a low profile cover-up. Sailors were, however, not the only vandals. Army personnel often outnumbered sailors. According to Commander Fogg, on June 8, 1943, hundreds of servicemen were "prowling downtown Los Angeles mostly on foot—disorderly— apparently on the prowl for Mexicans." By June 11, 1943, in a restricted memo, the navy and army recognized that the rioting resulted from "mob action. It is obvious that many soldiers are not aware of the serious nature of riot charges, which could carry the death sentence or a long prison term."[134]

On June 16 an item appeared in the *Los Angeles Times* from Mexico City, headlined: "Mexican Government Expects Damages for Zoot Suit Riot Victims." The article stated that "the Mexican government took a mildly firm stand on the rights of its nationals, emphasizing its conviction that American justice would grant 'innocent victims' their proper retribution." Federal authorities expressed concern and Mayor Fletcher Bowron assured Washington, D.C., that there was no racism involved. Soon afterwards Bowron ordered the Los Angeles police to stop using "cream-puff techniques." At the same time he ordered the formation of a committee to "study the problem." City officials and the Los Angeles press became exceedingly touchy about charges of racism. When Eleanor Roosevelt commented in her column that the riots had been caused by "longstanding discrimination against the Mexicans in the Southwest," on June 18 the *Los Angeles Times* reacted with the headline "Mrs. Roosevelt Blindly Stirs Race Discord." The article denied that racial discrimination had been a factor in the riots and charged that Mrs. Roosevelt's statement resembled propaganda used by the communists, stating that servicemen had looked for "costumes and not races." The article said that Angelenos were proud of their missions and of Olvera Street, "a bit of old Mexico," and concluded "We like Mexicans and think they like us."[135]

Governor Earl Warren formed a committee to investigate the riots. Participating on the committee were Attorney General Robert W. Kenny; Catholic Bishop Joseph T. McGucken, who served as chairman; Walter A. Gordon, Berkeley attorney; Leo Carrillo, screen actor; Karl Holton, director of the California Youth Authority.[136]

The committee issued a report that recommended punishment of all persons responsible for the riots—military and civilian alike. It took a left-handed slap at the press, recommending that newspapers minimize the use of names and photos of juveniles. Moreover, it called for a better educated and trained police department to work with Spanish-speaking youth.[137]

Little was done to implement the recommendations of the report, and most of the same conditions exist today in Los Angeles city and county. "The kid gloves are off!" approach of Sheriff Eugene Biscailuz has, if anything, hardened since the 1940s.

THE NEW ACTIVISM:
POLITICAL ACTIVISM AT THE GRASS-ROOTS LEVEL

After World War II Anglo-American society experienced unprecedented technological and social changes. The war brought changes within the Chicano community as well. Many for the first time perceived the contradictions in American democracy and, in view of the fact that they had just fought a war against Hitler's theories of Aryan supremacy, racism at home was even more intolerable than in the 1930s. Increasingly, Chicanos realized that they were entitled to full protection under the law and they wanted more out of life.

The battle fronts were fair employment, equal education, equal access to public facilities and full participation within the governance process. Past grievances did not disappear and police repression continued. Chicanos had an advantage over the past. Their population had become increasingly visible and their population had stabilized, with the overwhelming majority living in cities. The Chicanos sued to gain their rights and their organizations became more aggressive with their tactics becoming more mainstream American.

During and after the war it was common for Chicano servicemen not to be served in restaurants. In fact de facto exclusion of Mexicans from public facilities, schools, trade unions, juries, and voting remained the rule in many sections of the country. On May 20, 1946, the Chamber of Commerce of Tempe, Arizona, voted to admit Chicanos to the city swimming pool in response to pressure from a Chicano war veterans' group. Chicanos comprised 15 percent of the city. The First Regional Conference on Education of the Spanish-Speaking People in the Southwest took place at the University of Texas at Austin on December 13–15, 1945. George I. Sánchez of the University of Texas and A. L. Campa of the University of New Mexico took an active part in the proceedings. The conference condemned segregation.[138]

In 1946 Judge Paul J. McCormick in the U.S. District Court in southern California heard the *Méndez* v. *Westminister School District Case* and declared the segregation of Mexican children unconstitutional. On April 14, 1947, the Ninth U.S. Circuit Court of Appeals affirmed the decision stating that Mexicans and other children were entitled to "the equal protection of the laws," and that neither language nor race could be used as a reason to segregate them. On June 15, 1948, Judge Ben H. Rice, Jr., U.S. District Court, Western District of Texas, found in the *Delgado v. The Bastrop Independent School District* that the Mexican childrens' rights under the Fourteenth Amendment had been violated. These two cases set precedents for the historic *Brown* case in 1954.[139]

Attorney Gus C. García and Dr. George I. Sánchez led the fight against segregation. Both of these men participated in numerous cases against gerrymandering, homogeneous groupings, and other tactics used to segregate Mexicans. Chicanos once again demanded their rights. Ignacio López founded civic unity leagues in the small towns south of the big *barrio* of East Los Angeles—in the Chino, Ontario, and Pomona areas. During the war López headed the

Spanish department in the Office of Foreign Languages, Division of War Information, in Washington, D.C. and was the Spanish-speaking director of the Office of Coordinator of Inter-American Affairs in Los Angeles. His job was to get ethnic groups to support the war effort. In the East he organized European minorities into groups called liberty leagues, and on his return to Los Angeles he organized civic leagues among the Chicanos. Fred Ross from the American Council on Race Relations joined him. The leagues focused on the problems of poor Chicanos and stressed ethnic unity. The leagues did not promote radical revolution or confrontation politics, but appealed to the conscience and goodwill of the majority. They emphasized mass action, bloc voting and neighborhood protests. Organizers held meetings in homes, churches, and public buildings.[140]

The unity leagues differed from previous Chicano organizations in that they were not formed to meet the needs of the middle class nor were they trade unionist in orientation. Organizers designed them to stimulate political action among the grass-roots Chicanos. In Chino, California, for instance, the league elected Andrew Morales to the city council. They conducted intensive voter registration drives. Their tactics were to wait for the establishment to make a mistake, allow this mistake to precipitate a crisis, and then organize around the issue. They established unity leagues in San Bernardino and Riverside, California, where school discrimination became a prime issue.

The leagues in turn influenced the Industrial Areas Foundation (IAF) of the Back of the Yards area in South Chicago in the late 1940s. The IAF planned to work with Mexicans in Los Angeles. A group known as the Community Political Organization (CPO) formed in East Los Angeles at about the same time. Not wanting to be confused with the Communist party (CP) or partisan politics, it changed its name in 1947 to the Community Service Organization (CSO). The CSO evolved from Chicano steelworkers and the volunteers in Edward Roybal's unsuccessful bid for a Los Angeles city council seat in 1947. The IAF moved to Los Angeles and merged efforts with the CSO.[141]

These groups held open forums to discuss community problems, attracting many workingmen to their meetings. Fred Ross influenced the direction of the CSO, drawing on his experience with the civic unity leagues. Although the CSO was not political, it registered 12,000 new voters. This increase in registered Chicano voters helped elect Edward Roybal to the Los Angeles City Council in 1949—the first person of Mexican descent to serve on that body since 1881.

After Roybal's victory the CSO did not support another candidate for office. It concentrated on fighting housing discrimination, police brutality, and school segregation. In 1950 the CSO fielded

112 volunteer deputy registrars and within three months registered 32,000 new Latino voters. Voter registration was hazardous; many volunteers were harassed. The CSO gradually changed into a grass-roots "politically powerful organization that emphasized direct, mass action."[142]

The American GI Forum, founded in Corpus Christi, Texas, in 1948 by World War II veterans, fought discrimination. Upon returning from the war, Chicano GIs from Texas found that most Anglo-Americans there still considered them "greasers." Discrimination in housing, education, and employment was common and even veterans' organizations excluded Chicanos. When local authorities at Three Rivers, Texas refused to bury Félix Longoria, a Chicano war hero, and his body had to be taken outside his home state to Arlington Cemetery, Chicano veterans vowed that this would never happen again, and they organized under the leadership of Dr. Hector García. By the end of 1949 over 100 American GI Forum chapters had been organized. Eventually, forums spread to 23 states and had a total membership of over 20,000.[143] This nonpartisan organization promoted political and social reform. The key to the forums' success was the inclusion of the entire family through participation in ladies' auxiliaries and junior forums, although criticism has recently surfaced over the absence of women voting members.

Aside from education, politics, and discrimination, police brutality cases were of major importance to Chicano organizations. For instance, in September 1947 Bruno Cano, a member of the United Furniture Workers of America Local 576, was brutally beaten by Los Angeles police in East Los Angeles. Cano had attempted to stop police from assaulting three Mexican youths at a tavern. The United Furniture Workers of America Local 576, the Civil Rights Congress, and the American Veterans' Committee (Belvedere Chapter) protested Cano's beating. One of the officers, William Keyes, had a history of brutality; in 1947 he shot two Mexicans in the back. Nothing happened to Keyes in either those shootings or Cano's beating.

On March 10, 1948, Keyes struck again; the victim was 19-year-old Agustino Salcido. The victim had been drinking at a local bar where Keyes and his partner E. R. Sánchez, in plain clothes, were also drinking. Salcido knew Sánchez. According to Keyes and Sánchez, Salcido offered to sell them stolen watches. The officers arrested Salcido, but instead of taking him to the police station or to their car, they escorted him to "an empty, locked building" where they shot him. Salcido had only one watch on him which he had purchased that afternoon. At the coroner's inquest Keyes stated that the unarmed Salcido attempted to escape during interrogation. Witnesses contradicted Keyes, but the inquest exonerated him.[144]

After the inquest the Los Angeles police terrorized witnesses—jailing, beating, and running them out of town. On March

12 the Los Angeles CIO Council adopted a resolution calling for the prosecution of Keyes. On April 1 the CIO and community organizations held a "people's trial" attended by nearly 600 Chicanos.[145]

Leo Gallagher, attorney for the Civil Rights Congress, Oscar Castro, business agent for Local 576, and Ben Rinaldo, American Veterans' Committee, played leading roles. Keyes was found guilty. Several days later Guillermo Gallegos, who had witnessed the murder, signed a manslaughter complaint against Keyes. The district attorney had refused to prosecute Keyes. Judge Stanley Moffatt courageously accepted Gallego's complaint. Police retaliated by arresting Gallegos for "possession of marijuana." Officer Marvin Jacobsen of narcotics at one point in the interrogation asked Gallegos, "Who's behind all this?" and told him to run. In terror Gallegos responded, "For Christ's sake, don't shoot me through the back."[146]

At the preliminary trial defense attorney Joseph Scott red-baited Judge Moffat and the witnesses and attacked Leo Gallagher who appeared as a friend of the court, as a radical. Moffat found sufficient evidence to try Keyes and asked for a grand jury investigation as to why Keyes had not been prosecuted. The next day the *Hollywood Citizen-News* red-baited Moffat for running for Congress on the Henry Wallace ticket and for his role in the Keyes trial. The *Los Angeles Times* also denounced Moffat, asking for vigilante action against him. The Committee for Justice for Salcido was subjected to intense harassment. Meanwhile, the jury in the Gallegos trial ended deadlocked, seven for acquittal and five for conviction.[147]

Judge C. C. McDonald presided at Keyes's trial. The facts did not matter, for Keyes had waived a jury trial and McDonald was known as a law and order man. Although Scott did not rebut the evidence, and the prosecution proved that Keyes and Sánchez pumped bullets into Salcido, McDonald acquitted Keyes on the grounds that no evidence had been presented that the gun examined by the Police Scientific Investigation Bureau belonged to Keyes and that Gallegos had seen him fire only the last shot, which the court presumed was not the fatal shot. The prosecution, which had not wanted to prosecute in the first place, made mistakes as to the rules of evidence. Therefore Keyes was released on a technicality.[148]

OPTIMISTS IN A SEA OF APATHY

The Chicano population increased considerably in the 1950s. California's Mexican population almost doubled; Texas's Mexican population continued to grow and to migrate to other sections of the Southwest and to the Midwest. Hysteria and repression spread by

McCarthyism had a heavy impact on the community. The Korean War saw large numbers of Chicanos enter the armed forces. Chicanos, like other U.S. citizens, experienced the artificial prosperity of the first years of the decade and the recession after the Korean War in 1953.

The Chicano population benefited little from the nascent civil rights movement of the 1950s. The *Brown* decision of 1954 had no effect on schooling for Mexican-Americans. Not until the *Cisneros* case in 1970 did "a Federal district court. . . . [rule] that Mexican Americans constitute an identifiable ethnic minority with a past pattern of discrimination in Corpus Christi, Texas."[149] Authorities in fact took a stiffer stance toward Mexicans and it was not until the 1970s that the courts declared: "We see no reason to believe that ethnic segregation is no less detrimental than racial segregation."[150] In the *Keyes* case of 1973 the U.S. Supreme Court held that "negroes and Hispanos in Denver suffer identical discrimination in treatment when compared with the treatment afforded Anglo students."[151]

In the latter part of the 1940s, many Chicanos demanded that they be classified as caucasian on public records; they believed that they would then be treated as equals. The classification changed, but their status did not. Government bureaus continued to view them as the "Mexican problem"; the Los Angeles Police Department continued until 1950 to categorize Mexicans along with Indians as the red race.[152]

The GI Forum and other Chicano organizations fought segregation, filing cases against several school districts in Texas.[153] Victimized by separate and unequal schools, Chicanos in Texas applauded the *Brown* case and in larger numbers than Blacks or Whites approved of integration. A 1954 poll showed:

QUESTION	NEGROS	LATINS	OTHERS WHITES
Disobey the law	18%	11%	21%
Get around the law	10	8	31
Mix races gradually	22	30	31
Let all go to same schools now	40	47	11
No opinion	10	4	6

SOURCE: "Mexican-Americans Favor Negro School Integration," *G.I. Forum News Bulletin,* September-October, 1955.

Seventy-seven percent of all Mexicans surveyed supported immediate or gradual integration of Blacks versus 62 percent of the Blacks themselves. The Chicanos' own struggle for equal education conditioned their opinion.

In April 1955 suits were filed against the schools of Carrizo Springs and Kingsville. In Kingsville, Austin Elementary had been segregated since 1914 and was known as the "Mexican Ward School" with a 100 percent Chicano school population. Of the thirty-one Chicano teachers all but four taught in a 100 percent Mexican school.[154]

The GI Forum took a leading role in the prosecution of police brutality cases. In Mercedes, Texas, it brought enough pressure on June 20, 1953, to force the resignation of Darrill F. Holmes who intimidated George Saenz and his wife at their grocery store. As the result of police abuse Saenz had to be treated for a nervous condition. The Forum was also involved in the Jesse Ledesma case. On the afternoon of June 22, 1953, Austin police officer Bill Crow stopped Ledesma who suffered from insulin shock. Crow claimed Ledesma looked drunk and beat him up, inflicting a one-inch cut on the right side of his head and bruises on his legs, back and shoulders.[155]

On September 16, 1953, in Fort Worth, Officer Vernon Johnson shot Ernest L. García in the chest while delivering a court order for custody of a child. Johnson threatened members of the García family when they asked him if he had a warrant; the officer pulled a gun and pressed it against García's chest. Johnson claimed that he shot because he was afraid that the García family would mob him. The Forum lawyers handled the case and Johnson was indicted for aggravated assault.[156]

On May 3, 1954, the U.S. Supreme Court in a unanimous decision banned discrimination in juries. Peter Hernández had been found guilty of the murder of Joe Espinosa by an all-white jury in Edna, Texas. The jury sentenced him to life. This case was turned down by the Court of Criminal Appeals because, according to the court, Mexicans were white and therefore could not be treated as a class apart. Hernández appealed and the U.S. Supreme court found that for twenty-five years Mexicans had been treated as a class apart and that out of 6,000 citizens considered for jury duty a Mexican had never been selected. Peter Hernández was tried again; he pleaded guilty and was sentenced to twenty years.[157]

By the 1950s small changes had taken place. City councils in South Texas made slight improvements in "water, drainage, lights, and pavement."[158]

Chicano organizations brought about limited reforms. In Texas and elsewhere groups like the Forum and LULAC sensitized membership to the importance of organization and established nationwide networks which kindled a spirit of unity and nationalism. However, divisions prevented Chicanos from taking a unified stand. Members often became so loyal to their group that organizations such as LULAC and the GI Forum competed with one another instead of pursuing their common goals. The older organizations often opposed new organizations, such as PASSO, charging that the new group was too radical or not Chicano enough.[159]

Conditions created situations where certain individuals made outstanding contributions. Molly C. Galván, for instance, forged a position of leadership within the male dominated GI Forum. While others worked through the ladies' auxiliary, she functioned at a leadership level. Miss Galván, from Colorado Springs, at first worked as corresponding secretary. She then traveled to Utah where she organized a Forum chapter and a ladies' auxiliary in Ogden and a chapter in Salt Lake City. She returned on Forum business to Colorado occasionally. In October 1956 Galván was appointed national organizer for the Forum.

In 1957 she won a scholarship to the Fourteenth Annual Institute on Race Relations at Fisk University in Nashville, Tennessee. The institute trained minority leaders in problems, processes, and methods of achieving better group relations. Technique and strategies were emphasized. After this Miss Galván traveled to Texas and Wyoming conducting seminars in race relations. In Corpus Christi in August 1958 she succinctly stated her philosophy: "recognize the problems, accept them at their face value, discuss the solution and then act." Galván continued to travel the western states organizing for the Forum. In 1959 she left for Spain where she worked as a civilian for the U.S. Air Force.[160]

In the 1950s Los Angeles grew; Chicano life there mirrored experiences of Chicanos in other urban centers. Police established a pattern of repression. For the most part, as in cases such as the Salcido murder, officials gave officers *carte blanche*. In the "Bloody Christmas" case eight Los Angeles police on December 24, 1951, took seven young Chicanos out of their cells at the Lincoln Heights jail and brutally beat them. Danny Rodella, one of the prisoners, was sent to Los Angeles County General Hospital. Public outcry from the white, Black, and brown communities forced the courts to act and some of the officers were indicted and jailed.[161]

In February 1950 Los Angeles county sheriffs raided a baby shower at the home of Mrs. Natalia Gonzales. Sheriffs had given occupants three minutes to evacuate the premise. They arrested some fifty guests for charges ranging from disturbing the peace to resisting arrest. The Maravilla Chapter of the *Asociación Nacional México-Americana* petitioned the county supervisors, but were denied this right. Lieutenant Fimbres of the foreign relations bureau of the sheriff's department whitewashed the sheriffs. Virginia Ruiz and ANMA formed the Maravilla Defense Committee.[162]

On May 26, 1951, police raided a baptismal party at the home of Simon Fuentes. Officers received a call that the record player was too loud. They broke into the house without a warrant and assaulted the guests. A woman, eight months pregnant, and a handicapped man were thrown to the floor. Police broke Frank Rodríguez's leg when he went to the aid of the handicapped man. ANMA took an active role in this case.[163]

The CSO along with the American Civil Liberties Union took an active role in police brutality cases in East Los Angeles. Chicano activist Ralph Guzmán wrote in the *Eastside Sun* on September 24, 1953, "It is no secret that for years law and order in the Eastside of Los Angeles County has been maintained through fear and brutal treatment." Los Angeles newspapers whipped up hysteria against Mexicans. The 1953 recession further agitated nativist sentiments.[164]

Ralph Guzmán, in the *Eastside Sun*, on January 7, 1954, wrote, "It is becoming more and more difficult to walk through the streets of Los Angeles—and look Mexican!" On January 14, 1954, he wrote, "Basically, Eugene Biscailuz's idea to curb kid gangs is the evening roundup, a well known western drive." Guzmán then vehemently castigated the Los Angeles press for its irresponsibility. On May 8, 1953, Los Angeles deputy sheriffs Lester Moll and Kenneth Stiler beat David Hidalgo, age 15, while other deputies looked on as Hidalgo pleaded for mercy. Hidalgo's stepfather, Manuel Domínguez, pressed a civil suit against the Los Angeles county sheriff's department. The *Alianza Hispano-Americana* sponsored the case against the officers.[165]

Domínguez received a judgment two years later against the two deputy sheriffs with an award for damages of $1,000. In spite of the low award, the case represented an important victory since it was one of the first cases in which a Chicano won a civil action for damages against a law enforcement officer.

The *Alianza* handled the appeals in the murder and conspiracy conviction of Manuel Mata, Robert Márquez, and Ricardo Venegas. The three men were convicted of murdering William D. Cluff in a fight at Seventh and Broadway in Los Angeles on December 6, 1953. Cluff had intervened in a fight involving the three defendants and a marine, John W. Moore. Cluff died. The defense introduced expert medical testimony that Cluff had died of an enlarged heart, advanced arteriosclerosis of cerebral blood vessels, and arterial heart disease, and not of injuries inflicted during the fight. Los Angeles newspapers had inflamed public opinion and the three were convicted. After a series of appeals the defendants got a new trial.[166]

From about 1947 to the mid-1950s Los Angeles Chicanos were influenced by the Independent Progressive Party (IPP). By the late 1940s Mexicans had replaced the Jewish community in Boyle Heights. However, a small nucleus of the more progressive Jews either continued to live or function within the eastside community. Many of them gravitated to the Progressive Citizens of America which formed the core of the IPP which bolted the Democratic party in 1948 and ran Henry Wallace as a third party candidate. Progressive Latinos such as Richard Ibañez participated in these organizations and Ibañez was active in the IPP's functions. Unlike the Democratic party, the IPP supported Chicano candidates.[167]

The *Asociación Nacional México-Americana* had been founded in May 1949 in Grant County, New Mexico was closely associated with the IPP. Alfredo Montoya, a trade union organizer with the Mine, Mill and Smelters union, was its driving force. ANMA aggressively advocated human rights and had CIO backing. It launched its national organization in Albuquerque on August 14, 1949.

ANMA encouraged Mexicans to join unions. This national organization conducted drives outside the Southwest, in cities such as Chicago, Detroit, and other industrial centers. It sought links with the Puerto Rican colony. From the beginning the Catholic clergy labeled it communist and interfered with its campaigns.[168]

The IPP and ANMA were linked by an interlocking of membership and by issues. For instance, Virginia Ruiz, the national secretary of ANMA, became a delegate to the IPP convention in Chicago in 1950. The IPP supported Mexican candidates, such as Arthur O. Casas for assembly and Richard Ibañez for the superior court. Both ANMA and the IPP called for a cessation of hostilities in Korea.[169] The two groups also shared the harassment of reactionary elements in government.

Through 1952 ANMA was heavily involved with trade unions, and in the summer of that year Alfredo Montoya moved the national headquarters to Denver. By 1954 it made the U.S. attorney general's subversive list and even Chicano organizations red-baited it. Intense harassment undermined the organization and it faded away. The IPP also faded away and its members reverted to the Democratic party. Many Chicano activists joined the American Council of Spanish-Speaking People which held its founding convention at El Paso on May 18-19, 1951. Dr. George I. Sánchez called the convention. The *Alianza*, CSO, LULAC, the Texan GI Forum, and the Community Service Club of Colorado comprised the core group. Chicano leaders such as Gus García, Tony Ríos, Ignacio López, José Estrada, and Senator Dennis Chávez, Jr., of New Mexico attended the convention.[170]

Tibo J. Chávez, the lieutenant governor of New Mexico, was elected president of the council, and Dr. Sánchez served as its executive director. In 1952 the organization received a grant to be used to promote the civil rights of Chicanos from the Robert Marshall Foundation.[171]

The council worked closely with the *Alianza Hispano-Americana* in desegregation cases. In 1952, for instance, challenges were made in Glendale, Douglas, Miami, and Winslow, Arizona. In the case against Glendale and the Arizona Board of Education, they challenged segregation wherever it existed in Arizona. The Glendale board refused to go to court and be forced to integrate.[172]

In 1954 the *Alianza* initiated a suit against Winslow, Arizona, to open its swimming pool to Mexicans. Winslow officials settled the suit out of court. In 1955 the *Alianza* established a civil rights department and named Ralph Guzmán its director. In a desegregation case in El Centro, California, it cooperated with the National Association for the Advancement of Colored People. Black teachers were assigned to the two elementary schools which were predominately Mexican and Black. El Centro had avoided desegregation by allowing white students to transfer to an adjoining district which was overcrowded. A federal judge ruled that the plaintiffs must exhaust state courts before a federal court could hear the case, but the Ninth Circuit Court of Appeals reversed this decision and decided that El Centro practiced segregation of students and staff. This cooperation between the *Alianza* and the NAACP was significant since the *Alianza* itself had excluded Blacks. It indicated a change within the most traditional and nationalistic of Chicano groups.[173]

During the 1950s, urban *removal* continued to menace Chicanos. Los Angeles was the prototype, but other cities mirrored its experiences. In Los Angeles the eastside *barrio* came under attack by urban land grabbers engaged in freeway building, business enterprises, and urban renewal. Like poor people throughout the United States, they had settled in the older sections near the center of town. When plans for freeways were proposed, these sections were considered expendable. Government used the power of eminent domain to remove Chicanos so money interests could reap large profits. In the fall of 1953 the Mexican area was scarred by the San Bernardino, Santa Ana, and Long Beach freeways, and Chicanos protested the building of still another freeway through East Los Angeles. Unlike the residents of Beverly Hills, Chicanos were not able to stop the bulldozers; the $32 million Golden State wiped out another sector of the Mexican area. In 1957 the Pomona Freeway displaced thousands of Chicanos in the Hollenbeck area. The history of freeways through Los Angeles is one of plunder, fraud, and utter disregard for the lives and welfare of people. Land developers knew just where the routes were planned; the property of powerful corporate interests, such as the large Sears, Roebuck store and the *Los Angeles Times* facilities, was conveniently missed. Developers and politicians made millions.

In October 1957 the city removed Mexican homeowners from Chávez Ravine, near the center of Los Angeles, and gave over 300 acres of private land to Walter O'Malley, owner of the Dodgers baseball team. The Dodgers deal angered many people; many residents of Chávez Ravine resisted physically. In 1959 the county sheriff's department moved in and removed the Arechiga family. Councilman Ed Roybal condemned the action: "The eviction is the kind of thing you might expect in Nazi Germany or during the Spanish Inquisition." Supporters of the Arechigas protested to the city council. Victoria Augustian, a witness, pointed a finger at coun-

cil member Rosalind Wyman, who with Mayor Norris Poulson supported the giveaway. Poulson was a puppet of the Chandler family,
who owned the *Los Angeles Times*, which backed the giveaway.
During these years the Chicano community in central Los Angeles
was in effect under invasion. If the freeways and the giveaway were
not enough, other business interests actively grabbed land. For
instance, in 1958 a group under Dr. Leland J. Fuller proposed a $20
million medical and shopping area in the Boyle Heights district in
East Los Angeles. He called Boyle Heights a blighted area and
claimed that the renewal program would provide jobs, raise the
standard of living, and provide better housing. Fuller headed a
dummy group called the Boyle Heights Urban Renewal Committee
which released publicity showing the advantages of the move, and
sent out notices attempting to panic the people into selling. While
Fuller disclaimed association with the White Memorial Medical
Center, the list of associates of the center clearly linked him to it.[174]

Joseph Eli Kovner, publisher and editor of the *Eastside Sun*,
uncovered connections between the mayor's office, capitalist interests in Los Angeles, and urban renewal proposals in Watts,
Pacoima, Canoga Park, Bunker Hill, and Boyle Heights. (Watts is a
Black community and the other four predominantly Mexican.) Kovner cited a memo from the Sears Corporation to its executives,
instructing them to support urban renewal since the company had
an economic interest in protecting its investment. The presence of
too many minorities in an area depressed land values and discouraged the trade of white, middle-class customers. Urban renewal
insured construction of business sites and higher rent apartments
which inflated property values.[175]

Kovner, on July 24, 1958, in an *Eastside Sun* editorial, questioned the motives of Sears in sending out a survey letter to the
public. He charged that it paved the way for urban renewal by
scaring residents into selling and conditioning the results. Kovner
asked why Sears had never complained about the liquor stores and
bars in the Boyle Heights area. On July 31, 1958, the *Eastside Sun*
exposed the Boyle Heights Urban Renewal Committee plot to remove 480 homes north of Brooklyn between McDonnell and Med-
nick and to disperse over 4,000 people. Los Angeles county supervisor approval would be sought.

Actions of the neo-robber barons became so outlandish that De
Witt McCann, an aide to Mayor Poulson's Urban Renewal Committee, resigned, stating, "I don't want to be responsible for taking one
man's private property through the use of eminent domain and
giving it over to another private individual for his private gain."
Poulson and his associates displaced thousands of poor white senior citizens and Mexicans in Bunker Hill and turned over prime
land in the downtown section of the city to private developers.
Citizens of Bunker Hill lost their battle, but progressives derailed

the scheme which eventually would have handed all of Boyle Heights, City Terrace, and Belvedere to private developers. Mayor Norris Poulson, responded to the critics of urban renewal: "If you are not prepared to be part of this greatness, if you want Los Angeles to revert to pueblo status . . . then my best advice to you is to prepare to resettle elsewhere."[176]

City officials and especially the mayor were guilty of criminal negligence. The Los Angeles Community Redevelopment Administration's board of directors ordered Gilbert Morris, superintendent of building and safety, not to enforce safety regulations in the Bunker Hill area. Improvements would raise the value of property and the officials wanted to keep costs down. Poulson also instructed the commissioner of the Board of Building and Safety not to issue building permits. Consequently, buildings deteriorated. The inevitable occurred when a four-story apartment building collapsed; firemen saved the 200 occupants. Councilman Ed Roybal accused Poulson of playing politics with human lives.[177]

In 1959 activists backed the incorporation of East Los Angeles. Downey and the city of Commerce (which was not even a city yet) began to annex choice East Los Angeles which could have provided a tax base for an incorporated East Los Angeles.[178] This signaled the intensification of a struggle to maintain the territorial integrity of East Los Angeles that is still going on.

A handful of activists struggled for changes. Hank López unsuccessfully ran for California secretary of state. The Chicano community in 1958 prodded Governor Goodwin Knight into appointing Carlos Terán to a judgeship.[179] In 1958 Ed Roybal ran for the Los Angeles Board of Supervisors. After four recounts and evidence of voter intimidation, the election was stolen from him.[180] A year later, Lucy Baca unsuccessfully ran for the Los Angeles Board of Education.[181] That same year California established a Fair Employment Practices Commission, but the "liberal" Democratic Governor Pat Brown did not appoint a single Mexican to it.[182]

In the midwestern industrial cities, such as St. Paul, Chicago, Milwaukee, Detroit, Saginaw, Flint, Toledo, and East Lansing, the Chicano population became more aggressive. Chicago remained the largest Chicano city in the Midwest. In 1950 the census counted 24,000, but most conceded that this was a dramatic undercount, and the population surged during the 1950s.[183]

Urban renewal threatened the Chicago Chicano community. In 1947 the Chicago Land Commission was organized to supervise slum clearance and urban "removal." The flight of white families and industries to the suburbs had begun and was reflected in a loss of city jobs which greatly affected Chicanos.

Chicanos formed identifiable *barrios* in the Pilsen district and South Chicago. During this period the Chicago Democratic machine paid more attention to Chicanos. By the late 1950s, the

Puerto Rican population had grown sufficiently in the Midwest so that the two groups often competed for available resources.

In recognition of the growing importance of the Mexican community in Illinois, the Illinois Federation of Mexican-Americans (ILFOMA) was organized with the aid of state funds. In 1950 the Mexican American Council was organized to integrate Mexican residents into community life.

In 1951 the Mexican-American Council proved that Chicago policeman Michael Moretti had without provocation fatally shot two Chicanos and wounded another. Moretti, as a result of the council's work, was fired, charged with manslaughter, and jailed.

The Mexican-American Council began to lose support when a division occurred between its members and newer Mexican immigrants. Allegedly, Martín Ortiz, the council's chairman, had referred to himself as a representative spokesman of the "community." Salvador Herrera, president of the newly formed *El Comité Patriótico Mexicano* denounced Ortiz and stated emphatically that he did not represent the entire community. He threatened legal action against the council. José Chapa, a popular Chicago radio personality, also criticized Ortiz. The heavy flow of immigrants from Mexico and Texas to Chicago muted the assimilationist point of view and revitalized nationalism.

CONCLUSION

Throughout the nation there seemed to be no direction to the Chicanos' activism, and, in fact, after the Korean War the mood of most Anglo-Americans and minorities was apathetic. Capitalist interests kept the numerous Chicano communities in a state of siege. Many were intimidated by police authorities. Activists, frustrated over the lack of mass response in the face of blatant abuse, thought that it was hopeless and that the people did not have the energy to mobilize themselves. The 1960s proved them wrong.

NOTES

1. "Another Fight in Texas," *New York Times*, January 4, 1892; M. Romero, "The Garza Raid and Its Lessons," *North American Review* (Spring 1892): 327.
2. Romero, p. 324; "Mexico Wants Benavides Very Much," *New York Times*, February 23, 1893; "Benavides Said to Be an American," *New York Times*, February 28, 1893.
3. "Excitement in Juarez, Mexico," *New York Times*, November 13, 1893.
4. *New York Times*, November 18, 1893.
5. Edgar Greer Shelton, Jr., "Political Conditions Among Texas Mexicans Along the Rio Grande," (Master's thesis, University of Texas, 1946), pp. 7, 10, 14.
6. Shelton, pp. 14–15.
7. Edwin Larry Dickens, "The Political Role of Mexican-Americans in San Antonio" (Ph.D. dissertation, Texas Tech University, 1969), pp. 33–34.
8. Shelton, pp. 26–28, 32–36.
9. Shelton, pp. 39, 76–79.

10. Shelton, pp. 36–37.
11. Shelton, pp. 98, 123, 90.
12. Ellwyn R. Stoddard, *Mexican Americans* (New York: Random House, 1973), p. 10; Carolyn Zeleny, *Relations Between the Spanish-Americans and Anglo-Americans in New Mexico* (New York: Arno Press, 1974), pp. 147–148.
13. Zeleny, pp. 154–155, 157, 166.
14. Zeleny, pp. 176–177.
15. Zeleny, pp. 179, 187, 190, 192–193, 200–201, 216, 217.
16. Zeleny, pp. 218–219.
17. Zeleny, pp. 222–224, 229–230.
18. Carl Wittke, *We Built America*, rev. ed. (Cleveland: Case Western Reserve University, 1967), p. 466; Kaye Lyon Briegel, "*Alianza Hispano-Americana*, 1894–1965; a Mexican Fraternal Insurance Society" (Ph.D. dissertation, University of Southern California, 1974), pp. 12–15.
19. José Amado Hernández, "The Development of Mutual Aid Societies in the Chicano Community," *La Raza* 3, no. 2 (Summer Issue 1977): 15.
20. Meyer Weinberg, *Minority Students: A Research Appraisal* (Washington, D.C.: U.S. Department of Health, Education and Welfare, 1977), p. 286.
21. Arnoldo De Leon, "Blowout 1910 Style: A Chicano School Boycott in West Texas," *Texana* 12, no. 2 (November 1974): 124.
22. B. A. Hodges, *A History of the Mexican Mission Work* (1931), reprinted in Carlos E. Cortes, ed., *Church Views of the Mexican American* (New York: Arno Press, 1974), p. 5; De Leon, p. 124. The discussion of the San Angelo School segregation fight is based mainly on De Leon's work.
23. De Leon, p. 129.
24. Hodges, p. 5.
25. Hodges, pp. 5–7.
26. Ricardo Romo, "Mexican Workers in the City: Los Angeles, 1915–1930" (Ph.D. dissertation, University of California at Los Angeles, 1975), pp. 106–107.
27. Romo, pp. 56–57, 81–83.
28. *Regeneración* February 4, February 18, 1911.
29. Romo, pp. 109–111, 123.
30. Romo, p. 104.
31. Jay S. Stowell, *The Near Side of the Mexican Question* (Garden City, N.Y.: Doubleday, 1921), pp. 41, 44, 48.
32. Leo Grebler, Joan W. Moore, and Ralph C. Guzmán, *The Mexican American People: The Nation's Second Largest Minority* (New York: Free Press, 1970), p. 109.
33. See Américo Paredes, *With a Pistol in His Hand* (Austin: University of Texas Press, 1958).
34. José E. Limón, "*El Primer Congreso Mexicanista de 1911:* A Precursor to Contemporary Chicanismo," *Aztlán* (Spring and Fall 1974): 88.
35. Limón, p. 89.
36. *Regeneración*, August 5, 1911; *La Victim de los 'Civilizados,' " Regeneración*, August 26, 1911; Ricardo Flores Magón, "*A Salvar a un Inocente,*" *Regeneración*, September 9, 1911; "*En defensa de los Mexicanos,*" *Regeneración*, August 17, 1912.
37. Limón, pp. 86–89.
38. Limón, pp. 97–98.
39. Limón, pp. 92–93.
40. Stuart Jamieson, *Labor Unionism in American Agriculture* (New York: Arno Press, 1976), p. 261; *Regeneración*, February 10, February 17, March 9, May 11, 1912.
41. *Regeneración*, October 14, 1911.
42. *Regeneración*, March 18, March 25, 1911; see also *Regeneración*, February 4, February 11, 1911.
43. William M. Hager, "The Plan of San Diego. Unrest on the Texas Border in 1915," *Arizona and the West*, 5, no. 4 (Winter 1963): 330–336; Walter Prescott Webb, *The Texas Rangers*, 2nd ed. (Austin: University of Texas Press, 1965), p. 485; Juan Gómez-Quiñones, "*Plan de San Diego* Reviewed," *Aztlán* (Spring 1970): 125–126.
44. Hager, pp. 330, 336; Webb, p. 484; Charles C. Cumberland, "Border Raids in

the Lower Rio Grande Valley—1915," *Southwestern Historical Quarterly* 57 (January 1954): 290.

45. Cumberland, pp. 291–292, 294–295; Webb, pp. 478–479. Hager, p. 335, states between 50 and 200; the U.S. press claimed 3,000.
46. *Regeneración*, October 2, 1915.
47. *Regeneración*, October 2, 1915.
48. Quoted in Dickens, p. 38. Also see George Marvin, "The Quick and the Dead on the Border," *The World's Word* (January 1917): 295.
49. Webb, pp. 474, 475, 478.
50. Cumberland, pp. 286, 301, 306.
51. Miguel Tirado, "Mexican American Political Organization; the Key to Chicano Political Power," *Aztlán* (Spring 1970): 56.
52. Adela Sloss Vento, *Alonso S. Perales: His Struggle for the Rights of Mexican-Americans* (San Antonio: Artes Gráficas, 1977), p. vii.
53. Quoted in Tirado, p. 57; taken from the first LULAC constitution.
54. Vento, p. 27.
55. Paul Morgan and Vince Mayer, "The Spanish Speaking Population of Utah: From 1900 to 1935," Working Papers Toward a History of the Spanish Speaking in Utah, American West Center, Mexican-American Documentation Project (Salt Lake City: University of Utah, 1973), p. 54.
56. Taylor, p. 175; Lawrence A. Cardoso, "Mexican Emigration to the United States 1900–1930: An Analysis of Socio Economic Causes (Ph.D. dissertation, University of Connecticut, 1974), pp. 122–124.
57. Paul S. Taylor, *Mexican Labor in the United States*, vol. 1 (New York: Arno Press, 1970), pp. 84–85.
58. Hershel T. Manuel, *The Education of Mexican and Spanish-Speaking Children in Texas*, in Carlos E. Cortes, ed., *Education and the Mexican-American* (New York: Arno Press, 1974), pp. 82–83.
59. Manuel, p. 106.
60. Paul S. Taylor, *An American Mexican Frontier: Nueces County, Texas* (New York: Russell and Russell, 1971), p. 210.
61. Taylor, *Mexican Labor*, vol. 1, p. 75.
62. José Amado Hernández, dissertation manuscript on Mexican *mutualistas* in progress, University of California at Riverside.
63. Robin Fitzgerald Scott, "The Mexican-American in the Los Angeles Area, 1920–1950: From Acquiescence to Activity, (Ph.D. dissertation, University of Southern California, 1971), pp. 21–32.
64. Romo, p. 8.
65. Elizabeth Fuller, "The Mexican Housing Problem in Los Angeles," in Carlos E. Cortes, ed., *Perspectives on Mexican-American Life* (New York: Arno Press, 1974), p. 6; Mark Reisler, "Passing Through Our Egypt, Mexican Labor in the United States, 1900–1940" (Ph.D. dissertation, Cornell University, 1973), p. 153; Romo, p. 84.
66. Scott, p. 68.
67. Romo, pp. 95–96; Scott, p. 68.
68. Quoted in Romo, p. 95.
69. Merton E. Hill, *The Development of an Americanization Program in Ontario: the Board of Trustees of Chaffey Union High School and Chaffey Junior College, 1928*, in Carlos E. Cortes, ed., *Aspects of the Mexican-American Experience* (New York: Arno Press, 1976), pp. 76–101.
70. Romo, pp. 186–188.
71. Paul S. Taylor, "Crime and the Foreign Born: The Problem of the Mexican," in Carlos E. Cortes, ed., *The Mexican-American and the Law* (New York: Arno Press, 1974), p. 232.
72. *El Trabajo*, April 18, May 16, May 23, June 11, June 14, June 26, July 31, 1925.
73. Quoted in Taylor, "Crime and the Foreign Born," p. 232.
74. Taylor, "Crime and the Foreign Born," pp. 224, 225; Reisler, p. 194; Quoted in Taylor, "Crime and the Foreign Born," p. 235.
75. Paul Livingston Warnshuis, *Crime and Criminal Justice Among Mexicans of Illinois*, in Cortes, *The Mexican-American and the Law*, pp. 282–284.
76. Reisler, p. 195.
77. Warnshuis, p. 287. Ironically, the defendants in capital cases received a much

better class of representation than those committing minor offenses, who generally received inexperienced counsel. Warnshuis, p. 320, found that 71 of the 98 Mexican convicts were not literate in English; 83 of 98 were literate in Spanish, but self taught.

78. Louise Año Nuevo Kerr, "The Chicano Experience in Chicago: 1920–1970" (Ph. D. dissertation, University of Illinois at Chicago Circle, 1976), p. 39.

79. Kerr, p. 36; Mark Reisler, *By the Sweat of Their Brow: Mexican Immigrant Labor in the United States, 1900–1940* (Westport Conn.: Greenwood Press, 1976), pp. 141–142.

80. Kerr, p. 36.

81. Kerr, pp. 47, 49–50, 52, 53.

82. Kerr, pp. 54–58; Taylor, *Mexican Labor*, vol. 2, p. 135. For good contemporary accounts of Protestant missionary work see Cortes, *Church Views of the Mexican American*, esp. Vernon M. McCombs' essay "From Over the Border," pp. 91, 92, 135, 151.

83. Kerr, pp. 76–77. For a glimpse of life in Chicago, see Robert C. Jones and Louis Wilson, *The Mexican in Chicago*, in Cortes, *Church Views of the Mexican-American*.

84. Stanley A. West, *The Mexican Aztec Society: A Mexican-American Voluntary Association in Diachronic Perspective* (New York: Arno Press, 1976), pp. 98, 137, 139, 140. West, p. 98, lists 920 men, 29 women, and 7 children.

85. Barbara June Macklin, *Structural Stability and Cultural Change in a Mexican-American Community* (New York: Arno Press, 1976), p. 30.

86. Macklin, p. 30; "Minnesotans of Mexican Heritage," *Gopher Historian* 26, no. 1 (Fall 1971):7. *La Sociedad Mutualista Mexicana* was established soon afterwards in that city (Wittke, p. 466).

87. Morgan and Mayer, pp. 32–34, 41, 46–47, 50–52.

88. Erasmo Gamboa, "Chicanos in the Northwest: An Historical Perspective," *El Grito* (Summer 1973): 58–59, 60–62; Richard W. Slatta, "Chicanos in the Pacific Northwest: An Historical Overview of Oregon's Chicanos," *Aztlán* (Fall 1975): 328–329.

89. On March 6, 1979, Manuel Banda stated that Tom García, 33, the secretary of the YMCA, had had the idea for the MAM. García, who lived in Palo Alto, was the prime mover behind many activities. For more data on the MAM, see "Mexican-American Movement: Its Origins and Personnel," in the Angel Cano papers at California State University, Northridge/Chicano Studies, July 12, 1944, p. 4. (This collection is referred to hereafter as the Cano papers.)

90. "Mexican- American Movement," Cano papers, p. 3.

91. Albert R. Lozano, "Progress Through Education," Cano papers; *Forward*, October 28, 1945; "Felix Gutierrez, prominent youth worker, dies at 37, *Lincoln Heights Bulletin-News*, December 1, 1955; *Forward*, February 24, 1949; *Forum News Bulletin*, August 7, 1949.

92. The congress was first promoted by UCAPWA and *La Liga Obrera* of New Mexico.

93. Miguel Tirado, "Mexican American Community Political Organization: The Key to Chicano Political Power," in F. Chris García, *La Causa Politica: A Chicano Politics Reader* (Notre Dame, Ind.: University of Notre-Dame Press, 1974): F. Chris García, "Manitos and Chicanos in New Mexico Politics," in García, *La Causa Politica*.

94. Scott, pp. 147, 149, states that the goals of the congress were economic, social, and cultural advancement. Trade unions were active in the congress.

95. Luisa Morena, "Non-citizen Americans of the Southwest: Caravan of Sorrow," Cano papers, March 3, 1940.

96. Moreno, March 3, 1940.

97. Annie Reynolds, *The Education of Spanish-Speaking Children in Five Southwestern States*, U.S. Department of Interior Bulletin No. 11 (Washington, D.C.: 1933) in Carlos E. Cortes, ed., *Education and the Mexican-American* (New York: Arno Press, 1974), p. 13.

98. Ruth Lucretia Martínez, "The Unusual Mexican: A Study in Acculturation," (Master's thesis, Claremont College, 1942), pp. 36–38.

99. Martínez, pp. 38–39.

100. Kaye Lyon Briegel, "*Alianza Hispano-Americana* and Some Mexican-Ameri-

can Civil Rights Cases in the 1950s," in Manuel P. Servín, ed., *An Awakening Minority: The Mexican-Americans*, 2nd ed. (Beverly Hills, Calif.: Glencoe Press, 1974), p. 176.
101. Scott, pp. 148, 149.
102. Martha Cotera, *Profile of the Mexican-American Women* (Austin, Tex.: National Educational Laboratory, 1976), pp. 93–96.
103. Nick C. Vaca, "The Mexican-American in the Social Sciences, 1912–1970; Part II: 1936–1970," *El Grito* (Fall 1970): 18.
104. Ralph C. Guzmán, *The Political Socialization of the Mexican-American People* (New York: Arno Press, 1976), p. 89.
105. Ozzie G. Simmons, "Anglo-Americans and Mexicans in South Texas" (Ph.D. dissertation, Harvard University, 1952), pp. 246–277, 280–281.
106. Everett Ross Clinchy, Jr., *Equality of Opportunity for Latin-Americans in Texas* (New York: Arno Press, 1974), p. 43.
107. E. R. Fincher, *Spanish Americans as a Political Factor in New Mexico, 1912–1950* (New York: Arno Press, 1974), pp. 49, 53, 68, 69, 77.
108. Fincher, pp. 103–105, 107, 124.
109. Fincher, pp. 142, 146, 149–153, 160, 177.
110. Fincher, pp. 221, 224.
111. Kerr, pp. 69–74, 76–80.
112. Kerr, p. 83.
113. Kerr, pp. 95–96, 99, 101–104.
114. Raúl Morín, *Among the Valiant* (Alhambra, Calif.: Borden, 1966), p. 16; Scott, pp. 156, 195, 256, 261; Mauricio Mazón, "Social Upheaval in World War II. Zoot-Suiters and Servicemen in Los Angeles, 1943" (Ph.D. dissertation, University of California at Los Angeles, 1976), pp. 91–92.
115. Alonso Perales, *Are We Good Neighbors?* (New York: Arno Press, 1974), p. 79.
116. Scott, p. 195; Federal Bureau of Investigation, "Racial Conditions (Spanish-Mexican Activities) in Los Angeles Field Division," January 14, 1944, pp. 33–37. This report openly admits discrimination against Mexicans in employment in defense industries. Until 1943, many war industries refused employment to Mexicans. In one well-known company Mexicans were not made leadman because "employees work better under a white man." In the Bethlehem Steel shipyard only 300 of 7,450 employees were Mexican; at the California Shipbuilding Corporation less than 1,200 out of 43,000 were Mexican; and at the Western Pipe and Steel Corporation in Wilmington less than 700 out of 13,250 employees were Mexican. Special thanks are due to Dr. Russell Bartley of the History Department at the University of Wisconsin/Milwaukee, whose student had been provided access under the Freedom of Information Act, for allowing me to review the FBI files on the zoot-suit riots, from 1943–1945.
117. Ismael Dieppa. "The Zoot-Suit Riots Revisited: The Role of Private Philanthropy in Youth Problems of Mexican-Americans" (DSW dissertation, University of Southern California, 1973), p. 14; Harry Carlisle, *Citizens Without Rights* (Los Angeles: Los Angeles Committee for the Protection of the Foreign Born, n.d.), p. 6, states that 130,000 Japanese were uprooted, including 30,000 children and 70,000 persons born in the U.S.
118. "Editor's note," *Journal of Mexican-American History* (Fall 1974): 72.
119. "*Pachucos*" (Press release in the Sleepy Lagoon Defense Committee File), found in the Special Collections Library at the University of California at Los Angeles.
120. The FBI report cited earlier states, on pp. 40–41, that out of 2,547 Los Angeles Police Department officers, 22 (less than 1 percent) were of Spanish or Mexican descent. Out of 1,045 Los Angeles sheriff's office personnel, about 41 were of Spanish or Mexican extraction. There were three probation officers of Mexican or Latin extraction in Los Angeles County. See also Scott, p. 220.
121. Carey McWilliams, *North from Mexico* (New York: Greenwood Press, 1968), pp. 233–235. Interestingly, Deputy Sheriff Ed Durán Ayres was also an amateur historian who wrote a series of articles for the *Civic Center Sun* on "The Background of the History of California." Some of these articles appeared in the April 18, April 25, May 16, May 30, and June 6, 1940 issues of the paper. Throughout these articles Ayres seemed proud of the Hispano-Mexican heritage and gave no indicaton of his later negative conclusions about Mexicans.

On July 4, 1940, Ayres stated that Francisco López, the discoverer of gold in California in 1842, was a grand-uncle of "our own Sheriff, Eugene Biscailuz." On August 1, 1940, he wrote in glowing terms about the Aztecs, saying "Now . . . there is nothing Spanish about the Aztec eagle representing Mexico. It is 100 percent American." He also described "Astlan [sic]" General José Figueroa, one of the governors of California, as very proud of "his Aztec blood." Why his attitude changed 180 degrees in his testimony at the "Sleepy Lagoon trial" is a matter for speculation. There is some question whether Ayres even wrote the grand jury report. According to Guy Endore, the report was developed by the sheriffs, who signed Ayres's name. Also see Stephanie Dias, "The Zoot Suit Riots," (Pro-seminar paper, San Fernando Valley State College at Northridge, History Department, May 28, 1969), pp. 12–14; McWilliams, pp. 233–234.

122. Citizen's Committee for the Defense of Mexican-American Youth, *The Sleepy Lagoon Case*, Los Angeles, 1942, p. 21; Scott, p. 223; McWilliams, pp. 228–231. Two of the defendants demanded a separate trial and, on the basis of the same evidence, were acquitted (Citizen's Committee, pp. 7–8).

123. Scott, p. 225; McWilliams, pp. 232–233.

124. The report charged, on p. 44, that the Sleepy Lagoon Defense Committee "had attempted to create antagonism between the Spanish-Mexicans and local law enforcement"; the LAPD, according to the FBI, had done everything it could to improve relations.

125. Dieppa, p. 15, emphasizes the sex motive, stating that there were five servicemen to every girl. Mazón, pp. 149–150, quotes an incident reported by a black minister riding a streetcar, who observed two sailors from the South trying to get a Mexican girl's eye: "Boy, uh white man can git any gal he wants, can't he boy? Can't he get 'em if he wants 'em?" A great number of the servicemen were of southern extraction. See also McWilliams, p. 248. Mazón, p. 113, reports that on June 10, 1943, San Diego City Councilman Charles C. Dail wrote to Rear Admiral David W. Bagley, commandant of the 11th Naval District in San Diego, complaining about the conduct of servicemen, who "insulted and vilified civilians on public streets."

126. Mazón, pp. 16–19, breaks with the traditional analysis of the *pachuco* confrontations, stating that it was not frustration over losing battles that added to the servicemen's nervousness, but a reluctance to go overseas and become a statistic when they knew that the U.S. had already won the war. The riots became a way of rebelling against the "old men" who controlled the government. The *pachuco* became a scapegoat. Servicemen were also conditioned to view anyone who did not fall into step as disloyal. As time went on they became increasingly paranoid, hunting draft dodgers, pacifists, and communists.

127. McWilliams, pp. 244–254.

128. Dias, pp. 22–23.

129. McWilliams, pp. 246–247; *Los Angeles Times*, June 7, 1943.

130. McWilliams, pp. 248–252. *Time* Magazine, June 21, 1943; *PM*, June 10, 1943; Dieppa, p. 9.

131. FBI report, January 14, 1944. The *Eastside Journal*, June 9, 1943, wrote an editorial defending the zoot suits; it pointed out that 112 had been hospitalized, 150 hurt, and 12 treated in the hospitals. See also McWilliams, p. 250.

132. Ed Robbins, *PM*, June 9, 1943.

133. McWilliams, p. 251.

134. Mazón, pp. 114–118.

135. *Los Angeles Times*, June 10, 1943. Mazón, pp. 189–195, states that the authorities tried to make blacks the scapegoats for the riots. In a report to the commandant of the Eleventh Naval District on July 29, 1943, Commander Fogg, the senior patrol officer in Los Angeles, reported that "arrests [by the police] of members of the negro race had increased nearly 100 percent, compared with a year ago." In a memo written on October 16, 1943, Fogg described "an aggressive campaign sponsored by local, state and national representatives of the negro race. . . . to promote unrest and dis-satisfaction [sic] among the local negro population."

136. McGucken Report, California Legislature, Report and Recommendations of Citizens Committee on Civil Disturbances in Los Angeles, June 12, 1943, p. 1.

137. *Los Angeles Times*, July 10, 1943.
138. Pauline R. Kibbe, *Latin Americans in Texas* (New York: Arno Press, 1974), pp. 212, 214–215; "First Regional Conference on the Education of Spanish-Speaking people in the Southwest—A Report" (March 1946); *Image*, (Federation of Employed Latin American Descendents, Vallejo, California) FELAD, May 1976.
139. George Sánchez, "Concerning Segregation of Spanish-Speaking Children in the Public Schools," Inter-American Education Papers (Austin: University of Texas, 1951), reprinted in Cortes, *Education and the Mexican-American*, pp. 9–11.
140. Sánchez, pp. 13–19; Briegel, *"Alianza Hispano-Americana"* p. 175; Scott, p. 293; Ralph C. Guzmán, *The Political Socialization of the Mexican American People* (New York: Arno, 1976), pp. 138–139.
141. Guzmán, p. 139, states the Chicanos did not have anything to do with that organization; however, Chicanos were heavily involved in Back-of-the-Yards and lived in the area.
142. Guzmán, pp. 140, 141, 142. Through the CSO's efforts Ernesto Padilla was also elected to the city council of San Fernando, California.
143. Tony Castro, *Chicano Power: The Emergence of Mexican-Americans* (New York: Saturday Review Press, 1974), p. 188; Miguel Tirado, "The Mexican-American Minority's Participation in Voluntary Political Associations" (Ph.D. dissertation, Claremont Graduate School and University Center, 1970), p. 65.
144. Luis Arroyo, "Chicano Participation in Organized Labor: The CIO in Los Angeles, 1938–1950, An Extended Research Note," *Aztlán* 6, no. 2 (Summer 1975): 297; *Eastside Sun*, April 2, 1948. Keyes had shot four people in 18 months. See also Guy Endore, *Justice for Salcido* (Los Angeles: Civil Rights Congress of Los Angeles, 1948), pp. 5–9, 13. Salcido was hit four times—in the head from ear to ear, twice in the back of the head, and in the arm.
145. *Eastside Sun*, April 9, 1948.
146. *Eastside Sun*, April 9, 1948; August 22, 1947. Mexican screen star Margo Albert, wife of actor Eddie Albert, was very active in setting up the program. Also active in the people's court was Jack Berman of the Progressive Citizens of America. *Eastside Sun*, April 9, 1948. The IPP link to most leftist events is obvious. The Progressive Citizens of America, along with Councilman P. Christensen of the 9th Councilmatic District and Ed Elliot of the 44th Assembly District requested the suspension of Keyes, *Eastside Sun*, April 23, 1948. The American Jewish Congress protested the admitted shooting of an unarmed Mexican, "AJC Requests Action in Salcido Killing," *Eastside Sun*, July 23, 1948; See also Endore, p. 17.
147. Endore, pp. 19–21, 24. "Community Teachers Support Civil Rights Congress," an article in the *Eastside Sun*, April 30, 1948, criticized the *Times* editorial, stating that Mexicans historically suffered police brutality.
148. Endore, pp. 29–30.
149. Weinberg, pp. 286–287.
150. Quoted in Weinberg, p. 287.
151. Quoted in Weinberg, p. 287.
152. Patricia Rae Adler, "The 1943 Zoot-suit Riots: Brief Episode in a Long Conflict," in Servín, p. 146.
153. *G.I. Forum News Bulletin*, December 1953.
154. "Edgar Taken to Federal Court on Segregation," *G.I. Forum News Bulletin*, April 1955; *G.I. Forum News Bulletin*, January 1955.
155. "Mercedes Policeman Who Menaced Family Resigns as Result of G.I. Forum Pressure," *G.I. Forum News Bulletin*, June 15, 1953; June 15, 1963.
156. *G.I. Forum News Bulletin*, September 1953.
157. *G.I. Forum News Bulletin*, December 1953; May 1954; February–March, 1956.
158. Douglas E. Foley, Clarice Mota, Donald E. Post, and Ignacio Lozano, *From Peones to Politicos: Ethnic Relations in a South Texas Town, 1900–1977* (Austin: University of Texas Press, 1977), p. 94. Grebler et al., p. 218.
159. Foley et al., pp. 95, 96, 98.
160. Galván's career can be followed in a series of issues of the *G.I. Forum News Bulletin*–July 1954, August 1954, May–June 1955, August 1955, October 1956, June 1957, February 1958, June 1958, August 1958, July 1959, May 1961.

161. Briegel, *"Alianza Hispano-Americana* and Some Mexican Civil Rights Cases,"
p. 184, *Armando Morales*, "A Study of Mexican-American Perceptions of Law
Enforcement Policies and Practices in East Los Angeles" (DSW dissertation,
University of Southern California, 1972), p. 77. In August 1949 a "Committee
of 21" had been created in the Hollenbeck area to improve police-community
relations. It held two meetings and then faded away. (Morales, pp. 83–84.)
162. *Eastside Sun*, March 9, April 13, April 20, 1950.
163. "El Sereno Defense Group to Give Dance," *Eastside Sun*, July 12, 1951.
164. Ralph Guzmán, *Eastside Sun*, December 29, 1953.
165. Morales, p. 41; *Eastside Sun*, September 17, 1953; *G.I. Forum News Bulletin*,
February–March, 1956; Briegel, *"Alianza Hispano-Americana* and Some Mexican Civil Rights Cases," p. 184.
166. Briegel, *"Alianza Hispano-Americana* and Some Mexican Civil Rights Cases,"
p. 183.
167. *Eastside Sun*, September 5, 1947; Independent Progressive Party Is Launched
This Week in Eastside," *Eastside Sun*, November 14, 1947; "Jose Ramon
Chavez Woos IPP Support," *Eastside Sun*, March 26, 1948. José Ramón
Chávez was a member of Shipyard Workers Local 9 (CIO). See also "IPP
Announces Support for Candidate," *Eastside Sun*, March 18, 1949. The support was for Edward Roybal for Los Angeles city councilman.
168. Fincher, pp. 95–97.
169. *Eastside Sun*, February 16, April 20, July 20, 1950.
170. *Eastside Sun*, June 26, August 7, September 4, 1952.
171. "New Spanish Speaking Group Formed in Texas," *Eastside Sun*, May 31, 1951.
See also *Eastside Sun*, August 11, November 29, 1951; September 11, 1952.
172. Briegel, *"Alianza Hispano-Americana* and Some Mexican Civil Rights Cases,"
pp. 179–180.
173. Briegel, *"Alianza Hispano-Americana* and Some Mexican Civil Rights Cases,"
pp. 181–183; *Eastside Sun*, February 10, 1955.
174. Joseph Eli Kovner, "Route Would Slash Through Residential and Business
Districts; Protests Mount," *Eastside Sun*, October 1, 1953. See also *Eastside
Sun*, March 10, 1955; October 3, October 17, October 24, 1957; February 27,
December 30, 1958 and Joseph Eli Kovner, "The Arechiga Family Bodily
Evicted from Home in Chavez Ravine," *Eastside Sun*, May 14, 1959.
175. See the Joseph Eli Kovner articles in the *Eastside Sun*, April 10, April 17, April
24, May 1, May 8, May 15, June 6, June 12, June 26, July 3, July 17, July 24, and
July 31, 1958.
176. Joseph Eli Kovner, "Aide Quits in Bunker Hill Row," *Eastside Sun*, October 9,
1958; *Eastside Sun*, December 4, December 30, 1958; Joseph Eli Kovner,
"Resettle Elsewhere, Says Mayor 'If You Don't Want Urban Renewal,'" *Eastside Sun*, January 8, 1959.
177. Joseph Eli Kovner, "Brazen Politics Endangers Lives to Lower Property
Taxes," *Eastside Sun*, March 12, 1959. Bunker Hill cost the taxpayers $30
million to profit private individuals.
178. *Eastside Sun*, August 6, 1959.
179. *G.I. Forum News Bulletin*, January 1958.
180. *Belvedere Citizen*, November 6, November 13, November 20, and December 4,
1958.
181. *Eastside Sun*, March 26, 1959.
182. *G.I. Forum News Bulletin*, November–December, 1959.
183. Kerr, p. 8. Bertha Blair, Anne O. Lively, and Glen W. Trimble, in "Spanish-
Speaking Americans: Mexicans and Puerto Ricans in the United States," in
Cortes, *Church Views of the Mexican-American*, p. 28, state that the number
was 35,215, with only 1 percent Mexican born. Again this was probably an
undercount.

Chapter 11
Good-bye America

The 1960s represented a decade of both awareness and disillusionment. Many Chicanos who actively participated in the political life of the nation took a hard look at their assigned role in society, evaluated it, and then decided that they had had enough, so they bid good-bye to America.

THE CHICANO IN LIMBO

The U.S. census in 1960 reported that 3,464,999 Spanish-surnamed persons resided in the Southwest. Their per capita income was $968, compared to $2,047 for Anglos and $1,044 for other non-whites; 29.7 percent of the Spanish-surnamed population lived in deteriorated houses, versus 7.5 percent of the Anglos and 27.1 percent of the other nonwhites. The census further showed that the average size of the Spanish-surnamed family was 4.77 compared to 3.39 for Anglos and 4.54 for other nonwhites.[1] Unemployment was higher among Chicanos than among Anglos.

Chicanos were educationally at the bottom of the scale. The educational grade median for Spanish-surnamed persons over 14 years of age was 8.1, versus 12.0 for Anglos and 9.7 for other non-whites. Significantly, the grade median for the Spanish-surnamed in Texas was 4.8. Although Chicanos were not as strictly segregated as Blacks, the majority lived segregated from the Anglo community. Social segregation still existed and in places like Texas and eastern Oregon "No Mexicans Allowed" signs were common.[2]

What the census did not show was that a majority of Mexicans remained functionally illiterate. For the most part, Mexicans were packed into nonacademic programs from the first grade through junior high school; this left them ill-equipped to take academic courses in high school and killed learning motivation. On the basis of the census, one analyst observed: "That more education fails to improve the income position of Mexican-Americans in proportion to that of the majority is a matter of considerable social significance."[3]

Robert Coles, a medical doctor, and Harry Huge, an attorney, conducted an extensive investigation of the Chicano situation in San Antonio and other parts of Texas. In their article "Thorns on the Yellow Rose of Texas," they reported that Mexicans comprised 41.7 percent of the 700,000 people of San Antonio, and that two San

Antonios existed, one that was Anglo-American and the other that was Mexican. They further reported that city officials admitted that 28 percent of the families had an income of less than $3,000 per year, whereas 6 percent earned under $1,000. Coles and Huge painted a dismal picture of the city's west side:

> What San Antonio's officials spell out, we saw: unpaved, undrained streets; homes without water; homes with outdoor privies; homes that are nothing but rural shacks packed together in an urban ghetto that comprises 8 percent of San Antonio's land area, but whose residents must put up with a far higher percentage of suffering—32.3 percent of the city's infant deaths; 44.6 percent of its tuberculosis; and well over half its mid-wife deliveries. After we had gone from home to home on one street, we began to realize that in almost every way thousands of people are walled off—as in the ghettoes once present in Europe.[4]

Coles and Huge painted an equally dismal picture of the Chicanos' plight in the rest of Texas. Everywhere they went, the investigators found the same picture: poor political representation, poor education, and general poverty. They wrote that:

> Texaco had a net income of $754,386,000 in 1967. Gulf managed to reap $578,287,000 that year, and Sinclair, a modest $95,322,000. At the same time, as of November 1968, Texas, whose large cities and industrial wealth make it comparable to Michigan and Pennsylvania, ranks 47th among states in welfare payments per recipient.[5]

In one congressional district, during 1966, the poor received $244,000 in food assistance from the U.S. Department of Agriculture, while rich farmers (0.01 percent of the people) got $5,318,892 in benefits from that same department.[6] In short, the political and economic realities in Texas were that Chicanos were controlled by an oligarchy of white Anglo capitalists.

In California and the Southwest, activists mustered enough support to end the *bracero* program in 1964. César Chávez's small union grew and farm workers caught an emotional nerve.[7] The Chávez movement inspired activism among Chicanos everywhere.

Small civic groups emerged, most of which were concerned about the education gap. They advanced different reasons for the disparity. Many contended that Chicano students lagged behind Anglo students because of the language barrier; others blamed it on the lack of bilingual instruction; some blamed discrimination in the schools; while still others insisted it was the cultural conflict, which created a negative self-image in Chicano students. They advanced solutions: preschool education, bilingual programs, empathetic teachers, relevant materials, and more Chicano teachers.

The Chicano community soon became frustrated with the inaction of those in control. Chicano groups worked through the civil rights framework. They worked in the areas of housing, employment, police brutality, etc. They confined their methods to petitions and the courts; occasionally they took part in a sit-in. During this period, the groups, comprised mostly of volunteers, were small, but enthusiastic.

CHICANOS TEST THE POLITICAL PROCESS

In the 1960 presidential campaign Democratic politicians harnessed the Chicano vote for John Fitzgerald Kennedy. *Viva Kennedy* clubs worked feverishly throughout the Southwest. They conducted registration drives and produced significant results: the Kennedy-Johnson ticket would have lost Texas without the support of the Chicano bloc.[8] In California the Chicano vote also went to Kennedy, but Richard Nixon, a native of that state, won by a narrow margin. At that time, most political analysts conceded that the Chicano vote henceforth would play a larger role. Both the Mexican American Political Association (MAPA), prominent in California, and the Political Association of Spanish-Speaking Organizations (PASSO), active mainly in Texas, received considerable impetus as a result of the Chicano's political potential.[9]

While some persons of Mexican extraction filled high posts, such as federal Judge Harold Medina who was from Yucatán, Mexico, these men never identified with the masses of poor Chicanos and effectively served the interests of the rich.[10] In 1961 Henry B. González was elected to the U.S. Congress in San Antonio. The Chicano community won minor victories during the first half of the 1960s. In 1963 they briefly captured the city council of Crystal City, Texas. In 1964 Elizo (Kika) da la Garza of Texas was elected to the House and Joseph Montoya of New Mexico to the Senate.[11] The major victory was the abolishment of the poll tax in the mid-1960s in Texas; it had been on the books since the early 1900s.[12]

The illusion of power diminished with the appointment of Reynaldo Garza of Brownsville to the federal district court. He was the first Chicano in history to be appointed to the high court in Texas, but his appointment was a slap to the Chicano *politicos* who had worked for JFK. They believed that they would participate in the naming of officials. Garza's appointment demonstrated that the patronage was channeled through Lyndon B. Johnson. Garza had broken with the Democratic party in 1952 and 1956, and Chicanos generally considered him conservative.[13]

In 1962 MAPA was instrumental in electing John Moreno and Philip Soto to the California assembly, the first Chicanos to serve in seventy-five years. However, these victories were an illusion of power. They were defeated for reelection when East Los Angeles, Montebello, and Pico Rivera were reapportioned.[14]

In 1961 in a 3½ square mile area of unincorporated East Los

Angeles, residents attempted to create a Chicano city. Their proposal was voted down by a vote of 2563 for and 2884 against.[15] In 1962, one of the architects of the Dodgers deal, Los Angeles city Councilwoman Rosalind Wyman, proposed swapping Hazard Park for federally owned land in the Westwood area (an affluent area). Wyman represented the Westwood area and wanted the federal land so the city could build tennis courts for her constituents. Freeways had badly cut up parkland and a lack of green space existed in East Los Angeles, but this did not bother the proponents of the Hazard Park deal. Meanwhile, Councilman Ed Roybal successfully ran for Congress; although the council promised it would allow the voters to elect his replacement, it broke its word and appointed Gilbert Lindsay, a Black, leaving the Chicano community without a representative on the city council. The next year, in spite of opposition, the deal for most of Hazard Park was made. Chicano activists fought this giveaway finally winning in the courts nearly ten years later.[16]

In Los Angeles in 1963 Municipal Court Judge Leopoldo Sánchez stated that out of 5,000 appointments, Governor Edmund G. Brown, Sr. appointed fewer than 30 Chicanos; Brown had implied that no qualified Mexicans lived in California.[17]

The Chicano community in Chicago was further integrated into the Democratic machine. What potential voting the community had was funneled through its ward. The War on Poverty (to be discussed) served as another level of patronage which won support for the machine.

When John Chico, a leader in the steelworkers union of South Chicago, ran for the state constitutional convention in a special election in 1969, he was the first Mexican to run in that city. Chico had the support of the Tenth Ward Spanish-Speaking Democratic Organization, as well as the steelworkers union. He was considered a progressive, associated himself with the César Chávez movement, and openly identified with the Chicano movement. He and other Mexican unionists challenged the Tenth Ward organization which was part of the Daley machine. Although the challenge was unsuccessful in that Chico lost the election, the machine withheld all patronage from the Spanish-speaking organization and Chicano precincts were gerrymandered into two separate wards to dilute any power that they might have.[18]

When some 9,000 Mexicans were displaced by spreading freeways in the Near West Side, the Pilsen area became the largest *barrio*. Strong Chicano neighborhood organizations emerged, while at the same time more Chicanos joined traditional groups such as the Pilsen Neighbors. In spite of these changes, Mexicans by the mid-1960s in the Southwest and Midwest remained too poor to organize nationally or participate in the formal party structures.[19]

NATIONAL PROGRAMS RAISE EXPECTATIONS

The civil rights movement and the ghetto revolts of the mid-1960s greatly affected the direction of the newly instituted Economic Opportunity Act of 1964 and the subsequent War on Poverty. The act emphasized education and training programs: job corps, neighborhood youth corps, work-study and community-action programs.[20] Spin-offs were loans to farmers and small businessmen, as well as the formation of VISTA (Volunteers in Service to America). The War on Poverty supposedly attacked the causes of poverty through community participation. To understand the program, the mentality of President Lyndon B. Johnson must be understood. Johnson, a machine politician from Texas, was basically conservative. He had, however, been greatly influenced by Franklin D. Roosevelt and the New Deal. Fundamentally, the New Deal was aimed at preserving the capitalistic system in the United States and to insure a coalition of labor and ethnic peoples to support the Democratic party. Control of the national government was essential to perpetuating the Democratic party. Johnson was also influenced by Kennedy and his "New Frontier," which in many ways was a revival of idealism at home and abroad. Young people entered into the New Frontier's coalition, since they believed they could change society. They represented a large bloc vote. Basically, the program set up another patronage network. It bolstered the system through reformist measures. Groups like the GI Forum openly threw their fortunes behind LBJ. They saw the War on Poverty as a key to social awareness.[21] In 1966 the Forum sponsored Operation Service, Employment, and Redevelopment (SER), which was aimed at the disadvantaged in a few selected areas of the Southwest.[22]

Although programs were to service all poor people, from the beginning bureaucrats lacked an awareness of the problems of Chicanos. Indeed, many federal authorities did not even know what a Mexican looked like. As a consequence, most programs were directed at the Black community to the exclusion of Chicanos and other minorities. This neglect stiffened the resolve of many Chicanos to break the "Black-white syndrome," which was the tendency of most bureaucrats to look at U.S. society as Black and white, ignoring other races.[23]

On March 28, 1966, the Equal Employment Opportunity Commission held a meeting in Albuquerque, New Mexico, to investigate the Chicanos' employment problems. Approximately 50 Chicanos walked out because, although the commission advocated equal employment, it did not have one Mexican on its staff. Although these actions remained within the civil rights framework, they shook the stereotype of the docile Mexican. As a result of the walkout in Albuquerque and growing ferment among Chicanos, the federal government pacified the community in June 1967 by appointing Vicente Ximenes to the Equal Employment Opportunity Commission. Shortly thereafter he was named head of the newly created Interagency Committee on Mexican-American Affairs.[24] This office mollified middle-class activists, whose primary goal was to create better paying jobs for Chicanos.

Johnson had promised that he would hold a White House conference for Chicano leaders, but he feared that Chicanos would walk out of the conference and embarrass him politically. He did not keep his promise. Instead, in October 1967 he held cabinet committee hearings at El Paso, Texas. Johnson did not bother to invite the leading activists: César Chávez, Reies Tijerina, or Rodolfo "Corky" Gonzales. At El Paso he bused his Mexicans to the celebrations which returned the *Chamizal* to Mexico. (The *Chamizal* was a disputed section of land that was claimed by both the United States and Mexico. It must be added that it was an abandoned dump yard of little value.) Many Chicanos wondered if this had not been the main reason for the hearings since little else was accomplished. Activists boycotted and picketed the cabinet conference. They called their group *La Raza Unida*. Ernesto Galarza of San Jose, Corky Gonzales, and Reies Tijerina played leading roles in this opposition. Representatives of fifty Chicano organizations met at San Antonio and pledged support to the concept of *La Raza Unida;* about 1,200 people attended. To many observers, it was clear that the lid was about to blow off in the Chicano community.[25]

NEW NATIONALISM—THE YOUTH MOVEMENT

The thrust of the War on Poverty to obtain "maximum citizen participation" drove agency workers who competed with other government agencies to service all sectors of the community. Chicano youths became special targets. In 1966 the Los Angeles County Human Relations Council sponsored youth seminars and its fourth annual Chicano student conference at Camp Hess Kramer. Father John Luce hosted the Social Action Training Center at the Church of the Epiphany (Episcopal) in Lincoln Heights. Not long afterwards the Young Citizens for Community Action (YCCA) which later evolved into the Brown Berets was formed. By 1967 a handful of Chicano students were enrolled at East Los Angeles Community College (ELACC), Los Angeles State College (later California State University of Los Angeles), and the outlying city, state, and private colleges and universities. In early 1967 the Mexican-American Student Association (MASA) organized at ELACC. The campaign and later upset election of Dr. Julian Nava to the Los Angeles Board of Education inspired new hope in the community as well as further focusing on the importance of education to Chicanos.

On May 13, 1967 Chicano students met at Loyola University and founded the United Mexican-American Students (UMAS).

Most Chicano students were clearly influenced by the United Farm Workers. Its successes and tribulations became their own. On campus they joined with the Black student movement and the Students for a Democratic Society (SDS). By the fall of 1967 Chicano college student organizations spread throughout the country. Their priority was recruitment, but they were also involved in campus politics, participating in numerous antiwar rallies. Speakers such as Corky Gonzales and Reies López Tijerina added to their momentum. By December 16–17, 1967, the second general UMAS conference was held at the University of Southern California campus.[26]

In Northern California many Chicano groups called themselves the Mexican-American Student Confederation (MASC). In the south the size of the Chicano *barrios* tended to encourage students to focus on community issues, while the northern groups' greater involvement with politics on campus led to an emphasis on universal themes. Chicano student groups evolved elsewhere in the Southwest. As in California they were conditioned by regional differences. The centers of these student activities were Austin, Kingsville, San Antonio, Albuquerque, Tucson, etc.

Some writers have classified these students as cultural nationalists (which in itself is a generalization). It is true that some students went through cultural excesses; if it was not Chicano it had no value. They glorified the *bato loco*, the crazy dude on the corner, dressed in his baggy khakis, speaking a mixture of English and Spanish, and heavily into drugs and gang activity. To understand why students went through these excesses, the times must be examined. It was natural to glorify the *batos*, since in many ways they were the most oppressed elements of society. The 1960s were a time when students searched for causes and true believers were often fanatical in their zeal. This is often true of new converts— whether they be Catholics, Jesus followers, nationalists, or marxists. Nationalism in the case of Chicanos was a natural response to 120 years of political, economic, and cultural suppression. With incredible zeal students turned to their own campuses. Many institutions had made no effort to apply for funds under the Higher Education Act of 1965 which provided needy students with educational opportunity grants of $1,000 per needy student per academic year.[27] Students pressed the colleges to establish educational opportunity programs and formalize recruitment. At any campus with a half-dozen Chicano students they pressed school administrations for a Mexican-American studies (MAS) program and the admission of more Chicano students. Most students did not know what a MAS program entailed. Admittedly they were mirroring Black requests. But through raw energy by the fall of 1969 some fifty Mexican-American studies programs functioned in California alone—ranging from institutes and centers to departments.

The first program established was at Los Angeles State College in the fall of 1968. The administration made many promises, but gave minimal assistance and support. It allowed hostile faculties to badger inexperienced students in pseudo-democratic faculty committees and instructors in the program were rarely granted tenure. From the beginning the majority of the programs were set up to fail. The frustration of dealing with petty and bullying administrators added to student disillusionment and increased their alienation from the system.

From 1968 to 1971 the campuses provided a network which furnished information and provided the shock troops for the protests and marches of those years. Community newspapers such as *Inside Eastside* and *La Raza* (established in September 1967) became a source of information for students and community. They carried articles directed at high school students which articulated their grievances. In December 1967 Raúl Ruiz writing in *Inside Eastside*, entreated, "If you are a student at Lincoln you should be angry! You should demand! You should protest! You should organize for better education! This is your right! This is your life!" In January 1968 Lazaro Q. (Raúl Ruiz) wrote, "Picket, Brother, Picket." He criticized incompetent teachers and urged action: "Something is terribly wrong in Eastside schools and the young Chicano students are not to blame. . . . It is easy for students to organize walk-outs."[28]

Sal Castro, a teacher at Lincoln High School had considerable credibility among students. As early as September 1967, Castro, a charismatic speaker, addressed students at the Piranya Coffee House, making them aware of issues such as quality education, textbooks, and their right to learn. Discussions on strategies such as blow-outs (walkouts) were discussed among students and their energies were directed into positive channels. Clear goals were articulated. In March 1968 close to 10,000 Chicano students walked out of five Los Angeles high schools—Lincoln, Roosevelt, Garfield, Wilson, and Belmont. The schools were in East Los Angeles, with populations that were overwhelmingly Mexican. Chicanos' grievances and demands can be summarized as follows: Over 50 percent of the Chicano high school community was forced to drop out of school either through expulsion and transfers to other schools or simply because they had not been taught to read and thus failed their courses. Chicano schools were overcrowded and run down compared to Anglo and Black schools of the district. Many teachers openly discriminated against Chicanos and students wanted racist teachers removed. The curriculum was designed to obscure the Chicanos' culture and to condition students to be content with low-skilled jobs. Students demanded more Chicano teachers and administrators. The community formed the Educational Issues Coordinating Committee to support the walkouts and follow up on the demands.[29]

When students walked out, sheriff's deputies and police reacted by treating the protest as an insurrection; they broke up the demonstrations by beating students, and arrested those who did not move fast enough. Many activists were caught by surprise; however, in general, community organizations supported the walkout and condemned police brutality. Sal Castro had walked out with his students. He stated that he could not in good conscience remain inside the school, since the demands of his students were legitimate. Moreover, he condemned the schools for crippling Chicano children. Along with others, he was indicted by a Los Angeles grand jury on several charges, among them conspiracy to commit misdemeanors. After two years of appeals the courts found the charges unconstitutional. Castro was harassed by the California Department of Education, which attempted to revoke his credentials, and he was subject to frequent and arbitrary administrative transfers.[30]

The Los Angeles walkouts called national attention to the Chicano's plight in education and encouraged other walkouts throughout the Southwest and the Midwest. In March 120 students walked out in Denver. In April some 700 students walked out of Lanier High School in San Antonio, Texas, and shortly afterwards 600 walked out at Edgewood High School in the same city. Similar walkouts occurred in Santa Clara, California, Elsa and Abilene, Texas, and Phoenix, Arizona. Demands were for Mexican teachers, counselors, and courses and for better facilities. On May 5, 1970, Chicano students walked out of Delano Joint Union High. Protest centered around the denial of a Chicano speaker for an assembly. On the 7th police encircled the school. The walkout lasted until the end of the year when strikers were arrested as they attempted to enter graduation ceremonies. Police beat protesters and dragged them into paddywagons.[31]

Luis Váldez, of the *Teatro Campesino*, contributed to the spread of this new awareness. The *Teatro* used one-act plays to advertise the struggle of the farm worker and the Chicanos. They played *corridos* that popularized the Chicanos' struggle for liberation in the United States.

Another milestone was the publication of *El Grito: A Journal of Contemporary Mexican-American Thought* in the fall of 1967. The journal was organized by a group called *Quinto Sol* Publications, headed by Octavio Romano, a professor at the University of California at Berkeley. It published articles challenging Anglo-American scholarship and how it affected Chicanos. It carried scholarly articles, poetry, and art.

Youth made many symbolic changes during this period. Groups such as the Brown Berets, the Mexican-American Youth Organization (MAYO) in Texas, and other organizations adopted slogans and symbols that were accepted by older political activists.

For instance, the term *Chicano* historically had a pejorative meaning among the older generation; now youth embraced the term, rejecting the more established label of Mexican-American, which they said had been imposed upon them by the Anglo-American establishment. Idealistically the majority of campus groups changed their name to *El Movimiento Estudiantil Chicano de Aztlán* (MECHA) (The Chicano Student Movement of Aztlán). They dedicated themselves to a movement, devoting their efforts to the betterment of the underdogs of their community.[32]

In 1967 in East Los Angeles a group known as Young Citizens for Community Action (YCCA) was formed. The group was sponsored by an interfaith church organization, and its founding leader was David Sánchez, a teenager from an upper-lower-class family.[33] Four other Chicanos joined Sánchez as charter members. In time, the organization evolved from a community service club into a quasi "alert patrol," which assumed a defensive posture. Later in the year, the YCCA opened the coffee shop *La Piranya* to raise operating expenses.

The group changed its name to the Young Chicanos for Community Action. The members began to wear brown berets, and they took on a paramilitary stance. The YCCA became popularly known as the Brown Berets. Its militant profile attracted a large number of young Chicanos. Beret chapters spread throughout the Southwest and Midwest.

The Brown Berets' impact on the Chicano movement was greater than its influence in it. It aroused a fear in Anglo-Americans that a Chicano group would counter U.S. oppression with its own violence. Law enforcement authorities believed that the Brown Berets were capable of inspiring violent action in other groups. The Brown Berets panicked police officials and exposed their basic undemocratic attitudes toward Mexicans or groups attempting to achieve liberation. The police and sheriff's departments in Los Angeles abandoned reason in harassing, intimidating, and persecuting the Brown Berets in a way that few other Chicano organizations have experienced in recent times. Police and sheriff's deputies raided the Berets, infiltrated them, libeled and slandered them, and even encouraged countergroups to attack members. The objective was to destroy the Berets and to invalidate the membership in the eyes of the Anglo and Chicano communities.[34]

The Berets were thrown into the national limelight by the East Los Angeles school walkouts. Although there is little evidence that the organization took a leadership role in planning the walkouts, the police and sheriff's departments made it a scapegoat, branding the Brown Berets as outside agitators, while playing down the legitimate grievances of Chicano students. A grand jury later indicted thirteen Chicanos on conspiracy charges stemming from the walkouts and seven were Brown Berets. This case was appealed and declared unconstitutional, but only after three years of legal harassment. As the police and sheriff's repression increased, the popularity of the group spread.

Law enforcement agencies inundated the Berets with informers and special agents to entrap the members by encouraging acts of violence. They purposely subverted the Berets, keeping them in a state of flux and preventing the organization from solidifying.

Berets evolved into a radical group. Imbued with the politics of liberation, they dealt with the immediate needs of the *barrio*—food, housing, unemployment, education. Their philosophy was molded by the conflict and the street.

THE NEW LEADERS

Chicano leaders in general followed a different pattern from that of Black leadership. In the Black movement there were national leaders with large organizations and efficient staffs. In the Chicano movement César Chávez was the only leader of national prominence who had a large organization, and his organization was a trade union that promoted the interests of a specific interest group rather than Chicanos as a whole. The entire Chicano leadership pattern, in fact, closely resembled the pattern of the Mexican Revolution, where revolutionary juntas and local leaders emerged. These leaders took care of their home bases, and were supported by their own followers. Chávez, Gutiérrez, and Gonzales all adhered to this basic pattern, inspiring intense loyalty among their followers.

José Angel Gutiérrez

José Angel Gutiérrez rose to national prominence when only 22. In 1967 he and a group of fellow students founded the Mexican-American Youth Organization (MAYO) at St. Mary's College in San Antonio, Texas. MAYO was unique in that the membership was composed of activist organizers. Gutiérrez and Mario Compean, Nacho Pérez, and Willie Velásquez were the men who gave the organization an activist profile. Gutiérrez's approach was to attack the *gringo* establishment personally in order to create awareness among Chicanos as well as to call attention to their exploitation in Texas. His "Kill the *gringo*" statement made at a press conference caused considerable reaction among Anglo-Americans, who took the speech literally. Instantly, Gutiérrez became a controversial figure and was attacked by establishment Chicano politicians such as Congressman Henry B. González from San Antonio.

Activism in Texas hit a high note on March 30, 1969, at San Félipe Del Río (about 160 miles west of San Antonio) when some

2,000 Chicanos assembled to protest cancellation of a VISTA program by Governor Preston Smith at the request of three Val Verde county commissioners. VISTA workers had participated in a protest rally against the police's beating of Natividad Fuentes of Uvalde and his wife. At Del Río the people demanded reinstatement of the program and protested inequality, poverty, and police brutality throughout Texas. The GI Forum, LULAC, MAYO, and other organizations supported the mass rally. San Antonio County Commissioner Albert Peña taunted Congressman Henry B. González for not attending the rally.[35] Gutiérrez at the rally said, "We are fed up. We are going to move to do away with the injustices to the Chicano and if the 'gringo' doesn't get out of our way, we will stampede over him."[36] Participants pledged a commitment to cultural identity and condemned the racist system. They called it the Del Río Manifesto.

On June 20, 1969, Gutiérrez, accompanied by his young wife, Luz, and several young volunteers, returned to his hometown, Crystal City (population 8,500) to organize politically.[37]

Although Chicanos comprised over 85 percent of the region's population, an Anglo-American minority dominated the Winter Garden area. Gutiérrez knew that they could do nothing without organizing the people at the grass-roots level. The main tasks of MAYO were to increase awareness and then to confront the establishment. Anglo-Americans owned 95 percent of the land. In Zavala County the median family income was $1,754 a year; the agribusiness income in Dummit, La Salle, and Zavala counties totaled about $31 million. The median years of education for Chicanos was 2.3. On the school grounds a no-Spanish rule was vigorously enforced. Over 70 percent of the Chicano students dropped out of Crystal City High School. Few Mexicans held offices or were professionals. Those who received an education moved away. Anglo-Americans considered themselves racially and culturally superior to Chicanos. The Texas Rangers patrolled the area, terrorizing Mexicans. Adding to the plight of the Chicano was the fact that a substantial number of them were migrants who had to follow the crops. They left the Winter Garden area in late spring and did not return until the fall. Small hamlets of the area became ghost towns.[38]

Anglo authorities protected their privilege through fraud and intimidation at the polls and use of the Texas Rangers. Control of political parties was at the ballot box. The Democratic party, for example, held its primary elections shortly after most Chicanos left on their northern migration. At that time voters chose the man who would be the Democratic candidate, usually an Anglo-American. When Chicanos returned in time for the general elections, they had a choice between an Anglo-Republican or an Anglo-Democrat. Most Chicanos had been traditionally loyal to the Democratic party, and Gutiérrez knew that it would be difficult to get Mexicans to break with this tradition.[39]

A school crisis at Crystal City in November 1969 gave young volunteers the issue to organize Chicanos to confront the *gringo*. Chicano students presented demands to the Crystal City school board. They simply wanted relevant and quality education. Students were emotionally charged and were tired of injustices suffered at school. For example, for a girl to qualify as a candidate for homecoming queen, her parents had to be graduates of Crystal City High School. Not many Chicanos were eligible. The school board ignored students' demands and refused to discuss their grievances. By December tempers were high, and parents and students organized a school boycott. They formed picket lines and after several days 1,700 Chicano students walked out. They held meetings and a citizens' organization was formed. Chicanos decided at that time that they would take over the school board in the spring election of 1970. A spirit of solidarity developed that was exported to the surrounding areas. This activity polarized the community, putting issues and the enemy clearly into perspective.[40]

La Raza Unida party (LRUP) emerged from Gutiérrez's citizen group. Gutiérrez thus circumvented the two party system which dictated candidates. Chicanos could not always tell the difference between a good and a bad Anglo, but they knew the difference between a García and a Smith. Intensive organization took place during the first quarter of 1970. In April 1970 LRUP won four of the seven seats on the Crystal City Board of Education, and all of the Chicano city-council candidates were elected in Carrizo Springs, Cotulla, and Crystal City. In Cotulla the first Chicano mayor was elected. The box score for Chicanos in the Winter Garden area was fifteen elected with two new mayors, two school board majorities, and two city council majorities.[41] One *gringo* was elected.

Reies López Tijerina

Reies López Tijerina, or *El Tigre,* was the most charismatic of the Chicano leaders. Born on September 21, 1926, in farm fields close to Fall City, Texas, he lived a marginal existence with the Tijerina family, six sons and two daughters, following crops. Reies soon learned to hate his oppressors, especially Texas Rangers.

In 1942 a Baptist preacher interested him in the Bible. Subsequently, he attended a theological seminary. Eventually, he wandered into northern New Mexico. There he witnessed the poverty of New Mexicans. The more Tijerina learned about Bill Mundy, a rich agriculturalist in the area, and about the Catrons and the other Anglo-Americans who had robbed Mexicans of their land, the more interested he became in the land-grant question. He studied the Treaty of Guadalupe Hidalgo and became convinced that the national forest in Tierra Amarilla belonged to the *Pueblo de San Joaquín de Chama.* This was *ejido* land (communal or village land) that, according to Hispano-Mexican law, could not be sold and was to be held in common by the people. Villagers had the right to graze their animals and cut and gather timber in these forest lands. According to Tijerina, the U.S. government participated in frauds that deprived the people of the *ejido* lands. He got involved with the *Albiquiu* Corporation, an organization committed to the return of land grants to the New Mexicans.[42]

Tijerina called for the return of the land by any means necessary. In 1963 he incorporated *La Alianza Federal de Mercedes* (the Federal Alliance of Land Grants). It appealed to poor New Mexicans and to their lost dreams. *La Alianza* led marches on the state capital. On October 15, 1966, Tijerina and 350 members occupied the national forest campgrounds known as the Echo Amphitheatre and asserted the revival of the *ejido* rights of the *Pueblo de San Joaquín de Chama*, whose 1,400 acres lay mainly within the confines of the Kit Carson National Forest. The group elected a governing board reminiscent of the *ayuntamiento* of old and elected an *alcalde* (mayor), Francisco Salazar, a direct descendant of the founder of the pueblo. In less than a week state police, sheriff's deputies, and Rangers moved in. On October 22 *La Alianza* members took two Rangers into custody and tried them for trespassing and being a public nuisance. The court fined them and handed down a sentence of eleven months and twenty-one days in jail, then "mercifully" suspended the sentence.[43]

On November 6, 1967, Tijerina stood trial for the Amphitheatre affair.[44] Original charges included conspiracy, but the jury threw it out. It did convict him of two counts of assault and he was sentenced to two years in a state penitentiary, with five years' probation. Tijerina charged that the court convicted him for a political crime and that it had no jurisdiction. While appealing the conviction he was released on bond.

Tijerina's actions alienated the establishment under the leadership of Senator Joseph Montoya. His support dwindled in New Mexico. Many followers were frightened by his growing militancy.

While awaiting trial for the Amphitheatre incident, Tijerina entered Tierra Amarilla with the intention of making a citizen's arrest of District Attorney Alfonso Sánchez. There was a running gun battle, and Tijerina was pursued by what seemed the entire state. He was arrested. While on bail, he appeared at numerous protest rallies. Tijerina's uncompromising tactics gained him the admiration of militants and activists throughout the United States. In May and June 1968, Tijerina participated in the Poor People's Campaign. There, he proved to be an independent leader, threatening to pull the Chicano contingent out if Black organizers did not treat them as equals. In the fall he ran for governor of New Mexico on the People's Constitutional party ticket.[45]

Tijerina stood trial in late 1968 for the Tierra Amarilla raid. A key witness for the prosecution had been murdered, and it was rumored that Tijerina was responsible. District Attorney Sánchez made the prosecution of Tijerina a personal vendetta. Tijerina defended himself. Much of the trial centered around the right to make a citizen's arrest. Tijerina proved his points, and the jury entered a verdict of not guilty.[46]

In mid-February 1969 the Tenth Circuit Court of Appeals upheld the Amphitheatre conviction; Tijerina's lawyer immediately appealed to the Supreme Court. On June 5, 1969, *El Tigre* again attempted to occupy the Kit Carson National Forest at the Coyote Campsite. His wife, Patsy, and some of the participants burned a few signs. Two days later the Rangers and police arrested several of the liberators. Tijerina allegedly pointed a carbine at one of the Rangers, when deputies threatened his wife. Authorities charged him with aiding and abetting the destruction of U.S. Forest Service signs and assaulting and threatening a federal agent. The court sentenced him to three years in the federal penitentiary. On October 13, Chief Justice Burger refused to hear his appeal on the Amphitheatre case, and Tijerina went into prison to serve the two sentences concurrently. For seven months prison authorities isolated him from the other prisoners. Tijerina became a symbol; he had been convicted of political crimes, rather than of crimes against "society."[47] Tijerina was released in the summer of 1971.

Rodolfo "Corky" Gonzales

The most influential Chicano leader among the urban youth—students and *barrio batos*—was Rodolfo "Corky" Gonzales. Corky was born in Denver on June 18, 1928, son of migrant sugar beet workers. He came up the hard way—with his fists. A Golden Gloves champion who turned pro, he was a featherweight contender for the championship from 1947 to 1955.[48]

In 1957 he became the first Chicano district captain for the Democratic party. Two years later he entered the bail bonds business and opened an auto insurance agency. He kept active in the community, and in 1963 he organized *Los Voluntarios* (The Volunteers) which demonstrated against police brutality. In 1965 he became a director of one of the War on Poverty's youth programs. He was fired a year later for involvement in the Albuquerque FEPC walkout. Poverty officials viewed Corky as too zealous in defense of the Chicano community.[49] In 1966 he founded the Crusade for Justice, a community-based organization that emphasized total family involvement. His epic poem, "I am Joaquín," was probably the most inspiring piece of movement literature written in the 1960s. Its impact was immeasurable and Luis Váldez of the *Teatro Campesino* made it into a movie.

These accomplishments alone, however, did not explain

Corky's appeal to youth. He was a well-built, and beautifully tanned man, but there was something more that set Corky apart from the pack. Chávez appealed to the *campesino* (rural people); he understood them, and they followed him. The Texas Chicanos listened to Gutiérrez, for he articulated their frustrations. For a time, Tijerina represented a prophet who would deliver the lands back to their rightful owners. Corky represented the frustrations of the *bato* and the *barrio* youth, who were so intimidated by the public schools that they suffered from a mental block in speaking Spanish. Among the Chicanos of the Rio Grande Valley, the identity problem did not exist; the Chicanos knew that they were Mexicans, and they learned Spanish. It was different for the *barrio* dwellers. Schools menaced them. Corky understood this, and he understood the loss of identity when the Anglo teacher changed one's name from Rodolfo to Rudolph and when one is punished for speaking Spanish. All this is expressed in his poem *I Am Joaquín*.

The Crusade for Justice had a family organization. It included a school, a curio shop, a book store, and a social center. The school, *Tlatelolco, La Plaza de las Tres Culturas*, had about 200 students, from preschool to college. He worked to take community control of the public schools. He stated, "We intend to nationalize every school in our community." He published his own newspaper, *El Gallo: La Voz de la Justicia*.[50]

Corky realized that cultural awareness was imperative among the youth, and from the beginning he encouraged Chicano studies programs at colleges and universities. He said, "We realize that we have this tremendous lack of polished leadership that can handle all facets of organizing and creating a movement and bring it to a positive solution."[51]

On June 29, 1968, Corky headed a march on police headquarters to protest Patrolman Theodore Zavashlak's shooting and killing of 15-year-old Joseph Archuleta. In 1969 when students walked out of West Side High School Corky marched with parents in support. Corky and a number of other Chicanos were arrested when an altercation broke out at the demonstrations during the walkout. At the trial films proved that it was actually a "police riot," and defendants were acquitted.[52] In 1969 he called the First Annual Chicano Youth Conference at Denver. Gonzales was instrumental in establishing *La Raza Unida* party in Colorado, which ran candidates for state and local offices on November 4, 1970.

Católicos Por La Raza

In November 1969 opposition to the Catholic Church's neglect of Chicanos crystallized with the formation of *Católicos Por La Raza* (CPLR), led by Ricardo Cruz, a young law student from Loyola University Law School. The organization's members were infuriated over the closing, allegedly because of lack of funds, of Our Lady Queen of Girls' High School, which was predominantly Mexican. James Francis Cardinal McIntyre had just spent $4-million to build a cathedral in Los Angeles. The members were incensed at the church's refusal to involve itself in promoting social justice for Mexicans.

Although 65 percent of the Catholics in the Southwest were Mexicans, Mexicans had little voice in this institution. In 1969 fewer than 180 priests were of Mexican extraction and there were no Chicano bishops in the United States. The American church remained basically an Irish institution. In 1970 *La Raza* magazine researched the holdings of the church in Los Angeles County and estimated that it owned about $1 billion in real estate alone. Most of this property was tax free, and in other cases the church was an absentee landlord to the poor. The cardinal lived in a palace in one of the most exclusive districts of the city and was chauffeured in a Cadillac. The cardinal represented the establishment and the worldly possessions denounced by Christ.

On Christmas Eve of 1969 members of CPLR demonstrated in front of St. Basil's Cathedral. Picketing was peaceful and orderly. When the Mass began, demonstrators attempted to enter the church, but ushers locked them out. When a few gained entrance, sheriff's deputies met them. These "ushers" were armed, and they carried clubs, which they used to expel the demonstrators. Police units arrested twenty-one demonstrators, twenty of whom stood trial for disturbing the peace and assaults on police officers. Ricardo Cruz was convicted of a misdemeanor. On May 8, 1972, he began serving a 120-day sentence for his conviction.[53]

CPLR achieved national publicity. Chicanos throughout the Southwest supported it. Shortly afterwards, a Chicano bishop in Texas, Patrick Fernández Flores, was elevated to the post of auxiliary bishop. In 1978 he became Bishop of El Paso. Cardinal James Francis McIntyre retired, but not before, in a fit of anger, he told a group of Chicano students, "I was here before there were even Mexicans. I came to Los Angeles 21 years ago."[54]

In 1969 most activists had little hope that the church would change and looked on it as an enemy. However, changes were taking place among many of the Latino clergy, which would not become visible until the 1970s.

MAJOR DEMONSTRATIONS

The Chicano National Moratorium

The Vietnam war politicized the Chicano community. According to Ralph Guzmán, between January 1961 and February 1967, although the Chicano population officially numbered 10 to 12 percent of the total population of the Southwest, Chicanos comprised 19.4 percent of those from that area who were killed in Vietnam. From December 1967 to March 1969 Chicanos suffered 19 percent of all casualties from the Southwest. Chicanos from Texas sustained 25.2 percent of the casualties of that state.[55]

Chicano activists launched protests against the war. Rosalio Muñoz, a former student-body president at the University of California at Los Angeles, Sal Baldenegro, of the University of Arizona, and Ernesto Vigil, of the Crusade for Justice in Denver, were the first Chicanos to refuse induction.

In 1969 the Brown Berets formed the National Chicano Moratorium Committee and held its first demonstration on December 20, 1969 with 2,000 in attendance. Rosalio Muñoz joined as co-chairperson. On February 28, 1970, they staged another protest, with 6,000 Chicanos marching through the pouring rain.

In March 1970 Chicanos from all over the United States flocked to Denver to the Second Annual Chicano Youth Conference. They planned hundreds of local Chicano moratoria with the culmination to be a national moratorium in Los Angeles on August 29. Chicano youth organized demonstrations that ranged from a few hundred to several thousand participants. The events went off without a major incident. However, there were signs of police-community tension. On July 4, 1970, disturbances broke out at the East Los Angeles sheriff's substation during a demonstration protesting the deaths of six Mexican-American inmates in the preceding five months. There were 22 arrests, and it took some 250 deputies and the California Highway Patrol to quell the rebellion. One youth was shot and windows were broken along Whittier Boulevard.[56] The tension increased as August 29 neared.

On the morning of the 29th contingents from all over the United States arrived in East Los Angeles. By noon participants numbered between 20,000 and 30,000. *Conjuntos* (musical groups) blared out *corridos; Vívas* and yells filled the air; placards read: "*Raza sí, guerra no!*" "*Aztlán:* Love it or Leave it!" as sheriff's deputies lined the parade route. They stood helmeted, making no attempt to establish contact with marchers: no smiles, no small talk. The march ended peaceably and the parade turned into Laguna Park. Marchers settled down to enjoy the program; many had brought picnic lunches. Mexican music and Chicano children entertained those assembled.

A minor incident at a liquor store took place a block from Laguna Park when teenagers pilfered some soft drinks.[57] The police, instead of isolating this incident, rushed squad cars to the park and armed officers prepared to enter the park area. Deputies refused to communicate with monitors. Their demeanor caused a reaction, and a few marchers angrily threw objects at the police. Authorities saw that monitors were restraining the few protestors. The reasonable man could deduce that the presence of such a large number of police was causing the reaction. It became evident that the police had found an excuse to break up the demonstration.

Monitors begged police not to enter the park, explaining that there were many women and small children in the area. Deputies, in spite of this, rushed into the area, trapping men, women, and children and causing considerable panic. They wielded their clubs, trampled spectators, and clubbed those who did not move fast enough. In the main section of the park police surprised the crowd. Many did not know what had happened, for up to that time they had not heard a warning to disperse. Deputies fired tear-gas canisters. Participants admittedly hurled objects at the troops, maintaining that they did this in self-defense and others claiming that they acted simply out of hatred for what the police represented. By this time deputies numbered over 500. They moved in military formation, sweeping the park. Wreckage could be seen everywhere: baby strollers were trampled into the ground; Victor Mendoza, walking with a cane, frantically looked for his grandmother; four deputies beat a man in his sixties; tear gas filled the air.

According to Dr. James S. Koopman, a physician at the UCLA School of Medicine, Department of Pediatrics:

> Everyone was assembled peacefully at Laguna Park. My wife and I sat on the grass amongst diverse people. Immediately around us were little children playing with a puppy, an older woman with a cane, a pregnant woman with a small baby and a family eating hamburgers and french fries. The program began and after two speeches a Puerto Rican rhythm group was providing entertainment. The first sign of any disturbance I saw was when some people in the distance began to stand up. The loudspeaker calmly assured us that nothing was happening and that we should sit down. Seconds later I saw a row of gold helmets marching across the park, forcing everyone toward the high fences. The exit was too small for everyone to leave quickly. I, along with everyone else, panicked. The terrible tragedies of human stampedes in the soccer stadiums of Peru and Argentina were uppermost in my mind.[58]

Eventually, 1,200 officers occupied Laguna Park. Los Angeles police joined the sheriff's deputies, as did police units from surrounding communities,[59] extending the area of confrontation to Whittier Boulevard. Mass arrests followed. They kept prisoners chained in fours, in two buses at the East Los Angeles substation. Sheriff's deputies did not allow them to drink water or go to the bathroom for about four hours. Deputies maced the chained prisoners at least three times. A pregnant girl was manhandled by a deputy, and the deputies repeatedly maced the chained occupants of the bus.[60]

Deputies at Laguna Park shot at a Chicano when he allegedly ran a blockade; his car hit a telephone pole and he was electrocuted. A tear-gas canister exploded in a trash can, killing a 15-year-old boy. These events preceded the most controversial event of the day. Late in the afternoon Ruben Salazar and two coworkers from KMEX-TV, the Spanish language television station, stopped at the Silver Dollar Bar for a beer. Soon afterward deputies surrounded the bar, allegedly looking for a man with a rifle. When some occupants of the Silver Dollar attempted to leave, police forced them back into the premises. Police claimed that they then broadcast warnings for all occupants to come out; witnesses testified that they heard no warning. The suspect with the gun had been apprehended elsewhere and since released, but officers continued their activities at the Silver Dollar. They shot a ten-inch tear-gas projectile into the bar. The missile could pierce 7-inch plywood at 100 yards, and it struck Salazar in the head. Another shot filled the bar with gas. Customers made their way out of the establishment. About 5:30 PM Salazar's two colleagues frantically informed deputies that their friend was still in the bar. Deputies refused to listen, and not until two hours later was Salazar's body discovered.

In retrospect, observations of Danny Villanueva, general manager of KMEX-TV and former professional NFL football player, have a bearing on the case. Villanueva stated that Salazar had acted strangely the week before his death, putting many small details in order.[61] Salazar had commented to others that he was concerned about threats made to him by Police Chief Ed Davis. The newsman's problems had begun on July 16, 1970, when five Los Angeles detectives and two San Leandro police officers burst into the room of a hotel in downtown Los Angeles, shooting and killing two Mexican nationals, Guillermo, 22 and Beltrán, 23, now known as the Sánchez cousins. Police were hunting another man; it was a case of "mistaken identity." No warrant had been issued for the cousins. Police alleged that they shouted, "Police! Give up!" The Sánchez's spoke no English. One of the cousins was shot in the room; the other was shot to death while dangling from a window sill as he attempted to leave through a window.[62]

Ruben Salazar exposed the inconsistencies of police reports. Law enforcement officials called Salazar and ordered him to tone down his television coverage.[63] They alleged that he was inflaming the people. Salazar responded that he was merely reporting the facts. Police persisted that the Chicano community was not ready for this kind of analysis. Police authorities left, telling Salazar that they would get him if he continued his coverage. Salazar did not stop and at the time of his death was, in fact, working on a series of stories on the enforcement agencies in the Los Angeles area, entitled "What Progress in Thirty Years of Police Community Relations?"[64]

A federal grand jury brought in an indictment against the officers involved in the Sánchez shootings for violation of the civil rights of the two men. The City of Los Angeles paid for the defense of three of the police officers, which produced a storm of protest. The officers were acquitted by a federal court. An interesting sidelight is that the U.S. attorney who persisted in prosecuting the case resigned about a year later.[65] News media attributed this resignation to pressure and criticisms from Chief Ed Davis and Mayor Sam Yorty.

On September 10, 1970, a coroner's inquest probed the circumstances surrounding Ruben Salazar's death. In Los Angeles a coroner's inquest is generally informal, with seven jurors selected at random. A hearing officer without judicial standing is appointed. Because of general interest, local television stations cooperated in airing the entire proceedings. The hearing officer did not limit testimony to the death of Salazar and allowed the proceedings to begin with an edited film taken by the film crews of the sheriff's department. Officers testified as to the Chicano community's riotous nature. The hearing officer made no attempt to restrain deputies from introducing immaterial facts.

Chicano photographers saved the day. A series of photographs taken by *La Raza* reporters Raúl Ruiz and Joe Razo, eyewitnesses to the events at the Silver Dollar Bar, were shown. The photographs contradicted the testimony of the deputies. For example, deputies claimed that they did not force the occupants of the bar to return to the bar. Raúl Ruiz produced a photo that showed that they did. The hearing officer repeatedly attempted to limit Ruiz's testimony, and he questioned him at length. Shortly afterward *La Raza* published a special issue featuring the photos taken on August 29. The *Los Angeles Times* obtained permission from the *barrio* publication to reprint many of the photos.[66]

Four inquest jurors found "death at the hands of another"; the three remaining jurors decided on "death by accident." The *Los Angeles Times*, on October 8, 1970, interviewed the jurors. A majority juror, George W. Sherard, stated, "All seven jurors reached the rapid conclusion that the killing was unintended. Four of us felt . . . deputies expected they had a good chance of killing someone." Another juror, Betty J. Clements, added, "The main surprise to me was the deputies' lack of organization, their lack of consideration for innocent people. I like to go into cocktail lounges to have a drink. I'd certainly hate to think somebody was going to shoot teargas or anything else in there simply because somebody reported there was a man with a gun." This juror questioned deputies leaving Salazar's body in the bar for two hours and wondered whether they would have acted in the same manner in Beverly Hills.

Chicanos as well as many Anglos believed that Deputy Thomas Wilson would be tried. When Los Angeles District Attorney Evelle J. Younger announced on October 14, 1970, that he would not prosecute, many Chicanos charged that Younger did not prosecute because of political expediency. A candidate for California state attorney general (he was elected), he knew that the law-and-order mentality of Californians demanded this decision.

The *Los Angeles Times,* which usually supported Younger, criticized his actions in an editorial on October 16, 1970:

> So this is where the matter stands: an innocent man was killed by a weapon that should not have been used when it was used, but the public authorities assign no blame. One does not have to enter a legal argument over whether there was, or was not, sufficient evidence for prosecution of the deputy to observe that the decision not to prosecute leaves the public in the dark as to the facts it should know.

THE SIEGE CONTINUES

Police repression of Chicanos continued at a high level throughout 1970–1971. On September 16, 1970, a peaceful Mexican Independence parade ended in violence when police attacked the crowd as marchers reached the end of the parade route. Feelings ran high with many marchers carrying banners blaming the police for the murder of Ruben Salazar. Police accounts stated that teenagers had started the altercation between them and the Chicano community when the teenagers pelted police with rocks. According to the police, they ordered the crowd to disperse and when it failed to do so, they moved in to restore order. However, eyewitnesses state that officers broke into apartments, destroying furniture and beating up occupants. The press condemned the marchers. In fact, TV newscasters Baxter Ward and George Putnam were inflammatory. Both relied on police information; they had not been there.[67]

Before the January 9, 1971 demonstration in front of Parker Center in the city of Los Angeles, Chief Ed Davis openly baited activists. The demonstration began at Hollenbeck police station; leaders planned to picket the station as a protest against police brutality. The march had been organized by the Chicano Moratorium Committee, and Brown Berets acted as monitors. About 1,000 participated. No major incident occurred at Hollenbeck, but from the beginning the police intimidated marchers. At the First Street Bridge some marchers spilled into the street; police pushed them back onto sidewalks. Monitors cooled tempers. The main body reached Parker Center, the Los Angeles Police Department headquarters, and began to picket it. Police incited a riot and attacked demonstrators. Three hours later, when the melee was finally quelled, police had arrested thirty-two people. Again news media condemned Chicanos, with few questioning the methods of police or asking if they would have used similar vindictiveness in the west side of the city. Chief Davis blamed "swimming pool Communists" and the Brown Berets for the riot.[68]

Numerous smaller incidents occurred; however, the last major confrontation was on January 31, 1971. Contingents arrived at Belvedere Park in East Los Angeles from the four major *barrios* in the Los Angeles area. They had been baited before the rally by Sheriff Pitchess and Chief Davis. The demonstration was peaceful, and as the rally ended Rosalio Muñoz told the gathering of some 5,000 to disperse. A minority of the crowd, however, marched on the sheriff substation on Third Street and a confrontation occurred. According to Muñoz and others, although the sheriffs had maintained a low profile, they carefully orchestrated the confrontation. The crowd was heavily infiltrated by police provocateurs.

Protesters walked up Whittier Boulevard. They broke a few windows along the way, and tore down street signs.[69] At about 3:45 PM gunshots were heard at Whittier Boulevard, and the police moved in, shooting tear-gas at demonstrators. They fired shotguns into the crowd, and the protesters, in turn, hurled objects at police. The confrontation left one man dead, nineteen wounded by buckshot, two with stab wounds, and numerous with broken bones. Property damage climbed over $200,000. On February 4, the *Eastside Sun* quoted Pitchess, "This time they can't blame the disturbance on the department . . . because deputies were not in the area until after the burning and looting had started." Chicano leaders saw the problem in a different light. They stated that the trouble, in reality, had begun many months, if not years, before. At the crux of the problem was the question Ruben Salazar had posed: what progress in thirty years of police community relations?

POLICE SOLUTION TO UNREST

The police-community confrontations surrounding the August 29 demonstration were not unique. Considerable urban unrest existed among Chicanos during the mid-1960s, and if the Black community had not rebelled at Watts in 1965, the same thing would have occurred in East Los Angeles. In a 1964 survey among unemployed Chicanos in Los Angeles 90 percent of those interviewed felt that the fair employment legislation up to that time had produced no results whatsoever.[70] This feeling of hopelessness carried over into the streets.

On January 27, 1960, Chief William H. Parker had created a furor with a statement before the U.S. Civil Rights Commission: "Some of these people were here before we were but some are not far removed from the wild tribes of the district of the inner mountains of Mexico."[71] Parker underscored the attitude of the LAPD toward Mexicans. Parker claimed that 40 percent of the arrests in the city of Los Angeles were Black and 28 percent Mexican. Frank X. Paz led demonstrations against the police with over 500 attending a meeting of the Mexican-American Citizens Committee.[72] Dr.

R. J. Carreon, Jr., the token Chicano police commissioner, refused to attend the meeting stating that he had heard Parker's story and that the community should drop the issue. The community renewed its efforts to create a police review board. The American Civil Liberties Union, the NAACP, and the Mexican-American Citizens Committee joined to form the Committee for a Los Angeles Police Review Board.[73]

In East Los Angeles confrontations between Chicanos and police increased as the LAPD attempted to clamp down to discourage a Mexican Watts. In 1966 police called for a back-up crew when an angry crowd gathered as they attempted to make an arrest. Two warning shots were fired.[74] In July 1966 the Happy Valley Parents Association organized a surveillance of police. In September of that year the ACLU opened a center in East Los Angeles. From September 1966 to July 1968 it investigated 205 police abuse cases, with 152 filed by Chicanos.

In the summer of 1967 some 300 Chicanos attended a conference at Camp Hess Kramer on police-community relations. They asked for federal government intervention into the deteriorated relations between the police and the community in Los Angeles.[75] Federal intervention was not forthcoming and relations worsened. When the Chicano community began its massive mobilizations, the police solution to the growing unrest was a military one and military solutions involved subversion, provocation, and extensive use of secret police and spies.

During these years the Central Intelligence Agency (CIA), the FBI, and local law enforcement agencies became more paranoid. They provoked militants, investigated the personal lives of ordinary citizens, and kept files on those they considered suspect or subversive. In the process, they answered to no one. In the Los Angeles area the police agencies had become sacred cows that functioned beyond public control. While other segments of the city and county civil servant establishment went without pay raises, most law enforcement budget requests received approval, and police and sheriff's deputies received their raises as a matter of course. Any charge of police brutality or criticism of police transgressions was branded as subversive; Mayor Sam Yorty publicly denounced the accusations as communist-inspired. Furthermore, the only check on the Los Angeles Police Department was a police commission, which Yorty appointed.

The Los Angeles Police Department is one of the most professional police departments in the United States. Therein is the problem. It had become an elite guard dedicated to maintaining the status quo and protecting the privileged of the city. The only serious challenge to the power of this self-legitimizing agency became the Black and Chicano communities. The response of the police was to brand protest as communist-inspired and they reacted to crush the revolutionaries. In the process a secret police, along with a network of spies, was developed. Much of the story began to unfold with the defection of Louis Tackwood, a spy for the Los Angeles Police Department.

In October 1971 Louis Tackwood, a Black informer, stunned the Los Angeles public by testifying that the Criminal Conspiracy Section (CCS) of the Los Angeles Police Department paid him. He was assigned to a group of officers who, in cooperation with the FBI, planned to instigate a disruption by militants of the 1972 Republican convention in San Diego; they were to kill minor officials to force President Richard Nixon to use his powers to break the militant movement. Tackwood named Dan Mahoney (CCS) and Ed Birch (FBI) as those in charge of the operation. In private conversations he has also described the police use of drug pushers as informers in return for protection from prosecution.[76]

Officer Fernando Sumaya also worked as an undercover agent for the Los Angeles Police Department. In the fall semester of 1968 he attempted to infiltrate the United Mexican-American Student chapter at San Fernando Valley State College during campus protests there. He was ousted from the group because he was unknown and because he came on too strong. Sumaya then moved to East Los Angeles where he infiltrated the Brown Berets. In the spring of 1969 he was involved in the Biltmore Hotel affair, where Chicanos were accused of disrupting a speech by Governor Ronald Reagan at a Nuevas Vistas Education Conference, sponsored by the California Department of Education. Thirteen Chicanos were arrested on the charge of disturbing the peace; ten of the thirteen were charged with conspiracy to commit arson. After two years of appeals the defendants were tried. The key witness for the prosecution was Sumaya. The defendants all denied any involvement with the fires. Some charged that Sumaya set the fires. The jury found the defendants not guilty. Meanwhile, Carlos Montes, a Brown Beret, had left the area and he was not tried. He remained at large until the mid-1970s. After he was caught police continued to hound Montes. The LAPD destroyed records documenting Sumaya's role in the Biltmore fires. In spite of these inequities, in November 1979, a jury found Montes not guilty—evidently the jury questioned Sumaya's and the LAPD's suspect role.[77]

Most astounding was the testimony of Eustacio (Frank) Martínez, 23, in a press conference on January 31, 1972. He revealed that since July 1969 he had infiltrated Chicano groups. He was recruited by a federal agent for the Alcohol, Tobacco, and Firearms Division (ATF) of the Internal Revenue Service. In return for not being prosecuted for a federal firearms violation, he agreed to work as an informant and agent provocateur. During his service, he infiltrated the Mexican-American Youth Organization and the Brown Berets in Houston and Kingsville, Texas. He admitted that he committed acts of violence to provoke others. From September 1969 to October 1970 he participated in a protest march in Alice, Texas, and attempted to provoke a disruption "by jumping on a car and trying to cave its top in." He attempted to get militants to buy guns and to get police to cause violence. He was rebuked by the MAYO members.[78]

In October 1970 ATF agents sent him to Los Angeles where he worked for agents Fernando Ramos and Jim Riggs. Martínez began spreading rumors against Rosalio Muñoz, accusing him of being too soft, and in November 1970 Martínez ousted Muñoz and became chair of the Chicano Moratorium Committee. He continued in this capacity until March 1971, when he returned to Texas. There Martínez became a member of the Brown Berets and went around, according to informants, waving a carbine and advocating violent tactics. During his testimony Martínez named officers Valencia, Armas, Savillos, and Domínguez of the CCS as contacts. In other words, when Martínez took part in the Los Angeles riots on January 9 and 31, 1971, the Los Angeles police knew of his involvement. Upon his return from Texas he was instructed by Ramos and Riggs to infiltrate *La Casa de Carnalismo* to establish links between *Carnalismo* and the Chicano Liberation Front (CLF), which had been involved in numerous bombings. Martínez reported that the main functions of the group were to eliminate narcotics, to sponsor English classes, and to dispense food to the needy. He could find no links with CLF. The officers told him that his "information was a bunch of bullshit." He was to find evidence by any means necessary. They then instructed him to use his influence to get a heroin addict by the name of "Nacho" to infiltrate *Carnalismo*. Martínez refused to take part in the frameup. He finally became disillusioned when, on the first anniversary of the Chicano National Moratorium, agents told him to plead guilty to charges of inciting a riot. He had been promised protection from prosecution.[79]

Although newsmen did not question the reliability of Martínez's disclosures, they did not call for congressional investigations into the provocateur activities of federal and local agencies. Louis Tackwood and Frank Martínez were admitted provocateurs. The latter's role cast a shadow on the actions of the police in the Los Angeles Chicano rebellions. Local police authorities knew of Martínez's involvement with the moratorium. It is reasonable to speculate that they had other informants and provocateurs involved in the confrontations of 1970 and 1971 throughout the United States. What their role was is buried in the files of the secret police of the different branches of the federal and local police agencies. These are the aspects of history that remain closed to historians.

JUSTICE IN THE SOUTHWEST

According to *A Report of the United States Commission on Civil Rights: Mexican-Americans and the Administration of Justice in the Southwest,* published in March 1970, there was no civil or criminal justice for Chicanos. The official government report documented the Chicanos' inequality before the law. The report indicted Los Angeles police authorities, as well as the FBI, reinforcing a case of collusion between federal and local authorities in the repression of the Mexican community. Specific examples follow.

On September 1, 1968, Jess Domínguez, 41, Los Angeles, was looking for his teenage children in the early morning. He approached a police car and asked the officers for assistance. They answered: "We don't have any time for you Mexicans." Domínguez became indignant, whereupon officers beat him. At least 15 officers joined in the brutal beating of Domínguez. He was charged with assaulting an officer. Domínguez was badly bruised, could not move his jaw, and constantly vomited; subsequently, he underwent surgery. The FBI investigated and based on police reports, claimed that no investigation or prosecution of officers was warranted.[80]

On November 9, 1968, Salvador Barba, 13, was beaten by Los Angeles policemen and required 40 stitches in the head. An FBI investigation found that the facts of the case did not warrant the arrest of the officers involved. The findings of agents were based largely on Los Angeles Police Department reports.[81]

On May 5, 1969, Frank Gonzales, 14, Los Angeles, was skipping school when an officer called to him, and the boy ran away. Officer Thomas Parkham, suspended twice before—once for pointing a cocked pistol at a juvenile and another time for being drunk and disorderly while off duty—drew his gun. He claimed that he fired a warning shot before he fired at the boy. He was allowed to resign in lieu of disciplinary action. District Attorney Evelle Younger decided not to prosecute Parkham.[82]

On September 8, 1968, in Fairfield, California, Sergeant David Huff shot José Alvarado. The latter left a wife and five children. The chief of police would not meet with the community nor would he suspend Huff. The police claimed that Alvarado attacked five police officers with a meat cleaver. An enraged community formed the United Mexicans for Justice and questioned why no inquest had been conducted, why so many police could not disarm one man, why they had shot to kill, and why there had not been an investigation of Huff who had previously pistol-whipped a man.[83]

The report on the administration of justice bluntly states that police generally did not respect Mexicans. Ray Anaya, sheriff of Carlsbad, New Mexico, is quoted as saying, "An officer goes [to] a house of a man who has a long police record, knocks on the door, the wife opens the door, and [the officer] goes into the house [without a warrant]. If that were in another place in town, Riverside Drive, I am sure it would not happen. . . ."[84]

On September 2, 1969, Judge Gerald S. Chargin of Santa Clara County (California) Juvenile Court passed sentence on a 17-year-old Chicano, allegedly convicted of incest. Chargin stated:

> Mexican people, after 13 years of age, think is is perfectly all right to go out and act like an animal. We ought to send you out of the country— send you back to Mexico. You belong in prison for the rest of your life for doing things of this kind. You ought to commit suicide. That's what I think of people of this kind. You are lower than animals and haven't the right to live in organized society—just miserable, lousy, rotten people. Maybe Hitler was right. The animals in our society probably ought to be destroyed because they have no right to live among human beings.[85]

The defense attorney attempted to restrain Chargin, but the judge would not be silenced. A demonstration of over 1,000 people had little effect. Congressman Ed Roybal and Senator Joseph Montoya called for an investigation, as well as for the dismissal of Chargin. But despite this, Chargin was merely transferred to the civil division of the Superior Court.[86]

In 1970 Dr. Fred Logan, Jr., an osteopath, 31, was murdered by Sheriff Erick Bauch in Mathis, Texas. The doctor arrived in 1966 and made the mistake of socializing with Mexicans. The previous doctor had been run out of town. Chicanos were poor and could not pay for medical services which Logan often rendered free. In mid-1970 Anglo doctors refused a $167,000 grant from Health, Education, and Welfare for a clinic for the poor. Dr. Logan accepted. One day while drinking with Mexican friends, they fired blanks into the air. Bauch showed up and arrested Logan. "Six minutes later, the deputy sheriff put in a call for an ambulance. Logan, with two bullets from Bauch's .357 Magnum in his chest, was dead when the ambulance arrived on the scene. The official report—self-defense and attempted escape."[87]

Chicanos were excluded from trial juries and grand juries. Chicanos have been kept off trial juries by being excluded from the roll of prospective jurors. This exclusion was more prevalent in the "redneck" areas of the Southwest. Grand juries were selected by county judges. Judges in Los Angeles readily admitted that they submitted primarily names of prominent people. As a consequence, Chicanos often were judged by anti-Mexican Anglo-Americans who were convinced defendants were guilty before they stood trial. Even well-meaning Anglo-Americans were ill equipped to judge Chicanos, who lived under different social, economic, and cultural conditions from their own.

Mike Gonzales, an attorney in South Texas, said that in ten years of courtroom activity he had never seen a Chicano on a jury, even though the population in some areas was 85 percent Chicano.

R. P. Sánchez, a lawyer from McAllen, Texas, said that although Hidalgo County had a Mexican population of about 75 percent, only one or two Chicanos had served on juries. Similar data were collected in Phoenix and Tucson, Arizona. In Fort Summer, New Mexico, an area more than 60 percent Mexican-American, local Mexican-Americans stated that their peers just did not serve on juries. Public Defender Richard S. Buckley of Los Angeles said, "I recall very few Mexican-Americans on any juries I have tried in a period of 15 years." Pete Tijerina, an attorney from San Antonio, Texas, told of a case he attempted to try in Jourdantown, Texas, in March 1966. Tijerina stated that the town was 65 percent Mexican. Only one juror out of forty-eight listed was Mexican. The case was postponed until July when two Mexican-Americans were on the jury list, but it was found that one of them was dead. The case was again postponed until December. Five Chicanos were now on the list, but all five were peremptorily challenged by the insurance company. Tijerina's client was a Chicano.

The same pattern was repeated with grand juries. In the county of Los Angeles, where the Chicano population was about 1 million, only four Mexicans served on a grand jury in twelve years. In adjacent Orange County, which had over 44,000 Mexicans, only one had served in twelve years. Further investigation by the Commission on Civil Rights revealed that the grand juror who served was Spanish, and that no Chicano had served on the grand jury of Monterey County from 1938 through 1968.[88]

In the late 1960s the California Rural Legal Assistance (CRLA) unit was organized through federal grants. CRLA has a distinguished record in defending the rights of the poor. Although it did not handle criminal cases, it represented the poor in various other matters. In Kings County, California, for example, where growers received $10,179,917 *not* to produce crops and where the board of supervisors raised their annual salaries from $2,400 to $12,000, less than $6,000 was spent on food for the poor. The CRLA sued the county on behalf of the poor, charging that it was violating federal statutes. The poor could not have afforded to pay an attorney for such an action. As complaints mounted against the CRLA by reactionary elements such as the California growers, Governor Ronald Reagan became more incensed about the federal government's support of an agency that brought suits against private enterprise. In December 1970 Reagan vetoed the federal appropriation to CRLA. The matter was taken to Washington, and the CRLA was put on a year's probation, during which time their actions were to be reviewed. An investigation showed that the CRLA had done nothing improper. They continue to champion the underdog.[89]

The Mexican-American Legal Defense Fund (MALDF) was the victim of political pressure. Congressman Henry B. González was upset because money had been given to MAYO in Texas.[90]

González pressured the Ford Foundation to curtail grants to the Southwest Council of *La Raza* which was the funding agent through which the Ford Foundation went. González charged that they funded subversive organizations. Pressure was applied to limit the scope of MALDF's cases. As a consequence, the headquarters of MALDF was moved out of San Antonio. This seriously compromised the organization's effectiveness, since San Antonio was to Chicanos what Selma was to Blacks.

CONCLUSION

The decade began optimistically. Some Chicanos frequently referred to themselves as the "sleeping giant." Optimism turned to disillusionment, and then to bitterness as the Democratic party continued to exploit Chicanos by gerrymandering them, excluding them from government participation, and ignoring their needs. They were victimized by poverty and an inequitable criminal justice system. By the 1970s it was clear that even the small gains made by the Chicano community were checked by those in power to keep Chicanos in their place and were therefore illusory.

NOTES

1. Leo Grebler, Joan W. Moore, and Ralph C. Guzmán, *The Mexican-American People* (New York: Free Press, 1970), pp. 106, 126, 185, 251.
2. Grebler et al., pp. 143, 150, 236; Richard W. Slatta, "Chicanos in the Pacific Northwest: An Historical Overview of Oregon's Chicanos," *Aztlán* (Fall 1975): 335.
3. Grebler et al., p. 196.
4. Robert Coles and Harry Huge, "Thorns on the Yellow Rose of Texas," *New Republic* (April 19, 1969): 13–17.
5. Coles and Huge, p. 14.
6. Coles and Huge, p. 17.
7. Mark Day, *Forty Acres* (New York: Praeger, 1971), pp. 41–42.
8. Mark R. Levy and Michael S. Kramer, "Patterns of Chicano Voting Behavior," in F. Chris García, *La Causa Politica: A Chicano Politics Reader* (Notre Dame, Ind.: University of Notre Dame Press, 1974), p. 241.
9. Ralph C. Guzmán, *The Political Socialization of the Mexican-American People* (New York: Arno Press, 1976), p. 145; Carey McWilliams, *North from Mexico* (New York: Greenwood Press, 1968), pp. 15–16.
10. The *G.I. Forum News Bulletin*, March-April 1960, portrays Medina in another light.
11. "Revolt of the Masses," *Time* Magazine (April 12, 1963); Tony Castro, *Chicano Power: The Emergence of Mexican Americans* (New York: Saturday Review Press, 1974), p. 28.
12. Edwin Larry Dickens, "The Political Role of Mexican-Americans in San Antonio" (Ph.D. dissertation, Texas Tech University, 1969), p. 169.
13. *G.I. Forum News Bulletin*, June 1961. The October 1961 issue stated that Chicanos were dissatisfied with Kennedy's patronage policies.
14. Alberto Júarez, "The Emergence of El Partido de la Raza Unida: California's New Chicano Party," *Aztlán* 3, no. 2 (Fall 1972): 183.
15. Guzmán, p. 144; *Eastside Sun*, April 30, 1961.
16. *Eastside Sun*, July 26, 1962, January 31, 1963, July 9, August 12, 1965; "Hazard Park . . . That Classic Robin Hood Story in Reverse," *Eastside Sun*, March 13, 1969; *Eastside Sun*, May 29, 1969.

17. *G.I. Forum News Bulletin*, March 1963, September 1964.
18. Louise Año Nuevo Kerr, "The Chicano Experience in Chicago: 1920–1970" (Ph.D. dissertation, University of Illinois at Chicago Circle, 1976), pp. 183–184; William Kornblum, *Blue Collar Community* (Chicago: University of Chicago Press, 1974), pp. 161–182.
19. Kerr, pp. 192, 195; John Hart Lane, Jr., "Voluntary Associations Among Mexican Americans in San Antonio, Texas: Organization and Leadership Characteristics" (Ph.D. dissertation, University of Texas, 1968), p. 29.
20. Biliana María Ambrecht, "Politicization as a Legacy of the War on Poverty: A Study of Advisory Council Members in a Mexican American Community" (Ph.D. dissertation, University of California at Los Angeles, 1973), p. 1. Donald V. Kurtz, "Politics, Ethnicity, Integration: Mexican Americans in the War on Poverty" (Ph.D. dissertation, University of California, Davis, 1970) is an important study of the War on Poverty. It is a case study of the Border Community Action Council of San Diego County, California, in the border town of San Ysidro.
21. Greg Coronado, "Spanish-Speaking Organizations in Utah," in Paul Morgan and Vince Mayer, *Working Papers Toward a History of the Spanish Speaking in Utah* (Salt Lake City: American West Center, Mexican-American Documentation Project, University of Utah, 1973), p. 121.
22. Vernon M. Briggs, Jr., Walter Fogel, and Fred H. Schmidt, *The Chicano Worker* (Austin: University of Texas Press, 1977), p. 38; *Forumeer*, March 1967. This issue states that the Forum almost dropped sponsorship of SER because LBJ was hedging on the White House Conference.
23. The lack of service to the Mexican community led to a walkout of Chicano workers in Los Angeles. See "Chicano Caucus seeks freedom from poverty agency," *Belvedere Citizen*, January 7, 1971; "EYOA walkout goes on, urge settlement," *Belvedere Citizen*, November 18, 1971.
24. McWilliams, p. 17. I had extensive conversations with Miguel Montes and Louis García, both residents of San Fernando, California, who participated in the conference. They felt that what they did was a radical act, as did most Chicano activists at that time.
25. *Forumeer*, October 1967. The Forum supported the conference and said nothing about the demonstrations. See also Lane, p. 2; Richard Gardner, *Grito! Reies Tijerina and the New Mexico Land Grant War of 1967* (New York: Bobbs-Merrill, 1970), pp. 231–232.
26. Juan Gómez-Quiñones, *Mexican Students por La Raza: The Chicano Student Movement in Southern California, 1967–1977* (Santa Barbara, Calif.: Editorial La Causa, 1978), pp. 17–18, 22–23; Gerald Paul Rosen, "Political Ideology and the Chicano Movement: A Study of the Political Ideology of Activists in the Chicano Movement" (Ph.D. dissertation, University of California at Los Angeles, 1972), p. 248. Julian Nava was selected by a coalition of community organizations. This victory led to the later formation of the Congress of Mexican American Unity, in which youth played an active role. See "Community Endorsement Of Board of Education," *Eastside Sun*, January 29, 1967; "Calderon 'Peoples Choice' for Senator at Confab," *Eastside Sun*, February 29, 1968.
27. *Forumeer*, March 1966.
28. "Tragedy of Lincoln High," *Inside Eastside*, December 8–21, 1967; January 5–19, 1968.
29. Rosen, pp. 144, 43, 145.
30. Oscar Acosta, "The East L.A. 13 vs. the Superior Court," *El Grito* 3, no. 2 (Winter 1970): 14; Joan London and Henry Anderson, *So Shall Ye Reap* (New York: Crowell, 1971), p. 25.
31. William Parker Frisbie, "Militancy Among Mexican Americans: A Study of High School Students" (Ph.D. dissertation, University of North Carolina at Chapel Hill, 1972), pp. 4, 143. *Forumeer*, October, December 1968; Eugene Acosta Marín, "The Mexican American Community and Leadership of the Dominant Society in Arizona: A Study of Their Mutual Attitudes and Perspectives," (Ph.D. dissertation, U.S. International University, 1973), p. 12.
32. Chicano Coordinating Council for Higher Education, *El Plan de Santa Barbara: A Chicano Plan for Higher Education* (Oakland, Calif.: La Causa, 1969).

33. David Sánchez, *Expedition Through Aztlán* (La Puente, Calif.: Perspectiva Press, 1978).

34. Rona M. Fields and Charles J. Fox, "Viva La Raza: The Saga of the Brown Berets" (unpublished manuscript), was a source of information. Additional information was obtained by talking to members of the Brown Berets and to John Ortiz, an associate editor of *Regeneración*. Also see Rosen.

35. *Forumeer*, February, May 1969.

36. Quoted in Deluvina Hernández, "La Raza Satellite System," *Aztlán* 1, no. 1 (Spring 1970): 27; Castro, pp. 156–157.

37. José Angel Gutiérrez, "*Aztlán*: Chicano Revolt in the Winter Garden," *La Raza* 1, no. 4 (1971): 34–35.

38. Gutiérrez, p. 37. For a background study of Crystal City, see John Staples Shockley, *Chicano Revolt in a Texas Town* (Notre Dame, Ind.: University of Notre Dame Press, 1974).

39. Conversations with José Angel Gutiérrez.

40. Shockley, pp. 119, 120–121; Gutiérrez, pp. 39–40.

41. Gutiérrez, p. 40.

42. Gardner, p. 208; Peter Nabakov, *Tijerina and the Courthouse Raid* (Albuquerque: University of New Mexico Press, 1969), pp. 163–164; Nabokov, pp. 19, 28, 30; Gardner, pp. 66–84.

43. Gardner, pp. 129–130.

44. Clark Knowlton, "Guerillas of Rio Arriba: The New Mexico Land Wars," in F. Chris García, ed., *La Causa Politica: A Chicano Politics Reader* (Notre Dame, Ind.: University of Notre Dame Press, 1974), p. 333.

45. Nabokov, pp. 250, 256.

46. Nabokov, pp. 257–266; Gardner, pp. 265–279. Gardner presents a gripping account of the trial.

47. Gardner, p. 290.

48. Stan Steiner, *La Raza: The Mexican Americans* (New York: Harper & Row, 1969), pp. 378–392.

49. Christine Marín, *A Spokesman of the Mexican American Movement: Rodolfo "Corky" Gonzales and the Fight for Chicano Liberation, 1966–1972* (San Francisco: R & E Research Assc., 1977), pp. 1–3; *Forumeer*, November 1965; June 1966.

50. Marín, p. 5.

51. *The Militant*, December 4, 1970.

52. Marín, pp. 8, 10–11.

53. Interviews and conversations with Ricardo Cruz. Cruz passed the California bar, but had to fight to be certified because of his conviction. He is today practicing in East Los Angeles. See "Law Students Seek Signatures; Petition Protests Denial of Certification by Bar for Chicanos Active in Barrios," *Belvedere Citizen*, March 16, 1972.

54. Tapes in possession of the staff of *La Raza*. See "Catholic Archdiocese Issues Statement, Clarifies, Defines Role in Community, Government; Announce Inter-Parochial Council," *Belvedere Citizen*, February 19, 1970.

55. Ralph Guzmán, "Mexican American Casualties in Vietnam," *La Raza* 1, no. 1: 12. Most Chicano organizations supported the war in 1967, but by 1969 most were having second thoughts. The high mortality rate among Chicanos even sobered the *G.I. Forum* which had openly backed LBJ's war effort, *Forumeer*, November 1969. In "Population Control—Weeding Out Chicanos in Vietnam War?" *Forumeer*, April 1970, David Sierra asked why the United States should care about Vietnam if Australia did not. In the Southwest, out of 2,189 casualties, 316 were Chicanos. The article gave a good state-by-state rundown on casualties. An antiwar resolution was passed by the Forum during its June 26–28, 1970 convention, *Forumeer*, July 1970. A major reason for the change in position was the role of Chicano youth. See Ralph Guzmán, "Mexican-Americans have highest Vietnam death rate," *Belvedere Citizen*, October 16, 1969.

56. *The Belvedere Citizen*, July 9, 1970.

57. Armando Morales, *Ando Sangrando! I Am Bleeding* (Los Angeles: Congress of Mexican American Unity, 1971), p. 106.

58. Morales, p. 105.

59. In the spring of 1970 special units of the sheriff's department had been used to

put down student demonstrations near Santa Barbara. A grand jury investigation condemned the units' excessive use of force.

60. I was one of those arrested.
61. Villanueva made these remarks at the Los Angeles Valley Public Library in December 1970.
62. *Los Angeles Times*, July 17, 1970; Gene Blake and Howard Hertel, "Court Won't Drop Case Against Officers in 'Mistake' Slayings," *Los Angeles Times*, April 27, 1971.
63. This seems to be standard procedure for Davis. He called the managers of KTTV in Los Angeles after they showed films of the moratorium and ordered them not to show them again. A highly reliable source reports that although the management of Metromedia is conservative it resented this attempted censorship.
64. Letter from Manuel Ruiz, a member of the U.S. Commission on Civil Rights, to Herman Sillas, chairperson of the California State Advisory Committee to the Commission, September 14, 1970, in "A Report of the California State Advisory Committee to the U.S. Commission on Civil Rights: Police-Community Relations in East Los Angeles, California" (October 1970).
65. *New York Times*, December 18, 1971; *Los Angeles Times*, December 18, 1971.
66. *La Raza*, 3, Special Issue, (1970) is a classic. It contains a photo essay of the moratorium, documenting police repression.
67. Putnam's transcript on file.
68. Morales, p. 117; "Police Chief Davis claims Latin Youths being used by Reds," *Belvedere Citizen*, January 21, 1971.
69. *Eastside Sun*, February 4, 1971.
70. Gary A. Greenfield and Don B. Kates, Jr., "Mexican Americans, Racial Discrimination, and the Civil Rights Act of 1866," 5 *Cal Journal* (1975): 667.
71. Christopher Rand, *Los Angeles: The Ultimate City* (New York: Oxford University Press, 1967), p. 131; Joan W. Moore, *Mexican Americans*, 2nd ed. (Englewood Cliffs, N.J.: Prentice-Hall, 1976), p. 93; *G.I. Forum News Bulletin*, March-April 1960; *Eastside Sun*, February 4, 1960.
72. *Eastside Sun*, February 4, February 11, 1960.
73. *Eastside Sun*, February 11, 1960; "Roybal Comments on Crime Reports of East Los Angeles," *Eastside Sun*, March 10, 1960; "Police Maltreatment Subject at Conference at Biltmore Hotel," *Eastside Sun*, June 16, 1960.
74. Armando Morales, "A Study of Mexican American Perceptions of Law Enforcement Policies and Practices in East Los Angeles" (DSW dissertation, University of Southern California, 1972), p. 87.
75. Morales, "Study of Mexican American Perceptions," pp. 89, 90; *New York Times*, October 25, 1971.
76. A tape in the possession of a colleague who remains nameless for obvious reasons.
77. *Los Angeles Times*, July 27, August 18, 1971; *Valley News*, Van Nuys, California, November 27, 1979.
78. Frank Del Olmo, "Provoked Trouble for Lawmen, Chicano Informer Claims," *Los Angeles Times*, February 1, 1972; *Los Angeles Free Press* February 4–10, 1972.
79. *Los Angeles Free Press*, February 4–10, 1972. Throughout 1971 there was considerable unrest in East Los Angeles. A series of bombings took place, with a group calling itself the Chicano Liberation Front taking the credit. Banks, chain stores, government buildings, squad cars, etc. were targets. See "Chicano Liberation Front Group claims bombing credit," *Belvedere Citizen*, August 19, 1971. "Officials Probe, seek links in East LA bombings," *Belvedere Citizen*, May 6, 1971; "Roosevelt High bombings linked to series of explosions in area," *Belvedere Citizen*, June 10, 1971.
80. Morales, "Study of Mexican American Perceptions," pp. 103–104; U.S. Commission on Civil Rights, *Mexican Americans and Administration of Justice in the Southwest* (Washington, D.C.: U.S. Government Printing Office, 1970), pp. 4–5.
81. U.S. Commission on Civil Rights, p. 5; Morales, "Study of Mexican American Perceptions," pp. 105–106.

82. *La Raza* 1, no. 2 (1970): 18–19; Morales, "Study of Mexican American Perceptions," pp. 106–107.
83. *Forumeer,* October 1968.
84. U.S. Commission on Civil Rights, p. 9.
85. Quoted in Morales, p. 43.
86. *Forumeer,* January 19, 1970, "Roybal Demands Removal of San Jose Judge," *Belvedere Citizen,* October 16, 1969; "Judge's Intemperate Outburst Against Mexicans Investigated," *Eastside Sun,* October 9, 1969; *Forumeer,* March 1970.
87. Castro, pp. 52–54.
88. U.S. Commission on Civil Rights, pp. 37–38, 40; *Ideal,* February 15–28, 1970.
89. *Los Angeles Times,* February 7, 1972; *Justicia O* 1, no. 3 (January 1971).
90. Eugene Rodríguez, Jr., *Henry B. Gonzalez: A Political Profile* (New York: Arno Press, 1976). Henry B. González has been the highest ranking Chicano official in the state, but has refused to promote the candidacy of other Mexicans. He does not endorse anyone in the primaries, which is crucial to the nomination of a Chicano. He has also consistently branded any kind of human-rights protest as "reverse racism." A key to his character can be found in his family background. His father owned silver mines in Durango, which he lost when revolutionaries took them over. The family fled to San Antonio, where his father was managing editor of *La Prensa,* which catered to Mexican intellectuals and politicians.

Chapter 12
Born Again Democrats: The Age of the Brokers

Any analysis of the 1970s is incomplete at best; the closeness of events blurs the historian's focus. Generalizations made today may be riddled by exceptions within ten years as additional data becomes available. Who would have thought in 1972 that the tumultuous period between 1967 and 1971 would come to such an abrupt end? Activism after this point took a different form. The grinding down of the Vietnam war ended the fuel which fed the latter stages of the civil rights movement. With war no longer an issue many middle-class Americans lost interest in causes. The 1960s had resurrected a sense of justice in many Americans, but it had failed to make them political.

The end of the intense activism of the 1960s can be better understood by studying the political activism of the past sixty years which runs in cycles from times of action to leveling periods to reaction. Just before World War I reform movements flourished. During the war they were almost entirely wiped out by war time hysteria which demanded that Americans forget their social causes and support defense efforts. In the postwar period people wanted to forget causes. The mood changed to one of isolationism and nativism. The reaction saw a persecution of anything considered un-American. Reformers became unpopular and relatively few in number.

The economic conditions of the 1930s forced workers to strike. Because of massive discontent, reform legislation such as the National Labor Relations Act (the Wagner Act) was passed. However, the advent of another world war demanded everyone support the war effort and again militancy was denounced as un-American. And, again, the postwar era was dominated by reactionary forces: McCarthyism, the McCarran Act, and political regression. After the Korean conflict in 1953 President Dwight D. Eisenhower capitalized on public apathy and overtly catered to big business. Like President Warren G. Harding in the 1920s, Eisenhower represented the Anglo-American mainstream: conservative, pseudoreligious, and antiintellectual. Activists became unpopular, and many wondered if Americans had lost all sense of social conscience.

Various and complex forces introduced the turbulent 1960s; a young and charismatic president, anticolonial wars, the civil rights movement, the participation of youth, an unpopular war in Southeast Asia, all contributed to this new awareness. The 1960s represented a decade of causes. Chicano youth abandoned many of the traditional organizations and formed new groups. Nationalism dominated their rhetoric and they questioned assimilation into the Anglo-American mainstream. Along with other progressives, Chicanos fed the fires of a mass movement and inspired substantive reforms which would come under attack during the lull of the 1970s.

By 1973 the nation returned to a reactionary period. The abandonment by white America of the civil rights movement and the loss of the war issue muted activism. The news media also actively suppressed news of protest activities. Additionally, the government subverted militant groups by promoting factionalism and provoking incidents. Through large doses of federal funds it further compromised many former civil rights leaders. Meanwhile, a wide range of new causes—ecology, women, gays, and energy—took the focus from the central issue which affected Chicanos, and other poor folk—that of unequal distribution. The 1970s resembled the 1920s and 1950s which were periods of reaction, apathy, and normalcy.

THE AGENTS OF SOCIAL CONTROL

Before the 1970s most agents of social and political control were at the local level, functioning as ward bosses, political *patrones* (bosses), etc. The late 1960s and early 1970s saw the rise of the Chicano bureaucrats at the state and federal levels. This network served as a system of brokers—agents who go between the establishment power structure and the protesting group.

For the most part these brokers were individually sincere, hard working bureaucrats who believed that they served their community. However, their jobs and upward mobility depended on serving the system and not the people. In most instances they functioned within the Democratic and Republican parties. Democrats were more successful and their brokers delivered the majority of the Mexican vote. In 1968, for instance, 90 percent of the Chicano Texas vote went to Hubert Humphrey. Republicans generally did not bother to court the Mexican vote. However, census data showed the existence of a small middle class among Mexicans, many of whom shared class interests with Republicans. In fact, an analysis of the 1968 Texas presidential vote showed that if 5 percent more of the Chicano vote had gone to Nixon, he would have carried Texas.

Nixon supporters thus developed a Chicano strategy: "Their plan was simple: to woo Brown Middle America by providing high administration positions and more government jobs to Mexican-Americans and by doling out a bigger share of federal dollars to programs aimed at Mexican-Americans."[1] Nixonites referred to their strategy as the "Republicanization of the Mexican-American."

In 1969 Nixon replaced the Inter-agency Committee on Mexican-American Affairs with the Cabinet Committee on Opportunities for the Spanish-Speaking People. Nixon appointed Martin Castillo as its head. Castillo was forced to resign when Chicanos voted heavily for the Democrats in the 1970 California U.S. senatorial elections.[2]

Henry Ramírez of Whittier succeeded Castillo. He courted the Chicano middle-class.[3] In 1971 Nixon named Phillip V. Sánchez director of the Office of Economic Opportunity and Mrs. Romana A. Banuelos, a Los Angeles food manufacturer, treasurer of the United States.[4] By 1972 Nixon appointed fifty Chicanos to high ranking federal posts. Chicanos meanwhile were key in four states, Texas, California, New Mexico and Illinois, with 101 electoral votes.[5]

Nixon Chicanos joined the Committee to Re-Elect the President (CREEP) headed by Alex Armendaris of South Bend, Indiana. They became known as the "brown mafia."[6] They used federal grants to woo supporters and to punish those antagonistic to Nixon. Elaborate plans were also made to neutralize the newly created *La Raza Unida* party which appealed to lower income Chicanos and would thus necessarily siphon votes from the Democrats. According to memos, the brown mafia even talked about granting a pardon to Tijerina in return for his support.[7] During the last month of the campaign Democratic candidate George McGovern angrily accused Republicans of doing what Democrats had done for years—buying the loyalty of Chicanos through patronage and grants. McGovern specifically accused José Angel Gutiérrez of having espoused neutrality in the presidential election in return for a $1 million health clinic for Crystal City.[8] Gutiérrez denied the charges; he countered that the grant proposal had been developed in 1968, but due to Texas legislative restraint it had not been funded until 1972 when the Office of Economic Opportunity (OEO) approved the $397,206 grant. Gutiérrez defended the clinic, which was the first of its kind in South Texas; he pointed out that all communities received federal funding through school lunch programs, bilingual education, drainage, food stamps, and similar programs and asked why McGovern had singled out Crystal City.

Meanwhile, Henry Ramírez made it clear that if Nixon did not receive 20 percent of the Chicano vote, the administration would cut federal appointments to Chicanos and stop federal funding of Chicano projects. When Nixon received 31 percent of the Latino vote nationally, many expected increased patronage. Instead not only did the president move to dismantle the war on poverty, which he considered part of the Democratic party machine, but he also fired many of his Chicano loyalists.[9]

In 1973 Nixon added insult to injury by appointing Ann Armstrong, an Anglo-American, to the post of White House aide on domestic Latino Affairs. According to Nixon, she was qualified because "Mrs. Armstrong and her husband own a large ranch at Armstrong, Texas, an area populated extensively by Mexican-Americans."[10]

The brokerage system was not confined to the federal government; it was extensively used at the state and local levels. Foundations such as Ford relied extensively on a brokerage network. Organizations such as the National Council of La Raza (originally the Southwest Council of La Raza) and the Mexican-American Legal and Education Fund were created by Ford to serve as its broker. Again, the dangers are not only the control of individuals, but also the dependence of organizations on whatever kind of monies that are procured. The bottom line is that there is always the danger of becoming Carter Chicanos, Kennedy Chicanos, Nixon Chicanos, Ford Foundation Chicanos, etc., instead of advocates for change.

THE CREATION OF A CHICANO QUEBEC

The rise of the Chicano broker network is tied to the Chicano population explosion during the past two decades. Los Angeles, San Antonio, Houston, and Chicago all doubled their Chicano populations.[11] Between 1960 and 1970 Los Angeles County's Latinos increased from 576,716 to 1,228,595, an increase of 113 percent, while the Anglo population declined from 4,877,150 to 4,777, 904, a 2 percent drop.[12] (These figures do not take into account the census undercount or the large undocumented population.) The increase in Chicano population is a direct result of births. In Los Angeles County 76,619 Anglo babies were born in 1966 compared to 24,533 Latin and 17,461 Black. Eight years later the number of Anglo births declined to 41,940, Black births dropped to 16,173, while Latino births jumped to 45,113.[13]

A similar process has taken place in other Southwest cities. In 1960 Houston had the tenth largest concentration of Chicanos in the United States; by 1970 it had 212,000 Latinos, making it the fourth largest in the country. San Antonio was second with 385,000 and the San Francisco/Oakland area third with 362,900.[14] California led the nation with 3.2 million Latinos in 1970, followed by Texas with 2.3 million. As dramatic as the above figures appear, they are just the tip of the iceberg. The median age among Latinos in the mid-1970s was 20.7 versus the national median of 28.6, insuring a Latino population boom in the 1980s.[15] In San Antonio one-third of the Mexican population in 1972 was under 14.[16]

The Chicano community remained poor and powerless. The ruling political parties sponsored few Mexicans for elective offices. Activists responded by creating their own party. In Crystal City by 1972 *La Raza Unida* party had taken over the Board of Education and had swept city and county elections. At the state level the Texas RUP ran Ramsey Muñiz, a young attorney, for governor.[17] In Colorado, on March 30, 1970 Corky Gonzales announced the formation of the Colorado RUP.[18] By 1971 there was already talk about a national party. The two centers of activity were Colorado and Texas; rivalry between the RUP leaders from these states emerged. Meetings between Gutiérrez and Gonzales took place in the fall of 1971 in order to patch up differences. By the summer of 1972 arrangements were made for the first national RUP convention in El Paso in September.[19]

In California by July 1971 some 10,000 Californians had registered RUP.[20] The RUP there ran statewide candidates. In that month RUP Raúl Ruiz, a professor at California State University at Northridge and editor of *La Raza* magazine, ran for the assembly in the 48th District. He won 7.93 percent (2,778 votes) of the vote, siphoning enough votes from Democratic candidate Richard Alatorre, to give the election to Republican, Bill Brophy, 46.71 percent (16,346) to 42.17 percent (14,759). The Democrats were hurt most by of an independent Chicano party. Democrats accused the RUP of being neosegregationist.[21] In the next election for the 48th District the RUP did not run a candidate and Alatorre won. Alatorre proved to be one of the state's more progressive legislators, and in the long run, his first loss made him more independent of the party machine. The potential of the RUP to disrupt forced the Democrat machine to run Chicano candidates in other districts.

By 1972 22,358 persons registered RUP in Texas. They mainly came from the ranks of the Democratic party. The defection of Chicanos cost U.S. Senator Ralph Yarborough the Democratic primary in 1970; two years later Yarborough was forced into a primary race runoff for U.S. Senator by 536 votes. Yarborough was that many votes "shy of a clear majority with 49.987 percent of the popular vote."[22] He lost the runoff. Attempts to form an RUP in the Northwest and Midwest also took place, but the lack of large concentrations of Mexicans thwarted efforts to form a party.[23]

As September 1972 approached, there was considerable enthusiasm for the RUP El Paso convention. However, spirits were soon dampened as news arrived that Ricardo Falcón, 27, a party organizer from Fort Lupton, Colorado, had been murdered during an argument by Perry Brunson, a gas station owner in Orogrande, New Mexico (a local jury later acquitted Brunson).[24] Three thousand Chicanos attended the convention. Every major Chicano leader with the exception of César Chávez, attended (Chávez had endorsed McGovern).[25] Gonzales had called for an independent party which supported neither Democrats nor Republicans. He stood for "no compromise." Gutiérrez wanted to stay out of national politics until the RUP could consolidate at the local and state levels.[26] A power struggle developed between Gutiérrez and Gonzales. Gutiérrez was elected. A display of unity followed, but bitter feelings had developed which accentuated the differences between the two men.[27]

Gonzales was twenty years older than Gutiérrez and resented the *Tejanos'* brashness.[28] Gutiérrez came from a student background and from a small town; Gonzales was educated in the streets. He was from an urban *barrio*. Over the years Gonzales had developed a "no compromise" with the system attitude; Gutiérrez was a pragmatist, working within the Texas reality. Gonzales hated capitalism and the *gringo*, whereas Gutiérrez questioned who had the power and criticized the Chicanos' lack of access to it.

Individual perspectives played a part in separating the two men. When Gutiérrez negotiated with the Mexican government for cultural exchanges and scholarships, Gutiérrez saw it as the opening of a Chicano foreign policy, whereas Corky saw it as support for a facist Mexican government and a betrayal of the Mexican people. Corky also believed allegations about José Angel's complicity with CREEP.[29] Gutiérrez was infuriated that Gonzales had given the allegations credence, pointing out that the allegations were not that he had received payoffs, rather that CREEP thought about buying the Texas RUP off.

In the Texas gubernatorial elections that year the party's candidate, Ramsey Muñiz, ran a strong race, accumulating 214,118 votes (6.28 percent). In spite of a small budget and an antagonistic press, he had almost upset the Democrats whose candidate won over the Republican by 100,000 votes.[30] This strong showing qualified the RUP for the statewide ballot. Other states did not fare as well; in California so-called ideological differences split the different chapters. Meanwhile, the struggle between Gutiérrez and Gonzales continued. In 1974 the Colorado group bolted the national organization during a steering committee meeting in East Chicago. By the next year all hope of a national party ended.

During these years political activism declined to an all-time low. Unemployment, inflation, the national energy crisis, and apathy all contributed to a feeling of futility. In spite of this a small cadre continued to struggle. The RUP in November 1974 unsuccessfully attempted to incorporate East Los Angeles, an area with 105,033 residents, of whom 90,000 were Mexicans (the undocumented population not included). Numerous attempts since 1925 to incorporate the area had failed. Real estate, industrial, and business leaders mounted well-financed campaigns to beat incorporation efforts. Meanwhile, the area shrank with industry slicing off large sections and incorporating independently, thus depriving the people of East Los Angeles of a potential tax base if they incorporated their city. In 1974 the RUP joined other community groups in an effort to incorporate East Los Angeles. The drive lost 3,262, to 2,369.[31] In the race for city council positions RUP candidate Raúl Ruiz was the top vote getter receiving 1,138 votes.[32] The stakes were high, for without representation, the land grab continued.

The San Fernando Valley chapter also ran aggressive campaigns for city council, state assembly, and state senate. In the spring of 1978 Andrés Torres, a college professor, lost his race for the San Fernando city council by 80 votes. In the summer of 1978 the California RUP collected over 12,000 signatures in an effort to qualify the RUP on the statewide ballot. Torres ran for governor as a write-in candidate. Qualifying a third party in California was a nearly impossible task.

In New Mexico Juan José Peña, a Chicano studies professor at New Mexico Highlands University at Las Vegas led the RUP. The building of a third party was difficult because of the large number of people who depended on the two major parties. The two major parties fought any threat to their hegemony. The beneficiaries of the patronage system vehemently opposed any changes which threatened their livelihood.[33] State officials persecuted RUP members whom they characterized as un-American, radicals, and outsiders; corrupt officials in Río Arriba County conducted a campaign of terror against party members. As late as May 1976 deputy sheriffs in Río Arriba shot two RUP activists.[34]

Between 1970 and 1974 the RUP seemed invincible in Texas at the local level. Tangible gains were made. Crystal City served as a model for South Texas.[35] By 1974 cracks appeared. José Angel Gutiérrez, elected to the post of county judge in 1974, came under attack. In 1975 a Republican president cooperated with a Texas Democratic machine to stop grants to Chicano controlled cities. Crystal City had become overdependent on federal funds and felt the loss. José Angel had captured the city and county governments, but he failed to transfer the means of production to Chicano hands.

Gutiérrez had imported technicians to run schools and government. Many locals believed that the technicians would train them and then leave. With the loss of funds and opportunities, the locals increasingly criticized the outsiders whom they identified with Gutiérrez. A break occurred between Gutiérrez and the *barrio* club over patronage. When Gutiérrez did not deliver, he came under bitter personal attack.[36]

In April 1975 Gutiérrez and the RUP went to Cuba. He was then accused of creating a "Little Cuba" in Texas.[37] In 1976 Democratic Governor Dolph Briscoe stopped a $1.5 million grant to the Zavala County Economic Development Corporation from the U.S. Community Services Administration. The loss of this grant was a severe setback for Gutiérrez.[38]

The Texas RUP also lost momentum at the state level. The party depended on the popular appeal of Ramsey Muñiz, who in the 1974 election attracted one-third of the Chicano vote. In February 1977 the Texas RUP received a blow when Muñiz pleaded guilty to conspiracy in the sale of marijuana.[39]

Although Chicanos did not build a Chicano political force in Texas or anywhere else, the RUP did leave a legacy. Its major leader José Angel made mistakes; he did not achieve many of the ideals set in the late 1960s. However, according to one commentator, "If Gutiérrez has failed to establish socialism in Zavala County, he has at least succeeded in establishing democracy, something almost revolutionary in South Texas."[40] The RUP in Crystal City had established a bilingual program and Chicano students there for the first time in the city's history were college bound.[41] A significant change in attitude had taken place.

Proof of the change came in 1977 when the Lo Vaca Gathering Company shut off Crystal City's gas for nonpayment of $720,000 in back gas bills. Citizens protested the increase of rates from .35 per 1000 cubic feet of natural gas to $2.00. The raise in rates hit the poor. In Zavala County fifteen individuals owned 85 percent of the land and these capitalists supported Lo Vaca. When Lo Vaca president William Greeley ordered the gas shut off, ranchers immediately switched to electricity.[42] The different Chicano factions cooperated and doomsday predictions about Crystal City did not come about. The RUP had raised consciousness and had forced the Democratic party to promote Chicano candidates and issues.

Time also changed the activities of Rodolfo Corky Gonzales. The Colorado RUP was not as successful as the Texas party; it did not have the concentrated numbers that aided the Texas RUP. The party nevertheless pressured the Democratic machine to back Chicano candidates, with some elected officials owing their success to the RUP. The repression of local, state, and federal police, the assassination and arrest of key members, police provocation, disputes with the Italian mafia, and the raiding of his cadre by other organizations, all took a toll on Corky. During the 1970s Gonzales turned increasingly inward, consolidating the Crusade for Justice and concentrating more on his freedom school, *Tlatelolco*, which he had founded in 1970. Over the years the school became self-supporting, enrolling 160 students, from preschool through high school. While still participating in demonstrations, especially those against police brutality, he spent more time on the school and relied more and more on the loyalty of his wife Geraldine and their eight children and their spouses. Corky became more uncompromising with his principles which are described as a mixture of intense nationalism and socialism. His priority became the education of Chicano revolutionaries. Corky's "no compromise" approach sometimes placed him in conflict with other activists. There is no doubt that the 1970s had been tumultuous for him and the Crusade for Justice. However, they both endured.

CHICANO STUDIES: A LEGACY FROM HISTORY

During the latter part of the 1960s students applied pressure to institutionalize the study of Chicanos/Mexicanos and to admit and retain Chicano students. A byproduct was the establishment of Chicano studies programs and departments.[43] Although these programs were not the panacea that many of their founders hoped for, they did make significant contributions, graduating Chicanos from the universities and promoting scholarship. The many journals, articles, dissertations, and monographs published in the past ten years are a tribute to the student struggles.

In California alone over fifty programs functioned in 1969 and, in spite of the decline in the number of programs over the past ten years, the number that has survived is impressive. A number of the California state universities and colleges as well as the University of California system had departments, centers, or institutes; many of them grant a bachelor's degree in Chicano studies. The state universities at San Francisco and Fresno offer degrees in *La Raza* studies, and the Long Beach, Los Angeles, Northridge, San Diego, and Sonoma campuses have Chicano studies departments. Three campuses, San Jose, Los Angeles, and Northridge have master's degree programs in Chicano studies. At the University of California (with the exception of Berkeley which has a component in ethnic studies) the programs are basically centers. Both UCLA and Berkeley operate outstanding Chicano studies libraries and at UCLA the center publishes an excellent journal, *Aztlán*, and numerous monographs.

Outside of California, Washington State University and the University of Washington had small but functioning programs. The Mexican-American Center at the University of Texas at Austin has one of the finest libraries in the country and the center pressed the different departments into hiring Chicanos. Similar programs are found at the University of Houston, the University of Colorado at Boulder, and Alamosa State. Ironically, Chicano studies has had its toughest sledding in New Mexico. The Chicano studies programs at the University of New Mexico at Albuquerque and New Mexico Highland University at Las Vegas both were under constant attack by administrators, faculty, and politicians. Throughout the Southwest there were also excellent programs at the private universities and community colleges.

Chicano and Puerto Rican students in the Midwest often established Chicano/Boricua programs. Joint programs emerged at the University of Indiana, Wayne State (Detroit), and Iowa. Chicano studies departments or programs developed at the University of Minnesota, Notre Dame, and Michigan State University. Chicano student organizations functioned at almost every Ivy League and midwestern university.

At Santa Barbara, California, in the spring of 1969, students, faculty, and community issued the *Plan de Santa Barbara* which stated the goals, aspirations, and a place for action for Chicanos in higher education.[44] Although it was an idealistic document, for a long time it was the only guide that existed. Higher education responded to Chicano student demands by establishing paper programs which they funded out of soft money (special grant money which was not part of the regular university budget). The academic legitimacy of Chicano studies was openly questioned. Chicano faculty and students were treated like intruders. The programs which survived did so because of the sacrifices of students and faculty members. Those which did not succeed can blame a hostile administration. However, some Chicano faculty and students must also bear some of the blame. Student extremism often led to unnecessary sectarian fights which badly weakened the negotiating powers of the Chicano academic community. Faculty often pandered to student whims and, in many cases, did not demonstrate leadership.

As the student population boom and the fat budgets of the 1960s ended opportunistic administrators cut ethnic studies programs. The programs which were not institutionalized died; others have undergone a slow death.

The largest Chicano studies department was at California State University at Northridge.[45] The program had eighteen full-time professors, 80 percent of whom were tenured. The university did not draw from the large urban *barrios* that some of the other state universities do. In 1967 it only had seven Chicano students. By 1969 students forced university authorities to negotiate with student representatives, to commit themselves to recruiting 350 Chicanos annually, and to establish a Mexican-American studies department. The thirty Chicano students who attended CSUN at the time were ably led by Miguel Verdúgo. The curriculum developed at CSUN was interdisciplinary; the courses dealt with the Chicano/Mexicano in political science, history, literature, and other fields. The central objective was to keep students in college. The method was teaching skills through reinforcing identity and collective consciousness. The purpose was never to create super Chicanos; it was to prepare technicians to serve the people. This could only be done by equipping students with the skills to survive in other disciplines.

Time restraints prevent a full analysis of the development of Chicano studies at CSUN. As in the case of other universities and colleges, a documented history of the department is needed. The department followed the lead of the student movement. The students were involved in most movement issues such as war protests, police brutality, parent control of schools, forced sterilization, *Bakke*, the Chilean struggle. In addition the program developed an excellent music component which included several ballet *folklóricos*, a *mariache* group, a *conjunto jarocho*, and *Los Huicholos* (the latter specializes in the revolutionary folk music of all Latin America). CSUN has a *teatro*, a student newspaper, *El Popo*, and a Chicana Information Center. Its Operation Chicano Teacher, which specialized in training teachers, graduated over 300 Chicano teachers over 6 years. Chicano studies also developed a large number of community workers.

However, Northridge was the exception. Most programs at other campuses were not institutionalized, and when budget cuts were forced on the colleges and universities, administrators cut Chicano Studies programs as expendable. From the beginning, these programs had been doomed by ethnocentric and racist bureaucrats.

BILINGUAL EDUCATION

The struggle toward bilingual education preceded the struggle for Chicano studies. Chicanos tenaciously refused to surrender their right to their language and culture. The assertion of cultural rights was in many ways the most threatening aspect of the movement to Anglo-Americans, for many viewed such demands as subversive. Politicians and educators increasingly called for its elimination and a return to the Americanization of the child. The Bilingual Education Act of 1968, Title VII, provided the first federal funding for bilingual education.[46] In 1974 the historic *Lau v. Nichols* ruling institutionalized it. The suit was brought by San Francisco's Chinese community. In a unanimous decision the U.S. Supreme Court found that children who had a limited grasp of English were deprived of equal treatment when the schools did not meet the linguistic problems of those children. The decision was based on the Civil Rights Act of 1964.

In order to evaluate bilingual education, traditional American education as well as the attitudes of public educators toward the speaking of Spanish in the schools must be analyzed. In Castroville, California, in 1971, for example, Grambetta School had 500 students, 400 of whom were Mexican. At a school graduation two students and a guest speaker addressed the audience in Spanish. Judge Kenneth Blohm, a school trustee, stated, "It was a disgrace to let it happen." Leonard Shirrel, the board chair, said, "Before something like this happens again the board should know about it." Principal Paul Murray echoed, "It won't happen again."[47] This nativist sentiment is not isolated.

Bilingual education in fact was the antithesis of that of American public education in that it counteracts ethnocentricism.[48] American education espoused democracy while discouraging political dissent. Teachers were primarily agents of social control and the school reinforced the political system. In essence, it rejected any pedagogy which questioned the supremacy of the English language or the superiority of American institutions and culture. The speaking of Spanish or any other foreign language was viewed as deviant behavior. A study by William Jefferson Mathis found that

"students [Mexican] who have taken the traditional political socialization courses in American History and Civics and Government
tend to report lower acceptance of Chicano symbols and lower
scores on the Chicano political orientation."[49] Exposure to nontradi-
tional courses and symbols other than Anglo-American encouraged
the student to deviate from the norm and became more tolerant of
non–Anglo-American attitudes. This weakened the socialization
process.[50]

Harvard sociology professor Orlando Patterson, a Black, al-
leges that methods other than bilingual education would be more
effective to meet the need of the bilingual child. To Patterson the
uppermost task is to teach English to the child: "After nearly nine
years and more than half a billion dollars in federal funds . . . the
government has not demonstrated whether such instruction makes
much difference in the students' achievement, in their acquisition
of English, or in their attitudes toward school."[51] Patterson, however, ignores that Anglo-American education has failed Mexican
children for over 132 years.

The objective of bilingual education was not just to facilitate
the teaching of English to children who spoke only Spanish, but to
teach Latinos both languages and in the process counteract the
narrowness of the Anglo-American perception that only English
and Anglo-American values had worth. Through an appreciation of
Mexican culture, students would take pride in themselves and
counteract negative self-images. Bilingual education was intended
to decolonize the *pocho*, the U.S.-born Mexican, not to teach a new
language to the Mexican national. In the present form of most bilingual programs the *pocho* has been totally excluded. Administrators
of bilingual programs have sold out the *pocho* to court the favor of
nativist politicians by stating that bilingual education is just another way to teach English to Latinos and to Americanize the Spanish-speaking child.[52]

Chicanos were reluctant to criticize bilingual education because of the abuses in the school system itself. In California in the
early 1970s the U.S. Commission on Civil Rights found that 40
percent of the Chicano children in educationally and mentally retarded (EMR) classes were there because they did not speak English. Schools which discouraged the use of any Spanish in elementary classes ranged from a low of 13.5 percent in California to a high
of 66.4 percent in Texas. Students were punished for speaking
Spanish.[53]

On March 28, April 12, and September 12, 1973, Chicano students in Ysleta, Texas, walked out of school and charged that
teachers encouraged Anglo students to beat up Chicanos.[54] As late
as 1977 Chicanos in Tucson and other cities were fighting blatant
segregation in their schools. In 1972 Jesús Ortiz in Guadalupe,
California, was fired from his job and arrested by the INS because

he protested abuses of the school in that town.[55] On December 15, 1972, a Corpus Christi, Texas, coach stuck a 13-year-old Chicano's head in a commode.[56] In San Antonio two Chicano school teachers, Raúl Prado and Lorenzo Monroy, were suspended for criticizing the school administrator and participating in politics.[57]

The pupil-teacher ratios by ethnic groups were tragic:

STATE	CHICANO PUPIL-TEACHER	BLACK PUPIL-TEACHER	ANGLO PUPIL-TEACHER
Texas	98:1	31:1	19:1
California	172:1	50:1	21:1
New Mexico	58:1	48:1	16:1
Arizona	140:1	53:1	19:1
Colorado	144:1	45:1	20:1
Southwest	120:1	39:1	20:1

SOURCE: Adapted from U.S. Commission on Civil Rights, *Ethnic Isolation of Mexican Americans in the Public Schools of the Southwest*, Mexican American Education Study, Report I (Washington, D.C.: Government Printing Office, 1971), p. 42.

Efforts to close the educational gap were token. For example, the highly successful Chicano teacher training program at CSUN suffered a backlash when it attempted to place a sizable number of Chicano student teachers. Local master teachers refused to accept them, stating that they did not want to train their replacements. At the root of the backlash was that a teacher surplus developed and budget cutbacks were threatened. Middle-class Anglo-Americans had fewer children in the schools. This population was also getting older and its support for the schools lessened.

While the Anglos complained that their children were reading at a lower level, Mexicans complained that their children were not reading at all. The fact that Mexicans had a higher median of education in 1970 than in 1960 meant little. The bottom line was that they were not reading or writing better in 1970 than in 1960.[58] Unfortunately statistics were not available for all school districts where Chicano children attended. The Los Angeles City schools, however, had published mandatory state testing scores. In 1973 reading scores in selected Chicano and Anglo schools were as follows:

SCHOOL	PERCENT OF MINORITY STUDENTS IN SCHOOL	HIGHER FOURTH	MEDIAN	LOWER FOURTH
	PERCENTILE OF NATIONAL SCORE (0–100)			
Elementary (sixth grade)[a]				
Albion	98	28	18	7
Breed	99	35	19	10
Brooklyn	99	30	17	7
Haddon	84	29	17	7
Granada	8	77	54	34
Pacific Palisades	4	89	77	59
Reseda	18	72	51	43

[a]Spanish-speaking and so-called EMR (Educationally and Mentally Retarded) students did not take exams.

| | PERCENTILE OF NATIONAL SCORE (0–100) | | |
| | PERCENT OF MINORITY STUDENTS IN | HIGHER | | LOWER |
SCHOOL	SCHOOL	FOURTH	MEDIAN	FOURTH
Secondary (twelfth grade)[b]				
Garfield	98	26	15	5
Roosevelt	98	25	14	5
Lincoln	96	32	19	8
Taft	5	71	53	34
Palisades	15	80	58	38
El Camino Real	4	69	47	30

[b]ESL (English as a Second Language) students not included. By twelfth grade one-third of the Chicano students have dropped out.
SOURCE: Los Angeles Unified School District, *Summary Report, Mandatory State Testing Program,* Report 335, Fall, 1973.

The schools in the table were selected because they had a high concentration of Anglos or Mexicans. The Chicano high schools were picked because of their involvement in the walkouts. Scores have improved slightly since 1973 due to more programs, reviewing students for tests, and similar efforts, but the comparisons remain as dramatic.

Grades may be used to convey the illusion that the schools were doing well and to discourage community criticism. In all probability, in each of the schools those in the upper fourth of the reading scores received A's, the median B's, and the lower fourth C's and D's. In reading skills the upper fourth at Garfield read at the 26th percentile whereas a D student in the lower fourth at Taft High School was at the 34th percentile.[59] In 1973 no bilingual programs functioned at the high school level in Los Angeles; such scores indicate that after over 132 years of teaching in English the schools were failing. This is true of school districts across the nation.[60]

Current desegregation programs have greatly affected the Chicano community, splitting many progressives. The integration struggle is very much part of Chicanos' history. For instance, the GI Forum filed over 200 lawsuits in the 25 years preceding 1973 in efforts to stop board discrimination against Mexican-Americans. A large percentage of these suits were to obtain equal and quality education for Chicanos. Nevertheless, there were problems in integration, least of which was teachers who were not trained to teach Chicanos and had deep-seated prejudices toward them. Moreover, integration was not in the hands of the people or even the elected boards of education, but in the hands of school bureaucracies. In addition in the massive Los Angeles City school system of close to 600,000 students, as of 1977 the school population was 38 percent Latino, 33 percent Anglo, and 25 percent Black.[61]

Bilingual education must, however, be analyzed and criticized; often schools of higher education applied for government funds although they did not have qualified bilingual personnel to teach adequately or to supervise teacher training. In most cases universities hired nontenured faculty. At the school level unqualified Anglo teachers were employed; often Spanish-speaking aides did the teaching with English-speaking teachers "supervising" them.

More tragic was the network of brokers which bilingual education created. Often grants were awarded to friends rather than to programs that had the resources to train bilingual teachers. A classic example was the elimination of Dr. Ernesto Galarza's bilingual institute by the funding of a parallel consultant firm. Galarza had traditionally been viewed as a radical by authorities because he had asked hard questions as to not only how the teacher taught, but *why?* Dr. John Molina, the national director of Bilingual Education, favored his friends who had submitted proposals which paralleled Galarza's and in June 1975 the Molina group received $1,044,000. The defunding of his group did not end Galarza's problems. In February of 1977 students in his course at Santa Cruz on research into bilingual programs investigated bilingual education in San José. On February 4, 1977 Olivia Martínez, director of the San José Bilingual Consortium, wrote to Dr. Angus Taylor, chancellor of the University of California at Santa Cruz, accusing Dr. Galarza's students of political activities and threatening that if this activity was not stopped, the school districts involved in her consortium might not accept student teachers from Santa Cruz.[62] Galarza's experience exposed the basic problem of Anglo-American education. It is run by political appointees who have converted it into a commodity. The granting of funds depends more on the wrapping paper than on what is in the package.

CHICANO POLITICS OF THE 1970s: BORN AGAIN DEMOCRATS

By the late 1970s Chicano political potential still remained untapped.[63] Of those who did vote 86 percent registered as Democrats more out of tradition than conviction.[64] For the most part the left remained isolated in a political ghetto, in part due to their sectarianism and in part because of the youth and transiency of leftist organizations.

Chicano representation in the state legislatures as of March 1973 is shown in the following table.

STATE	TOTAL NUMBER OF REPRESEN-TATIVES	NUMBER OF CHICANO REPRESEN-TATIVES	PERCENTAGE OF CHICANO REPRESEN-TATIVES	PERCENTAGE OF CHICANOS IN TOTAL POPULATION
Arizona	90	11	11.1	18.8
California	118	5	4.2	15.5
Colorado	100	4	4.0	13.0
New Mexico	112	32	34.0	40.1
Texas	181	10	5.5	18.4

SOURCE: F. Chris García and Rudolph O. de la Garza, *The Chicano Political Experience: Three Perspectives* (North Scituate, Mass.: Duxbury Press, 1977), p. 107.

Although Los Angeles County had a massive Chicano population, they remained unrepresented in the Los Angeles City Council and Board of Supervisors.[65]

What representation Chicanos had was often inferior. For instance, in Kika de la Garza's congressional district in South Texas 25,000 people lived without potable water and he "appeared uninterested in alleviating the condition." Ninety to 95 percent of federal funds were channeled to support the Anglos who constituted only 25 percent of the district.[66] Both de la Garza and Congressman Henry B. González in 1974 voted against extending the benefits of the voting rights act to Chicanos. Raúl Castro was elected governor of Arizona in 1974, but spent most of his time supporting the state's right-to-work law and placating Anglo conservatives.[67] In 1977, he resigned under a cloud to take the ambassadorship to Argentina.[68]

Only in San Antonio, Texas, were significant victories won. The San Antonio City Council in the spring of April 1977 stood balanced with five Chicanos, five Anglos, and one Black.[69] In District 5 Bernardo Eureste won over Dario Chapa because of the endorsement of the Committee Organized for Public Service (COPS), a Catholic lay group organized along the model of Saul Alinsky's community action program. This marked the entrance of a more progressive Catholic church related group into politics.[70] In another race St. Philips College counselor Rudy Ortiz overpowered Bob Thompson.[71]

These election victories were labeled as progressive by all groups including *La Raza Unida*. Ortiz, who served as mayor pro tem in 1978, publicly condemned the INS, supported the undocumented worker, and participated in demonstrating against the *Bakke* decision (to be discussed) which threatened affirmative action and minority university admissions programs. Ortiz and the council instructed the city attorney to file a friend-of-the-court brief against *Bakke*.[72]

The victory was significant since it marked a break with the city machine. Henry B. González's victory in the early 1960s depended in great part on the grace of Vice President Lyndon B.

Johnson who neutralized Sheriff Owen Kilday. González won 12 to 1 in Mexican precincts and 9 to 1 in Black, while his opponent John Goode won 6 to 1 in Anglo precincts. In the 1977 effort Mexicans won on the issues.[73]

On the national scene Latinos are continuing their Democratic party habit. For instance, in 1972, although Nixon made inroads, a majority still went Democrat. In 1976 President Gerald Ford made an active bid for Chicano votes. He had a good chance since ex-Governor Jimmy Carter did not have a good image among Chicano voters. The Hispanic Committee for President Ford was formed.[74] However, the Latino vote swung back to the Democrats:

	WHITE VOTERS	JEWISH VOTERS	BLACK VOTERS	LATINO VOTERS	LABOR VOTERS
Percentage for Carter	48	68	91	81	70
Percentage for Ford	52	32	9	19	30

SOURCE: Andrew Hernandez, *The Latin Vote in the 1976 Presidential Election*, (San Antonio, Tex.: Southwest Voter Registration Education Project, 1977), p. 18.

Considering that the large number of unregistered Chicano voters would most probably have gone Democrat and that the party had a candidate *unattractive* to Chicanos the trend was clear:

> The 205,800 vote plurality that Latinos gave Carter was almost twice his winning margin for Texas. Had President Ford been able to capture 40 percent of the Latino vote, Ford would have carried Texas with a 14,141 vote margin and received Texas' 26 electoral votes.[75]

Sheer numbers in 1976 made the Chicano vote vital. The results intensified organizational efforts in the Chicano community and Carter through appointments built his network of brokers within that community.

Immediately after the election Carter appointed "his Mexicans." Chicanos lacked a national political organization and had little input into the appointments. Consequently the appointees were entirely beholden to Carter.[76] The appointment of Leonel Castillo to head the INS was by far the most controversial. As the 1980 elections approached Carter made many more Chicano appointments, indicating the growing importance of the "Mexican vote." Unfortunately none of the appointees showed much independence in advocating the rights of Chicanos.

In Texas, many former *Raza Unida* activists joined MAD (Mexican-American Democrats) and, according to many observers, they were now "Born Again Democrats."[77] Clearly attempts to work within the system while engaging in alternative politics had failed; however, so had traditional politics.

THE BARRIOS

Congestion increased in the Chicano *barrios* during the 1970s. In the housing projects of San Bernardino, California baby gang members (12- to 14-year-olds) ran extortion rackets and elsewhere gang activity reached alarming proportions. Freeways, urban renewal, blight, and the bulldozers moved out many small homeowners, while high interest rates and high building costs quickly wiped out the rest. Slum conditions were not new to the *barrios*. In Los Angeles as early as 1905 slum conditions were serious, and, as usual, city authorities solved the problem by appointing a commission to study the problem.[78]

In Los Angeles freeways and urban renewal were a problem not only for eastsiders but also for the northeast communities such as Lincoln Heights and Highland Park where the Pasadena, Glendale, and Long Beach freeways all bulldozed Mexican homes.[79] Similar conditions prevailed in Chicano *barrios* throughout the Southwest and Midwest. Chicanos served as caretakers and when the property, usually near the civic center, became too valuable, capitalist speculators expropriated the land, claiming that the *barrios* were blighted. Improvements were frustrated by high construction costs, red-lining (lending policies), "high-risk" insurance rates, and yearly increases in property taxes based on an inflated property evaluation.[80]

Committees to fight urban renewal formed in *barrios* such as El Paso, Texas. Carmen Félix headed *El Comité Por la Preservación del Barrio* which was also known as *La Campaña*. In May 1978 members attempted to lobby Housing and Urban Development Secretary Patricia Harris to oppose the city's redevelopment program.[81] In June 1978 *La Campaña* held community meetings to educate the public to the fact that the city wanted to use urban development grants (UDAG) to buy *barrio* land to construct a parking garage near the civic center. *La Campaña* charged collusion between bankers and politicians.[82] The El Paso struggle mirrored that of poor people throughout the United States who fought losing battles with contractors, bankers, developers and politicians who actively encroached on their space in order to make fantastic profits.[83] The struggle against urban land grabs today represents the greatest threat to the building of stable Chicano communities.

Individual alienation also increased during the 1970s. This frustration was illustrated by Ricardo Chávez-Ortiz, a 36-year-old immigrant from Mexico and father of eight children who in 1972, skyjacked a Frontier Airlines plane over New Mexico with an unloaded .22. The landing in Los Angeles received extensive media coverage. Chávez-Ortiz's demands startled the public. According to *Los Angeles Times* reporter Frank Del Olmo:

No other hijacker has demanded and gotten what the 36-year-old Mexican national did—live broadcast time in which to voice the frustrations of a man who feared the world would not listen to his problems, and those of his people, under any other circumstances.[84]

He spoke for thirty-five minutes in Spanish over radio station KWKW and KMEX-TV.

After his arrest he turned to the airplane captain and said, "Forgive me, captain ... forgive me ... I never had an intention of hurting anyone." His bail was placed at $500,000. Unemployment, racial discrimination, the war, and pollution had driven Chávez-Ortiz to a desperate action.[85] A jury convicted Chávez-Ortiz of piracy and he received a life sentence.[86] He remained in jail until 1978 when he apologized and left for Mexico. He had served twice the time of a rapist or an armed robber and three times the time of a Watergate conspirator.[87]

An example of direct collective action took place on September 1, 1976, when over thirty Chicano villagers at Chilili, New Mexico, (35 miles southeast of Albuquerque) halted construction of a road near their village. They objected to the road because it would attract tourists, developers, and rich speculators. They had taken their case to the U.S. Supreme Court to protect themselves against the Chilili Cooperative Association which was granted $85,000 from the state to develop a recreation park.[88]

The association, a private corporation, had been formed in 1942 by residents of Chilili to obtain Federal Housing Administration (FHA) loans. Outsiders infiltrated it, such as Leo Dow. Under the management of unscrupulous speculators communal lands declined from 30,000 to 5,000 acres; originally, the land grant amounted to 42,000 acres. Opponents were threatened and intimidated. In 1973 Chicanos formed *El Comité Para Reformar y Preservar Las Tierras de La Merced de Chilili* (The Committee to Reform and Preserve the Lands of the Chilili Land Grant).[89]

On September 5, 1975, they blockaded roads leading to *La Jara* Estates. A restraining order was issued. In May 1977 they again blockaded the roads leading to *La Jara* Estates and declared the land off limits to Anglo outsiders. Their motto was *"Guerra, justicia para Chilili."* The action ended with the arrest of about fifteen protesters by twenty-five armed deputies. This did not end the conflict and in July seven more were arrested. The State Supreme Court found that the road was legal.[90]

GROWING AWARENESS OF THE CHICANAS' STRUGGLE

While Chicanas have always played a prominent role in the movement, the growth of the Chicano population and the women's movement demanded a clearer statement of the Chicanas' role in society. In 1970 many Chicano organizations began women's caucuses. In that year the Mexican-American National Issues Conference in Sacramento sponsored a workshop on women. Participants at the workshop voted to become *La Comisión Feminil Mexicana*.[91] From this conference, Chicanas continued to communicate, and in May 1971 *La Conferencia de Mujeres Por La Raza* was in Houston, Texas, hosting over 600 Chicanas from 23 states. Participants stressed that the enemy was the system and not the Chicano male.[92] Among other issues discussed were experiments that the Southwest Foundation for Research and Education had conducted on Chicana women in the westside of San Antonio, using a nonbirth-control drug which resulted in ten unwanted pregnancies. Many women were upset at the sponsorship of the YWCA and about 40 percent walked out because they considered that association racist. Interest in Chicana issues spread throughout the Southwest and Midwest.[93] Francisca Flores, a veteran activist from the 1950s and 1960s, organized the Chicana Service Action Center at Los Angeles; it was one of the first antipoverty agencies to service *barrio* women.[94]

Because of Chicana activists, welfare agencies paid more attention to servicing Chicanos who made up 16 percent of the welfare clients and had only 4 percent of the social welfare staff.[95] Alicía Escalante laid much of the groundwork. In 1967 she established the East Los Angeles Welfare Rights Organization. Escalante pulled the East Los Angeles chapter out of the National Welfare Rights Organization because the organization did not respond to Chicano issues. She founded the Chicano National Welfare Rights Organization. In 1973 she and Francisca Flores, among others, spearheaded opposition to the Talmadge Amendment to the Social Security Act.[96] It required mothers on public assistance who had children over six to register with the state employment office and to report every two weeks until they got a job. No provisions were made for child care. The Welfare Rights Organization stated that it was the right of every mother to stay at home with her child. It also condemned Nixon for vetoing a child care bill in 1971.

Chicanas became more aggressive in asserting their rights to control their bodies. The issues of abortion and birth control were discussed at length. Women were also instrumental in educating Chicanos that rape was not a sex crime, but one of brutality. They followed the case of Inez García, 32, with interest. Although the judge and press referred to Inez as Mexican, she was of Cuban and Puerto Rican ancestry. Two drug addicts, Miguel Jiménez, 21, and Louie Castillo, 17, raped her twice and beat up her companion, Fred Medrano. Fifteen minutes later she picked up a .22 rifle and shot Jiménez, a 300-pound man, who had held her down. She was convicted largely due to the prejudices of the judge and jury of second degree murder in October 1975. The California Court of

Appeals overturned the case because of erroneous jury instructions. In her second trial Inez was acquitted.[97]

During the 1970s the issue of involuntary sterilization surfaced. The Department of Health, Education and Welfare had funded the sterilization of poor women since 1966.[98] As the argument that Third World women have too many babies became more popular, sterilizations became more widespread. Studies showed that one-third of all Puerto Rican women on the island and 3,046 Native American women treated at the obstetric wards of the U.S. Indian Health Service hospitals in Albuquerque, Phoenix, Oklahoma City, and Aberdeen, South Dakota, from 1973 to 1976 alone, had been sterilized.[99] According to Dr. Bernard Rosenfeld, between July 1968 and July 1970 elective hysterectomies jumped 742 percent at the Women's Hospital of Los Angeles County Medical Center; elective tubal ligations increased 476 percent and tubal ligations after delivery 115 percent.[100] These increases were attributed to an unwritten policy of the staff and administration. Doctors were encouraged to get their patients to consent to tubal ligations.[101] Rosenfeld stated that the attitude of his fellow physicians was "deep seated personal beliefs regarding overpopulation, coupled with a particular physician's belief as to what an 'ideal' number of children for any family should be." Frustrated by the millions spent on welfare, they set out to do something about it.

Rosenfeld also attributed sterilization abuses to the "incredible arrogance of medical power," its belief that "the doctor knows best." One doctor, questioned about sterilizing a 19-year-old girl, responded, "I want to ask every one of these girls if they want their tubes tied. I don't care how old they are. . . . remember everyone you get to get her tubes tied now means less work for some poor son of a bitch next time." Another doctor told Rosenfeld "if we're going to pay for them we should control them." Rosenfeld interviewed more than fifty physicians at USC/Los Angeles County Hospital from medical schools throughout the nation. Two wire service reporters accompanied him and corroborated his interviews. Some doctors bragged that they would wait until "the anesthesia started to wear off" and they would go into their pitch. A consensus existed that most medical schools pushed sterilization. A doctor trained in the Southwest School told Rosenfeld, "I just don't think it's good for them to drive around in a 1950 Chevy full of kids." Dr. Juan Nieto, 25-year-old Chicano intern, confirmed Rosenfeld's findings. According to Nieto they would start right in on the mother in the delivery room, urging her to have her tubes tied. He was convinced that the Spanish-speaking women often did not understand what was happening. Both Nieto and Rosenfeld stated that the county hospitals are training institutions and many interns want to perform sterilization operations for practice. They would rather perform a hysterectomy than a tubal ligation because it is more challenging.[102]

A probe disclosed that USC/Los Angeles County Hospital authorities ignored many of the federal guidelines which had been implemented as the result of the sterilization of two Black girls, 12 and 14, in Montgomery, Alabama.[103]

As a result of protests led by Chicanas, attention was brought to the issue of involuntary sterilization and restraints were placed on hospitals.

During the 1970s the case of Olga Talamantes, 23, from Gilroy, California, inspired admiration. In 1973 Olga was arrested in Argentina while visiting foreign students there. She had participated in Chicano activities at the University of California at Santa Cruz. On November 11, 1974, she and twelve others were accused of being members of a left-wing *Peronista* group. The U.S. embassy in Argentina dragged its feet, and for nearly eighteen months Olga remained in prison where she was beaten and tortured and finally forced to confess after two days of continuous electric shocks. She never informed on her friends. In San Antonio, at a nationwide immigration conference in November 1977, Olga stated that a vision of the future, an ideology , gave her courage to resist. Another time she stated, "I learned once more that my imprisonment is but a small part of the historical yearning for freedom." Olga was released because of international pressure on both the U.S. and Argentine governments.[104]

Throughout the decade Chicana visibility increased within the movement. Activity was not limited to the activist sector but spread to professional groups such as the Mexican-American Business and Professional Women's Club, the League of Mexican-American Women. The Hispanic Women's Council worked toward more assimilative goals. Just as in the case of the Chicano movement and society as a whole, class differences between Chicana groups resulted in variant goals. For example, the question of female mobility was a priority among middle-class women, whereas among poor women more basic needs such as health, unemployment, and other economic factors were priorities. They both agreed on issues such as day care. Poorer women also tended to work more within local organizations which included both sexes and on issues involving the entire community rather than through organizations limited to feminist issues.

THE CATHOLIC CHURCH: THE THEOLOGY OF COLLECTIVE SALVATION

The Catholic church as an institution did not change during the 1970s, but many Latino priests and nuns did. Most Chicano activists failed to appreciate the nationalism among Latino priests and nuns or the growing influence of radical trends within the Latin American church which have affected Chicano clergy in the United

States. The theology of liberation* encouraged priests and nuns to look after the material well-being of their congregations. The UFW and the civil rights movements also had an impact.

Many Catholics were angered that it took the church five years to take a stand on the UFW strikes, while the Protestant Migrant Ministry had been heavily committed from the beginning. Not until 1970, when the grape strike ended, did five U.S. bishops form the Committee on Farm Labor Disputes to mediate between the union and the growers.[105] When *Católicos Por La Raza* protested on Christmas Eve 1969, bitter recriminations followed. Some clergy at first became defensive, but many questioned the contradictions both within and outside the church.

The failure of the church to make any official statement after the killing of Ruben Salazar on August 29, 1970, angered many priests and nuns. In February 1970 *Padres Asociados Por Derechos Religiosos Educativos y Sociales* (PADRES) held its first national congress in Tucson, Arizona. The main demand of this group was for more Chicano bishops. On May 5, 1970, Fr. Patrick Flores of Pasadena, Texas, was ordained auxiliary bishop of San Antonio. He was the first Chicano appointed to the rank of bishop. Soon afterwards Msgr. Gilbert Chávez was named auxiliary bishop of San Diego, the first Chicano named to the rank of bishop in California. Ironically, about that time a series of articles were published by Catholic authorities commenting on the lack of qualified Chicano priests to assume "executive" positions.

An organization of nuns called *Hermanas* (sisters) was formed. A prime mover was Sister Gregoria Ortega, a community leader who supported the Chicano students' walkouts in Abilene, Texas, in the fall of 1969. Sister Gregoria championed human rights causes in West Texas for two years; she was expelled from two dioceses.

An increasing number of priests and nuns were influenced by the theology of liberation of Paulo Freire and Gustavo Gutiérrez. Under the leadership of Bishop Flores the Mexican-American Cultural Center (MACC) was established in San Antonio. Under the direction of Fr. Sergio Elizondo it trained priests, nuns, and lay persons to better serve Chicanos.[106] MACC brought radical priests and scholars from Latin America and the United States to lecture to the participants.

During this period many priests and nuns identified more closely with Chicano issues such as the farm workers, the undocumented, and prison reform. On May 25, 1972 Juan A. Arzube, a native of Ecuador, was ordained auxiliary bishop in Los Angeles.

---

*A philosophy which merges Christian and Marxist thought, emphasizing that the role of the church is both spiritual and material and that salvation is a collective endeavor instead of an individual affair.

He later officiated at a mass for Ricardo Chávez-Ortiz and his family and supported many community activities.[107]

In 1974 open opposition to the hierarchy developed over a vacancy in the diocese of Santa Fe and some priests and nuns threatened schism if the church did not fill that post with a Chicano. Rumblings also occurred among the lay constituency. Confrontation was averted when the Reverend Robert F. Sánchez was appointed archbishop—the first New Mexican to occupy that post. Two years later Manuel Moreno was named auxiliary bishop of Los Angeles. That year, while attending the annual Latin American Bishops Conference in Quito, Ecuador, Archbishop Sánchez along with Patrick Flores, Gilbert Chávez, Juan Arzube, and thirty-three Latin bishops were jailed on charges of subversion.[108]

In 1977 PADRES took a more aggressive stance under the leadership of Fr. Ralph Ruiz of San Antonio and Fr. Alberto Gallegos of Chicago, the national chair of the group. They demanded that one of their own be appointed to the board of the U.S. Catholic Conference. In August 1977 a conference of U.S. Latino bishops drew up a list of grievances which startled many. They condemned institutional and personal racism from both within and without the church; discrimination in language, culture, and education, political underrepresentation, poor housing, and few job opportunities; they also condemned the economic system which valued profit over human worth.[109]

In May 1978 Patrick Flores was appointed bishop of El Paso, Texas. He was the most aggressive and innovative of the Chicano bishops. Flores had founded MACC and raised $500,000 annually for its support. He was also instrumental in organizing the Communities Organized for Public Service (COPS) which was sponsored by San Antonio Mexican parishes to bring about social change through the involvement of grass-roots people. COPS organizers received training from Saul Alinsky's Industrial Areas Foundation in Chicago. Ernesto Cortés, Jr. played a leadership role in founding the organization.

COPS took on the City of San Antonio, forcing the city council to build curbs and drainage ditches in the *barrios*. It protested the using of $1.3 million in federal funds for the Pecan Valley Country Club, lobbied the governor and state legislature to allot more money to the San Antonio schools, and led the fight to elect progressive city councilmen who would represent the poor. COPS threatened the Anglo establishment which had for years controlled the city for the few. They in turn baited COPS and accused it of being power hungry.[110] COPS represented a radical departure from the 1960s.

In Los Angeles a similar organization, United Neighborhood Organizations (UNO), was organized in 1975 by Bishop Arzube when he saw COPS in action. It included a coalition of twenty-two

Catholic parishes and ten Protestant churches and was headed by Fr. Luis Olivares of Our Lady of Solitude Catholic Church. Two thousand packed the auditorium of East Los Angeles Community College at California state senate subcommittee hearings on insurance rates, during which UNO members protested the high automobile insurance rates for East Los Angeles.[111] UNO emulated COPS, even sending their staff to Alinsky's Industrial Areas Foundation in Chicago for training. Cortés, the San Antonio organizer, played a key role. However, unlike the San Antonio organization, the Los Angeles group was led by priests.

UNO did not appear to be as well disciplined or as political as COPS. As of mid-1979 it shunned electoral politics. This was understandable since in San Antonio the archdiocese gave COPS much more support. In Los Angeles Cardinal Timothy Manning verged on being a reactionary and kept a tight lid on his Mexican and Latin clergy. However, UNO showed no signs of weakening when on October 7, 1979, it drew between 4,000 and 5,000 participants at its annual convention. Another difference is that MACC has had a radicalizing influence on the COPS' leadership; UNO has not enjoyed this ideological reinforcement. It is too soon to make a judgement as to which way UNO and COPS will go. Their continued growth could contribute greatly to progressive gains for the Chicano community.

CHICANOS IN THE MIDWEST

By the 1970s, because of their numbers and militancy, Midwest Chicanos became a force within the movement. The 1970 U.S. census counted 225,923 Mexicans in the states of Ohio, Indiana, Illinois, Michigan, Wisconsin, Minnesota, Iowa, Missouri, Nebraska, and Kansas which was a serious undercount with the actual figures closer to 500,000 and expected to double by the end of the decade.[112] Mexicans arrived in the Midwest via the Texas-Mexican migrant stream and through direct documented and undocumented settlement from Mexico. They remained attracted by the higher paying jobs in the heavy industries of that region.[113] High unemployment in the Southwest drove Chicanos further north.

Cultural identity played a major role in unifying Chicanos of diverse urban centers of the Midwest. Unlike most Chicanos in the Southwest, Chicanos in the Midwest have had to adjust to other Latin groups who began to arrive after World War II. Living in proximity with Puerto Ricans, they found it necessary to coalesce with the *Boricua*. The term Latino was more common in that section of the nation. The *barrios* in the different Midwest cities followed the patterns set by preceding immigrant groups. For example, Chicago historically had neighborhoods with strong traditional and ethnic identities, and Mexicans there have followed that pattern. In contrast Flint, Michigan, has no identifiable *barrio* and the Chicano population is dispersed throughout the city. There is a network of church and organizational contacts which helped sustain an identity.[114]

While nationalism and militancy declined in the Southwest during the 1970s, Midwest Chicano students pushed for more services and struggled to maintain their identity. The student movement differed from state to state. In many cases university authorities recruited a disproportionate number of students from Texas and often totally neglected development of the local Chicano population. Authorities did not want to build a cadre of militants in their own backyard. Gradually this situation changed somewhat as universities responded to Chicano demands that they service the region before recruiting elsewhere.

Poverty agencies played a more prestigious role than in the Southwest, especially in places like Wisconsin where Chicanos look to these agencies for service, jobs, and leadership. LULAC and the GI Forum remained strong, especially with their sponsorship of SER manpower programs. *La Raza Unida* in the Midwest generally was not a party, but an issue-oriented organization which sponsored demonstrations and was closely allied to the migrant cause. In many states it became a poverty agency. Other organizations formed to promote the interests of Chicanos were the United Migrant Opportunity Services (UMOS) in Wisconsin, the Latin American Union for Civil Rights (LAUCR) in Milwaukee, the United Mexican-Americans in South Bend, Indiana, and the Midwest Council of *La Raza* in Notre Dame, Indiana.[115] Bureaus relating to the Spanish speaking were established by the state governments of Minnesota, Iowa, Wisconsin, Illinois, Michigan, and Indiana as a result of community pressure. *Las fiestas patrias*, Mexican holidays, are actively celebrated throughout the region.

The 1970 census listed Detroit's Chicano population as close to 27,000; activists claim it was as high as 50,000. That figure expected to double in the 1970s to give Detroit one of the largest concentrations of Mexicans in the Midwest. The city had a smaller, but highly visible Puerto Rican community which occupied the same neighborhoods as Chicanos. Other Michigan cities with sizable Mexican populations were Adrian, Flint, Grand Rapids, Lansing, and Saginaw.

In most Midwestern states Chicano migrant labor continued to play an important role. For instance, during the peak of the 1970 picking season between 12,000 and 13,000 migrant workers labored in Minnesota. This count excluded children and nonworking family members. Nearly all migrants were from Texas. In Minnesota the former migrant population stabilized. By the 1970s many owned their own farms, while others became factory workers, salespeople, government workers, and even professionals. A similar pattern existed in Milwaukee where the migrant fallout continued to swell the Mexican community which still centered in the South Side around Sixth and National.[116]

Chicago continued to house the largest concentration of Chicanos in the Midwest. Unlike most other Midwestern cities it had a large concentration of Mexican nationals. Visitors from the Southwest were struck by the energy of the Chicago Chicano population, especially when walking down the center of 18th Street in the Pilsen district. Signs in Spanish and neon lights attracted the visitor and Mexican cafes served food which surpassed that of many places in the Southwest. The district also had many murals depicting past and present Chicano struggles. Chicanos successfully pressured local school authorities to name the high school Benito Juárez. Since the 1920s this had been the largest Chicano *barrio* and served as a port of entry for Mexicans.[117]

Occupations in Pilsen were not those of the highly unionized industrial sectors such as found in Back of the Yards and South Chicago. Ethnic identification tended to be much stronger than union ties as in South Chicago. Workers in Pilsen remained largely unskilled, working mainly in light industry and the hotels and restaurants. Pilsen was the poorest of the Mexican *barrios* and in 1970 it ranked fifty-ninth out of the seventy-six Chicago communities in measures of education and job levels, income, rents, home values, and others.[118] Through the years urban renewal projects victimized residents. Construction and expansion of the University of Illinois Chicago Circle Campus wiped out half of the Pilsen resident's homes, but the *barrio* continued to exist and grow.

El Centro de la Causa (the Center of the Cause) served as a community-based organization. In the early 1970s the Mexican American Council on Education (MACE) and the Brown Berets functioned out of the center's facilities. *Casa Aztlán* functioned in Pilsen and housed the Benito Juárez Health Center.[119] In the late 1970s *Mujeres Latinas en Acción* established an independent center featuring counseling and a crash pad for runaway Latinas.

Communities in Back of the Yards and South Chicago continued. Mexicans worked in meat packing and steel. By the 1970s they played a more significant role in community politics. In Back of the Yards Mexicans were a necessary component of the multiethnic coalition since 1939.[120] William Kornblum described the growing importance of the Chicano in South Chicago.[121] In this area the United Steel Workers of America (AFL-CIO) dominated the life of residents. Ethnic division in the area often prevented worker unity. Chicanos lived in the Irondale and Millgate *barrios*, and territoriality often prevented unity between the two Mexican communities. Kornblum stated that "The Mexicans of South Chicago are on the verge of becoming full participants in the negotiations of primary groups in community institutions." Mexicans in the past concentrated their efforts in churches and *mutualistas;* however, in the 1970s they turned increasingly to politics and unions. According to a study by the Center for Urban Affairs of Northwestern University:

> Mexicans have taken a position between ethnic and working class ideologies in their approach to political issues. Mobilization around the issues of elections takes the form of an "ethnic vote" which appears to be ethnic only in its composition, not purpose. Rather, ethnicity is the way in which economic class positions take shape in South Chicago.[122]

In South Chicago the Chicano population in the steel plants was relatively small in comparison to European ethnics and Blacks. In union politics it amounted to only about 15 percent. Its importance was that it was the swing vote. Mexican steelworkers increasingly cooperated with Blacks and progressives to challenge the union leadership which was composed of the older ethnics and was often reactionary.[123]

Despite the gerrymandering of Chicano *barrios* in the 10th Ward the Democratic machinery has been forced to include Mexicans in the party network. For instance, at the 1972 presidential convention Carmen Chico was an active delegate, "the first woman from the Mexican neighborhoods to achieve prominence in the politics of metropolitan Chicago."[124]

Factors frustrating Mexican unity in Chicago were the dispersal of Chicano *barrios* throughout the city and their intense territorial loyalties. There were also class differences. Machine politics firmly locked political action into the wards. Although the Chicano population was large, it was unorganized. There was no strong central organization to bind many of the small interest groups together. LULAC was the best known Chicano organization and it did not have a history of coalition politics. The study by the Center of Urban Affairs found that Latinos in general identified the common issues of education, housing, and employment as their main concerns. Job discrimination was a primary concern, since Chicanos throughout the city were well aware that they were the last hired and first fired.[125] Chicago's problems and concerns were similar to those of the region. The Chicano population in the cities of the Midwest increased in importance and size, giving the Chicanos in the United States a national forum.

HUMAN RIGHTS, 1970s

In the late 1970s President Jimmy Carter attacked the lack of human rights in communist countries but ignored the indiscriminate killings and gross violations of human rights in the United States. Following a White House conference between the president and Latinos, Al Pérez, a Mexican-American Legal Defense Fund attorney, criticized the Carter Administration for insisting on looking at each police brutality case individually.[126] By looking at each case as an isolated incident, by refusing to see or to remember similarities among cases, Carter disregarded the pattern of violence directed toward an identifiable group of people.

In the 1970s police-Chicano relations worsened because of the economic crisis; in 1976 the official rate of inflation was 5.5 percent, and almost 8 percent were unemployed.[127] With the percentage of unemployed Mexican youths reaching 30 percent in many urban *barrios,* discontent increased.

The attitude of law enforcement officials was clear. The report to the grand jury during the Sleepy Lagoon case of the 1940s had characterized Mexicans as genetically violent; in 1960 Los Angeles Police Chief William Parker stated that Mexicans were wild Indians; in 1970 J. Edgar Hoover said, "You never have to bother about a President being shot by Puerto Ricans or Mexicans. They don't shoot very straight. But if they come to you with a knife, beware."[128] Joseph Wambaugh, author and former member of the Los Angeles Police Department, stated in an interview on KABC-TV on May 18, 1977, that racism existed in the department and that "young macho men trained in violence wanted to exercise their trade." According to Wambaugh, from the moment a man became an officer too much emphasis was put on violence on the street and on the hazards of police work. An "acute defensive mechanism built up," and officers were prepared for war.

Police brutality was not past history. The violence of past decades continued in the 1970s. On June 23, 1970, Hank Coca from Santa Clara County arrived in Los Angeles. He was a furniture store owner and had made automobile reservations with Hertz. He had a credit card, but his driving license was defective. Six officers, without giving him an opportunity to identify himself, handcuffed and arrested him, stating, "Police just don't take any chances with Mexicans in Los Angeles these days." They baited and insulted Coca and on the way to the Venice station an officer told him, "You Mexican son-of-a-bitch, I wish you'd start running! Then I could kill you or beat the shit out of you! I could book you for resisting arrest, assaulting an officer, anything!" The police officer then hit Coca. At the station the desk sergeant immediately released Coca.[129]

In 1972 in Blythe, California, 200 Chicanos stormed the police station when an off-duty police officer, named Richard Krupp, shot Mario Barreras, 23, following a motorcycle accident. When Barreras attempted to leave the scene of the accident, Krupp chased him. Upon stopping Barreras, "Krupp stepped out of his Datsun pick-up camper with a gun in his hand, walked directly to the passenger side of the vehicle, opened the door, leaned over, aimed at the youth's head and fired at point blank range."[130]

On March 17, 1973 Denver police stormed into the Crusade for Justice, alleging snipers had fired at them. They killed Luis H. Martínez, 20, active in the Colorado RUP and wounded nineteen others. The confrontation began when Martínez was stopped in front of the Crusade headquarters. An explosion ripped the side of the apartment; police claimed Crusade members had dynamite. Twelve officers were injured and thirty-six Chicanos were arrested.[131]

In the summer of 1973 Dallas police officer Darryl L. Cain, 30, questioned Santos Rodríguez, 12, and his brother David, 13, about a gas station burglary. Cain pulled out his revolver and attempted to scare Santos into answering questions. "Cain pulled his pistol and pointed it at the back of Santos' head. The .357 magnum went off." Several thousand marched in protest to City Hall where a riot broke out. Cain admitted playing Russian roulette and he was convicted of criminal homicide and sentenced to five years. The Chicano community was infuriated. Cain received another trial in 1976 and was again convicted and received another light sentence.[132] While the case was on appeal, Darryl Cain remained in the streets.

In June 1975 three Texas Alcoholic Beverage Commission officers, two Department of Safety highway patrolmen, and a Frio County deputy sheriff beat Modesto Rodríguez for his support of the Voting Rights Act.[133] In July 1975 four police savagely beat Manuel Ortega in San Pablo, California. He had received a call that his son Donicio, 20, had been arrested, charged with drunkenness. When Ortega requested a blood test for his son, the police refused. When he offered to put up bail, the police refused. After this another son told a police officer, "I'd like to get you without that badge." The police officer lunged at the boy; Ortega intervened and pushed his son out of the door. He was kicked and beaten with billy clubs and flashlights until he cried out, "Kill me." Ortega was tried on two counts of battery and one count of resisting arrest by an all-white jury.[134]

On September 14, 1975 Chief of Police Frank Hayes took Ricardo Morales, 27, of Castroville, Texas, to an isolated field and murdered him. Before shooting Morales, Hayes threatened him, "I've already killed one Mexican and I'm going to kill me another." After shotgunning Morales to death, he had his wife and daughter drive Morales' corpse 400 miles where they buried him. When they were returning to Castroville, they were caught. Police became suspicious when they stopped their car and found a pool of fresh blood in the trunk. Hayes was convicted of "murder by aggravated assault" and he received two to ten years; his wife received probation. The Justice Department, after considerable community pressure, reopened the Hayes case with the possibility of trying him for the violation of Morales' civil rights. The case set a precedent, because since 1959 the U.S. attorney general had not intervened once a state court rendered a judgement. While awaiting a civil rights trial, Hayes remained free on a $1,000 bond. A federal court finally convicted Hayes, sentencing him to a life term.[135]

On November 29, 1975, Lorenzo Verdugo, 25, was found hanged in Huntington Park jail (Los Angeles County). Authorities detained him because he did not have papers. He had died of a ruptured trachea which was the result of a blow, not of hanging. The Mexican American Political Association (MAPA) and the Mexican consulate asked for an investigation which was not granted.[136]

In San Jose, California, officers Don Edwards and Craig Smith killed Danny Trevino, 29, who had been drunk, but unarmed.[137] Two months of demonstrations followed with fifty-two organizations demanding justice. In Oakland, California, officer Michael Cogley allegedly accidentally shot José Barlow Benavidez. For two years community groups attempted to get justice with no success.[138] On February 20, 1977, in San Antonio Juan Zepeda, 42, died in jail as the result of injuries inflicted by a blackjack.[139] In the spring of 1977 Eduardo Prieto, 23, of El Paso underwent surgery for a ruptured testicle. Two police officers, a man and a woman, beat him up and dragged him into a car. The head of Internal Affairs Division refused to say if the accused officers were still working.[140]

In 1977 city council member, Pat Russell pressured the Los Angeles Police Department for a report on police shootings over the past two years. In 1975 and 1976 police shredded complaint files against police with the approval of the city attorney's office, destroying documents which showed a pattern of Los Angeles Police Department violence. The LAPD and the city attorney's office had entered into a conspiracy to destroy evidence. Judge George W. Trammell called the incident "tarnishment of our system of criminal justice which is rarely seen in our courts."[141]

In 1977 five Houston policemen beat José Campos Torres, 23, and threw him into the Buffalo bayou, where he drowned. On the 8th of May police arrested Campos Torres at a bar. Considerable tension existed between Chicanos, which comprised 25 percent of the city, and the Houston police department. Terry W. Denson, 27, Alan D. Nichols, 26, Eugene Elliot, 20, James Janish, 22, and Stephen Orlando, 21, participated in the beating. Campos Torres's family learned about the death of their son on television.

Stephen Orlando and Terry Denson were found guilty of misdemeanor negligent homicide. An all-Anglo jury ordered probation. The sentence was a $2,000 fine and a year in jail. The judge excused the convicted defendants from paying the fine and serving their light sentence. In a federal trial for the violation of Campos Torres's civil rights, Denson, Orlando, and Janish were sentenced to one year in jail. A riot broke out on May 5, 1978, at a protest rally.[142]

On May 18, 1977 Juan Veloz Zuñiga, 33, was beaten to death by

Hudspeth County Sheriff Claymon McCutcheon. Texas Rangers investigated the death. On May 15, 1977 Veloz Zuñiga, on his way to Odessa where he worked as a plumber's assistant, was detained by INS officers who handed him over to the Texas Department of Public Safety which charged him with drunk driving, a tail light violation, and no license. At Fort Hancock a judge fined Veloz Zuñiga $240 and sentenced him to three days in jail. In jail Veloz Zuñiga became depressed and began crying for his wife and children. The sheriff took a sawed off cue stick and stated, "I'm going to shut him [Zuñiga] up once and for all." He hit him three times in the head. An autopsy exonerated McCutcheon; however, a pathologist questioned the validity of the autopsy. The grand jury took no action. John Ainsworth, a grand juror, told a group of several people, "If I've got to stay at that courthouse all day and all night, they're not going to do anything to Claymon." Other prisoners stated that Veloz Zuñiga was not having a fit, but was scared. They told reporters that the sheriff, a DPS officer, and another deputy stood by while McCutcheon beat Veloz Zuñiga's brains out. "McCutcheon hit him with a tremendous shot in the head and the man went down on one knee. When he started to get up, McCutcheon hit him again and the blood just began spurting out of Zuñiga's head." The DPS officer then maced him and choked him with his knee.[143]

This pattern of police violence continued through the remainder of 1977 and into 1978. The reader must remember that the cases of police brutality reported in this text are but a fraction of those suffered by Mexicans in the United States.[144]

REVERSE DISCRIMINATION: AN ANGLO-AMERICAN ILLUSION

Affirmative action and equal opportunity programs which were acceptable during the 1960s, a time of economic prosperity, came under attack in the 1970s, an era of inflation and unemployment. Involved in intense competition for jobs in low paying public servant professions such as teachers and librarians, majority groups were no longer tolerant of efforts to add new groups, the minorities, to the competition. In medicine practices of the American Medical Association limited the number of doctors produced at a time when more qualified people, both from the majority and minority communities, were graduating from college.[145] So-called taxpayer revolts also limited government spending and eliminated jobs. As a consequence of educational opportunity programs more minority group members were qualified for the few available jobs; affirmative action programs gave them some of these jobs and allowed others to pursue higher education to become qualified. Unsuccessful whites, blaming their inability to move upward on minorities, charged that affirmative action was "reverse discrimination."

The California Supreme Court on September 16, 1976 decided *Bakke* v. *The Regents of the University of California* in favor of the plaintiff; it struck down the special admissions program at the medical school at the University of California at Davis. During 1973 and 1974 Allan Bakke, a 34-year-old white engineer, applied to thirteen medical schools and was rejected because of his age. Bakke came from a lower-middle-class background; his father was a mailman and his mother a teacher. Peter Storandt, an assistant to the dean for admissions, encouraged Bakke to challenge the university's special admissions program and referred Bakke to two lawyers who specialized in medical law.[146]

The Davis special admissions program had set aside 16 out of 100 places for disadvantaged students. The Davis Medical School, founded in 1968, had no special admissions program until 1970. In 1968 and 1969 it admitted 2 Blacks and 1 Latino; from 1970 to 1974, under the special program, it admitted 33 Latinos, 26 Blacks, and 1 Native American.

Judge F. Leslie Manker heard the case. The defendants agreed to a trial based solely on the written evidence. Based on scant evidence, Manker found that Bakke had been unconstitutionally denied equal protection under the Fourteenth Amendment because of his race. The California Supreme Court upheld this decision. The media meanwhile conditioned the public to accept this reversal in the commitment to integrate minorities economically by calling student affirmative action programs "reverse discrimination."

Many activists were surprised when Jewish organizations, such as the American Jewish Congress, the American Jewish Committee, and the Anti-Defamation League, which had been at the forefront of combating racism, actively supported *Bakke*. While the abandonment of liberal causes by middle-class whites had been anticipated, minorities had not expected the defection of Jewish organizations. Jews had also been victimized by Anglo-American racists and nativists. Jewish leaders explained that their stand was consistent with their opposition to quotas which limited the number of Jews admitted to professional schools. Minorities angrily retorted that this situation was different, since it was not imposing a ceiling, but establishing a minimum. Minorities charged that Jewish organizations were responding to the growing conservatism among the Jewish middle-class who were increasingly fearful that minorities would interfere with their dream that their children would become professionals just as they were threatened by high taxes and school busing programs which would take their children back to the ghettoes from which many had escaped.

The loss of the support of Jewish organizations hurt minorities since they had been influential in raising funds for liberal causes, brought organizational skill to the struggle, and they had considerable political lobbying power. Their defection along with the *Bakke* decision encouraged racist administrators of graduate schools to severely cut back on the admissions of minorities.

The active backing by Jewish organizations of the *Bakke* case did not represent the entire Jewish community. Many Jews condemned the stand of the ADL. The stand of Jewish organizations must be put into the context of middle-class self-interests which were no different from those of white Americans or, for that matter, the middle-class interests of many minority group members.

Even California Supreme Court Justice Stanley Mosk, once a liberal, made a 180 degree turnabout. In his opinion he claimed that there had been no history of discrimination at the University of California. According to Mosk, an admission of past discrimination was essential to Davis's case. The University of California, however, had not attempted to prove past discrimination at the University of California. This is ironical since much of the student turmoil of the 1960s had focused on this same issue. As late as 1967 fewer than a dozen Chicanos attended either the University of California's Los Angeles or Berkeley campus. At Davis "until 1972, all minority students coming to Davis received penicillin shots on arrival, a prophylactic measure against disease, according to health service officials."[147] Moreover, Mosk only had to look at the disparity between Anglos and minorities in order to judge if there was a history of discrimination. In 1975 in California there was 1 Anglo lawyer for every 530 Anglos, 1 Asian lawyer for every 1,750 Asians, 1 Black lawyer for every 3,441 Blacks, 1 Latino lawyer for every 9,482 Latinos, and 1 Native American lawyer for every 50,000 Native Americans.[148]

The primary care physician-to-patient ratio for Latinos in California was 1:21,245, Blacks 1:4,028, Native Americans 1:7,539, and Anglos 1:990.[149] The media distorted the question of qualifications. At no point was the admission of unqualified minorities at issue. For example, in both law and medicine minority students had graduated from four-year accredited institutions. "The average LSAT score of admitted minority students is now higher than or equal to the median score of students at 80 percent of the nation's law schools." All students were required to pass state certification examinations, as well as satisfactorily completing the medical school's curriculum.[150]

Special assistance is and always has been given to groups and individuals, but attitudes toward that assistance definitely change according to who is receiving it. Payments to the business community and the rich are subsidies, tariffs, taxbreaks, etc., while payments to the poor are referred to as welfare. Preference to rich applicants whose families have heavily endowed the university goes unnoticed and uncriticized, but admissions of minorities becomes "reverse discrimination."[151]

A *Bakke* spin-off case was that of Rita Greenwald Clancey. Allegedly Mrs. Clancey, age 22, was disadvantaged because she immigrated to the United States at the age of 14, speaking only Hungarian and Russian. Her family was on welfare because her father underwent brain surgery. Her father had been a bookkeeper in the Soviet Union. His education was therefore superior to that of minorities in the United States who, for the most part, attended segregated schools. A judge issued an order admitting Clancey to Davis Medical School; her lawyer husband continued to pay the bills.[152]

The U.S. Supreme Court on June 28, 1978, announced its 5–4 decision upholding *Bakke*; it ruled that Davis had gone too far in 1973 and 1974 in setting numerical quotas and that affirmative action policies were all right as long as they did not use quotas that set specific numbers. Unlike the lower court, it based its decision on a violation of the 1964 U.S. Civil Rights Act. The court approved nonquota affirmative action programs. Justice Thurgood Marshall dissented, stating that the court had come "full circle," returning to the time after the Civil War when the courts stopped congressional efforts to initiate programs to assist former slaves to gain the rights of full citizenship. The court left matters up in the air, and it encouraged racist university administrations and faculties throughout the United States not to admit minorities.[153]

In addition to *Bakke*, California's Proposition 13 has had far-reaching effects. Besides further unveiling a basic selfishness of middle-class Americans, it also demonstrated a certain gullibility of the public who believed that landlords or private industry would pass on windfall profits to renters. Essentially Proposition 13 limited taxing of property to a set percentage, rolling back assessed evaluations to 1975 levels. Major benefactors of 13 were commercial property owners, large farmers, and industry. The proposition passed in June of 1978. Its immediate effects were softened by the state which passed on billions of dollars of surplus tax money to county and city agencies to prevent massive layoffs. However, this money will not be forthcoming in future years and without new revenue these agencies will be forced to lay off even more workers; 83 percent of the 9,042 Latinos working for the County of Los Angeles have been hired in the past five years and will be the first to go.

In both the county and city library systems of Los Angeles there are fewer than a dozen Mexican librarians; all will probably lose their jobs if additional state revenues are not forthcoming.[154] This also applies to teaching where the majority of Chicano teachers in California have been certified since 1972. Chicano teachers have remained somewhat untouched only because of the large amounts of bilingual and special funds.[155] Proposition 13, even more than *Bakke*, has the potential of wiping out a generation of public servants which the Chicano community has produced over years of struggle.

CONCLUSION

The problems confronting Chicanos have changed from decade to decade. A historical memory of this struggle is important to produce unity within the group in order to force changes within a frozen society that had relegated the majority of Chicanos to blue-collar occupations or unemployment. A historical memory separates *homo sapiens* from other animals. It allows them to build on the past. Therefore, the more that Chicanos know about their past, the more they will be able to participate in the future. The 1980s promise to provide a special challenge when conditions will again resemble those of the turbulent 1960s. The basic differences between the 1960s and 1980s are that the Chicano population has doubled; its sizable population in the Midwest gives it a national base; and the largeness of its brokerage system which, for good or bad, insures its visibility. Which direction the Chicano movement takes will in great part depend on unity. Because of the lack of a national media controlled by Chicanos or effective national institutions, that unity will in great part depend on the historical consciousness that develops among the masses of Mexicans in the United States.

NOTES

1. Tony Castro, *Chicano Power: The Emergence of Mexican Americans* (New York: Saturday Review Press, 1974), pp. 198–199.
2. Castro, pp. 199–200.
3. Richard Santillán, *La Raza Unida* (Los Angeles: Tlaquila, 1973), p. 80; Castro, p. 103. Ramírez had been director of the division of Mexican-American Studies of the U.S. Commission on Civil Rights.
4. Santillán, pp. 80–81. On October 6, 1972, the INS raided the Banuelos factory. Banuelos was employing undocumented workers.
5. Castro, pp. 200–201.
6. Frank Del Olmo, "Watergate Panel Calls 4 Mexican-Americans," *Los Angeles Times*, June 5, 1974; Report of the Senate Select Committee on Presidential Activities, *The Senate Watergate Reports* (New York: Dell, 1974), vol. 1, pp. 345–372.
7. Castro, pp. 202–203.
8. With California and Colorado already committed to remaining neutral, buying Gutiérrez's neutrality would have been useless. See "La Raza Platform Prohibits Support of Non-Chicanos," *Los Angeles Times*, July 4, 1972; Cindy Parmenter, "La Raza Unida Plans Outlined," *Denver Post*, June 20, 1974. Jim Wood in "La Raza Sought Nixon Cash," *San Antonio Express*, November 18, 1973.
9. Castro, pp. 7–8, 210.
10. "Top Woman Aide Gets U.S. Latin Position," *Los Angeles Times*, March 8, 1977; "Spanish-Speaking Aid Hits Cutbacks," *Santa Fe New Mexican*, March 26, 1973. By this date Henry Ramírez was beginning to have second thoughts.
11. Vernon M. Briggs, Jr., Walter Fogel, and Fred H. Schmidt, *The Chicano Worker* (Austin: University of Texas Press, 1977), pp. 8, 10.

12. Regional Planning Commission, County of Los Angeles, California, 1972. A basic problem with the 1970 census was that there were no specific guidelines for counting Mexicans such as there were for counting blacks. Chicano organizations fought for guidelines since they realized that all funding was based on numbers. See *Los Angeles Times*, March 8, 1972; Edward Murguia, *Assimilation, Colonialism and the Mexican American People* (Austin: Center for Mexican American Studies, University of Texas, 1975), p. 43; Ray Hebert, "L.A. County Latin Population Grows 113 percent," *Los Angeles Times*, August 18, 1972; *Forumeer*, February 1970; Frank Del Olmo, "Spanish-Origin Census Figure Revised by U.S., "*Los Angeles Times*, January 15, 1974; "Census Hikes Spanish Count," *Denver Post*, January 16, 1974; "State Gains 643,000 Latins," *San Francisco Chronicle*, May 11, 1974; Citizens of Spanish Origin Gain in U.S.," *San Antonio Express*, March 31, 1974.

13. "Births, Los Angeles County, 1966–1974," Chicano Resource Center, Clippings, East Los Angeles County Library Branch; Regional Planning Commission.

14. For a good rundown of the Texas count, see Nell Fenner Grover, "S.A.'s Spanish Speakers Highest Concentration in State," *San Antonio Express*, August 10, 1972. For a good rundown of the San Francisco count, see Ralph Crail, "What the 1970 Census Showed About Bay Area," *San Francisco Chronicle*, August 3, 1972.

15. "Census of Spanish Origin Population Shows Most Live in Southwest Area," *El Paso Times*, March 23, 1976.

16. *Denver Post*, May 13, 1973.

17. John Staples Shockley, *Chicano Revolt in a Texas Town* (Notre Dame, Ind.: University of Notre Dame Press, 1974), pp. 202–203.

18. Christine Marín, *A Spokesman of the Mexican American Movement: Rodolfo "Corky" Gonzales and the Fight for Chicano Liberation, 1966–1972* (San Francisco: R & E Research Assc., 1977), p. 17.

19. Marín, pp. 24–26.

20. Santillán, p. 57.

21. Santillán, pp. 84–86.

22. Castro, pp. 16, 23.

23. Castro, pp. 42–44; *Denver Post*, August 31, September 1, 1972; Edna Vega, "Brunson Acquitted in Falcon Killing," *Forumeer*, December 1972.

24. Santillán, pp. 98–99, 103–104.

25. "Raza Unida Party Enters Presidential Politics," *Arizona Republic*, September 2, 1972; "Raza Unida Urges Bilingual Education, Stays Neutral on President," *Arizona Republic*, September 4, 1972; "Raza Unida Vows Fight for Self-determination," *Arizona Republic*, September 5, 1972.

26. Marín, p. 29.

27. "La Raza Meet, Split Hinted," *Denver Post*, September 3, 1972; "La Raza Unida Won't Support McGovern," *Denver Post*, September 4, 1972; "Gonzales Loses Chair Election 256–175," *Denver Post*, September 4, 1972.

28. Castro, p. 134.

29. See Tony Castro, "Nixon Strategy May Haunt La Raza," *Reporter Lead-In*, (March 1974): 1–2.

30. Castro, *Chicano Power*, pp. 21–33.

31. Jorge García, "Incorporation of East Los Angeles 1974, Part One," *La Raza Magazine* (Summer 1977): 29–33, García, the chairperson of Chicano studies at California State University at Northridge, was an RUP candidate for city council.

32. Frank Del Olmo, "Early Returns Show East L.A. Incorporation Measure Failing," *Los Angeles Times*, November 6, 1974; "L.A.'s Huge Chicano Section Divided by Social Prejudice and Freeways," *Arizona Republic*, November 28, 1974; Frank Del Olmo, "Defeat of East L.A. Plan Laid to Fear of High Property Tax," *Los Angeles Times*, November 7, 1974.

33. F. Chris García, "Manitos and Chicanos in New Mexico Politics," in F. Chris García, *La Causa Politica: A Chicano Politics Reader* (Notre Dame, Ind.: University of Notre Dame Press, 1974), pp. 275–276.

34. "Man Shot; 2 Arrested in La Raza Incident," *Albuquerque Journal*, May 22, 1976.

35. Tom Curtis, "Politics: Raza Desunida," *Texas Monthly* (February 1977): 102.
36. Curtis, p. 102.
37. " 'Little Cuba' Battleground Expands," *San Antonio Express,* January 7, 1977; Kemper Diehl, "State Crystal Probe Threatens Big Grant," *San Antonio Express,* September 5, 1976; "Zavala Grant Suit to Begin," *San Antonio Express,* October 1, 1976; Jerry Deal, "Feds Probe Zavala Agency," *San Antonio Express,* October 10, 1976; Jerry Deal, "Raza Chief Fighting for Political Life," *San Antonio Express,* April 12, 1976.
38. Jerry Deal, "Big Zavala Grant Gets a Congressional Eye-balling," *San Antonio Express,* August 29, 1976; Jerry Deal, "Gutierrez Denies Grant Charges," *San Antonio Express,* August 25, 1976.
39. Bill Mintz, "Muniz Sentenced to Five-Year Prison Term," *San Antonio Express,* March 3, 1977; "Ramsey Muniz Surrenders, Expected in Court," *El Paso Times,* August 2, 1976.
40. Curtis, p. 160.
41. Curtis, p. 132.
42. Jerry Deal, "Crystal City Posts Guards on Gas," *San Antonio Express,* July 20, 1977; Dick Merkel, "Crystal Loses Gas Fight," *San Antonio Express,* July 21, 1977; Gregorio Barrios, "The View from Crystal City on Gas Case," *San Antonio Express,* July 29, 1977; "Crystal City Residents Describe Struggle With Lo-Vaca," *Chicano Times* August 19–September 1, 1977; Chavel López, "Lo-Vaca Co. Leaves Crystal City with No Gas," *Sin Fronteras,* October 1977.
43. Alternative colleges such as D-Q University at Davis, California, Jacinto Treviño in South Texas, and Colegio César Chávez in Oregon will not be discussed.
44. *El Plan de Santa Barbara: A Chicano Plan for Higher Education* (Oakland, Calif.: La Causa Publications, 1969).
45. See Ronald W. López and Darryl D. Enos, *Chicanos and Public Higher Education in California* (Sacramento: Joint Committee on the Master Plan for Higher Education, California Legislature, December 1972).
46. According to Congressman Edward Roybal, Lyndon Johnson was actually responsible for the passage of the act. Johnson had been a teacher in a Chicano school and said that students could not learn because of the language problems. He told Roybal and Senator Ralph Yarborough that he wanted the act while on a flight to Mexico.
47. *Forumeer,* August 1971.
48. William Jefferson Mathis, "Political Socialization in a Mexican American High School" (Ph.D. dissertation, University of Texas, 1973), pp. 7, 35, 67–68.
49. Mathis, p. 112.
50. Phillip Lee Paris, "The Mexican American Informal Policy and the Political Socialization of Brown Students: A Case Study in Ventura County" (Ph.D. dissertation, University of Southern California, 1973), p. vii. Paris's study shows that the poorer and more rural Mexicans are, the more apt they are to express ethnic awareness and political unity. Jacqueline Jo Ann Taylor, "Ethnic Identity and Upward Mobility of Mexican-Americans in Tucson (Ph.D. dissertation, University of Arizona, Tucson, 1973), pp. 160–162, talks about the school system's tracking of Chicanos into vocational education and discouraging them from going to college in the 1950s, children were humiliated when they spoke Spanish. For a study of Chicano medical students, see David Emmet Hayes-Bautista, "Becoming Chicano: A 'Disassimilation' Theory of Transformation of Ethnic Identity" (Ph.D. dissertation, University of California, San Francisco, 1974).
51. Keith J. Henderson, "Bilingual Education Programs Spawning Flood of Questions," *Albuquerque Journal,* June 11, 1978; See also, Briggs et al., p. 21; Myer Weinberg, *Minority Students: A Research Appraisal* (Washington, D.C.: U.S. Department of Health, Education and Welfare, 1977), p. 287.
52. According to the U.S. Commission on Civil Rights, *The Excluded Student: Educational Practices Affecting Mexican Americans in the Southwest,* Mexican American Education Study, Report iii (Washington, D.C.: Government Printing Office, 1972), bilingual education reached only 2.7 percent of the entire Chicano population. The 1970 U.S. census stated that over 2.6 million Latinos, 70 percent of them born in the U.S., listed Spanish as their principal

language. Data tabulated on p. 34 of the report dramatically demonstrated the lack of Chicano/Mexican-heritage courses actually taught.

PERCENTAGE OF CHICANO SECONDARY-SCHOOL CHILDREN ENROLLED IN

	CHICANO HISTORY COURSES	MEXICAN HISTORY COURSES
Arizona	1.4	1.1
California	0.7	0.5
Colorado	0.7	0.8
New Mexico	0.8	1.7
Texas	0.5	1.7
Southwest	0.7	0.9

53. U.S. Commission on Civil Rights, pp. 13–16, 19.
54. "Student Says Anti-Chicano Feelings of Ysleta Faculty Stirred Walkout," *El Paso Times*, January 22, 1974.
55. *Los Angeles Times*, May 21, 1972.
56. "Coach Dunks 13 Year Old in Commode," *Chicano Times*, January 26–February 9, 1973.
57. Liz Sweet, "Outspoken Teachers Are Suspended," *San Antonio Express*, May 7, 1977.
58. Joan W. Moore, *Mexican Americans*, 2nd ed., (Englewood Cliffs, N.J.: Prentice-Hall, 1976), p. 35.
59. *Los Angeles Times*, June 20, 1977. At Colton Junior High School, which was 70-percent Mexican, 70 percent of the test scores were below average in 1977.
60. Moore, p. 70.
61. William Trombley and Jack McCurdy, "L.A. School Board Rejects Citizens Panel Proposals," *Los Angeles Times*, January 18, 1977; Jonathan Kirsh, "White Heat; Behind the Panic Over Busing in Our Public Schools," *New West* (February 14, 1977): 47.
62. Ernesto Galarza, Statement submitted to the Subcommittee on Elementary, Secondary, and Vocational Educaton of the House Committee on Education and Labor, Hearings on Title VII, Bilingual Education Program, Washington, D.C., San Jose, June 3, 1977; Olivia Martínez, director of the San Jose Bilingual Consortium, letter to Dr. Angus Taylor, chancellor of University of California at Santa Cruz, February 4, 1977; Galarza letter to Taylor, February 17, 1977; Galarza letter to Mrs. Terry Pockets, April 27, 1977.
63. In California there were 1,290,870 Latinos of voting age, with over half of them unregistered; in Texas there were 800,424, with 421, 845 unregistered. Arnold Sawislak, "Political Parties Seek Untapped Latino Vote," *Albuquerque Journal*, February 24, 1976. In 1972 44.4 percent of the Spanish-origin citizens of voting age were registered to vote versus 65.5 percent of the blacks and 73.4 percent of the anglo (Briggs et al., p. 25).
64. F. Chris García and Rudolph de la Garza, *The Chicano Political Experience: Three Perspectives* (North Scituate, Mass.: Duxbury Press, 1977), p. 135; Ed Curda, "Racist Remarks by Aspirant Bring Laughter, Incredulity," *El Paso Times*, March 17, 1977.
65. "3 million Chicanos Voiceless in California," *Forumeer*, October 1971. In California in 1971 out of 15,650 elected and appointed officials 310, or 1.98 percent, were Chicanos. None of the 46 state officials and none of the advisors to the governor were Mexican.
66. Castro, *Chicano Power*, p. 106.
67. Don Bolles, "Raul Castro Scoffs at Reports He'll Put Latinos in Top Offices," *Arizona Republic*, October 16, 1974.
68. Ben Cole, "Castro Takes Oath as Ambassador to Buenos Aires," *Arizona Republic*, October 21, 1977.
69. "San Antonio Gets Ethnic Balanced Council," *El Paso Times*, April 14, 1977.
70. Sara Martinez, "COPS Backing Looks Like Key in District 5," *San Antonio Express*, April 4, 1977; Sara Martinez, "Eureste Wallops Chapa," *San Antonio Express*, April 14, 1977.

71. James McCory, "Cockrell Sails Past Monfrey," *San Antonio Express*, April 15, 1977.

72. Vicki Davidson, "Bakke Case Angers Ortiz," *San Antonio Express*, October 8, 1977. David McLemore, "Bakke Decision Protested," *San Antonio Express*, October 8, 1977; "Marchers Rap Bakke Ruling," *San Antonio Express*, June 30, 1978; Kemper Diehl, "Ortiz: From Poverty to Power," *San Antonio Express*, June 19, 1977.

73. James McCory, "HBG, the Man and the Myth," *San Antonio Express*, January 6, 1974.

74. Frank Del Olmo, "Ford Intensifies Bid for Latino Votes! Woos Chicano Leaders Nava, Gallegos, Ochoa in Visit Here," *Los Angeles Times*, October 12, 1976; Frank Del Olmo, "Latino Farm Unit to Support Ford," *Los Angeles Times*, October 15, 1976.

75. Andrew Hernández, *The Latin Vote in the 1976 Presidential Election* (San Antonio, Tex.: Southwest Voter Registration Education Project, 1977), p. 9. Starting in 1975 the Southwest voter registration project registered over 160,000 Latinos. In 1976, 4,947,000 Latinos were eligible to register and vote. Approximately 2,735,700 were actually registered and 1,887,600 actually voted. (Hernández, pp. i, 1–2.)

76. Ellen Hume, "Carter to Name 13 More Latin Aides—Roybal," *Los Angeles Times*, March 8, 1977; "Increase Seen in Minorities Getting Top Federal Jobs," *Albuquerque Journal*, May 12, 1977.

77. Joe Quintana, "Texas MAD Convention Way in El Paso," *El Paso Times*, July 2, 1977.

78. *Environmental Impact Report for the Northeast Los Angeles District Plan* (Los Angeles: Department of City Planning, 1974), p. 7.

79. *Environmental Impact Report*, pp. 8, 30.

80. *Boyle Heights Community: Background Report*; City Plan Case 23186 (Los Angeles: Dept. of City Planning; 1974), p. 28.

81. Tom Butler, "Eight Barrio Families Planning Last Stand," *El Paso Times*, February 2, 1977; Tom Butler, "South Side Housing Breeds Anger; Factions Clash, and No One Wins," *El Paso Times*, April 26, 1977; Tom Butler, "Southside EP: Dark Quarter Housed in Squalor," *El Paso Times*, April 24, 1977; Ron Dusek, "EP Professor: Crime Supports Households," *El Paso Times*, May 6, 1977; Ron Dusek, "La Campana Says HUD Hears Protests," *El Paso Times*, June 1, 1978.

82. Jessica Watson, "La Campana Stresses Alternative Plan," *El Paso Times*, June 21, 1978.

83. During the 1970s displacement took place under various community improvement programs, such as the Home Owner's Modernization Effort (H.O.M.E.), and the Model Cities program. An objective study of these programs has not been made. Arthur Montoya of the *Eastside Sun* is a constant critic of these urban, removal (renewal) programs.

84. "Hijack Defense to Put Stress on Ills of South," *Los Angeles Times*, July 6, 1972. Joan Sweeney, "Latin Hijacks Jet in L.A., Surrenders After Radio Protest," *Los Angeles Times*, April 14, 1972.

85. Frank Del Olmo, "Hijacking Trial Opens, Plane Crewmen Testify," *Los Angeles Times*, July 19, 1972; Frank Del Olmo, "Hijacked Jet to Save America and World, Chavez-Ortiz Says," *Los Angeles Times*, July 19, 1972.

86. Frank Del Olmo, "Chavez-Ortiz Convicted of Air Piracy, Receives Life In Prison," *Los Angeles Times*, July 24, 1972; *Denver Post*, November 30, 1972.

87. "Defend Ricardo Chávez Ortiz," *La Raza* (Summer 1977): 48.

88. La Federación Land Committee, *The Fight for the Chicano Nation: Chilili Defends Right to Land* (no publisher listed)(1976), p. 1.

89. La Federación Land Committee, p. 2.

90. "Chilili Take-Over Ends in Arrests," *Chicano Times*, July 1–15, 1977; Mike Lilley, "Chilili Road is Reopened; 15 Arrested," *Albuquerque Journal*, May 20, 1977; "Chilili Road Surveyors Not Opposed," *Albuguerque Journal*, May 26, 1977; Betty Childers, "New Road Closure Hearing Set," *Albuquerque Journal*, May 20, 1977; Mike Gallagher, "Chilili Dispute Troubles Deputy," *Albuquerque Journal*, May 26, 1977; "Chilili Road Surveyors Not Opposed," *Albuquerque Journal*, May 26, 1977; Betty Childers, "Seven Arrested at Chilili Trial," *Albuquerque Journal*, July 38, 1977; "Ruling on Chilili Road Reversed by High Court," *Albuquerque Journal*, February 28, 1978.

91. Francisca Flores, "Mexican-American Women Ponder Future Role of the Chicana," *Eastside Sun*, July 1, 1971.

92. "Chicanas Meet at Houston: La Confederación de Mujeres in Houston, May 28–30," *Forumeer*, July 1971; Martha Cotera, *Profile on the Mexican American Women* (Austin: National Educational Laboratory Publishers, 1976), p. 183. See also Rosaura Sánchez and Rosa Martínez, eds., *Essays on la Mujer* (Los Angeles: Chicano Studies Center, University of California at Los Angeles, 1977), esp. Judith Sweeney, "Chicanas History: A Review of the Literature," and Cotera, 183; Sonia A. López, "The Role of the Chicana within the Student Movement"; Arlene Stewart, "*Las Mujeres de Aztlán:* A Consultation with Elderly Mexican American Women in a Sociological Historical Perspective" (Ph.D. dissertation, California School of Professional Psychology, 1973), p. 77.

93. See Cotera, pp. 184–188, for a list of resultant conferences. The *Comisión Feminil Mexicana* had been formed on October 11, 1970, and it played a leading role in calling the spring 1971 Chicana conference. See Dorinda Moreno, ed., *La Mujer en Pie de Lucha* (San Francisco, Espina Del Norte, 1973); Cotera, pp. 183–184.

94. The early Chicana conferences of the 1970s owe a debt to Francisca Flores, who pioneered concern over women's issues. In the mid-1960s she established *La Carta Editorial*, the Mexican American Women's League, and later the magazine *Regeneración*. "Women's Club to Confer Achievement Awards," *Belvedere Citizen*, May 7, 1964; "Twelve Women Honored at Women's League," *Belvedere Citizen*, April 1, 1965; "Chicana Action Service Center opens Fri., Sept. 8," *Belvedere Citizen*, August 31, 1972. The Chicana Action Service Center was first funded under a grant to the *Comisión Feminil Mexicana*.

95. Jim Wood, "Report on Bias Against Latinos in Welfare," *San Francisco Chronicle*, July 2, 1972.

96. Cotera, pp. 108–109.

97. "Inez Garcia Gains Victory," *Sin Fronteras*, January 1976; "Justice," *La Gente*, March 1976; *San Francisco Chronicle*, January 4, 1976; "The Book Report: Inez Garcia, A Tale of 2 Rapes," *Los Angeles Times*, April 2, 1976; "Acquitted in Her Second Trial," *San Francisco Chronicle*, March 5, 1977.

98. Norma Solis, "Do Doctors Abuse Low-Income Women?" *Chicano Times* April 15–29, 1977.

99. "Doctor Raps Sterilization of Indian Women," *Los Angeles Times*, May 22, 1977; "Puerto Rican Doctor Denounces Sterilization," *Sin Fronteras*, May 1976. Dr. Helen Rodrigues, head of pediatrics at Lincoln Hospital in San Francisco, said that by 1968 35 percent of the women in Puerto Rico had been sterilized.

100. Bernard Rosenfeld, Sidney M. Wolfe, and Robert E. McGarrah, Jr., *A Health Research Group Study on Surgical Sterilization: Present Abuses and Proposed Regulation* (Washington, D.C.: Public Citizens, 1973), p. 1.

101. Rosenfeld et al., p. 7.

102. Quoted in Robert Kistler, "Women 'Pushed' into Sterilization, Doctor Charges," *Los Angeles Times*, December 2, 1974.

103. Robert Kistler, "Many U.S. Rules on Sterilization Abuses Ignored Here," *Los Angeles Times*, December 3, 1974. See also Georgina Torres Rizk, "Sterilization Abuses Against Chicanos in Los Angeles," Published by the Los Angeles Center for Law and Justice, December 2, 1976. Richard Siggins, "Coerced Sterilization: A National Civil Conspiracy to Commit Genocide upon the Poor?" (Loyola University School of Law, January 15, 1977), p. 12.

104. Quoted in *Vision* (San Diego State University, Spring 1976): 44; *San Francisco Chronicle*, February 17, March 29, 1976.

105. Castro, *Chicano Power*, p. 109.

106. "PADRES and the Selection of the Bishop," PADRES (May 1974): 7, 9–10; "The Chicanos Campaign for a Better Deal," *Business Week* (May 29, 1971): 48. See also Patricia Hynds, "The Chicano and the Catholic Church in Los Angeles Since 1969: Progress—Reality or Mirage?" (Seminar paper, Chicano Studies 501, California State University at Northridge, 1978), p. 9. PADRES was formed in 1968.

107. *Los Angeles Times*, May 6, 1972. Arzube also appeared at the California bar legal hearings for Ricardo Cruz, leader of *Católicos por la Raza*, who was being

denied admission to the California bar because he had been convicted and served time for CPLR activities.

108. Job Schuleer, "New Archbishop Sets Precedent," *Santa Fe New Mexican*, July 25, 1974. Two years later, PADRES quit the powerful National Federation of Priests Councils because it was not responsive to Latinos, *San Antonio Express*, March 24, 1976. See also Russell Chandler, "2 Auxiliary Bishops Named to Aid Manning," *Los Angeles Times*, December 21, 1976; "Quito Troops Seize Bishop Flores," *San Antonio Express*, August 14, 1976.

109. *La Raza Habla*, New Mexico State University (March 1977): 1–2, 4; "Bishops List Injustices," *Albuquerque Journal*, August 22, 1977.

110. David Hendricks, "Flores Leaves City He 'Loves,' " *San Antonio Express*, April 5, 1978; Calvin Trillin, "U.S. Journal: San Antonio. Some Elements of Power," *New Yorker* (May 2, 1977): 94–95, 97; Vickie Davidson, "5000 Mass for Third S.A. COPS Convention, *San Antonio Express*, November 22, 1976; *San Antonio Express*, October 16, October 26, 1976; James McCory, "COPS Hit as Raiders of Union," *San Antonio Express*, December 29, 1976; Sara Martínez and David McLemore, "COPS, Sutton Like 10-1 Plan," *San Antonio Express*, January 9, 1977; Roddy Stinson, " 'Get COPS Month' Should Be Discontinued," *San Antonio Express*, July 12, 1977.

111. Lee Harris, "2000 Protest High Auto Insurance Rates," *Los Angeles Times*, May 7, 1977; Frank Del Olmo, "Community Coalition Mobilizing East Los Angeles," *Los Angeles Times*, December 26, 1977.

112. Gilbert Cardenas, "*Los Desarraigados:* Chicanos in the Midwestern Region of the United States," *Aztlán* 7, no. 2 (Summer 1976): 155, 172, 183–184.

113. Leobardo F. Estrada, "A Demographic Comparison of the Mexican Origin Population in the Midwest and Southwest," *Aztlán* (Summer 1976): 226–227. In 1970 the median income for Chicano males in Texas was $3,885; in Michigan it was $7,466.

114. In Flint the Mexicans who work for the auto plants may earn over $20,000 a year, working six days a week and often 12-hour shifts. This has often compromised their struggle and, in fact, has deterred many local Chicano youths from pursuing a higher education. The fact that the black population (about 130,000) is some twenty times larger than the Mexican population has made it extremely difficult for Chicano or Latino agencies to obtain funds. In spite of these obstacles, Chicanos such as Lilia Alvarado have continued to struggle to maintain an activist profile.

115. Ricardo Parra, Victor Ríos, and Armando Gutiérrez, "Chicano Organizations in the Midwest: Past, Present and Possibilities," *Aztlán* (Summer 1976): 239; Miriam J. Wells, "From the Field to Foundry: Mexican American Adaptive Strategies in a Small Wisconsin Town" (Ph.D. dissertation, University of Wisconsin, 1975), pp. 253–254; John Gurda, *The Latin Community on Milwaukee's Near South Side* (Milwaukee: Milwaukee Urban Observatory, University of Wisconsin at Milwaukee, 1976), p. 18.

116. *Gopher Historian* (Fall 1971): 13; Gurda, pp. 7–11.

117. John Walton and Luis M. Salces, *The Political Organization of Chicago's Latino Communities* (Evanston, Ill.: Center for Urban Affairs, Northwestern University, 1977), pp. 3, 17–18. In 1970 247,857 Latinos were officially counted in Chicago and 324,215 in the metropolitan area.

118. Walton and Salces, pp. 18, 22.

119. Louise Año Nuevo Kerr, "The Chicano Experience in Chicago: 1920–1970" (Ph.D. dissertation, University of Illinois at Chicago Circle, 1976), pp. 196, 197.

120. Walton, and Salces, p. 25.

121. William Kornblum, *Blue Collar Community* (Chicago: University of Chicago Press, 1974).

122. Walton and Salces, p. 28.

123. Kornblum, pp. 30, 39, 116.

124. Kornblum, pp. 217–218.

125. Walton and Salces, pp. 57, 96–97.

126. Roger Langley, "Hispanics Bitter After Meeting at White House," *San Antonio Express*, June 7, 1978.

127. *The Iron Fist and the Velvet Glove*, 2nd ed. (Berkeley, Calif.: Center for Re-

search on Criminal Justice, 1977), p. 176.
128. Quoted in *La Raza Habla* (March 1977). For an excellent study, see Armando Morales, "A Study of Mexican American Perceptions of Law Enforcement Policies and Practices in East Los Angeles," (DSW dissertation, University of Southern California, 1972).
129. *Forumeer*, April 1971.
130. "Shooting Death of Latin Sets Off Riot in Blythe," *Los Angeles Times*, May 20, 1972; *Forumeer*, July 1972.
131. Castro, *Chicano Power*, pp. 55–57; George Lane, "Police Actions; Condemned, Lauded," *Denver Post*, February 18, 1973; "4 Face D.A. Charges in Gun Battle Case," *Denver Post*, March 27, 1973.
132. *Los Angeles Times*, July 25, 1973; *Arizona Republic*, July 29, November 16, 1973; Castro; *Chicano Power*, p. 219. See also Shirley Achor, *Mexican American in a Dallas Barrio* (Tucson: University of Arizona Press, 1978), pp. 102–108; *San Antonio Express*, April 21, 1976; March 10, 1977.
133. *San Antonio Express*, June 18, 1977.
134. *FELAD-Image* (Federation of Employed Latin American Descendants, Vallejo, California) August, December 1975.
135. Rick Scott, "Morales Killing Still Stirs Ire," *San Antonio Express*, October 30, 1976; *San Antonio Express*, February 2, February 24, 1977; *El Paso Times*, February 24, 1977; Bill Mintz, "Frank Hayes Indictment Dismissal Being Sought," *San Antonio Express*, March 24, 1977; *San Antonio Express*, February 18, 1978.
136. *Sin Fronteras*, January, February 1976.
137. *Sin Fronteras*, February 1976; Rich Carroll, "COPS Cleared in Slaying of Chicano," *San Francisco Chronicle*, April 3, 1976.
138. *Sin Fronteras*, July 1976; "U.S. Clears Oakland Cop in Killing," *San Francisco Chronicle*, May 25, 1978.
139. "Probe into Mark Villanueva, Texas Jail Death," *San Antonio Express*, March 15, 1977.
140. Gregory James and Tom Butler, "Beating Investigation Ordered," *El Paso Times*, April 6, April 8, 1977.
141. Narda Zacchino, "Davis Flays Channel 7's Masked Officer Interview," *Los Angeles Times*, May 12, 1977; Gene Blake and Michael A. Levett, "Pines Acts to Avoid Conflict of Interest," *Los Angeles Times*, May 11, 1977; Gene Blake, "Ex Pines Aide Changes Story on Files," *Los Angeles Times*, May 31, 1977; Gene Blake, "File-Shredding Case Testimony Disrupted," *Los Angeles Times*, June 1, 1977; Gene Blake, "Judge in Shredding Case Charges Perjury in Perez," *Los Angeles Times*, June 3, 1977; Gene Blake, "Final 16 Cases Dismissed in File-Shredding Controversy," *Los Angeles Times*, June 14, 1977.
142. Nicholas C. Chriss, "5 Houston Police Officers Suspended in Beating, Drowning of Mexican-American," *Los Angeles Times*, May 13, 1977; *Chicano Times*, May 20–June 3, 1977; *Los Angeles Times*, October 8, 1977; *El Paso Times*, October 8, October 11, 1977; *Los Angeles Times*, March 29, May 9, 1978.
143. Allen Pusey, "Sheriff Claims Prisoner Went Berserk," *El Paso Times*, May 20, 1977; *El Paso Times*, May 21, May 24, May 25, June 1, 1977; Allen Pusey, "Pathologist Doubts Hudspeth Jail Death Autopsy," *El Paso Times*, June 4, 1977; Allen Pusey, "Juan Veloz Zuñiga Was Just Wanting to Get to His Job," *El Paso Times*, June 5, 1977; Allen Pusey, "Ex-Hudspeth Prisoners Claim Seeing Beatings," *El Paso Times*, June 12, 1977.
144. See Howard S. Erlanger, in collaboration with Fred Persity, "Estrangement, Machismo, and Gang Violence," (unpublished paper written for the National Insitute of Mental Health, Madison, Wisc. 1977). See "Cases Compiled by the Mexican American Legal Defense and Educational Fund," parts 1 and 2 of the Case Summaries (San Francisco: Mexican American Legal Defense and Education Fund, 1978) for an excellent summary of 56 Police brutality cases in which Maldef has been involved.
145. Minority Admissions Summer Project, sponsored by the National Lawyers Guild and the National Congress of Black Lawyers, *Affirmative Action in Crisis; A Handbook for Activists* (Detroit, 1977) hereafter referred to as *Minority Admissions*. See also Marian Kromkowiki and Izetta Bright, "Affirmative Action History and Results," in Minority Admissions, p. 2. In 1910, 7 of the 155

medical schools in the United States were black. An AMA study by Abraham Flexner found that its members did not have the high incomes they "deserved." The study recommended that the AMA upgrade all the medical schools or close most of them; 124 of the 155 were closed, including 5 of the 7 black schools.

146. William Trombley, "Court Rejects College Plans for Minorities," *Los Angeles Times*, September 17, 1976. For basic documents, including the California Supreme Court's transcripts, see Carlos Manuel Haro, ed., *The Bakke Decision: The Question of Chicano Access to Higher Education*, Chicano Studies Center Document No. 4 (Los Angeles: University of California at Los Angeles, 1976); Ronald D. Moskowitz, "The Man Behind the Storm," *San Francisco Chronicle*, June 29, 1978; Steven Schear, "Bakke: A Lesson in Minimal Adversity," in Minority Admissions, p. 49. See *Minority Admissions*, pp. 21–23, for an annotated chronology of events and dates surrounding *Bakke*.

147. Bonnie K. Solow, "Past Discrimination at the University of California," in Minority Admissions, pp. 55–65. A newspaper report quotes Mosk as saying that "the legal issues of the case would have changed if UC had justified a minority admissions program by saying it had discriminated against minorities in the past." Had the university done so, Mosk said, he would have ruled differently, since under Title VII of Civil Rights Act of 1964 minorities would be entitled to preference if they had previously been discriminated against, "A Rare Mosk Comment on Bakke Case," *San Francisco Chronicle*, June 10, 1977. Apparently, Mosk and his friends had forgotten their utterances in 1950s and 1960s.

148. Celeste Durant, "California Bar Exam—Pain and Trauma Twice a Year," *Los Angeles Times*, August 27, 1978.

149. Robert Montoya, "Minority Health Professional Development: An Issue of Freedom of Choice for Young Anglo Health Professionals," paper presented at the Annual Convention of the American Medical Student Association, Atlanta, Ga., March 4, 1978, p. 4.

150. Sharon Blackman, "Bakke Boogaloo," in *Minority Admissions*, pp. 27–28.

151. Minorities resented that the press dwelled on the cliché "reverse discrimination" and did not object to class discrimination common to all medical schools. For example Davis Medical School dean C. John Tupper had intervened in the admissions procedure on behalf of five wealthy applicants in 1973 alone, *People's World*, October 8, 1977.

152. "The Other Bakke," *Newsweek* (October 24, 1977).

153. John Fogarty, "Race Can Still Be a Factor," *San Francisco Chronicle*, June 29, 1978.

154. Ronald L. Soble, "Minorities' Leaders Expect Setback If Proposition 13 Wins," *Los Angeles Times*, June 5, 1978. As of March 1978 the Los Angeles County Library system operated at 75 percent of the 1977 level and prepared to lay off 1,000 employees in the event it did not receive state bail out money.

155. California School Finance Reform Project, printout, July 1978. For example, the Los Angeles Unified School System receives close to $64 million annually from state and federal sources for bilingual education. If this money was not forthcoming, the number of layoffs would be devastating.

Index